Theory of
Industrial Economics

To Elke,
who is always my co-author

Theory of Industrial Economics

Clement G. Krouse

Basil Blackwell

First published 1990

Basil Blackwell, Inc.
3 Cambridge Center
Cambridge, Massachusetts, 02142, USA

Basil Blackwell Ltd
108 Cowley Road, Oxford, OX4 1JF, UK

Library of Congress Cataloging in Publication Data
Krouse, Clement G.
  Theory of industrial economics.

  Includes bibliographical references.
  1. Industrial organization (Economic theory) I. Title
HD2326.K76 1990   338.5   89-18147
ISBN 1-55786-029-7

British Library Cataloguing in Publication Data
A CIP catalogue record for this book is available from the British Library.

Typeset in 10 on 12 pt Times
by KEYTEC, Bridport, Dorset
Printed in Great Britain

Contents

Preface

This is a text in economic analysis. Its purpose is to set out systematically the theoretical foundations underlying the economics of industrial markets. The long list of references which make up the final pages of the text is a clear indication not only of the scope of the material, but also of my debt to others for their ideas. I would, however, like to specifically express my gratitude to those colleagues who have read and commented on early drafts of the manuscript: William Comanor, Ted Frech, Stanley Ornstein, Ivan Png, Eric Rasmusen, and Stanley Reynolds deserve particular mention in this regard. David Li and Lee Motley were careful and cheerful student readers. In addition, an acknowledgment is again due to my friend J. Fred Weston for his intellectual support. I also appreciate the patience of Becky Davis, David Alix, and Bee Hanson, whose TROFF skills brought some order out of a chaotic first draft. Finally, there is a salute to Bryan, who says he will peruse, but not study, this sort of thing.

Clement G. Krouse
Santa Barbara, CA

Introductory Note

What is written here concerns economic theory generally and the economic theory of markets specifically. The nature of competition, the determinants and welfare effects of market structure, the variety of products that will be produced, and the price and sales policies of suppliers are indicative of the topics addressed. This is the usual stuff of the industrial economics field.

Perhaps the most widely noted shortcoming of traditional industrial economics has been the tendency to move too rapidly from economic analysis to empirical study and policy prescription. That impatience with building solidly on underlying theory has changed in the last decade. Compared with earlier work, recent research makes systematic use of microeconomic theory in a way which recognizes that industry history matters, that the costs of information in part determine what is preferred and what is supplied, and that competition is a dynamic process. Property rights, moral hazard, transaction costs, and complex contractual arrangements, both implicit and explicit, are more carefully considered, and the structure and solution concepts of game theory are used to unify these things.

While there have been these important advances, very little of this has found its way into modern texts. This book is written in response to these observations. That does not mean that this is a compendium. Of necessity topics have been dealt with selectively in both their depth and their breadth. Despite this, I have attempted to cover the major issues along with solution concepts and principles of analysis. While the theories that are addressed in this way generally lead to testable implications, this is not always the case. Some analyses are included largely because they provide a basis for further study by offering insight and simplicity to otherwise complex and confused topics.

The treatment of topics found in the following pages differs from most prior work in three ways. First, I am able to draw on extensive literature in dynamic models of competition that was not available a decade ago. That is a major advantage in the analysis of industrial markets. Second, rather than viewing microeconomic theory and institutional description as being in essential conflict, I am inclined to think of these as complements which jointly contribute to our understanding. When the opportunity arises, the solution *concept* is tailored to what is actual in an industry. Third, I have attempted to be explicit, sometimes painfully, about the "rules of play" in each analysis and to point to those which are at the heart of any startling results.

The table of contents provides a clear view of the specific topics covered and their sequence. While some old issues are considered, this is meant primarily to sharpen the reader's understanding of recent developments. As to how these things unfold, the book gives more or less equal weight to the logical structure of the theory and its results. Because these are sufficient tasks in themselves, there are only introductory comments concerning empirical tests of the regularities that are deduced and policy implications are briefly noted, and not dealt with in detail. The material is theoretical in this sense, but it is not designed to require extensive mathematical abstraction. This is in part because new ideas and results are introduced step by step (some will say laboriously) and in part because a large number of applied examples (E) are developed. There are also longer and more integrative supplementary examples (SE) at the ends of the chapters (except chapters 1 and 2). Finally, to limit the required techniques some ideas are not presented in their most rigorous or most general form when there appear to be rapidly diminishing returns to mathematical precision. Graduate students with a good foundation in microeconomic theory and standard mathematical skills should therefore find the material within their reach.

The material covered in chapters 1 and 2 is background, but it is essential and must be understood by the reader at the onset. There are also some "wrinkles" which cast these things in a way more immediate to the problems in industrial economics. That explains the prominent location of this material instead of the alternative and slighted appendix position. Chapters 3 and 9 are the centrepieces of the book. In chapter 3 the classical conjectural variation approach to timeless oligopoly models is developed. Inappropriate dynamic interpretations of the models are noted and there is an alternative interpretation of conjectural variations as representations of the static Nash solution concept. Some two-stage applications of the models are finally developed, each with one market date and a prior, prescient choice of strategy variable. These notions of static oligopoly equilibria with differentiated products are used in chapters 4–6, and the concepts are applied to discriminatory pricing in chapter 7. In chapter 8 the durable goods monopoly is dealt with and a bridge to the explicitly dynamic models of the remaining chapters is provided. The fundamental concepts in the game-theoretic representation of oligopoly are outlined in chapter 9. Special attention is given to refinements of the Nash solution concept which are appropriate to a dynamic treatment of repeated and other multistage games with and without complete information. Entry and exit as repeated and multistage dynamic games are described in chapters 10 and 11, and chapter 12 looks at how variations on the rules of play in oligopoly games cause competitive processes to have monopoly outcomes. Finally, chapters 13 and 14 deal with markets in which costs of pre-purchase and post-purchase quality determination are important. Chapters 3 and 9 must be read; thereafter the reader can choose as he or she will.

Examples

Figures

Part I

Foundations

1 Demand and Consumer Welfare

The economic theory of demand concerns the manner in which individuals make consumption decisions. Underlying this theory is a simple principle of rationality: each consumer chooses the most preferred bundle of commodities from those which are feasible. The theory's complexity, and its essential structure, becomes evident when specifying feasible commodity bundles, reasonable preference orderings, and rules of exchange, and in turn understanding the implications of these specifications.

To see in general terms how this theory develops consider the usual static and certain market exchange economy and focus on a typical individual's consumption choice. Let $m = 1, 2, \ldots, M$ consumption commodities be well defined, measurable, and continuously divisible. A consumption plan for the individual is given by the M vector $z = [z_1 z_2 \ldots z_M]$, which lists amounts z_m of each commodity chosen. A particular plan is said to be **technically feasible** when it lies within a consumption possibility set Z. While this set may generally depend on the trading skills and characteristics of the individual, more commonly it is used to reflect the limitations on trade imposed by the physical nature of the commodities and/or the organization of markets. Omitting extraordinary restrictions and assuming that the individual does not contribute to production, it is usual to take Z as all nonnegative consumptions.

To account for prior exchange providing value at the current date, each consumer is assigned a nonnegative endowment of the commodities $\bar{z} = [\bar{z}_1 \bar{z}_2 \ldots \bar{z}_M]$. Market exchange using these endowed commodities, to fashion a preferred plan of consumption, occurs at fixed rates of exchange given by the nonnegative prices $p = [p_1 p_2 \ldots p_M]$. A limitation on trade provides the second constraint: a consumption plan is said to be **feasible in exchange** for some individual if its value at these prices does not exceed that of his endowment $\bar{z}$:

$$\sum_m p_m z_m \leqslant \sum_m p_m \bar{z}_m \equiv y$$

where y is called income. When giving attention to the theory of individual demand, a smallness argument is usually employed with the result that prices and income are taken as exogenously given data and referred to as the **data set**.

The individual's preferences are generally restricted in such a way that they can be represented by a real scalar-valued utility function $u(z_1, z_2, \ldots, z_M)$. This function represents preferences in the following sense: for two plans z, $z^1 \in Z$, $u(z) > u(z^1)$ iff the individual strictly prefers z to z^1, $u(z) = u(z^1)$ iff there is indifference to the plans, and $u(z) < u(z^1)$ iff z^1 is strictly preferred to z. The individual is said to be **rational** if, from among the feasible consumption plans, he chooses that which yields the greatest value for u.

An **individual equilibrium** is described by the consumption plan z^0 maximizing u subject to the technical and economic feasibility constraints. As we will show later, an equilibrium plan exists uniquely under reasonable convexity assumptions concerning preferences (and the individual's utility function) and the constraint sets. Associated with the individual's equilibrium is a vector of functions $d(p, y)$ whose components are real scalar-valued demand functions $d_m(p, y) = z_m^0$ that determine the consumption amounts for various values of the parameters p and y (given the preferences expressed by u). For each commodity, the aggregation of these demands across individual yields a market demand. For a given array of products, the theory of markets is concerned with the division of this aggregate demand among producing firms under various rules of interaction. When firms interact over many periods and can introduce new product variations, this division of demand is doubly complex. The properties of the resulting "multimarket" equilibrium reflect this complexity.

1.1   Individual Equilibrium

Given that consumer preferences are reflexive, transitive, continuous, and strongly monotonic, there exists a continuous order-preserving utility function.[1] Assuming further that these preferences are strictly convex and nonsatiable, the utility function is strictly quasi-concave and the budget constraint is binding at each individual's consumptive optimum. When all these conditions obtain and the utility function is suitably differentiable, classical optimization procedures using the calculus are employed to derive the individual equilibrium.

1.1.1   Utility and Demand

If it is assumed that the optimal consumption plan for the individual lies in the interior of the consumption set, that optimum can be derived from the stationarity conditions of the problem (s.t. indicates "subject to"):

$$\max_z u(z) \text{ s.t. } \sum_m p_m z_m = y \tag{1.1}$$

Proceeding in this usual way, we have the associated Lagrange form

$$L(z, \lambda) = u(z) - \lambda \left(\sum_m p_m z_m - y \right) \tag{1.2}$$

---

[1] The details of such a representation are fully developed by Herstein and Milnor (1953); see also Arrow and Hahn (1971, pp. 80–7).

with multiplier λ and, by differentiation, the standard first-order conditions[2]

$$u_m(z) - \lambda p_m = 0 \qquad m = 1, 2, \ldots, M \tag{1.3a}$$

$$\sum_m p_m z_m - y = 0 \tag{1.3b}$$

The subscripts to u here indicate partial derivatives, for example $u_m(z)$ is the marginal utility of commodity m at z.

The optimal consumption plan – the solution values of (1.3) – generally depends on the exogenous price and income parameters. The function which relates p and y to the *optimal* consumption $z_m{}^0 = d_m(p, y^0)$ is referred to as the consumer's **demand function** for each good m. In turn, the optimal value of utility at given prices and income is derived by substituting these demands in u to produce

$$U(p, y) = U\{z^0(p, y)\} = \left\{ \max_z u(z) \text{ s.t. } \sum_m p_m z_m \leqslant y \right\}$$

$U(p, y)$ is called the **indirect utility function** as it depends on the elements of the data set – the prices and income.

It is usual to eliminate the multiplier by rearranging the stationarity conditions (1.3) in the form

$$-\left(\frac{dz_l}{dz_m} \right)_u = \frac{u_m(z^0)}{u_l(z^0)} = \frac{p_m}{p_l} \qquad \text{for all } l, m = 1, 2, \ldots, M \tag{1.4}$$

In this relationship the ratio of marginal utilities is termed the individual's **rate of commodity substitution** between goods l and m (at constant utility), and the price ratio is the market **exchange rate of substitution**.

E1.1

Utility and Demand

Consider the case of two goods and assume that individual preferences are given by $u(z_1, z_2) = z_1 z_2$. Stationarity conditions (1.3) then have the specific form

$$z_2{}^0 = \lambda^0 p_1$$

$$z_1{}^0 = \lambda^0 p_2$$

$$p_1 z_2{}^0 + p_2 z_2{}^0 = y$$

Here, $z_2{}^0/z_1{}^0 = p_1/p_2$ corresponds to equation (1.4) where the ratio of quantities is the rate of commodity substitution and the ratio of prices is the market rate of exchange.

Solving, the optimal values are

$$\lambda^0 = \frac{y}{2p_1 p_2}$$

---

[2] Second-order conditions require that the utility function is strictly quasi-concave (that is, the upper level set of u is supported by the budget hyperplane), see Arrow and Hahn, (1971).

with the demand functions

$$z_1{}^0 = \frac{y}{2p_1}$$

$$z_2{}^0 = \frac{y}{2p_2}$$

Note that the quantity demanded of each commodity depends only (and inversely) on its own price in this particular case. More generally, *all* prices would appear in each demand function.[3]

Equivalent Utilities. The numbers assigned by the utility function to various bundles reflect the order of the bundles in the consumer's preference. The specific numbers assigned, as long as they are order preserving in this way, have no other meaning. This suggests that a consumer's preference can be represented by more than one such function. That is, given a utility function $u(z)$ we can form a new utility function $v\{u(z)\}$, where v is a monotonic increasing transformation of u. Not only does v preserve the u ordering of z, it leads to the same optimal bundle for the individual. To clarify this, consider the optimization problem $\max_z v\{u(z)\}$ s.t. $\Sigma_m p_m z_m \leq y$ and the associated stationarity conditions

$$v_u u_m - \lambda p_m = 0 \qquad \text{for all } m$$

$$\sum_m p_m z_m - y = 0$$

where, again, λ is the Lagrange multiplier and v_u is the obvious derivative. Since v is an increasing monotonic transformation, $v_u > 0$ and these equations imply (1.4). The stationarity conditions and the optimal consumption plan z^0 are thus invariant to the choice of utility functions as long as the utility functions represent the same underlying preference ordering.[4]

1.1.2   Income Effects

What meaning can be given to λ^0, the optimal value of the Lagrange multiplier? An answer comes when rewriting (1.3) as

$$\frac{\partial u(z^0)}{\partial z_m} = \lambda^0 p_m$$

Since p_m is a constant, this can be rearranged to yield

$$\frac{\partial u(z^0)}{\partial(p_m z_m)} = \lambda^0 \tag{1.5}$$

Here, the product $p_m z_m$ is the expenditure on good m at the individual's

---

[3] See section 1.3.2 for an explanation of the interdependence found here.

[4] The reader can quickly show that the second-order conditions for the maximum are also unaffected by the transformation.

consumptive optimum. Since this expression holds for all commodities, the incremental dollar spent on each must provide the same increment to utility, that is,

$$\frac{\partial u(z^0)}{\partial y} = \lambda^0 \tag{1.6}$$

Thus, λ^0 is the **marginal utility of income** (at the optimum), that is, the conversion rate between income and utility.[5]

E1.2

Marginal Utility of Income

The envelope theorem provides a direct way to the results given by (1.6). Let $L(z, \lambda) = u(z) - \lambda(\Sigma_m p_m z_m - y)$ again be the Lagrange function associated with the utility maximization problem. At an interior optimum the consumption choices depend on the price and income parameters, which we write as

$$L\{z^0(p, y), \lambda^0\} = U(p, y)$$

$$= u\{z^0(p, y)\} - \lambda^0 \left(\sum_m p_m z_m^0 - y \right)$$

Once more, the superscript zero indicates optimal values and $U(p, y)$ is the indirect utility. As this expression holds identically it can be differentiated with respect to income, holding prices constant, to yield

$$\frac{\partial L(z^0, \lambda^0)}{\partial y} = \frac{\partial U}{\partial y} = \left(\frac{\partial u(z^0)}{\partial z} - \lambda^0 p_m \right) \frac{\partial z^0}{\partial y} + \lambda^0$$

At the optimum $\partial u(z^0)/\partial z = \lambda^0 p_m$, and this expression simplifies to

$$\frac{\partial U}{\partial y} = \lambda^0$$

which is again (1.6).

Elasticity of Income. When utility is strictly increasing in the consumption of each good (nonsatiation), the budget restriction $\Sigma_m p_m z_m = y$ will hold identically at the consumer optimum. At constant prices this can the be differentiated to yield

$$\sum_m p_m \frac{\partial z_m}{\partial y} = 1$$

Multiplying and dividing each term by z_m/y puts this in the elasicity form

---

[5] An alternative way to this result is to rewrite (1.5) as $\lambda^0 = \{\partial u(z^0)/\partial z_m\}/p_m$ and note that $1/p_m$ is the quantity of good m that can be purchased with \$1.

$$\sum_m \frac{p_m z_m}{y} \left(\frac{\partial z_m}{\partial y} \frac{y}{z_m} \right) = 1$$

which can be rewritten as

$$\sum_m s_m \eta_m = 1 \tag{1.7}$$

where $s_m = (p_m z_m / y)$ is the **expenditure share** and $\eta_m = (\partial z_m / \partial y)(y / z_m)$ is the **income elasticity of demand** for each commodity m. Thus, for any system of demand equations arising from a well-formed utility maximization problem, the expenditure share-weighted average of income elasticities must equal unity.

There are some standard ways of characterizing commodities by their income elasticities. Commodities with income elasticities less than zero, where the demand falls with increases in income, are said to be **inferior**. The usual case is that of **normal** goods, where demand increases with income. Note that these elasticities are properties of the demand at a given point so that the classification of a good as inferior or normal generally changes with changes in prices and income. This is seen clearly in the graph of quantity demanded and income (holding prices fixed), which is called the **Engel curve**. Obviously, a good is normal in the region where its Engel curve is positively sloped, and conversely.

1.1.3   Demand Functions: Some Special Cases

Demand functions must possess specific properties when they arise from a well-formed utility maximization problem. For example, it was noted above that the budget restriction requires that the share-weighted income elasticities of demand must be unity. In addition to such general requirements, which are further outlined below, specific restrictions on the underlying utility functions produce demand functions with properties which are analytically useful. The nature of some common restrictions made in this regard, and the resulting relationship between utility and demand functions, is considered in sections 1.2 and 1.3. As a basis for that analysis, two generally useful properties of functions are first noted.

Homogeneity. A function $f(z) = f(z_1, z_2, \ldots, z_m)$ is said to be **homogeneous of degree κ in z** iff

$$f(tz_1, tz_2, \ldots, tz_m) = t^\kappa f(z_1, z_2, \ldots, z_m)$$

where t is a positive constant. That is, when each variable of a homogeneous function is multiplied by the same constant it is possible to factor that constant to some power from the function. When f is homogeneous it is of particular note that $f(0) = 0$, so that homogeneous functions have graphs necessarily passing through the origin. In the specific case where $\kappa = 1$ the function f is said to be **linearly homogeneous** (or to exhibit **constant returns to scale**) and proportionate changes in the arguments lead to an identical proportionate change in the value of f. A second interesting instance occurs when $\kappa = 0$: f is homogeneous of degree zero and proportionate changes in its arguments leave the value of the function unaltered.

E1.3 ───

Demand is Linearly Homogeneous in Prices and Income

Demand functions are homogeneous of degree zero in prices and income:

$$d_m(tp, ty) = t^0 d_m(p, y) = d_m(p, y)$$

for all m. This result follows from several simple steps. First, multiply prices and income in the first-order conditions (1.3) to yield

$$\frac{u_m(z^0)}{u_l(z^0)} = \frac{tp_m}{tp_l}$$

and

$$\sum_m tp_m - ty = 0$$

The result is obvious: factoring t from these expressions leaves the quantity demanded unchanged. The homogeneity of demand functions is not at all surprising since neither the utility function (by definition) nor the budget set are affected by proportionate changes in the data set parameters.

═══

Homotheticity. Related to the homogeneity of a function is the concept of homotheticity. Specifically, a function $F(\xi)$ is said to be **homothetic** is there is a transformation of variables such that

$$F(\xi) \equiv F(f(z))$$

where F is a positive, finite, continuous, and strictly monotonic increasing function of one variable with $F(0) = 0$, and f is a homogeneous function of z. Homogeneous functions are homothetic (but the converse is not generally true). Homotheticity is of interest because functions exhibiting this property have ratios of first derivatives which depend only on the ratio of quantities. That is,

$$\frac{\partial F/\partial z_1}{\partial F/\partial z_2} = g_{12}\left(\frac{z_2}{z_1}, \frac{z_3}{z_1}, \ldots, \frac{z_M}{z_1}\right) \tag{1.8}$$

where g_{12} is a function pertaining to the case of goods 1 and 2.[6] This condition corresponds to the geometric property where tangents of the level contours of F are parallel along the intersection of any given ray emanating from the origin.

For example, when the individual's utility function is homothetic the locus of tangents between indifference levels and budget lines (of constant slope) lies along a single ray from the origin: as a result, the rate of commodity substitution u_l/u_m depends only on the ratio of consumption amounts z_l/z_m. This further implies that, with given commodity prices, the relative share of each consumer's expenditure allocated to any commodities z_l and z_m must be constant as income changes. (Obviously, $p_l z_l/p_m z_m$ is constant when there are fixed prices and a

─────────────────

[6] See Rader (1972, ch. 6) for the proof.

constant z_l/z_m ratio.) This is the well-known result that with homothetic utility the share of each commodity in the total expenditure of the individual is independent of income and depends only on *relative* prices. That is, if s_m is an appropriate function of p_1/p_2, then

$$\frac{p_m z_m}{y} = s_m\left(\frac{p_l}{p_m}\right)$$

and therefore

$$p_m z_m = y s_m\left(\frac{p_l}{p_m}\right) \tag{1.9}$$

Finally, from this last equation it is clear that homotheticity of the demand function implies the following:

1   $\partial(p_m z_m)/\partial y$ is independent of y (the marginal propensity to expend on each good m is independent of income);
2   $\partial(\ln z_m)/\partial(\ln y^0) = 1$ (unit income elasticity of demand for each good m).

E1.4

Special Utilities and Associated Demands

One frequently employed utility function is the two-commodity quadratic form $u(z_1, z_2) = z_1 z_2 + z_1^2 z_2^2$. Clearly u is not homogeneous in this case; it is homothetic, however, since a change of variables $\xi = z_1 z_2$ produces $u(z_1, z_2) = \xi + \xi^2$, where ξ is a homogeneous function of the z. (Note, moreover, that $\partial u/\partial \xi = 1 + 2\xi \neq 0$, since consumption is nonnegative.) For this specific case the slope of each indifference curve becomes

$$-\frac{u_1}{u_2} = -\frac{z_2 + 2z_1 z_2^2}{z_1 + 2z_1^2 z_2} = -\frac{z_2}{z_1}\left(\frac{1 + 2z_1 z_2}{1 + 2z_1 z_2}\right)$$

$$= -\frac{z_2}{z_1}$$

Using the notation of equation (1.8), $u_1/u_2 = g_{12}(z_1, z_2) = z_2/z_1$, so that the function g_{12} is homogeneous of degree zero. In turn, the indifference (level) contours of u have the same slope at all points along every ray from the origin.

A second frequently used utility function is based on the multiplicative form $u(z) = z_1 z_2 \ldots z_m$. For reasons which will shortly become clear, two generalizations are then made. First z_1 is replaced by $z_1 - \alpha_1$, and similarly with z_2, z_3, etc. Next it is usual to introduce exponents β_1, β_2, etc. and take the (monotone increasing) logarithmic transformation to obtain

$$u(z) = \sum_m \beta_m \ln(z_m - \alpha_m) \tag{1.10}$$

With the normalization $\sum_m \beta_m = 1$ the stationarity conditions corresponding to (1.3) are then

$$\beta_l = \lambda p_l(z_l - \alpha_l) \tag{1.11a}$$

$$\sum_m \beta_m = \lambda \sum_m p_m(z_m - \alpha_m) = 1 \tag{1.11b}$$

$$\lambda = \frac{1}{y - \Sigma_m p_m \alpha_m} \tag{1.11c}$$

In these equations all values of λ and z are understood to be those at the consumptive optimum, but the superscript zero is omitted as a notational convenience. Using (1.11a) and (1.11c) to eliminate λ gives

$$\beta_l = \frac{p_l(z_l - \alpha_l)}{y - z_m p_m \alpha_m}$$

which can be solved as follows:

$$p_l z_l = p_l \alpha_l + \beta_l \left(y - \sum_m p_m \alpha_m \right) \tag{1.12}$$

This is commonly referred to as the **linear expenditure system**: the expenditure on each good l depends linearly on income and prices. It is easily shown, and is of special importance, that the income consumption curve and the Engel curve are linear in this case, but that neither goes through the origin.[7] Thus, while result 1 noted above obtains for the linear expenditure system, result 2 does not. That is, the utility function given by (1.10) is not homothetic.

1.2   Duality

Recall the original utility maximization problem and suppose that z^0, providing utility u^0, is the solution with given income level and commodity prices. When underlying preferences are strictly convex, so that level contours of utility also have this strict convexity, there exists only one point z^0 on level contour u^0 at which the budget hyperplane $\Sigma_m p_m z_m = y$ is tangent. Figure 1.1 illustrates this solution for two goods. This uniqueness also means that the utility maximizing consumption z^0 is the unique solution to the problem of minimizing the expenditures associated with producing the utility level u^0, and the minimum expenditure must be y. That is, if the solution to $\max_z u(z)$ s.t. $\Sigma_m p_m z_m \le y$ is z^0 and this yields $u(z^0) = u^0$, then the solution to the problem $\min_z \Sigma_m p_m z_m$ s.t. $u(z) = u^0$ must be z^0 and the resulting expenditure is at the same level $y = \Sigma_m p_m z_m^0$. In this sense it is usual to say that these minimization and maximization problems are **dual** to each other. The importance of this duality in both the theory and application of demand economics is our next subject.

1.2.1   Indirect Utility

The indirect utility function depends only on prices and income:

---

[7] The reader can also show that the income consumption curve goes through point $(\alpha_1, \alpha_2, \ldots, \alpha_m)$ and the Engel curve for good m has $(\alpha_m \Sigma_m p_m \alpha_m)$ as an intersection.

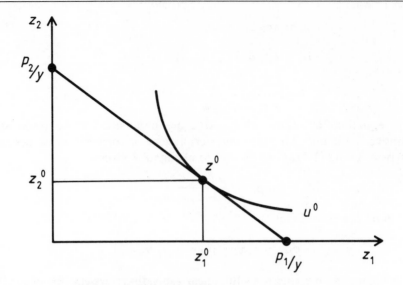

Figure 1.1
Utility maximization, expenditure minimization

$$U(p, y) = \left\{ \max_z u(z) \text{ s.t. } \sum_m p_m z_m = y \right\} \tag{1.13}$$

The reader can immediately see that the degree zero homogeneity of the demand functions in prices and income means that the indirect utility function will also have this same homogeneity. Diewert (1978) has shown, and it is intuitive from the geometry of figure 1.1, that the indirect function $U(\cdot)$ has the following properties.

    U1 It is continuous at all positive prices when u is continuous in the z.
    U2 It is nonincreasing and quasi-convex in p with fixed y.
    U3 Given nonsatiation, it is strictly increasing in y with fixed p.

E1.5 ──

Utility and Indirect Utility

Recall E1.1 and the demand functions

$$z_1{}^0 = \frac{y}{2p_1}$$

$$z_2{}^0 = \frac{y}{2p_2}$$

associated with the direct utility $u(z_1, z_2) = z_1 z_2$. Substituting these solution values in u gives the indirect utility function

$$U(p, y) = \frac{y^2}{4p_1 p_2} \tag{1.14}$$

Note that this indirect utility satisfies the above conditions **U1–U3**.

The demand functions of section 1.1.1 were derived from the $M + 1$ stationarity conditions associated with the utility maximization problem. It is easy to see that obtaining explicit solutions by this technique would be difficult when M is large and the solution equations are nonlinear. In fact, for many reasonable, even simple, specifications of utility it is extremely difficult to analytically express the demand functions in this manner. A derivative property of the indirect utility function is at times useful in achieving such solutions without having to deal with large systems of simultaneous equations.

Roy's Identity. Let $U(p, y)$ be a suitably differentiable indirect utility function. Then, ordinary demand functions are given by the ratio of derivatives

$$z_m = d_m(p, y^0) = - \frac{\partial U(p, y)/\partial p_m}{\partial U(p, y)/\partial y} \tag{1.15}$$

for each commodity m. Proof of the identity is straightforward. Suppose that z^0 is the consumptive optimum with parameters p and y, that is, $z^0 = d(p, y^0)$. The following identities then obtain:

$$u^0 \equiv u(z^0) \equiv u\{d(p, y^0)\} \equiv U(p, y^0)$$

If we next let $y(p, u^0)$ indicate that level of income which, at prices p, just allows the individual to reach utility level u^0, then

$$u^0 \equiv U\{p, y(p, u^0)\} \tag{1.16}$$

also holds identically. This expression can then be differentiated to yield

$$0 = \frac{\partial U(p, y^0)}{\partial p_m} + \frac{\partial U(p, y^0)}{\partial y} \frac{\partial y(p, u^0)}{\partial p_m} \tag{1.17}$$

Substituting $z_m^0 = \partial y(p, u^0)/\partial p_m$ from the budget constraint finally gives

$$z_m^0 = - \frac{\partial U(p, y^0)/\partial p_m}{\partial U(p, y^0)/\partial y}$$

As this holds for all prices and income, Roy's identity is proved.

E1.6 ───

Addilog Utility, Roy's Identity, and Demand

Let $U(p, y) = \Sigma_m \, \alpha_m(y/p_m)^{\beta_m}$, which is the indirect addilog utility function first used by Houthakker (1960). Then, for each commodity l,

$$\frac{\partial U}{\partial p_l} = - \frac{\alpha_l \beta_l y (y/p_l)^{\beta_l - 1}}{p_l^2}$$

$$\frac{\partial U}{\partial y} = \sum_m \left(\frac{\alpha_m \beta_m}{p_m} \frac{y}{p_m} \right)^{\beta_m - 1}$$

Using Roy's identity gives the ordinary demand for good l as

$$z_l = \frac{\alpha_l \beta_l y^{\beta_l - 1} p_l^{-\beta_l + 1}}{\sum_m \alpha_m \beta_m y^{\beta_m - 1} p_m^{-\beta_m}}$$

1.2.2 Expenditure Function

$U(p, y)$ is strictly increasing with y (nonsatiation), it is possible to solve for y as a function of the level of utility. This "inverse" is commonly referred to as the consumer **expenditure function**. The essential properties of the expenditure function are evident from the dual problem

$$\min_z \sum_m p_m z_m \text{ s.t. } u(z) \geq u \tag{1.18}$$

which determines the consumption plan minimizing the consumer's expenditure subject to the constraint that utility attain at least the level u. The solution vector z^* of this problem depends on prices and the value of u, that is

$$z^* = h(p, u) \quad \text{with } m\text{th element} \quad z_m^* = h_m(p, u) \tag{1.19}$$

It should be apparent that the z^* solution to the minimization problem (1.18) at given prices p and utility u is also the solution to the original utility maximization problem (1.1). (The geometry of figure 1.1 is helpful here.) To go through the steps briefly, let $u = u(z^0)$ where z^0 solves the utility maximization problem (1.1). Then the stationarity conditions associated with (1.18) are, for each m,

$$p_m - \gamma u_m = 0 \tag{1.20a}$$

and

$$u(z) - u(z^0) = 0 \tag{1.20b}$$

where γ is the Lagrange multiplier. For two commodities l and m equation (1.20a) gives

$$\frac{u_m(z^*)}{u_l(z^*)} = \frac{p_m}{p_l} \tag{1.21}$$

This expression, however, is identical with that arising from the stationarity conditions of the utility maximization problem – recall (1.3) – and so we must have $z^* = z^0$. The expenditure minimization problem (1.6) produces the same solution conditions as the utility maximization problem (1.1).

Based on this equivalence of problems, it is usual to provide an equivalent definition of the expenditure function as

$$E(p, u) = \min_z \sum_m p_m z_m \text{ s.t. } u(z) \geq u \tag{1.22}$$

Diewert (1978) has shown, and it is intuitive from the geometry of figure 1.1, that $E(p, u)$ has the following properties.

El It is nondecreasing, continuous, and concave in p.
E2 It is linearly homogeneous in p.
E3 It is strictly increasing in u (with nonsatiation).

Perhaps the most important use of the expenditure function is based on the following derivative property.

Hotelling's Theorem. If the expenditure function is differentiable, then the individual's optimal consumption plan is given as

$$z_m{}^0 = h_m(p, u) = \frac{\partial E(p, u)}{\partial p_m} \qquad (1.23)$$

for each commodity m.

The proof proceeds by letting z^0 be optimal at specific prices p and utility level u: $z_m{}^0 = h_m(p, u)$ for each m. Then $E(p, u) = \Sigma_l p_l z_l{}^0$ holds as an identity and can be differentiated to give

$$\sum_l E_l(p, u) \, dp_l + E_u(p, u) \, du = \sum_l (z_l \, dp_l + p_l \, dz_l) \qquad (1.24)$$

with $E_l(\cdot) = \partial E(\cdot)/\partial p_l$ for all l. Using (1.20a) the fact that $du = 0$ is required to keep utility at level u, and setting $dp_l = 0$ for all $l \neq m$ (leaving only p_m to vary) proves the theorem.

1.2.3　Income-compensated Demand

The function $h_m(p, u)$ of (1.19) and (1.23) is generally referred to as the Hicks (income) **compensated demand curve** for commodity m, for it determines the optimal consumption of m for variations in p_m holding the prices of other commodities *and* the individual's level of utility (real income) constant. As p_m varies, holding utility constant means it is generally necessary to vary money income y, which explains the (income) compensated qualifier for the demand.

E1.7 ⸻

Utility, Expenditure Function, and Compensated Demand

Restrict attention to two commodities and let utility be given by $u(z) = z_1 z_2$. As shown in E1.1, the ordinary demand functions associated with this specification are

$$z_1{}^0 = d_1(p, y) = \frac{y}{2p_1}$$

$$z_2{}^0 = d_2(p, y) = \frac{y}{2p_2}$$

There is also the associated indirect utility

$$U(p, y) = \frac{y^2}{4p_1 p_2}$$

derived in E1.5. Inverting this gives the expenditure function

$$E(p, u) = 2(p_1 p_2 u)^{1/2}$$

In turn, there are the compensated demand curves

$$z_1^0 = h_1(p, u) = \frac{\partial E(p, u)}{\partial p_1} = \left(\frac{p_2 u}{p_1}\right)^{1/2}$$

$$z_2^0 = h_2(p, u) = \frac{\partial E(p, u)}{\partial p_2} = \left(\frac{p_1 u}{p_2}\right)^{1/2}$$

Note carefully the differences between compensated and ordinary demands.

With continuous strictly convex indifference contours it is easily shown that the (income) compensated demand for each commodity m is a decreasing function of its own price p_m. That is, as p_m rises and y is simultaneously adjusted to keep the utility level constant, the individual's optimal consumption of good m falls. Additional properties of $h_m(\cdot)$, and its relationship to the conventional demand $d_m(\cdot)$, are generally based on a decomposition of the impact of a price change into two "effects."

1.2.4   Income and Substitution Effects

Suppose that z^0 maximizes utility with specific prices p and money income y and let $u^0 = u(z^0)$. Then at these values

$$h_m(p, u^0) \equiv d_m(p, E(p, u^0)) \tag{1.25}$$

holds as an identity. Differentiating this with respect to p_l and evaluating the derivatives at p gives

$$\frac{\partial h_m(p, u^0)}{\partial p_l} = \frac{\partial d_m(p, y^0)}{\partial p_l} + \frac{\partial d_m(p, y^0)}{\partial y} \frac{\partial E(p, u^0)}{\partial p_l} \tag{1.26}$$

Recall from Hotelling's theorem that $\partial E(p, u^0)/\partial p_l = z_l^0$. Substituting this in (1.26) and rearranging yields what is commonly referred to as the **Slutsky equation**:

$$\frac{\partial d_m(p, y)}{\partial p_l} = \frac{\partial h_m(p, u^0)}{\partial p_l} - z_l^0 \frac{\partial d_m(p, y)}{\partial y} \tag{1.27}$$

If we let $l \equiv m$, the Slutsky equtaion decomposes the effects of an own-price change on the individual's consumption of that commodity into two parts:

$$\Delta z_m \approx \frac{\partial h_m}{\partial p_m} \Delta p_m - \frac{\partial d_m}{\partial y} z_m \Delta p_m \tag{1.28}$$

The individual's overall change in demand Δz_m can be thought of as arising from a **substitution effect** $(\partial h_m/\partial p_m)\Delta p_m$ and an **income effect** $(\partial d_m/\partial y)z_m\Delta p_m$. This second effect is the variation (in quantity demanded) arising from the change in the individual's *real* income brought about by the price change. A price decrease leads to an increase in the individual's purchasing power, and he will generally adjust his demand in response to this increase. In contrast, the substitution effect is that part of the quantity variation which arises because (holding real income constant) relative price changes generally induce consumption changes.

For completeness we note (a) that both the income and substitution effect result from a single price change, (b) that the sum of these two effects is equal to the actual (observed) change in quantity demanded, and (c) that the income effect is a *quantity* change induced by a change in a *price*.

Relative Slopes. Look again at the Slutsky equation, with $m \equiv l$. For a normal good the income compensation will be negative with own-price decreases and, conversely, positive with own-price increases. As a result, in the neighborhood of the optimal consumption $z_m{}^0$ the absolute slope of the compensated demand curve $h_m(p, u^0)$ will be greater than that of the ordinary demand $d_m(p, y)$. Figure 1.2 illustrates this condition. For an inferior good these relative slopes are, of course, reversed.

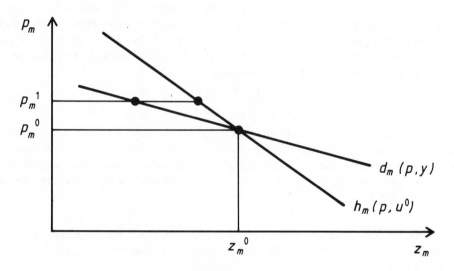

Figure 1.2
Ordinary and compensated demands

E1.8 ───

Slutsky Equation: Elasticity Form

Multiply the Slutsky equation (1.27) by $p_l/z_m{}^0$ and, in turn, multiply the income effect term by y/y. Dropping the function arguments to simplify the notation then gives

$$\frac{\partial d_m}{\partial p_l}\frac{p_l}{z_m{}^0} = \frac{\partial h_m}{\partial p_l}\frac{p_l}{z_m{}^0} - \frac{p_l z_m{}^0}{y}\frac{y}{z_m{}^0}\frac{\partial d_m}{\partial y}$$

These terms are easily recognized as elasticities and we write

$$\varepsilon_{ml} = \varepsilon_{ml}^* - s_l\eta_m$$

where, using the obvious notation, ε_{ml} is the p_l elasticity of commodity m ordinary demand, ε_{ml}^* is the p_l elasticity of commodity m compensated demand, s_l is the expenditure share of commodity l, and η_m is the income elasticity of commodity m.

Slutsky Symmetry and Definiteness. It is common to write the Slutsky equations in vector-matrix form as

$$\left[\frac{\partial d_m}{\partial p_l}\right] = \left[\frac{\partial h_m}{\partial p_l}\right] - \left[\frac{\partial d_m}{\partial y}\right]z^0 \tag{1.29}$$

where $[\partial d_m/\partial p_l]$ and $[\partial h_m/\partial p_l]$ are $M \times M$ matrices with the indicated entries, $[\partial d_m/\partial y]$ is an $M \times 1$ column vector of derivatives with respect to income, and z^0 is an $M \times 1$ row vector of equilibrium quantities. The matrix $[\partial h_m/\partial p_l]$ contains the substitution effects of the price change. This matrix has two key properties. First, it is symmetric. To show this, recall that $h_m = \partial E/\partial p_m$, which in turn gives $\partial h_m/\partial p_l = \partial^2 E/\partial p_m\partial p_l$. As the order of partial differentiation is irrelevant for suitably continuous functions,

$$\frac{\partial h_m}{\partial p_l} = \frac{\partial^2 E}{\partial p_m\partial p_l} = \frac{\partial^2 E}{\partial p_l\partial p_m} = \frac{\partial h_l}{\partial p_m} \tag{1.30}$$

That is, with the compensated demand, cross-substitution effects are identical (the matrix of substitution effects is symmetric). Secondly, the matrix of substitution effects is negative semidefinite. This follows immediately from the fact that $\partial h_m/\partial p_l = \partial^2 E/\partial p_m\partial p_l$ and the expenditure function is concave in prices (recall E1).

Substitutes and Complements. The symmetry of the compensated demand cross-substitution effect and the Slutsky equation implies that, for *ordinary* demand curves,

$$\frac{\partial d_m}{\partial p_l} + z_l{}^0\frac{\partial d_m}{\partial y} = \frac{\partial d_l}{\partial p_m} + z_m{}^0\frac{\partial d_l}{\partial y} \tag{1.31}$$

for all l and m. Pairs of goods for which $\partial d_m/\partial p_l > 0$ are termed **gross substitutes**, and they are termed **gross complements** when that inequality is reversed. While this categorization is commonly used, it is unsatisfactory in many applications because the gross effect that a change in p_l has on the demand for commodity m includes (as is evident in the Slutsky equation) an income effect which is unrelated to fundamental complementarity or substitutability. A pair of commodities can be found to be gross complements, for example, even when totally unrelated to each other (steaks and automobile gasoline come to mind) simply because the income effect of a rise in the price of one results in a decline in demand for the other.

A second difficulty with the gross substitutability (complementarity) definition is its potential inconsistency. Because income effects need not be symmetrical, it might be that $\partial d_m/\partial p_l > 0$ while $\partial d_l/\partial p_m < 0$ – that is, commodities l and m might be either substitutes or complements depending on which price change is considered.

For these reasons it is useful in many circumstances not to use gross substitutability or complementarity based on the ordinary demand function, but to employ instead the notion of (Hicks–Allen) **net substitutability** $\partial h_m/\partial p_l = \partial h_l/\partial p_m > 0$ or **complementarity** $\partial h_m/\partial p_l = \partial h_l/\partial p_m < 0$, defined on the cross-effects associated with the compensated demand curve. It is of note that, while net cross-substitution effects are symmetrical, the associated elasticities are not:

$$\varepsilon^*_{lm} = \frac{\partial h_l}{\partial p_m} \frac{p_m}{z_l{}^0} \neq \frac{\partial h_m}{\partial p_l} \frac{p_l}{z_m{}^0} = \varepsilon^*_{ml}$$

An alternative frequently used measure of elasticity, termed the **Allen–Uzawa elasticity of substitution**, is given by the ratio

$$\xi^*_{lm} = \frac{\varepsilon^*_{lm}}{s_m}$$

and does have the property of symmetry ($\xi^*_{lm} = \xi^*_{ml}$), as the reader can quickly show. For the two-commodity case, Goldman and Uzawa (1964) show that ξ^*_{lm} measures the inverse of the curvature of the indifference contour, with high ξ^*_{lm} implying a nearly straight contour.

E1.9

Quadratic Utility and Linear Demand

Consider the frequently used quadratic strictly concave utility function

$$u(z_1, z_2) = a_1 z_1 + a_2 z_2 - \frac{b_1 z_1{}^2 + 2dz_1 z_2 + b_2 z_2{}^2}{2} \tag{1.32}$$

where parameters a_i and b_i are positive ($i = 1, 2$), $b_1 b_2 - d^2 > 0$, and $a_i b_j - a_i d > 0$ for $i \neq j$. This utility gives rise to linear ordinary demands, which explains its frequent use. The associated inverse demands are

$$p_1 = a_1 - b_1 z_1 - dz_2 \tag{1.33a}$$

$$p_2 = a_2 - dz_1 - b_2 z_2 \tag{1.33b}$$

for positive prices. It is straightforward to show that the goods are gross substitutes or complements according to whether the parameter d is respectively greater or less than zero. Moreover, the ordinary demand for each good is always negatively sloped and increases (decreases) with increases in the prices of the other good when the goods are substitutes (complements). For the "symmetric case," where $a_1 = a_2$ and $b_1 = b_2 = d$, the goods are perfect substitutes as expected. Finally, when $a_1 = a_2$ it is usual to use d/b_1b_2 as a measure of substitutability; this index ranges from zero when the goods are independent $(d = 0)$ to unity when they are perfect substitutes $(b_1 = b_2 = d)$.

1.3   Separability

It is usual in industrial economics analyses to deal only with a subset of firms in the economy. Generally, these are firms producing a collection of goods which are more or less good substitutes in demand for one another – an "industry."[8] This is the method of Marshallian partial equilibrium analysis, where price cross-effects with other goods are generally set aside as being of second order in importance. The basis in theory for this independence assumption lies in a separation of commodities in the consumer's utility function. More exactly, we say that the utility function $\hat{u}(z)$ is **(weakly) separable** into commodity groups a and b if it can be written in the form

$$\hat{u}(z) = \hat{u}(u^a(z^a)), u^b(z^b)) \tag{1.34}$$

where the vectors $z^a = [z_1 z_2 \ldots z_n]$ and $z^b = [z_{n+1} z_{n+1} \ldots z_M]$ define the commodities of the two groups, and $u^a(\cdot)$ and $u^b(\cdot)$ are subutility functions exclusively associated with z^a and z^b, rspectively. It is required that the utility function $u(\cdot)$ possess the usual continuity, strict quasi-concavity, and differentiability properties in "commodities" u^a and u^b, and in turn these subutilities must possess similar properties in their commodity arguments. In what way is separability in utility related to industry analyses?

1.3.1   Decomposition and Independence

Given that commodities are separable in utility as in (1.34), the individual's choice problem can be written as

$$\max_z u(u^a(z^a), u^b(z^b)) \tag{1.35a}$$

$$\text{s.t.} \sum_j p_j z_j + \sum_k p_k z_k = y \tag{1.35b}$$

where the $j = 1, 2, \ldots, n$ and $k = n + 1, n + 2, \ldots, M$ subscripts respectively index commodities in groups a and b. It is instructive to solve this problem in stages.

To begin this process, fix the quantities in group b at some specific levels, say $\bar{z}^b = [\bar{z}_{N+1} \bar{z}_{N+2} \ldots \bar{z}_M]$. Associated with this vector of consumptions there is an expenditure $\Sigma_k p_k \bar{z}_k = \bar{y}^b$ and some subutility value $u^b(\bar{z}^b)$. If $\bar{z}^b$ is in fact chosen to maximize u^b with the $\bar{y}^b$ income restriction (at fixed prices), then in the usual way there is an "indirect subutility" function $U^b(p^b, \bar{y}^b)$ with the

---

[8] There is also the question of "substitutability in supply," which is considered in chapter 2.

standard properties (here p^b is the vector of group b commodity prices). In turn, the consumer's problem becomes

$$\max_{z_j} \hat{u}(u^a(z^a), U^b(p^b, \bar{y}^b)) \tag{1.36a}$$

$$\text{s.t. } \sum_j p_j z_j = y - \bar{y}^b \equiv y^a \tag{1.36b}$$

Given y and $\bar{y}^b$, then y^a is also fixed and (1.36) has a solution equivalent to that occurring in the problem

$$\max_{z_j} u^a(z^a) \tag{1.37a}$$

$$\text{s.t. } \sum_j p_j z_j = y^a \tag{1.37b}$$

since u is increasing in u^a. The solution can be written as **conditional demand functions** for the commodities of group a, that is,

$$z_j = \hat{d}_j(p, y) = d_j(p^a, y^a) \tag{1.38}$$

for each commodity j in the group. It is important to note that these conditional demands are expressed only as a function of the prices p^a of commodities in the group and the expenditures y^a allocated to the group.

We must be careful not to misunderstand this independence. It is *not* the case that the demand for commodities in group a, for example, is entirely independent of the prices of commodities in group b or of total expenditures. Rather, it is only that total expenditures and the prices of commodities outside the group enter into the group a conditional demands by their effect on the group a expenditure y^a. This means only that, given that y^a is taken to be fixed, we can then ignore the prices of all commodities outside the group.

E1.10

Separable Utility

The implications of the separability structure can be further clarified by considering several derivatives. Particularly, differentiate the conditional demands (1.38) with respect to the price p_k of a commodity not in group a and total income to obtain

$$\frac{\partial z_j}{\partial p_k} = \frac{\partial d_j}{\partial y^a} \frac{\partial y^a}{\partial p_k} \tag{1.39a}$$

$$\frac{\partial z_j}{\partial y} = \frac{\partial d_j}{\partial y^a} \frac{\partial y^a}{\partial y} \tag{1.39b}$$

for every j in a. These equations again recognize the "external" effect on z_j demand only through y^a. Dividing and rearranging terms gives (when $\partial y^a / \partial y \neq 0$)

$$\frac{\partial z_j}{\partial p_k} = \frac{\partial y^a/\partial p_k}{\partial y^a/\partial y} \frac{\partial z_j}{\partial y}$$

$$= \theta^a \frac{\partial z_j}{\partial y} \tag{1.40}$$

where θ^a is a factor of proportionality which is the same for all goods in group a (but is dependent on the specific price of commodity k). Using some second commodity in group a, call it l, we obtain

$$\frac{\partial z_l/\partial p_k}{\partial z_j/\partial p_k} = \frac{\partial z_l/\partial y}{\partial z_j/\partial y} \tag{1.41}$$

The ratio of external price effects on any two group a commodities is equal to the ratio of total expenditure effects.

Decomposition by Separation. It helps our intuition to note briefly the two-step process lying behind the solution of the general problem (1.35). For an arbitrary $y^a > 0$, the first step is to solve the problem (1.37), which yields the indirect subutility $U^a(p^a, y^a)$. A similar problem solved for group b yields $U^b(p^b, y^b)$. There is, in turn, the second-level problem where the group income allocation y^a is the choice variable

$$\max_{y^a} u(U^a(p^a, y^a), U^b(p^b, y - y^a)) \tag{1.42}$$

The solution y^{a0} to this problem and then the calculation $y^{b0} = y - y^{a0}$ provide the income levels to be used in the "commodity problems" of the form (1.37) which finally yield the optimal z^{a0} and z^{b0}.

1.3.2   Quasi-linear Utility

Focus now on two commodities, 1 and 2, and assume that all other commmodities, represented by a bundle 0, enter additivity into the consumer's utility function, that is,

$$\hat{u}(z_0, z_1, z_2) = u(z_1, z_2) + z_0 \tag{1.43}$$

The subutility u is assumed to have the usual monotone increasing strict concavity in z_1 and z_2, but in contrast $\hat{u}$ exhibits constant marginal utility in z_0. Because of the additivity, $\hat{u}$ is said to be **strongly separable** in the two subutilities, and, because we deal with a single "all other" commodity, without loss of generality that subutility function can be chosen to be linear. It is in turn usual to say that $\hat{u}$ is *quasi-linear*, or is linear in the "all other" commodity z_0.

The quasi-linear utility is to be maximized subject to the budget constraint

$$p_1 z_1 + p_2 z_2 + z_0 = y \tag{1.44}$$

where commodity zero is chosen as numeraire. Stationarity conditions for a solution are

$$u_1 - \lambda p_1 = 0 \tag{1.45a}$$

$$u_2 - \lambda p_2 = 0 \qquad (1.45b)$$

$$1 - \lambda = 0 \qquad (1.45c)$$

and the original budget constraint. As a consquence of the quasi-linearity, the marginal utilities of commodities 1 and 2 are also the marginal subutilities: $\hat{u}_1 \equiv u_1$ and $\hat{u}_2 \equiv u_2$. Moreover, upon eliminating λ, we obtain $u_1(\cdot) = p_1$ and $u_2(\cdot) = p_2$ at the optimum: the marginal utilities of goods 1 and 2 are simply adjusted to equal their price (again, with z_0 as numeraire).

Quasi-linear Indirect Utility. Let the demands $z_1{}^0 = d_1(p_1, p_2)$ and $z_2{}^0 = d_2(p_1, p_2)$ solve the stationarity conditions (1.45). Because prices equal marginal utilities in the way indicated, these demands are independent of the income level y. As a result, the budget constraint determines the optimal consumption of the "outside good" simply as

$$z_0{}^0 = y - p_1 d_1(p_1, p_2) \, p_2 d_2(p_1, p_2)$$

Substituting for $z_0{}^0$, $z_1{}^0$, and $z_2{}^0$ in (1.43) produces the indirect utility

$$U(p_1, p_2, y^0) = \{u(d_1(p_1, p_2), d_2(p_1, p_2))$$
$$- p_1 d_1(p_1, p_2) - p_2 d_2(p_1, p_2)\} + y$$
$$= V(p_1, p_2) + y \qquad (1.46)$$

which is additive and linear in y, or also *quasi-linear*. It is because of this linearity in income that the quasi-linear utility (1.43) is frequently referred to as the case of "constant marginal utility of income."

E1.11 ——————————————————————————————

Quasi-linear Utility and Quasi-linear Indirect Utility

A case of limited practical use, but with some interesting analytical properties, is that where utility is quasi-linear and of the specific form $\hat{u}(z) = z_1{}^2 z_2 + z_0$. The associated demand functions for goods 1 and 2 are quickly shown to be

$$z_2{}^0 = \frac{p_1}{2p_2{}^{1/2}}$$
$$z_1{}^0 = p_2{}^{1/2}$$

The budget constraint in turn solves for the optimal z_0:

$$z_0{}^0 = y - \frac{3p_1 p_2{}^{1/2}}{2} \geqslant 0$$

Then the indirect utility function resulting from the obvious substitutions is

$$U(p_1, p_2, y^0) = - p_1 p_2{}^{1/2} + y$$

It is important to observe that U is additive, linear, and increasing in y, and a decreasing function of the prices. That is, U is quasi-linear in the same sense that $\hat{u}$ is.

1.4   Consumer Welfare

It is frequently of interest to determine whether some specific industry reorganization or trade practice improves or diminishes consumer welfare. For example, the level of advertising used by a firm may have economic benefits, such as decreasing the consumer costs of search. Against these benefits there are the increased costs to the firm of the advertising and, perhaps, a higher product price at equilibrium. How should these several benefits and costs be compared? In part the answer depends on the welfare gain or loss associated with the price change. Measuring this welfare effect is straightforward task, as the essential tools for the analysis are now at our disposal.

1.4.1   Compensating Variation

Suppose that the price of some commodity m is increased while all other prices are held constant. As remarked earlier, it is possible to compensate the individual for such a price change by varying his (money) income. Of particular interest is the level of compensation which is necessary to exactly "balance" the price change in the sense that the individual's utility is unaffected, so that he is indifferent between the original and post-change (with compensation) positions. Restricting attention to two commodities with initial prices (p_1^0, p_2^0), suppose that p_1^0 changes to $p_1^1 > p_1^0$ with p_2^0 held constant. The utility preserving compensation can then be represented as the change in expenditures.[9]

$$CV(\Delta p_1, u^0) \equiv E(p_1^1, p_2^0, u^0) - E(p_1^0, p_2^0, u^0) \tag{1.47}$$

where the utility level $u^0(p_1^0, p_2^0, y^0)$ is associated with the original prices (p_1^0, p_2^0) and income y^0 and $E(\cdot)$ is the expenditure function. $CV(\Delta p_1, u^0)$ is defined as the **compensating variation** (income compensation) associated with the indicated price change Δp_1.[10] Thinking of this change as a sequence of small changes we have, in turn,

$$CV(\Delta p_1, u^0) = \int_{p_1^0}^{p_1^1} \frac{\partial E(p_1, p_2^0, u^0)}{\partial p_1} \, dp_1$$

$$= \int_{p_1^0}^{p_1^1} h_1(p_1, p_2^0, u^0) \, dp_1 \tag{1.48}$$

where we use the relationship between the expenditure and the compensated demand functions from (1.21). That is, the compensating variation for a price change in some single price is the enclosed area bounded by the compensated demand curve and the associated price lines.

In figure 1.3 the compensating variation is indicated by the shaded area $p_1^0 p_1^1 BA$. Note also in the figure that the compensating variation is positive:

---

[9] More generally, p_2 can be thought of as the vector of all prices except that of commodity 1.

[10] There is also the complementary **equivalent variation**: the amount of income necessary to compensate an individual if an economic change did not occur to make him as well off as if it did. That is, $E(p_1^1, p_2^0, u^1) - E(p_1^0, p_2^0, u^1)$ measures the equivalent variation. The difference between the concepts is the level of utility at which the expenditure difference is measured: the compensating variation is based on the *original* utility level and the equvalent variation is based on the *final* level.

income compensation must be paid to the consumer to make him as well off at the higher price for commodity 1. If money income in this amount is *not* paid, then the price increase is said to impose a welfare loss equal to the compensating variation. An alternative expression for CV is therefore

$$U(p_1{}^1, p_2{}^0, y^0 + CV) = U(p_1{}^0, p_2{}^0, y^0) \tag{1.49}$$

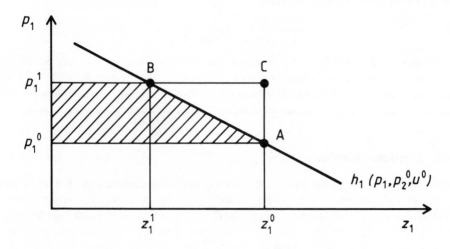

Figure 1.3
Compensating variation

E1.12 ———————————————————————————

Compensated Demand and Compensating Variation

Consider the consumer with utility $u(z_1, z_2) = z_1 z_2 + z_0$ and the associated ordinary demands, indirect utility, expenditure function, and compensated demands:

$$z_1 = \frac{y}{2p_1}$$

$$z_2 = \frac{y}{2p_2}$$

$$U(p, y) = \frac{y^2}{4p_1 p_2}$$

$$E(p, u) = 2(p_1 p_2 u)^{1/2}$$

$$h_1(p, u) = \left(\frac{p_2 u}{p_1}\right)^{1/2}$$

Let $y = \$10$, $p_1{}^0 = \$2$, and $p_2{}^0 = \$1$ be initial conditions, giving (Marshallian) demands $z_1{}^0 = 2.5$ and $z_2{}^0 = 5$, and the utility $u^0 = 12.5$. Note in turn that

$E(p^0, u^0) = 2\{2(12.5)\}^{1/2} = 10 = y^0$, which checks, as does $h_1(p^0, u^0) = (12.5/2)^{1/2} = 2.5 = z_1^0$.

Suppose now that the price of commodity 1 rises to $p_1^1 = 3$. Using (1.47) we can calculate the compensating variation as

$$CV = 2(3 \times 1 \times 12.5)^{1/2} - 2(2 \times 1 \times 12.5)^{1/2} = 2.247$$

Using (1.49), alternatively, we have

$$\frac{(10 + CV)^2}{4 \times 3 \times 1} = \frac{10^2}{4 \times 2 \times 1}$$

which also solves for CV = 2.247. If we were to award the individual $2.247 as the price of commodity 1 increases from $2 to $3 (other things being equal) his utility would remain unchanged; otherwise he incurs a $2.247 welfare loss.

1.4.2 Consumer Surplus

A practical difficulty with the compensating variation measure is that it cannot be calculated without information concerning the consumer's compensated demand curve or, equivalently, his indirect utility. In applied economic analysis we will have at best an estimate of the ordinary demand curve for a commodity, and it is therefore useful to measure the welfare effects of a price change on this basis. In this regard, it is usual to use the (Marshallian) **consumer surplus**, defined as the area "under" the ordinary demand equation between two prices:

$$CS(\Delta p_1, y^0) = \int_{p_1^0}^{p_1^1} d_1(p_1, p_2^0, y^0) \, dp_1$$

$$= - \int_{p_1^0}^{p_1^1} \frac{\partial U(p_1, p_2^0, y^0)/\partial p_1}{\partial U(p_1, p_2^0, y^0)/\partial y} \, dp_1 \qquad (1.50)$$

where the final equation uses Roy's identity.

The consumer surplus integral differs from that defining the compensating variation in equation (1.48). To keep the individual at the same indifference level in (1.48), the income level (which enters both numerator and denominator in (1.50)) must be constantly adjusted along the path of the price change from p_1^0 to p_1^1. This produces the difference between ordinary demand (consumer surplus) and compensated demand (compensating variation) (see figure 1.2).

Compensating Variation and Consumer Surplus. In general $CS(\Delta p_1, y^0)$ and $CV(\Delta p_1, u^0)$ do not provide the same measure of welfare. This difference is apparent from a slight rearrangement of the Slutsky equation

$$\frac{\partial h_1(p_1, p_2^0, u^0)}{\partial p_1} - \frac{\partial d_1(p_1, p_2^0, y^0)}{\partial p_1} = z_1 \frac{\partial z_1(p_1, p_2^0, y^0)}{\partial y} \qquad (1.51)$$

Notice that the compensated and ordinary demands will be identical, and $CS(\Delta p_1, y^0) = CV(\Delta p_1, u^0)$ if the two derivatives on the left-hand side are equal. From Roy's identity, a *sufficient* condition for the right-hand side of (1.51) to equal zero (and therefore for the compensated and ordinary demands to be identical) is that both $\partial^2 U(p_1, p_2{}^0, y^0)/\partial y \partial p_1 = 0$ and $\partial^2 U(p_1, p_2{}^0, y^0)/\partial y^2 = 0$. These conditions obviously occur when there is constant marginal utility of income.[11]

E1.13 ──

Consumers' Surplus

Note from Roy's identity that

$$d_1(p, y) = - \frac{\partial U(p, y)/\partial p_1}{\partial U(p, y)/\partial y}$$

so that

$$CS = \int_{p_1{}^0}^{p_1{}^1} d_1(p, y^0) = - \int_{p_1{}^0}^{p_1{}^1} \frac{\partial U(p, y)/\partial p_1}{\partial U(p, y)/\partial y} \, dp_1$$

If the marginal utility of income is constant, the integral can be evaluated as

$$CS = \frac{U(p_1{}^1, p_2{}^0, y^0) - U(p_1{}^0, p_2{}^0, y)}{\partial v(p^0, y^0)/\partial y}$$

Suppose now that the underlying utility function is quasi-linear in some numeraire commodity z_0. Then, from section 1.3.2, indirect utility is of the form $U(p_1, p_2, y) = V(p_1, p_2) + y$. The marginal utility of income is constant in this case, and, using Roy's identity, the demand for good 1 is given simply as the negative of the derivative of V. In turn, the integral of demand is just $V(p_1, p_2)$ and consumer surplus measures the price change directly in terms of utility.

══

---

[11] Willig (1976) and Varian (1978, ch. 7) show that, even when the marginal utility is not exactly constant, the percentage difference $(CV - CS)/CS$ is of the order $\eta CS/2y$, which is probably small in practice. See chapter 2, section 2.4, for a similar proof.

2 Production and Cost, Competition and Monopoly

There are two general paradigms by which industrial markets have been studied. The model economy in the first paradigm is described by specific collections of agents, producers, and consumers along with production and exchange technologies. Despite their prominence, the pivotal unit of analysis is not these agents but an omnipresent *central auctioneer* who directs all exchange activity and otherwise manages the business of the economy. The way in which the auctioneer goes about his work in this first market paradigm is critical and deserves early attention.

Walrasian Paradigm. As the label suggests, the auctioneer conducts an auction. Initially, a tentative set of exchange rates among tradable goods is called out. Using this information, agents make plans for production and consumption decisions. Being generally different from endowments, these plans provide an incentive for each agent to enter into trade. A provisional *trading plan*, which lists buy and sell orders (quantities) at the announced rates of exchange, is fashioned by each agent subject to the requirement that the value of the commodities offered for sale equal the value of those offered to buy (at the announced rates of exchange). The central auctioneer collects these trading plans and then sums up the individual offers to determine whether or not these are consistent in the aggregate (that is, whether or not the total quantity demanded equals the total quantity offered for sale). If the aggregate totals are consistent, the tentative rates of commodity exchange are declared final, all trades are executed, and production and consumption are carried out. These equilibrium levels of production, exchange, and consumption constitute the observed events of the economy.

If in aggregating the individual plans the total supply is not equal to total demand, the central auctioneer announces a new set of exchange rates which will encourage increased production and decreased consumption of commmodities for which there is excess demand, and conversely for those for which there is excess supply. In turn, agents reformulate production and consumption plans and issue revised (tentative) trading plans. The auctioneer aggregates these just as before and again compares total supply and demand for each commodity. If these are equal then all plans are executed; otherwise the process continues, with information being transmitted between the auctioneer and the agents on rates of exchange and trading plans.

This is the **Walrasian** view of the economic system. It is, to be sure, an abstract picture of real economies, with the centralized coordination of trading plans and the execution of trading contracts both being unrealistic devices. More generally, individuals buy and sell goods in many markets, dealing directly with other individuals and using a single commodity of account.

Marshallian Paradigm. The above comments do not mean that the Walrasian paradigm is irrelevant for purposes of economic analysis. It is a useful model in answering some questions, but to understand the economics of industrial organization something more is usually needed – something that will provide more detail and greater intuition about actual production and exchange decisions and their institutional setting. For this reason, the alternative **Marshallian** paradigm is usually adopted. This approach differs from that of Walras principally in that it makes use of separate markets wherein different commodities are traded. With M commodities there are $M - 1$ markets, one for each commodity except for a commodity of account (numeraire). Given that each commodity is traded in a distinct market, it is then usual to analyze price and quantity (and quality) decisions in terms of demand and supply conditions that pertain to each separate market. (This is not proper in the Walrasian paradigm, since only a single general market obtains there and the demand and supply of every commodity is necessarily expressed in terms of the demand and supply of every other.) Using the Marshallian assumptions we are therefore able to focus attention on the behavior of individuals in their consumption activity and (collections of) individuals in their production activity. In particular, we can focus on the decision behavior of specific firms and industries as in this chapter.

2.1 Theory of the Firm

We begin with a static and certain market economy in which $j = 1, 2, \ldots, J$ firms are the sole source of production. Each firm selects from a given list of $k = 1, 2, \ldots, K$ factors as inputs in a transformation process creating consumption commodities as outputs. To be specific, let $x_k{}^j \geq 0$ be the quantity of factor k used by firm j; there is, in turn, the **factor plan** $x^j = [x_1{}^j x_2{}^j \ldots x_k{}^j]$ listing j's selection of all K factors. On the output side it is convenient for the moment to assume that each firm j produces just one good (commodity), which is measured in quantity by z^j. A **production plan** $[z^j \ x^j]$ for firm is a $(K + 1)$-vector associating an output level with a factor plan. The technology of the firm is, in turn, described by the feasible set of such production plans.

In this early development it is sufficient and convenient to deal with a typical producer. Thus, where there is little chance of misunderstanding, the firm superscript is omitted and we write the scalar $z = z^j$ and the K-vector $x = x^i$.

2.1.1 Technology

An investigation of the technical details of production is not required for our present purposes. All that are important are the inviolate constraints which technology imposes on the choice of production plans. Such an imposition can be quite simple: we need only list those production plans which represent technically feasible transformations of inputs into outputs, and exclude those which do not. Plans which are feasible, by whatever rules the technology imposes, are said to belong to a **production set** $F(z, x)$. While for some purposes this is the most direct way of specifying the technology of production, it is useful here to reverse our thinking somewhat and, for each given output level, deal with the associated **factor requirements** set

$$X(z) = \{x \geq 0 | [z \ x] \in F(z, x)\} \tag{2.1}$$

Although we will not say much about the limits of the firm's technology, some minimal usual assumptions can be made. These are stated as properties of $X(z)$ as follows.

> X1 **Regularity:** every $z \geq 0$ can be produced by some vector of inputs, and if $x = 0$, then $z = 0$. Moreover, $X(z)$ is a closed subset of $R_+{}^K$.
>
> X2 **Free disposal:** if x is in $X(z)$ then so are all $\hat{x}$ when $\hat{x} \geq x$.[1]
>
> X3 **Strict convexity:** if x and $\hat{x}$ both produce z, then the inputs $\theta x + (1 - \theta)\hat{x}$, where $0 \leq \theta \leq 1$, can also produce z. Moreover, if $0 < \theta < 1$ then a quantity $\hat{z} > z$ is produced by the combination.

Technical Efficiency. Not all the technically feasible production plans given by $F(z, x)$ are of interest, for some may require greater factor quantities to produce a given (or smaller) output than others. For this reason, it is usual to further restrict attention to plans which produce the maximum level of output for each given factor plan. More exactly, a production plan $[z^* \ x^*] \in F(z, x)$ is said to be **technically efficient** if there exists no other plan $[\hat{z} \ \hat{x}] \in F(z, x)$ where $\hat{z} \geq z^*$ and $\hat{x} \leq x^*$. While in general equilibrium analyses it is often convenient to deal with the production set without a prior restriction to technically efficient plans, that will not be the case here and we will explicitly impose such efficiency in production at the onset. The restriction is generally part of the definition of a production function either directly or by the description of its level contours.[2]

The **production function**

$$z = f(x) \geq 0 \tag{2.2}$$

describes technically efficient production plans when $f(\cdot)$ identifies only the maximum feasible output level for any input vector. It is usual to assume that f has continous partial derivatives of at least second order, with all first partial derivatives being nonnegative over the relevant range of output. Associated with $f(x)$ there are level contours, termed **isoquants**, given by

$$L(z) = \{x \geq 0 \mid z = f(x) \text{ is satisfied for the given output } z\} \tag{2.3}$$

When the production technology satisfies conditions X1–X3 and only technically efficient plans are considered, the resulting $f(x)$ is said to be a

---

[1] By $\hat{x} \geq x$ we mean that every element of $\hat{x}$ is at least as large as every element of x.

[2] We will not inquire here into the conditions that the production set must satisfy in order to define a suitable production function. See Malinvaud (1972, pp. 48–61).

neoclassical production function. Unless stated otherwise, we will assume these neoclassical properties.

Leontieff and Cobb–Douglas Technologies

A variety of specific restrictions can be placed on the firm's technology. One broad class occurs when it is required that factors be used only in fixed proportions. Such **Leontieff** production technologies, with two factors x_1 and x_2, have the following description:

$$f(x_1, x_2) = \min[\alpha x_1, \beta x_2]$$

and

$$L(z) = \{x_1, x_2 \geqslant 0 \mid z = \min[\alpha x_1, \beta x_2]\}$$

with $\alpha, \beta \geqslant 0$ as parameters.

More generally, the technology is assumed to permit substitutions among inputs. One of the simplest and most frequently used cases in this regard is the **Cobb–Douglas** production technology which, again with two factors, is described by

$$f(x_1, x_2) = x_1{}^\alpha x_2{}^{1-\alpha}$$

and

$$L(z) = \{x_1, x_2 \geqslant 0 \mid y = x_1{}^\alpha x_2{}^{1-\alpha}\}$$

In this case, $0 < \alpha < 1$ is the single parameter of the technology and the rate at which x_1 can be substituted for x_2 to produce a fixed output level is given by the differential

$$df = \alpha x_1{}^{\alpha-1} x_2{}^{1-\alpha} \, dx_1 + (1 - \alpha) x_1{}^\alpha x_2{}^{-\alpha} \, dx_2 = 0$$

which solves for

$$\frac{dx_2}{dx_1} = -\frac{\alpha}{1 - \alpha} \frac{x_2}{x_1}$$

2.1.2 Maximizing Output, Minimizing Cost

Suppose that factors are purchased competitively at constant unit prices $r_k(k = 1, 2, \ldots, K)$. Then the **cost equation**

$$c(x, r) = \sum_k r_k x_k \tag{2.4}$$

determines the firm's total cost of using any given input combination. Because factor prices are fixed, all factor combinations which lead to the same cost lie on an **isocost (hyper)plane**.

Economic Efficiency. The production function defines technically efficient factor combinations – the minimum amount of any factor that will provide a specific level of output given the level of other factors. **Economically efficient** production plans satisfy this technical standard and, as an added requirement, provide minimum cost for any given output level. That is, any given output $z > 0$ and factor combination $x > 0$ describes an economically efficient plan iff they jointly solve

$$\min_k \sum r_k x_k \text{ s.t. } f(x) = z \tag{2.5}$$

Stationarity conditions for this problem are

$$r_k - \lambda f_k = 0 \qquad \text{for all } k \tag{2.6}$$

and the original constraint.[3] λ is the usual Lagrange multiplier and the K derivatives $f_k = \partial f(x)/\partial x_k$ are **marginal (physical) products** of the factors (in producing output). Dividing any two of these solution equations gives

$$\frac{f_k}{f_l} = \frac{r_k}{r_l} \tag{2.7}$$

At the optimum, the ratio of marginal products equals the ratio of factor prices.

The slope of the isoquants, termed the **rate of technical substitution** (RTS), is the rate at which factors can be substituted in the production process to keep output constant. The RTS is everywhere equal to the ratio of marginal products.[4]

Duality. A problem related to minimizing costs subject to producing a given output level is that which maximizes output subject to a cost constraint:

$$\max_x f(x) \text{ s.t. } \sum_k r_k x_k = c \tag{2.8}$$

where c is some given cost level. Stationarity conditions for this solution are

$$f_k - \lambda r_k = 0 \qquad \text{for all } k \tag{2.9}$$

---

[3] With constant factor prices, strict convexity of the isoquants (strictly quasi-concave f) assures sufficiency and solution uniqueness.

[4] This can be shown quite easily using two inputs x_1 and x_2 and a differentiable and continuous production function $z = f(x_1, x_2)$. For this case, the isoquant associated with specific quantity z^* can be written as $x_2 = g(x_1, z)$ where g is decreasing in x_1. That is, $g(x_1, z^*)$ is the minimum quantity of x_2 that produces z^* when factor 1 is used in amount x_1. Substituting this in the production function gives $z^* = f(x_1, g(x_1, z))$. As this holds identically, it can be differentiated by x_1 to yield

$$\frac{\partial f(x_1, g(x_1, z^*))}{\partial x_1} + \frac{\partial f(x_1, g(x_1, z^*))}{\partial g(x_1, z^*)} \frac{dg(x_1, z^*)}{dx_1} = 0$$

Rearranging and substituting this last expression gives

$$-\frac{dg(x_1, z^*)}{dx_1} = \frac{\partial f(x_1, x_2)/\partial x_1}{\partial f(x_1, x_2)/\partial x_2}$$

The left-hand side is the negative of the isoquant slope, the RTS of x_1 for x_2 to maintain z^*. The right-hand side is the ratio of marginal products for factors 1 and 2. More generally,

$$RTS_{k,l}(x) = \frac{\partial f(x)/\partial x_k}{\partial f(x)/\partial x_l} \qquad \text{for all } k \text{ and } l$$

and the original cost constraint. Dividing any two of equations (2.9) again implies the equality of the marginal product ratio and the factor price ratio, which is identical with the solution conditions for the constrained cost minimization.

The ratio of marginal products (RTS) is everywhere the slope of the isoquant. Thus, in the constrained cost minimization problem the geometric interpretation of the optimality condition is that the firm adopts the factor plan where the (minimum) isocost hyperplane is just tangent to the given isoquant (see figure 2.1). For the constrained output maximization, the geometric interpretation is similar, but "inverted": the firm adopts the factor plan where the (greatest) isoquant is just tangent to the given isocost. The linearity of costs in the factors and the strict convexity of the isoquants guarantee a unique solution to each of these problems. It is apparent, moreover, that when the minimum cost – determined from equation (2.5) – is used in the constrained output maximization problem, then the optimal input vector will be identical for the two problems. That is, if the solution of $\{\max_x f(x) \text{ s.t. } \Sigma_k r_k x_k = c^0\}$ is x^0 and this implies an output level $z^0 = f(x^0)$, then the solution of $\{\min_x \Sigma_k r_k x_k \text{ s.t. } f(x) = z^0\}$ must also be x^0 and implies $c^0 = \Sigma_k r_k x_k^0$. Because of this relationship, these two problems are said to be **dual** to each other.

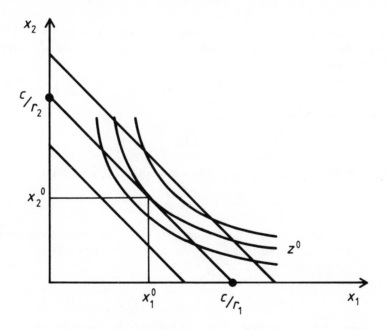

Figure 2.1
Cost and production duality

2.1.3   Costs and Duality

The cost-minimizing combination of factors, the solution to equation (2.5), obviously depends on the output level and factor prices, that is,

$$x_k{}^0 = d_k(z, r) \qquad \text{for all factors } k \qquad (2.10)$$

Each $d_k(\cdot)$ derives from the equations (2.9) and can be thought of as a **conditional factor demand function** (conditional on the output z). Substituting these in the cost equation (2.4) defines the **cost function**[5]

$$c(z, r) = \sum_k r_k d_k(z, r) \qquad (2.11)$$

Note that $c(z, r)$ is the firm's *minimum* cost of producing z with given factor prices r, assuming that the firm is constrained to some given technology $z = f(x)$.

E2.2 ──

Marginal Cost and Marginal Physical Product

The properties of the cost function are clearly related to those of the underlying production technology. To see this, differentiate (2.11) to give

$$c'(z, r) \equiv \frac{\partial c(z, r)}{\partial z} = r_1 \frac{\partial d_1}{\partial z} + r_2 \frac{\partial d_2}{\partial z} \qquad (2.12)$$

for the case of two inputs. Here, $c'(z, r)$ defines the firm's marginal cost, that is, the total cost rate of change with output. Using d_1 and d_2, write the production function as

$$f(d_1(z, r), d_2(z, r)) = z$$

and differentiate to yield

$$\frac{\partial f}{\partial x_1} \frac{\partial d_1}{\partial z} + \frac{\partial f}{\partial x_2} \frac{\partial d_2}{\partial z} = 1 \qquad (2.13)$$

Substituting for the marginal products from the optimality condition (2.6) gives

$$r_1 \frac{\partial d_1}{dz} + r_2 \frac{\partial d_2}{\partial z} = \lambda^0$$

where λ^0 is the value of the Lagrange multiplier at the optimum. Comparing this last equation with (2.12) note that $\lambda^0 = c'(z, r)$. Finally, substituting $c'(z, r)$ for λ^0 gives

$$c'(z, r) = \frac{r_1}{\partial f/\partial x_1} = \frac{r_2}{\partial f/\partial x_2} \qquad (2.14)$$

These equations inform us that, when production is optimal, $c'(z, r)$ equals factor price divided by marginal product for every factor. This is an explicit relationship between the firm's production technology (function) and its cost (function).

══

[5] $c(z, r)$ is perhaps best termed an *indirect* cost function (for example, recall the definition of the indirect utility in chapter 1). It is usual, however, to drop the "indirect" label so that we must then distinguish between the cost function of inputs and output.

It is of importance that the cost function, being derived from the cost minimization problem subject to the production function constraint, must reflect the limitations (and opportunities) of the underlying technology. Our intent is to show that the duality relationship provides a straightforward basis for determining the properties of any cost function from that of the underlying technology, and conversely. The following "derivative property" is a useful intermediate result in this regard.

> **Shepard's lemma.** (Derivative Property of the Cost Function) (Shepard, 1953). Let $d_k(z, r)$ be the conditional factor k demand. When $c(z, r)$ is differentiable at positive prices r and output z,
>
> $$d_k(z, r) = \frac{\partial c(z, r)}{\partial r_k} \qquad \text{for all } k \qquad (2.15)$$

Proof of this proposition is omitted here as it is analytically similar to that given for Hotelling's theorem in section 1.2.1.

E2.3

Production and Cost Duality

It is generally possible to identify the production technology of the firm from a knowledge of its cost function. To see this in a simple context, consider a cost function dependent on only two factors

$$c(z, r) = z r_1^{\alpha} r_2^{1-\alpha}$$

Using the derivative property gives conditional demands

$$x_1(r, z) = \frac{\partial c}{\partial r_1} = \alpha z \frac{r_2}{r_1}^{1-\alpha} \qquad (2.16a)$$

$$x_2(r, z) = \frac{\partial c}{\partial r_2} = (1 - \alpha) z \frac{r_2}{r_1}^{-\alpha} \qquad (2.16b)$$

Solving these for the price ratio yields

$$\frac{r_2}{r_1} = \frac{x_1}{\alpha z}^{1/(1-\alpha)} \qquad (2.17a)$$

and

$$\frac{r_2}{r_1} = \left\{ \frac{x_2}{z(1 - \alpha)} \right\}^{-1/\alpha} \qquad (2.17b)$$

respectively. Equating the right-hand sides of these and solving for the output z finally gives

$$z = A x_1^{\alpha} x_2^{1-\alpha}$$

where $A = 1\{\alpha^{\alpha}(1 - \alpha)^{1-\alpha}\}$. This, as the reader will recall, is simply the Cobb–Douglas production technology.

Costs Linear in Output. When the production function exhibits constant returns to scale (is linearly homogeneous), it is intuitive that the cost function is linear in quantity produced. That intuition is supported by the above example and is more generally correct. To confirm this, suppose that $\hat{x}$ is the minimum cost combination producing one unit of output, that is $c(1, r) = \Sigma_k r_k \hat{x}_k$. If it is assumed that the technology has constant returns, then $z\hat{x}$ is a feasible factor combination for producing the alternative quantity z. If we can show that $\hat{x}$ is also the minimum cost factor combination for z, then the linearity relationship is proved. We proceed by contradiction. Suppose that some different combination x^* produces z more cheaply at prices r, that is, $\Sigma_k r_k x_k^* < \Sigma_k r_k (z x_k)$. If this were true, then $\Sigma_k r_k (x_k^*/z) < \Sigma_k r_k \hat{x}_k$ would hold for strictly positive outputs. This inequality, however, contradicts the definition of $\hat{x}$ as the minimum cost method of producing one unit. Thus, when the production function has constant returns to scale, the cost function can be written multiplicatively as $c(z, r) = zc(1, r)$.

Because of the underlying relationship between homogeneous and homothetic functions it is natural to ask next about the form of the cost function when the production function is homothetic. To answer this question, begin with the general homothetic technology $z = F(f(x))$ where f is linearly homogeneous and $F' = \partial F/\partial f > 0$. Let $\omega = F^{-1}(z) = f(x)$. Then the cost function for ω can be written as

$$c(\omega, r) = \omega c(1, r) = c(1, r)F^{-1}(z) \qquad (2.18)$$

from the homogeneous case. That is, with homothetic production functions the associated cost functions are separable (multiplicative) functions of output and factor prices. The linearly homogeneous production function is, of course, simply a special instance where F^{-1} exhibits strict proportionality.

2.1.4 Profit Maximization

For many purposes it is simplest to analyze firm behavior in terms of revenues and costs expressed as a function of output. In such analyses the notions of marginal cost function $c'(\cdot)$ and average cost function $AC(\cdot)$ arise naturally. There are defined simply as

$$c'(z, r) \equiv \frac{\partial c(z, r)}{\partial z} \qquad (2.19a)$$

and

$$AC(z, r) \equiv \frac{c(z, r)}{z} \qquad (2.19b)$$

Since this last equation holds identically it can be differentiated to yield

$$c'(z, r) = AC(z, r) + \frac{\partial AC(z, r)}{\partial z} \qquad (2.20)$$

which relates the two cost functions.

The output-constrained cost minimization problem examined above determines the least expensive means of producing any prescribed output. It does not fully determine the firm's profit maximum. However, using the cost function which results from that earlier cost minimization, profit maximization becomes a straightforward task. Profits written in terms of the output level are given by $\pi(z) = p(z)z - c(z, r)$, and the problem is

$$\max_{z}\{p(z)z - c(z, r)\} \qquad (2.21)$$

where $p(z)$ is the inverse demand facing the firm and $p(z)z$ are revenues. The associated stationarity condition is the well-known requirement that the output level equate marginal revenue and marginal cost:[6]

$$p(z) + z\,\frac{\partial p(z)}{\partial z} = c'(z, r) \qquad (2.22a)$$

Dividing by marginal cost and rearranging gives

$$\frac{p(z) - c'(z, r)}{p(z)} = \frac{1}{\eta_F} \qquad (2.22b)$$

where η_F is the price elasticity of the *firm's* demand. The left-hand side of this last equation, the excess of price over marginal cost divided by price, is usually called the firm's **Lerner index**. Thus, at the output level which maximizes the firm's profit, the firm's Lerner index is equal to the inverse of its demand elasticity. Firms in a competitive market are price-takers in the sense that price equals marginal revenue on all units sold. This, in turn, requires that $\eta_F = \infty$ and the optimal output level for price-taking firms occurs with price equal to marginal cost.

Finally, it is important to note that the firm has an option not recognized by the stationarity condition (2.22). It can discontinue production and accept a loss limited by its fixed cost. This decision will be optimal if the maximum profits from producing any positive output level are negative and greater absolutely than fixed cost. Let F indicate fixed cost and define $\text{ATC} = \{c(z, r) + F\}/z$ as the average total cost. The firm will produce at a loss only if that loss is less than fixed cost, for revenues in excess of average cost allow the firm to cover a portion of its fixed cost.

2.2 Derived Demand

Up to this point the firm's profits have been expressed in terms of its output level using the cost function. It is also usual to write profits in terms of the factors employed and prices:

$$\pi(x; r, p) = pf(x) - \sum_{k} r_k x_k \qquad (2.23)$$

which uses the production function. The conditions for maximum profits in terms of factor employment follow from this form. Suppose that $f(x)$ has the usual neoclassical properties and the firm is a taker of both the product and factor prices. Then conditions for an interior optimum in factors are

---

[6] The second-order condition requires that the marginal cost intersect the marginal revenue from below.

$$p \frac{\partial f(x)}{\partial x_k} = r_k \qquad \text{for all } k \qquad (2.24a)$$

This condition can be written more simply as

$$\frac{\partial f(x)}{\partial x_k} = r_k^* \qquad \text{for all } k \qquad (2.24b)$$

where $r_k^* = r_k/p$ define **normalized factor prices**. In turn, define **normalized profits** π^* as

$$\pi^* \equiv \frac{\pi}{p} \equiv f(x) - \sum_k r_k^* x_k \qquad (2.25)$$

Equations (2.24) can be solved for the factor demand functions

$$x_k{}^0 = d_k(r^*) \qquad \text{for all } k \qquad (2.26)$$

and these can then be substituted in (2.25) to give the **indirect normalized profit function**

$$\pi^0(r^*) = f\{d_1(r^*) \ldots d_k(r^*)\} - \sum_k r_k^* d_k(r^*) \qquad (2.27)$$

The reader can readily show (see the analogy with indirect utility in section 1.2.1) that π^0 is decreasing and convex in the normalized factor prices.[7]

2.2.1   Unconditional Factor Demands

In section 2.1.2 conditional factor demands were derived from the firm's cost minimization problem (with given output). Shepard's lemma, the derivative property of the cost function, was the basis of that derivation. Associated with the firm's "higher level" profit maximization problem there are also factor demand functions (of prices) given by (2.26), but since output is variable in this problem the derived demands are unconditional. A useful result in deriving these unconditional demands in a more direct way than the simultaneous solution of equations (2.24) is the following.

Derivative Property of the Profit Function. Let (2.27) define the firm's indirect normalized profit function. Then

$$x_k^* = - \frac{\partial \pi^0(r^*)}{\partial r_k^*} \qquad \text{for all factors } k \qquad (2.28)$$

The proof is straighforward. Since (2.27) holds identically, differentiate π^0 with respect to r_k^*. Doing this and using the optimality condition (2.24b) provides the result. The importance of equation (2.28) is that it yields the firm's factor demands as a function only of the exogenously given factor prices r^*.

In deriving factor demands, there are several advantages of working with π^0 rather than the production function. First, equation (2.28) makes it possible to derive factor demand functions directly from arbitrary specifications of π^0 without an explicit specification of the production function – and hence without

---

[7] Diewert (1978) provides the detailed proof.

the need to solve equations (2.24b) simultaneously. As we will see below this is helpful in applied analyses and provides flexibility in econometric studies. Second, using π^0 as a basis for deriving factor demands assures us that the resulting specifications are consistent with profit maximization under an admissable technology. The reader should be cautioned, however, that an assumption of competitive factor and product markets has been used to reach this result.[8]

E2.4

Derived Factor Demand

It is helpful to repeat the above derivations for a specific case. Consider the (short-run) Cobb–Douglas production function with variable factors of production x_1 and x_2 and fixed factor $\bar{x}_3$:

$$z = A x_1{}^{\alpha} x_2{}^{\alpha 2} \bar{x}_3{}^{\alpha 3} \tag{2.29}$$

with $\alpha_1 + \alpha_2 = \beta < 1$. The associated profit function when normalized and written in logarithmic form is

$$\ln \pi^0 = \ln A^* + \alpha_1^* \ln r_1^* + \alpha_2^* \ln r_2^* + \alpha_3^* \ln \bar{x}_3^* \tag{2.30a}$$

where the following parameters are defined

$$A^* \equiv (1 - p) \; \frac{\alpha_1{}^{\alpha_1/(1-\beta)} \alpha_2{}^{\alpha_2/(1-\beta)}}{A^{1-\beta}} \tag{2.30b}$$

$$\alpha_k^* \equiv - \frac{\alpha_k}{1 - \beta} < 0 \qquad k = 1, 2 \tag{2.30c}$$

$$\alpha_3^* \equiv \frac{\alpha_3}{1 - \beta} > 0 \tag{2.30d}$$

The derivative property of π^0 yields the derived (variable) factor demands immediately as

$$x_k{}^0 = \frac{\partial \pi^0}{\partial r_k^*} \qquad k = 1, 2 \tag{2.31}$$

Multiplying by r_k^*/π^0 and rearranging gives the logarithmic (elasticity) form

$$\frac{\partial \ln \pi^0}{\partial r_k^*} = - \frac{r_k^* x_k{}^0}{\pi^0} \qquad k = 1, 2 \tag{2.32}$$

For the Cobb–Douglas production function specifically, (2.30) can then be rewritten

$$\alpha_k^* = - \frac{r_k^* x_k{}^0}{\pi^0} \qquad k = 1, 2 \tag{2.33}$$

Because of their linearity and simplicity, equations (2.33) and (2.30) are

---

[8] In estimating the derived demands (2.28) it is usual to also estimate the π^0 function. The restriction that common parameters be equal in these equations increases the precision of resulting estimates.

frequently used as estimating equations in cross-sectional analyses. (Note that the α_k^* parameters appear in all equations.)

2.2.2   Elasticities of Substitution

Recall from Shephard's lemma (2.15) that that *conditional* demand for factor k (as a function of output) is

$$d_k(z, r) = \frac{\partial c(z, r)}{\partial r_k} \qquad \text{for all } k \qquad (2.34)$$

From this it follows that, for any two factors l and k,

$$\frac{\partial x_k}{\partial r_l} = \frac{\partial c(z, r)}{\partial r_k \partial r_l} = \frac{\partial x_l}{\partial r_k} \qquad (2.35)$$

that is, the cross-effect of price on factor demands is "symmetric." Using c_{kl} to indicate the partial derivative of cost, it is instructive to write this relationship in its elasticity form:

$$\varepsilon'_{kl} \equiv \frac{\partial \ln x_k}{\partial \ln r_l} = \frac{r_l}{x_k} \frac{\partial x_k}{\partial r_l} = c_{kl} \frac{r_l}{x_k} \qquad (2.36)$$

Here ε'_{kl} is the output constant, factor l, price (cross-) elasticity of factor k demand. It is usual to refer to ε'_{kl} as the kl **substitution elasticity**. This is not to be confused with the corresponding Allen–Uzawa **elasticity of substitution**, which is

$$\sigma_{kl} = \frac{\varepsilon'_{kl}}{s_l} \qquad (2.37)$$

where $s_l = r_l x_l / c$ is again the share of factor l in total cost. While ε'_{kl} generally need not equal ε'_{lk}, this symmetry does obtain for the elasticity of substitution

$$\sigma_{kl} = \frac{\partial x_k}{\partial r_l} \frac{r_l}{x_k} \frac{c}{r_l x_l} = \frac{c_{kl} c}{c_k c_l} = \sigma_{lk} \qquad (2.38)$$

where $\partial c / \partial x_k = c_k$ and similarly for factor l.

E2.5

Translog Flexible Form

Econometric studies of firm (and industry) costs are frequently based on the **translog** function

$$\ln c(z, r) = \alpha_0 + \alpha_z \ln z + \frac{1}{2} \alpha_{zz} (\ln z)^2 +$$

$$+ \sum_k \alpha_k \ln r_k + \frac{1}{2} \sum_k \sum_l \alpha_{kl} \ln r_k \ln r_l + \sum_k \alpha_{kz} \ln z \ln r_k \quad (2.39)$$

The popularity of this function is based on two facts. First, the function should fit most data "well," since it is derived as a local second-order approximation to an arbitrary cost function (in logarithmic form). Second, related to the fact that the approximation is by a second-order Taylor series, it is a "flexible" form which does not a priori impose particular productivity and scale restrictions, but rather permits these aspects to be established by the parameter values.

Because the parameters pertain to partial derivatives of the underlying cost function it is required that $\alpha_{kl} = \alpha_{lk}$ when that function is continuous. Moreover in order for (2.39) to correspond to a neoclassical production technology the cost function must also be homogeneous of degree one in factor prices, which further requires

$$\sum_k \alpha_k = 1 \tag{2.40a}$$

$$\sum_k \alpha_{kz} = 0 \tag{2.40b}$$

$$\sum_k \alpha_{kl} = \sum_l \alpha_{kl} = \sum_k \sum_l \alpha_{kl} = 0 \tag{2.40c}$$

While the conditional factor demands associated with the translog cost function are not linear in the parameters, the factor share equations are, and therefore these are also used as estimating equations. To see this, note that Shepard's lemma expressed in logarithmic form is

$$\frac{\partial \ln c}{\partial \ln r_k} = \frac{r_k x_k}{c} = s_k \tag{2.41}$$

For the translog cost function, this yields

$$\frac{\partial \ln c}{\partial \ln r_k} = \alpha_k + \alpha_{zk} \ln z + \sum_l \alpha_{kl} \ln r_l \tag{2.42}$$

Equating the right-hand sides of the last two expressions gives the factor share equations which are linear in the parameters

$$s_k = \alpha_k + \alpha_{zk} \ln z + \sum_l \alpha_{kl} \ln r_l \tag{2.43}$$

Using (2.38), it is also usual to note that Allen–Uzawa elasticities of substitution take the specific forms

$$\sigma_{kl} = \frac{\alpha_{kl} + s_k s_l}{s_k s_l} \tag{2.44a}$$

$$\sigma_{kk} = \frac{\alpha_{kk} - s_k(s_k - 1)}{s_k^2} \tag{2.44b}$$

The elasticities can be calculated from parameter estimates and factor share data. In turn, it is also straightforward to calculate $\varepsilon'_{kk} = \sigma_{kk} s_k$, which is the own-price elasticity. It is particularly important that these elasticities are not constrained by the translog specification, but depend on the α parameters and the factor cost shares to be determined.

Finally, decreasing average cost can be measured as the proportional change in cost associated with a proportional change in output

$$\frac{\partial \ln c}{\partial \ln z} = \alpha_z + \alpha_{zz} \ln z + \sum_k \alpha_{kz} \ln r_k$$

which also depends on parameter estimates and the output level. Note that $\partial \ln c / \partial \ln z = MC/AC$ (MC is marginal cost), which is less than unity with scale economies and greater than unity with diseconomies.

Economies of Scale. Continuing to limit attention to firms producing a single output, it is said that the cost function is **subadditive** up to z^* if

$$c(z^*) < c(z) + c(z^* - z) \tag{2.45}$$

for all z such that $0 < z < z^*$. A sufficient condition for subadditivity is **economies of scale**; that is,[9]

$$c(\lambda z^*) < \lambda c(z^*) \tag{2.46}$$

for all $\lambda > 1$ and $z^* > 0$. Dividing both sides of the inequality by λz^* gives

$$\frac{c(\lambda z^*)}{\lambda z^*} < \frac{c(z^*)}{z^*}$$

Economies of scale imply that average total cost is a decreasing function of output about z^*. Finally, when a cost function is such that average cost falls for all z, it exhibits strict subadditivity: $c(z_0)/z_0 > c(z)/z$ and $c(z - z_0)/(z - z_0) > c(z)/z$ implies $c(z_0) + c(z - z_0) > c(z)\{z_0/z + (z - z_0)/z\} = c(z)$. The converse case, where all the above inequalities involving the cost function are reversed and average cost is rising, is termed **diseconomies of scale**.

Four sources of scale economies are usually noted. The first is purely technical, depending on the geometric area–volume relationships between the materials required for certain kinds of equipment and the equipment's capacity (Bain, 1954, Pratten, 1971). Roughly, it is observed that in many manufacturing processes the rate of output depends on the value of tanks, pipes, etc., but the cost of this equipment depends simply on the area of the material used in their construction. This leads to a fall in unit costs, as the output increases with the cube of the dimension of the equipment whereas costs increase with the square of the dimension. The second source of scale economies is based on the gains from specialization and from the division of labor (Stigler, 1951, 1958). For example, individual workers can be used in the specific tasks which best match their skills and can further concentrate on a narrower range of tasks as the scale of operation expands. When such specialized factors are only available in indivisible units, these factors can be more intensively employed with an increase in the scale of operations. The third source of scale economies has been termed the "principle of bulk transactions" by Florence (1972; see also Williamson, 1973). The notion here is that the costs associated with exchange transactions do not rise proportionately with the scale of the transaction. The fourth

---

[9] The sufficiency of scale economies is limited to the single-product case. For the multiproduct case see Baumol et al. (1982).

source of scale economies arises from risk and the operation of large numbers. Termed "stochastic returns to scale" by Haldi and Whitcomb (1967), the idea is based on the fact that optimal factor replacement inventories do not rise proportionately with the number of units of a given factor subject to random failure.

Against these sources of scale economies are offsetting tendencies for unit costs to rise with increasing scale. These sources of diseconomies include the increasing costs of accurately transmitting information through a more extensive administration, and assuring that decisions are properly implemented, and the difficulties larger organizations pose for industrial relations (Williamson, 1973, 1975).

2.3 Competitive Market Analysis

At a short-run profit maximum the price-taking firm produces where price equals marginal cost when price is in excess of the minimum average variable cost $\text{AVC} = c(z)/z$. If we let $z^s(p)$ be the inverse of the stationarity condition $p = \text{MC}(z)$, where z^s is the short-run quantity, then

$$z^s = z^s(p) \qquad \text{for } p \geq \text{min AVC} \qquad (2.47)$$

$$z^s = 0 \qquad \text{for } p < \text{min AVC}$$

define the firm's **short-run supply function**.[10] In turn, *industry* short-run supply is obtained as the sum of the quantities supplied by constituent firms:

$$\text{SRS}(p) = \sum_j z_j{}^s(p) \qquad (2.48)$$

2.3.1 Market Equilibrium

To keep demand and supply quantities clearly apart, denote the market (or aggregate) demand function for z by

$$z^d = D(p) \qquad (2.49)$$

$D(p)$ is constructed as the (quantity) sum of the individual consumer demand functions. While it is possible that some individuals may have positively sloped demands, this is quite improbable in the aggregate and we will assume $dD(p)/dp < 0$.

In the short-run, a **market equilibrium** is attained at the price where quantities demanded and supplied are equal:

$$D(p) = \text{SRS}(p) \qquad (2.50)$$

The usual details of this equilibrium are set out in figure 2.2. The cost schedules of a typical producer j are given in figure 2.2(a), and the market demand and supply schedules are given in figure 2.2(b). As an illustration, suppose that there

---

[10] Second-order conditions for the firm's profit maximum require that the marginal cost be rising, so that z^s must be an increasing function of market price.

are 100 identical producers like that in figure 2.2(a). Then the short-run market equilibrium is reached at price p^0 where $D(p^0) = \text{SRS}(p^0)$ and quantities $z_j{}^0$ and $z^0 = 100z_j{}^0$ obtain for the firm and the market respectively. In this specific case, each firm is making positive profits since $p^0 - \text{AC}(z_j{}^0) > 0$.

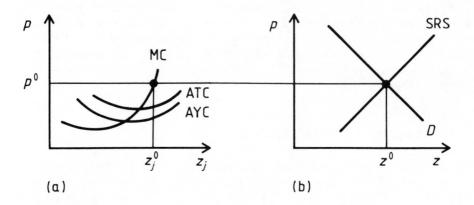

(a)   (b)

Figure 2.2
Short-run competitive equilibrium: (a) firm; (b) market

Free Entry. The long-run market equilibrium with identical producers is slightly more complicated. When each producer, extant and potential, has equal access to all markets and technologies, we say that there is **free entry**. In this case the firms have identical costs and the long-run supply is

$$\text{LRS}(p, J) = Jz(p) \qquad (2.51)$$

where J is the number of actual producers. Equating aggregate demand and supply gives

$$\text{LRS}(p, J) = D(p) \qquad (2.52a)$$

which can be solved for the market equilibrium price as a function of J:

$$p^0 = p^0(J) \qquad (2.52b)$$

The second part of the long-run equilibrium conditions are those which determine J.

New firms will have an incentive to enter the market when positive profits can be obtained post-entry. Similarly, there will be exit when existing firms are earning negative profits. Long-run equilibrium must therefore satisfy several conditions: (a) equality of aggregate demand and supply; (b) profit-maximizing firms; (c) the free-entry long-run stipulation that no producer has any incentive to enter or exit the market. If indivisibilities are neglected and it is assumed that the firms are small relative to the market, (c) implies that each (identical) firm earns zero profits at the industry long-run equilibrium.[11]

---

[11] The equilibrium number of firms is found by dividing the aggregate supply of firms by aggregate demand at the price where zero profits are earned. If this number is nonintegral, the market does not clear exactly. This integer problem is well known (Arrow and Hahn, 1971, ch. 7).

The analytical steps leading to the equilibrium solution are straightforward. To begin, the (maximum) profits of each firm j can be expressed as a function of the market price: $\pi_j = \pi_j(p)$. Using (2.52) this gives $\pi_j = \pi_j(p^0(J))$, that is, each firm's profits are a function of the number of firms producing. Thus the zero-profit equilibrium condition means that

$$\pi_j = \pi_j(p^0(J)) = 0 \qquad \text{for each } j \qquad (2.53)$$

which can be solved for J^0, the equilibrium number of firms. Equations (2.53) and (2.52a) form a system of two equations which yield solutions for the two unknowns p^0 and J. Finally, as profits are maximized at p^0 and z_j^0 (for each j), the locus of equilibrium price p^0 and $z^0 = Jz_j^0$ (as the market demand shifts) defines the long-run market supply schedule.

Long-run Supply. The long-run market supply schedule is, by the above construction, based only on the output of actual firms, and not on the supplies of would-be producers. To see this clearly and further clarify the relationship between short- and long-run industry supply, think of an industry made up of price-takers at long-run equilibrium with demand D_1, a fixed number of firms J_1, and an associated short-run market supply SRS_1. Figure 2.3 illustrates the case, with prevailing price p_0 clearing the market at quantity z^{01}. Every firm (say j, as shows in figure 2.3(a)) earns zero profits. Suppose now that industry demand shifts to D_2. In the short run, before the entry of new firms, existing firms supply the new output by using their existing (fixed) assets **intensively**, producing with rising marginal cost. In this case, SRS_1 is the short-run industry supply, p' is the short-run equilibrium price, and each firm earns positive profits.

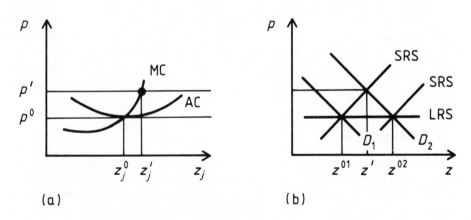

Figure 2.3
Long-run supply: (a) firm; (b) market

Attracted by these profits, new firms enter the industry causing the short-run supply schedule to shift "outward." Suppose that the entry leaves J_2 firms in the market, giving SRS_2. Note that both SRS_1 and SRS_2 are based on a fixed number of firms. In contrast, the LRS is obtained by solving for the J which, for given demand, yields zero profits. (The unique zero-profit J, of course, defines a single SRS.) Since profits are zero for every point on the LRS, the price corresponding to a long-run equilibrium output must be the average cost of producing the output. With firms identical and small relative to the market, this means that the LRS is horizontal. It also means that the LRS is the industry's average cost curve. (In contrast, the SRS is the industry's short-run marginal cost.) Finally, note that the long-run increment $z^{02} - z^{01}$ to industry output is produced **extensively**, that is, with the entry of new firms each producing at minimum average cost. In fact, all units of output along the LRS are produced extensively.

Standard Long-run Supply. Three key, and usual, assumptions have been used in the construction of the LRS. First, it was assumed that all firms, existing and potential, possessed identical cost schedules. This is again the **free-entry** condition based on a presumption that information about production technologies and market opportunities is freely available and no factors are in limited supply. Every entering firm can exactly replicate existing ones. (For the converse situation, where entry is absolutely restricted, a shift in industry demand yields incremental output produced intensively in both the long run and the short run. As a result, beyond the output level Jz^*, where z^* is the quantity for which AC is minimized for each existing firm, the LRS and SRS are identical.)

The second key assumption in the above analysis is that the AC schedules of the firms are U-shaped. If, alternatively, each firm had constant AC, then (with or without free entry), the LRS would be horizontal, profits would be zero, and the number of firms would be indeterminate. Strictly increasing average costs with free entry would produce an equilibrium with each firm infinitesimally small, which is usually thought to be an uninteresting case.[12]

The third assumption underlying the constant long-run supply arises because we have considered only factors internal to the firm and the entry and exit of firms to determine the industry supply function. Alternatively, there are those effects which are external to the individual firm, but internal to the industry as a whole, which act to determine industry supply. The external effects may yield economies or diseconomies and come from either "pecuniary" or "technological" sources.

2.3.2 External Effects

Pecuniary external economies, or diseconomies, occur when the link between industry output and the firm's cost function arises from changes in the market prices of production factors. In contrast, **technological external economies**, or diseconomies, occur when the link between industry output and the firm's cost function arises from changes in the physical production possibilities (a change in the production set). For example, an external technology economy is often thought to occur in the process of advertising a relatively new product. Each firm's advertising contains some information concerning the generic features of

---

[12] There is also the possibility of decreasing average cost. If firms acted as price-takers in this case each would earn negative profits, as $p = \text{MC} < \text{AC}$. Probably, a single producer (or some small number of producers) will survive in this case and the price-taking assumption would be questionable.

the product which, it is said, acts in turn to increase the efficiency of every other firm's advertising. In this case, the fact that other firms advertise decreases the cost of advertising for a given firm. (External technological diseconomies might also occur after some large number of firms advertise.)

E2.6

External Economies

Consider an industry with (only) two price-taking firms. Let z_1 and z_2 be the outputs of these firms and $z = z_1 + z_2$ indicate the industry total. Suppose that the firms have cost functions given by

$$c_1 = \alpha z_1^2 + \delta z_1 z$$

$$c_2 = \beta z_2^2 + \delta z_2 z$$

where α, $\beta > 0$. Note that when $\delta > 0$ there are external diseconomies (greater industry output z implies greater cost for each individual firm), and conversely for $\delta < 0$. Note also that the average cost of firm 1 is $AC = \alpha z_1 + \beta(1/m_1)$, where m_1 is its market share. Stationarity conditions for the joint profit maximum are

$$p - 2\alpha z_1 = \delta z$$

$$p - 2\beta z_2 = \delta z$$

Solving these equations simultaneously yields the supply schedules

$$z_1^0 = \frac{\beta p}{2\alpha\beta + \delta(\alpha + \beta)}$$

$$z_2^0 = \frac{\alpha p}{2\alpha\beta + \delta(\alpha + \beta)}$$

which are linear in price. In turn, the industry short-run supply schedule is

$$SRS = \frac{(\alpha + \beta)p}{2\alpha\beta + \delta(\alpha + \beta)}$$

In the $\delta > 0$ case, with external diseconomies, this supply schedule will have a positive slope, with supply more inelastic (upward sloping) than would obtain in the absence of the external effect. The LRS also slopes upward in this instance as the min(AC) for each firm is at a higher level with increased industry output. In the $\delta < 0$ external economies case, the supply schedule can have either a positive or a negative slope depending on the absolute values of the two terms in the denominator. The LRS will have a negative slope, however, as the external economies reduce each firm's min(AC).

2.3.3 The Ricardian Case

The symmetry assumption, that all existing and potential firms have identical cost functions, is convenient but not required for the price-taker equilibrium.

The presence of different individual skills and other scarce resources (fertile land, for example) implies that some firms may have lower marginal cost (greater efficiency) at all levels of output. Suppose that each firm differs only slightly from its more and less efficient neighbors so that there is an efficiency continuum. Arrange firms from highest to lowest according to their efficiency level. For any given demand, only so many of these firms will be actual producers, depending on their efficiency. At long-run equilibrium the equality of industry supply and demand will be such that the prevailing industry price will just equal the min(AC) of the highest-cost firm – and that firm will earn zero profits. Lower-cost inframarginal firms have $p = MC > AC$ at their optimal output and earn positive economic profits at the equilibrium. Firms outside the industry have no incentive to enter, for at the prevailing industry price their higher min(AC) is greater than the prevailing equilibrium price. However, a shift out in industry demand will establish a new industry equilibrium where some new higher-cost marginal firm has price = min(AC). Obviously, the industry LRS in this case is upward sloping in contrast with the "constant cost" symmetrical case.

E2.7

Ricardian Competitive Equilibrium

Consider an industry with two categories of firms. For convenience, let there be 100 firms in each category. The low-cost firms have total costs

$$c_1 = 0.03z_1^3 - 0.6z_1^2 + 5z_1$$

and high-cost firms have total costs

$$c_h = 0.03z_h^3 - 0.6z_h^2 + 10z_h$$

where l and h indicate low cost and high cost respectively. Note that $\min\{AC_l(z_l)\} = 2$ and $\min\{AC_h(z_h)\} = 7$. Using the marginal cost functions, supply schedules are

$$z_1^0 = 0 \qquad\qquad \text{for } p < 2$$

$$= \frac{1.2 + \{1.44 - 0.36(5 - p)\}^{1/2}}{0.18} \qquad \text{for } p \geqslant 2$$

$$z_h^0 = 0 \qquad\qquad \text{for } p < 7$$

$$= \frac{1.2 + \{1.44 - 0.36(10 - p)\}^{1/2}}{0.18} \qquad \text{for } p \geqslant 7$$

Since there are 100 firms in each category, the industry supply function has three distinct segments:

$$\text{LRS}_1 = 0 \qquad\qquad \text{for } 0 \leqslant p < 2$$

$$\text{LRS}_2 = 100 \left[\frac{1.2 + \{1.44 - 0.36(5 - p)\}^{1/2}}{0.18} \right] \qquad \text{for } 2 \leqslant p < 7$$

$$LRS = LRS_2 + 100 \left[\frac{1.2 + \{1.44 - 0.36(10 - p)\}^{1/2}}{0.18} \right] \qquad \text{for } 7 \leqslant p$$

Suppose further that the industry demand is given by $D = 1000 - 100p$. Then the relevant portion of the supply is LRS_2. Setting $LRS_2 = D(p)$ gives $p^0 = 6.5$, and $100z_1{}^0 = 350$. Each low-cost producer sells 3.5 units, making a profit of $(6.5 - 4.5) \times 3.5 = \$7.0$. No high-cost firm is in the market since $\min(AC_h) = 7 > p^0$.

2.4 Monopoly

The usual "theory of monopoly" is not a theory of how firms acquire and sustain monopoly. Rather, it is a theory about how price is determined after it is found, or assumed, that some firm has a market to itself.[13] This freedom from interaction with other firms comes by the usual assumption that there is a fixed market demand and the seller can choose price–quantity pairs from that schedule.

This theory of monopoly pricing is straightforward and is developed below. The theory of how firms acquire and sustain monopoly, of some degree, is a much more complex subject. To a large extent this theory of *competition for monopoly* under static and dynamic conditions, under complete and incomplete information, under various technologies and political environments, and using a variety of strategy variables is the stuff of the remainder of this book. While the following theory of monopoly pricing is well defined, precise, and generally lacking in application, the theory of competition for monopoly has loose ends, complexity, and a rich empirical and policy content.

2.4.1 Monopoly Pricing

Let $p = p(z)$ be the inverse market demand facing a single-product monopolist, and hold all other prices in the model economy fixed. Further, let the monopolist have costs $c(z)$. The stationarity condition for a profit maximum to result under a pure price policy (no discrimination) is then

$$\frac{\partial \pi(z)}{\partial z} = p(z) + z \frac{\partial p(z)}{\partial z} - \frac{\partial c(z)}{\partial z} = 0 \qquad (2.54a)$$

which solves for

$$\frac{p - c'}{p} = \frac{1}{\eta} \qquad (2.54b)$$

---

[13] It is usual to think of two forms of monopoly. In *closed monopolies* the seller's right to some trade is franchised and protected by government. This was Adam Smith's (1937, pp. 600–21) original concept of the matter and seems to explain why the classical theory of monopoly has such little concern for questions of existence and sustainability. In contrast, with *open monopolies* sellers are not (exogenously) awarded rights to trade so that existence and sustainability are central questions.

where c' is the marginal cost and $\eta = -(p/z)(\partial z/\partial p)$ is the elasticity of market demand.[14] At the profit maximum the monopolist's price–cost margin $(p - c')/p$ equals the inverse of its (the *market's*) demand elasticity. The more inelastic is the market demand, say from an outward shift, the greater is the price–cost margin.

It is usual to distinguish among monopolies, saying that one expresses more **monopoly power** than another. The basis for this distinction is generally the price–cost margin: more specifically, it is said that a seller with a greater margin has greater monopoly power. In turn, the more inelastic is the demand, *ceteris paribus*, the greater is the monopoly power.[15]

2.4.2   Monopoly and Welfare

The first question to be considered here is routine, but important. What is the loss in consumer value associated with a monopoly restriction in output and price increase? There is almost uniform agreement on the proper quantity to be measured in this regard. It is the (dollar) amount that the consumer would require to be just as well off after the price increase as before. The reader will recall from section 1.4 that this is Hick's compensating variation (CV). While there is this agreement in principle about what is to be measured, there are some "how to" questions about which opinions differ.

Since Dupuit, it has been usual to use the consumer surplus (CS) area, to the left of the conventional (money income constant) demand, as a surrogate for the CV associated with a price change. As we saw in section 1.4, a sufficient condition for CV and CS to be equal is for individuals to have constant marginal utility of income. When that constancy does not exactly obtain all is not lost, however, for as we shall show below the percentage error in using CS rather than CV is generally small given that (a) the income elasticity of demand is small and/or (b) the proportion of the consumers' income spent on the good is small. It is generally thought that this approximation error will be less than the error involved in estimating the demand function in most applications.

The CV–CS approximation is only one aspect of the difficulty in measuring monopoly loss. We are not generally interested in the entire CV, but only in the residual "triangle" which corresponds to the excess of the CV over the additional profits captured with any monopoly increase in price. That only this residual is of concern is based on the fact that the monopoly profits are not a social loss, but instead a wealth transfer with distributional consequences.

---

[14] Sufficient conditions for the maximum are (2.54), negatively sloped demand, and rising marginal cost.

[15] It is interesting to note Samuelson's (1967) comments after his development of the theory of the monopoly firm: ". . . It is important to realize just how much content there is to a particular economic theory. As far as the single firm is concerned, everything fundamental which can be said is implied in the statement that at equilibrium there must exist no movement by which the firm can improve its profits; i.e. $\Delta\pi \leqslant 0$ for all movements of variables possible to the firm. In the case of continuity certain necessary relations of differential coefficients (marginal equivalences) are implied. Moreover, assuming certain specific forms to our functions (independences of prices, *et cetera*), it is possible to deduce formally the implications of the equilibrium position . . . . It appears that no more than this can be validly stated" (Samuelson, 1967, p. 81).

Unfortunately, measuring the monopoly output loss by this residual is not as straightforward as the simple subtraction seems at first glance. After briefly reviewing the relationship between CS and CV as background and developing some notation, we turn to this issue.

Compensating Variation and Consumer Surplus, Again. Recall the model of consumer choice from sections 1.1 and 1.2, beginning with the utility maximization problem

$$U(p, y) \equiv \left\{ \max_z u(z) \text{ s.t. } \sum_m p_m z_m = y \right\} \qquad (2.55a)$$

Here u is a monotone increasing strictly quasi-concave utility, z is the M-vector of goods with prices p, and y is income. The indirect utility function of prices and income, $U(p, y)$, is defined by the problem solution. There is a corresponding dual problem which minimizes expenditures[16]

$$E(p, u) \equiv \left\{ \max_z \sum_m p_m z_m \text{ s.t. } u(z) = u \right\} \qquad (2.55b)$$

and defines the expenditure function of prices and utility $E(p, u)$.

Our principal interest in $E(p, u)$ is its derivative property

$$h_m(p, u) = \frac{\partial E(p, u)}{\partial p_m} \qquad (2.56)$$

for all goods $m = 1, 2, \ldots, M$. The $h_m(p, u)$ are (Hicks's) income-compensating demands, which generally contrast with the (Marshall, conventional) uncompensated demands $d_m(p, y)$. These conventional demands also arise from a derivative property, but of the indirect utility function:

$$d_m(p, y) = - \frac{\partial U(p, y)/\partial p_m}{\partial U(p, y)/\partial y} \qquad (2.57)$$

While the compensated and uncompensated demands take on the same value at the maximum level of utility, other fundamental differences between these functions give rise to important differences between the CV and CS measures.

To understand the exact nature of these differences, consider an exogenous shift in the price vector from some initial values p^0 to a new value p^1 The compensating variation $CV(p^0, p^1, y^0)$ is the least income (paid or received) necessary to keep the individual indifferent between (p^0, y^0) and the final situation $(p^1, y^0 + CV)$. That is,

$$CV(p^0, p^1, y^0) = E(p^1, u^0) - E(p^0, u^0)$$
$$= E(p^1, u^0) - y^0 \qquad (2.58)$$

where $u^0 = U(p^0, y^0)$. Notice that the *initial* utility level u^0 is the basis of comparison here. When thinking of a single price change, say in good 1 only, this compensating variation is unambiguous and is given by

$$CV(p^0, p^1, y^0) = \int_{p_1^0}^{p_1^1} h_1(p, u^0) \, dp_1 \qquad (2.59)$$

---

[16] See equation (1.22) and the discussion immediately following it for a list of the important properties of $E(p, u)$.

where $h_1(p, u^0) = \partial E(p, u^0)/\partial p_1$. The CV is simply the area under the compensated demand curve between the prices. CS is by definition something different: it is the area under the conventional uncompensated demand between the price changes, that is,

$$\text{CS}(p^0, p^1, y^0) = \int_{p_1^0}^{p_1^1} d_1(p, y^0)\, dp \tag{2.60}$$

where[17]

$$d_1(p, y^0) = -\frac{\partial U(p, y^0)/\partial p_1}{\partial U(p, y^0)/\partial y}$$

A comparison of (2.59) and (2.60) reveals the essential difference between the CV and CS. To keep the individual at utility level u^0 when constructing the CV, the nominal income y must be adjusted (compensation made) along the path of price change. In contrast, when measuring CS income is kept constant at y^0 in both the numerator and denominator of d_1. This difference is seen clearly in the Slutsky equation[18]

$$\frac{\partial h_1(p, u^0)}{\partial p_1} - \frac{\partial p_1(p, y^0)}{\partial p_1} = z_1 \frac{\partial d_1(p, y^0)}{\partial y} \tag{2.61}$$

The slopes of h_1 and d_1 will be the same, and for small price changes CV will equal CS only when the income effect of the price change $\partial d_1(p, y^0)/\partial t$ is zero. With regard to the derivative property of the indirect utility, an apparent sufficiency condition for this is that both $\partial^2 U(p, y^0)/\partial y \partial p$ and $\partial^2 U(p, y^0)/\partial y^2$ equal zero. That is, it is sufficient that there be constant marginal utility of income.[19]

E2.8

Compensating Variation with Constant Income Elasticity

In welfare analyses a constant income elasticity for the conventional demand is frequently assumed. To understand why this specification is so popular, consider the following developments. Let $\eta_1 > 0$ be the constant income elasticity of good 1:

$$\frac{\partial d_1(p_1, y)}{\partial y} \frac{y}{d_1(p_1, y)} \equiv \eta_1 \tag{2.62}$$

Integrating from y^0 gives the demand[20]

$$d_1(p_1, y) = d_1(p_1, y^0) \left(\frac{y}{y^0}\right)^{\eta_1} \tag{2.63}$$

Since compensated and uncompensated demands are equal at the consumer optimum, using the derivative property of the expenditure function gives

[17] The CV and CS are illustrated in figure 1.2.
[18] This relationship was developed in section 1.2.4; see equation (1.27) specifically.
[19] Recall section 1.4.2.
[20] Hausman (1981) provides details for this and the following calculations.

$$\frac{\partial E(p, u^0)}{\partial p_1} = d_1(p_1, y^0) \left\{ \frac{E(p, u^0)}{y^0} \right\}^{\eta_1}$$

where u^0 is the utility at the optimum. Using this expression, solve for the uncompensated demand

$$d_1(p_1, y^0) = y_0^{\eta_1} E(p, y^0)^{-\eta_1} \frac{\partial E(p, u^0)}{\partial p_1}$$

Integrating under d_1 gives the consumer surplus

$$CS(p^0, p^1, y^0) = y_0^{\eta_1} \int_{p_1^0}^{p_1^1} E(p, u^0)^{-\eta_1} \frac{\partial E(p, u^0)}{\partial p_1} \, dp_1 \qquad (2.64)$$

which can be solved for $E(p^1, u^0)$ to yield

$$E(p^1, u^0) = y^0 \left\{ 1 + \frac{(1 - \eta_1)CS}{y^0} \right\}^{-(1-\eta_1)} \qquad \eta_1 \neq 1 \qquad (2.65a)$$

$$E(p^1, u^0) = y^0 \exp\left(\frac{CS}{y^0}\right) \qquad \eta_1 = 1 \qquad (2.65b)$$

where we use $y^0 = E(p^0, u^0)$. Since $CV(p^0, p^1, u^0) = E(p^1, u^0) - y^0$, it is straightforward to substitute for $E(p^1, u^0)$ from (2.65) to give the CV as a function of CS:

$$CV = y^0 \left[\left\{ 1 + \frac{(1 - \eta_1)CS)}{y^0} \right\}^{-(1-\eta_1)} - 1 \right] \qquad \eta_1 \neq 1 \qquad (2.66a)$$

$$CV = y^0 \left\{ \exp\left(\frac{CS}{y^0}\right) - 1 \right\} \qquad \eta_1 = 1 \qquad (2.66b)$$

In these expressions we understand that the CV and CS are both measured between p^0 and p^1.

For the constant income elasticity case, the CV is a monotone increasing function of CS. The exact size of the difference between the two is a function only of initial income y^0 and the constant income elasticity η_1. The popularity of welfare analyses with η_1 restricted to being constant thus comes from the ability to use CS and the conventional demand to reach consistent qualitative (ordering) results. Then, to change to the exact CV measure only requires simple computations using one of the expressions (2.66).

An Approximation Result. Willig (1976) has derived bounds on the percentage difference between CV and CS when the income elasticity is not constant. We can reach his results by considering the upper and lower values that η_1 can take in equation (2.66a). To simplify the notation, let $\delta = (1 - \eta_1)CS/y^0$ in that expression and approximate the bracketed term $(1 + \delta)^{1-\eta_1}$ by a second-order Taylor series (Willig, 1976, p. 593):

$$(1 + \delta)^{1-\eta_1} \approx 1 + \frac{1 + \delta}{1 - \eta_1} + \frac{\eta_1 \delta^2}{2(1 - \eta_1)^2} \qquad (2.67)$$

Substituting the right-hand side of this in (2.66a) and solving gives the percentage difference

$$\frac{CV - CS}{CS} \approx \eta_1 \frac{CS}{2y^0} \tag{2.68}$$

For the left-hand side to be small and CS to be a useful surrogate for CV requires the product of η_1 and CS/y^0 to be small. Since (a) CS/y^0 is the proportionate change in real income due to the price change (which should generally be small) and (b) η_1 will probably be in the neighborhood of 1.0, the right-hand side of (2.68) will generally be small and the CS will be a good surrogate for CV.

E2.9

Direct Calculation of Compensating Variation

The CV can be derived exactly in some simple situations. The derivation begins with the observed conventional demand function and proceeds by the following steps: (a) use the derivative property (2.57) and integrate to derive the associated indirect utility function; (b) invert it to produce the expenditure function; (c) using either the definition (2.58) of CV or the derivative property of $E(\cdot)$ from (2.56) calculate the CV.[21]

Following Hausman (1981), this technique can be illustrated using the linear demand function

$$z_1 = \alpha p_1 + \delta y + \gamma \tag{2.69}$$

where $\alpha \leqslant 0$, $\delta \geqslant 0$, and $\gamma \geqslant 0$ are constants and both p_1 and y are deflated by the single other composite good price.[22] Roy's identity implies

$$\alpha p_1 + \delta y + \gamma = -\frac{\partial U(p, y)/\partial p_1}{\partial U(p, y)/\partial y} \tag{2.70}$$

Using the implicit function theorem, along a price path which remains at constant utility we have

$$\frac{dE(p_1, u^0)}{dp_1} = \alpha p_1 + \delta y + \gamma \tag{2.71}$$

where $E(p_1, u^0)$ is the income compensation function. Integrating gives

$$E(p_1, u^0) = k \exp(\delta p_1) - \frac{1}{\delta}\left(\alpha p_1 + \frac{\alpha}{\delta} + \gamma\right) \tag{2.72}$$

where k is the constant of integration depending on the utility level. It is convenient to let k be the utility index and then solve for it as a function of price and income. In this way we have

$$U(p_1, y) = \exp(\delta p_1)\left\{y + \frac{1}{\delta}\left(\alpha p_1 + \frac{\alpha}{\delta} + \gamma\right)\right\} \tag{2.73}$$

---

[21] Recall from section 1.2 that for demand functions satisfying the Slutsky equation the integration indicated here is possible.

[22] Good 1 and the composite good are here assumed to be weakly separable in the utility function (see section 1.3).

The reader can verify that the indirect utility satisfies the required properties: it is (a) continuous and homogeneous of degree zero in prices and income (again, the composite good is numeraire), (b) decreasing in prices since $\alpha \leqslant 0$, (c) increasing in income since $\delta \geqslant 0$, and (d) satisfies the Slutsky conditions.

Hausman (1981) considers the following approximate demand for gasoline:

$$z_1 = -14.22p_1 + 0.082y + 4.95$$

He further chooses a mean income of $720 and $p^0 = \$0.75$ (which gives a price elasticity of 0.2 and income elasticity of 1.1, both of which appear reasonable). For a price increase to $p^1 = \$1.50$, equation (2.73) can be used to calculate the associated CV. In this regard, note that

$$CV(p_1{}^1, p_1{}^0, u_1) = E(p_1{}^1, u_0) - E(p_1{}^0, u_0)$$

$$= u_0 \exp\{\delta(p_1{}^1 - p_1{}^0)\} - \frac{\alpha}{\delta}(p_1{}^1 - p_1{}^0)$$

where the second equality uses (2.73). Substituting for u_0 from (2.72) and using the various parameter values set out above gives CV = \$37.17. Finally, the CS can be calculated in a straightforward way from the conventional demand as \$35.97. A little arithmetic reveals a (relatively small) 3.2 percent difference in these measures.

Producers' Surplus. In a private ownership market economy individuals receive value not only in their role as consumer but also from their ownership shares in productive enterprises. In the aggregate, and ignoring any drains in distribution, the value received by individuals from ownership just equals the sum of producers' profits and factor rents. It is usual to refer to this sum as the **producers' surplus** (PS):

$$PS = p(z^*)z^* - \int_0^{z^*} c'(z)\,dz \qquad (2.74)$$

where $c'(z)$ is the usual marginal cost function. Integrating gives

$$PS = p(z^*)z^* - c(z^*) + F \qquad (2.75)$$

where F indicates fixed costs.

E2.10 ——————————————————————

Ramsey Prices

In a homogeneous goods industry the presence of increasing returns in production creates difficulties in using perfect competition as a benchmark for social efficiency. Prices set equal to marginal cost in this case will lead to losses (in the absence of lump-sum subsidies and/or some form of price discrimination). It has been frequently suggested that a **second-best** pricing policy, where prices are chosen to maximize total consumer surplus subject to a profit (producer surplus) constraint, be adopted (for example, Baumol and Bradford, 1970). These second-best conditions are easily developed.

Consider a simple model with $j = 1$, 2 commodities and $i = 1$, 2 consumer classes. We seek regulated prices $p = [p_1 p_2]$ which maximize the total consumer surplus $CS(p)$:

$$CS(p) = CS_1(p) + CS_2(p) \tag{2.76}$$

where CS_i is the consumer surplus of consumer class i, from both goods, written as a function of prices. Let $CS(p)$ be strictly convex in p and suppose that the demands for the two goods are independent, which means that it is possible to simply write

$$CS_i(p) = CS_{i1}(p_1) + CS_{i2}(p_2) \tag{2.77}$$

where CS_{ij} is the surplus of class i derived from good j.

The firm's profit from producing both goods is

$$\pi(p) = pz - c_1(z_1) - c_2(z_2) \tag{2.78}$$

where $z = [z_1 z_2]$ is the vector of inputs and $c_j(z_j)$ is the cost of producing z_j. The profit function is assumed to be strictly concave in p. We seek the solution to

$$\max_p CS(p) \quad \text{s.t. } \pi(p) \geq \pi^* \tag{2.79}$$

where π^* is some "fair" profit level. (This, for example, might be the problem worked by a regulatory agency setting tariffs in the public interest while permitting the regulated firm to earn a competitive return.) At the optimum the constraint is binding and stationarity yields the *second-best* conditions (for each j)

$$\frac{p_j - c_j'}{p_j} = \frac{\lambda^*}{\eta_j} \tag{2.80}$$

Here, λ is the Lagrange multiplier, $\lambda^* = (\lambda - 1)/\lambda$ is termed the **Ramsey number**, and c_j' and η_j are marginal cost and own-price elasticity respectively. Note that λ^* is common to both goods.

The second-best qualifier arises in this case because the prices maximize CS only to the extent that they *first* satisfy the profit constraint. Note that these second-best prices depend on marginal costs, demand elasticities, and the Ramsey number. Other things being equal, the greater is η_j the closer price should be to marginal cost. If the elasticities in question are equal, it is easily shown that all prices should stand in direct proportion to marginal costs. When the p_j satisfy the second-best condition (2.80) they are referred to as **Ramsey prices**.

2.4.3   Monopoly Output Loss

Figure 2.4 illustrates compensated demand $h_m(p, u)$, the conventional demand $d_m(p, y)$, and the marginal cost (MC) schedules for a normal good. With a monoply restriction in output and a price increase from p_0 to p_1, the value forgone by individuals *as consumers* is the area under h_m and between these prices. Our immediate interest lies not with this CV, but more exactly with the **monopoly output loss** (M$_z$L) defined (in a partial equilibrium framework) as the compensating variation less the profits earned by the restriction in output. The monopoly profit is to be subtracted from the CV as that quantity has only distributional implications, with the loss to individuals as consumers being gained by individuals as producers.[23] Thus, M$_z$L is a **deadweight loss** in the sense that its value is foregone, captured by no one, with the increase in price. How is M$_z$L to be measured? For the p^0 to p^1 price change the CV is represented by the collected area $1 + 2 + 3 + 4 + 5$ in figure 2.4. To calculate M$_z$L it is only necessary to subtract the monopoly profits earned after the price increase from this CV area.[24] What are those profits?

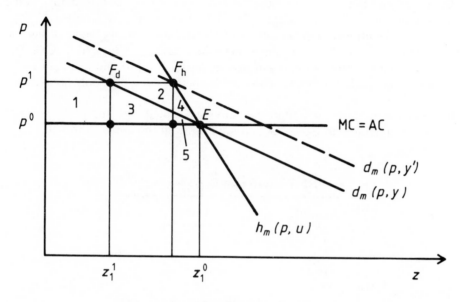

Figure 2.4
Monopoly output loss

Suppose as a first case that the monopoly profit, when taken as income by individuals, does not appreciably affect either their income or the conventional demand. Ignoring general equilibrium interactions, this is often termed the

---

[23] Not much is known about the distribution of monopoly profits. In a preliminary analysis Comanor and Smiley (1975) conclude that "... past and current degrees of monopoly have had a major impact on the current degree of inequality in (the household wealth) distribution." Their rough estimate for the United States is that in 1962 the wealthiest 0.27 percent of households would have a share of between 3 and 10 percent of wealth in the absence of monopoly profits, compared with the recorded share of 18 percent.

[24] In figure 2.4 the monopolist's marginal costs are assumed constant. With rising marginal cost the restriction in output would also result in a loss of factor rents (the area above the marginal cost, below the initial price, and between the output levels). Thus, more generally, the monopoly loss would also have to subtract this loss in rents to individuals as producers. Doing so alters none of the following results.

"two-class" assumption: producers (those taking the monopoly profits as income) are distinct individuals from consumers so that the incremental profit income does not affect the demand for the good. Because the distribution of monopoly profits does not add to *consumer* income in this case, $d_m(p, y)$ is both the pre- and post-change demand and area 1 in figure 2.4 stands as monopoly profits. Alternatively, suppose that the payout of profits increases the income to consumers to some level y' so that $d_m(p, y')$ is the post-change conventional demand. In this case the monopoly profits are represented by the collected area $1 + 2 + 3$ in figure 2.4. While the monopoly profits will usually bring with them some income effect, the tradition in industrial economics has been to rely on some version of the two-class assumption which leaves the conventional demand function unshifted with the price change. This tradition, following Marshall's (1920, p. 503) notion of "compromise benefit," would have us take area 1 as the monopoly profits.[25] We will generally follow that tradition here.

Because conventional demand curves are observable and the general basis of applied analyses, it is usual to approximate M_zL using CS instead of CV. The result is termed the **monopoly output loss surrogate** (M_zLS) and is measured by CS less the monopoly profits, which is the triangle made up of only areas 3 and 5.

In summary, the several welfare measures associated with the p^0 to p^1 price increase are illustrated in figure 2.4 and built up from the areas 1 through 5 as in table 2.1.

Table 2.1 Welfare measures

Measure	Area
CV	$1 + 2 + 3 + 4 + 5$
CS	$1 + 3 + 5$
M_zL	$2 + 3 + 4 + 5$
M_zLS	$3 + 5$

What error results from using M_zLS instead of M_zL? When the income elasticity is small, the *percentage* difference (CV–CS)/CS between CV and CS is also small. In figure 2.4 this is a statement that the ratio of areas $(2 + 4)/(1 + 3 + 5)$ is small. In contrast, the percentage difference in monopoly loss arising from using M_zLS instead of M_zL is $(M_zL - M_zLS)/M_zLS$, or the area $(2 + 4)/(3 + 5)$. There is a potentially important difference between the two approximations: note that area 1 is in the denominator for the CS approximation to CV but not for the M_zLS approximation to M_zL. As a result, in those situations where area 1 is relatively large, CS may be a good approximation to CV while M_zLS will be a poor approximation to M_zL.

---

[25] Note, however, that this tradition introduces an inconsistency, as it compares E and F_h in one aspect of the welfare calculation and E and F_d in the other. That is, the post-change equilibrium is taken to be at both F_h and F_d.

E2.11

Calculating Deadweight Loss using Consumer Surplus

Recall E2.10 where, with the linear demand function given by $z_1 = -14.22p_1 + 0.082y + 4.95$, income of $y = 720$, and a price increase from $p_1{}^0 = 0.75$ to $p_1{}^1 = 1.50$, the calculated value changes were $CV = 37.17$ and $CS = 35.99$. If the above demand is used, the price changes induce quantity changes of $z_1{}^0 = 53.33$ (at $p_1{}^0 = 0.75$) and $z_1{}^1 = 42.66$ (at $p_1{}^1 = 1.50$). This implies a monopoly profit measured by area 1 in figure 2.4 of $\pi^m = (42.66)(1.50 - 0.75) = 31.99$ and, in turn, this gives

$$M_zL = CV - \pi^m = 5.18$$

$$M_zLS = CS - \pi^m = 4.00$$

or $(M_zL - M_zLS)/M_zLS = 27.5$ percent difference. While the CS is in this case a good surrogate for CV, M_zLS is a rather poor surrogate for the true loss associated with the price increase.

In the case where marginal utility of income is small and the compensated and conventional demands are nearly coincidental, a glance at figure 2.4 reveals that the areas 2 and 4 will be small relative to areas 3 an 5, and M_zLS will be a better approximation to M_zL. When using M_zLS as a surrogate for M_zL, such an assumption must be made.

2.4.4 Rent Seeking

Adam Smith offered three general reasons why monopoly could be inconsistent with maximizing the "wealth of nations." First, he argued (Smith, 1937, p. 546) that the monopolist's ". . . stock would be deranged." We have measured this loss by M_zL. Second, he expressed concern that firms would expend resources to acquire and secure monopoly rents that otherwise could be used to social advantage. His third condemnation was that monopolies are prone to be technically inefficient: to him, they seemed not to produce as much as could be obtained from their factors of production.[26]

Tullock (1967) and Posner (1975) have addressed Smith's second source of inefficiency, arguing that the M_zL as defined above in an inadequate welfare measure in many monopoly situations. They follow Smith's argument that the possibility of obtaining a monopoly position will lead to resources being spent to that end, and the opportunity cost of these resources adds to the social cost of monopoly. When the competing firms are identical, each will expend up to their

---

[26] Liebenstein (1966) has recently termed his third source of loss *X inefficiency*, arguing that it arises principally from the monopolist's lack of motivation. Despite the presumption of Smith and Leibenstein, there is no systematic evidence that this is an important consideration in modern economies: see Shelton (1967), Comanor and Leibenstein (1969), Liebenstein (1973), Stigler (1965), Primeaux (1977), and Alchian (1982).

expected rents from the monopoly to capture and hold the monopoly. Posner (1975, p. 812) notes, for example.[27]

> . . .If ten firms are vying for a monopoly having a present value of $1 million and each of them has an equal chance of obtaining it and is risk neutral, each will spend $100,000 (assuming constant costs) on trying to obtain the monopoly. Only one will succeed and *his* costs will be much smaller than the monopoly profits, but the total costs of obtaining the monopoly – counting losers' expenditures as well as winners' – will be the same as under certainty.

Competition among equally skilled firms for the monopoly, when it has no socially valuable byproducts, then converts the monopoly profits into social losses. Stated in this way, it is clear that Smith's second source of inefficiency is built on two separate notions: (a) *rent dissipation*, the total expenditure by firms to obtain and sustain monopoly profit is equal to the level of that profit; (b) *wastefulness*, the expenditure lacks social value. Corresponding to these, there are two usual qualifications to the argument that the opportunity cost of resources spent in competing for monopoly are a cost of monopoly. Related to (b), wastefulness, when firms attempt to capture a monopoly by competing directly for customers, profits will necessarily be dissipated in the combination of price, product features, and conditions of sale *most highly valued* by consumers. This suggests that waste will be small.[28] Related to the rent-dissipation effect (a), even if the byproducts of the competition have no social value, the profits will not be fully dissipated (transformed to a social loss) to the extent that there are inframarginal firms in the competition. There are two frequently mentioned cases in this regard: (1) when there are different costs of organizing the firm to compete in the rent-seeking process; (2) when a monopoly franchise is periodically assigned the incumbent generally possesses an advantage in the renewal.[29]

E2.12

Deadweight Loss in the US Economy: Some Estimates

Ignoring the social cost of rent-seeking and assuming zero income effects, Harberger (1954) roughly estimated the M_2L using 73 US manufacturing sectors and 1924–28 data. His approach was to calculate the partial equilibrium loss arising in each sector and then add these together.

His specific method of calculation was based on the simple geometry illustrated in figure 2.5. There, the demand is assumed to be linear over the relevant range, making M_2L simply equal to the triangle ABC. This can be

---

[27] It is to be stressed that Posner assumes risk neutrality. Hillman and Katz (1984) have shown that the rent-seeking loss will be reduced if the firms are risk averse and the risks are large.

[28] Rice and Ulen (1981) argue specifically that the byproducts of the competitive rent-seeking will generally have substantial social value. See also Williamson (1968), McGee (1971), and Fisher (1985).

[29] See the detailed arguments of Demsetz (1968b) and Rogerson (1982) on this point.

approximated by $M_zL = 1/2\Delta p\Delta z$ where Harberger measures Δp and Δz as deviations from the competitive price and output respectively. If we let $\theta = \Delta p/p^0$, then $\eta = (\Delta z/z^0)\theta$ is the demand elasticity and, in turn,

$$M_zL = \frac{1}{2(pz)\theta^2\eta} \qquad (2.81)$$

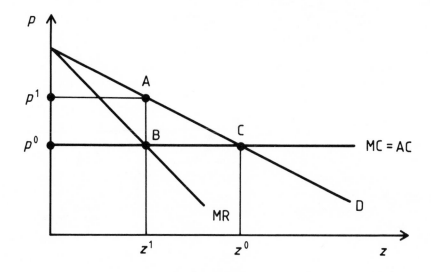

Figure 2.5
Welfare loss measurement

Harberger calculated each manufacturing sector's profit deviation from the manufacturing average and then expressed this as a percentage of revenues to obtain a rough estimate of θ. Adopting a demand elasticity of unity for each sector, the M_zL simplifies to $1/2\theta^2$ times the sector's revenues pz. Further, assuming that all output was sold in consumer final-good markets, Harberger calculated a monopoly loss of the order of 0.1 percent of gross national product (GNP).

Stigler (1956) argued that key errors in Harberger's estimation procedures made his final results questionable. Of particular concern to Stigler was (a) the fact that rational monopolists always produce in the output range where demand elasticity is greater than unity, (b) the reported profits used by Harberger omitted many sources of monopoly returns disguised as "costs," such as patent royalties and executive salaries, and (c) for many monopolists some "intangibles" are (improperly) counted among assets, reducing the recorded profits-to-assets ratio. Schwartzman (1960), Kamerschen (1966), and (using firm-level data) Worcester (1973) later refined and extended Harberger's original calculations, producing maximum loss estimates of 0.3 percent of GNP. Bergson (1973) has argued that the neglect of cross-demand elasticities in the calculations render the results meaningless (see, however, Carson (1975) and Worcester (1975) for critical comments on Bergson's conclusions).[30]

Using data from 1963 in eight "cartelized" industries Posner (1975) calculated M_zL *including* the monopoly rent area using roughly the method of Hargberger. He found the social cost of monopoly to be between 5 and 24 percent of revenues in the cases considered.

---

[30] Cowling and Mueller (1978), using 1968–9 data for 103 corporations, provide estimates for the United Kingdom. They find relatively large losses.

Part II

Theory of Markets

3 Oligopoly: Classical Equilibrium Concepts

Classical market analyses are concerned with the polar cases of competition and monopoly. In these situations each seller finds its best decision by straightforward maximization, with no attention being given to other market participants. In contrast, oligopoly markets are characterized by nonnegligible interdependences among active (and inactive) firms. The decisions of an oligopolistic firm, whether in output, advertising, product quality, etc., generally depend on the decisions of its rivals in trade. Moreover, the interdependence is circular: each oligopolist's optimal decision depends on its rivals' decisions, and each rival's decisions depend on its rivals' decisions, and so on. Cournot (1838) was the first to systematically describe the market interaction of firms in this manner and to develop a solution procedure for the resulting equilibrium.

Despite its rather obscure beginning, Cournot's solution concept has become a central part of modern oligopoly theory. The intuitive appeal and simplicity of the concept as well as the tractability it brings to analyses are reasons for its prominence. Consider the rivalry between two firms. The solution concept focuses on the properties of decision functions, $\alpha^*(\beta)$ for firm 1 and $\beta^*(\alpha)$ for firm 2, which are *best replies* to the actions of their respective rivals in the sense that

$$\pi_1(\alpha^*(\beta), \beta) \geq \pi_1(\alpha, \beta) \qquad \text{for all admissible } \alpha$$

$$\pi_2(\alpha, \beta^*(\alpha)) \geq \pi_2(\alpha, \beta) \qquad \text{for all admissible } \beta \tag{3.1}$$

where α is firm 1's action and $\pi_1(\cdot)$ is its payoff; β and $\pi_2(\cdot)$ similarly pertain to firm 2. As an analytical device, Cournot imagined the decisions to occur in a sequential manner, beginning with firm 1 observing 2's trial action β and, at the same time, firm 2 observing firm 1's action α. On that basis, new trial decisions are calculated and simultaneously announced: firm 1 shifts its choice from α to $\alpha^*(\beta)$ and 2 shifts from β to $\beta^*(\alpha)$. Repeating this, the firms next reply with $\alpha^*(\beta^*(\alpha))$ and $\beta^*(\alpha^*(\beta))$, and so forth. Cournot described the *equilibrium* point of these trials as the set of decisions (α^0, β^0) with the property that each firm's belief about the level of its rival's action is correct when each employs its best reply; that is, the α^0 and β^0 are such that

$$\pi_1(\alpha^0, \beta^0) \geq \pi_1(\alpha, \beta^0) \qquad \text{for all admissible } \alpha$$

$$\pi_2(\alpha^0, \beta^0) \geq \pi_2(\alpha^0, \beta) \qquad \text{for all admissible } \beta \qquad (3.2)$$

Interpreting α and β as firm output quantities and π as profits, he regarded this as the appropriate market outcome for a duopoly.[1]

Nearly a century later Nash (1950) described a similar set of equilibrium conditions. Because of the greater rigor and generality of his analysis, it is now understood that this solution concept applies to a much broader range of oligopoly behavior than Cournot had originally considered. For this reason analyses proceeding in this way are generally said to employ the *Nash solution concept* and the stopping points are called *Nash equilibria*. In this chapter we consider a series of oligopolistic industries and a series of variations on the Nash solution concept. In each case we ask about the properties of the resulting market equilibrium.

3.1   Conjectures and Reactions

While dealing with oligopoly generally, for the moment it simplifies our task to focus on duopoly – the two-seller case. Particular attention is given to duopolists selling differentiated products and choosing output quantities. In later sections the analysis is at times specialized to homogeneous products and generalized to other choice variables and greater numbers of firms.[2] A final and much more restrictive condition is that the analyses are at first confined to models with only one market date. The principal limitation of these static analyses is that they bring with them a myopia where no firm has any incentive to consider the effects of its current actions on either its future opportunities or those of its rivals.[3]

It is usual to imagine Cournot's analysis as involving a **symmetric pre-market process** which, when thought through to its end result, yields the (observed) market decisions of the firms. The imagined process, or "thought experiment," begins at stage $t_0 - \delta_1$ $(\delta_1 > 0)$, when it is assumed that the duopolists simultaneously, and without prior consultation, announce *trial* decisions for implementation at a forthcoming market data t_0. After this first announcement, at a later stage $t_0 - \delta_2$ $(0 < \delta_2 < \delta_1)$, the firms evaluate their trial decisions in light of their rival's planned move and issue (again simultaneously and separate-

---

[1] We note here, and emphasize later, that the equilibrium point defines the only market event. The prior decision process of the firms set out above represents only an analytical device for reaching the equilibrium.

[2] Chapters 10 and 11 deal with entry, making the number of active firms endogenous to the analysis.

[3] The obvious rationale for a single-period model is that there is in fact only one market date before the end of the economy. Alternatively, we might imagine that there are markets opening and closing over a number of dates, but the firm must choose a single value for its decision variables and never change it. (In this case the firms' profits are measured by the present value of its market payoffs.) Both the single-period horizon model and the single-decision alternative are obviously artificial and provide little to choose between. The reason for using either is that much of what is learned can be transferred to more complex dynamic situations, as we do in later sections and chapters.

ly) announcements of adjustments. The process continues with a sequence of such adjustments until the equilibrium conditions (3.2) obtain. These conditions mark time t_0, when markets open and transactions in fact occur with the firms' equilibrium decisions.[4] While it will be clear below, it is nonetheless important enough to give prior notification that each seller's conjectures about its rival's adjustments in this thought experiment are critical in determining the final market equilibrium point.[5]

3.1.1 Conjectural Equilibria

The starting point is the usual demand and cost conditions. For each firm $j = 1$, 2 there are prices p_j and quantities z_j. These are jointly related by the demand functions

$$z_j = z_j(p_1, p_2) \tag{3.3a}$$

or the associated inverse demands

$$p_j = p_j(z_1, z_2) \tag{3.3b}$$

Throughout, these functions are assumed to be continuous and differentiable, and to relate own prices and quantities inversely. For each commodity there is also a finite "choke" price $\bar{p}_j = p_j(0, z_k)$, which leads to zero sales – note that $\bar{p}_j$ depends on p_k. (We use firm k as the rival firm when speaking of firm j. Thus, references to j and k generally mean for j, $k = 1$, 2 with $j \neq k$.) Using the notation $z = [z_1 z_2]$ and $p = [p_1 p_2]$, at times it is convenient to write $z = z(p)$ and $p = p(z)$ as a shorthand for equations (3.3). On the supply side, the cost of production for each firm j will be denoted by the function $c_j(z_j)$, with marginal costs positive and nondecreasing: $c'_j \equiv dc_j(z_j)/dz_j > 0$ and $c''_j \equiv d^2c_j(z_j)/dz_j^2 \geq 0$ when $z_j > 0$.

Each firm is presumed to maximize profits given by

$$\pi_j(z) = z_j p_j(z) - c_j(z_j) \qquad j = 1, 2 \tag{3.4}$$

Here, the firms' decision variables are output quantities. We continue with this case for the moment, for it is the usual textbook case. In later sections it will be clear why it may be important to extend the analysis to other decision variables and how that can be done.

Conjectural Variations. The "problem" of oligopoly is evident in (3.4), for the profit function π_1 depends not only on z_1 but also on z_2, and similarly π_2

---

[4] This pre-market process is akin to the well-known Walrasian tatonnement process. There, a vector of normalized prices is called out at random by a central auctioneer and then modified if supply and demand are not equal for all goods. When consumers are price-takers the equilibrium occurs where the excess demand (the difference between tentatively offered demand and supply) is zero for each good. As here, the Walrasian tatonnement process is simply offered as a method of solving a system of equations and economic questions about the out-of-equilibrium adjustment process and properties of is convergence are left unresolved.

[5] That transactions occur only at a single market date means that we do not here consider retaliation in the future for the present actions by either of the sellers. It also means that we rule out tacit collusion signaled by the nature of decisions over time.

depends on z_1 as well as z_2 It is usual to resolve this interdependence by supposing that each firm forms expectations, or conjectures, about how its rival will respond to changes in its own output. However these conjectures are characterized, our interest is limited to solution points where each firm's conjecture about the level of its rival's output is correct and there will be no further actions or reactions. As we will see below, this will require the choice problems of the firms to be solved simultaneously. This leads to a second usual aspect of an equilibrium: firms maximize profits. This requires the stationarity conditions[6]

$$v_j(z; \gamma_{kj}) \equiv \frac{d\pi_j(z)}{dz_j} = \frac{\partial \pi_j}{\partial z_j} + \frac{\partial \pi_j}{\partial z_k} \frac{dz_k^e}{dz_j} \tag{3.5}$$

$$= \left[\{p_j(z) - c_j'(z_j)\} + z_j \frac{\partial p_j(z)}{\partial z_j} \right] + \gamma_{kj} z_j \frac{\partial p_j(z)}{\partial z_k} = 0$$

where the **conjectural variation** (derivative)

$$\gamma_{kj} \equiv \frac{dz_k^e(z_j)}{dz_j}$$

reflects the change in z_k expected by firm j for some small change in its own output.[7] If firm j were to ignore, or not anticipate, any reaction by other firms, then $\gamma_{kj} = 0$ and $v_j = \partial \pi_j / \partial z_j$. More generally, the stationarity function v_j depends on the conjectural variation γ_{kj} weighted by the output decision times the indicated cross-partial derivative. To complete the solution, note also that the second-order condition associated with (3.5) is

$$\frac{d^2 \pi_j}{dz_j^2} = \frac{\partial v_j}{\partial z_j} + \frac{\partial v_j}{\partial z_k} \frac{\partial z_k^e}{\partial z_j} \tag{3.6}$$

$$= \mu_{jj} + \gamma_{kj} \mu_{jk} < 0$$

where μ_{jj} and μ_{jk} are the obvious partial derivatives of v_j.

Zero and Nonzero Conjectural Variations. The model developed above is static (or, more exactly, timeless): firms maximize profits, not the discounted value of some profit stream, and all decisions and events occur at a single (unnoted) date. Yet the conjectural variations of the model suggest that, although the firms simultaneously choose an action, each firm responds to the actions of others. To respond in the fashion of the conjectural variations would seem to require that one firm move after some other firm (in time). Such an action–reaction sequence is, of course, inconsistent with the static nature of the model. Because there is no (time) opportunity for responses, the only logically consistent conjectural variations are those with identically zero value, that is $\gamma_{kj} = 0$.

A second view of the conjectural variation approach, which also permits

---

[6] Given the regularity of the cost and demand functions and the concavity of the profit function, equations (3.5) and (3.6) to follow are both necessary and sufficient for an interior profit maximum.

[7] Bowley (1924) introduced the notion of the conjectural variation, arguing that the prior models of Cournot and Bertrand (discussed below) are special cases of a more general "... conjectures basis for oligopoly."

rational nonzero conjectural variations, is often employed in analysis. This view is essentially that favored by Marshack and Selten (1974, p. 5):

> ... our approach follows the "conjectural" approach of classical oligopoly theory. In the equilibria we study, each firm is content with its actions in the sense that it prefers them to what it believes would be the *end result* of deviating from them. It conjectures what others responses to its deviations would be and effectively assumes the others responses are *instantaneous*.

By this view firms can hold nonzero conjectural variations, but in their "minds" they immediately simulate the action–response sequence of the pre-market process, as a "thought experiment," and act only where the conjectural variations take on zero value at the end result of that sequence.[8] While this presumes a high level of abstraction and rationality, it is in fact not any more than needs to be assumed with zero conjectural variations.

An alternative and complementary view of nonzero conjectural variations is that they are *representations* of zero conjectural variations resulting from different strategy variables. For example, some nonzero conjecture in quantity might be equivalent to a zero conjecture in prices. This possibility is based on the fact (to be shown in section 3.2) that under mild restrictions every equilibrium arrived at using nonzero conjectural variations in one strategy variable (quantity, as above, or price, or advertising, . . .) corresponds to an equilibrium arrived at using zero conjectural variations in some other strategy variable. Thus we are able to transform a model industry involving nonzero conjectural variations into an equivalent industry with zero conjectural variations. This means that, as *solution concepts*, the zero and nonzero conjectural variations are equivalent (given due care in the selection of strategy variable and conjectural variation).

If the zero and nonzero conjectural variations have this correspondence, why bother at all with the nonzero case? There are several reasons. First, in many situations it will be much easier to gauge the behavior assumed of the firm (say the extent of monopoly power) by the specification of nonzero conjectural variations than it will be by the specification of zero conjectural variations in some strategy variable. Second, and related to that, at times it will be analytically easier to characterize different kinds of firm behavior by inducing variations on parameters of the conjectural variation function than by changing strategy variables in a zero conjectural variations model. Third, since nonzero conjecture models are not "wrong," there is some value in developing them here as they are commonly used in the literature (see Kamien and Schwartz, 1983, and Dixit, 1986, for surveys).

Conjectural Equilibrium. For the moment suppose that there are $j = 1, 2, \ldots, J$ firms. Then a **conjectural equilibrium** (CE) occurs at the simultaneous solution of equations (3.5). Let $z^0 = [z_1{}^0 z_2{}^0 \ldots z_J{}^0]$ be some (feasible) vector of outputs, and let $[z^0 : z_j]$ be the specific vector z^0 with the

---

[8] Existence and uniqueness of the end result, or equilibrium, are considered below.

$z_j{}^0$ entry replaced by z_j. This separates the choice of firm j from that of the other firms. Then z^0 is an **equilibrium output vector** if it is technically feasible and $\pi_j(z^0) \geq \pi_j(z^0 : z_j)$ for all z_j and every j. For the interior solutions of interest this requires the stationarity condition $v_j(z^0; \gamma_j) = 0$ to hold simultaneously for all firms j, where γ_j is the $(J - 1)$-vector of firm j conjectural variations.[9] The solution of the J stationarity equations occurs where each firm's output decision is optimal given the output decisions of all other firms and the conjectural variations.

Reaction Functions. The independent solution of the stationarity conditions (3.5) defines **reaction functions**

$$z_j = r_j(z_k; \gamma_{kj}) \tag{3.7}$$

for each duopolist $j = 1, 2$.[10] Given some decision z_k by its rival, $r_j(z_k; \gamma_{kj})$ determines the optimal output reaction of firm j, which explains why (3.7) is also frequently, and descriptively, referred to as the **best reply function** and the z_j value taken on by the function is then called j's **best reply** (for the given z_k). Using these ideas, the CE associated with the specific conjectures γ_{kj} is a feasible output pair $(z_1{}^0, z_2{}^0)$ lying at the intersection of the reaction functions: that is, $z_j{}^0 = r_j(z_k{}^0; \gamma_{kj})$ for each j. The properties of r_j depend on the conjectural variation γ_{kj}, as noted explicitly, as well as on the demand and cost functions.

E3.1

Pre-market Process

Consider duopolists producing a homogeneous product which is solid in a market with linear inverse demand $p = a - b(z_1 + z_2)$. Let the firms have increasing convex cost functions $c_1(z_1)$ and $c_2(z_2)$. There are, in turn, the profit functions

$$\pi_1 = \{a - b(z_1 + z_2)\}z_1 - c_1(z_1)$$

$$\pi_2 = \{a - b(z_1 + z_2)\}z_2 - c_2(z_2)$$

To step through the *solution procedure* (thought experiment) imagined by the pre-market process we first index successive solution stages $n = 0, 1, \ldots$ until equilibrium is reached. The stationarity conditions (3.5) which pertain to each iteration $n - 1$ and govern the *imagined*, or *trial*, decisions for iteration n are

$$a - b\left\{2z_{1,n} + z_{1,n}\frac{dz_2{}^c(z_{1,n})}{dz_1}\right\} - bz_{2,n-1} - c_1' = 0$$

$$a - b\left\{2z_{2,n} + z_{2,n}\frac{dz_1{}^c(z_{2,n})}{dz_2}\right\} - bz_{1,n-1} - c_2' = 0$$

---

[9] The CE definition here assumes output quantities to be the decision variables of the firms. That is not a general restriction as will be made clear in section 3.2. The definition might also make allowance for the entry and exit of firms and sustainable profit levels. These issues are considered as we proceed.

[10] No, with zero conjectural variations these are not called "nonreaction" functions.

Suppose further that the conjectural variations for both firms are equal to the same constant γ at each stage and the marginal costs are positive constants. Then the associated reaction functions are derived from the solution of these equations as

$$z_{1,n} = \frac{(a - c_1') - bz_{2,n-1}}{(2 + \gamma)b}$$

$$z_{2,n} = \frac{(a - c_2') - bz_{1,n-1}}{(2 + \gamma)b}$$

respectively. Note that the form of the reaction functions depends not only on the demand and cost functions, but also on the conjectural variations.

To illustrate the process, consider the following specific parameter values: $a = 100$, $b = 1$, $c_1' = 10$, $c_2' = 20$, and zero conjectures $\gamma = 0$. These give $z_{1,n} = 45 - 0.5z_{2,n-1}$ and $z_{2,n} = 40 - 0.5z_{1,n-1}$ as reaction functions. Beginning with initial levels $z_{1,0} = 20$ and $z_{2,0} = 20$, the following iteration of pre-market (trial) decisions would then occur:

	$z_{1,n}$	$z_{2,n}$
$n = 1$	35	30
$n = 2$	30	22.5
$n = 3$	33.75	25
$n = 4$	32.5	23.125
$n = 5$	33.44	23.75
$n = 10$	33.32	23.33
$n = 20$	33.33	23.33

As n increases, the trial choices are seen to converge to equilibrium values 33.33 and 23.33 for firms 1 and 2 respectively. (This convergence is assured by a stability condition noted below.) The reader can quickly verify that these CE values are also given by the intersection (simultaneous solution) of the reaction functions.[11] The reader can also see that the pre-market process is just a solution procedure for determining the only relevant economic event – the final equilibrium point.

3.1.2 Equilibrium Existence, Uniqueness, and Stability

The existence and uniqueness of a conjectural equilibrium are not addressed by the CE definition. Rather, these issues turn on whether the reaction functions of the firms intersect at positive quantities and, if so, intersect one or more times. Existence and uniqueness thus depend upon those things which determine the properties of the reaction functions: the underlying conditions of demand and cost *and* the conjectural variations.

[11] In contrast with the view adopted here, Cyert and DeGroot (1973) model the adjustment process as an *actual* sequence of market decisions which converge to a steady state for the industry. Specifically, in their analysis time is discrete and the actual output decisions are staggered: one firm makes its output decision in the even-numbered period and the other in the odd-numbered period. It is important to their solution that the decisions occur in sequence. Thus a firm choosing its output at any date knows that, during the market period immediately following, its rival will keep its output unchanged.

E3.2

Equilibrium Existence and Uniqueness

Some problems associated with a CE can be illustrated with a specific heterogeneous duopoly example. Let firms 1 and 2 have the inverse demands

$$p_1 = \xi - \frac{z_1 z_2}{2}$$

$$p_2 = 1 - z_1 - \frac{z_2}{2}$$

The constant $\xi > 0$ can be thought of as a product quality parameter which scales firm 1's demand. For simplicity, assume further that both goods are produced with zero costs. Profit functions are therefore

$$\pi_1(z_1, z_2) = \xi z_1 - \frac{z_1^2 z_2}{2}$$

$$\pi_2(z_1, z_2) = z_2 - z_1 z_2 - \frac{z_2^2}{2}$$

Suppose that the firms choose output quantities and, as an additional simplification, let there be zero conjectural variations in quantity: $\gamma_{jk} = \gamma_{kj} = 0$. The stationarity of profits then occurs where

$$v_1(z_1, z_2) \equiv \xi - z_1 z_2 = 0$$

$$v_2(z_1, z_2) \equiv 1 - z_1 - z_2 = 0$$

These conditions produce the reaction functions

$$r_1(z_2) = \xi/z_2$$

$$r_2(z_1) = 1 - z_1$$

which are rectangular hyperbolic and linear respectively as illustrated in figure 3.1.

Figure 3.1 also indicates the three solution possibilities depending on the specific value taken by ξ. The reader can quickly show that when $\xi = 1/4$ the reaction functions have just one intersection (a tangency) at the point C where $z_1 = z_2 = 1/2$. In contrast, when $\xi > 1/4$ there is no intersection and no solution. Finally, when $\xi < 1/4$ there are two possible equilibria at points C' and C'', which solves the problem of existence but not that of uniqueness.

Stability Conditions. It is said that a CE is (locally) **stable** when, starting from some neighboring point, the appropriate pre-market process asymptotically converges to the equilibrium point. Conversely, unstable points are those which do not converge in this way. As a basis for choosing among multiple equilibria, it is often argued that unstable points should be dismissed.[12] Some care must be

[12] See, for example, Theocharis (1960), Fisher (1961), Hahn (1962), Hadar (1966), Okuguchi (1969), and, more recently, Seade (1980a), Brander and Lewis (1986), and Dixit (1986)

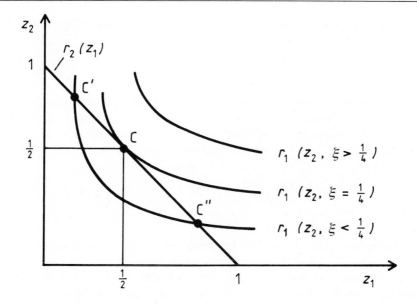

Figure 3.1
Duopoly equilibria

exercised here, for the models under investigation are static (there is only one market event and all variables and parameters have exactly the same date) and stability is inherently a dynamic property. Stability must be related then to the only "dynamic aspect" of the analysis: the solution procedure. Although simultaneous direct solution of equations (3.5) yields all equilibria, stable and unstable, the stability criterion asks that we reject those solutions which cannot be reached using one particular technique (pre-market process) for solving these equations. Given that our economic interest is only with the solutions of (3.5), there is no economic rationale for ignoring some solutions simply because they cannot be produced by some analytical procedure. What then is stability all about?

At this point it is helpful to remind the reader, as Lancaster (1968, ch. 12) has, that ". . . There is no fundamental theory concerning the behavior of economic decision makers out-of-equilibrium; there are only theories of equilibrium behavior." Having said that, he leaves us also to note that out-of-equilibrium theory about oligopolistic behavior is being proposed in stability analyses. If we are comfortable with treating the static oligopoly models in an *ad hoc* dynamic fashion by thinking of the pre-market process as an actual out-of-equilibrium adjustment mechanism for small displacements, then the stability conditions to be developed below are acceptable. If we are inclined to reject out-of-equilibrium descriptions out of hand, then these stability conditions are irrelevant. As the conditions are employed more than occasionally in the literature, it is instructive to briefly set them out here.

To this end, think of a specific adjustment process in which each firm increases its output in the neighborhood of an equilibrium iff it perceives (using whatever conjectures are appropriate) that an increase in profits will result.[13] That is, for each j there is the kinematic equation

$$\dot{z}_j \equiv \frac{dz_j}{dt} = k_j v_j \qquad (3.8a)$$

where $k_j > 0$ is an adjustment-rate parameter and v_j is the stationarity function defined by (3.5). Suppose that the adjustment rate is common across firms, $k_j = k > 0$, and think of a small shock or perturbation (dz_1, dz_2) about the equilibrium point $(z_1{}^0, z_2{}^0)$. A linearization of the kinematic equations about this point gives

$$\begin{bmatrix} \dot{z}_1 \\ \dot{z}_2 \end{bmatrix} = k \begin{bmatrix} v_{11} & v_{12} \\ v_{21} & v_{22} \end{bmatrix} \begin{bmatrix} dz_1 \\ dz_2 \end{bmatrix} \qquad (3.8b)$$

where $v_{jk} \equiv dv_j(z^0)/dz_k$.

The equilibrium point is said to be **stable** when the perturbation brings the motion described by these differential equations (asymptotically) back to rest. It is well known that this motion property occurs iff the coefficient matrix $[v_{jk}]$ has eigenvalues with negative real parts, which is equivalent to the following principal minor and full determinant sign conditions (see, for example, Timothy and Bona, 1968, section 6.6, or Benavie 1972, ch. 4):

$$v_{11} < 0 \qquad v_{22} < 0 \qquad (3.9a)$$

$$D \equiv v_{11}v_{22} - v_{12}v_{21} > 0 \qquad (3.9b)$$

For the special case where the conjectural variations are all zero, these conditions reduce to $\mu_{11} < 0$, $\mu_{22} < 0$, and $D = \mu_{11}\mu_{22} - \mu_{12}\mu_{21} > 0$.[14] We delay further comment on these stability conditions until heterogeneous products are introduced in section 3.1.5.

3.1.3   Nash conjectures and equilibrium

The first level of complexity in specifying an oligopoly solution is the identification of the strategy variable(s). For the moment, we limit attention to a single variable (scalar) for each form. In doing so it is not required that this variable be the same for each firm. For example, firm j in choosing output may form its conjecture with respect to firm k's price, while firm k may choose revenues based on a conjecture concerning firm j's advertising reaction. Despite these possibilities, it is usual to let the decision variables be identical for all firms. If one firm chooses quantity and makes conjectures about other firms' quantity responses, then it is usual to let all firms act in that way, and similarly for price or any other decision variable. (In section 3.3 several cases are considered where one firm chooses price and the other quantity. A duopoly where each firm has two strategy variables is considered in SE3.1)

---

[13] It is worth emphasizing that stability here is stated in terms of the effect of *quantity* changes on profits. Other decision variables might be used as shown in section 3.1.3 below.

[14] For the duopoly situation set out in E3.2 above, the reader can quickly show that stability required $z_2{}^0 > z_1{}^0 > 0$.

Nash Conjectures. Suppose that the strategy variables s_j and s_k are chosen by firms j and k respectively. In turn, let $s_j = [s_j{}^1 s_j{}^2 \ldots s_j{}^N]$ indicate the N possible **strategies** available to each duopolist j, and let $S = [s_1 s_2]$ indicate the collection of all such strategies. A **strategy combination** $s \in S$ represents a collection of strategy choices, one for each firm. Given that these strategy variables are adopted, we are still left to choose the functional form of the conjectural variation: that is, what is $\gamma_{kj}(s)$ in the expression $d(s_k)^c/ds_j = \gamma_{kj}(s)$? **Zero conjectures**, where $\gamma_{kj}(s) \equiv 0$, is the most frequent assumption (recall the discussion of section 3.1.1).[15] Because of Nash's detailed study of this case, these are generally labeled **Nash conjectures** and the associated conjectural equilibrium is called a **Nash equilibrium** (NE).[16] When the Nash solution concept is confined to output strategies and $dz_k{}^c/dz_j = 0$ obtains, we say more exactly that the conjectures are *Nash-in-quantity*, and when $dp_k{}^c/dp_j = 0$ the analysis is said to be *Nash-in-price*. More generally, there are *Nash-in-s* analyses.[17]

A common alternative to Nash conjectures are the **constant conjectures** $\gamma_{kj}(s) = \text{const} \neq 0$. Less frequently used are analyses where the $\gamma_{kj}(s)$ have complex linear and nonlinear forms. While it appears that such complex expressions would bring greater realism to the analysis of real-world oligopolies, that is not generally so. The reason for this is a *correspondence proposition*: if mild regularity conditions on the functions involved (to be noted below), are assumed with an appropriate change of strategy variable every conjectural equilibrium corresponds to a Nash equilibrium. As a first example of this proposition, we will show later that a homogeneous duopoly with nonzero quantity conjectures $dz_k{}^c/dz_j = -1$ for each firm has an equilibrium equivalent to a Nash-in-price duopoly. The general correspondence proposition, set out in section 3.2 below, means that Nash-in-s analyses and equilibria are quite general if due consideration is given to the choice of strategy variable.

It is instructive to work our way to a systematic statement and demonstration of the correspondence proposition by several steps. First, and related to issues raised earlier, we shall note the conditions under which a unique equilibrium exists for a Nash-in-s oligopoly. The nature of these conditions provides additional motivation (beyond simplicity) for limiting attention to NE. Then it is shown as an intermediate results that corresponding to every CE there is an

---

[15] There is some possibility for confusion here. The conjectual variations are derivatives, presumably of some underlying conjectures function. It might be thought that zero conjectures means that this conjectures function is identically zero. That is not necessary. The underlying conjectures function is (almost) never considered, and the terms conjectures and conjectural variations are generally used equivalently, as here.

[16] For completeness we again spell out the solution concept, which is now labeled the **Nash solution concept**. Let $v_j(s) = 0$, $v_k(s) = 0$ be the stationarity conditions for a duopoly with zero conjectural variations in s. Associated with these conditions are reaction function equations $r_j(s_k) = s_j$ and $r_k(s_j) = s_k$. Let $s_j{}^0$ and $s_k{}^0$ simultaneously solve these reaction function equations. This solution has the best response property $\pi_j(s_j{}^0, s_k{}^0) \geq \pi_j(s_j, s_k{}^0)$ and $\pi_k(s_j{}^0, s_k{}^0) \geq \pi_j(s_j{}^0, s_k)$ for all admissible s_j and s_k. (The duopoly equilibrium is extended to any number of firms in a straightforward way.)

[17] For emphasis: $dz_k{}^c/dz_j = 0$ indicates *two* conditions, as we use j, $k = 1$, 2, with $j \neq k$. That is, the zero conjecture is held by both firms. A similar duplicity holds for price, or any other strategy variable. More generally, with J firms the Nash-in-s conjectures hold for *all pairs* of firms.

equivalent CE (assuming rather standard conditions) where the conjectural variations are constant functions: $\gamma(s) = $ const. Finally, and as additional background for the correspondence proposition, some properties of the Nash-in-quantity and Nash-in-price oligopoly solutions are set out.

Nash Equilibrium Existence and Uniqueness. If an NE exists and is unique, then a **Nash solution** for the oligopoly is said to obtain. Friedman (1977, theorem 7.1) has shown that an NE exists in strategy variables s_j when (a) the number of firms J is finite, (b) the admissable values for each s_j are a convex subset of finite dimensional Euclidean space, (c) the profit payoff π_j of each firm j is continuous and bounded for all feasible strategies by all firms and (d) π_j is quasi-concave in s_j. For example, the Nash-in-quantity conjectural equilibrium exists when J is finite, output quantities are positive and chosen from the (closed and bounded) interval $[0, \bar{z}_j]$, where $\bar{z}_j$ solves $p_j(\bar{z}_j) = 0$ and $p_j(0)$ is finite, cost functions are continuous and bounded for all firms, and the demand facing each firm is weakly concave and marginal costs are increasing in z_j (making π_j strictly concave in z_j). These are standard specifications in formal analyses.

Although an equilibrium exists under the above conditions, it need not be unique as demonstrated in E3.2. Friedman (1977, p. 71) presents perhaps the most general sufficient conditions for uniqueness, which assures the stability of the equilibrium – recall equations (3.9). The condition is based on the link between stability and uniqueness: if an equilibrium exists and is *globally* stable, then it must also be unique. Global stability requires equilibrium convergence by some kinematic process from *any* feasible starting point.

Stability in Prices. While the stability conditions are usually expressed using quantities as the strategy variables, as in (3.9) this is not necessary. Any change of variables that leaves the profit function suitably differentiable and continuous means that similar conditions will obtain in the new strategy variables. For example, consider duopolist j's profits written in terms of price as

$$\pi_j^*(p) = p_j z_j(p) - c_j\{z_j(p)\} \tag{3.10a}$$

where the asterisk denotes the price dependence. The associated stationarity condition is

$$v_j^*(p; \lambda_{kj}^*) = \frac{d\pi_j^*(p)}{dp_j} = \frac{\partial \pi_j^*(p)}{\partial p_j} + \gamma_{kj}^* p_j \frac{\partial z_j}{\partial p_k} = 0 \tag{3.10b}$$

where $\gamma_{kj}^* \equiv dp_k{}^e/dp_j$ is the conjectural variation in price. Stability is now associated with an adjustment process in which each firm increases its *price* in the neighborhood of the equilibrium iff it perceives an increase in profits to result. This directly follows the development of section 3.1.1, and the stability conditions in price have a form similar to those in quantity:

$$v_{11}^* < 0 \qquad v_{22}^* < 0 \tag{3.11a}$$

$$D^* \equiv v_{11}^* v_{22}^* - v_{12}^* v_{21}^* > 0 \tag{3.11b}$$

where $v_{jk}^* = dv_j^*/dp_k$. With Nash-in-price conjectures these conditions simplify to $\mu_{11}^* < 0$, $\mu_{22}^* < 0$, and $D = \mu_{11}^* \mu_{22}^* - \mu_{12}^* \mu_{21}^* > 0$.

Constant Conjectural Variations. The importance of the conjectural variations cannot be minimized, for with the "proper" choice of such functions a wide range of equilibrium points can be reached. For example, consider a duopoly where the firms use quantity as their strategy variable, the cost function $c_j(z_j)$ of each firm is increasing and strictly convex with $c_j'(0) = 0$, and the demand for each $z_j \geq 0$ is decreasing with $\partial^2 p_j/\partial z_j{}^2 < 0$. In this case a choice of constant conjectural variations can always be made to cause any admissible output pair to be a CE.

Proof of this proposition is based on an output pair $\hat{z}_1$, $\hat{z}_2 \geq 0$. Suppose that this pair is arrived at as a CE with some, perhaps complex, expression of conjectures. Then the pair of *constants* $\hat{\alpha}_1$ and $\hat{\alpha}_2$ chosen to solve the stationarity conditions

$$p_1(\hat{z}_1, \hat{z}_2) + \hat{z}_1 \frac{\partial p_1(\hat{z}_1, \hat{z}_2)}{\partial z_1} (1 + \hat{\alpha}_1) = c_1'(\hat{z}_1)$$

$$p_2(\hat{z}_1, \hat{z}_2) + \hat{z}_2 \frac{\partial p_2(\hat{z}_1, \hat{z}_2)}{\partial z_2} (1 + \hat{\alpha}_2) = c_2'(\hat{z}_2)$$

are constant conjectural variations associated with the $(\hat{z}_1, \hat{z}_2)$ CE. The indicated properties of demand and cost functions assure that the second-order maximum conditions hold globally and that an $\hat{\alpha}$ solution pair exists.

E3.3 _____

Conjectures and the Size Distribution of Firms

Consider again a homogeneous oligopoly with industry output $z = \Sigma_j z_j$ and define the aggregate conjecture

$$\gamma_j \equiv \frac{dz^e}{dz_j} = 1 + \sum_{k \neq j} \gamma_{kj} \tag{3.12}$$

where each $\gamma_{kj} \equiv dz_k{}^e/dz_j$ is positive. Suppose that for $dz_j > 0$ other firms are expected to increase their output at most by the same rate that j does. These conditions imply $0 < \gamma_j \leq J$, but the γ_j need not be constants. Following Kamien and Schwartz (1983), define

$$\frac{1}{\Gamma} = \sum_j \frac{1}{\gamma_j} \tag{3.13}$$

that is, Γ is the $(1/J)$th harmonic mean of the γ_j, which we will term the harmonic sum. Since $0 < \gamma_j \leq J$, then $1/\Gamma \geq J/J$ or $0 < \Gamma \leq 1$.

If we use γ_j, each firm j's profit-maximizing condition becomes

$$z_j \gamma_j \frac{dp(z)}{dz} + p(z) - c_j' = 0$$

From this we see that, when marginal costs are the same for each firm, $z_j \gamma_j$ will be the same for each and therefore $z_j = \gamma_1 z_1/\gamma_j$. In turn we have $z = \Sigma_j z_j = \gamma_1 z_1/\Gamma$ and, finally,

$$\frac{z_j}{z} = \frac{\Gamma}{\gamma_j} \tag{3.14}$$

Each firm's share of the industry output equals its share in the harmonic sum of conjectural variations for the total industry. Different conjectures give rise to different market shares, with each (otherwise identical) firm's share varying directly with the conjectural variations of its rivals and inversely with its own.

Reminder. The stationarity functions v_j and associated reaction functions r_j depend upon the conjectural variations. While this dependence has been explicit in the notation to this point, it is usual in the literature to simplify the notation by omitting this argument in the functions. We will follow that simplified notation hereafter.

3.1.4 Cournot and Bertrand

If the conjectures (strategy variables with Nash conjectures) are so critical to the oligopoly solution, then how should they be specified? Unfortunately there are no hard-and-fast rules. Instead, the choice involves a large dose of the economist's art. Some intuition about what makes sense and what is tractable comes from understanding the specifications that have appeared in the literature. Surely the most frequently used models are those of Cournot and Bertrand with homogeneous products, and these make a good starting point.

Cournot Conjectural Equilibrium. As we noted earlier, the first conjectural variation model of duopoly was developed by Cournot (1838). Cournot dealt with the homogeneous goods case and adopted the view that each duopolist determines its output level taking the prevailing *output level* of its rival constant – the Nash-in-output conjectures. Specifically, the Cournot conjectures imply $\gamma_{kj} \equiv dz_k^c/dz_j = 0$. This greatly simplifies the stationarity conditions (3.5) to $v_j = \partial \pi_j / \partial z_j = 0$, giving

$$p - c_j'(z_j) = -z_j \frac{\partial p(z)}{\partial z_j} > 0 \qquad (3.15a)$$

with the rightmost inequality holding when $z_j > 0$ and $\partial p(z)/\partial z_j < 0$. Associated with these stationarity conditions are the Cournot reaction functions

$$z_j = r_j^c(z_k) \qquad (3.15b)$$

Let $z_j^c = [z_1^c z_2^c]$ indicate the simultaneous solution to (3.15b). This Cournot conjectural equilibrium (CCE) has the Nash solution property that neither firm k can increase its profits by choosing an output different from z_k^c, *given* that its rival chooses $z_j^c (j \neq k)$.

Cournot Conjectural Equilibrium and Pareto Optimality. Note from (3.15a) that at the CCE the price of each firm facing a negatively sloped demand and producing a positive quantity is greater than its marginal cost. Thus an economy cannot be at a Pareto optimum if it contains some industry at a CCE. To see this more clearly, suppose that the CCE conditions obtain with each firm providing strictly positive quantities. In this case inequality (3.15a) informs us that a simultaneous small reduction in the outputs of each firm would increase the profits of each. In this way we find an output vector $z^* = [z_1^* z_2^*]$ which yields strictly greater profits for each firm than occur at the CCE.

The fact that the CCE is, in this sense, inside the profit possibility frontier (in output space) also raises an objection to it: the firms, acting in an accommodating way, can do better than the CCE allows. We reserve further discussion concerning the incentives for, and difficulties with, such accommodation until chapters 9 and 12.

E3.4 ───

Reaction Functions Depend on Demand and Cost

The standard case with Cournot oligopoly is to assume that reaction functions are negatively sloped on the quantity plane. What demand and cost conditions assure this?

Using the usual notation we write the problems of two identical homogeneous-good duopolists $j = 1, 2$ as

$$\max_{z_j} \{p(z)z_j - c(z_j)\}$$

With Cournot conjectures the stationarity conditions are given by (3.15a), which we write here as

$$v_j \equiv p(z) + p'(z)z_j - c'(z_j) = 0$$

In turn, the slopes of the Cournot reaction functions are obtained by implicit differentiation of this stationarity condition. Along firm 1's (Cournot) reaction function $r_1^c(z_2)$,

$$\left[\frac{dz_2}{dz_1}\right]_{r_1^c} = -\frac{\mu_{11}}{\mu_{12}}$$

$$= -\frac{p' + p''z_1 + p' - c''(z_1)}{p' + p''z_1} < -1 \quad (3.16a)$$

Along $r_2^c(z_1)$

$$\left[\frac{dz_1}{dz_1}\right]_{r_2^c} = -\frac{\mu_{21}}{\mu_{22}}$$

$$= -\frac{p' + p''z_2}{p' + p''z_2 + p' - c''(z_2)} > -1 \quad (3.16b)$$

These derivatives inform us of the two usual conditions for negatively sloped reaction functions (on the quantity plane): (a) $p' < 0$ and $(p' + p''z_j) < 0$, that is, there are negatively sloped demand curves which are either concave or not "too" convex; (b) marginal cost is rising, $c'' > 0$. Moreover, under these conditions the reaction functions intersect only once. This is obvious geometrically, with z_1 on the horizontal axis, since 1's reaction function is always steeper than a line with slope -1 while firm 2's is always flatter.

Solution Technique and Solution Concept. It is frequently noted, as a criticism, that the proprietors in the Cournot pre-market process behave in an unusual manner out of equilibrium. At every stage of that behavioral process each assumes that its rivals will not react, although this conjecture is repeatedly shown to be false. In this sense it is said that Cournot firms have no capacity for learning from past misconjectures. Their saving grace, however, is that by persisting in this misguided way an equilibrium is reached where their conjectures are finally satisfied. While the Cournot adjustment process has this troubling aspect out of equilibrium, it is important to note again that (except in the discussion of stability conditions) the sole purpose of the pre-market process and reaction functions is to provide an analytical procedure for deriving the equilibrium and *not* to describe an *actual* sequence of behavior. Thus, any perverseness in the pre-market process is to be viewed simply as a property of the technique used to solve the oligopoly problem and not of any economic importance. More particularly, any such perverse behavior does not invalidate Cournot as a *solution* (or *equilibrium*) *concept*.

Bertrand Conjectural Equilibrium. Cournot's theory of oligopoly received little attention for nearly half a century after its original publication. Bertrand (1883) and Edgeworth (1881, 1897), in the first published reviews of Cournot's treatise, changed that permanently. While acknowledging the importance of the basic Cournot solution concept, both reviewers objected to the central role that Cournot gave to output choice. Instead, Bertrand argued that oligopolists generally, and well owners in particular, controlled prices and smoothed sales by the use of inventory. In this way it was argued that price rather than the production level should be the choice for the firm's strategy variable. With this variation on Cournot, Bertrand fashioned a Nash-in-price theory of homogeneous oligopoly. The critical aspect of his analysis is of course that, with identical products and perfect information, the firm posting the lowest price sells to the entire market.

Bertrand's underlying conviction was that the price would fall to the competitive level, even in duopoly. Assuming that the rivals had identical costs and that each had sufficient capacity to alone supply the market demand at all relevant prices, Bertrand argued simply that if firm j sets some price p_j greater than marginal cost, its rival firm k would choose a price just less than p_j, but greater than marginal cost, and sell to all purchasers. Similarly, firm j would undercut firm k to recapture the market and so forth. The only equilibrium would be that where price equals marignal cost for each firm.

Bertrand's equilibrium point can also be thought of as arising from the choice of output quantities. Suppose that every firm conjectures that, for its own output change, rivals will adjust their output in a compensatory way to leave the market price unchanged. For example, in a duopoly producing a homogeneous product a change in output dz_j by firm j is conjectured to bring about a rival output change $dz_k^c = -dz_j$, leaving aggregate industry output and thereby price unaffected. This implies *output* conjectural variations $\gamma_{kj} = dz_k^c(z_j)/dz_j = -1$ and the optimality condition (3.5) in turn becomes

$$\{p - c_j'(z_j)\} + z_j \left\{ \frac{\partial p(z)}{dz_j} - \frac{\partial p(z)}{dz_k} \right\} = 0 \qquad (3.17)$$

Since the goods are homogeneous, the derivative of the demand is the same for both outputs and (3.17) reduces to

$$p = c_j'(z_j) \tag{3.18}$$

For each firm price is equal to marginal cost at a Bertrand conjectural equilibrium (BCE). This is in contrast with the CCE where, recalling equation (3.9), the equilibrium generally obtains with price in excess of marginal cost for each duopolist. It is to be emphasized that the specification of conjectures affects the resulting equilibrium quantities (and prices) in a potentially important way.

Because each firm produces the output where market price equals its marginal cost, the homogeneous-good BCE is frequently referred to as the *competitive conjectures* solution.[18] When there is equal access to technologies and factors of production, the cost functions of the firms are identical and (3.18) is a necessary condition for a *perfectly* competitive equilibrium. When the cost functions differ in the cross-section of firms, (3.18) is a necessary condition for a competitive equilibrium of the Ricardian sort (see section 2.3.3). In this second case each firm adjusts its output so that its marginal cost equals the common market price and entry provides that the marginal firms earns zero profits.

Although it is not immediately clear from the above analysis, the BCE results from discontinuities in the firm demands. To see this, suppose that the firms have identical and constant costs $c_j'(\cdot) = c'$ (see Novshek and Sonnenschein, 1980, for a detailed analysis). Because the goods are homogeneous, if buyers are fully informed about prices each will give his trade to the firm with the lowest price

$$z_j(p_j, p_k) = z(p_j) \qquad \text{for } p_j < p_k$$

or

$$z_j(p_j, p_k) = 0 \qquad \text{for } p_j > p_k$$

where $z_j(\cdot)$ is j's demand and $z(\cdot)$ is the market demand. The discontinuity is now clear: one firm captures the entire market if its price is less than its rival's, and it sells nothing if it has a higher price. When the firms set identical prices, on average each will serve half the market:

$$z_j(p_j, p_k) = \frac{z(p_j)}{2} \qquad \text{for } p_j = p_k$$

In the above situation the only Nash equilibrium that can occur is $p_j^0 = p_k^0 = c'$. If $p_j > p_k > c'$, firm j sells nothing and earns zero profit. A small price reduction to undercut firm k would give j the entire market and positive profits. Therefore firm j undercuts. Firm k reasons similarly and also undercuts when it is profitable. The undercutting just becomes unprofitable for both firms when prices are equal to each other and to marginal cost, which marks the end of the competitive process and the equilibrium.

---

[18] It is to be emphasized that this result obtains only with homogeneous goods. The heterogeneous-good case is analyzed in section 3.1.3. below.

E3.5

Bertrand Duopoly with Capacity Constraints

Edgeworth (1897) proposed a variation on the Bertrand analysis which, he argued, solved the "paradox" that homogeneous-good oligopolists acting with Nash-in-price conjectures reach the price-equals-marginal-cost competitive equilibrium regardless of their numbers. Unfortunately, his analysis leaves the industry without an equilibrium. Edgeworth presumed that at every (common) market price each firm would serve half the market and (what is critical to his analysis) that neither had sufficient capacity to serve its half of the market when the price was equal to the marginal cost. Let $\bar{z}_1$ and $\bar{z}_2$ indicate these output constraints on the firms and, as Edgeworth, assume that both firms produce with zero marginal cost.

Edgeworth's analysis was based on each firm's incentive to undercut its rival's price. To begin, he noted that if the duopolists collude they set a price p^m and produce quantities $z_j{}^m < \bar{z}_j$ where MR = MC = 0. If the firms act noncooperatively, however, each has an incentive to shave its price relative to its rival. Suppose that firm 1 has unused capacity $\bar{z}_1 - z_1{}^m$ that is not sold at price p^m. If it could sell these units at a fractionally lower price, still greater than the zero marginal cost, it could increase its profits. A small price cut below p^m in fact makes sense to firm 1 *given* it conjectures that firm 2 will not respond with a price change. Firm 2 does respond, however, using similar logic, it lowers its price fractionally below the lowered price of firm 1. Edgeworth argued that the undercutting process continues until the price $\bar{p} > 0$ is reached where each firm produces at its capacity $\bar{z}_1 = \bar{z}_2$ At this level neither firm would gain by further undercutting since neither could serve the new customers.

While it appears that $\bar{p}$ is an equilibrium, Edgeworth argued that it is not. By acting in the undercutting fashion the firms have moved to output levels where marginal revenue is in fact negative (despite the Bertrand conjecture which "promises" positive marginal revenue). Edgeworth argued that, being disappointed by the profit level at $\bar{p}$, one firm would seize the chance to raise its price back to the more profitable p^m, hoping that its rival would follow. Once the firm has done that, however, Edgeworth maintained that the rival would instead raise its price to some small amount less than p^m and another round of undercutting adjustments would take place. Edgeworth concluded that the price would oscillate between p^m and $\bar{p}$, and outputs and profits would be subject to these cycles. For further analysis of this solution see SE9.1 and SE9.2.

3.1.5 Competitive Equilibrium

With homogeneous firms there are two usual bases for competitive (price-taking) behavior and a competitive equilibrium: Bertrand conjectures and, when the number of firms is infinite, Cournot conjectures. To see how these situations develop, consider $j = 1, 2, \ldots, J$ oligopolists producing a homogeneous good. The demand and cost functions again have the standard properties set out in section 3.1.1. Each firm's stationarity point, corresponding to (3.15), occurs with

$$\frac{d\pi_j}{dz_j} = p(z) + z_j \frac{dp}{dz} \frac{dz^e}{dz_j} - c'_j = 0 \tag{3.19}$$

where $p(z)$ is the inverse market demand and $z = \Sigma_j z_j$. It is instructive to restate the conjecture as

$$\frac{dz^e}{dz_j} = \frac{dz_j}{dz_j} + \frac{d(\Sigma_{k \neq j} z_k{}^e)}{dz_j} \equiv 1 + \gamma_j \tag{3.20}$$

The right-hand side defines γ_j as firm j's conjecture concerning the output of *all other* firms. Substituting this in (3.19) and rearranging gives

$$\frac{p - c'_j}{p} = \frac{s_j(1 + \gamma_j)}{\eta} \tag{3.21}$$

where $s_j = z_j/z$ is j's market share and $\eta = -(p/z)(dz/dp)$ is the *market* demand elasticity. It is usual to refer to $(p - c'_j)/p$ as firm j's **price–cost margin**. The inverse of the right-hand side term, $\eta_j \equiv \eta/s_j(1 + \gamma_j)$, is the elasticity of demand for firm j. The denominator of this last expression, the product of the market share and the conjectural variation, "divides" or "scales" the market demand elasticity to the firm level.

For the limiting case where $\gamma_j = -1$ the conjectures are Bertrand. This price-taking behavior occurs as η_j becomes infinite and price becomes equal to marginal cost. For Cournot conjectures, $\gamma_j = 0$, the elasticity of firm demand is $\eta_j = \eta/s_j$, and the price–cost margin reduces to $s_j(1/\eta)$. In this case price-taking behavior obtains in the limit as the number of identical firms becomes infinitely large: s_j goes to zero, η_j becomes infinite, and again price equals marginal cost.[19]

As a case for comparison, suppose that each firm acts in a way that, if it changes output, it anticipates all others will follow. More exactly, each firm j with market share s_j expects its rivals (collectively) to react to any change it makes according to their (collective) shares of the market relative to his. This implies the conjectural variation $\gamma_j = (1 - s_j)/s_j$, and (3.21) becomes

$$\frac{p - c'_j}{p} = \frac{1}{\eta} \tag{3.22}$$

The price–cost margin of each firm is equal and equal to the inverse of the market demand elasticity. If the firms have different cost functions in this case, their market shares will differ. "Low-cost" firms will have greater shares and "high-cost" firms will hold back their output to maximize joint profits.[20]

Note, finally, that the numerator of (3.21) is of the form

[19] Ruffin (1971) refers to this Cournot case as "quasi-competitive" to distinguish it from the Bertrand case. Note also that the Cournot result hinges on the fact that firms are identical, so that with entry the market share of each decreases to zero. Novshek (1980) and Roberts (1980) show that if the technology of the firms is not convex, an expansion in the number of firms leads to an increase in price since costs also rise. For larger J in these cases, the Cournot equilibrium moves further away from the competitive equilibrium. (If there are fixed costs, note also that a zero-profit equilibrium fixes the upper bound on J.)

[20] Armentano (1972) and Posner (1976) have argued that these differences in market shares are a major source of difficulty in maintaining a collusive agreement. See also section 12.2.

$$s_j(1 + \gamma_j) = s_j \frac{dz^e}{dz_j} = \frac{z_j}{z} \frac{dz^e}{dz_j}$$

which is the *elasticity* conjectured by firm j concerning the industry output response to its own output change. With homogeneous goods, where price depends only on total industry output, this elasticity measures the impact firm j believes that it can exert on price. In a monopoly this elasticity is unity, if the firms are price-takers then the elasticity is zero, and in the Cournot case with a finite number of identical firms the elasticity is simply equal to each firm's market share.

3.1.6   Heterogeneous Products and Conjectural Variations

Think now of a model economy with two sectors. In the first, duopolists produce differentiated products. The second "all other goods" sector competitively provides a numeraire (composite) good. Suppose further that consumers in this economy have preferences which satisfy conditions for aggregation and, moreover, the aggregate utility is separable and linear in the numeraire good, that is $u(z) + z_0$ where the "outside" good 0 is the competitive numeraire and u is the subutility for $z = [z_1 z_2]$. We can therefore focus on the duopolists 1 and 2 without concern for price linkages with outside goods (recall section 1.3).

Cournot and Bertrand themselves considered homogeneous oligopolies, but this is not a general restriction although some details of the analysis and equilibria are affected when heterogeneous products are produced. To investigate these details assume that the products of the firms are differentiated and the applicable inverse demand functions $p_j(z)$ are both downward sloping $(\partial p_j/\partial z_j < 0)$. The products can be either substitutes $(\partial p_j/\partial z_k < 0)$ or complements $(\partial p_j/\partial z_k > 0)$. There is, in addition, the associated demand function $z_j(p)$, which is also negatively sloped and indicates substitutes when $\partial z_j/\partial p_k > 0$ and complements when $\partial z_j/\partial p_k < 0$. These functions, we assume, arise from solutions to well-formed consumer problems with concave utility so that $\partial p_j/\partial z_k = \partial p_k/\partial z_j$ (Slutsky symmetry) and $(\partial p_j/\partial z_j)/(\partial p_k/\partial z_k) - (\partial p_j/\partial z_k)/(\partial p_k/\partial z_j) > 0$ (definiteness) hold (recall section 1.3.2). To complete the notation let $c_j(z_j)$ be the increasing and convex cost function of each firm j.

We will use the profit functions of the firms in terms of both quantities

$$\pi_j(z) = p_j(z)z_j - c_j(z_j) \tag{3.23a}$$

and prices

$$\pi_j^*(p) = p_j z_j(p) - c_j\{z_j(p)\} \tag{3.23b}$$

In the quantity case, note again that the *partial* derivative $\partial \pi_j/\partial z_j$ is not usually the marginal profit perceived by the firm. In addition to this direct effect, each firm's output change is linked to those of its rival by the conjectural variation $\gamma_{kj} \equiv \partial z_k^e/\partial z_j$. A similar relationship obtains for marginal profit with respect to price and the price conjectures $\gamma_{kj}^* \equiv dp_k^e/dp_j$. In turn, the quantity and price stationarity conditions are

$$v_j(z) \equiv p_j + z_j \left(\frac{\partial p_j}{\partial z_j} + \frac{\partial p_j}{\partial z_k} \gamma_{kj} \right) - \frac{\partial c_j}{\partial z_j} = 0 \tag{3.24a}$$

$$v_j^*(p) \equiv z_j + p_j \left(\frac{\partial z_j}{\partial p_j} + \frac{\partial z_j}{\partial p_k} \gamma_{kj}^* \right) - \frac{\partial c_j}{\partial z_j} \frac{\partial z_j}{\partial p_j} = 0 \tag{3.24b}$$

respectively, and so we have that the second-order condition associated with (3.24a) is

$$v_{jj} = 2\frac{\partial p_j}{\partial z_j} + 2\frac{\partial p_j}{\partial z_h} \gamma_{kj} + z_j \left(\frac{\partial^2 p_j}{\partial z_j^2} + 2\frac{\partial^2 p_j}{\partial z_j \partial z_k} \gamma_{kj} + \frac{\partial^2 p_j}{\partial z_k^2} \gamma_{kj}^2 \right)$$

$$+ z_j \frac{\partial p_j}{\partial z_k} \left(\frac{\partial \gamma_{kj}}{\partial z_j} + \frac{\partial \gamma_{kj}}{\partial z_k} \gamma_{kj} \right) - \frac{d^2 c_j}{d z_j^2} < 0$$

Grouping terms with and without γ_{kj}, this expression reduces to

$$v_{jj}(z) = \mu_{jj}(z) + \gamma_{kj}\mu_{jk}(z) < 0 \tag{3.25a}$$

Note that γ_{kj} is considered here to be a function of the outputs. A similar calculation yields

$$v_{jj}^*(p) = \mu_{jj}^*(p) + \gamma_{kj}^*\mu_{jk}^*(p) < 0 \tag{3.25b}$$

For the case of zero conjectures ($\gamma_{kj} = 0$ in quantities and $\gamma_{kj}^* = 0$ in prices) these conditions simplify to $v_{jj} = \mu_{jj} < 0$ and $v_{jj}^* = \mu_{jj}^* < 0$.

Four Common Cases. As is now well understood by the reader, there is a range of equilibria depending on the specific conjectures which are adopted by the firms. Four of the more usual specifications are listed below in their equivalent *quantity* forms (see Bramness, 1979, for a more detailed catalogue).

1. Competitive: each firm j perceives its own price to remain constant as it changes its own output ($dp_j^e/dz_j = 0$). Using the implicit function theorem on $p_j(z) = $ const, this implies

$$\gamma_{kj} = - \frac{\partial p_j/\partial z_j}{\partial p_j/\partial z_k)} \tag{3.26a}$$

2. Cournot (quantity competition): each firm j perceives its rival's output to be unaffected by changes in its own output ($dz_k^e/dz_j = 0$), that is,

$$\gamma_{kj} = 0 \tag{3.26b}$$

3. Bertrand (price competition):[21] Each firm j perceives its rival's price to remain constant for changes in its own price $p_j(dp_k^e/dp_j = \gamma_{kj}^* = 0)$. Using the implicit function theorem on $p_k(z) = $ const, this implies

$$\gamma_{kj} = - \frac{\partial p_k/\partial z_j}{\partial p_k/\partial z_k} \tag{3.26c}$$

4. Market shares (collusion): each firm j perceives that a percentage output

---

[21] Although Cournot and Bertrand originally dealt with homogeneous goods, these labels are commonly attached to the Nash-in-quantity and Nash-in-price conjectures respectively, even with heterogeneous goods. The labels "quantity competition" and "price competition" respectively are also frequently used for these cases.

change dz_j/z_j will bring about the same output response dz_k^e/z_k from its rival:[22]

$$\gamma_{kj} = \frac{z_k}{z_j} \tag{3.26d}$$

for z_j, $z_k > 0$ in equilibrium.

When the conjectures are expressed in quantity form, as in equation (3.26a), the stationarity condition (3.24a) is appropriate. Since v_j implicitly defines the optimal output response of firm j as a function of firm k's output, it yields the usual reaction function: $z_j = r_j(z_k)$ solves (3.24a).

The slope of the reaction function can be calculated by differentiating (3.24a) implicitly. Along $r_j(z_k)$ we have $(\partial v_j/\partial z_j)\,dz_j + (\partial v_j/\partial z_k)\,dz_k = 0$, and therefore

$$r_j'(z) \equiv \frac{\partial r_j(z_k)}{\partial z_k} = \left(\frac{dz_j}{dz_k}\right)_{r_j} = -\frac{\mu_{jk}}{\mu_{jj}} \tag{3.27a}$$

It should be emphasized that this slope generally depends on the particular specification of the conjecture γ_{kj}.

Cournot (Quantity Competition). Suppose that the conjectures are Nash in quantity. Then $v_{jj} = \mu_{jj} < 0$, from the second-order condition (3.25a), and the Cournot reaction function r_j^c is downward sloping iff $\mu_{jk} = \partial p_j/\partial z_k + z_j \partial^2 p_j/\partial z_j \partial z_k < 0$. This last inequality can be quickly shown to obtain in the frequently employed case where (a) demand curves are linear (so that the second partial derivatives of the demand are zero) and (b) the products are substitutes. In this case, $\mu_{jk} = \partial p_j/\partial z_k < 0$ and each firm's output response is decreasing in its rival's output (recall E3.4).

With z_2 on the vertical axis and z_1 on the horizontal, the slopes of the Cournot reaction functions are, using (3.27a),

$$\left(\frac{dz_2}{dz_1}\right)_{r_1^c} = -\frac{\mu_{11}}{\mu_{12}}$$

along r_1^c and

$$\left(\frac{dz_2}{dz_1}\right)_{r_2^c} = -\frac{\mu_{21}}{\mu_{22}}$$

along r_2^c. Suppose that the slopes of both reaction functions are negative and r_1^c is *absolutely greater* in slope than r_2^c. Then the above two equations imply $\mu_{11}/\mu_{12} > \mu_{21}/\mu_{22}$. Using the second-order condition for profit maximization $\mu_{jj} < 0$ and the negative slope condition $\mu_{jk} < 0$ in turn implies $\mu_{11}\mu_{22} - \mu_{12}\mu_{21} > 0$. (When the slopes of r_1^c and r_2^c are reversed the converse is true.) The reader will recognize the left-hand side of this last inequality as D from stability conditions (3.9) with $\gamma_{kj} = 0$. Therefore the Cournot equilibrium with substitutes is stable iff firm 2's reaction function intersects that of firm 1 from below (on the z_2, z_1 plane). The reader can now note that the equilibrium

---

[22] With a little differentiation and algebra the reader can show that when there is Slutsky symmetry in demand ($\partial p_j/\partial z_k = \partial p_k/\partial z_j$) the market shares equilibrium is the same as that obtained under collusion, that is, when maximizing joint profits $\pi_1 + \pi_2$ with respect to both outputs.

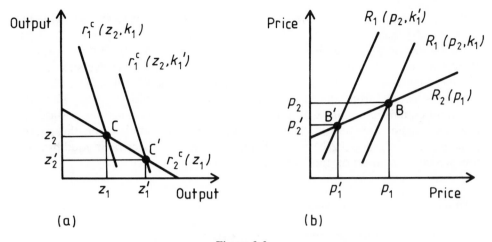

Figure 3.2
Equilibrium comparative statics: (a) Cournot equilibrium; (b) Bertrand equilibrium

points C and C′ in figure 3.1. are stable, but point C″ is not.[23] In figure 3.2(a) both C and C′ are stable Cournot equilibrium points.

Bertrand (Price Competition). A similar analysis of reaction functions obtains in prices. The stationarity condition $v_j^*(p) = 0$ implicitly defines the best price response p_j as a function of p_k, that is, $p_j = R_j(p_k)$ solves (3.24b). In turn, there is the slope

$$R_j' = \frac{\partial R_j(p_k)}{\partial p_k} = -\left(\frac{dp_j}{dp_k}\right)_{R_j} = \frac{\mu_{jk}^*}{\mu_{jj}^*} \qquad (3.27b)$$

Suppose that conjectures are Nash in price. Then $v_{jj}^* = \mu_{jj}^* < 0$, from the second-order condition (3.25b), and the reaction function (now in price space) is positively sloped iff $\mu_{jk}^* = -z_j \partial^2 z_j/\partial p_j \partial p_k + \partial z_j/\partial p_k > 0$. With linear demand and substitutes, for example, the Bertrand reaction functions $R_j{}^b$ are positively sloped. More generally, with substitutes a sufficient condition for the positive slope is $\partial^2 z_j/\partial p_j \partial p_k < 0$. Even when these conditions do not obtain, the *standard assumption* is that the relative signs and magnitudes are such that $\mu_{jk}^* > 0$, making the Bertrand reaction functions *upward* sloping on the price plane.[24]

With p_2 on the vertical axis and p_1 on the horizontal axis, the slopes of the Bertrand reaction functions are, using (3.27b),

$$\left(\frac{dp_2}{dp_1}\right)_{R_1{}^b} = -\frac{\mu_{11}^*}{\mu_{12}^*}$$

along $R_1{}^b$ and

$$\left(\frac{dp_2}{dp_1}\right)_{R_2{}^b} = -\frac{\mu_{21}^*}{\mu_{22}^*}$$

[23] With complements, stability alternatively requires positive slopes with r_1^c greater in slope than r_2^c.

[24] Note that even with complements μ_{jk}^* may be positive and the reaction functions positively sloping in prices.

along $R_2{}^b$. Suppose that the reaction functions are positively sloped, with the slope of $R_1{}^b$ *greater* than that of $R_2{}^b$. As a result, $(-\mu_{11}^*/\mu_{12}^*) > (-\mu_{21}^*/\mu_{22}^*)$. Cross-multiplying – note the second-order condition $\mu_{jj}^* < 0$ and the positive slope condition $\mu_{jk}^* > 0$ – in turn implies $\mu_{11}^*\mu_{22}^* - \mu_{12}^*\mu_{21}^* > 0$. (Reversing slopes, the converse is true.) The reader will recognize the left-hand side of this last inequality as D^* from the stability condition (3.11b) with $\gamma_{kj}^* = 0$. Thus the Bertrand equilibrium point with positively sloping reaction functions is stable iff firm 1's reaction function intersects that of firm 2 from below (on the p_2, p_1 price plane). In figure 3.2(b) points B and B′ are stable Bertrand equilibria for the two different reaction functions of firm 1.

E3.6 ───

Reaction Functions in Price and Quantity

Starting with the conditions (3.27) and the differential of the demand function $dz_j = (\partial z_j/\partial p_j)\,dp_j + (\partial z_j/\partial p_k)\,dp_k$, a little algebra produces the slope of the reaction function on the price plane in terms of that on the quantity plane:[25]

$$R_j' = \frac{r_j'(\partial z_k/\partial p_k) - (\partial z_j/\partial p_k)}{r_j'(\partial z_k/\partial p_j) - (\partial z_j/\partial p_j)} \tag{3.28}$$

From this relationship, note that when the reaction functions are negatively sloped on the quantity plane ($r_j' < 0$), own-demands are negatively sloped, and the goods are complements ($\partial z_j/\partial p_k > 0$), the reaction functions on the price plane are also negatively sloped ($R_j' < 0$). It is important to understand that (3.28) links the reaction function slope on the price and quantity planes for the single specification of conjectures adopted in the stationarity conditions; it does not link Bertrand and Cournot conjectures on the two planes.

═══

3.1.7   Comparative Statics of Conjectural Equilibra

For each firm j let κ_j indicate a parameter of the cost function: $c_j(z_j, \kappa_j)$. It is usual to think of κ_j as plant capacity (capital), but that specific interpretation is not necessary.[26] Using the stationarity conditions (3.24a), we obtain the differential change in equilibrium outputs arising from a change in the κ as

$$\mu_{11}\,dz_1 + \mu_{12}\,dz_2 = \frac{\partial c_1'}{\partial \kappa_1}\,d\kappa_1 \tag{3.29a}$$

$$\mu_{21}\,dz_1 + \mu_{22}\,dz_2 = \frac{\partial c_2'}{\partial \kappa_2}\,d\kappa_2 \tag{3.29b}$$

---

[25] For emphasis: $R_j(\cdot)$ indicates a reaction function in prices, while $r_j(\cdot)$ is in terms of quantities.

[26] A per unit tax and investments in product development can also be thought of in this way. To see this second case, suppose that each firm's product provides valued consumer services measured by ξ and let $p(\xi)$ be the associated inverse demand. These services are assumed to be "bundled in" with the product. With z the quantity of the product output, $c(z)$ the usual cost function, and $f(\kappa)$ the quantity of the services per unit z, $\xi = f(\kappa)z$ and the cost of delivering services ξ is $c(\xi/f(\kappa)) \equiv \bar{c}(\xi, \kappa)$.

with c'_j again indicating marginal cost. These equations solve for the output changes

$$dz_1 = \left(\mu_{22} \frac{\partial c'_1}{\partial \kappa_1} d\kappa_1 + \mu_{11} \frac{\partial r_1}{\partial z_2} \frac{\partial c'_2}{\partial \kappa_2} d\kappa_2\right)\Big/D \qquad (3.30a)$$

$$dz_2 = \left(\mu_{11} \frac{\partial c'_2}{\partial \kappa_2} d\kappa_2 + \mu_{22} \frac{\partial r_2}{\partial z_1} \frac{\partial c'_1}{\partial \kappa_1} d\kappa_1\right)\Big/D \qquad (3.30b)$$

where $D \equiv \mu_{11}\mu_{22} - \mu_{12}\mu_{21}$ is the determinant arising in the stability conditions, and we use the reaction function slope given by (3.27a).

A situation frequently of interest occurs when only one parameter, say κ_1, changes. In this case, note that

$$dz_1 = \left(\mu_{22} \frac{\partial c'_1}{\partial \kappa_1} d\kappa_1\right)\Big/D \qquad (3.31a)$$

$$dz_2 = \left(\mu_{22} \frac{\partial r_2}{\partial z_1} \frac{\partial c'_1}{\partial \kappa_1} d\kappa_1\right)\Big/D \qquad (3.31b)$$

When the stability conditions $\mu_{22}/D < 0$ hold (recall (3.9)) and the effect of a greater capital level is to decrease marginal cost, then $dz_1 > 0$: a greater plant capacity κ_1 implies an increase in firm 1's output. When, in addition, the goods are substitutes and the reaction functions are negatively sloped on the quantity plane, $dz_2 < 0$: greater κ_1 yields a decrease in firm 2's output.[27] These results are illustrated in figure 3.2(a) with the reaction function shift from $r_1{}^c(z_2, \kappa_1)$ to $r_1{}^c(z_2, \kappa'_1)$ brought about by $\kappa'_1 > \kappa_1$. Dividing (3.31b) by (3.31a), it is finally of interest to observe that (again with κ_2 constant)

$$\frac{dz_2}{dz_1} = \frac{\partial r_2}{\partial z_1} \qquad (3.32)$$

that is, the displaced equilibrium moves along the r_2 reaction function as indicated by points C and C′ in figure 3.2(a).

Price Effects. The analysis with price as the strategic variable develops in a way parallel to that of the quantity case. Corresponding to equations (3.31) there are the comparative statics results

$$dp_1 = \left(\mu_{22}^* \frac{\partial c'_1}{\partial \kappa_1} \frac{\partial z_1}{\partial p_1} d\kappa_1\right)\Big/D^* \qquad (3.33a)$$

$$dp_2 = \left(\mu_{22}^* \frac{\partial R_2}{\partial p_1} \frac{\partial c'_1}{\partial \kappa_1} \frac{\partial z_1}{\partial p_1} d\kappa_1\right)\Big/D^*. \qquad (3.33b)$$

where D^* is given by (3.11b). The presence of the demand slope term $\partial z_1/\partial p_1$ in these expressions is to retain the cost change as a function of *output* (marginal cost). Consider (3.33a) assuming that the stability conditions holds, own-demands are negatively sloped, and marginal cost decreases in κ_1. In this case $dp_1/d\kappa_1 < 0$. Thus, for positively sloping reaction functions on the price

---

[27] Despite the disdain for stability conditions voiced in section 3.1.2, the reader now sees their key role in signing comparative statics results. To the extent that the stability conditions are irrelevant, the sign results presented here require an alternative explanation.

plane, (3.33b) implies $dp_2/d\kappa_1 > 0$. An increase in firm 1's capital decreases the equilibrium price of *both* firms. Finally, dividing conditions (3.33) gives

$$\frac{dp_2}{dp_1} = \frac{\partial R_2}{\partial p_1} \tag{3.34}$$

that is, the displaced equilibrium moves along the R_2 reaction function as illustrated in figure 3.2(b) for $\kappa_1' > \kappa_1$.

3.2   Strategy Variables and Nash Solutions

Look back to the specification of conjectures set out in equations (3.26). What is of interest here is that those conjectures, whether originally stated in terms of prices or revenues, were finally expressed in terms of quantities. For example, the Nash-in-price conjectures of the Bertrand case $dp_k^e/dp_j = 0$ were alternatively stated in terms of outputs as $dz_k^e/dz_j = -(\partial p_k/\partial z_j)/(\partial p_j/\partial z_j)$. These transformations focus our attention on a critical aspect of the Nash solution concept. That concept, and finally the Nash equilibrium, is based on the requirement that each firm chooses a strategy which maximizes its payoff when the strategy selected by all other firms is held constant. While this assumed lack of interaction appears contrary to the recognized interdependence typical of oligopoly, it is not: if one firm anticipates a (nonzero) reaction on the part of its rivals, then all that is necessary is to define the strategy variable in such a way that the reaction becomes part of it. For example, the nonzero conjectures in quantities $dz_k^e/dz_j = -(\partial p_k/\partial z_j)/(\partial p_j/\partial z_j)$ appear to be inconsistent with the Nash solution concept, but the restatement of these conjectures in terms of price yields an equivalent model consistent with the Nash concept.

These observations lead to a general and important result: under certain regularity conditions (noted below), every conjectural equilibrium corresponds to a Nash equilibrium in some (usually different) strategic variable, and conversely. The proof of this correspondence is straightforward. Restricting attention to a duopoly, let

$$\frac{d\sigma_j^e}{d\sigma_k} = \gamma_{jk}(\sigma) \neq 0 \tag{3.35}$$

indicate complex conjectures in strategy variables $\sigma = [\sigma_1\sigma_2]$ for which a unique equilibrium exists and for which we wish to find the equivalent Nash conjectures and equilibrium. Consider the new strategy variables $s = [s_1s_2]$ defined by the functions $s_j = f_j(\sigma)$. Associated with these identities are the derivatives

$$\frac{ds_j}{d\sigma_j} = \frac{\partial f_j}{\partial \sigma_j} + \frac{df_j}{\partial \sigma_k}\frac{d\sigma_k}{d\sigma_j} \tag{3.36}$$

Take the ratio of these two equations. When the conjectures in s are Nash ($ds_k^e/ds_j = 0$), then this ratio will equal zero. Solving leads to the corresponding σ conjectures

$$\gamma_{kj} \equiv \frac{d\sigma_k^e}{d\sigma_j} = -\frac{\partial f_j/\partial \sigma_j}{\partial f_j/\partial \sigma_k} \tag{3.37}$$

which are two differential equations in the functions f_1 and f_2. When these functions are suitably regular,[28] these equations have a solution and any CE in z can therefore be transformed to an equivalent Nash equilibrium in the strategy variables s defined by the f solutions.

E3.7

Zero and Nonzero Conjectures Equivalence

Suppose that the following output conjectural variations obtain (with $z_j \neq 0$):

$$\frac{dz_1{}^c}{dz_2} = \gamma_{12}(z_1, z_2) = \frac{-2z_1}{z_2} \qquad (3.38a)$$

$$\frac{dz_2{}^c}{dz_1} = \gamma_{21}(z_1, z_2) = \frac{-2z_2}{z_1} \qquad (3.38b)$$

The corresponding form for equations (3.37) becomes

$$\frac{\partial f_2/\partial z_2}{\partial f_2/\partial z_1} = \frac{2z_1}{z_2} \qquad (3.39a)$$

$$\frac{\partial f_1/\partial z_1}{\partial f_1/\partial z_2} = \frac{2z_2}{z_1} \qquad (3.39b)$$

which can be solved for the functions f_1 and f_2. A little trial and error quickly produces the transforming strategy variables

$$s_1 = \frac{z_1{}^2 z_2}{2} \qquad (3.40a)$$

$$s_2 = \frac{z_2{}^2 z_1}{2} \qquad (3.40b)$$

It is left as an exercise for the reader to show that the conjectural equilibrium with the quantity conjectures (3.38) is identical with the Nash equilibrium with strategy variables s_1 and s_2 defined by (3.40).

3.3 Cournot and Bertrand: Choice of Type

A Cournot conjectural equilibrium requires that each firm choose a (nonnegative) quantity to maximize profits, taking the output of its rivals as constant. With $j = 1, 2, \ldots, J$ firms producing a homogeneous product this means that each firm j behaves as a monopolist with respect to the *residual* demand schedule

$$z_j{}^{cr}(p) = z(p) = \sum_{k \neq j} z_k \qquad (3.41)$$

---

[28] There are several sufficiency conditions for the existence of a solution to the differential equations (3.37). One of the simplest is that the equations satisfy a Lipschitz condition (see Lee and Marcus, 1968, ch. 1).

where $z(p)$ is the market demand and $\Sigma_{k\neq j}z_k$ is the output of all rivals, a quantity that firm j perceives to be constant. Firm j's conjecture that it cannot affect the quantity sold by its rivals is equivalent to the belief that these rivals have irrevocable contracts to supply the quantity $\Sigma_{k\neq j}z_k$ to buyers at all market prices. When supply contracts of this kind are used, or perceived to be used, it is usual to say that there is (static) **quantity competition** and a Cournot–Nash equilibrium results. Using this notation, an output plan $[z_1{}^c z_2{}^c \ldots z_j{}^c]$ is then a CCE if, for each j, $z_j{}^c \geqslant 0$ maximizes

$$\pi(z_j : z^c) \equiv z_j p(z_j{}^{cr}) - c(z_j) \tag{3.42}$$

where $p = p(z_j{}^{cr})$ is the inverse demand associated with (3.41), $c(\cdot)$ is the common cost function, and $(z_j : z^c)$ is the notation for the J-tuple of equilibrium outputs with z_j replacing $z_j{}^c$. Grossman (1981) illustrates these ideas with a simple entry example as follows.

E3.8

Barriers to Entry with Quantity Competition

Suppose that the market demand for a particular product is $z(p)$ and there is a corresponding inverse demand $p(z)$. Suppose further that every firm choosing to sell the product has the same average cost as shown in figure 3.3. If one such firm, say k, produces the monopoly output level $z_k{}^m$, then with Cournot conjectures the residual demand $z_j{}^{cr}(p) = z(p) - z_k{}^m$ is faced by every potential entrant j. In the figure the inverse market demand $p(z)$ and average cost $AC(z_j)$ are contructed in such a way that the inverse residual demand schedule

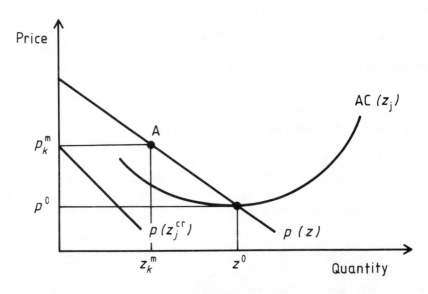

Figure 3.3
Entry barriers: quantity competition

$p(z_j^{cr})$ lies (at all prices) to the left of the average cost curve. Under these conditions the CCE occurs with one firm producing the monopoly level and all other producing zero. Even though there is free entry in the sense that all firms have equal access to markets, technologies, and factors, an incumbent monopolist deters entry in this case since, with the Cournot conjectures, no other firm foresees production as being profitable (Modigliani, 1958, provides a detailed analysis of this case).

In the above example each would-be producer assumes that, should he produce, the incumbent monopolist will retain all its existing trade. This Cournot conjecture has no fundamental economic rationale. On the contrary, it seems more likely that some potential producer would instead approach buyers with a price-stipulating contract, offering to meet their demand at prices less than the monopolist charges.[29] If the buyers are not contractually bound to purchase quantity z_j^m from the monopolist and the monopolist will not lower its price below p^m, then the would-be producer will attract the entire market trade with such an offer. When price-stipulating contracts are used, or are perceived to be used, in this way it is usual to say that there is (static) **price competition** and a Bertrand–Nash equilibrium results. As Grossman (1981) has emphasized, such contracts result in a residual demand schedule with important differences from that which occurs with quantity competition. Specifically,

$$z_j^{br}(p) = 0 \qquad \text{if } p_j > p_k \text{ for some firm } k$$

$$= z(p)/J' \qquad \text{if } p_j \leqslant p_k \text{ and } J' \text{ firms set price } p_j \quad (3.43)$$

Using this residual demand specification, a BCE is a collection of J prices $[p_1^b p_2^b \ldots p_j^b]$ such that, for each firm j, p_j^b solves

$$\max[p_j z_j^{br}(p_j : p^b) - c\{z_j^{br}(p_j : p^b)\}]$$

where $(p_j : p^b)$ is the notation for the J-tuple of equilibrium prices with p_j replacing p_j^b.

E3.9

Barriers to Entry with Price Competition

As the residual demand with price competition differs from that with quantity competition it will generally have different implications for conditions of entry. Figure 3.4 reveals these differences for the homogeneous-goods case. As before, $p(z_j^{cr})$ is the entrant's inverse residual demand with quantity competition when the incumbent firm k chooses price p^m. In contrast, with price competition the entrant's inverse demand $p(z_j^{br})$ is zero for p_j above p_k^m, one-half the market demand for $p_j = p_k^m$, and the entire market demand for $p_j < p_k^m$. In this case

---

[29] This is precisely the argument Bertrand offered for his revision of Cournot's analysis.

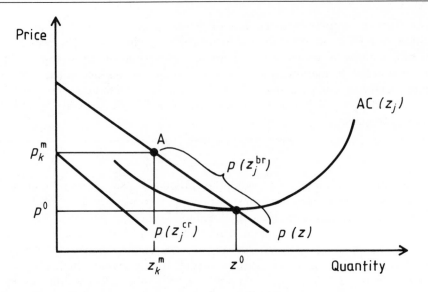

Figure 3.4
Entry barriers: price competition

the price p_k^m is not a barrier to entry, since an entrant can shade price slightly and capture the entire trade. Rather, the entry-deterring price is the competitive price p^0.

Bertrand conjectures produce competition which is *as if* an incumbent cannot make a binding contract to customers, and thus it gives up its trade to entrants. Cournot conjectures produces competition which is *as if* an incumbent makes a binding commitment with its customers that leaves only a (perhaps unprofitably small) residual available for the entrant.

By choosing to fix its price (regardless of the quantity supplied) by contract, a firm induces its rival to have Bertrand conjectures. Alternatively, a firm choosing to fix its quantity (regardless of its selling price) by contract induces its rival to have Cournot conjectures. Intermediate cases obtain and we might more generally think of every firm's offer to sell as a function specifying supply at various prices. By this view, the (Bertrand) price contract corresponds to a horizontal supply schedule, as the firm agrees to supply any quantity at a quoted price, and the (Cournot) quantity contract corresponds to the polar vertical supply schedule, as the firm agrees to supply a fixed quantity at all market prices. A variety of alternative supply contracts and equilibria obviously lie between the polar Bertrand and Cournot cases.

3.3.1   Choice of Contract Type

For duopolies in which identical firms produce a homogeneous good the Bertrand equilibrium price equals marginal cost and the Cournot equilibrium price is above that. With differentiated products the Bertrand price is above marginal cost, but the Cournot prices are even greater.[30] For this reason it is common to think of the CCE as expressing greater monopoly power than the BCE. Does this in turn mean that firms will always choose Cournot quantity-setting contracts?

Two-stage Interaction. An answer to this question can be formulated by considering the following two-stage decision sequence:

1 (contract type choice) at stage $t - 1$ the firms (simultaneously) choose a contract type (price or quantity) without knowledge of the type chosen by their rival;
2 (price or quantity choice) at the following stage t the choices of contract type are publicly announced and each firm then chooses the maximum-profit price or quantity respectively, depending on whether price or quantity contracts are adopted.

It bears emphasizing that stage $t - 1$ is not a market date in this sequence, as exchange does not take place at that time. At stage t trading occurs and we seek the appropriate Nash equilibrium. The firms' choice (and maximum payoff) at the market stage depends strongly on the contract type choices at the prior stage. In a duopoly there are four possible equilibria.[31] First, both duopolists might choose price contracts, in which case the standard BCE occurs at market stage t. The value of this outcome to each duopolist j is measured by its profits $\pi_j{}^b$. If both duopolists choose quantity contracts, the standard CCE then occurs and the equilibrium prices and quantities imply profits $\pi_j{}^c$ for each j. These BCE and CCE results follows exactly as in section 3.1. Moreover, because we assume that both firms have full information and are fully rational, the profits can be calculated for each case and compared at $t - 1$.

In addition to these standard cases, there are two possible "cross strategies": where firm 1 chooses to offer one type of contract and firm 2 chooses the other. When firm 1 adopts the Bertrand conjecture (firm 2 uses the price contract) and firm 2 adopts Cournot (firm 1 uses the quantity contract) the cross-strategy is labeled bc, and conversely for cb. Table 3.1 indicates the four possible cases. The Cournot (c) and Bertrand (b) solutions have been developed above, which leaves only the bc and cb crossed cases to be analyzed and compared. That task is simplified by a duality in analytical structure between the Cournot and Bertrand models. It is to that duality which we first turn.

---

[30] Compare (3.15) and (3.18) for the homogeneous-good case and (3.24a) and (3.24b) for heterogeneous goods. SE3.5 fully develops these various price relationships for linear demand and constant marginal cost. The reason for this relationship of price to cost is that firms have less incentive to price above marginal cost with Bertrand competition since their perceived demand elasticity is greater than it is with Cournot competition.

[31] Analyses of Cournot–Bertrand strategy choice in duopoly have been performed by Bylka and Komar (1975), Hathaway and Rickard (1979), Cheng (1984), Singh and Vives (1984), and Vives (1985).

Table 3.1 Contract Strategies

		Firm 2: contract type	
		Quantity	*Price*
Firm 1:	*Quantity*	c	bc
contract type	*Price*	cb	b

3.3.2 Cournot and Bertrand Duality

It is helpful to quickly review the assumed demand and cost conditions. Again, let $p = [p_1 p_2]$ and $z = [z_1 z_2]$. The inverse demands $p_j = p_j(z)$ are twice continuously differentiable, downward sloping in own-quantities, and have (symmetric) cross-effects with $\partial p_j/\partial z_k = \partial p_k/\partial z_j$ positive for complements and negative for substitutes. The corresponding demand functions $z_j = z_j(p)$ are also downward sloping in own-prices and have (symmetric) cross-effects with $\partial z_k/\partial p_j = \partial z_j/\partial p_k$ positive for substitutes and negative for complements. Assume further that marginal costs for the firms are positive and constant and, without loss of generality, let this constant be zero (otherwise, define prices as net of marginal costs).

Under these conditions each firm j's profits can be written in terms of either quantities $\pi_j(z) = p_j(z)z_j$ or prices $\pi_j^*(p) = p_j z_j(p_j)$. With Cournot contracts, firms choose outputs to solve $\partial \pi_j/\partial z_j = p_j + z_j\{\partial p_j(z)/\partial z_j\} = 0$; with Bertrand contracts, prices are alternatively chosen to solve $\partial \pi_j^*/\partial p_j = z_j + p_j\{\partial z_j(p)/\partial p_j\} = 0$. On inspection it is seen that these problems have a *dual* structure in the sense that the *analytical form* of one solution derives from the other when replacing z_j with p_j and $p_j(\cdot)$ with $z_j(\cdot)$, or conversely. There is only one slight complication: $\partial z_j/\partial p_k$ and $\partial p_j/\partial z_k$ have opposite signs, and as these derivatives are involved in the price and quantity stationarity conditions respectively, duality requires something more. Cournot oligopoly with *substitutes* is the dual of Bertrand oligopoly with *complements*. [32]

It is important to understand that duality is in analytical structure alone. Duality means that, given demand and cost conditions, if we know the Cournot solution equations we can immediately write down the Bertrand solution equations. This is done by exchanging prices and quantities and exchanging substitutes and complements (that is, exchanging $-\partial p_j/\partial z_k$ with $\partial z_j/\partial p_k$). It should be noted that duality does *not* mean that the Cournot equilibrium quantities, and corresponding prices, are those that occur in the dual Bertrand equilibrium.

---

[32] This duality was first recognized by Sonnenschein (1968) for the case of homogeneous products. See also Friedman (1977) and Hathaway and Rickard (1979). We assume here than the two equilibria exist uniquely.

E3.10 ===

Bertrand and Cournot Duality

The duality of the BCE and the CCE can be illustrated for the frequently used case of linear demands and inverse demands. Specifically, let the inverse demands be

$$p_1 = a_1 - b_1 z_1 - dz_2 \tag{3.44a}$$

$$p_2 = a_2 - b_2 z_2 - dz_1 \tag{3.44b}$$

where a_j, b_j, and d are parameters. For these functions to result from the maximization of a strictly concave utility it is required that $b_j > 0$ and $b_1 b_2 - d^2 > 0$. In addition, for prices and quantities to be nonnegative the parameters must be such that $a_j > 0$ and $a_j b_j - a_j d > 0$ (recall E1.9). If we define four new parameters $\gamma = b_1 b_2 - d^2$, $\alpha_j = (a_j b_k - a_k d)/\gamma$, $\beta_k = b_j/\gamma$, and $\delta = d/\gamma$, the demand functions themselves can be written as

$$z_1 = \alpha_1 - \beta_1 p_1 + \delta p_2 \tag{3.45a}$$

$$z_2 = \alpha_2 - \beta_2 p_2 + \delta p_1 \tag{3.45b}$$

The products are substitutes, independent, or complements in this case depending on whether $\delta > 0$, $\delta = 0$, or $\delta < 0$ respectively. The reader will also note that when $a_1 = a_2$ and $b_1 = b_2 = d$ the products are perfect substitutes. Finally, when $a_1 = a_2$ it is common to use $d^2/b_1 b_2$ as an index of product differentiation since this expression uniformly increases from zero to unity as the goods range from being independent to perfect substitutes.

On the supply side, it is assumed that the duopolists produce under conditions of constant marginal costs. Without loss of generality assume that this marginal cost is zero (otherwise define the price as net of marginal cost.)[33] That gives $\pi_j = p_j z_j$, which is symmetric in price and output variables.

Duality in Equilibria. In arriving at the CCE and BCE, Cournot duopolists set output quantities and Bertrand duopolists set prices. In the linear demand case this means that Cournot firm 1 maximizes $(a_1 - b_1 z_1 - dz_2)z_1$ by choosing z_1, with z_2 given and Bertrand firm 1 maximizes $(\alpha_1 - \beta_1 p_1 + \delta p_2)p_1$ by choosing p_1, with p_2 given. Note the duality in maximands: one can be derived from the other by simply substituting z_j for p_j, α_j for a_j, β_j for b_j, and $-\delta$ for d, or conversely. Cournot duopolists with substitute products $(d > 0)$ face a problem having the same analytical structure as Bertrand duopolists with complements $(\delta < 0)$.

The duality in maximand carries over directly to a duality in CCE and BCE. More generally, it is straightforward to write down Cournot reaction functions, optimal strategies, solution points, and profits directly from the dual Bertrand case, and vice versa. For example, the reader can quickly show that Bertrand

---

[33] Using this redefined net price in the demand and inverse demand functions requires only that the original parameter a_j be redefined as $a_j - c_j'$ and the original α_j be redefined as $\alpha_j + c_j'(-\beta_j + \delta)$. In the following sections we will generally use these redefinitions.

reaction function of firm 1 (given price p_2) to be $R_1{}^b = (\alpha_1 + \delta p_2)/2\beta_1$. The corresponding Cournot reaction function of firm 1 (given output z_2) can then be written simply by making the duality substitutions: $r_1{}^c = (a_1 - dz_2)/2b_1$.

When the goods are substitutes the reaction functions have a negative slope (on the quantity plane) for the Cournot duopolists and a positive slope (on the price plane) for Bertrand duopolists.[34] Moreover, the linearity of these functions assures that they will intersect only once (with an appropriate choice of parameters) and therefore provide only one equilibrium for each case.[35] SE3.5 provides BCE and CCE solution details.

3.3.3   Dominant Strategies

We are now ready to analyze the duopolists' choice of type. It is helpful to start with the result. Under conditions which guarantee unique equilibria for all four (c, cb, bc, b) strategy pairs the following conditions are met.

> 1 Cournot prices are greater than Bertrand prices, which with negatively sloped demands implies that Cournot quantities are less than Bertrand quantities.
> 2 In the two-stage interaction both firms will choose the Cournot type if their products are substitutes and both will choose the Bertrand type if their products are complements – cross-strategies will not be adopted.

We work our way to these results in several steps. While Cournot conjectures and reactions are usually stated in quantity terms and Bertrand conjectures and reactions in prices, it is now clear that these are not essential requirements (recall E3.6). In fact, when speaking of cross-strategies, it is convenient to carry out the analysis uniformly in terms of either prices or quantities. We adopt prices in the following analysis and translate the Cournot reaction functions to price terms. (Again, the superscripts b and c indicate Bertrand and Cournot cases respectively, and r and R indicate reaction functions in quantity and price respectively). Using the inverse demand, and following the development of (3.28), the Cournot quantity reaction $z_j(p) = r_j{}^c\{z_k(p)\}$ solves for the Cournot price reaction $p_j = R_j{}^c(p_k)$.

For the moment, suppose that the duopolists produce substitute goods. Further let both the Bertrand and Cournot reaction functions have positive slope on the price plane with pairwise intersections of $R_1{}^c(p)$, $R_2{}^c(p)$, $R_1{}^b(p)$, and $R_2{}^b(p)$ occurring uniquely as shown in figure 3.5.[36] The intersection of $R_1{}^c$ and

---

[34] The reader can show that this is a special case of equations (3.19).

[35] Stability conditions for the equilibrium are easily shown to be $\mu_{jj} = -2b_j < 0$, $D = 4b_1b_2 - d^2 > 0$ and $\mu_{jj}^* = -2\beta_j < 0$, $D^* = 4\beta_1\beta_2 - \delta^2 > 0$ (for the Cournot and Bertrand cases respectively). These conditions are assured by the concavity of the quadratic utility underlying the linear demands.

[36] Recall E3.5, which describes necessary and sufficient conditions for $dR_j{}^b/dp_k > 0$. Singh and Vives (1984, appendix 2) and Cheng (1985) give sufficient conditions for $dR_j{}^c/dp_k > 0$ and the unique pairwise intersections. Briefly, the existence and uniqueness conditions are that the Bertrand and Cournot reaction functions have slopes of less than unity in absolute value and the stability conditions (3.9) and (3.11) obtain.

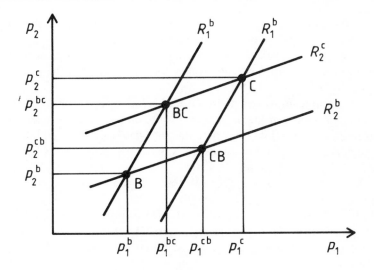

Figure 3.5
Bertrand–Cournot equilibria

$R_2{}^c$ gives the Cournot equilibrium point; $R_1{}^b$ and $R_2{}^b$ intersect at the Bertrand equilibrium. The cross-strategy pairs are also as suspected: the intersection of $R_1{}^c$ and $R_2{}^b$ determines the cb equilibrium, and $R_1{}^b$ and $R_2{}^c$ intersect at the bc equilibrium. These equilibria will immediately be described in terms of price, but the demand functions yield corresponding equilibrium quantities and, in turn, equilibrium profits can be calculated. While the choice of Cournot or Bertrand type by the firms will finally be based on the profit opportunities provided in the four possible equilibria, a key intermediate result concerns the relationship betwen Cournot and Bertrand prices as developed in the following steps.

Step 1. Cournot stationarity (in prices) requires

$$\frac{d\pi_j^*(p)}{dp_j} = \frac{\partial\pi_j^*(p)}{\partial p_j} + \left(p_j\frac{\partial z_j}{\partial p_k}\frac{dp_k{}^c}{dp_j}\right) = 0$$

where

$$\frac{dp_k{}^c}{dp_j} = -\frac{\partial z_k/\partial p_j}{\partial z_k/\partial p_k}$$

for the zero quantity conjectures. With negatively sloped own-demands and substitutes the term in parentheses must be negative and therefore $\partial\pi_j^*(R_j{}^c(p_k), p_k)/\partial p_j > 0$. Thus $R_j{}^c(p_k) > R_j{}^b(p_k)$. That is, each firm's Cournot best-response price (given its rival's price) is always greater than the Bertrand best-response price. As this holds uniformly, for all values of the rival price, the Cournot reaction function in price "lies above" the Bertrand reaction function as illustrated in figure 3.5.

Step 2. Since $R_j{}^c > R_j{}^b$ and the reaction functions are upward sloping, each firm j's Cournot equilibrium price must be greater than all other equilibrium prices: $p_1^c > p_1^{cb}$, p_1^{bc}, p_1^b, and $p_2^c > p_2^{cb}$, p_2^{bc}, p_2^b. By a similar argument $p_1^{cb} > p_1^b$ and $p_2^{bc} > p_2^b$. These results are indicated by the C, BC, CB and B equilibria shown in figure 3.5. Thus, regardless of the type choice of firm k, firm j's decision to play the Cournot type gives it a greater equilibrium price.

Step 3. The implications of these price relationships for profits are as expected. Cournot behavior yields greater profits under all cases when the goods are substitutes. To prove this, note first that the profit of firm 1 increases along R_1^b as p_2 increases, because the goods are substitutes, and thus $\pi_1^{bc} > \pi_1^b$ since $p_2^{bc} > p_2^b$. In addition, from the stationarity condition $d\pi_1^*(R_1^c(p_2), p_2)/dp_2 = z_2 \partial p_1(z)/\partial z_1$ of the Cournot problem, the profit of firm 1 must increase along R_1^c as p_2 increases. Thus, $\pi_1^c > \pi_1^{cb}$ since $p_2^c > p_2^{cb}$. Finally, since firm 1's profits are increasing in p_1 and increasing with decreases in p_2, then $p_1^{cb} > p_1^{bc}$ and $p_2^{bc} > p_2^{cb}$ imply $\pi_1^{cb} > \pi_2^{bc}$. Firms 1 and 2 can be reversed in the above arguments (and cb replaced with bc) to give the firm 2 profit rankings.

The alternative complementary products case derives from the above analysis using Cournot–Bertrand duality. It is left to the reader to interchange prices and quantities, substitutes and complements, and Cournot and Bertrand types.

Once more, with substitute goods, the equilibrium prices occurring with quantity contracts are greater than those occurring with price contracts in all four strategy cases and therefore the two-stage interaction has a Cournot solution. Conversely, if the goods are complements, the Bertrand solution dominates. Cross-strategies are not optimal.

E3.11 ───

Cournot and Bertrand Dominance

The above results for dominant strategies can be illustrated using the linear demand and constant cost conditions set out in E3.10. Consider first the bc situation, where duopolist 2 chooses $z_2 \geqslant 0$ to maximize its profits $p_2 z_2 = (\alpha_2 + \delta p_1 - z_2)z_2/\beta_2$, taking the rival's price p_1 as given. The (Cournot) reaction function for 2, derived in the usual way, is $z_2 = (\alpha_2 + \delta p_1)/2\beta_2$. Because of the linearity in demand, when the duopolists' products are substitutes (complements), the function has a positive (negative) slope. Firm 1's problem is the Bertrand dual: it chooses $p_1 \geqslant 0$ to maximize $p_1 z_1$, with its rival's quantity z_2 taken as given. The duality of the problems immediately yields 1's (Bertrand) reaction function $p_1 = (a_1 - dz_2)/2\beta_2$, which has a positive (negative) slope for substitutes (complements). The two linear reaction functions intersect once, providing a unique bc equilibrium with prices and outputs[37]

$$p_1^{bc} = \frac{2\alpha_1\beta_1 + \alpha_2\delta}{\varepsilon} \tag{3.46a}$$

[37] See Singh and Vives (1984) for detailed calculations of these and all formulae in this example.

$$z_1{}^{bc} = \frac{\theta p_1{}^{bc}}{\beta_2} \tag{3.46b}$$

$$p_2{}^{bc} = \frac{2\alpha_2\beta_1 + \alpha_1\delta - \alpha_2\delta^2}{\beta_2/\varepsilon} \tag{3.46c}$$

$$z_2{}^{bc} = \beta_2 p_2{}^{bc} \tag{3.46d}$$

Here, $\varepsilon = 4\beta_1\beta_2 - 3\delta^2$ and $\theta = \beta_1\beta_2 - \delta^2$ are composite parameters.

The second crossed case cb is analogous. When firm 1 selects the quantity contract and firm 2 the price contract, then 1 uses a Bertrand reaction function and 2 uses a Cournot reaction function. The symmetry with the bc case immediately gives the cb equilibrium prices and outputs

$$p_1{}^{cb} = \frac{2\alpha_1\beta_2 + \alpha_2\delta - \alpha_1\delta^2/\beta_1}{\varepsilon} \tag{3.47a}$$

$$z_1{}^{cb} = \beta_1 p_1{}^{cb} \tag{3.47b}$$

$$p_2{}^{cb} = \frac{2\alpha_2\beta_1 + \alpha_1\delta}{\varepsilon} \tag{3.47c}$$

$$z_2{}^{cb} = \frac{\theta p_2{}^{cb}}{\beta_1} \tag{3.47d}$$

With these calculations as background it is straightforward to show that, given a linear demand and constant costs, the Nash equilibrium strategy choice for each firm is the quantity (price) contract type when the products are substitutes (complements). The proof can be sketched briefly for firm 1, with that for firm 2 following by symmetry. Using the appropriate prices and outputs, we obtain the following profit functions.[38]

$$\pi_1{}^c = \frac{\theta(p_1{}^c)^2}{\beta_2} \tag{3.48a}$$

$$\pi_1{}^b = \beta_1(p_1{}^b)^2 \tag{3.48b}$$

$$\pi_1{}^{bc} = \frac{\theta(p_1{}^{bc})^2}{\beta_2} \tag{3.48c}$$

$$\pi_1{}^{cb} = \beta_1(p_1{}^{cb})^2 \tag{3.48d}$$

Note first that the profits have a useful symmetry in ratios:

$$\frac{\pi_1{}^c}{\pi_1{}^{cb}} = \frac{\pi_1{}^b}{\pi_1{}^{bc}} = \frac{(4 - \psi^2)^2}{(4 - \psi^2)^2 - \psi^6} \tag{3.49}$$

where $\psi = \delta^2/\beta_1\beta_2$. Moreover, these ratios are greater than unity for $\psi \neq 0$ and therefore

$$\pi_1{}^c > \pi_1{}^{cb} \qquad \pi_1{}^b > \pi_1{}^{bc} \tag{3.50}$$

Next, form the ratio

---

[38] The Cournot prices $p_j{}^c$ and outputs $z_j{}^c$ and the Bertrand prices $p_j{}^b$ and outputs $z_j{}^b$ are left for the reader to derive. See SE3.5 for help.

$$\frac{\pi_1{}^{cb}}{\pi_1{}^{b}} = \frac{1 - \alpha_1\delta^2/\beta_1(2\alpha_1\beta_2 + \alpha_2\delta)}{1 - 2\delta^2/(4\beta_1\beta_2 - \delta^2)} \tag{3.51}$$

which is greater than unity iff $\delta > 0$. As a final case, note that the ratio

$$\frac{\pi_1{}^{bc}}{\pi_1{}^{c}} = \frac{1 - \delta^2/\beta_1\beta_2}{1 - \{\alpha_1\delta^2/\beta_1(2\alpha_1\beta_2 + \alpha_2\delta)\} - \{1 - \{2\delta^2/(4\beta_1\beta_2 - \delta^2)\}}$$

is greater than unity iff $\delta > 0$. Combining these results gives

$$\pi_1{}^{c} > \pi_1{}^{cb} > \pi_1{}^{b} > \pi_1{}^{bc} \qquad \text{when } \delta > 0 \text{ (substitutes)} \tag{3.52a}$$

$$\pi_1{}^{b} > \pi_1{}^{bc} > \pi_1{}^{c} > \pi_1{}^{cb} \qquad \text{when } \delta < 0 \text{ (complements)} \tag{3.52b}$$

It is a dominant strategy for firm 1 to choose Cournot when the products are substitutes, for then $\pi_1{}^{cb} > \pi_1{}^{b}$ and $\pi_1{}^{c} > \pi_1{}^{bc}$. Conversely, it is a dominant strategy for firm 1 to choose Bertrand with complements, for then $\pi_1{}^{b} > \pi_1{}^{cb}$ and $\pi_1{}^{bc} > \pi_1{}^{c}$.

3.4   Stackelberg: Leaders and Followers

The usual story told with the application of either Cournot or Bertrand conjectures involves firms of nearly identical products, technologies, and information. Stackelberg (1934) objected to such a foundation for oligopoly analysis since it was, by his assertion, "widely known" that most industries had one firm (or group) as the market leader with others acting in a follower role. Moreover, Stackelberg was quite specific about the behavior that he thought was exhibited by these firms. A **follower** firm, which he described as being small relative to the market, acts exactly in the fashion of Cournot. In contrast, the large **leader** firm knows that its rival uses the Cournot conjecture and reaction function and acts to take advantage of this knowledge. Using quantities as strategy variables, the leader firm j is therefore characterized as maximizing

$$\pi_j = \pi_j(z_j, r_k{}^{c}(z_j)) \tag{3.53}$$

where $r_k{}^{c}(z_j)$ is the Cournot reaction function of the follower. Stackelberg further assumed that the leader firm possesses full knowledge of its rival's demand and cost functions so that the conjectured reaction $r_k{}^{c}(z_j)$ holds without error. Note that, by these assumptions, the leader's payoff in (3.53) is written simply in terms of its own output level z_j.

Asymmetric Information. The Stackelberg analysis is built on an asymmetry in information. Specifically, the leader–follower roles only make sense if the leader firm j announces its quantity decision first and, knowing that information, follower firm k then makes its decision. Because of this we think of the Stackelberg model as occurring in a two-stage interaction with two decision dates but a single market. In this interaction the follower maximizes profit behaving in a Cournot fashion; the leader's advantage is that it knows the followers act with Cournot reaction functions and makes its decision based on this knowledge.

E3.12

Quantity Decisions in Sequence: Stackelberg Leaders and Followers

As a simple illustration of leader–follower behavior, consider two firms, 1 and 2, producing a homogeneous good. Suppose further that firm 1 can select from (only) three discrete output levels z_1^1, z_1^2, and z_1^3 and, similarly, firm 2 can select only from z_2^1, z_2^2, and z_2^3. Let the profits received by the firms with the various choices be as given in table 3.2. The columns represent firm 2's output choices and the rows represent the choice of firm 1. The first entry in each cell corresponds to firm 1's profits, and the second entry is the profits of firm 2. For example, if the combination of output decisions is (z_1^2, z_2^3), then firm 1 receives 11 in profits and firm 2 receives 7.

Table 3.2 Discrete payoffs

	z_2^1	z_2^2	z_2^3
z_1^2	(8, 10)	(5, 10)	(8, 11)
z_1^2	(7, 5)	(8, 6)	(11, 7)
z_1^3	(5, 6)	(9, 9)	(12, 6)

In Stackelberg rivalry the follower is held to act rationally in the sense that, given the leader's decision, it chooses optimally. Thus, each firm's reaction set is defined as the collection of decision pairs according to which that firm reacts optimally to every possible choice by its rival. For example, from the data given in table 3.2, the reaction set of firm 1 when firm 2 is the leader is the set of pairs (z_2^1, z_1^1), (z_2^2, z_1^3), and (z_2^3, z_1^3): if firm 2 chooses z_2^1 then 1 chooses z_1^1, and so on. From this set of pairs the highest payoff for the leader firm 2 occurs with (z_2^1, z_1^1). Thus, leader firm 2 chooses z_2^1, follower firm 1 then optimally chooses z_1^1, and the profits are $\pi_2 = 10$ and $\pi_1 = 8$ at equilibrium.

The reader can quickly show that (z_1^2, z_2^3) are the Stackelberg equilibrium decisions in the converse situation, with firm 1 as *leader*. Note finally that the Cournot–Nash decision pair for table 3.2 is (z_1^3, z_2^2) and that, for this example, both leaders in the alternative Stackelberg situations obtain better payoffs than in the Cournot equilibrium and both followers are worse off.

3.4.1 Stackelberg Equilibria

The key properties of the Stackelberg equilibrium can be illustrated graphically. In figure 3.6 isoprofit contours for the two firms (labeled $\bar{\pi}_j$) and the usual Cournot reaction functions (labeled r_j^c) are indicated on the (z_1, z_2) output plane.[39] The reaction function of firm 2 intersects the vertical axis at z_2^m, the

[39] We assume strictly concave isoprofit contours, negatively sloping linear reaction functions, and a stable CCE.

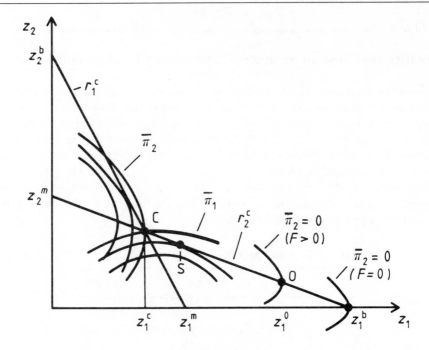

Figure 3.6
Stackelberg equilibria with fixed cost

quantity at which 2's profits are maximized given $z_1 = 0$ (this is the usual monopoly output for firm 2). If we assume that firm 2 has no fixed cost, the point where its reaction meets the horizontal axis yields both zero quantity and zero profits. The axes points of firm 1's reaction function have a similar interpretation. The intersection of r_1^c and r_2^c at point C defines the CCE. In contrast, when firm 1 is the Stackelberg leader and firm 2 is the follower, the point S defines the equilibrium point. At S, firm 1 maximizes its profits given the known Cournot reactions of firm 2. Using the above assumptions, this occurs at the tangency of firm 1's isoprofit contour with r_2^c. It is also possible to note conditions under which no such tangency solution will occur and therefore the equilibrium point will lie at the z_1^b and $z_2 = 0$ corner (see Osborne, 1973, for details of this case).

A second set of interesting possibilities occurs with the incidence of fixed cost and scale economies. Following Dixit (1980), continue with firm 1 as leader and assume that a potential entrant firm 2 has a single available technology that requires given (nonzero) fixed costs and constant marginal cost. Assume further that with these costs firm 2 now reaches a level of zero profits at point 0 on its reaction function as shown in figure 3.6. If firm 1 had a prevailing output greater than z_1^0 (and less than z_1^b), then firm 2's best reply would no longer be given by r_2^c. Instead, it would remain inactive. That is, firm 2's reaction function is discontinuous with segments $z_2^m 0$ and $z_1^0 z_1^b$ as shown in the figure. The point of discontinuity at 0, or z_1^0, depends on the level of fixed cost that firm 2 must incur on entry. If this fixed cost is so large that z_1^0 lies to the left of z_1^m, then the Stackelberg equilibrium will occur at $z_1{}^m$ with no entry. If $z_1{}^0$ is to the left of $z_1{}^c$, then the Cournot–Nash equilibrium too will result without entry. Such possibilities are considered in detail in chapters 10 and 11. Our present concern is otherwise, with the prior choice of type by the firms. Who will be leader, and who follower?

3.4.2 Choice of Leader–follower Type

We again consider duopolists involved in a two-stage interaction. As in section 3.2, at the pre-market stage $t - 1$ each firm chooses one of two possible types, but rather than choosing price and quantity contract types, now let the duopolists choose either a Stackelberg leader or follower role. These choices are assumed to occur simultaneously, with each firm announcing its type at the same moment and without prior consultation or cooperation. Because of prohibitive switching costs, the choices are considered to be final. Given its leader or follower choice, at the subsequent market stage t each firm chooses that output level which provides it with maximum profits. These maxima depend on the types chosen (as well as on demand and cost conditions).

Four Cases. Assume that the firms have the information and ability at stage $t - 1$ to calculate the maximum stage t profits that would arise under their various type decisions. This calculation will be the basis of the type decision and in a duopoly four outcomes are then possible: $\pi_j{}^c$, where both firms choose the follower Cournot type; $\pi_j{}^s$, where both firms choose to be leaders, which is labeled as the Stackelberg (s) choice; $\pi_j{}^{lf}$, where firm 1 chooses leader and firm 2 chooses follower; $\pi_j{}^{fl}$, where firm 1 chooses follower and firm 2 chooses leader. These possibilities are tabulated in table 3.3.

Table 3.3 Profitability and Choice of Type

| | *Firm 2* | |
	Follower	*Leader*
Firm 1		
Follower	$\pi_j{}^c$	$\pi_j{}^{fl}$
Leader	$\pi_j{}^{lf}$	$\pi_j{}^s$

Figure 3.7 outlines the solution of these models when we take the products of the duopolists to be substitutes, as von Stackelberg did.[40] When both firm adopt the follower type the usual CCE occurs at point C, where $r_1{}^c(z_2)$ and $r_2{}^c(z_1)$ intersect. In the lf case firm 1 adopts the leader type while firm 2 is a follower. Firm 1 can exploit firm 2's willingness to respond to, but not directly determine, firm 1's output. By moving from $z_1{}^c$ to $z_1{}^{lf}$ firm 1 selects the rate of output to maximize profits, knowing that its rival will move along a Cournot reaction function $r_2{}^c(z_1)$. Because the products are substitutes, firm 1's profits now

---

[40] The existence of a unique equilibrium with each choice of type is assumed.

exceed those at the usual Cournot equilibrium ($\pi_1{}^{lf} > \pi_1{}^c$) and firm 2's profits are decreased.

Reversing firm types only requires some minor relabeling. In the fl asymmetrical case, firm 2 selects $z_2{}^{fl}$ to maximize its profits while form 1 moves on $r_1{}^c(z_2)$. Similarly, $\pi_2{}^{fl} > \pi_2{}^c$ and $\pi_1{}^c > \pi_1{}^{fl}$. Being the leader appears to be profitable.

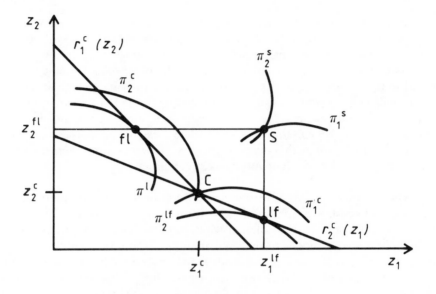

Figure 3.7
Stackelberg duopoly

Stackelberg "Disequilibrium." In the fourth case, which Stackelberg saw as most likely, it is assumed that *both* firms will seek the increased profits from being the leader. This seems reasonable as, given that each firm takes the type of the other as fixed, leadership is the best response for each firm. The logic of that choice, however, is derived to some extent from a fallacy of composition. The difficulty with the Stackelberg case arises because each firm expects its rival to act as a follower and adjust along a Cournot reaction function, but rivals also have leadership conjectures and do not react in the Cournot fashion. When both duopolists adopt the leader type, the quantity pair ($z_1{}^l$, $z_2{}^l$) is produced. While firm 1 expects profits $\pi_1{}^{lf}$ it in fact receives the smaller amount $\pi_1{}^s$ indicated in figure 3.7; firm 2 similarly expects $\pi_2{}^{fl}$ and receives the smaller $\pi_2{}^s$. The figure also indicates that $\pi_1{}^s < \pi_1{}^c$ and $\pi_2{}^s < \pi_2{}^c$, making the leader–leader case the worst possible outcome.

For the above reasons, point ($z_1{}^{fl}$, $z_2{}^{fl}$) is commonly termed the Stackelberg *disequilibrium*. While in a two-stage analysis it is a conjectural equilibrium for the industry, that is an uncomfortable result as it is dominated by the Cournot solution. Because of this it is usual to presume that an equilibrium will finally emerge based on more complex rules of interaction, with one firm submitting to the leadership of its rival or both adopting Cournot-type follower roles.[41] In section 9.3 several forms of "dominant-strategy" equilibria are systematically considered as solutions to such situations.

E3.13

Stackelberg Duopoly Solution

Some details of the Stackelberg analysis are clarified by considering a heterogeneous duopoly with the specific (inverse) demand and cost functions

$$p_1 = 48 - 2z_1 - z_2 \qquad c_1 = z_1^2 \tag{3.54a}$$

$$p_2 = 40 - 2z_2 - z_1 \qquad c_2 = 2z_2^2 \tag{3.54b}$$

The Cournot reaction functions, derived in the usual way, are

$$r_2^c(z_1) = 5 - \frac{z_1}{8} \tag{3.55a}$$

$$r_1^c(z_2) = 8 - \frac{z_2}{6} \tag{3.55b}$$

These give $z_1^c = 7.32$ and $z_2^c = 4.085$ as the CCE and, in turn, imply the following prices and profits:

$$p_1^c = 29.28 \qquad \pi_1^c = 160.75$$

$$p_2^c = 24.51 \qquad \pi_2^c = 66.75$$

Next, consider the lf case (firm 1 as leader, firm 2 as follower). Firm 1 determines its maximum profits by substituting firm 2's reaction into its profit function. Doing so yields

$$\pi_1^{lf}(z_1, r_2^c(z_1)) = \left(48 - 2z_1 - 5 + \frac{z_1}{8}\right)z_1 - z_1^2 \tag{3.56}$$

The stationarity point occurs at $z_1^{lf} = 7.48$. Substituting this into firm 2's reaction function gives $z_2^{lf} = 4.065$. Using the demand and cost function again yields lfCE profits of

$$\pi_1^{lf} = 160.78$$

$$\pi_2^{lf} = 66.10$$

The fl case (firm 2 leader, firm 1 follower) proceeds in an exactly analogous manner. This solves for $z_1^{fl} = 7.305$ and $z_2^{fl} = 4.17$ as the flCE quantities; associated profits are $\pi_1^{fl} = 160.08$ and $\pi_2^{fl} = 66.78$. The final leader–leader case

---

[41] See Ono (1981) and Friedman (1977, p. 80) for preliminary analyses of the choice of leader–follower roles in this model. Both support Schelling's (1960, p. 231) comment that such price leadership is ". . . an unprofitable distinction evaded by the apparent follower and assumed perforce by the apparent leader." Under the conditions of his model, Ono shows that the less efficient (higher-cost) firm will in fact optimally act as leader and the more efficient (lower-cost) firms will be followers. In this sense the "dominant" firm is not the leader.

occurs where firm 2's output is at the leadership level (given still that it believes that firm 2 will act as a follower) and firm 2 similarly produces it leadership level. That is, $z_1{}^s = 7.48$ and $z_2{}^s = 4.17$, which in turn gives profits $\pi_1{}^s = 159.99$ and $\pi_2{}^s = 66.05$.

3.4.3   Dominant–firm Price Leadership

The basic leader–follower framework is often adapted to strategic variables other than quantity. One frequently used variant is the dominant-firm price-leadership model.[42] In this case, the leader (dominant) firm establishes a price with full knowledge that the follower (fringe) firm (or firms acting as a group) will react as a price-taker.[43] For the price leader j the profit function then is

$$\pi_j = \pi_j(p_j, r_k^*(p_j)) \tag{3.57}$$

where $z_k = r_k^*(p_j)$ is the follower firm k's *quantity* reaction taking the *price* p_j to be fixed. Again, the sequence of pre-market moves (and information), where the leader announces prices and then followers react, is suggested by the analysis.

The key operational aspect of the price-leadership model is that the dominant firm establishes the prevailing price and fringe firms sell all they choose at that price. This means, in turn, that the dominant firm sells the difference between the fringe supply and the market demand at the established price. Given this construction of demand functions, what price does the dominant firm establish? Figure 3.8 illustrates that choice, assuming as usual that the leader knows the cost and demand conditions of the followers so that the reaction function $r_k^*(p_j)$ is in fact correct.

In the figure DD indicates the market demand, S_f is the supply schedule of the price-taking (competitive) fringe, and MC is the marginal cost of the dominant firm. The first step is to determine the demand facing the dominant firm. To do so, consider a range of prices for the dominant firm, calculate the fringe supply for each price, and then subtract that from the total demand at each price (respectively). This residual is the quantity demanded from the dominant firm over the range of prices.

For example, consider the price $\bar{p}$ in the figure. At that price the competitive fringe supplies the entire market and the dominant firm sells nothing. Similarly, at prices greater than $\bar{p}$ the fringe supplies the total demand. Therefore $\bar{p}$ is the vertical intercept for the dominant-firm demand schedule. Consider next some

---

[42] A wide variety of price-leadership models have appeared in the literature. See, for example, Forchheimer (1908), Nichol (1930), Stigler (1947), Markham (1951), Lanzilotti (1958), and Bain (1960). Scherer (1982) has classified these into three types. In addition to the dominant-firm model developed here, there is "collusive price leadership," where the principal firms of the industry establish the monopoly price which is followed by the minor firms, and "barometric price leadership," where the (low-cost) leader's price adjustments are followed by rivals, usually to a competitive level.

[43] Price leadership is only one (perhaps unnecessary) aspect of "dominance." More generally, see Encaoua et al. (1984) and Geroski and Jacquemin (1984).

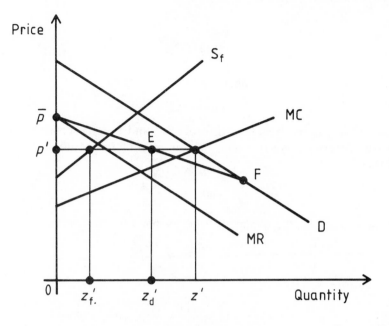

Figure 3.8
Dominant-firm price leadership

price $p^1 < \bar{p}$. The fringe supplies z_f^1 units at this price, the total demand is z^1, and the dominant-firm output is the difference $z_d^1 = z^1 - z_f^1$. The quantity z_d^1 determines point E on the dominant-firm demand schedule. Other points on this demand are developed in a similar way, giving the schedule $\bar{p}$EFD as shown. Associated with this demand is the marginal revenue schedule MR. With MR, the dominant firm maximizes profits in the usual way, setting MR = MC at price p^1.[44] The following numerical example illustrates these developments.

E3.14

Dominant-firm Price Leadership

Consider an industry in which there is one dominant firm (the "leader") and a number of smaller firms (the "fringe"). The firms in the fringe act like pure competitors, choosing their outputs on the basis of the price set by the dominant firm. The market behavior of the fringe is, as a result, given by their supply function, which is simply the appropriate sum of their marginal cost schedules (recall section 2.3).

Assume the following specific functions for market demand

$$z = \frac{a}{p} - b \tag{3.58}$$

[44] An analysis of the monopoly power possessed by the dominant firm and its implications for social welfare are delayed until chapter 12 and SE12.3 in particular.

fringe supply

$$z_f = d - \frac{e}{p} \tag{3.59}$$

and total variable cost of the dominant firm

$$\text{TVC} = c z_d \tag{3.60}$$

where $z_d = z - z_f$ is the dominant-firm output, and c is the constant marginal cost. All parameters are positive and, to assure an interior solution, it is further required that

$$\frac{a}{b} > \frac{e}{d} \quad \text{and} \quad c < \frac{a + e}{b + d}$$

Under these conditions, the dominant firm's demand function is

$$z_d = z - z_f = \frac{a}{p} - b - d - \frac{e}{p} \tag{3.61}$$

In turn, its profits are given by

$$\pi_d = a + e - (b + d)p - c\left\{\frac{a + e}{p} - (b + d)\right\} - F \tag{3.62}$$

where F is fixed cost. For the dominant firm the stationarity point for a maximum requires

$$(b + d)p^2 = c(a + e)$$

Solving this for the market price yields

$$p = \left\{\frac{c(a + e)}{b + d}\right\}^{1/2} \tag{3.63}$$

Substituting this price in (3.59) gives the fringe supply and similar substitutions in (3.61) and (3.62) give the dominant-firm output and profit.

Dominant-firm Decline. Worcester (1957), Gaskins (1971), Ono (1981), and others have argued that dominant firms following the above strategy will naturally decline over time. Roughly, their idea is that entrants are attracted to the industry by the profits gathered by the incumbents. On entry, these firms become part of the competitive fringe. The larger is the fringe, the smaller is the residual demand facing the dominant firm, the smaller is its output share, and the smaller are its profits. When dominant firms have no cost advantage, it is argued that this process of decline continues until all firms are on the same footing and adopt the same strategies.[45] Geroski (1986) summarizes a substantial empirical literature which supports an "optimally managed" decline where the dominant firm realizes the inevitability of the process and controls the rate of

---

[45] See Geroski and Jacequemin (1984), who express several reservations to this development.

new entry by "moderation" of price. Entry is dealt with systematically in chapters 10 and 11.

Supplementary examples

SE3.1 Research and Development and Quantity Equilibrium Strategies

Dasgupta and Stiglitz (1980b) construct a model of homogeneous oligopoly with a Nash equilibrium in output and research and development (R&D) strategy variables. Their purpose is to explain several aspects of technological competition. Although they adopt two strategy variables for each firm, their model and analysis are not doubly complex.

The effect of technological innovation is to reduce the firms' cost; specifically, if firm j spends $\kappa_j \geq 0$ on R&D its unit cost is $c(\kappa_j)$, where $c' < 0$, $c'' > 0$, and $c(0) = \infty$. That is, there are positive but decreasing returns to R&D. On the demand side, $j = 1, 2, \ldots, J$ firms, each producing $z_j \geq 0$, supply the industry output $z \equiv \Sigma_j z_j$ with prices determined by the negatively sloped industry demand function $p(z)$. Consider specifically the isoelastic forms

$$p(z) = \sigma z^{-\eta} \qquad \sigma, \eta > 0 \tag{3.64a}$$

$$c(\kappa_j) = \alpha \kappa_j^{-\beta} \qquad \alpha, \beta > 0 \tag{3.64b}$$

Note that the unit cost function is identical for all firms. The parameter σ measures the size of the market and α measures the size of the industry's R&D base. Parameters η and β have the usual elasticity interpretations.

The J firms are considered to choose R&D and output levels (the strategy variables) simultaneously to maximize profits. For a typical firm j the profit function is given by

$$\pi_j = z_j(\sigma z^{-\eta} - \alpha \kappa_j^{-\beta}) - \kappa_j \tag{3.65}$$

Since the firms enter into the model symmetrically (output is homogeneous and R&D opportunities are identical), consider only a symmetric equilibrium in the z_j and κ_j by requiring that these choices be the same for all active firms. The stationarity conditions are

$$\frac{\partial \pi_j}{\partial z_j} = 0 \tag{3.66a}$$

and

$$\frac{\partial \pi_j}{\partial \kappa_j} = 0 \tag{3.66b}$$

for each j. Using these necessary conditions and routine (but tedious) calculations the reader can derive the symmetric equilibrium output $z_j^0 = z^0/J$ and R&D $\kappa_j^0 = \kappa^0$ as functions of the parameters J, α, β, σ, and η:[46]

---

[46] Dasgupta and Stiglitz (1980b, appendix D) show that an equilibrium exists if $\eta < J \leq \eta(1 + \beta)/\beta$ and $\eta(1 + \beta)/\beta > 1$.

$$z_j{}^0 = \frac{1}{\alpha\beta} \left\{ \sigma\left(\frac{\beta}{J}\right)^{\eta} \alpha^{\eta-1} \left(\frac{1-\eta}{J}\right) \right\}^{(1+\beta/\eta-\beta(1\eta))} \tag{3.66c}$$

$$\kappa_j{}^0 = \left\{ \sigma\left(\frac{\beta}{J}\right)^{\eta} \beta^{\eta-1} \left(\frac{1-\eta}{J}\right) \right\}^{1/\{\eta-\beta(1\eta)\}} \tag{3.66d}$$

Notice that $\kappa_j{}^0(J+1) < \kappa_j{}^0(J)$ and $z_j{}^0(J+1) > z_j{}^0(J)$: as the number of firms increases, total industry output increases and the R&D per firm decreases (Loury, 1979, derives similar results.) The R&D decisions of firms are considered in greater detail in chapter 11.

SE3.2   Merger Incentives in Quantity Competition

A merger is a binding agreement among firms to maximize joint profits by correlating strategies and, if required, making side payments. Analytically, merger analysis leads us to compare a Nash equilibrium in a given J-firm coalition with one in a "less fine" coalition. The Cournot-Nash solution concept is easily applied to this situation. Pre- and post-merger analyses of the industry CCE can then be used as a basis for measuring the effects of the merger, as in the following case suggested by Salant, et al. (1983).

Suppose that, at some initial stage, there are J identical firms in an industry, and consider a merger of $\kappa + 1 \leq J$ of these. To focus on the question of merger for monopoly, not efficiency, we assume that there are no firm-specific fixed costs and that marginal costs of production are constant. Let $\pi(J)$ be the profits of each (identical) firm at the (symmetric and assumed unique) CCE in the pre-merger market. Similarly, let $\pi^m(J, \kappa)$ indicate the profits of the merged group of $\kappa + 1$ firms in the (also assumed unique) CCE post-merger market. As a final item of notation, denote by

$$\Delta\pi(J, \kappa) = \pi^m(J, \kappa) - (\kappa + 1)\pi(J)$$
$$= \pi(J - \kappa) - (\kappa + 1)\pi(J) \tag{3.67}$$

the change in profits (across equilibria) of the $\kappa + 1$ firms coming with the merger. The equality $\pi^m(J, \kappa) = \pi(J - \kappa)$ used in (3.67) is the result of the constant average and marginal cost assumption.

Suppose further that there is a linear market demand $p = \alpha - z$, where $\alpha \geq 0$ is a parameter and z is the sum of the outputs of the firms. Also, let c be the constant marginal costs. Then

$$\pi(J) = \frac{\alpha - c}{(J + 1)^2} \tag{3.68}$$

can easily be derived as the pre-merger CCE profits of each firm. Since marginal costs are constant, the merged firms behave exactly like the $J - \kappa$ other firms post-merger. Thus the post-merger CCE has per firm profits of

$$\pi(J - \kappa) = \frac{\alpha - c}{(J - \kappa + 1)^2} \tag{3.69}$$

Subtracting (3.68), weighted by $\kappa + 1$, yields the profit change across equilibria:

$$\Delta\pi(J, \kappa) = \left(\frac{\alpha - c}{J - \kappa + 1}\right)^2 + (\kappa + 1)\left(\frac{\alpha - c}{J + 1}\right)^2 \tag{3.70}$$

This last equation with J and κ treated parametrically sets out the conditions under which the merger yields increased profits to the firms involved. Straightforward differentiation shows that $\partial\Delta\pi(J, \kappa)/\partial\kappa < 0$ for $\kappa = 0$ and $\partial^2\Delta\pi(J, \kappa)/\partial\kappa^2 > 0$ for $\kappa > 0$. Thus, depending on the pre-merger value $\Delta\pi(J, 0)$, we have the counter-intuitive result that a merger of some (significant) number of firms *may* reduce the profits of the merged group relative to the sum of their pre-merger profits.[47] Because the rivalry is Cournot, if (say) two firms merge, the output of the new firm will be lower than the original combined output. This occurs because with Cournot conjectures the two previously independent profit-maximizing firms each ignored the negative external effects of their output decisions on the other, while when merged they do not.

SE3.3 Proportional Conjectures

While the most frequently used conjectural variation specifications are those of Cournot and Bertrand, conjectures based on proportionality rules have appeared from time to time (see, for example, Cowling and Waterson, 1976, Clarke and Davies, 1983).

To illustrate these, consider a heterogeneous duopoly with firms j, $k = 1$, 2 and $j \neq k$. Let $p_j(z_j, z_k)$ be the inverse demand facing firm j and let $c_j(z_j)$ be its cost function. The proportional conjectures most commonly used are those associated with the following:

1 quantities

$$\frac{dz_k^e}{dz_j} = \frac{z_k}{z_j} \tag{3.71}$$

2 prices

$$\frac{dp_k^e}{dp_j} = \frac{p_k}{p_j} \tag{3.72a}$$

which can also be expressed in quantity terms as

$$\frac{dz_k^e}{dz_j} = \frac{z_k}{z_j} \frac{\eta_{jj} - \eta_{kj}}{\eta_{kk} - \eta_{jk}} \tag{3.72b}$$

where the $\eta_{jk} = (\partial p_j/\partial z_k)(z_k/p_j)$ are elasticities;

3 revenues

$$\frac{d(p_k z_k)^e}{d(p_j z_j)} = \frac{p_k z_k}{p_j z_j} \tag{3.73a}$$

---

[47] Deneckere and Davidson (1985) have shown that mergers generally will be profitable when the original firms produce differentiated products and the merged firm continues to offer all the products of the constituent firms. Perry and Porter (1985) also find incentives to merge, even with homogeneous oligopoly, when there are cost advantages of firm size relative to the asset size of all firms.

which can also be expressed in quantity terms as

$$\frac{dz_k^c}{dz_j} = \frac{z_k}{z_j}\left(1 + \frac{\eta_{jj} - \eta_{kj}}{1 + \eta_{kk} - \eta_{jk}}\right) \tag{3.73b}$$

where the $\eta_{jk} = (\partial p_j/\partial z_k)(z_k/p_j)$ are the usual cross-elasticies of demand.

It is left as an exercise for the reader to prove the quantity-equivalent expression for price and revenue conjectures.

SE3.4   Kinked Demand and Rigid Prices

The kinked demand curve model purports to describe differentiated oligopoly markets in which product prices do not generally change over extended periods, even with significant changes in demand and supply conditions.[48] For each firm j and its rival k, the conjectural assumptions of this model can be stated in price as

$$\frac{dp_k^c(p_j)}{dp_j} = 0 \qquad \text{for } dp_j > 0 \tag{3.74a}$$

$$\frac{dp_k^c(p_j)}{dp_j} > 0 \qquad \text{for } dp_j < 0 \tag{3.74b}$$

The usual geometric analysis of the model is given in figure 3.9, where z_1 represents the prevailing output of duopolist 1 at price p_1 and $MC_1 \equiv c_1'$ is its

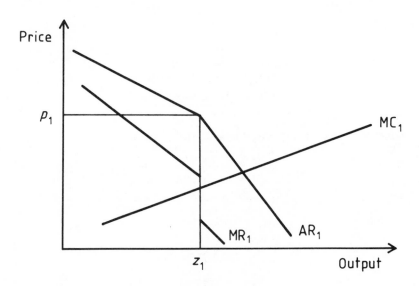

Figure 3.9
Kinked demand oligopoly

[48] The originators of this idea are Galbraith (1936) and, more systematically, Sweezy (1939).

marginal cost schedule. AR_1 and MR_1 are the (perceived) average and marginal revenues of firm 1, based on the given conjectures, expressed as a function of z_1. It is of importance that at the prevailing market price and output a "kink" appears in AR_1, because of the asymmetrical conjectures (3.74), and there is a corresponding discontinuity in MR_1. With the discontinuity in marginal revenue the usual stationarity conditions ($MR = MC$) are replaced by the inequality that marginal cost lie between the upper and lower points of marginal revenue. This means that variations in marginal cost between these limit points do not result in price variations.

The profit maxima and equilibrium are easily determined, however, since decreases in firm 1's output imply $MR_1 > MC_1$ and increases imply $MR_1 < MC_1$. It is of particular note that, given the MR_1 discontinuity, changes in supply and demand may occur without accompanying changes in the market price. For example, if the MR_1 schedule shifts without intersecting MC_1, then p_1 will not change. Similarly, shifts in the MC_1 schedule which do not result in its intersection with MR_1 also leave p_1 unaffected.[49]

SE3.5 Price and Quantity Competition with Linear Demand

Linear demand schedules are frequently used in the analysis of Bertrand and Cournot oligopolies. As this assumption produces rather specialized results, it is helpful to review these cases here. Recall the notation and the linear inverse demand functions of E3.10

$$p_1 = a_1 - b_1 z_1 - d z_2 \tag{3.75a}$$

$$p_2 = a_2 - b_2 z_2 - d z_1 \tag{3.75b}$$

and the associated demands

$$z_1 = \alpha_1 - \beta_1 p_1 + \delta p_2 \tag{3.76a}$$

$$z_2 = \alpha_2 - \beta_2 p_2 + \delta p_1 \tag{3.76b}$$

It is usual to deal with the "symmetric" case where $a_j = a$ and $b_j = b$ for $j = 1$, 2. To further simplify, let marginal cost again be constant and, as in E3.10, define the price p_j as net of this constant cost. For $d = 0$ the products are independent, giving Bertrand and Cournot equilibrium prices $p_j^b = p_j^c = \alpha/2\beta$ and quantities $z_j^b = z_j^c = a/2b$. Alternatively, when $d = b > 0$ the products are perfect substitutes (homogeneous duopoly). In this case the Bertrand equilibrium occurs at $p_j^b = 0$, where price equals marginal cost, and the Cournot equilibrium is at $z_j^c = a/3b$. In turn, there are equilibrium price and output differences of

$$p_j^c - p_j^b = \frac{a_j d}{4 b_1 b_2 - d^2} \geq 0 \tag{3.77a}$$

$$z_j^c - z_j^c = \frac{\alpha_j \delta}{4\beta_1\beta_2 - \delta^2} \geq 0 \tag{3.77b}$$

---

[49] See Stigler (1949a, 1978), who criticizes the kinked demand curve model for its "undue" simplicity and lack of empirical support. Stiglitz (1984) provides an alternative view.

These inequalities inform us that Cournot duopolists, regardless of the substitutability or complementarity of their products, never have a lower price nor a greater output quantity than Bertrand duopolists (assuming, as we have, that the firms possess similar demand and cost structures). Moreover, the differences in price and output that do occur are a function of the extent to which the products of the duopolists differ. That is, for the case where $a_1 = a_2$ the index of product differentiation is d^2/b_1b_2 and the price difference becomes

$$p_j^c - p_j^b = \frac{a_j}{d\{4(b_1b_2/d^2) - 1\}} \tag{3.78}$$

As the index goes to zero, and its inverse becomes larger, the goods become more independent and the Cournot–Bertrand price (and output) difference goes to zero. Conversely, with greater product and substitutability the price and output differences become greater.

SE3.6   Monopoly Power and Uncertainty

Robson (1981) has shown that a simple (but commonly used) form of demand uncertainty causes existence problems for the Cournot equilibrium but not for the Bertrand equilibrium.

The proof begins with a J-firm homogeneous oligopoly producing total output $z = z_1 + z_2 + .. + z_J$. Let the market demand be linear and subject to an additive random noise ε:

$$z = a - bp + \varepsilon \tag{3.79}$$

where $E(\varepsilon) = E(\varepsilon|p) = 0$ and $E(\varepsilon^2) = \sigma^2 \geqslant 0$. Suppose further that the firms have constant (and identical) marginal cost, and think of the price p as though it were net of that cost so that $p = 0$ implies price equal to marginal cost.

The firms can choose one of two strategy types: the linear supply function (LSF)

$$z_j = \alpha_j + \beta_j p$$

or the Bertrand price contract (B)

$$p_j = \delta_j$$

where α_j, β_j, and δ_j are positive constants for each j. The LSF strategy type is a linear extension of the quantity contract and implies Cournot behavior when $\beta_j = 0$. More generally, the choice of LSF strategy requires the selection of the α_j and β_j parameters. Strategy type B is the usual Bertrand price contract where p_j is the price firm j chooses to charge all who would purchase from it.

Consider first an equilibrium with all firms having adopted LSF-type strategies. Further, let the firms be risk neutral and let each maximize expected profits

$$E\pi_j = E((\alpha_j + \beta_j p)p) \tag{3.80}$$

Using the LSF definition and (3.79) we can eliminate z and specify prices as

$$p = \frac{a - \alpha_1 - \alpha_2 \ldots - \alpha_J + \varepsilon}{b + \beta_1 + \beta_2 \ldots + \beta_J}$$

Substituting this expression in $E\pi_j$ and taking the expectation gives

$$E\pi_j = \alpha_j \frac{A}{B} + \beta_j \frac{A^2 + \sigma^2}{B^2} \tag{3.81}$$

where $A \equiv a - \Sigma_j \alpha_j$ and $B \equiv b + \Sigma_j \beta_j \neq 0$.

At the linear supply function conjectural equilibrium (LSFCE) each firm j maximizes $E\pi_j$ with respect to α_j and β_j, holding the strategies of other firms constant. Without loss of generality choose firm J for analysis. The optimal α_J requires

$$\frac{\partial E\pi_J}{\partial \alpha_J} = \frac{A - \alpha_J}{B} - \frac{2\beta_J A}{B^2} = 0 \tag{3.82}$$

or

$$\alpha_J = \frac{(a - \alpha_1 \dots - \alpha_{J-1})(b + \beta_1 \dots + \beta_J)}{2(b + \beta_1 \dots + \beta_{J-1})} \tag{3.83}$$

The reader can verify that $E\pi_J$ is strictly concave in α_J when $\beta_1 + \beta_2 + \dots + \beta_{J-1} < b$. Next we consider the stationarity conditions for β_J:

$$\frac{\partial E\pi_J}{\partial \beta_J} = -\frac{A\alpha_J}{B^2} + \frac{A^2 + \sigma^2}{B^2} + \frac{2\beta_J(A^2 + \sigma^2)}{B^3} = 0 \tag{3.84}$$

Suppose, for the moment, that the market demand is certain ($\sigma^2 = 0$). When, in addition, the LSF strategies are symmetrical we have $\beta_j = \beta$ for all j and (3.84) reduces to

$$\alpha = \alpha_j = \frac{a\{b + (J + 2)\beta\}}{(J + 1)b + J(J + 3)\beta} \tag{3.85}$$

Then, for the Cournot case with $\beta = 0$,

$$\alpha^c = \frac{a}{J + 1} = z_j \tag{3.86}$$

$$z^c = \Sigma z_j = \frac{aJ}{J + 1} \tag{3.87}$$

$$p^c = \frac{a}{(j + 1)b} \tag{3.88}$$

Suppose now that the market demand is subject to uncertainty so that $\sigma^2 > 0$. In this case the stationarity conditions (3.84) imply $\beta_J = b - \beta_1 \dots - \beta_{J-1}$. As this equality must hold for all firms, $\beta_j = \beta$ for each j, and, in turn, $(J - 2)\beta = b$ is required. For the duopoly case ($J = 2$), these last conditions cannot be simultaneously satisfied and an LSFCE does not exist. For the more general case with $J > 2$, $\beta = b/(J - 2)$ which is inconsistent with the second-order concavity requirements for $E\pi_j$ in α_j since

$$(J - 1)\beta = \frac{J - 1}{J - 2} b > b \tag{3.89}$$

Thus an LSFCE does not exist for $J > 2$.

If any firm adopts the price contract then all other firms will also, and the BCE is such that $p_j = 0$ for all j. Once more, firms are competitive price-takers and the competitive equilibrium obtains with price equal to marginal cost.

SE3.7   Raising Rivals' Costs

Consider Cournot duopolists j and k producing a homogeneous good with constant unit costs c_j and c_k respectively and facing a linear demand

$$p_j = \alpha - \beta(z_j + z_k) \tag{3.90}$$

The Cournot equilibrium occurs with

$$z_j{}^c = \frac{\alpha - 2c_j + c_k}{3\beta} \tag{3.91a}$$

$$\pi_j{}^c = \frac{(\alpha - 2c_j + c_k)^2}{9\beta} \tag{3.91b}$$

Two points are of special note about the equilibrium conditions. First, and directly observable, the greater is c_k, the greater is firm j's equilibrium output and profit. Other things being equal, each firm would prefer to face a rival with greater cost. The second notable fact concerns the effect of the changes in c_k on $\pi_j{}^c$ and $\pi_k{}^c$. A little differentiation and algebra gives

$$\frac{\partial \pi_j{}^c}{\partial c_k} = -\frac{1}{2} \frac{z_j{}^c}{z_k{}^c} \frac{\partial \pi_k{}^c}{\partial c_k} \tag{3.92}$$

For small increases in c_k, firm j's gain is greater than firm k's loss provided that $z_j{}^c > 2z_k{}^c > 0$. Thus, if j has more than twice the market share that k has, it would be willing to incur investment costs to increase its rival's costs, and the amount of money it would spend in this way is greater than that which would be optimally spent by k to hold its cost down. At the center of this result is a price effect: when c_k increases the market equilibrium price increases, and this provides a greater gain to the firm selling the largest number of units.

Krattenmaker and Salop (1986) describe a variety of business practices which can be designed with the intent of raising rivals' costs in this way. One group of such practices concerns exclusive dealing contracts with either a factor supplier or a product distributor–retailer. In the case of factor supply, suppose that firm j, with a sufficiently large market share, enters into an exclusive dealing contract with the low-cost supplier of a factor used by both itself and its rival. In exchange for the right to supply all j's requirements the low-cost dealer agrees not to sell to rival firm k. More exactly, the low-cost supplier, calculating the net value of its factor to k, will not accept the exclusion arrangement unless it receives at least that amount from j. If the arrangement is made, this leaves firm k to purchase only from high-cost suppliers, thus raising its cost.

For the linear demand case above, (3.92) informs us that the amount j would pay to the factor supplier as incentive for the exclusive dealing arrangement is greater than the amount firm k would offer to thwart it. That leaves the success of this arrangement, from j's perspective, to hinge on whether alternative suppliers will be sufficiently high in their cost that firm k's cost increase will offset that of firm j.

Dominant-firm Price-leadership Version. Salop and Sheffman (1983) develop the argument of raising rivals' cost in the context of a dominant-firm price-leadership model, rather than the Cournot duopoly suggested above. Their analysis is easily reconstructed. Let z indicate the quantity supplied in the market by the dominant firm. Suppose that the dominant firm has available to it some exclusionary variable x which raises its own cost $c(z, x)$ and simultaneously that of the rival fringe. This external effect is captured in the fringe supply schedule $S(p, x)$. Specifically, we assume $\partial c/\partial x > 0$ and $\partial S/\partial x < 0$: more exclusion increases the cost of the dominant firm and reduces the fringe supply at any price. The dominant firm solves the problem (recall section 3.4.3)

$$\max_{p,x} \{pz - c(z, x)\} \text{ s.t. } z = D(p) - S(p, x) \tag{3.93}$$

where $D(p)$ is the industry demand. From the stationarity conditions it can be shown that a sufficient condition for exclusion to be practised $(x > 0)$ is

$$-\frac{\partial S/\partial x}{\partial S/\partial p} > \frac{\partial c/\partial z}{z} \left\{ \frac{1}{1 + m\eta/(1 - m)\varepsilon_f} \right\} \tag{3.94}$$

where $m = z/D(p)$ is the dominant firm's market share, η is the price elasticity of industry demand, and ε_f is the price elasticity of fringe supply (see SE12.3 for further details). Feasible and optimal exclusion requires the fringe's change in marginal cost induced by x (the left-hand side of (3.94), to be greater than the induced change in the average cost of the dominant firm times the factor in braces (which includes market shares and elasticities as indicated). Other things being equal, the greater is the dominant firm's market share and the market elasticity of demand the more likely is the exclusion to occur. Conversely, the smaller is the fringe elasticity of supply the greater is the likelihood of exclusion.

4 The Demand for Differentiated Products

While market analyses often focus on situations where products are homogeneous, a moment's reflection assures us that this is generally not a reasonable restriction in modern economies. Consumers have diverse preferences and firms routinely face a choice not only of what quantity to produce, but what the product design should be. The optimal choices, doubly complex in this way, depend on the limits of production (relating factor usage, quantity, and product variety) and the details of consumer demand for both quantity and variety. The nature of this complexity and the degree to which firms differentiate their products are central problems in industrial economics. In this chapter we begin an analysis of these problems by setting out some fundamentals of the demand for product variety. Production is added in chapter 5 and a range of market equilibria in differentiated product markets are considered. An analysis of the welfare implications of these equilibria follows in chapter 6.

Products can be differentiated in two basic ways. First, in an economy with complete information, product differences arise because of variations in physical properties, in the terms and conditions of sale, and in the manner in which the products are used by different consumers. In this case buyers and sellers know exactly, and agree on, every attribute of every product. As a result two products can differ in market exchange if and only if their attributes actually differ. In contrast, there is the more usual case with incomplete and costly market information, where consumers only know the attributes of products imperfectly and the extent of the information possessed generally differs between buyer and seller and among the buyers. In this case product differentiation is defined from the buyer's viewpoint, which is to say that two products are differentiated if the buyer's *perceptions* of their attributes are different. There are, for example, the special cases where (a) all products are in fact identical in all relevant respects, yet they are differentiated by diverse consumer perceptions, or (b) the products are in fact different but because consumers are completely uninformed they are perceived as identical.

In this chapter and the next we shall mostly consider the first (and simplest) case with complete information. The demand and supply of differentiated products in model economies with costly and imperfect information are dealt with systematically in chapters 13 and 14.

Models of Differentiation. The earliest attempts at developing a theory of product differentiation and variety treated different variations of "a good" as if they were different goods. It was then a short step to deal with sellers as isolated monopolists and leave systematic consideration of product rivalry outside the analysis.[1] While the resulting theory is analytically compact and elegant, unless more is said about the rate at which individuals substitute among varieties of the good as relative prices change, the empirical content of the theory is limited. Exemplary functional forms for utilities which parametrically describe product varieties and specify consumers' rates of substitution have recently been identified. These permit industry equilibria in prices, outputs, and product variety to be derived in quite specific terms and compared for various configurations of producing firms. In the most widely used version of this model product varieties are symmetrical in the sense that each is an equally good substitute for all others. While the model seems complex because the dimensionality of the product space is expanded each time a new variety appears, the symmetry allows the dimension number to summarize the extent of variety and much of what is important about the demand for both quality and quantity.

The most frequently employed models of product differentiation do not generally impose this degree of product symmetry, but instead are based on variations of the geographic location analysis developed by Hotelling (1929). In these so-called spatial models the number of firms and their locations (read product varieties) typically exceed the dimensionality of the product space. On the demand side there are two central assumptions: each consumer is assumed (a) to have an ideal variety and (b) to suffer increasing disutility as less ideal product brands are consumed. A key implication of these assumptions is that brands compete only with those adjacent to themselves.

The standard extension of the basic spatial model is based on the presumption that the traded products in themselves do not provide value, but are instead a vehicle for bundling the more fundamental "characteristics" that are of interest to consumers. In turn, each good is described by its location in an N-dimensional space of characteristics. The technology of firms then describes the characteristic bundles that can be produced with various factor combinations and at various costs. Consumers also have a "location" in the characteristics space, describing their most preferred bundle, and there is a "consumption technology" indicating the ways in which individuals can and cannot combine the products to create preferred bundles of characteristics. The final component in these analyses is a disutility measure which diminishes the value of product choices distant from the consumer's location. It is models of this kind that are addressed in the final sections of this chapter.

The first systematic analysis of product differentiation was the monopolistic competition model of Chamberlin (1933). For this reason, and because of the

---

[1] Joan Robinson (1933) in her treatise on imperfect competition used one variant of this approach: ". . . The demand curve for the individual firm may be conceived to show the full effect upon the sales of that firm which results from any change in the price which it charges, whether it causes a change in the prices charged by the others or not. It is not our purpose to consider this question in detail. Once the demand curve for the firm is drawn, the technique of analysis can be brought to play, whatever the assumption on which the demand curve was drawn up" (Robinson, 1933, p. 21).

detail and large number of studies that have been developed in this context, it is usual to use monopolistic competition (or some variant of it) as the benchmark for product differentiation analyses. The reader will be reminded of this as we often refer to this model.

4.1   Demand with Spatial Differentiation

If, for example, automobiles were a single commodity, then individuals could not distinguish the output of one firm from another. The concept and importance of a differentiated product begins with the converse of this observation and two facts. The converse is that products are said to be differentiated when consumers do not all view them as perfect substitutes at a common price. The facts are well known. First, because of differing technologies the products of different firms are rarely alike in all important respects, even when they are in the same "industry." Second, consumers differ in their preferences for the various outputs so that the price difference which would cause any given consumer to be at the margin between any pair of products generally differs in the cross-section of consumers.[2]

Industry Analysis. When such differentiation occurs it is common to use products of the same basic "kind" to constitute a group for analysis. Following Chamberlin (1933), is it usual to define an *industry* by the group of products within which cross-elasticities of demand are positive and significant (but such cross-elasticities are small across groups). Despite its popularity, there are several well-known problems with such a definition. First, it ignores firms (actual and potential) having production facilities capable of being readily converted to the production of commodities which are good substitutes in demand. Such high "elasticity in supply" can be very important, for example in determining the degree of rivalry among firms.[3] Thus, while it is usual to think of an industry on the basis of substitutability in demand, this may be inappropriate when the firms (would-be and actual) who supply the demand substitutes do not also cover the range of those offering good substitutability in supply.[4]

The second difficulty in defining an industry on the basis of clusters in demand cross-elasticities is that clusters with clear separating gaps do not generally occur. Most goods are interconnected in some way, and various quite unexpected groups of goods can be empirically linked in gross substitutability. Triffin (1940), Stigler (1949a), Bishop (1952), and others have suggested circuitous ways in which, for example, beef steaks and gasoline can be placed in

---

[2] Again, products may acquire such differentiation on either a real or perceived basis related to functional characteristics, terms and conditions of sale, ancillary services, manner of use, etc.

[3] Demsetz (1968b) and Posner (1976) stress the importance of supply elasticity in the definition of industries for antitrust purposes.

[4] The UK and US Standard Industry Classification (SIC) schema are largely based on supply substitutability. As a result firms in the same SIC "industry" are more or less related by their technical processes and raw material usage.

the same industry by the usual cross-elasticity measures.[5]

In practice there is generally no unambiguous way of defining the extent of an industry along the demand and supply substitutability scale. The definition finally depends on the purpose for which the economic analysis is intended and the applied economist's art.[6] In the present analyses, we sidestep these issues and assume that demands are generated by utility functions of the form $\hat{u}(u(z), z_0)$, where z is the vector of outputs under consideration and the utility $\hat{u}$ is separable in the subutility u and the "outside" goods z_0. All actual and potential producers of the z goods are then said to belong to the industry under consideration.[7] While they are all industry members, the firms may nonetheless differ in the exact details of the commodities they produce and in the costs of production and distribution.

4.1.1 Location and Transportation

Consider an industry in which firms produce functionally identical products, albeit at different geographic locations. The locational possibilities are represented by a **market line**, for example as shown along the horizontal axis in figure 4.1. For the moment we shall assume there are just three firms 1, 2, and 3

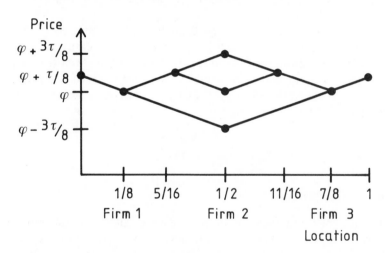

Figure 4.1
Market areas

---

[5] For example, Stigler (1949a, p. 15) notes that "It is perfectly plausible . . . that the group (industry) contains only one firm or, on the contrary, that it includes all firms in the economy. This latter possibility can readily follow from the asymmetry of substitution relationships among firms: taking any one product as our point of departure, each substitute has in turn its substitutes, so that the adjacent cross-elasticities may not diminish, and even increase, as we move further away from the 'basic' firm in some technological or geographical sense."

[6] Key practical issues in market definition are described by Weiss (1972), Elzinga and Hogarty (1973), Posner (1976, pp. 125–33), Boyer (1979), and Schmalensee (1979b).

[7] Recall from section 1.3.2 that the link between such an outside good and those in the considered industry is then only through an income effect, and not directly by prices or other product aspects.

located as indicated 1/8, 1/2, and 7/8 of the distance from one end of the market. In this case, firm 2 has firms 1 and 3 as neighbors, firm 1 has only 2 as a neighbor, and similarly firm 3 has only 2 as a neighbor. For simplicity, consumers are assumed to be (a) uniformly distributed along the market, (b) identical except for their location, and (c) perfectly elastic in price, with each purchasing exactly one unit of the lowest-priced good delivered to his location. That portion of the consumer's income not spent on one of these goods is spent on the outside good.

Preconditions. There are two preconditions for spatial markets to be of interest. The first is a significant cost of transportation. If the movement of goods were costless, the location of production would be irrelevant; from a buyer's perspective, a firm situated thousands of miles away would be equivalent to a rival next door. Nontrivial transportation costs give the spatial firm an advantage in dealing with nearby customers.

The second necessary feature of the spatial model is that the firms exhibit some initial range of outputs where their average production costs fall. If the average costs did not fall, there would be no incentive for firms to concentrate production at given locations. Rather, they would be widely distributed, filling every consumer's location. In turn, there would be no transportation and therefore no spatial model.

Location is, however, an interesting distinction when these two preconditions occur. The transportation cost which is then relevant can easily be incorporated in the analysis. To each product's **mill price** ϕ we assume, as a first approximation, that there is a constant (and uniform across firms) transportation cost τ added per unit distance in delivery. That is, the **delivered price** p is related to mill price by the simple accounting rule

$$p_j = \phi_j + \tau l \tag{4.1}$$

for each firm j when delivering a distance l.

4.1.2 Spatial Competition

Taking the number and location of the firms as given for the moment, it is straightforward to follow Hotelling and develop the Nash-in-price equilibrium for the three-firm model. The first step is the construction of firm demand schedules. For this we refer to the market line in figure 4.1 and focus on firm 2, holding the mill price of rivals 1 and 3 fixed at $\phi_1 = \phi_3 = \phi$ while letting ϕ_2 vary.

Suppose at the onset that 2 also sets a mill price equal to ϕ, in turn selling to those "close-in" consumers lying midway between 1/8 and 1/2 (at 5/16) on the "left" and 1/2 and 7/8 (at 11/16) on the "right". With the uniform prices, buyers between 5/16 and 11/16 have a lower delivered price from firm 2 and, all other things being equal, they will purchase from him. Those individuals at location 5/16 and 11/16, the *marginal* consumers, are indifferent between firm 2 and firms 1 and 3 respectively. The 5/16–11/16 line segment (including end-points) is termed firm 2's **market area**.

Suppose next that firm 2 lowers its mill price below ϕ in an effort to extend its trade. For $\phi_2 \leqslant \phi$, the market area of firm 2 is given by the distance l (moving outward in both directions from its location) which satisfies the condition $\phi_2 = \phi - \tau l$. Given ϕ and τ, smaller values of ϕ_2 permit greater values of l; that is, a decrease in ϕ_2 leads firm 2 to sales gain at the expense of competing firms 1 and 3. For some value of ϕ_2 just slightly above $\phi - 3\tau/8$, firm 1 retains all the consumers located between zero and 1/8 and the few to the "right" of 1/8 where its delivered price is less than that of firm 2. Firm 3 serves a similar market segment on the other side of firm 2. At $\phi_2 = \phi - 3\tau/8$, *all* consumers at 1/8 *and* less are just indifferent to purchasing from firm 1 or 2. Something special occurs when ϕ_2 falls by any small amount less than $\phi - 3\tau/8$: these previously indifferent consumers, *as a group*, switch to firm 2. A similar abrupt switch occurs on firm 2's right, there involving firm 3 and the entire market segment at and beyond 7/4. The "switch" occurs when the firm sets a mill price such that its delivered price at a rival's location is less than that rival's mill price. In this case it is said that the rival is eliminated by **mill-price undercutting**.[8]

Things proceed more usually and smoothly as firm 2 increases its price above ϕ. It continuously loses customers until $\phi_2 > \phi + 3\tau/8$, at which point all consumers prefer the outputs of firms 1 and 3 to that of firm 2.

The Nash-in-price (perceived) demand curve facing firm 2 is illustrated in figure 4.2. Note particularly that at $\phi_2 = \phi - 3\tau/8$ the undercutting segment EE' indicates the switch from 3/4 to the entire market.

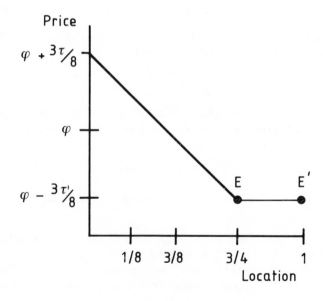

Figure 4.2
Nash-in-price demand

---

[8] Salop (1979b) refers to these as "zap" prices, as they remove neighbors from the trade.

E4.1

Demand in a Linear Spatial Model

Hotelling dealt extensively with the case of two firms, thinking of these as shop-owners and the market line segment as "main street." Figure 4.3 is the basis for his analysis. Following Hotelling, let the line segment have length $L = l_1 + m_1 + m_2 + l_2$, where l_j is the distance firm j is from the end of the street and m_j is the distance firm j is from the specific customer located at point A in the figure.[9]

Figure 4.3
Hotelling "main street"

Suppose, to begin with, that the customer at location A is marginal to the two firms, that is, he is just indifferent to the products of the firms delivered to his location. In this case

$$\phi_1 + \tau m_1 = \phi_2 + \tau m_2 \tag{4.2}$$

Letting j indicate one firm and k the other, solve (4.2) for k's location m_k and then substitute this in the market length identity to give

$$m_j = \frac{\delta\tau - (\phi_j - \phi_k)}{2\tau} \tag{4.3}$$

Here, $\delta = L - l_1 - l_2$ is the distance between the firms. If we assume, with Hotelling, that each firm's production cost is zero, then the profit of each is just $\phi_j(l_j + m_j)$ or, using (4.3),[10]

$$\pi_j = \phi_j(l_j + m_j)$$

$$= \frac{(\delta + 2l_j)\phi_j\tau - \phi_j{}^2 + \phi_j\phi_k}{2\tau} \tag{4.4}$$

Note that the profit is expressed as a function of the fixed location parameters and transportation costs as well as the prices.

Hotelling described the industry's "rest position" using the Nash solution concept in prices. This requires solving the two stationarity conditions

$$\frac{\partial\pi_j}{\partial\phi_j} = (\delta + 2l_j)\tau - 2\phi_j + \phi_k = 0 \qquad j \neq k = 1, 2 \tag{4.5a}$$

---

[9] Hotelling uses street length L, but it is a simple matter to choose $L = 1$ and express all other lengths relatively.

[10] The quantity $l_j + m_j$ is just firm j's unit sales.

for equilibrium prices. Doing so gives

$$\phi_j = \tau\left(L + \frac{l_j - l_k}{3}\right) \qquad (4.5b)$$

In turn, the unit sales of the firms at these prices are given by substituting (4.5b) in (4.3) and solving for $l_j + m_j$:

$$l_j + m_j = \frac{L + (l_j - l_k)/3}{2} \qquad (4.5c)$$

Finally, substituting for m_j from (4.3) and letting z_j indicate quantity sold gives the demand functions

$$z_j = \frac{L + l_j - l_k - (\phi_j - \phi_k)/\tau}{2} \qquad (4.6)$$

(Again, j, $k = 1$, 2 and $j \neq k$.) It is to be stressed that these are the demand schedules *perceived* by the firms, as they are based on the Nash-in-price conjectures which hold true only *at* the equilibrium point.

The demands (4.6) are linear in prices, with negative slopes equal to $1/2\tau$ in own-price. The locations of the firms determine the intercept of the demand functions and, as expected, j's quantity is increasing in k's price. Finally, note that the demands are continuous in both prices as long as neither firm undercuts the other.

Hotelling's lesson is simple: even given functionally identical products, spatial differentiation and nontrivial transportation costs permit unequal product prices and give rise to (perceived) demands which are possibly quite inelastic functions of these prices.

4.1.3 "Competitive" Equilibrium

Up to this point, the number and locations of firms have been held fixed. Only prices have been variable and determined in equilibrium. More generally, it is also possible to include location among the firm's decision values. We might, for example, ask what locations would be employed at a "competitive" equilibrium where the rivalry among firms causes the average total cost of servicing consumers to be minimized. To investigate this case let total costs be given by

$$c(l) = F + cl \qquad (4.7)$$

where F indicates fixed cost, l is the length of the market line serviced, and c is constant average (and marginal) production cost. For example, a single (monopoly) firm located at the center of the market would have average total costs

$$a(l) = c + \frac{F}{l} + \frac{\tau l}{4} \qquad (4.8)$$

where $c + F/l$ are average production costs and $\tau l/4$ is the average distribution cost.[11]

---

[11] Total distribution costs are $\int_0^{l/2} \tau l \, dl = \tau l^2/8$ for each "half" of the market so that the average is $(\tau l^2/8)/(l/2)$.

Consider alternatively the equilibrium occurring where firms are uniformly spaced a distance l^* apart such that average costs are minimized; that is, where

$$l^* = \operatorname*{argmin}_{l}\left(c + \frac{F}{l} + \frac{\tau l}{4}\right) \tag{4.9}$$

The stationarity condition giving this minimum is

$$\frac{\tau}{4} = \frac{F}{(l^*)^2}$$

which yields

$$l^* = 2\left(\frac{F}{\tau}\right)^{1/2} \tag{4.10}$$

This result is as expected: the spacing of the firms is directly related to the level of fixed cost, inversely related to transport cost, and independent of the unit production cost. Moreover, since the firms are identical, the solution is symmetrical.

It is important to observe in the above case that each firm can raise its price by some small amount and, even though it will lose some trade, it will not lose it all. Aside from the discontinuities at prices where undercutting just occurs, each firm's demand is negatively sloped and not necessarily small relative to the market demand. While some have termed the resulting equilibrium "competitive," this must be done with qualification as firms do not face *perfectly* elastic demands. Instead, the equilibrium has elements of both competition and monopoly.[12] Chamberlin (1933) was the first to extensively describe the properties of equilibria in which product variety is central to the analysis, and it is to his particular model that we turn.

4.2   Competition with Differentiated Products

While there are many common elements between Chamberlin's theory of monopolistic competition and Hotelling's spatial model, there are also key differences. First, in Chamberlin's analysis the demand of every firm always (at all quantities) varies continuously with the prices of other firms. Specifically, there is no price level where one firm undercuts another with an abrupt discontinuous gain in trade. Second, Chamberlin thought of the competition among firms as symmetric: a price change by any seller affected the demand of *all* others. Despite these conditions Chamberlin was only suggestive and descriptive, not explicit and precise, about the source of product differentiation.

---

[12] By monopoly we mean only that the firm faces a less than perfectly elastic demand. This definition, while now common, is at some odds with the classical use. For John Stuart Mill a monopolist was any seller receiving payments beyond that needed to induce it to supply its product (rent) (Mill, 1965, p. 416). Adam Smith applied the term monopoly to any seller who traded its wares in a closed market. Smith thus found the colonial trade of English merchants to be a monopoly, despite the fact that he found that there was no collusion in the trade, the number of sellers was large, and each seller saw itself at the "mercy" of other firms' low prices (Smith, 1937, pp. 600–20).

He did not, for example, generally think of a single dimension (such as the location of production) along which differentiation occurs and with which consumers express differing preferences.

Instead, Chamberlin began simply with a group of ". . . monopolists selling similar, but not exactly the same, products." He metaphorically argued that the consumer demand for any given product was dependent on the specific characteristics of that product and the prices of rival products. By his assertions, these formed the basis of a "well-behaved" demand function $z_j(p_j, \bar{p}_j)$ and a profit objective

$$\max[z_j(p_j, \bar{p}_j)p_j - c(z_j)] \qquad (4.11)$$

where z_j is j's output, $\bar{p}_j = [p_1 p_2 \ldots p_{j-1} p_{j+1} \ldots p_J]$ is the $(J-1)$-vector of prices for rival firms, and $c(z_j)$ is j's total cost function.[13]

As an industry equilibrium, Chamberlin described the Nash-in-price solution with $j = 1, 2, \ldots, J$ firms. We can be somewhat more systematic here than he was half a century ago. At the profit maximum, each firm j chooses the price $p_j{}^0$ satisfying the stationarity condition

$$z_j(p_j{}^0, \bar{p}_j) + \frac{\partial z_j(p_j{}^0, \bar{p}_j)}{\partial p_j} p_j - c'(z_j) \frac{\partial z_j(p_j{}^0, \bar{p}_j)}{\partial p_j} = 0 \qquad (4.12)$$

where $c'(\cdot)$ is the marginal cost function. At the monopolistic competition equilibrium this stationarity condition must hold when every other firm uses its best reply in price, that is, when

$$z_j(p_j{}^0, \bar{p}_j{}^0) + \frac{\partial z_j(p_j{}^0, \bar{p}_j{}^0)}{\partial p_j} p_j - c'(z_j(p_j{}^0, \bar{p}_j{}^0)) \frac{\partial z_j(p_j{}^0, \bar{p}_j{}^0)}{\partial p_j} = 0 \quad (4.13a)$$

for all j. Dividing by the partial derivative in this last expression, it is evident that each firm chooses a price where its *perceived* marginal revenue is equal to its marginal cost. Again, by the "perceived" qualifier we understand that it is the demand curve, and associated marginal revenue, based on each firm's (Bertrand) Nash-in-price conjectures.[14]

Suppose that necessary short-run conditions (4.12) and (4.13a) are satisfied. If any firm is then making positive profits, Chamberlin argued that new firms would enter the industry to sell close substitutes for its product. This, he maintained, would shift the firm's demand "inward" and reduce its profit. With free entry, the long-run monopolistic competition equilibrium has the entry process continue until all profits are zero, that is, until price is just equal to average cost for every firm j:

$$p_j{}^0 = \frac{c(z_j)}{z_j} \qquad (4.13b)$$

At the equilibrium there is no level of perceived demand where positive profits can be obtained by any firm. Conversely, Chamberlin reasoned that exit would occur if negative profits were to result, so that the equilibrium condition (4.13b) stipulates exactly zero profits.

---

[13] All firms are assumed to have identical cost functions – the "uniformity" assumption – despite the fact that their products are not identical.

[14] Chamberlin labeled the perceived (inverse) demand dd and the actual demand DD in his analysis and these schedules are still generally referred to using these notations.

The long-run monopolistically competitive equilibrium with free entry is illustrated in figure 4.4. There, dd represents the Nash-in-price perceived demand of the representative firm; the less elastic DD (at the prevailing price and output pair) incorporates whatever reactions competing firms would in fact make. The MR schedule is the marginal revenue associated with dd. AC and MC indicate average and marginal cost respectively. Note that the profit-maximizing condition $MR = MC$ obtains at the zero-profit output, where $AC = p$ and the AC and dd schedules are tangent: $p = c/z$ and $\partial p/\partial z = \partial(c/z)/\partial z$ jointly imply $mr = (\partial z/\partial p)p + z = mc$.

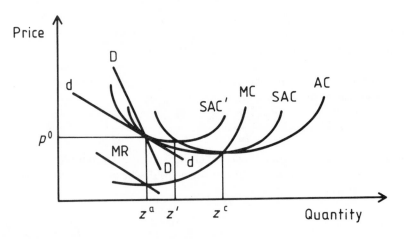

Figure 4.4
Monopolistic competition equilibrium

Excess Capacity and Brand Proliferation. Perhaps the most widely noted aspect of the long-run (free-entry) equilibrium in monopolistic competition is that of **excess capacity**: the representative firm's equilibrium output z^0 is less than that which minimizes its unit cost. This means that the firm will charge a price that exceeds both its (long-run) marginal cost and the competitive price. It also means that the firm will build a scale of plant less than the "technically optimal" scale. In figure 4.4 the chosen plant scale is represented by SAC', while the technically optimal scale is given by SAC.[15] If the quantity z^0 were produced by firms with plant scale SAC, then fewer firms would be necessary. Alternatively, if z^0 were produced by firms operating with SAC', but at the minimum unit cost for that scale, then again fewer firms would be necessary. Because of this, the monopolistic competition equilibrium with excess capacity is frequently said to result in **brand proliferation** (too many firms) and under-utilized plants. It is to be emphasized here that brand proliferation is simply a statement about the number of firms and the level of average cost, as given above. As we will see clearly in chapter 6, section 6.2, it is *not* a statement that the monopolistically competitive equilibrium over- or under-supplies brands relative to the number

---

[15] With plant scale SAC', the quantity z' is technically the most efficient. For this reason it is usual to distinguish the $z^0 z'$ and $z' z^c$ parts of the overall $z^0 z^c$ excess capacity.

which is socially optimal (measured by the sum of consumer and producer surplus).

E4.2

Excess Capacity and Demand Increasing Costs

In the most complete version of Chamberlin's theory firms are permitted to choose *demand increasing costs*, such as advertising, as well as price. For this case Demsetz (1959, 1964) has argued that there is the possibility that average total cost (average production plus average demand increasing cost) will be minimized at equilibrium. An analysis of this possibility is instructive.

Consider a representative firm and use the following usual notation: p indicates price, α indicates advertising messages, ξ is a quality index, γ indicates the constant cost per advertising message, $z = z(p, \alpha, \xi)$ is the demand function, and $c(\xi, z)$ is the production cost function. The demand function $z(\cdot)$ is assumed to incorporate Nash-in-price conjectures and thus correspond to the dd perceived demand of Chamberlin. Profits are given by $\pi = pz - c - \alpha\gamma$ and the free-entry equilibrium leads to $\pi = 0$. The stationarity conditions for maximum profits are

$$\pi_p = pz_p + z - c_z z_p = 0 \tag{4.14a}$$

$$\pi_\alpha = pz_\alpha - c_z z_\alpha - \gamma = 0 \tag{4.14b}$$

$$\pi_\xi = pz_\xi - c_z z_\xi - c_\xi = 0 \tag{4.14c}$$

where the subscripts indicate partial derivatives. We assume interior solutions for all variables.

With the above notation the firm's average total costs are given by

$$A = \frac{c(z, \xi) + \alpha\gamma}{z} \tag{4.15}$$

In turn, the minimum of A occurs with

$$z^2 A_p = zc_z z_p - (c + \alpha\gamma)z_p = 0 \tag{4.16a}$$

$$z^2 A_\alpha = z(c_z z_\alpha + \gamma) - (c + \alpha\gamma)z_\alpha = 0 \tag{4.16b}$$

$$z^2 A_\xi = z(c_z z_\xi + c_\xi) - (c + \alpha\gamma)z_\xi = 0 \tag{4.16c}$$

Holding price constant, from the above equations Schmalensee (1972b) has noted that (a) $\pi_\alpha = 0$ and $\pi = 0$ implies $A_\alpha = 0$, and (b) $\pi_\xi = 0$ and $\pi = 0$ implies $A_\xi = 0$. That is, given p, the advertising and quality conditions for a profit maximum with zero profits are identical with the advertising and quality conditions for A to be at its minimum.

When price can vary the above results change. Substituting (4.14a) and the zero-profit conditions in (4.16a) gives $A_p = 1$. From the chain rule there is $A_p = A_z z_p$ and therefore $A_z z_p = 1$ or $A_z = 1/z_p$. This is, of course, just part of the tangency condition shown in figure 4.4, where the demand and average cost function have the same slope at equilibrium. It means that if z_p is negatively sloped then the equilibrium occurs where A could be lowered by increases in output. There is "excess capacity" in monopolistic competition. Again, a further clarification of excess capacity, and especially its implications for social welfare, are given in chapter 6 and E6.4 specifically.

Integer Problem. Although the free-entry zero-profit (tangency) equilibrium shown in figure 4.4 is that which Chamberlin proposed for monopolistically competitive markets, it must be looked upon only as an approximation. Because of fixed costs, the entry of some last single firm can cause the profits of producing firms to go from a strictly positive to a strictly negative level. While we might try to save the zero-profit condition by arguing that firms are very small relative to the market, when pushed to the necessary limits this denies the presence of fixed costs. When fixed costs are not arbitrarily small, it might then be that no (integer) number of firms can produce a zero-profit equilibrium. This **integer problem**, first noted by Kaldor (1935), has no real solution in the standard Chamberlinian model (for related comments see chapter 5, section 5.6). Rather, it is usual to neglect this difficulty and, when the number of producing firms is large, to treat the zero-profit equilibrium as an approximation result.

4.2.1 Fixed Cost and Equilibrium Variety

The entry of firms was imagined by Chamberlin to fill the gaps in the spectrum of available goods by attracting consumers "symmetrically" from extant sellers to a new brand which might better suit their tastes. In the absence of fixed costs a result much like perfect competition would occur at the end-point of such entry: the market would be filled with a complete spectrum of product varieties in the sense that each consumer would have his particular tastes satisfied. Monopolistic competition was intended by Chamberlin to deal with the converse case, where the presence of fixed costs and scale economies are important and the equilibrium generally involves a compromise which leaves many consumer types with purchases that do not exactly match their most preferred choice. Presumably, the cost savings from an increased scale of production and lower equilibrium prices offsets the utility losses from not receiving the product most preferred.[16]

---

[16] The existence of fixed costs is well recognized in the industrial economics literature. Fixed costs are often said to arise from indivisibilities in physical capital as well as from factors such as research and development, advertising, and promotion (Bain, 1956, pp. 142–3, 216; Biggadike, 1976, ch. 4; Scherer, 1980, ch. 4). These costs may also arise as expenditures necessary to establish the firm as a credible and reliable enterprise to both factor suppliers and consumers (Chandler, 1969; Williamson, 1975). Direct evidence of scale economies includes statistical estimates of production and cost functions (Walters, 1963; Needham, 1969; Johnston, 1974) and engineering analyses (Scherer et al., 1975). Indirect evidence includes estimates using the survivor principle (Stigler, 1958), the relative consistency of industry concentration ratios over time (Mueller and Hamm, 1974), and the cross-sectional consistency of concentration ratios (Pryor, 1972).

E4.3

Automobile Style Changes and Scale Economies

It is frequently argued that the rapidity of style changes in the automobile industry has been responsible for the resulting high concentration in the industry (see, for example, Menge, 1962). Briefly, the argument goes as follows. The dies used in the manufacture of automobiles, as inserts in large metal stamping presses, must be carefully tailored to a particular body style. The dies represent major discrete investments; they are discrete in the sense that they necessarily take on a given final form when used to produce either a very small or a very large number of bodies. The result is that if larger firms change body style frequently and therefore change dies frequently, and small firms follow this lead, the die cost per automobile produced will be much higher for firms producing the smaller rate of output. Given industry price, rapid style changes involving very expensive die changes, it is argued, will drive small firms from production.

Whether or not the argument holds depends on a variety of facts. The critical requirement is that style change costs are independent of the level of the firm's output, resulting in scale economies.[17] It is also necessary that style be such an important element in demand that smaller firms will be forced to change body style with the same frequency as large firms. Finally, it is required that there be a fixed industry price to which all firms must adhere, so that the firms changing bodies less frequently cannot shade price to compensate.[18]

At this point it should be noted that the economies of scale arising with the change in the automobile body style also arise with advertising, R&D, or any other category of cost that is independent of the firm's rate of output.

Fixed Cost, Supply, and Demand. The specific manner in which fixed cost determines product variety in monopolistic competition can be seen using an analysis suggested by Rosen (1974). To begin, suppose that products can differ only along a single *quality* dimension and, at a given price, all consumers prefer more quality to less. It also simplifies matters to assume that actual and would-be producers have the same cost function

---

[17] McGee (1973) reports that the "fixed" stamping machine and die costs can be altered somewhat depending on planned volumes, but not by much.

[18] Fisher et al. (1962) provide estimates of the costs of automobile model changes between 1949 and 1960. Their research compares prices in 1949 with those in 1960 for given automobiles while controlling for automobile length, weight, horsepower, transmission, and other characteristics. They estimated that $454 (1960 dollars) would have been saved per 1960 automobile if automobile size and horsepower had not been changed during the period. This saving would have been $116 if additional optional equipment had not been added. Of specific interest relative to the style change theory of concentration, they also estimated that an additional $99 per car would have been saved if the automobile manufacturers had not retooled and changed automobile body styles annually. (Fisher et al. did not maintain that the 1960 automobiles were not superior in unmeasured, but possibly substantive, respects and that this may have caused their estimates to be high.) If Fisher et al. were correct and market prices were competitively determined, then a smaller firm would have been able to price $99 less on average and avoid the style change.

$$C = F + c(\xi)z \qquad (4.17)$$

where F is fixed cost and $c(\xi)$ is the constant marginal cost of production which depends on the quality variable ξ. Higher quality leads to greater production costs and this occurs at an increasing rate: $dc(\xi)/d\xi > 0$ and $d^2c(\xi)/d\xi^2 > 0$. The *minimum supply price* necessary for any firm to break even on a product of quality ξ is

$$p^s(z; \xi) = \frac{F}{z} + c(\xi) \qquad (4.18)$$

With a larger number of buyers each shares a smaller fraction of the fixed cost. Thus $p^s(\cdot)$ is decreasing in output z for any given quality level ξ, and, for fixed z, $p^s(\cdot)$ is increasing and convex in ξ.

On the demand side, suppose further that each consumer buys just one unit of the product and each belongs to one of two types. Let there be z_1 individuals of type 1 and z_2 of type 2, with the difference being that type 2 individuals place greater value on the quality attribute and are therefore inclined to pay a higher price for any given level of ξ (per unit output).

Separating and Pooling Equilibria. One possible market equilibrium under the above assumptions would have two product varieties being offered: one with quality ξ_1 satisfying the type 1 consumers and a second of higher quality ξ_2 satisfying those of type 2. After entry, sellers offering quality level ξ_1 sell for $p_1^s = F/z_1 + c(\xi_1)$, and similarly those offering ξ_2 sell for $p_2^s = F/z_2 + c(\xi_2)$. All firms earn zero profits. If it is assumed that there are more type 1 buyers than type 2 buyers ($z_1 > z_2$), then no type 1 buyer has an incentive to switch to the higher type 2 quality since the value he places on the additional quality is less than the increment in price. Conversely, buyers of type 2 have no incentive to switch to the ξ_2 product. Because of the lack of incentive to switch, the price–quality bundles are said to be **incentive compatible**. Finally, note that at these prices the sellers are also satisfied as they recover full costs. This is called a **two-good (separating) equilibrium**.

Figure 4.5 illustrates such an equilibrium. The contours $\bar{U}^1$ and $\bar{U}^2$ indicate combinations of price and quality which give type 1 and 2 consumers respectively a fixed utility index. These sloped upward and are strictly concave, as we assume diminishing marginal utility for quality.[19] The $p^s(\xi)$ minimum supply schedules derive from (4.18) with $c(\xi)$ increasing and strictly convex in ξ and quantities z_1 and z_2 fixed. The difference between the $p_1^s(\xi)$ and $p_2^s(\xi)$ schedules is simply due to the difference between the quantities z_1 and z_2: since $z_1 > z_2$, the $p_1^s(\xi)$ schedule lies everywhere below $p_2^s(\xi)$.

The cross-hatched area (the preferred set) "above" the intersection of $\bar{U}^1$ and $\bar{U}^2$ suggests a second possible equilibrium. If we now permit a new product variety offering a price–quality combination falling anywhere in the shaded area, consumers of both type 1 and 2 will switch to that new and preferred good, and the old goods with ξ_1 and ξ_2 will disappear from the market. The result is a **single-good (pooling) equilibrium**. The critical question is whether or not the

---

[19] Moreover, the contours intersect only once. The importance of this "single-crossing" property is made clear in chapter 7, section 7.3.

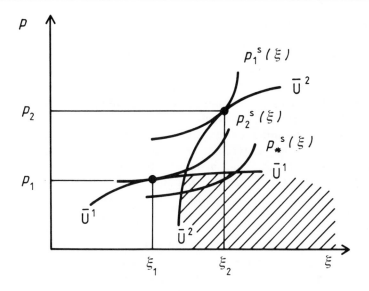

Figure 4.5
Separating equilibrium

prices that can be established in this preferred set permit such a product to cover its cost. To see the condition necessary for this, let $z_* = z_1 + z_2$ be the quantity of a single product of quality level ξ sold to both types. Then the single-good equilibrium will occur if the minimum supply price schedule

$$p_*^s(\xi) = \frac{F}{z_*} + c(\xi) \tag{4.19}$$

includes price–quality combinations which are *simultaneously* more preferred by type 1 buyers than $\bar{U}^1$ and more preferred by type 2 buyers than $\bar{U}^2$. The schedule $p_*^s(\xi)$ in figure 4.5 illustrates such a case as it has many points in the jointly preferred set (shaded area).

What aspects of technology and the market will allow a single good to drive out all others? Two are particularly notable in this model. The first and most obvious is the size of the fixed cost. Other things being equal, the greater is the fixed cost of production the more likely it is that a pooling equilibrium will occur. To see this, note that at any quality level the rate by which the p_s schedule rises with F is inversely related to quantity: $dp^s/dF = 1/z$. Given $z_* = z_1 + z_2$, this means that increases in F shifts up the supply schedules more for the separate type 1 and type 2 goods than for the single-good alternative. As a result the greater is the fixed cost the greater are the savings from producing just one good; that is, the larger F is, the greater is the difference between $F/(z_1 + z_2)$ and either F/z_1 or F/z_2.

Second, the relative number of individuals in the type 1 and type 2 groups will affect the likelihood of the single-good equilibrium. When, for example, z_1 is much greater than z_2 the p_*^s supply schedule will be only slightly below that for p_1^s and the chance that p_*^s will have any points in the preferred set will be diminished (see figure 4.5).

4.3   Localization of Competition

In Hotelling's original spatial model each firm competes in the market only with adjoining suppliers – those immediately to its right and left whose mill price it has not undercut. Chamberlin's theory of monopolistic competition was not intended to deal with market situations in which competition is "localized" in this strict fashion. Chamberlin instead imagined a "symmetric" market in which each firm faced a large number of quite small competitors. This large-numbers competition was, in fact, the rationale he offered for assuming Nash-in-price conjectures. Chamberlin thus had in mind a fundamentally different concept of products and consumer demand than that set out by Hotelling. What was that concept? A large measure of discontent with monopolistic competition was expressed in the early literature because Chamberlin failed to specify in detail a theory of demand consistent with his analysis.[20]

Archibald and Rosenbluth (1975) and others have more recently constructed theories of demand with, more or less, the properties asserted by Chamberlin. These analyses are based on the Lancaster (1966) characteristics model of consumption, where consumers are assumed (as a primitive) to have preferences for bundles of characteristics and the demand for goods is derived from the underlying demand for characteristics. For example, the demand for oranges is thought to derive from fundamental demands for characteristics of nutrition, taste, nonperishability, etc.

The key advantage of the Lancaster approach is that it leads to objective ways of defining products by their characteristic composition. Personal preferences need not be weighed. Of course, the objectivity requires that characteristics be quantitatively measurable, and while at times problematic this is generally manageable.[21] Other technical problems are avoided by assuming that characteristics are continuously variable.

E4.4 _____

Characteristics and Industries

In Lancaster's characteristic model each consumer's utility is a function of characteristics, which suggests that we define a product group, or industry, on that basis. A commodity with positive amounts of some specific set of characteristics and insignificant amounts of others is in the group; otherwise, it is not. Commodities in the group are then distinguished by their characteristic proportions and scale.

In this regard, perhaps the most frequently used definition of industries is based on the derivation of characteristics from goods by the linear **combinable-in-use** consumption technology proposed by Lancaster. He requires characteristic bundles to be formed in the fashion

---

[20] For a review of this criticism see Archibald (1961). A variety of other criticisms, and defenses, of the monopolistic competition model are reprinted in Rowley (1972).

[21] Good examples of characteristic measurement techniques are Griliches (1961, 1971), Hall (1971), Gorman (1980), and Bresnahan (1981a).

$$\zeta = Bz \qquad (4.20)$$

where ζ is an N-vector of characteristics, z is an M-vector of goods, and B is an $N \times M$ matrix of constant (technology) coefficients. (To avoid uninteresting problems it is also assumed that $M > N$.) Suppose that B can be arranged as (essentially) a block diagonal matrix. The goods within a block then have a set of common characteristics unlike those in other blocks. Such blocks of goods can be thought of as constituting "industries." Note that such an industry definition is not based on consumer preferences, utility functions, or cross-elasticities as is usual. Further, the definition does not mean that there are no substitution possibilities in consumption (based on prices, income, and preferences) between goods in one block and those in another. That would be precluded only on the assumption of a properly separable utility function, where the matrix of marginal rates of characteristics consumption are also block diagonal.[22] Lancaster (1966, 1975) and Archibald et al. (1986) provide further details of this method for defining industries and some problems.

4.3.1 Characteristics and Commodity Demand

Consider the two-space of characteristics in figure 4.6. There, each of the rays 01, 02, 03, 04, 05, and 06 represents different proportions of the two characteristics ζ_1 and ζ_2. Each such proportion defines a distinct commodity and product differentiation is measured by the angle each ray makes with the horizontal. The consumption possibilities are bounded by commodity 1, which contains characteristic ζ_2 only, and commodity 6, which contains only ζ_1. Points along any commodity ray indicate the scale of consumption. For example, the specific

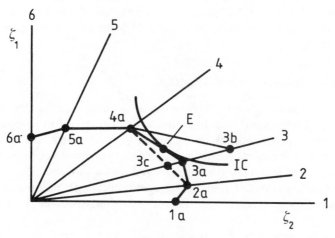

Figure 4.6
Market opportunity set

---

[22] In addition to such demand conditions, partial equilibrium analysis requires an industry definition where production factor prices are independent, such as occurs in a constant-cost industry.

bundles (locations) in the characteristics space given by 1a, 2a, 3a, ..., 6a represent amounts of commodities 1–6 respectively that can be obtained with some common unit expenditure.

Following Archibald and Rosenbluth, and Lancaster, for the moment let us assume that differentiated commodities are linearly **combinable in use** by individuals. This means, for example, that one laundry detergent with high sudsing and low bleaching can be combined (blended) after purchase with a low-sudsing high-bleaching alternative to produce intermediate amounts of these characteristics. The linear consumption technology also implies that, if the sudsing and bleaching measures for these two products are [6 1] and [2 5] respectively at the unit expenditures location of these goods, some individual could also devote half this expenditure to each and "self-produce" the intermediate bundle [4 3]. There are no claims here that this is a pervasive consumption technology, only that it is instructive to think through its implications.

With commodities combinable in use and a linear consumption technology, the **market opportunity set**, that is, the characteristic bundles that are feasible in exchange, is a convex set whose extreme points are the unit expenditure vectors and the origin. [23] In turn, the **frontier** of this set is that subset of points which cannot be purchased with less than the full unit expenditure. For example, in figure 4.6 the market opportunity set includes the bundles given in the area enclosed by 0, 1a, 2a, ..., 6a, and the frontier of the set is given by the line segments joining the points 1a, 2a, ..., 6a. Commodities are said to be **neighbors** if all characteristic bundles which arise as convex combinations of the commodities lie on the market opportunity frontier. In figure 4.6, commodities 2 and 3 are neighbors, for example, but 2 and 4 are not.

The characteristic bundle purchased by any given consumer can be determined using indifference contours defined over fundamental (ζ_1, ζ_2) bundles. In figure 4.6, IC indicates one such contour. With the given product prices and unit expenditure, the tangency optimum occurs at point E where a convex combination of commodities 3 and 4 is chosen. It is apparent from the geometry of the two-characteristic case that each consumer will form optimal bundles of at most two commodities. [24]

4.3.2 Combinable-in-use Demand Functions

Changes in a commodity's price give rise to a change in its unit expenditure vector. In turn, price changes in all commodities will result in changes in all the unit expenditure vector lengths and a movement in all line segments of the market opportunity frontier. A change in just one commodity's price results only in the length of one unit vector being changed and a movement in only the two line segments of the frontier joining the commodity with its neighbors. As the price of commodity 3 increases, for instance, the length of vector 3a shortens. [25]

---

[23] Except in very special cases, the market opportunity set is a convex combination using only nonnegative quantities.

[24] Note that, with the prices given in figure 4.6, commodities 1 and 6 will not be purchased by any individual.

[25] A change in the design, the characteristic composition, of commodity 3 leads to a change in the slope of the 03 ray.

It is in this last fashion that we attempt to build up the properties of the Nash-in-price perceived demand of Chamberlinian monopolistic competition.

In figure 4.6 assume that there is a small price decrease for commodity 3 and that all other commodities have fixed prices and therefore fixed unit expenditure vectors. The segments of the frontier affected by this particular price change are those indicated by 4a–3a and 3a–2a. As the price of 3 is decreased, the tangency solution for the representative consumer first moves continuously with more of 3 being purchased at the expense of 4. There is, however, a critical price indicated by the unit expenditure 3b where the purchase of commodity 4 ceases, since a bundle of commodities 5 and 3 will provide a superior characteristic combination with the unit expenditure.[26] In a reverse manner, increases in 3's price will cause quantity shifts from 3 to 4 for the consumer. At the price which implies unit expenditure 3c, a second critical point is reached. Further price decreases will leave consumers better off if they purchase a bundle made up of commodities 2 and 4 along the broken-line segment 2a–4a and commodity 3 will no longer be purchased.[27] The consumer demand schedule generated in this way has the general form given in figure 4.7. There are negatively sloped portions along which the consumer demands bundles of two neighboring commodities, with discontinuities in demand at those prices where the neighbor relationship changes and quantities change abruptly.[28]

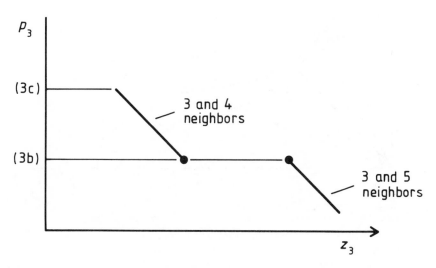

Figure 4.7
Demand with commodities combinable in use

---

[26] To produce 3b using commodities 4 and 5 requires holding "negative amounts" of one of these constituents. While for some commodities a "negative" holding may make sense, this does not seem to be a uniformly reasonable assumption. This has been a recurring criticism of combinable-in-use characteristic models.

[27] When 3 has a critical price greater than that given by 3c it is "excluded" from the market so that 2 and 4 then become neighbors (and segment 2a–4a is on the market opportunity frontier).

[28] These correspond to the mill price undercutting points in the Hotelling spatial model (Archibald and Rosenbluth, 1975).

4.3.3   Commodities not Combinable in Use

In the above analysis the extent of competition is quite limited. Each product competes only with its neighbor in any range of price, even though there may be a large number of sellers of products combining characteristics ζ_1 and ζ_2. This, as we noted earlier, is not the monopolistically competitive situation imagined by Chamberlin.[29] Might the localized competition arise simply because the commodities were assumed to be combinable in use?

This possibility is considered in figure 4.8 where four commodities are available (1, 2, 3, and 4 as indicated), again with just two characteristics ζ_1 and ζ_2. Vectors 1a, 2a, 3a, and 4a indicate unit expenditure amounts, and IC is once more the indifference contour of the characteristics for the representative individual. (Ignore IC′ for the moment.) Commodity 2 is chosen at 2a for the obvious reason.

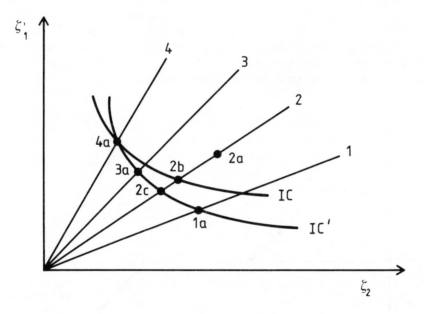

Figure 4.8
Demand in monopolistic competition

What happens to the consumption of commodity 2 as its price changes? For price increases the unit expenditure vector for 2 becomes shorter. In what seems to be the more likely case where self-production is not possible (buying half a pair of black size 7 shoes and half a pair of white size 3 shoes is not equivalent to buying a grey size 5 pair), the consumption opportunities of interest are

---

[29] It can be seen that competition is not localized with two characteristics when many commodities fall on the same straight-line segment of the market opportunity frontier. This, however, produces an instability, for a small change in the price of any of the firms in the mid-portion of a segment, say, eliminates all others (except those two at the "end" of the line segment). This acute form of competition is not that imagined by Chamberlin.

limited to those given by the unit consumption vectors and not (interior) convex combinations of them.[30] In this case, and still restricting attention to the individual with indifference contour IC, the price implied by unit expenditure 2b becomes critical, for at any price below that the consumer will shift his trade to commodity 4, at 4a. If all individuals were identical, then the demand for good 2 would be perfectly inelastic until the 2b price were reached and then it would jump to zero. At the specific price implied by 2b, however, goods 2 and 4 are perfect substitutes and competition is localized.

Diversity in consumer preferences changes things considerably. For example, as the price of 2 is decreased to the level indicated by 2c, the (different) individual with IC′ shifts from commodity 2 to commodity 3, at 3a. More generally, with a continuum of consumers with diverse ζ_1 and ζ_2 preferences, switches will occur between all commodity pairs and they will occur smoothly as price is changed. Competition will not be localized in this case. With this state of affairs the dd demand of monopolistic competition will be everywhere continuous (see Hart, 1985a, and Archibald et al., 1986, for details).

4.3.4   Localization and the Number of Characteristics

It is also possible that the combinable-in-use consumption technology itself yields nonlocalized rivalry when there are a large number of characteristics. Archibald and Rosenbluth (1975) have specifically shown that, when the number of combinable product characteristics is four or more, the number of neighbors for any brand can be of the order of $J/2$ (J is, again, the number of firms in the industry). In this case a large number of firms in the industry means a large number of competitors *on average*.[31] The degree of localization thus turns on several questions of fact.[32] Unfortunately, industrial economists have made few systematic efforts to measure localization.

Supplementary examples

SE4.1   Spatial Competition: Fixed Prices, Market Areas, and Border Prices

Perhaps the most frequently used model of spatial competition is based on the **Loeschian** assumption that firms set price as if they were monopolists within their own *fixed* market area (see, for example, Loesch, 1954; Beckman, 1970; Stern, 1972). This contrasts with Hotelling's Nash-in-price assumption, where each firm conjectures that its rivals leave their price unchanged. A third

---

[30] That is, the market opportunity frontier is now only those unit expenditures and excludes the line segments joining them.

[31] Roughly, the polygon formed when there are four or more characteristics has $J + (J + 2)(J - 2)/4$ edges. The *average* number of neighbors per firm is twice this divided by the number of firms, or $(J + 4)/2 - (2/J)$. This average number of competitors approaches $J/2$ as J increases. See Archibald and Rosenbluth (1975, pp. 580–82) for details.

[32] See Schmalensee (1978b), who argues that localization of competition occurs in ready-to-eat cereals despite the large number of product characteristics.

frequently considered case, developed by Greenhut and Ohta (1972), occurs where each firm assumes that only the price to the marginal consumer, at the boundary of its market area (the so-called "border price"), is fixed. Some equilibrium differences caused by these differences in conjectural variations can be briefly noted.

In every spatial model consumers buy from the firm offering the lowest delivered price. The boundary point of two neighboring firms occurs where they offer identical delivered prices. For example, two firms j and k a distance δ apart have their boundary a distance l away (from j) when

$$\phi_j + \tau l = \phi_k + \tau(\delta - l)$$

or when

$$l = \frac{\phi_k - \phi_j + \tau\delta}{2\tau} \tag{4.21}$$

If the two firms set the same price then they share the intervening market equally and $l = \delta/2$. If firm j raises its price relative to firm k, then under the Loeschian assumption the market areas must remain unchanged. The only way that this can occur is if the rival firm k also raises its price; that is, the Loeschian assumption if that $dp_k/dp_j = 1$. From (4.21) we therefore obtain for this case

$$\frac{dl}{dp_j} = \frac{1}{2\tau}\left(\frac{dp_k}{dp_j} - 1\right) \tag{4.22}$$

Since $dp_k/dp_j = 1$, then $dl/dp_j = 0$, which is the Loeschian case. In contrast, the Hotelling–Chamberlin assumption is $dp_k/dp_j = 0$, which yields $dl/dp_j = -1/2\tau$. Firm j perceives its market area to shrink when it raises its price. Finally, under the Greenhut and Ohta specification of spatial "competition," the border price can remain constant only if an increase by firm j leads to an exactly offsetting decrease in price by its rival k. In this case the border point changes since $dl/dp_j = -1/\tau$; again, firm j's market area shrinks, and it shrinks at a faster rate than in the Nash-in-price competition.

SE4.2   The Technology of Product Characteristics

It is straightforward to extend the usual theory of the firm to account for the production of characteristics. To begin, suppose that there are a finite number of characteristics $m = 1, 2, \ldots, M$. A specific commodity j is then described by the M-vector

$$\zeta_j = [\zeta_{j1}\zeta_{j2} \ldots \zeta_{jM}] \tag{4.23}$$

where ζ_{jm} is the amount of characteristic m per unit of the commodity. For simplicity, let each commodity be associated with just one of the $j = 1, 2, \ldots, J$ firms.

We assume that the characteristic composition of every commodity can be represented by a *design parameter* α_j. Changes in the choice of α_j by firm j will in general result in changes in each characteristic element of ζ_j, and we write

$\zeta_j(\alpha_j)$ to reflect this. Compared with α_j, some $\alpha_j' > \alpha_j$ may increase the amount of some characteristic while decreasing others. Because of this, it would be too restrictive to require that heterogeneous individuals unanimously prefer the α_j' choice to α_j. If, however, a change in α_j just happens to increase the amounts of each (desirable) characteristic, then we say that the commodity's *quality* is increased and, regarding this change, there is unanimous agreement.

The technology of each firm j is specified by an implicit production function

$$f_j(\alpha_j, z_j; x_j) = 0 \tag{4.24}$$

where x_j is a vector of $n = 1, 2, \ldots, N$ factor quantities. To assure an appropriate solution to the firm's problem, f_j should exhibit concavity in α_j as well as the usual concavity in output and factor inputs. For some given inputs, f_j sets out the maximum output z_j consistent with each α_j. The profit function follows in the usual way:

$$\pi_j(\alpha_j, z_j; x_j) = p_j(\alpha_j, z_j)z_j - \sum_n r_n x_{jn} \tag{4.25}$$

where the r_n are (constant) factor prices and $p_j(\alpha_j, z_j)$ is the inverse demand function. Maximizing these profits with respect to α_j, z_j, and x_j subject to (4.24) completes the theory of the firm.

SE4.3 Product Characteristics in Exchange and Hedonic Prices

The theory of consumer behavior is also easily restated in the combinable characteristics framework. Initially, suppose that each consumer's preferences over characteristics exhibit the usual nonsatiation and quasi-concavity properties. These are then properties of the utility function

$$u_i(\zeta_{i1}, \zeta_{i2}, \ldots, \zeta_{iM}) \tag{4.26}$$

When commodities are combinable in use, consumers can be thought of as selecting commodities to produce a characteristic bundle ζ_i with elements

$$\zeta_{im} = \sum_j (\beta_j{}^i z_j)\zeta_{jm} \tag{4.27}$$

where $\beta_j{}^i$ is the fraction of j's output chosen by individual i.

Consumers select bundles which maximize utility subject to the budget constraint

$$\sum_j \beta_j{}^i(p_j z_j) = W^i \tag{4.28}$$

where W^i is i's wealth. The stationarity point of the maximization problem is given by

$$\sum_m \frac{\partial u_i}{\partial \zeta_{im}} \zeta_{jm} - \lambda_i p_j = 0 \tag{4.29}$$

where λ_i is the Lagrange multiplier. This can be written as

$$\sum_m \mu_{im}\zeta_{jm} = p_j \tag{4.30}$$

where $\mu_{im} = (\partial u_i/\partial \zeta_{im})/\lambda_i$ has an interpretation as the implicit (shadow) price individual i assigns to each characteristic. For each consumer, the price of a commodity is equal to the sum of its characteristics weighted by these implicit prices per unit characteristic.

Write (4.30) in vector–matrix notation as $p = \mu_i \zeta$ where p is a $1 \times J$ vector of market prices, μ_i is a $1 \times M$ vector of i's implicit prices of the M characteristics, and ζ is an $M \times J$ coefficient matrix tabulating the characteristic composition of the J products. If we assume that (a) there are as many characteristics as commodities and (b) the vector of characteristics supplied by any commodity cannot be written as linear combinations of other commodities, then ζ has an inverse and we write $\mu_i = p\zeta^{-1}$: the implicit prices are the same for all individuals in market equilibrium. These common μ_i prices are usually referred to as **hedonic prices** for the characteristics.[33]

---

[33] See Griliches (1961, 1971) for a variety of examples of the estimation of hedonic prices.

5 Equilibria in Differentiated Product Markets

The first equilibrium theory of product variety came with Chamberlin's monopolistic competition. His analysis was designed to capture two central features of a modern market economy: the differentiation of products which, he argued, gives rise to inelastic firm demands, and a process of entry whereby each new brand causes a shift in the incumbents' demand curves until zero profits are earned. Because of free entry the equilibrium number of firms (brands) occurs where the average revenue function for each is just tangent to its average cost function. Because of the differentiation in products this tangency occurs with falling average cost, to the "left" of the minimum. When compared with the classical competitive equilibrium, it is usual to note that Chamberlin's results imply excess capacity, price above marginal cost, and an excess number of brands (recall section 4.3). Chamberlin found these conditions to be "sort of ideal" given the underlying differences in consumer preferences and the resulting demand for product variety. In contrast, many commentators have found the equilibrium conditions to reflect the inefficiency of monopoly and the pejorative "excess" qualifiers have persisted in the traditional view.

The lack of detail in Chamberlin's specification of demand has been a recurring concern with the monopolistic competition equilibrium and particularly with its implications for efficiency. As a result, that specification has received attention in recent differentiated product models. While these newer models have various forms, they fall into two essential types. The first is based more or less on the spatial analogy that we know from chapter 4. Products are indivisible and small price differences cause consumers to make discrete switches among the available brands. The equilibrium properties of this kind of model are studied first, in sections 5.1 and 5.2. The second model type is more classical in the sense that products are continuously divisible and variations in price lead only to adjustments on a continuous margin in each consumer's optimal bundle of brands. The equilibrium properties of this model are studied in section 5.3. There are crucial differences in these model types: in the assumptions made about consumer preferences, in the nature of the products offered for sale, in the form of brand competition and the concept of equilibrium, and in the implications for equilibrium brand varieties. These differences, and some similarities, are discussed in several final sections of this chapter. The welfare implications of the various equilibria are considered in chapter 6.

5.1   Equilibrium Locations in Spatial Competition

What product varieties will be produced? An early, indirect answer to this question was given by Hotelling in the context of his original main street model. He considered the equilibrium locations (read product varieties) for duopolists choosing location and price in sequence in a two-stage game. He imagined the location decisions to be made simultaneously at the first stage, with each duopolist knowing the equilibrium prices that will then occur at the second stage for every admissible choice of location. In this context, Hotelling argued that identical duopolists would choose price equal to (the constant) average production cost and back-to-back locations at the center of the linear market. The argument used by Hotelling in reaching this result is straightforward: if either firm is located away from the center, its rival will locate just next to it on the side which gives it the advantage with the larger fraction of the market.[1] Equilibrium locations (product varieties) are minimally differentiated. Because of that, the two-stage spatial model of Hotelling is frequently said to give rise to a **principle of minimum differentiation**.

The robustness of the minimal differentiation result has been questioned on several grounds. First, it has been shown that when price undercutting strategies are permitted the principle does not define equilibrium price strategies in the second-stage price game nor, in turn, location strategies in the first-stage game (Smithies, 1941; Eaton and Lipsey, 1976, 1978; Novshek, 1980). This failure of an equilibrium to exist is related directly to the abruptness of the demand change with mill price undercutting and the associated discontinuities in price reaction functions. We deal with this issue in section 5.1.1. The nonexistence problem can be "corrected" by alternative specifications of the model. For example, in contrast with Hotelling's linearity assumption, the case where transportation costs are strictly convex in distance is analyzed in section 5.1.2. That is not a trivial change in the model, for the resulting location equilibrium then occurs with the firms located near the ends of the market, just the opposite of Hotelling's minimum differentiation result. Section 5.1.3 then returns to the case of linear transport costs but rules out, on a priori grounds, the mill price undercutting strategies which prevent the original Hotelling solution.[2] Two final sections consider location choices when there are prohibitive relocation costs and firms enter the market sequentially.

5.1.1   Hotelling's Results: Recognizing Undercutting Strategies

The first question to be asked concerns the impact of mill price undercutting on the existence of the Hotelling locational equilibrium. This means that we begin

[1] Eaton and Lipsey (1975) note that his result does not exactly extend beyond two firms. However, they do report a tendency for "local clustering" of groups of firms in the large-number case.

[2] As another possibility, which we do not address here, de Palma et al. (1985) show that sufficient heterogeneity in consumer demand is capable of reducing the abruptness of mill price undercutting and thus allows Hotelling's minimal differentiation as an equilibrium result.

with two firms and the basic main street model set out in E4.1. On a market line having length L, firms 1 and 2 produce and sell a functionally identical product. As shown in figure 4.3, the firms are located at distances l_1 and l_2 from the (left and right respectively) ends of the market line. The restrictions $l_1 + l_2 \leqslant L$ and $l_1, \ l_2 \geqslant 0$ determine feasible locations, with $\delta = L - l_1 - l_2 \geqslant 0$ being the distance between firms. Production costs are assumed to be zero. On the demand side, consumers are uniformly distributed along the market line and each purchases a single unit of the lowest-priced commodity delivered to its location. Mill and delivered prices are related by a constant transportation cost per unit distance:

$$p_j = \phi_j + \tau l \tag{5.1}$$

which repeats the earlier equation (4.1).

Given that locations l_1 and l_2 have been selected in the first stage of the game, at the second stage the strategies of the firms are positive mill prices ϕ_1 and ϕ_2. Allowing for undercutting, the profit function varies according to three possibilities. For each j, $k = 1, 2$ $(j \neq k)$

$$\pi_j(\phi_j, \phi_k) = l_j\phi_j + \frac{\delta\phi_j}{2} + \frac{1}{2\tau}\phi_j\phi_k - \frac{1}{2\tau}\phi_j^2 \qquad \text{for } |\phi_j - \phi_k| \leqslant \tau\delta \tag{5.2a}$$

$$\pi_j(\phi_j, \phi_k) = L\phi_j \qquad \text{for } \phi_k > \phi_j + \tau\delta \tag{5.2b}$$

$$\pi_j(\phi_j, \phi_k) = 0 \qquad \text{for } \phi_j > \phi_k + \tau\delta \tag{5.2c}$$

In the demand segment (5.2a) there is no undercutting and the firms have the same marginal consumer. In (5.2b) firm j undercuts k and sells to the whole market. Finally, in (5.2c) the converse case holds with firm k undercutting j so that j sells nothing. It is evident from these equations that there is a discontinuity in demand functions, and this carries to the profit functions at the point where each firm just undercuts the mill price of its rival. It is this discontinuity which poses the equilibrium existence problem

A Nash-in-price equilibrium for the above situation (given locations) is a price pair (ϕ_1^*, ϕ_2^*) such that ϕ_1^* is a best reply to ϕ_2^* and conversely. d'Aspremont et al. (1979) have shown that such an equilibrium exists if[3]

$$(3L + l_j - l_k)^2 \geqslant 12L(l_j + 2l_k) \tag{5.3}$$

These two weak inequality conditions are based on the necessity for an equilibrium point to satisfy the strict inequality $|\phi_j^* - \phi_k^*| < \tau\delta$,[4] and for the mill prices to maximize the profit function (5.2a) for each firm.

---

[3] When $\delta = 0$ and the firms occupy the same location, the model degenerates to the "no-differentiation" homogeneous duopoly of Bertrand. As shown in chapter 3 the Nash equilibrium in this case has $\phi_1^* = \phi_2^* = 0$ (again, production costs are assumed to be zero).

[4] Necessity is shown by contradiction. Take the specific instance where $|\phi_1^* - \phi_2^*| > \tau\delta$. In this case the firm setting the greater (positive) mill price receives zero profit (see (5.2c)). This leaves the firm to better itself by raising its mill price just to the delivered price of its rival (at that distant location). This, however, contradicts the fact that (ϕ_1^*, ϕ_2^*) is an equilibrium.

Suppose alternatively that $|\phi_1^* - \phi_2^*| = \tau\delta$ and, particularly, $\phi_2^* = \phi_1^* + \tau\delta$. When $\phi_1^* = 0$ in this case, firm 1 earns zero profit, but it can better that by raising it to a level less than $\phi_2^* + \tau\delta$. When $\phi_1^* > 0$, there are two possibilities. In the first, firm 1 takes the entire trade, which means that firm 2 may increase profits by decreasing its price. In the second, firm 1 takes only a fraction of the trade but is then capable of slightly lowering price to take the entire trade and increase profits. By either possibility there is a contradiction and therefore $|\phi_1^* - \phi_2^*| < \tau\delta$ is required.

Proof that (5.3) is required at an equilibrium begins with the stationarity conditions associated with the profit function (5.2a):

$$\phi_j^* = \tfrac{1}{3}\tau(3L + l_j - l_k) \tag{5.4}$$

For ϕ_j^* to be an equilibrium choice for firm j it must maximize $\pi_j(\phi_j, \phi_j^*)$ for all $\phi_j \geq 0$. Thus, given l_1 and l_2, the following inequality must hold for any $\varepsilon > 0$:

$$\pi_j(\phi_j^*, \phi_k^*) = \frac{\tau}{18}(3L + l_j - l_k)^2 \geq L(\phi_k^* - \tau\delta - \varepsilon) \tag{5.5}$$

where the rightmost expression is j's profit should it set a delivered price ε less than ϕ_k^*. Rearrangement of this inequality gives (5.3),[5] which informs us that an equilibrium exists in the basic Hotelling model only when sellers are "far enough" apart. For example, if $L = 1$ and $l_j = 0.3$, then (5.3) requires $l_k \geq 0.92$ ($\delta = 0.62$).

The reason for the minimal distance restriction, which we might call a *principle of product diversity*, lies in the size of gains possible when undercutting a rival. To see this, suppose that firm 2 lower its price (with firm 1's held constant). As ϕ_2 falls, the marginal consumer comes closer to firm 1. When ϕ_2 reaches the level $\phi_2 = \phi_1 - \tau\delta$, the marginal consumers are, at once, all those individuals at firm 1's location and beyond, and any further (small) decrease in ϕ_2 allows it to capture all that remaining trade. When l_1 is large, it is more attractive for firm 2 to undercut in this way (since there is a greater market to be served by doing so) rather than choosing a price to just satisfy the stationarity condition (5.4). Therefore each firm protects itself against its rival's undercutting by making the associated gains small, that is, by moving to a distant end of the market. Hotelling reached his minimum differentiation result by ignoring the potentially large gains associated with such undercutting strategies.

Note, finally that, if attention is restricted only to **symmetric spatial equilibrium**, that is, where $l_1 = l_2$, the locational requirements (5.3) for existence simplify to

$$L/4 \geq l_1 = l_2 \tag{5.6}$$

The duopolists must be located in the "outer quartiles" of the market line for a symmetric Nash equilibrium in prices to obtain.

5.1.2 Convex Transportation Costs

Suppose now that the unit transportation cost function of the spatial model is strictly convex rather than linear.[6] More specifically, let these costs be quadratic in the distance τl^2 between the consumer and the firm. The key feature of this specification is that market areas do not change discontinuously with mill price undercutting. Even though a firm may be undercut at its location, it can still have a delivered price advantage in the market area remote from the undercut-

---

[5] The sufficiency of (5.3) requires that the prices given by (5.4) imply $|\phi_j^* - \phi_k^*| < \tau\delta$, which is straightforward to show.

[6] Lane (1980) develops a two-product-characteristic model with a nonlinear distance measure which is unique to each consumer.

ter. Since a large gain to abrupt undercutting was the factor keeping firms apart with linear transportation costs, do the firms tend to locate closer together with quadratic costs? That is, keeping all other aspects of the analysis the same, we ask whether the above locational constraints on the existence of a market equilibrium still obtain

Again, the demand functions facing firm j are given in three parts corresponding to sharing the market, being the sole seller, and selling nothing. Respectively, these take the forms

$$z_j(\phi_j, \phi_k) = l_j + \frac{\phi_k - \phi_j}{2\tau\delta} + \frac{\delta}{2} \qquad \text{for } 0 \le l_j + \frac{\phi_k - \phi_j}{2\tau\delta} + \frac{\delta}{2} \le L \qquad (5.7a)$$

$$z_j(\phi_j, \phi_k) = L \qquad \text{for } l_j + \frac{\phi_k - \phi_j}{2\tau\delta} + \frac{\delta}{2} > L \qquad (5.7b)$$

$$z_j(\phi_j, \phi_k) = 0 \qquad \text{for } l_j + \frac{\phi_k - \phi_j}{2\tau\delta} + \frac{\delta}{2} < 0 \qquad (5.7c)$$

These demand functions differ from those with linear transportation costs as a comparison with equations (5.2) indicates.

Continuing with the assumption that marginal cost of production is zero, note that the profit function for each firm j has the same basic form

$$\pi_j(\phi_j, \phi_k) = \phi_j z_j(\phi_j, \phi_k) \qquad (5.8)$$

where $z_j(\cdot)$ is given by possibilities (5.7). The Nash equilibrium in prices is to be determined for all admissible locations $L - l_1 - l_2 \ge 0$ and $l_1, l_2 \ge 0$. Inspection of the profit function for all three of possibilities (5.7) quickly indicates that (5.7a) is the relevant case and solution prices are given by market sharing. That is, for both firms j

$$\phi_j^* = \tau\delta\left(L + \frac{l_j - l_k}{3}\right) \qquad (5.9)$$

Note that the prices are functions of the distances l_j and l_k. Substituting (5.9) and (5.7a) in (5.8) and differentiating shows that the derivatives $\partial \pi_j(\phi_j^*, \phi_k^*)/\partial l_j$ are everywhere negative; that is, the sellers locate as far as possible from each other. This is exactly the opposite of Hotelling's minimum differentiation result. When costs increase at an increasing rate with distance, not only is there no abrupt jump in demand with undercutting, but maximal product differentiation occurs.[7]

E5.1

Equilibrium Prices and Quadratic Transportation Costs

Suppose that there are $j = 1, 2, \ldots, J$ equally spaced firms with each adjacent pair a fixed distance δ apart. Let the market have unit length ($L = 1$) so that $\delta = 1/J$, and let transportation costs be quadratic in distance ($\tau = l^2$). At the

---

[7] D'Aspremont et al. (1979) show that the Nash-in-price maximal differentiation solution exists and is unique under the conditions set out here.

symmetric equilibrium competition will be localized with each firm j competing with its neighbors $j - 1$ and $j + 1$. At the market boundary between j and $j - 1$ the delivered prices will be such that

$$\phi_l + (\theta_j - l_-)^2 = \phi_{j-1} + (\theta_{j-1} - l_-)^2 \tag{5.10}$$

where θ_j and θ_{j-1} are the locations of the two firms and l_- is the location of this market boundary. Solving for l_- gives

$$l_- = \frac{\phi_j - \phi_{j-1}}{2\delta} - \frac{\delta}{2} + \theta_{j-1} \tag{5.11a}$$

where $\delta = \theta_{j+1} - \theta_j$ is the distance between brands. In an analgous way the location of the boundary between j and $j + 1$, call it l_+, is

$$l_+ = \frac{\phi_{j+1} - \phi_j}{2\delta} + \frac{\delta}{2} + \theta_j \tag{5.11b}$$

The extent of j's market area is $l_+ - l_-$. Further supposing that there is a uniform density of customers, ω, along the market line, the quantity demanded from j is $\omega(l_+ - l_-)$, or

$$z_j = \frac{\omega(\phi_{j-1} + \phi_{j+1} + 2\delta^2 - 2\phi_j)}{2\delta} \tag{5.12}$$

If we assume that production costs are in the quadratic form $c(z_j) = F + az_j^2$, j's profit is

$$\pi_j = \phi_j z_j - az_j^2 - F \tag{5.13}$$

which is strictly concave in the mill price. The Nash equilibrium in prices is in part described by the stationarity points of the π_j, which solve for

$$\phi_j^* = \frac{(\phi_{j+1}^* + \phi_{j-1}^* + 2\delta^2)(\delta + 2a\omega)}{4(\delta + a\omega)} \tag{5.14}$$

When it is further required that the equilibrium be symmetric, the price set by every firm is equal and given by

$$\phi^* = \delta(\delta + 2a\omega) \tag{5.15}$$

Notice that, given the symmetric locations of the firms, the equilibrium price is increasing in marginal cost a and consumer density ω, and decreasing in the number of firms ($\delta = 1/J$).

5.1.3 Modified Zero Conjectures

Consider again the spatial model with *linear* transportation costs and, with that, mill price undercutting strategies which lead to equilibrium product diversity. In analyses of this case, Eaton and Lipsey (1978), Novshek (1980), and Carruthers (1981) have argued that admissible price strategies should a priori dismiss undercutting when firms have foresight and constant marginal production cost.[8]

---

[8] See Graitson (1980) for a related restriction on the strategy space in purely locational models.

The rationale offered for this exclusion focuses on two neighboring firms j and k and the observation that firm j will prefer a mill price ϕ_j between its marginal cost c and the delivered price of k's product (at j's location), that is,

$$c \leqslant \phi_j \leqslant \phi_k + \tau\delta \qquad (5.16)$$

In contrast, for k to sell at j's location with a profit requires

$$\phi_j > \phi_k + \tau\delta \geqslant c \qquad (5.17)$$

With the strict inequality and a common cost, firm j can always choose a profitable mill price such that (5.17) will not hold. Because of this, k should never choose to undercut j. That is, *with foresight* each firm will conclude that it cannot drive its neighbor out of the market by undercutting, at least as long as that neighbor has the option of selling some amount at a price above (a common) incremental production cost.

The a priori limitation to no-undercutting strategies is frequently referred to as the "modified zero conjectural variation" rule: each firm takes the strategy of rivals as fixed only when its own strategy does not involve undercutting. Each firm, moreover, believes that no rival will allow itself to be undercut, as those rivals will simply reduce price if this is attempted.[9] The modified strategy rule can be thought of as an attempt to dismiss expectations lacking foresight by a modification of the Nash solution concept. It in turn averts possible discontinuities in the underlying demand and reaction functions and, with linear transportation cost, is also implies Hotelling's minimal product differentiation.[10]

5.1.4 Sequential Location, Immobility, and Foresight

A recurring complaint concerning spatial models centers on the assumption that location (product design) can be costlessly adjusted. While the free-mobility assumption is a critical determinant of the symmetric model equilibria that have been developed up to this point, it may be an inappropriate assumption when the spatial analogy is intended to deal with differentiated products (see, for example, Schmalensee, 1979). Even casual knowledge of the costs associated with research and development, retooling, new advertising, plant alterations, etc, are enough to suggest important cases where the costs of relocation (product redesign, new market development) can be significant.

When these relocation costs are nontrivial, it has been argued that an appropriate model of oligopoly would be one in which location decisions are made ". . . once-and-for-all, one firm at a time, with firms being aware of the relative permanence of their decisions and thus taking some care to anticipate the decision rules firms entering later in the sequence will follow" (Prescott and Visscher, 1977, p. 378). The so-called "perfect expectations" or "foresight" models of sequential location are standards in this approach (see, for example, Hay, 1976; Prescott and Visscher, 1977; Novshek, 1980; Lane, 1980; Eaton and

---

[9] Novshek (1980) gives full conditions for the existence of a zero-profit equilibrium with these modified conjectures and shows that, if this modification is absent a free-entry equilibrium will not generally exist.

[10] However, when these costs are strictly convex greater equilibrium diversity will occur.

Wooders, 1985). These are generally variants of Hotelling's original model which differ principally in the larger number of firms considered and their process of location choice.

Foresight in Sequential Entry. Consider a two-stage model. At the second, market, stage the firms' locations are given and Nash equilibrium prices are determined (as a function of the locations). In turn, each firm's profit can be written as a function of location alone. These "indirect" profit functions are then used in the first, strategic stage to determine the Nash equilibrium as the $j = 1, 2, \ldots, J$ firms locate sequentially once and for all.[11] What locations will be chosen by the firms? As the location process extends over time, some additional structure is necessary to answer this question. This structure is required to specify the information available to existing and entering firms at every state of the industry's development. Specifically, we will assume that each firm makes its first-stage location decision in order to maximize profits given the following **foresight**:

   1 it knows the location of firms already in the market;
   2 it knows that, in the end, J firms will have entered;
   3 it knows that later entering firms will locate to maximize profits;
   4 it knows the rules of the second-stage market game.

Location Equilibrium with Foresight. To avoid side issues, consider a simple model economy with I consumers residing uniformly along a market of unit length. Firms enter by adopting a location in this market. Let the number of firms be fixed exogenously at J and index them so that firm j indicates the jth to enter, occupying location $0 \leq l_j \leq 1$. The sequential nature of the entry with the foresight implied by assumptions 2 and 3 suggests that the equilibrium solution should proceed by backward induction, in the fashion of dynamic programming. That is, we begin with the Jth (last) firm to enter, determine its optimal location, and then work in a reverse order to find optimal locations for earlier entrants.[12]

Consider first the location choice of the last firm J. The foresight assumption in this case means that J knows the locations of all prior entrants $L_{J-1} \equiv [l_1 l_2 \ldots l_{J-1}]$. Given this knowledge, J calculates the Nash equilibrium price that would obtain for all choices of its own location choice. Let $p_j^*(p_J; L_{J-1})$ be the resulting price function relating the locations chosen by the firms to the equilibrium price of each firm j[13] and let $p^*(l_J; L_{J-1})$ be the associated J-vector of prices, one for each firm. The price function p^* is exactly known by foresight assumption 4. With p^*, firm J's profits can be written

---

[11] This is the model set-up used by Prescott and Visscher (1977), Lane (1980), and Anderson (1987). Anderson uses Stackelberg play in prices at the market stage, while the other studies use simultaneous Bertrand play. Recall also that the original two-stage Hotelling model assumes that the firms *simultaneously* choose location at the first stage.

[12] The equilibrium derived in the sequential entry game will possess the subgame perfection property (see chapter 9, section 9.4).

[13] The existence of a unique set of prices requires that the market game satisfy certain regularity conditions as, for example, imposed by Lane (1980) and Anderson (1987).

"indirectly" in terms of the locations alone as

$$\pi_j^*(l_j; L_{J-1}) \equiv \pi_j(p^*(l_j; L_{J-1}), l_j, L_{J-1}) \tag{5.18}$$

In turn, J's choice

$$l_j^*(L_{J-1}) = \max_{l_j} \pi_L^* \tag{5.19}$$

specifies its optimal location as a function of the locations of its predecessors.[14] The problem facing firm $J - 1$ is slightly different as it must consider not only the given locations of its predecessors, but also the implications of J's subsequent entry. The foresight assumptions mean two things at this point. First, firm $J - 1$ knows the locations of its predecessor; it accurately observes L_{J-2}. Second, $J - 1$ knows that its successor J will choose a location given by the function $l_j^*(L_{J-1})$. Writing L_{J-1} as $(l_{J-1}; L_{J-2})$ we have firm $(J - 1)$'s profit function

$$\pi_{J-1}^*(l_{J-2}; L_{J-2}) \equiv \pi_{J-1}(l_{J-1}; p^*(L_J), L_{J-2}, l_j^*(l_{J-1}; L_{J-2})) \tag{5.20}$$

In turn, $J - 1$'s solution

$$l_{J-1}^*(L_{J-2}) = \max_{l_{J-1}} \pi_{J-1}^* \tag{5.21}$$

specifies its optimal location given the location of its predecessors.

In a similar way firm $(J - k)$'s location solution is given by

$$l_{J-k}^*(L_{J-k+1}) = \max_{l_{J-k}} \pi_{J-k}^*(l_{J-k}; L_{J-k-1}) \qquad k = 2, 3, \ldots, J - 2 \tag{5.22a}$$

and, finally,

$$l_1^* = \max_{l_1} \pi_1^*(l_1) \tag{5.22b}$$

The recursive solution procedure determines each firm's profit function and optimal location rule in terms of the locations adopted by its predecessors. The first firm to enter thinks only of its own location, given the optimal location rules of its successors. With appropriate regularity in the functions the set of functions $\{l_j^*\}$ determines the locational equilibrium. Then, the final Nash-in-price market solution is found using the price function $p^*(L_J)$.

Lane (1980) has studied the foresighted sequential location problem for several special functional forms for demand and cost. While closed-form analytical solutions were generally not possible, constructive numerical results using the above recursive solution procedure yielded some central tendencies: (a) although the firms are otherwise equal, those which enter early on in the sequential location process are able to use their additional freedom of choice to obtain higher equilibrium profits than their successors; (b) the initial entry locations are in the center of the market, and later entrants then fill out toward the extremes; (c) equilibrium prices and profits vary inversely with the number of firms J, that is, the intensity of rivalry measured by the price–cost margin is increased as firms become closer together and vie for consumers more in price than location.

---

[14] Given the restrictions on l_j, continuity and concavity of π^* are sufficient for the existence of the function l_j^* (see Lane, 1980). These conditions are assumed here.

5.1.5   Sequential Myopic Entry

In contrast with perfect foresight, there is the more standard **myopic** decision rule in which the entrant at any stage of the sequential entry game simply maximizes its immediate profits by locating, relative to existing firms, at the midpoint of the largest vacant market interval (see, for example, Prescott and Visscher, 1977, example 3, Eaton and Lipsey, 1978, 1979). How does the market develop in this case? Let J^* be the endogenously determined equilibrium number of (identical and myopic) firms to sequentially enter (still with prohibitive relocation costs) a market over which consumers are uniformly distributed. For a given demand it is usual to show that the extent of scale economies determines J^* and the equilibrium profits of the firms, and that the firms will be evenly spaced about such a market.

Consider, for example, the market given by the circle with unit circumference shown in figure 5.1. Let the firms enter the market sequentially using the myopic location rule. The first firm's decision is moot; suppose it locates at l_1. The next firm then locates at the center of the largest market then vacant, at l_2. Firms 3 and 4 will act similarly, locating at l_3 and l_4. In the next "round," and assuming that it is still profitable to do so, firms will locate at l_5, l_6, l_7, and l_8 as indicated in the figure, doubling the number of firms in the market. Each of the identical firms earns the same profit at this point. If it is profitable for some entrant firm to locate between any of the incumbents at this juncture, then it will also be profitable for firms to locate between every pair of incumbents and the number of firms will again double.[15] The equilibrium number of firms, and the profits of these firms, will be determined when the entry of another firm in the largest vacant arc yields negative profits to the entrant.

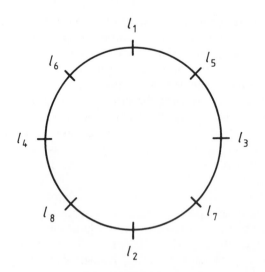

Figure 5.1
Sequential, myopic entry

[15] Let $\pi(J)$, $J = 2^n (n = 1, 2, \ldots)$ indicate the profits of a typical firm with J total firms in the industry. Then $\pi(2J) = \pi(J + k)$ where $k < J$.

E5.2

Barriers to Entry in Ready-to-eat Cereals

Using a myopic location model Schmalensee (1978b) has argued that the US ready-to-eat cereal manufacturers have prohibitively high costs in relocating brands and have used this fact to deter entry in the sense that the equilibrium number of brands is less than that number J^c which gives the firms zero profits. Roughly, his argument goes as follows. Suppose that J firms are symmetrically located about the circular market, with $J^c \leqslant J \leqslant J^c/2$, and the firms earn positive profits. Further, suppose that each firm produces just one brand (there are no scope economies) and the number J is such that net revenues per firm are less than fixed (brand) cost: $\bar{\pi} < F$. In this case a new entrant will perceive entry as unprofitable if it believes that the existing firms will not relocate their products after entry. If undercutting strategies are omitted and identical pricing is assumed, the entrant's myopic choice of location would be the middle of the space between any two existing brands, leaving it a distance $1/2J$ from each neighbor. As far as any single entrant is concerned, this is as if there were twice as many firms in the market. The entrant's location is thus less profitable than any existing brand and, as it must incur fixed costs on entry, it would suffer a loss (since $\bar{\pi} < F$).

5.2   Symmetric Equilibrium in a Spatial Model

The spatial model to be investigated here involves two industries. The first produces the differentiated commodity of specific concern; the second is a competitive industry producing everything else – a homogeneous composite commodity to be called the **outside good**. It is usual to simplify the analysis by assuming that each of the differentiated commodities is made up of just two characteristics, with θ_j indicating the characteristic ratio for the commodity of each firm $j = 1, 2, \ldots, J$.[16] Some technical difficulties can also be avoided at the ends of the differentiated product spectrum by further assuming that the product space in θ_j is measured along a circle of unit circumference.[17] In turn, each brand θ_j is given a location on the unit circle.

5.2.1   Preferences and Utility

Underlying the spatial model is the presumption that consumers have most preferred (ideal) characteristic bundles. For example, when speaking of soda drinks this might be specific amounts of sweetness and tartness. For the typical consumer let $0 \leqslant \theta^0 \leqslant 1$ indicate the ideal ratio of these characteristics – his

[16] Each θ_j defines a (different) ray in the two-dimensional characteristic space. Recall, for example, figure 4.5.

[17] A line extending infinitely to the right and left of some reference point is at times also used for this purpose (see Stern, 1972).

location on the unit circle. As E5.3 below demonstrates, this is consistent with the fact that each consumer's utility is separable in the differentiated commodity and the outside (numeraire) good: $u(\theta_j, \theta^0) + z_0$. As a convenience it is further assumed that the I consumers are uniformly located about the circular market. Each consumer purchases at most one unit of one kind of the differentiated commodity, so that the **utility surplus** associated with the choice of brand θ_j can be measured as $u(\theta_j, \theta^0) - p_j$, where p_j is j's price. The consumer then chooses one unit of the differentiated commodity to maximize

$$\max_j \{u(\theta_j, \theta^0) - p_j\} \geq \mu \qquad (5.23)$$

where μ is the constant surplus provided by the outside good. If the inequality does not hold for any j, then all the consumer's income $\bar{y}$ is allocated to the outside good. Otherwise, when some specific brand j is best and purchased at price p_j, only the residual $\bar{y} - p_j > 0$ is available to the outside good.

The analogy with a spatial model is completed by assuming that the consumer's disutility in taking any brand θ_j different from θ^0 is directly related to the shortest arc length on the circular market between these locations. If this disutility is assumed to be one of constant proportionality, then

$$u(\theta_j, \theta^0) = \mu^0 - \tau|\theta_j - \theta^0|$$

where $\tau > 0$ is the constant disutility per unit arc length and μ^0 is the utility of the ideal θ^0.[18] Given these conditions the individual's choice problem can be rewritten compactly as[19]

$$\max_j (v - \tau l_j - p_j) \geq 0 \qquad (5.24)$$

where we use the notation $v \equiv \mu^0 - \mu > 0$ and $l_j \equiv |\theta_j - \theta^0|$.

E5.3 ══

Location in Characteristic Space: Some Restrictions on Utility

The link between spatial and product variety models is critically dependent on the fact that each consumer has a "location" in characteristics space – an ideal bundle. This need not always be the case with preferences, as the following variation on the analysis by Archibald et al. (1986) shows.

Continuing with the assumption that the differentiated good is made up of just two characteristics ζ_1 and ζ_2, suppose that the aggregate utility is given by $u(\zeta_1, \zeta_2, z_0)$ – again, the outside good is measured by z_0. Let u have the standard properties and let θ indicate the ratio of ζ_1 and ζ_2 in any one of the differentiated goods. Further, for any given θ, let $f_1(\theta)$ and $f_2(\theta)$ indicate amounts of ζ_1 and ζ_2 respectively in each unit of the differentiated good. In turn, define the indirect utility

[18] Lane (1980) develops a spatial analogy model in which each consumer's measure of disutility is a nonlinear function of the distance between product variants and is unique to each individual. His results follow those of section 5.1.4, where convex "transportation" costs were considered.

[19] This is the demand model used by Lerner and Singer (1937), Hirshleifer (1972), Salop (1979b), Salant (1980), and Economides (1981).

$$U(\theta, p, y) = \max_{z, z_0} \{u(zf_1(\theta), zf_2(\theta), z_0)\} \text{ s.t. } pz + z_0 = y \qquad (5.25)$$

where z is the amount of the differentiated good chosen and y is income. $U(\theta, p, y)$ has the usual quasi-concavity and is decreasing in p and increasing in y. Assuming that $u(\zeta_1, \zeta_2, z_0)$ has level contours which are asymptotic to the axis in the (ζ_1, ζ_2) space, we show the level contours of U in θ and p in figure 5.2(a). When ζ_1 and ζ_2 are weakly separable from the outside good in u, then there are no price effects, the optimal choice of θ is independent of z_0 (and y), and the consumer has a unique ideal bundle θ^0 as illustrated in the figure.

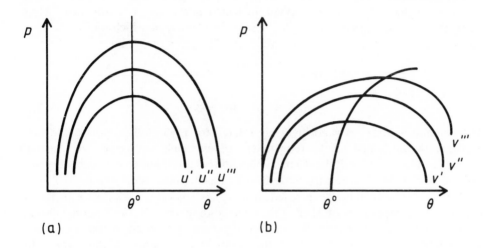

Figure 5.2
Separable utility: (a) spatial analog; (b) no spatial analog

Figure 5.2(b), in contrast, illustrates the case where the inside and outside goods are not separable – that is, it is *not* possible to write $u(\zeta_1, \zeta_2, z_0) = \hat{u}(f(\zeta_1, \zeta_2), h(z_0))$. In this case, the ideal θ depends on the choice of z_0 and y in equation (5.25). There is, as a result, no ideal bundle, no fixed location for the consumer, and no simple link from spatial models to product differentiation.

5.2.2   Demand[20]

Monopoly. We begin with J firms uniquely located about the circular market. Focus on one of these firms and suppose that all others have locations remote enough at prevailing prices that there are no price interactions with the considered firm. In the monopoly case the considered firm's market area when

---

[20] This and the following section on market equilibria generally follow Salop (1979b).

charging price p is made up of those consumers whose preferences lie within a distance l^* given by[21]

$$l^* = \frac{v - p}{\tau} \qquad (5.26)$$

Individuals more distant than l^* on either side of the firm, but not "close enough" to the remote other sellers of the differentiated product, find the outside good to be a better value. That is, in this between-firm "gap" consumers do not purchase any of the various brands of the differentiated good, but instead allocate all their income to the outside good.

As the I customers are uniformly distributed along the unit circle market, l^* is also the fraction of the total population which purchases from the firm. Thus, when the firm sets price p in (5.26) it sells $2Il^*$ units, of which half come from the region to its right and half from the left. This gives the demand function

$$z^m(p) = \frac{2I(v - p)}{\tau} \qquad \text{for } p < v \qquad (5.27a)$$

$$z^m(p) = 0 \qquad \text{for } p \geq v \qquad (5.27b)$$

The demand is linear in (and inversely related to) price and proportional to the total population. Further, the (constant) rate at which consumers are lost with increases in p is $-(2/\tau)I$. Lost consumers shift their trade to the outside good, and the firm gives up its entire trade to the outside good when $p \geq v$.

The concept of demand expressed in (5.27) is somewhat restrictive in that it ignores the competition of rival sellers by holding them in sufficiently remote portions of the circular market. Because the firm is isolated in this way, these expressions are said to represent the *monopoly demand* of the firm. This explains the superscript m in (5.27).

Monopolistic Competition. Suppose now that the other sellers of the good are closer in, so that with relative price changes the firm gains (or gives up) its trade at the expense of these rivals and not of the outside good. In this *monopolistically competitive* case our attention is restricted to *symmetric* conditions where the firms (brands) are equally spaced about the unit circle market (product space) and each charges the same price.[22] With J sellers this means that each is located $1/J$ from its right and left neighbor. Because of this symmetry it is convenient to focus on one firm and its rivals to the immediate left and right.

---

[21] We drop the typical firm j subscripts here as a convenience.

[22] We follow Chamberlin (1933) and Salop (1979b) in this assumption. While this is a legitimate method for showing the existence of equilibrium, the reader must be careful not to compare the symmetric equilibria of various markets (say, in a welfare analysis) unless it can be further demonstrated that nonsymmetric equilibria do not exist. The location symmetry may arise in several ways. With the sequential entry of identical firms the symmetry may occur because relocation is costless after each entry (with or without foresight) or, when relocation costs are prohibitively large, the symmetry may occur with the firms choosing location myopically (as in section 5.1.5). Alternatively, the symmetry may come from a model in which identical fully rational firms make their price and location decisions simultaneously once and for all. This simultaneous case seems to be most consistent with the other aspects of the model to be developed and so we evoke that specific assumption at times.

Let this firm choose the price p while its rivals independently set $\bar{p}$. That is, all firms sell using price contracts with Nash-in-price conjectures. As a result of the symmetry assumption the locations of the marginal consumers – those individuals indifferent to the product of the given firm and its neighbors – are given by the l-solution to

$$v - \tau l - p = v - \tau\left(\frac{1}{J} - l\right) - \bar{p} \tag{5.28}$$

This determines one-half of the **market area** for the firm as a function of its own price, and the rivals' fixed $\bar{p}$, given by the distance

$$l^{**} = \frac{\bar{p} + \tau/J - p}{2\tau} \tag{5.29}$$

to both its right and its left. In turn, the quantity demanded from the firm is

$$z^c(p; \bar{p}) = 2Il^{**} = I\frac{\bar{p} + \tau/J - p}{\tau} \tag{5.30}$$

where the superscript c indicates this monopolistically competitive segment.

On comparing (5.27) and (5.30) we see that the constant slope of $-\tau/2I$ developed for the monopoly demand segment is just half of the slope $-\tau/I$ of the monopolistically competitive demand segment. The overall linear-segmented demand for the typical firm thus has a three-part form:

$$
\begin{aligned}
z(p; \bar{p}, J) &= 0 && \text{for } p \geqslant v \\
&= \frac{2I}{\tau}(v - p) && \text{for } p \geqslant 2v - \bar{\jmath} - \frac{\tau}{J} \\
&= \frac{I}{\tau}\left(\bar{p} + \frac{\tau}{J} - p\right) && \text{for } p \leqslant 2v - \bar{p} - \frac{\tau}{J}
\end{aligned} \tag{5.31}
$$

These segments "fit together" as illustrated in figure 5.3, producing a kink in the overall inverse demand schedule at point k where the switch from monopoly to monopolistically competitive segments occurs.[23]

When the firm sets its price above v it sells nothing. For prices just below v buyers are attracted from the outside good according to the monopoly demand (5.27a) at the rate $-\tau/2I$, at the kink price $2v - \bar{p} - \tau/J$ consumers are just indifferent to the firm's brand and to those of its left and right neighbors, and at lower prices the firm captures consumers from these neighbors at the higher rate $-\tau/I$ (again, assuming that the neighbors hold their price fixed). The kink occurs just at the boundary of these demand segments and depends on the parameters I, J, v, τ, and $\bar{p}$. As will be seen below, the kink price depends inversely on the market equilibrium values of the parameters $\bar{p}$ and J.

Supercompetition. The figure also illustrates a final **supercompetitive** region of demand. This occurs at the levels of price and quantity where the given firm

[23] It is of interest that the kink in the demand does not arise here because of asymmetrical conjectures as in chapter 3, E3.4. Rather, the kink occurs because consumers purchase at most one unit of the commodity. Salop (1979b) has argued that, for the case where consumers at each location have smooth negatively sloped demands, there is no kink, but a smooth transition between segments.

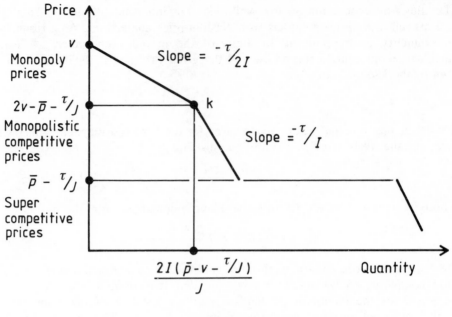

Figure 5.3
Firm demand

undercuts its neighbors. Specifically, at prices some small amount less than $\bar{p} - \tau/J$ the firm abruptly captures the entire trade of its immediate neighbors and enters into monopolistic competition with more distant firms.

Market Areas. Figure 5.4 illustrates the various market situation. In figure 5.4(a) firms 1 and 2 are located opposite from each other on the circular market. Both firms are pricing monopolistically, producing gaps aa' and bb' (the short arc lengths) in which consumers choose *only* the outside good. Individuals along the larger arc ab purchase one unit of good 1 and, after that expenditure, their residual income is allocated to the outside good. A similar situation obtains for individuals in firm 2's market area a'b'. If either firm were to lower price a small amount to extend its monopoly market area, the consumers gained would be from the outside good and not the inside good.

In figure 5.4(b) firm 1 has lowered its price sufficiently relative to the outside good and firm 2 to extend its market over the greater arc length cc'. Note in this case that there are no gaps in the market between firms 1 and 2: all consumers buy one or the other of the inside goods (with residual income then used to purchase the outside good). While all consumers are served, the firms are not quite in competition for the marginal consumer. However, any further price decrease by one firm j relative to its neighbor firm k will result in such competition, as the increase in j's market area then comes directly from a decrease in k's area. Finally, if some firms 3 and 4 were in the market previously, then figure 5.4(b) implies that they have been undercut by firm 1's supercompetitive pricing.

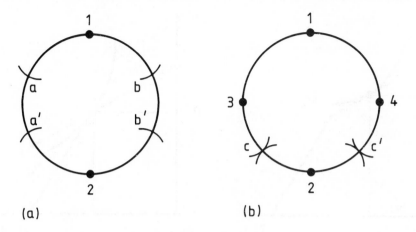

Figure 5.4
Market areas: (a) monopoly; (b) monopolistically competitive

5.2.3 Symmetric Equilibria

Following Salop (1979b) we restrict attention to Nash-in-price equilibria where firms are equidistant along the market circle (symmetric locations) and each firm earns zero profits (long run with free entry and no "integer" problem). When the disutility cost τ is constant we would expect firms to employ aggressive undercutting strategies (recall section 5.1.1). To exclude that possibility it is also assumed that firms adopt the modified zero conjectures developed in section 5.1.3: not only does each firm view the price of other firms as fixed, but it also believes that no other firm will allow itself to be undersold at its own location. This eliminates any supercompetitive segment of demand as an equilibrium outcome.

Given the above conditions there are three possible Nash-in-price equilibria. These can be cataloged by superimposing the firm's average cost schedule on the kinked demand and identifying the three possible (zero-profit) tangencies. The cases are illustrated in figure 5.5. and have the following properties.[24]

> **Monopoly equilibrium** (figure 5.5(a)): each firm serves only close-in customers – those inside the distance l^* given by (5.26). Consumers falling in the gaps between firms do not purchase the differentiated good as they prefer the outside good. These gaps separate the monopoly market areas of the sellers.
>
> **Kinked equilibrium** (figure 5.5(b)): each firm continues as a monopolist in the sense that demand conditions (5.26) and (5.27) obtain, but now the "gap" contains zero customers. Every customer buys one unit of some brand of the differentiated commodity.
>
> **Monopolistically competitive equilibrium** (figure 5.5.(c)): the market areas of the firms now share common boundaries given by l^{**} from (5.29) and

---

[24] The demand kink and marginal revenue discontinuity pose some problems for the existence of an equilibrium; see Roberts and Sonnenshein (1977) and Salop (1979b) for details and examples.

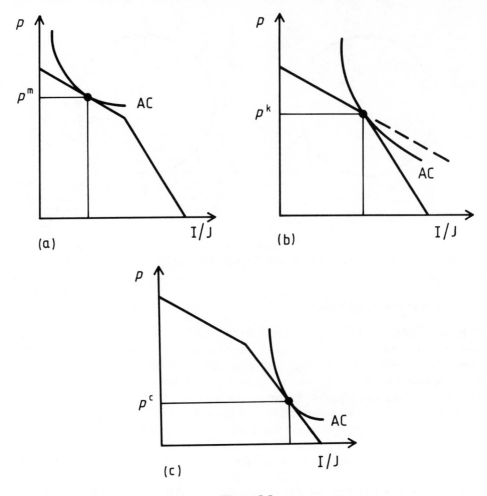

Figure 5.5
Family of equilibria: (a) monopoly; (b) kinked; (c) competitive

each firm competes for marginal consumers with immediate right and left neighbors.

Equilibrium Prices and Outputs. The market equilibrium has the usual two properties: prices and quantities maximize profits for each firm and the number of firms is determined such that these maximum profits are zero. These conditions require respectively that (a) marginal revenue and marginal costs satisfy

$$p + z\frac{\mathrm{d}p}{\mathrm{d}z} \leqslant c \tag{5.32a}$$

with the inequality holding only at the kinked equilibrium (which is not a tangency solution), and (b) average revenue and average cost are equal

$$p = c + \frac{F}{z} \tag{5.32b}$$

In addition, the symmetry of the equilibrium implies equal market shares:

$$z = I/J \tag{5.32c}$$

These three equations are solved jointly using $dp/dz = -\tau/2I$ from (5.27a) in the monopoly case and $dp/dz = -\tau/I$ from (5.29) in the monopolistically competitive case. Making these substitutions in (5.32a) using z from (5.32b), and rearranging gives the equilibrium number of firms, the price–cost margin, and the output per firm

$$J^m = \left(\frac{\tau I}{2F}\right)^{1/2} \tag{5.33a}$$

$$p^m - c = \frac{\tau}{2J^m} = \left(\frac{\tau F}{2I}\right)^{1/2} \tag{5.33b}$$

$$z^m = \frac{I}{J^m} = \left(\frac{2FI}{\tau}\right)^{1/2} \tag{5.33c}$$

for the monopoly solution. At the monopolistically competitive equilibrium similar manipulations give

$$J^c = \left(\frac{\tau I}{F}\right)^{1/2} \tag{5.34a}$$

$$p^c - c = \frac{\tau}{J^c} = \left(\frac{\tau F}{I}\right)^{1/2} \tag{5.34b}$$

$$z^c = \frac{I}{J^c} = \left(\frac{FI}{\tau}\right)^{1/2} \tag{5.34c}$$

The comparative static properties of the τ, F, and I parameters are evident from the above equations. In both the monopoly and the monopolistic competition cases a large disutility rate τ for nonideal brands leads to a greater equilibrium number of firms and a greater price–cost margin. Greater fixed cost reduces the number of firms and increases the price–cost margin (as the advantages of scale economies are reduced relative to the consumer's value of having a more preferred variety). Finally, note that as the size of the market increases with I, the number of firms increases (without bound), the price–cost margins decrease, the output of each firm increases, and the market share (which is always equal to $1/J$) decreases.

At the kinked equilibrium the calculations are slightly different. Since (5.32a) holds with inequality at the kink, the associated equilibrium price is given directly by the monopolistic demand function. That is,

$$p^k = v - \frac{\tau}{I} z = v - \frac{\tau}{J^k} \tag{5.35a}$$

This condition, along with the price and average cost equality, implies an equilibrium number of firms which solves

$$\frac{F}{I} J^k + \frac{\tau}{J^k} = v - c \tag{5.35b}$$

and by symmetry we again have

$$z^k = \frac{I}{J^k} \tag{5.35c}$$

For the kinked equilibrium number of firms, the quadratic form in (5.35b) yields

$$J^k = \frac{(v - c) \pm \{(v - c)^2 - (4F\tau/I)\}^{1/2}}{2F/I}$$

which is not a simple expression. Nonetheless, some useful bounds can be derived. To this end, note first that at the monopoly equilibrium

$$v - c \geqslant \left(\frac{2\tau F}{I}\right)^{1/2} = \frac{\tau}{J^m} \tag{5.36}$$

Monopoly profits are

$$\pi^m = \left(v - \frac{\tau z}{2I} - c\right)z - F$$

which has a maximum at $z^* = I(v - c)/\tau$. Substituting this in π^m gives the equilibrium profits

$$\pi^{m^\circ} = \frac{I(v - c)^2}{2\tau} - F$$

Nonnegative equilibrium profits then satisfy (5.36). Because of their relative slopes, at the monopolistically competitive equilibrium the price p^c must lie below (the extension of) the monopoly demand curve as indicated in figure 5.4(b). This requires $v - \frac{1}{2}(\tau/I)(I/J^c) > p^c$. Using (5.34b) with this condition then gives

$$v - c \geqslant \left(\frac{9\tau F}{4I}\right)^{1/2} = \frac{3\tau}{2J^c} \tag{5.37}$$

The last two inequalities imply that the kinked equilibrium must be such that

$$\left(\frac{2\tau F}{I}\right)^{1/2} \leqslant v - c \leqslant \left(\frac{9\tau F}{4I}\right)^{1/2} \tag{5.38}$$

Finally, using (5.33b) and (5.34b) in (5.38) yields

$$\frac{\tau}{v - c} \leqslant J^k \leqslant \frac{3\tau}{2(v - c)} \tag{5.39}$$

Equilibrium and Optimal Variety. For the moment consider only the monopolistically competitive demand segment and symmetric equilibrium. (Analyses of the monopoly and kinked equilibrium run in a parallel fashion.) If there are J firms each attracting $J/2$ consumers away, then aggregate surplus is given by

$$W(J) = 2JI \int_0^{J/2} (v - \tau l - c)\, dl - JF \tag{5.40}$$

The welfare optimum number of firms maximizes W. Using the usual stationarity condition gives $J^* = (\tau I/F)^{1/2}/2$ as the optimal product variety. Note that $J^c = 2J^*$: there is an "excess" of these monopolistically competitive brands (brand "proliferation"), just as suggested by the traditional view of Chamberlin's excess capacity. The reader should take this as a tentative result, which is not robust to slight variations in the model specifications. Detailed comments on the extent and optimality of product variety are reserved for chapter 6.

5.2.4 Horizontal Product Differentiation

Consumers have heterogeneous preferences. If a specific single price were fixed for all product varieties in the above analysis, there would *not* be uniform agreement among consumers about the preference ordering of the varieties. In the above spatial model this has been assured by (a) assuming that each consumer has his own ideal product (location in characteristics space) and (b) having nontrivial disutility costs associated with choices of nonideal brands. The competition among firms occurs with variations in relative price as that permits any seller to make its product variety a better or worse substitute for any other and thereby alter consumption choices. When consumer preferences are expressed and product competition operates in this manner **horizontal product differentiation** is said to exist.

5.3 The Symmetric Substitution Model

Among the criticisms of the spatial model of monopolistic competition are the strong localization of competition it implies and the fact that the equilibrium results rely critically on the unobservable parameters θ and τ. These criticisms are avoided, but not without introducing other difficulties, by a somewhat more neoclassical model. The beginning point for this alternative is the recognition that the convexity of indifference contours over brands is in fact a precise expression of each consumer's preference for variety. To construct an operational theory of demand for variety then, all that is necessary is to be explicit and reasonable about these rates of substitution.[25]

Underlying Assumptions. Studies proceeding in this way are generally built on two key assumptions: (a) differences across individuals are limited to those which permit equilibrium prices and outputs to be determined by an aggregate utility function $\hat{u}(z, z_0)$, where $z = [z_1 z_2 \ldots z_J]$ is the vector of perfectly divisible outputs of firms $j = 1, 2, \ldots, J$ and z_0 is a composite outside good;[26] (b) $\hat{u}$ is separable and has the general form

$$\hat{u}(z, z_0) = u\left(\sum_j z_j^{\sigma}\right) + z_0 \tag{5.41}$$

where u is the subutility defined over the commodities of concern.[27] It is also

---

[25] Equilibrium variety will, of course, depend not only on the demand for variety but also on its cost. The conditions of supply are made explicit below.

[26] Detailed conditions on individual utilities for such aggregation are given by Pollack (1971) and Gorman (1976).

[27] Dixit and Stiglitz (1977), Spence (1977a), O. Hart, (1983, 1985a, b), Sattinger (1984), and Yarrow (1985) have used utilities of this general form.

required that $0 < \sigma \leq 1$, so that u is increasing and concave in each z_j. The analysis is simplified if we ignore economies of scope and let each product (brand) be supplied by just one single-product firm. Thus j indexes both product varieties and firms.

The Value of Variety. Notice in the subutility u that the consumption of different brands is not generally treated with indifference; if it were, then we would specifically have $\sigma \equiv 1$ and there would be consumer indifference as to how any given industry output was made up by the individual brands. Thus in the demand model the parameter σ defines the (exogenously given) value consumers (in aggregate) place on brand differentiation. As the same σ pertains to each brand, the value of brand differentiation will be symmetric. Our first task is to be rather more precise about these things.

Given the constant marginal utility of the numeraire (z_0), the inverse demand function associated with (5.41) is, for each j,

$$p_j = \frac{\partial \hat{u}}{\partial z_j} = \sigma u' z_j^{\sigma-1} \tag{5.42}$$

where $u' = \partial u / \partial (\Sigma_j z_j^{\sigma})$. Because of the particular form of the utility these demands have several notable properties. First, they are symmetric in the sense that increments in the output of any brand will have the same scale effect on the demand for all other brands (through u'): competition is not localized. Second, at positive (finite) prices for any brand, positive amounts will be demanded. And, finally from (5.42) we have $z_j/z_k = (p_j/p_k)^{1-\sigma}$ so that there are no income effects on relative brand consumptions.

While these properties of the utility are somewhat restrictive, they do not appear to be unreasonable and there are important accompanying advantages. Of first interest is the form of the associated price cross-elasticities (for brands j and l)

$$\eta_{lj} = -\frac{z_j}{p_l} \frac{\partial p_l}{\partial z_j} = -\frac{\sigma u'' z_j^{\sigma}}{u'} \tag{5.43a}$$

$$= \sigma s_j E$$

where $E = u'' \Sigma_k z_k^{\sigma} / u'$ is the elasticity of the marginal subutility and $s_j = z_j^{\sigma} / \Sigma_k z_k^{\sigma}$ is a utility form of market share. Note from the right-hand side of this expression that every competing brand l has the same price cross-elasticity with brand j. In turn, the price own-elasticities are

$$\eta_{jj} = -\frac{z_j}{p_j} \frac{\partial p_j}{\partial z_j} = 1 - \sigma + \eta_{lj} = 1 + \sigma(s_j E - 1) \tag{5.43b}$$

which depends on the market parameters σ and E and the firm's share s_j. As a brand's share increases its demand becomes more elastic.

The formulae for η_{lj} and η_{jj} indicate the specific way in which the preference parameter σ measures brand substitutability (or, conversely, measures the consumer's desired degree of brand diversity): when $\sigma = 1$ the cross- and own-elasticities are equal, making all brands perfect substitutes (diversity is not valued by consumers); alternatively, when $0 < \sigma < 1$ the goods are not seen as substitutes and diversity is of value, with smaller σ implying greater value. In this case the division of a given quantity of industry output uniformly over more brands increases consumer welfare.

E5.4

Constant Elasticity of Substitution Utility and Brand Preference

A specific form of the utility function (5.41) that is frequently adopted is that having constant elasticity of substutition:

$$\hat{u}(z, z_0) = \left(\sum_j z_j{}^\sigma \right)^\theta + z_0$$

with parameters $0 < \sigma \leqslant 1$ and $0 < \theta < 1$. The system of inverse demands is given by

$$p_j(z) = \frac{\partial \hat{u}}{\partial z_j} = \sigma\theta\left(\sum_k z_k{}^\sigma \right)^{\theta-1} z_j{}^{\sigma-1}$$

for all j. Again, consumers purchase additional units of each commodity until marginal utility and price are equal, and there is declining marginal utility for each commodity as a function of the quantities of all others (since $\theta < 1$).

Note also that this specification implies an elasticity of substitution between any two commodities which is the same and given by $\delta = 1/(1 - \sigma)$. Again, commodities are homogeneous in the limiting case where $\sigma = 1$ (indifference contours are then hyperplanes). When $\sigma < 1$ the commodities are imperfect substitutes and spreading a given industry output over more products increases the value of $\hat{u}$. This unlimited benefit of diversity is usually offset, in a full equilibrium model, by economies of scale.

5.3.1   Demand with a Change of Variables

A change of variables at this point leads to some simplifications that are helpful in deriving the demand functions of individual firms. Specifically, let

$$v_j \equiv z_j{}^\sigma \tag{5.44a}$$

and

$$v \equiv \sum_j v_j = \sum_j z_j{}^\sigma \tag{5.44b}$$

It is usual to call v_j the *v*-**output** or **utility product** of firm j, and similarly v is called the *v*-output, or utility product, of the industry. Associated with these new variables is a *v*-**demand** identified by substituting (5.41) in (5.42) to produce the revenue function

$$p_j z_j = (\sigma u' z_j{}^{\sigma-1}) z_j = \sigma u' z_j{}^\sigma = \rho(v) v_j \tag{5.45}$$

where $\rho(v) \equiv \sigma u'(v)$, the price per unit v_j, is the industry inverse demand for v.

The advantage of the change in variables is evident at this point: since $u(z) = u(v_1 + v_2 + \ldots + v_J) = u(v)$, there is the equivalent utility function $u(z) = v_1 + v_2 + \ldots + v_J = v$. Thus each firm j, which produces a differentiated commodity measured in units by z_j, can be equivalently thought of as producing a commodity measured in v_j units which is a perfect substitute for the v-output of every other firm. Consistent with this homogeneity, the v-market price is the same for all firms and depends only on the aggregate industry v-output. The change to products measured linearly in terms of their utility value thus leaves the effects of product differentiation to arise only in the cost functions of the firms and, in turn, the conditions of supply.

5.3.2 Utility Product Supply

To make the question of optimal product variety interesting it is assumed that each firm produces with increasing returns (recall chapter 4, section 4.2.1). This is done most simply by letting each firm j's total costs be made up of fixed and variable components:

$$TC_j = F + cz_j \tag{5.46}$$

where the fixed cost F and marginal cost c are common to all firms. In turn, average (total) cost $a_j = F/z_j + c$ uniformly declines with output. Making the change of variables to the v-product gives

$$TC_j = F + cv_j^{1/\sigma} \tag{5.47}$$

If $\sigma < 1$, then $1/\sigma > 1$ and each firm's average total cost takes on the usual U-shape in units of the v-product, in contrast with the uniform decline in z_j. Each firm's v-**capacity**, that is, its v-output level at minimum average cost, is given by[28]

$$v_j^* = \text{argmin } a(v_j) \tag{5.48}$$

$$= \left(\frac{F}{c} \frac{\sigma}{1 - \sigma} \right)^{\sigma}$$

The assumption of identical cost structures for the differentiated products z_j gives identical cost structures and capacity levels in v-products. Finally, the associated capacity level in z-output is $z_j^* = (v_j^*)^{1/\sigma} = (F/c)\sigma/(1 - \sigma)$.

Two factors, the ratio of fixed to variable costs and the (diversity) parameter σ of the aggregate utility, determine the v-capacity. In accord with our intuition, this capacity is an increasing function of the firm's ratio of fixed to variable (unit) costs. Moreover, as $\sigma \to 1$ and products become better substitutes, the v-capacity of the firms increases. Alternatively, the more differentiated are the products the smaller is the v-capacity. In short, product differentiation can be analyzed in an equivalent utility product homogeneous-goods framework with the degree of differentiation having its effect simply (and only) through the capacity of the firms to produce the v-product. That, however, leaves us with the question as to the relationship between v-capacity and equilibrium product variety.

[28] The minimum of average cost is only one definition of capacity. This definition and three alternatives are discussed by Stigler (1966, pp. 156–8). Phillips (1963) considers the practical problems in measuring capacity in its various forms.

5.3.3 Market Equilibrium

The equilibrium for the homogeneous v-market can be developed in the usual way. Making the (inverse) change of variables from (ρ, v) to (p, z) then yields the corresponding equilibrium in the original differentiated goods market.

We can, of course, continue to use the Nash solution concept in the v-market. One possibilitiy in this regard would be to adopt the Nash-in-price solution. In this homogeneous-goods case the free-entry equilibrium yields the usual competitive results: the equilibrium price ρ^* will equal average and marginal cost; the industry v-ouput (call it v^*) can be determined from the v-demand (at this price); finally, the equilibrium number of zero-profit firms follows as the ratio v^*/v_j^*. (Again, the integer problem is ignored). This competitive (in v) equilibrium will induce a large number of firms (and therefore a large number of differentiated products in the original market) whenever the v-capacity of the firms is small relative to the market.

The reader can also see that the Cournot–Nash equilibrium in the homogeneous good v-market proceeds in the standard way. Of particular interest in this solution is the fact that smaller v-capacities imply a greater number of firms and, in the usual way, this forces the Cournot solution closer to the competitive result (recall chapter 3, section 3.1).

Detailed properties of the equilibria, and especially the correspondence of equilibrium product variety to the socially optimal level, are considered in chapter 6.

E5.5

Correspondence between Physical and Utility Product Markets

A numerical example is helpful in understanding the correspondence between z- and v-product markets. Let the aggregate utility have the specific form

$$\hat{u}(z, z_0) = 10^3 \left(\sum_k z_k^{0.5} \right)^{0.5} + z_0 \tag{5.49}$$

and assume that the total cost function of each firm has fixed and variable components given by

$$\mathrm{TC}_j = 4 + 2z_j \tag{5.50}$$

From (5.42) derive the demand function for each firm j's output:

$$p_j = \frac{\partial \hat{u}}{\partial z_j} = \frac{10^3}{4z_j^{0.5}(\sum_k z_k^{0.5})^{0.5}} \tag{5.51}$$

Define the v-product as $v_j = z_j^{0.5}$ and further let $v = \sum_k v_k$. Using these definitions we can transform price and revenue functions as $p_j = 10^3/(4v_j v^{0.5})$ and $p_j z_j = 10^3 v_j/4v^{0.5}$. In turn, the price of the homogeneous v-product is

$$\rho = \frac{10^3}{4v^{0.5}} \tag{5.52}$$

Note also that the cost function is transformed as

$$TC_j = 4 + 2v_j^2 \qquad (5.53)$$

Each firm's v-capacity can then be calculated from (5.48), giving

$$v_j^* = \left(\frac{4}{2}\frac{0.5}{05}\right)^{0.5} = 1.414 \qquad (5.54)$$

Putting these parts together gives the profit function

$$\pi_j(v_j, v) = \frac{10^3 v_j}{4v^{0.5}} - (4 + 2v_j^2) \qquad (5.55)$$

We look for the zero-profit Nash equilibrium where each firm takes the market price, and therefore v, to be unaffected by its own output decision. In this case the relevant stationarity condition is

$$\frac{\partial \pi_j}{\partial v_j} = \frac{10^3}{4v^{0.5}} - 4v_j = 0 \qquad (5.56)$$

Since the firms produce a homogeneous v-product, $Jv_j = v$ where J is the number of active firms. Substituting this in the profit stationarity condition gives

$$v_j^3 = \frac{10^6}{256J} \qquad (5.57)$$

At equilibrium the output level and number of firms is limited by this expression. In turn, the equilibrium number of firms is determined by the zero-profit condition. Using (5.55) and a little algebra gives

$$J = \frac{10^6 v_j}{\{8(2 + v_j^2)\}^2} \qquad (5.58)$$

Substituting this in the stationarity condition (5.57) finally yields the equilibrium output per firm

$$v_j^3 = \frac{\{8(2 + v_j^2)\}^2}{256v_j} \qquad (5.59)$$

which solves for $v_j^0 = 1.414$. Given that the firms are price-takers, it is not surprising that each produces at the minimum of average total cost (recall that $v_j^* = 1.414$ also). The equilibrium number of firms and the v-product price can immediately be calculated:

$$J^0 = \frac{10^6}{256(1.414)^3} = 1381 \qquad \rho^0 = \frac{10^3}{4(1381 \times 1.414)^{0.5}} = 5.6$$

The v-market equilibrium conditions are easily transformed back to the heterogeneous z-market to give $z_j^0 = 2$ and $p_J^0 = 4$.

5.4   Horizontal and Vertical Differentiation

The addition of product differentiation greatly increases the amount of information that firms employ and the expectations that they must form concerning their rivals. In a homogeneous oligopoly only the aggregate supply and the aggregate supply response of rivals are important to the firm; in contrast, with differentiated products the firm must not only give weight to each rival's output or price response, but is must also consider additional strategy variables for each. Because of the dimensionality it has frequently been suggested that nonprice competition generally dominates the effects of price competition (on which economists have traditionally focused). (See, for example, Porter, 1981). These nonprice effects are diminished, however, when competition is localized and only a small number of rivals and variables are of concern to any given firm.

Horizontal and Vertical Differentiation. The degree to which competition is localized in any market turns on a variety of factors, as we first noted in chapter 4, section 4.3. These factors have generally been grouped, or organized, into two modeling approaches. The first leads to what is called **horizontal product differentiation** (recall section 5.2.4). This case occurs when the products of the firms, if offered at the same price, are ordered differently in preference by consumers, as they value the characteristic bundles of the products differently.

Spatial models generally exhibit horizontal product differentiation when (a) the products and consumers have specific locations in characteristics space, (b) the number of relevant characteristics is small and there is a distance measure in that space, and (c) there is a measure of disutility which is increasing in distance. For example, the model developed in section 5.2 was of this kind. Even when the number of firms becomes very large in such models, each firm will have only a small number of neighbors who are directly affected by its strategy choices. Competition is localized, and the demand curve facing each firm is not perfectely elastic.[29]

A second approach to product specification, termed **vertical product differentiation**, occurs when the products of firms, if offered at the same price, are ordered in preference in exactly the same way by every consumer. In this case all the relevant characteristics of different products can be summarized by a single (scalar) **quality index**, with products of greater quality being preferred to those of lesser quality by all consumers.[30]

Although the spatial models that have been developed to this point have all exhibited the properties of horizontal differentiation, this need not be the case. Recall, for instance, Hotelling's main street example from chapter 4, section 4.1. The essentials of that model with two firms selling homogeneous products and located at points l_1 and l_2 interior to the $[0, 1]$ market are illustrated in figure 5.6(a). The alternative case where the sellers, for whatever reason, are not permitted to be located "in" the market area but must service their clientele from an outside location, is illustrated in figure 5.4(b). In the figure 5.6(a) the products are horizontally differentiated. Each consumer is serviced with a

---

[29] For completeness we note that the localization of competition in this spatial model depends in part on the fact that consumers have full information about product prices and locations. In chapter 13, and section 13.2 specifically, we relax the full information assumption and show how nonlocalized competition generally results.

[30] Scalar quality measures have been widely used in analysis. For example, Panzar (1973) and Schmalensee (1977) use frequency of service as the product quality index for the airline industry, Smallwood and Conlisk (1979) and Schmalensee (1978a) use frequency of a product's being found unsatisfactory, and Dixit and Stiglitz (1977) use "range" of choice.

transportation cost, and when equal mill prices are set by the firms consumers located closer to firm 1 choose its products and those closer to firm 2 choose its product. In contrast, in figure 5.6(b) the products are vertically differentiated: at equal mill prices consumers in the market area uniformly prefer product 1 over product 2, since each then has a lower delivered price.

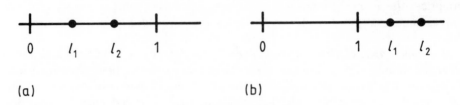

(a)   (b)

Figure 5.6
Differentiation in spatial markets: (a) horizontal; (b) vertical

5.5   Vertical Production Differentiation

E5.6

Quality-differentiated Products with Consumers Located by Income

The model of differentiated product demand can be built up from differences which occur in (and the spatial analogy is with respect to) consumer incomes, not consumer tastes as in section 5.2 (see, for example, Jaskold-Gabszewski and Thisse, 1979, Shaked and Sutton, 1982, 1983). To follow this idea, consider a continuum of consumers over the unit interval $[0, 1]$ where each consumer $i \in [0, 1]$ has income given by $yi(y > 0$ is a constant). Without loss of generality choose $y = 1$. The result of these assumptions is to differentiate consumers only by income as measured by their location in the $[0, 1]$ interval.

   The model economy has two commodities: the one under consideration, which we will call the "good," and the usual composite "outside" commodity. Consumer income not spent on the good is allocated to the outside composite. Suppose further that each consumer purchases at most one indivisible unit of the good which is available at quality levels measured by the parameter $\xi > 0$. It may be helpful to think of some standard product and to let the quality difference among brands of this good arise from the level of services offered, such as delivery time, credit conditions, or provisions for installation and repair. Whatever its source, quality is assumed to be perfectly observable.

   Utility, Income, and Demand. Let the consumers have identical tastes with utility functions $u(\xi, i - p)$, where $i - p$ is the income remaining after purchasing one unit of the good of quality ξ at price p. To further simplify, suppose that the utility is multiplicative:

$$u(\xi, i - p) = v(\xi)(i - p) \tag{5.60a}$$

It is required that $\partial v/\partial \xi > 0$ so that, other things being equal, goods of higher quality are preferred. Notice that, at given prices, consumers with greater income receive greater utility from a good of given quality. Finally, let

$$u(0, i) = v_0 i \qquad v_0 > 0 \tag{5.60b}$$

when none of the good is purchased. In this circumstance the consumer allocates all his income to the purchase of the outside composite.

One Quality. As a first case consider two firms who choose to sell goods of the same quality ξ. With perfect information the goods must have the same price if both are sold. A consumer with specific income $\bar{i}$ is indifferent between purchasing and not purchasing the output of one of these firms at price p when

$$v_0 \bar{i} = v(\xi)(\bar{i} - p)$$

This *separating income* is given explicitly by

$$\bar{i} = \frac{p v(\xi)}{v(\xi) - v_0}$$

Consumers with income $i > \bar{i}$ will purchase the commodity and those with $i < \bar{i}$ will not. As a result the total demand for the good will be given by $1 - \bar{i}$, or

$$D(p, \xi) = 1 - \frac{p v(\xi)}{v(\xi) - v_0}$$

Low- and High-quality Separating Income. Suppose next that the two sellers choose different qualities for their products. The low-quality firm l supplies ξ_l and the high-quality firm h supplies ξ_h. Let the respective product prices be given by p_h and p_l. With the simplifying notation $v(\xi_h) \equiv v_h$ and similarly for v_l, the consumer i^* is just indifferent between these two products when

$$v_l(i^* - p_l) = v_h(i^* - p_h)$$

which implies $p_h > p_l$ since $v_h > v_l$. This indifference relationship solves for

$$i^* = \frac{v_h}{v_h - v_l} p_h - \frac{v_l}{v_h - v_l} p_l \tag{5.61a}$$

From these expressions note that $v_h > v_l$ (and, in turn, $p_h > p_l$) implies that consumers with income less that i^* will prefer low quality and that those with greater income will prefer high quality.

Not all the consumers with $i < i^*$ will purchase the low-quality good, however. Some may prefer to allocate their entire income to the outside good. The consumer i^0 who is indifferent to the low-quality good and the outside good satisfies

$$v_0 i^0 = v_l(i^0 - p_l)$$

which solves for

$$i^0 = \frac{v_l}{v_l - v_0} p_l \tag{5.61b}$$

The final demands for the low- and high-quality goods follow directly from the above boundary conditions. Demand for the high-quality good is

$$D_h(p_h; p_l) = 1 - i^* \tag{5.62a}$$

where i^* is given by (5.61a), and demand for the low-quality good is

$$D_l(p_l; p_h) = i^* - i^0 \tag{5.62b}$$

where i^0 is given by (5.61b).

If the price and quality of every brand of a product is costlessly observable, then brands of the same quality but with different prices cannot both have positive sales. Similarly, no two brands of the same price but different quality will both be purchased. However, more generally, the nature of demand depends on how price and quality vary in the cross-section of vertically differentiated brands. This, in turn, depends on the relationship between consumers' willingness to pay for quality improvements, the increase in unit variable cost associated with such improvements, and the rules by which firms play the market game. A variant of the model developed above, in E5.6, where consumers differ only in income, is helpful in developing these relationships.

On the demand side, let us now assume that $v(\xi) = \xi$ so that each consumer i with income y_i derives utility

$$u(\xi_j, p_j) = (y_i - p_j)\xi_j \geq 0 \tag{5.63}$$

when purchasing brand j at price p_j and quality level ξ_j. Again, any residual $y_i - p_j$ is spent on the outside good, which gives constant utility ξ_0 per unit. When no inside good is purchased the consumer receives utility $y_i\xi_0$ and we take $p_0 = 0$. Let $0 < \underline{y} \leq y_i \leq \bar{y}$ for all i.

Finally, assume that the model economy has J products, numbered by ascending quality so that $\xi_J > \xi_{J-1} > \ldots > \xi_1$, and I consumers, numbered by ascending income so that $y_I > y_{I-1} > \ldots > y_1$.

Income and Brand Choice. In (5.63) individuals differ only by their income, so that in a comparison of products individual choices will be a function only of that single distinguishing factor. Moreover, the form of the utility function (5.63) makes quality a superior good in the sense that the consumers' willingness to pay for any quality level is increasing with income. This leads us to ask about the levels of income which separate the preference for brands of different quality.

An individual with specific income y_j^* is indifferent between brand j and brand $j - 1$, which is next lowest in quality, when

$$(y_j^* - p_j)\xi_j = (y_j^* - p_{j-1})\xi_{j-1} \tag{5.64a}$$

or, defining the relative quality measure $\alpha_j \equiv \xi_j/(\xi_j - \xi_{j-1}) > 1$, when

$$y_j^* = \alpha_j p_j + (1 - \alpha_j)p_{j-1} \tag{5.64b}$$

Note from (5.64a) that the quality ordering $\xi_j > \xi_{j-1}$ implies a similar price ordering $p_j > p_{j-1}$ if the assumed indifference point obtains. The immediate implication of the ascending quality and price structure is a set of separating income levels such that $y_J^* > y_{J-1}^* > \ldots > y_1^*$. The implication is that individuals with incomes greater than y_J^* purchase brand J, those with incomes between y_j^* and y_{j-1}^* purchase brand $j - 1$, and those with incomes less than y_1^* purchase the outside good only (none of the considered brands).

Figure 5.7 illustrates these purchase decisions along the income line. In the figure individuals with incomes between y and y_2^* purchase brand 1, between y_2^* and y_3^* they purchase brand 2, and so forth.[31] In this situation the individual with the highest income at $\bar{y}$ purchases the highest-quality brand. This need not always be the case. If the price p_J of the highest-quality good is too high, then $\bar{y}$ can lie to the left of y_J^* (but to the right of y_{J-1}) and brand J will not be taken at all. In another extreme case, the prices of all brands may be raised to the point where $\bar{y} < y_1^*$, so that none of the inside brands is purchased (all income is allocated to the outside good).

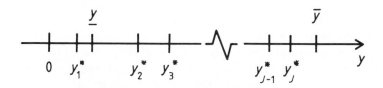

Figure 5.7
Income and brand choice

Equilibrium Varieties. In the above situation, and in figure 5.7 specifically, suppose for the moment that the consumers are uniformly distributed over the $[\,\underline{y}, \bar{y}]$ interval. Since y_J^* lies close to $\bar{y}$ in the figure we can conclude that the highest-quality brand J receives a relatively small share of the market. To the extent that the distribution of consumers changes and/or the price of J is lowered, moving y_J^* along the income line, then market shares and numbers of varieties sold can change.

The analytics of such changes are easy to trace out. Consider the high-quality product J and, to keep things straightforward, assume that the prices of its rivals are equal to their marginal costs and ordered so that $p_{J-1} > p_{J-2} > \ldots > p_1$. Suppose now that firm J alone discovers a technology which allows it to produce its product at a lower (constant) unit cost. Under these conditions assume further that J chooses to lower its price to yield the separating income y_J^* illustrated in figure 5.8. On doing this, firm J sells to all customers with incomes between y_J^* and $\bar{y}$, firm 2 sells within the $y_2^*-y_J^*$ line segment, and firm 1 sells within the $y-y_2^*$ segment. In this case, the lower price and high quality of J exclude brands 3 through $J - 1$ from the market.[32]

---

[31] Note also that if the lower income level $\underline{y}$ is less than y_1^* then those individuals with $y_i \leqslant y_1^*$ will purchase the outside good; for $y_1^* \leqslant y \leqslant y_2^*$, only those individuals with income in the interval $\underline{y} \leqslant y_i \leqslant y_2^*$ purchase good 1, and so forth.

[32] We assume here that rival firms have set their price equal to (constant) marginal cost and none can reduce price.

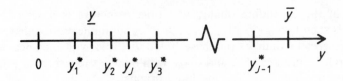

Figure 5.8
Uniform income distribution

More generally, the price J chooses with the new technology and its specific location y_J^* will depend on its level of unit cost, the price–quality positions y^* of its rivals, and the distribution of consumers by income (which also measures their willingness to pay for quality in this model). To follow one case, suppose that the distribution of consumers is skewed toward lower incomes as in figure 5.9(a). With its lower cost, firm J will be inclined to lower its price to capture the larger number of consumers at the low-income end of the market. As illustrated, the lower p_J and y_J^* exclude all but two rivals from the market. Figure 5.9(b) illustrates an alternative case, with a distribution of consumers skewed toward high incomes. Here, firm J will find it optimal to set a higher price (relative to the situation in figure 5.9(a)), for it can capture a large market share with a wider price–cost margin. The result, as illustrated, is that only one firm is excluded by J's technological innovation.

E5.7

Vertical Differentiation Fixes Maximal Number of Firms

For the utility function (5.63) and a uniform distribution of consumers, Shaked and Sutton (1982, 1983) have derived an upper bound on the number of firms that can be profitable in a Nash-in-price industry equilibrium. Their development is followed here. There is also a final note on a key equilibrium difference in product variety between vertically and horizontally differentiated product markets.

Quality Separation by Income. Let ω indicate the density of consumer incomes uniformly spread over $[\underline{y}, \bar{y}]$. From the above analyses we know that in this case the sales of any firm $1 < j < J$ are equal to $(y_{j+1}^* - y_j^*)\omega \geqslant 0$. For the high-quality firm J, sales are $(\bar{y} - y_J^*)\omega \geqslant 0$, and the low-quality firms sells $(y_2^* - \max[\underline{y}, y_1])\omega \geqslant 0$. If $\phi_j \equiv p_j - c_j$ is the price–cost margin, the firm profit functions are

$$\pi_J = \phi_J(\bar{y} - y_J^*)\omega \geqslant 0 \tag{5.65a}$$

$$\pi_j = \phi_j(y_{j+1}^* - y_j^*)\omega \geqslant 0 \qquad \text{for } 1 < j < J \tag{5.65b}$$

$$\pi_1 = \phi_1(y_2^* - \max[\underline{y}, y_1^*])\omega \geqslant 0 \tag{5.65c}$$

The stationarity conditions associated with these profit functions and a Nash-in-price equilibrium are respectively

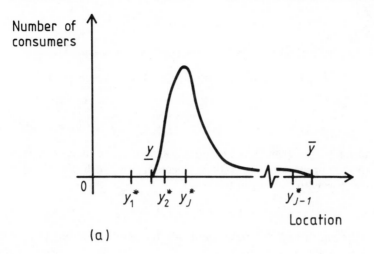

(a)

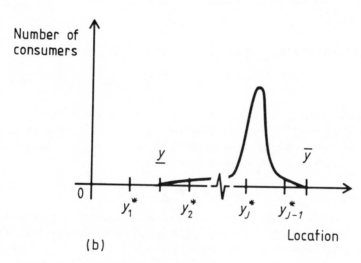

(b)

Figure 5.9
Skewed income: (a) low incomes; (b) high incomes

$$(\bar{y} - y_J^*) - \phi_J \alpha_J = 0 \tag{5.66a}$$

$$(y_{j+1}^* - y_j^*) + \phi_j(1 - \alpha_{j+1} - \alpha_j) = 0 \tag{5.66b}$$

$$y_2^* - \underline{y} - \phi_1(1 - \alpha_2) = 0 \qquad \text{for } y_1^* < \underline{y} \tag{5.66c}$$

$$y_2^* - y_1^* - \phi_1(1 - \alpha_2 - \alpha_1) = 0 \qquad \text{for } y_1^* > \underline{y} \tag{5.66c'}$$

Suppose that the $k + 1$ firms $J, J - 1, \ldots, J - k$ have positive market shares at equilibrium; this implies $y_{J-k+1}^* > \underline{y}$. By subtracting (5.63b) from the stationarity conditions for these $k + 1$ firms and rearranging, the following recursive forms for the solution y^* are derived:

$$\bar{y} = 2y_J^* + \phi_J(\alpha_J - 1) \tag{5.67a}$$

$$y_J^* = 2y_{J-1}^* + \phi_{J-1}(\alpha_J - 1) + \phi_{J-2}(\alpha_{J-1} - 1) \tag{5.67b}$$

$$y_{J-1}^* = 2y_{J-2}^* + \phi_{J-2}(\alpha_{J-1} - 1) + \phi_{J-3}(\alpha_{J-2} - 1) \tag{5.67c}$$

and so forth until

$$y_{J-k+2}^* = 2y_{J-k+1}^* + \phi_{J-k+1}(\alpha_{J-k+2} - 1) + \phi_{J-k}(\alpha_{J-k+1} - 1) \tag{5.67d}$$

Now substitute y_{J-k+1}^* from this last equation into its predecessor, and then for y_{J-k+2} from that predecessor into its predecessor, and so forth. These successive substitutions stop with (5.67a) in the form

$$\bar{y} = 2^k y_{J-k+1}^* + \Sigma \tag{5.68}$$

where Σ is the sum of *all* the right-hand side terms of equations (5.67) involving ϕ and α. Since each $\phi_j \geq 0$ and each $\alpha_j < 1$, $\Sigma \geq 0$ and we have the inequality

$$\bar{y} > 2^k y_{J-k-1}^* \tag{5.69}$$

From the original assertion that $y_{J-k-1} > y$ this finally gives

$$\bar{y}/\underline{y} > 2^k \tag{5.70}$$

Equilibrium Bounds on the Number of Firms. If the converse of this last equality holds, $\bar{y}/y < 2^k$, then y cannot be less than y_{J-k+1}^* and, in turn, brand $J - k$ cannot have a positive market share. That is, not more than k firms can have positive market shares, where k solves

$$\bar{y} < 2^k \underline{y} \tag{5.71}$$

For example, no more than two firms can be sustained by the Nash-in-price industry equilibrium (with a uniform distribution of consumer) when the range of incomes is narrowed to the extent that $\bar{y} < 4 \underline{y}$.

Consider a two-stage game in which firms choose their quality level sequentially in the first stage and reach a Nash-in-price equilibrium in the second stage. Suppose that entry costs do not depend on quality and let $\bar{y} < 4y$ so that at most two firms will enter. The first firm to enter will select the highest quality. The second will select some lesser quality (still greater than the quality ξ_0 of the outside good). It will not imitate the high quality of the first firm, for that will lead to zero profits in homogeneous-good Bertrand play. Thus in this case a perfect equilibrium is reached with differentiated products.

Shaked and Sutton emphasize that, as long as $\bar{y}$ and $\underline{y}$ are strictly positive and bounded, the number of product varieties than can be sustained at the industry equilibrium is bounded from above. Moreover, this upper bound on varieties is independent of the size of the market (since the result does not depend on ω). In this vertical differentiation case it is simply the diversity of consumers (in income) which provides the demand for product variety. For example, if the maximal number of products were available in the industry and then some higher-quality product were to enter, price competition would force (at least) the lowest-quality product out as it is the income distribution alone which fixes the maximal number of brands.[33] This, they note, is in contrast with the product variety which results with horizontally differentiated products where (unbounded) increases in market size bring with it an (unbounded) increase in the number of varieties – recall equations (5.36) and (5.37) and the discussion thereafter.

5.6 Monopolistic Competition More Precisely

To this point the label "monopolistic competition" has been used somewhat loosely, requiring simply that there be a large number of firms selling differentiated products. Chamberlin, however, had a rather precise desiderata in mind for a monopolistically competitive industry:

1 *Large numbers*: many firms producing differentiated products.
2 *Smallness or independence*: each firm small in the sense that it believes that its price decisions do not elicit rival price reactions.
3 *Market power*: each firm faces a relatively inelastic demand.
4 *Free entry*: at equilibrium (marginal) firms earn zero profits.

Despite the intuitive appeal of this set of conditions, jointly imposed they present difficulties.[34] With the number of firms finite, the smallness condition cannot precisely obtain. And, in the limit as the number of firms increases it is difficult to preserve the requirement of monopoly power. The challenge is to capture all these conditions in one model.

At first glance it would seem that some sort of localization in competition would be needed. On this belief, the horizontal differentiation model of section 5.2, where localization persists even as the number of firms becomes arbitrarily large, has often been referred to as being monopolistically competitive. The problem with this case is that each firm has only a small number of neighbors who are affected by its decisions – even when the total number of firms in the industry is large – and the basis for the *smallness* condition is unclear. It is usual to sidestep this implication of localization, assume the requisite independence, and in turn take such models to "essentially" yield a monopolistically competitive equilibrium.

The symmetric substitutes model of section 5.3 comes somewhat closer to Chamberlin's desiderata. The specification of aggregate utility in that model is such that as the number of brands becomes infinitely large the demand for each remains constant in elasticity (and therefore expresses monopoly power even with large numbers.) The problem, however, is that when each (active) firm produces a strictly positive quantity, the utility itself becomes unbounded with the unlimited increase in brands. This is problematic, as it leaves the number of

---

[33] Shaked and Sutton (1983) note that if the conditions of a Nash-in-quantity equilibrium obtain (in contrast with the Nash-in-price equilibrium here), then much weaker results follow as the competition is less intense.

[34] Stigler (1949a, b) and Demsetz (1959, 1964) were early commentators on these problems.

brands determined essentially by aggregate wealth with preferences serving only a trivial role.

Specialization of Preferences and Search Costs. Although we have in the usual manner referred to the models of section 5.2 and 5.3 as monopolistically competitive, it is seen that some qualifications must be attached to that labeling. Additional restrictions must be placed on the basic model of section 5.3 to more exactly satisfy Chamberlin's desiderata. In this regard, one recent tack has been to restrict each consumer's interest to a fixed finite subset of potential brands (see Sattinger, 1984; Hart, 1985a; Perloff and Salop, 1985). Such a specialization in preferences limits the substitutability among brands such that in the limit as the number of brands becomes large and each firm becomes negligibly small, the firms still face demands with finite elasticity (Hart, 1985a, provides details).

While the above specialization of preferences analytically resolves the inconsistency among the Chamberlin desiderata, it is a rather arbitrary imposition. Moreover, it implies, uncomfortably, that with an increase in available brands the consumer does not find increasingly close substitutes for any given brand. An alternative to this restriction has been recently proposed by Wolinsky (1984, 1986). In his model information imperfections and search costs limit the number of brands any consumer will optimally consider. This in turn limits intrabrand substitutability (localization of competition) and finally preserves the monopoly power of each firm, even when each becomes small relative to the total market.

E5.8

Demand Elasticity and Number of Brands

Does the elasticity of the firm's demand remain constant as the number of rival brands increases, or does the elasticity increase? When the market is larger and there are more competing substitutes, do the substitutes become more competitive or do they stay the same "distance" apart? Are four refrigerator brands in a market twice the size closer substitutes for each other than two brands in the original market?

A simple specific case is helpful in understanding the issues involved in the above questions. Consider two aggregate utility functions of the form

$$u(z) = az - \frac{bz^2}{J} - \frac{\varepsilon}{J}\left(\sum_j z_j^2 - \frac{z^2}{J}\right) \tag{5.72a}$$

$$u(z) = az - \frac{bz^2}{J} - \frac{\varepsilon'}{J}\left(\sum_j z_j^2 - \frac{z^2}{J}\right) \tag{5.72b}$$

where J is the number of brands, $z = \Sigma z_j$, and $\varepsilon' = \varepsilon J$. (These quadratic utilities are defined only for the range where marginal utility is not negative.) In both utilities the effect of product differentiation comes through the variance expressed by the $(\cdot)$ term. In the utility function (5.72a) the variance is controlled by ε. The consumer prefers increased variety, for as the number of brands increase they become progressively closer substitutes. In the alternative case (5.72b) the introduction of the extra J in $\varepsilon' = \varepsilon J$ helps to keep the products apart.

The reader can easily write out the demand in terms of price for these cases, in turn develop the profit functions, and finally solve for the Nash-in-price equilibrium. This procedure yields

$$z_j = \frac{a - \bar{p}}{2b} - \frac{J}{2\varepsilon}(p_j - \bar{p}) \tag{5.73}$$

$$p_j = \frac{J(J-1)bc + \varepsilon(Ja + c)}{J(J-1)bc + \varepsilon(J+1)} \tag{5.74}$$

where c is the marginal cost and $\bar{p}$ is the average rival price. Note first that as J becomes large, the firm's price approaches its marginal cost (the competitive price). However, when ε is replaced by εJ, notice that

$$p_j = \frac{(J-1)bc + \varepsilon(Ja + c)}{(J-1)b + \varepsilon(J+1)} \tag{5.74'}$$

In this case as J becomes large p_j approaches $(bc + \varepsilon a)/(b + \varepsilon)$: even though price will decrease with more competitors, it does not approach that of the competitive equilibrium. Instead, a term involving ε remains, indicating that there is always a measure of monopoly power present. The reader should compare this with the standard Cournot equilibrium results when J increases given in section 3.1.4.

Supplementary examples

SE5.1 Consumer Location and Surplus

Consider the unit circle market, taking the number of symmetrically placed firms to be fixed at J. Focus on a specific firm and let it choose price p while its $J - 1$ rivals all hold their priced fixed at $\bar{p}$. It is convenient to label that specific firm 0 and say that it produces brand 0. Consumers are again uniformly distributed over the market and have the preference structure developed above. Assume further that J is large enough and the prices are low enough for all neighboring brands to be in competition. What is the ranking of the various brands by net surplus for any given individual, and how is this affected by the firms' choice of price? The answer to this question will be important, for example, when buyers have imperfect information and the probability that they will choose any brand in a search process depends on its rank.

A buyer located a distance l from brand 0 receives $v - \tau l - p$ net surplus when he purchases that brand. How this net surplus compares with that for other brands clearly depends upon the price p, the rival firms' prices $\bar{p}$, and the given consumer's location. Since the rival brands are assumed to set the same price, every consumer ranks these simply by their relative distance from his location. That is, where brand 0 lies in its ranking depends on p (relative to $\bar{p}$) and the consumer's distance l from 0.

Following Grossman and Shapiro (1984), figure 5.10 illustrates how these various factors interact. The net surplus is plotted on the vertical axis and the location, measured as the distance from the firm 0, is plotted horizontally. (This figure and much of our analysis is limited to the semicircle, say, clockwise from firm 0. However, at appropriate points we will use the symmetry of the market to complete the analysis.) Note that firm 0's closest neighbor is located at distance $1/J$, its next-closest at $2/J$, etc. because of the imposed symmetry. Consumers situated at the locations of these rival firms receive net surplus $v - \bar{p}$. For increases or decreases in the distance l away from $1/J$, for example, the net surplus of that firm's brand decreases at the disutility rate (slope) τ. In the figure, the schedule marked $v - \bar{p} - \tau|1/J - l|$ indicates this net surplus for various consumer locations. Similar schedules obtain for the rival brands located at $2/J$, $3/J$, etc., as also indicated in the figure.

Brand Ranking by Surplus. Figure 5.10 helps in determining the surplus ranking of brands. Consider, for example, consumers located at l^*. They receive the greatest net surplus from the brand at $2/J$, the brand at $1/J$ provides the next-greatest net surplus, then comes the brand at $3/J$, and finally there is brand 0. All these net surpluses depend on the brand prices. For example, for brand 0 to rank first in net surplus for the l^* consumers it would have to lower its price below p' as shown in the figure.

For any price, say p, the consumer locations $l_1, l_2, l_3, \ldots$, at which net surplus schedules intersect represent the critical points where consumer rankings change. To the "left" of l_1, for example, brand 0 has greater net surplus than its nearest rival; that ordering reverses beyond l_1. The location l_2 similarly indicates the consumer's location where brand 0's net surplus falls below that of the brand offered by the firm positioned at $2/J$, and so forth.

Demand for Brands. Algebraic expressions for the consumer locations $l_1, l_2, l_3, \ldots$ can be derived using the geometry of figure 5.10. The consumer at the

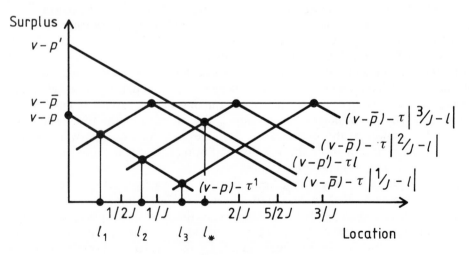

Figure 5.10
Surplus and location

margin between brand 0 and that situated at $1/J$ is located a distance l_1 which solve

$$v - p - \tau l_1 = v - \bar{p} - \tau\left(\frac{1}{J} - l_1\right)$$

or

$$l_1(p, \bar{p}) = \frac{\bar{p} - p}{2\tau} + \frac{1}{2J} \tag{5.75}$$

Because of the symmetry of the market, the total number of consumers who rank brand 0 first in net surplus is $2Il_1$, or

$$I_1 \equiv 2Il_1 = I\left(\frac{\bar{p} - p}{\tau} + \frac{1}{J}\right) \tag{5.76}$$

where I is the total number of consumers along the market.[35] Similarly, l_2 is given by those consumers at the margin between brand 0 and that located $2/J$ away, so that

$$v - p - \tau l_2 = v - \bar{p} - \tau\left(\frac{2}{J} - l_2\right)$$

and

$$l_2 = \frac{\bar{p} - p}{2\tau} + \frac{1}{J} \tag{5.77a}$$

In turn, the number of consumers ranking brand 0 second is

$$I_2 \equiv 2I(l_2 - l_1) = I/J \tag{5.77b}$$

Proceeding by induction, we have for the kth-removed neighbor

$$l_k = \frac{\bar{p} - p}{2\tau} + \frac{k}{2J} \qquad k = 1, 2, \ldots, J - 1 \tag{5.78a}$$

and

$$I_k \equiv I/J \qquad k = 2, 3, \ldots, J - 1 \tag{5.78b}$$

The last group is of course given as a remainder, that is,

$$l_J \equiv \frac{1}{2} - \frac{\bar{p} - p}{2\tau} + \frac{J}{2J} \tag{5.79a}$$

and

$$I_J = I - \sum_k I_k + I\left(\frac{1}{J} - \frac{\bar{p} - p}{\tau}\right) \tag{5.79b}$$

SE5.2   Demand for Brands with Quadratic Disutility

We consider a model of horizontal product differentiation where the disutility associated with the nonideal brand is quadratic in its distance from the

---

[35] These N_1 consumers in fact purchase brand 0, so that equation (5.76) is the brand 0 demand function with perfect information.

consumer's ideal. Of particular interest is the impact of this nonlinearity on product demand.

Suppose that there are two sellers ($j = 1, 2$) and let $0 \leqslant \theta_j \leqslant 1$ indicate the ratio of two relevant characteristics in the brands. As usual consumers are considered to lie uniformly along a market line. Each consumes one unit of the product depending on his preference relative to the characteristic composition of the brands and the prices being charged. Specifically, some consumer i located at $0 \leqslant \theta_i \leqslant 1$ when selecting brand θ_j receives surplus $\{v - p_j - \alpha|\theta_i - \theta_j| - \beta(\theta_i - \theta_j)^2\}$ where v is i's reservation demand price, p_j is the price of brand j, and $\alpha, \beta > 0$ are constants. The disutility associated with using a nonideal brand is quadratic in the "distance" between the ideal brand and the brand taken. Without loss of generality let v be zero (alternatively, all prices can be thought of as "net" of v).

Piecewise Linear Demand. Following the layout of figure 5.11, we consider the firms to be located symmetrically in the market, each the same distance δ from the center point $1/2$. Consumers buy that brand which yields the greatest net surplus. This means that the demand faced by each firm is conditional on the price charged by its rival. Let $\theta^*(p_1, p_2)$ be the location of the marginal consumer, that is, that person just indifferent to the two brands. $\theta^*(p_1, p_2)$ derives from the solution of

$$p_1 + \alpha|\theta_1 - \theta^*| + \beta(\theta_1 - \theta^*)^2 = p_2 + \alpha|\theta_2 - \theta^*| + \beta(\theta_2 - \theta^*)^2$$

All consumers residing between 0 and θ^* choose brand 1, while those between θ^* and 1 choose brand 2. The demand function for firm 1 is piecewise linear with five price domains whose end-points depend on the θ^* location relative to the points 0, θ_1, θ_2, and 1.

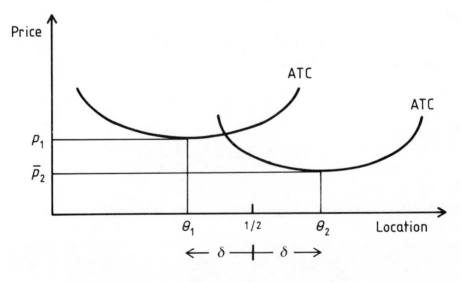

Figure 5.11
Market areas

Suppose that the price set by firm 2 is $\bar{p}_2$; then the demand faced by firm 1 is $z_1 = Id_1(p_1, \bar{p}_2)$ where there are I consumers along the $[0, 1]$ interval and

$$d_1(p_1 - \bar{p}_2) = 0 \qquad\qquad \text{for } p_1 \geq p_1{}^{a} \qquad (5.80a)$$

$$= \frac{\bar{p}_2 - p_1 + 2\delta(\alpha + \beta)}{4\delta\beta} \qquad \text{for } p_1{}^{a} > p_1 \geq p_1{}^{b} \qquad (5.80b)$$

$$= \frac{\bar{p}_2 - p_1 + \alpha + 2\delta\beta}{2(2\delta\beta + \alpha)} \qquad \text{for } p_1{}^{b} > p_1 \geq p_1{}^{c} \qquad (5.80c)$$

$$= \frac{\bar{p}_2 - p_1 + 2\delta(\alpha - \beta)}{4\delta\beta} \qquad \text{for } p_1{}^{c} > p_1 \geq p_1{}^{d} \qquad (5.80d)$$

$$= 1 \qquad\qquad \text{for } p^{d} > p_1 \geq 0 \qquad (5.80e)$$

with the boundary prices given by

$$p_1{}^{a} = \bar{p}_2 + 2\delta(\alpha + \beta)$$
$$p_1{}^{b} = \bar{p}_2 + 2\delta(\alpha + \delta\beta)$$
$$p_1{}^{c} = \bar{p}_2 - 2\delta(\alpha - \delta\beta)$$
$$p_1{}^{d} = \bar{p}_2 - 2\delta(\alpha + \beta)$$

The piecewise linear demand is illustrated in figure 5.12.

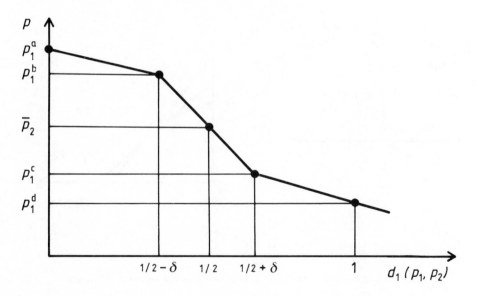

Figure 5.12
Firm 1's demand

It is of interest that a kink occurs in the demand at the price $p_1 = p_1{}^{c}$, where firm 1's market boundary is just at firm 2's location $\frac{1}{2} + \delta$. Similarly, when the boundary is just at 1's location $\frac{1}{2} - \delta$, with $p_1 = p_1{}^{b}$, there is also a kink. An analogous Nash-in-price demand schedule obtains for firm 2. Note finally that the same continuity, piecewise linearity, and attendant lack of concavity obtains for the firm's profit functions.

SE5.3   Vertical Differentiation and Demand for Quality

Suppose that, say, refrigerators differ by a scalar measure called quality. Let all consumers agree about the quality of each brand, but differ in their willingness to pay for this quality. Further, assume that every consumer has a constant marginal rate of substitution between brand quality and all other goods. For simplicity, let that rate be uniformly distributed in the cross-section of individuals.

Consumer Demand. Figure 5.13(a) sets out the one-dimensional market based on the above assumptions.[36] Consumers are located according to their strength of brand preference λ along the horizontal axis, with the vertical dividing marks indicating the consumer that is marginal between any two brands. For example, the individual located at λ_{32} is indifferent between products 3 and 2: those just to the right of that prefer product 3 and those just to the left prefer brand 2. Note also that, if the price of brand 2 were to be lowered, the individual at λ_{32} would then strictly prefer 2 and some other consumer to his right would then be marginal between brands 2 and 3.

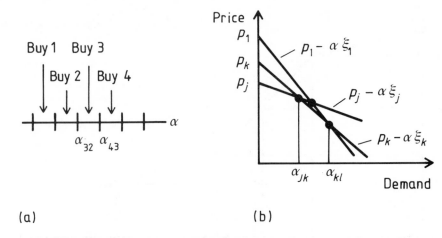

(a)   (b)

Figure 5.13
Consumer demand for brands: (a) one-dimensional market; (b) demand

Suppose further that each consumers's preference has the specific form:

$$u(\xi, y; \lambda) = y + \lambda\xi \qquad \text{if any brand } \xi \text{ is purchased} \tag{5.81}$$
$$= g(u; \lambda) \qquad \text{otherwise}$$

---

[36] This example is adapted from Bresnahan's (1981b) model of automobile demand.

where ξ indicates quality and y is the (constant) value of the money spent on the outside good. Moreover, it is assumed that λ is uniformly distributed with density ω on the market interval. The function $g(\cdot)$ measures the utility of the outside good to individuals with parameters y and λ. Clearly, the consumer with parameter λ will select the brand j with price p_j which maximizes $\lambda \xi_j - p_j$, provided that it chooses any brand instead of the outside good.

Market Demand for Given Brand. To aggregate individual demands into a "total industry" demand, it is necessary to first find the λ parameter of the consumers just indifferent to the various brands. To this end, let brands j and k have price and quality pairs (p_j, ξ_j) and (p_k, ξ_k) and suppose that k is the next higher brand in quality $(\xi_j < \xi_k)$. The consumer with rate of substitution λ_{jk} is indifferent to these brands when prices and qualities are such that

$$\lambda_{jk} \xi_k - p_k = \lambda_{jk} \xi_j - p_j$$

This condition can be solved for

$$\lambda_{jk} = \frac{p_k - p_j}{\xi_k - \xi_j} \tag{5.82}$$

Every consumer with a greater λ will prefer brand k, and those with a lower λ will prefer j.

The demand for brand k is made up of the line segment with end points given by the consumer marginal to k and j (the next brand below it in quality) and the consumer marginal to k and l (the brand next above it in quality). Equation (5.82) locates the jk marginal consumer. If it is assumed that there is a brand of higher quality than k, and kl marginal consumer can be found in exactly the same way. Brand k is purchased only by consumers lying in the interval $[\lambda_{jk}, \lambda_{kl}]$. With the uniform density of consumers, this then implies a demand function for k given by

$$z_k = \omega(\lambda_{kl} - \lambda_{jk}) \tag{5.83}$$

$$= \omega \left(\frac{p_l - p_k}{\xi_l - \xi_k} - \frac{p_k - p_j}{\xi_k - \xi_j} \right)$$

From this expression it is seen that the quality difference $\xi_k - \xi_j$ measures the strength of the k and j brands as substitutes. As this difference becomes smaller, the cross-derivative $\partial z_k / \partial p_j = \omega/(\xi_k - \xi_j)$ becomes closer (in absolute value) to the own-derivative $\partial z_k / \partial p_k = -\omega\{1/(\xi_k - \xi_j) - 1/(\xi_l - \xi_k)\}$.

The choices of consumers among brands j, k, and l are depicted in figure 5.12(b) with brand price on the vertical axis. The three lines set out the utility received by consumers of different taste as the prices of the three brands vary. For example, brand k is purchased by those consumers in the indicated λ_{jk}–λ_{kl} interval, as it is there that k yields greatest utility (smallest $p - \lambda\xi$). To the left of λ_{jk} brand j is chosen and to the right of λ_{kl} brand l is chosen.

SE5.4 Two Sectors, One Monopolistically Competitive

In this example we investigate how capacity, number of firms, and prices in a monopolistically competitive industry can depend on production in a second competitive sector. The economy is made up of individuals having identical preferences represented by

$$U = \left\{ \left(\sum_j z_j^{\sigma} \right)^{1/\sigma} \right\}^{\gamma} z_0^{1-\gamma} \tag{5.84}$$

with parameters $0 < \sigma \leq 1$ and $0 < \gamma < 1$. Here, z_0 is the quantity of the commodity produced in a second competitive market sector. The z_j, $j = 1, 2, \ldots, J$, are quantities of a heterogeneous variety produced under conditions of monopolistic competition. By this specification the elasticity of substitution between z_0 and *each* variety j is identical and equal to γ. In turn, the substitutability between every distinct pair of varieties j and k is symmetric and constant.

Production Technology. For the monopolistically competitive industry, suppose that each firm produces using a fixed-proportion technology with capital limitational:

$$z_j = 0 \qquad \text{for } \kappa_j < \kappa^*$$
$$= L_j/\beta \qquad \text{for } \kappa_j \geq \kappa^* \tag{5.85}$$

where κ_j is j's capital stock, ι^* is known as the *minimum efficient capital scale* (MES), L_j is the labor input, and $1/\beta$ is the (constant) marginal product of labor. Associated with this technology is the linear cost function

$$\text{TC}_j = \phi\kappa^* + \omega\beta z_j \tag{5.86}$$

for $z_j > 0$. Here, r is the constant unit cost of capital and ω similarly pertains to the labor factor. Since there are increasing returns in the production of each variety, assume that each firm specializes its production and j is then used to index both firms and varieties. In the competitive sector we alternatively assume that there are variable proportions in production given by a Cobb–Douglas technology

$$z_0 = \kappa_0^{\alpha} L_0^{1-\alpha} \tag{5.87}$$

where κ_0 and L_0 are capital and labor quantities respectively. Finally, assume that there is free entry into both the monopolistically competitive and the competitive sectors.

Consumer Demand. The stationarity conditions for the consumers' problems give the inverse demands

$$p_j = \frac{\gamma}{1 - \gamma} \frac{z_0 z_j^{\sigma-1}}{\Sigma_k z_k^{\sigma}} \tag{5.88}$$

(recall (5.64)).[37] Because the z_j enters symmetrically in the utility function and the cost structures of the monopolistically competitive firms are identical, there will be a symmetric equilibrium in output and price. Let $z_j = z$ and $p_j = p$ as a notational convenience. In this case (5.88) becomes

---

[37] Let z_0 be numeraire; then the stationarity of U with respect to z_0 yields $z_0 = 1/[(1 - \gamma)\{\Sigma_j(z_j^{\sigma})^{1/\sigma}\}^{\gamma}]$ which is used in (5.88).

$$p = \frac{\gamma}{1 - \gamma} \frac{z_0}{zJ} \tag{5.89}$$

In turn, each variety j has an own-elasticity of

$$\eta = \frac{1}{1 - \sigma + 1/J} \tag{5.90a}$$

If J is large, then as an approximation we have

$$\eta = \frac{1}{1 - \sigma} \tag{5.90b}$$

Firm Optimum. Each monopolistically competitive firm sets marginal revenue equal to marginal cost, which gives

$$\text{MR} = p\left(1 - \frac{1}{\eta}\right) = \beta\omega = \text{MC}$$

and, using (5.90b) there is an optimal price

$$p = \frac{\omega\beta}{\sigma} \tag{5.91}$$

for each firm.

Industry Equilibrium. Hold this result aside for the moment and look at the implications of the free-entry conditions. First, the profits of the monopolistically competitive firms can be written as

$$\pi_j = p_j z_j - \phi\kappa^* - \omega\beta z_j$$

Solving this for z_j at the free-entry equilibrium gives

$$z_j = \frac{\phi\kappa^*}{\omega\beta} \frac{\gamma}{1 - \gamma} \tag{5.92}$$

Notice that the larger is the MES, the larger will be the equilibrium z_j.

For the competitive industry it is easily shown that profit maximization requires

$$\omega L_0 = (1 - \alpha)z_0$$

$$\phi\kappa_0 = \alpha z_0$$

If there is a fixed stock of capital $\bar{\kappa}$ and labor $\bar{L}$ in the economy, then the conservation conditions

$$\bar{\kappa} = \kappa_0 + J\kappa_j^* \tag{5.93a}$$

$$\bar{L} = L_0 + JL_j \tag{5.93a}$$

must also be satisfied. Using these constraints in (5.90)–(5.92) finally gives

$$J = \frac{\bar{\kappa}}{\kappa^*} \frac{1}{1 + \psi} \tag{5.94}$$

where $\psi \equiv \alpha(1 - \gamma)/\gamma(1 - \sigma)$. The number of firms (brands) in the monopolistic competitive industry depends directly on the total capital stock and inversely on the MES, with parameters as indicated by ψ.

6 Product Variety and Welfare

A central, but often ignored, function of a market economy is the selection of product designs. When there are increasing returns in production a range of products sufficient to satisfy the tastes of diverse individuals is generally not optimal. The tradeoff is between quantity and variety: resources that can be saved by producing fewer product varieties and, with increasing returns, larger quantities of each will reach a level which offsets the consumers' disutility of reduced variety (see Makowski, 1980a, 1980b, and Ostroy, 1980, for several counter-examples). The economic calculus of this offsetting process is the focus of this chapter. Of particular interest is the level of product variety which is socially optimal and the industry conditions which provide that level.

We begin in the simplest way by considering the pure monopolist's choice of quality for a single product. In this analysis it is at once discovered that a fundamental problem in the provision of quality is that a (nondiscriminatory) market price conveys information about the value attached to product quality only by the marginal consumer and generally not by either *infra*marginal or *extra*marginal consumers. As sellers use market price as a basis for their production decisions, the properties of demand leading to the over- and under-supply of quality can be cataloged. That catalog and background completed, the final sections of the chapter address related problems in the supply of product variety. This analysis focuses on the tradeoff between consumer benefits, which generally increase with variety, and production efficiency which, because of scale economies, decreases with greater variety. Very briefly, the result is that there is no general relationship between socially optimal and equilibrium varieties. Whether or not variety will be over- or under-supplied in market equilibrium depends on a wide range of details by which the model economy is specified.

6.1 Monopoly and Product Selection

We begin with a single-firm monopolist whose product enters separably into an aggregate utility function

$$U(z, \xi; z_0) = u(z, \xi) + z_0 \tag{6.1}$$

where z is the monopolist's output level, ξ is its quality parameter, and z_0 is an all-other-products numeraire.[1] The utility U and subutility u are assumed to be continuous, differentiable, and strictly increasing and concave in both z and ξ. Because of the quasi-linearity, the inverse demand for z is given simply by the marginal utility

$$p(z, \xi) = \frac{\partial u(z, \xi)}{\partial z}$$

The particular variety of product offered by the monopolist is given by its specific choice of quality ξ.

6.1.1 Optimal and Equilibrium Quality

The monopolist's price, quantity, and product quality levels are **socially optimal** when they maximize aggregate surplus, which is the sum of consumer and producer surpluses.[2] For fixed ξ, the consumer surplus at output level z is given in the usual way by

$$\text{CS}(z, \xi) = \int_0^z p(s, \xi)\,\text{d}s - zp(z, \xi) \tag{6.2}$$

Producer surplus also has a simple expression: if we let $c(z, \xi)$ be the firm's cost of producing quantity z with quality ξ, then

$$\Pi(z, \xi) = zp(z, \xi) - c(z, \xi) \tag{6.3}$$

The expression for **aggregate surplus** $W(z, \xi) \equiv \text{CS}(z, \xi) + \Pi(z, \xi)$ derives from these definitions:

$$W(z, \xi) = \int_0^z p(s, \xi)\,\text{d}s - c(z, \xi) \tag{6.4}$$

which assumes that profits are fully disbursed to consumers (without drains). Let $W(z, \xi)$ be increasing and concave in both its arguments with $W(0, \xi) = W(z, 0) = 0$. Socially optimal choices of z and ξ maximize W.

Quantity Choice. Hold the monopolist's choice of product quality fixed at some specific level $\hat{\xi}$ for the moment and suppose that W has an interior maximum with respect to quantity, which is derived from the condition

$$\frac{\partial W(z, \hat{\xi})}{\partial z} = p(z, \hat{\xi}) - \frac{\partial c(z, \hat{\xi})}{\partial z} = 0 \tag{6.5}$$

Not surprisingly, this is the usual condition of price equality with marginal cost. We will refer to the quantity z solving this equation and maximizing aggregate surplus as *optimal* (for the given $\hat{\xi}$).

For the same given $\hat{\xi}$ and a monopolist using a pure (nondiscriminatory) price policy, profits are maximized otherwise, where price is generally in excess of

---

[1] Again, this is the case of vertical product differentiation; recall section 5.4.

[2] Recall from section 1.4 that the marginal utility of income is constant with specification 6.1 so that consumer surplus is an exact measure of compensating variation here.

marginal cost and determined by

$$p(z, \hat{\xi}) - \frac{\partial c(z, \xi)}{\partial z} = -z\frac{\partial p(z, \hat{\xi})}{\partial z} > 0 \tag{6.6}$$

The differences between (6.5) and (6.6) is the basis of the usual welfare loss associated with the monopolist's output decision. That loss is measured by M_zL and discussed at length in section 2.4. The z satisfying the maximum profit condition (6.6) is called the *equilibrium* quantity (again, for the given $\hat{\xi}$).

Quality Choice. Less well known are the welfare implications associated with potential differences between the firm's profit-maximizing choice of quality and the socially optimal level. This can be uncovered quite readily, however. Following Spence (1975), consider some specific output level $\hat{z}$ and note that W has a stationarity point with respect to ξ when

$$\frac{\partial W(\hat{z}, \xi)}{\partial \xi} = \hat{z}\{\bar{u}(\hat{z}, \xi) - \kappa(\hat{z}, \xi)\} = 0 \tag{6.7a}$$

where

$$\bar{u}(\hat{z}, \xi) \equiv \frac{1}{\hat{z}} \int_0^{\hat{z}} \frac{\partial p(s, \xi)}{\partial \xi} \, ds \tag{6.7b}$$

is the market's average value of incremental quality (averaged over the $\hat{z}$ units) and

$$\kappa(\hat{z}, \xi) \equiv \frac{1}{\hat{z}} \frac{\partial c(\hat{z}, \xi)}{\partial \xi} \tag{6.7c}$$

is the corresponding average cost of incremental quality. At the optimal margin, the *average* value of quality is equal to its *average* cost. In contrast, the profit maximum occurs with ξ such that

$$\frac{\partial \Pi(\hat{z}, \xi)}{\partial \xi} = \hat{z}\{\mu(\hat{z}, \xi) - \kappa(\hat{z}, \xi)\} = 0 \tag{6.8a}$$

where

$$\mu(\hat{z}, \xi) \equiv \frac{\partial p(\hat{z}, \xi)}{\partial \xi} \tag{6.8b}$$

is the market's *marginal* value of quality (at $\hat{z}$). It bears emphasizing that it is the value of marginal *quality* $\partial p(z, \xi)/\partial \xi$ at a fixed level of output appearing in the μ and $\bar{u}$ expressions and *not* the usual value of the marginal *quantity* $\partial p(z, \xi)/\partial z$ at fixed quality. That is, the key derivative here is *not* the usual slope of the inverse demand function.

Comparing (6.7a) and (6.8a), it is seen that the socially optimal level of quality is chosen by the monopolist only in the special case where average and marginal valuations of quality are equal: $\bar{u}(\hat{z}, \xi) = \mu(\hat{z}, \xi)$. (Again, $\hat{z}$ is fixed here; it can be chosen as profit maximizing, but that is not necessary for the moment.) What is the form of the quality bias when $\bar{u}(\hat{z}, \xi) \neq \mu(\hat{z}, \xi)$? Spence (1975) considers these questions as follows. Note first that $\partial W/\partial \xi = \partial CS/\partial \xi + \partial \Pi/\partial \xi$. With $\partial \Pi(\hat{z}, \xi)/\partial \xi = 0$,

$$\text{sgn}\left(\frac{\partial W}{\partial \xi}\right) = \text{sgn}\left(\frac{\partial CS}{\partial \xi}\right) = \text{sgn}\{\bar{u}(\hat{z}, \xi) - \mu(\hat{z}, \xi)\} \tag{6.9}$$

where the derivative of consumer surplus is a straightforward calculation using (6.2). Aggregate surplus is increasing in quality for $\bar{\mu}(\hat{z}, \xi) > \mu(\hat{z}, \xi)$, and in this case, the profit-maximizing firm under-supplies quality relative to the social optimum. Conversely, for $\bar{\mu}(\hat{z}, \xi) < \mu(\hat{z}, \xi)$ quality is over-supplied. Since the manner in which the marginal value of incremental quality $\mu(z, \xi)$ varies with output determines the average–marginal relationship at $\hat{z}$, it also determines whether quality is over- or under-supplied: when $\mu(z, \xi)$ falls uniformly with increasing z ($\partial\mu/\partial z = \partial^2 p/\partial\xi\partial z < 0$), then $\bar{\mu}(\hat{z}, \xi) > \mu(\hat{z}, \xi)$ and, conversely, when $\mu(z, \xi)$ increases uniformly with z up to $\hat{z}$ ($\partial\mu/\partial z > 0$), then $\bar{\mu}(\hat{z}, \xi) < \mu(\hat{z}, \xi)$.

Figure 6.1 illustrates these cases. Note in the figure that the level of quality ξ is held fixed throughout and *only* quantity changes generate the $\bar{\mu}$ and μ schedules.

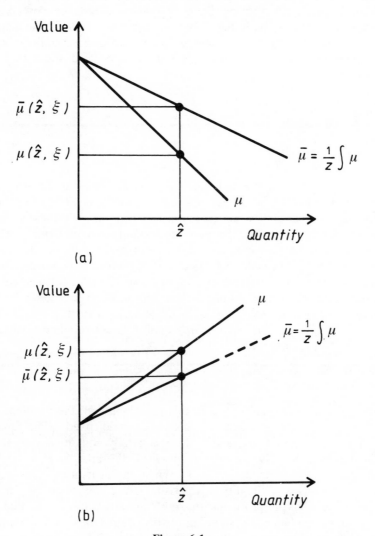

Figure 6.1
Valuation of quality as quantity changes: (a) $\partial\mu(z, \xi)/\partial z < 0$; (b) $\partial\mu(z, \xi)/\partial z > 0$

The above results can be made somewhat more intuitive by thinking of a small discrete change in quality. Consider specifically a monopolist deciding whether or not to increase the quality of its product by some small amount while holding its output constant. If it decides on the increase, this will lead to changes in both its revenues and its costs. Costs go up by Δc, the value of the product increases at the margin by $\Delta p(z)$, and concomitantly revenues go up by the amount $z\Delta p(z)$. The decision to increase quality and set off this chain of events depends as usual on whether or not it is profitable, that is, whether or not $z\Delta p(z) > \Delta c$. When the monopolist's decision is based on maximum profits and price is determined in the usual way, the quality choice is generally inconsistent with the welfare optimal choice which should be based on whether the gross benefit of the quality change $\int_0^z \Delta p(s)\,ds$ exceeds its total cost or equivalently, given z is fixed, whether the average benefit of the quality change $(1/z)\int_0^z \Delta p(s)\,ds$ exceeds the increment it brings to average cost $\Delta c/z$. This social value is identical with the firm's revenue only when the valuation of quality at the margin equals its average value. Otherwise, quality is under- or over-supplied. Unfortunately, nothing general can be said about this average–marginal relationship.

E6.1

The Value of Quality

A specific numerical example helps in fixing the above ideas. Let the monopolist's inverse demand be given by $p = \xi - \beta z^\delta$ with β, $\delta > 0$. For this case straightforward calculations using (6.7b) and (6.8b) show that $\bar{\mu} = 1$ and $\mu = 1$. Changes in quality only shift the inverse demand intercept and therefore the valuation of *each* unit, marginal and inframarginal, changes identically. For every z, quality is optimally supplied by the profit-maximizing monopolist regardless of the demand parameters β and δ. Specifically, for a linear demand ($\delta = 1$) the values of μ and $\bar{\mu}$ do not depend on the slope parameter β.

Suppose, alternatively, that $p = \xi(1 - \beta z^\delta)$, again with β, $\delta > 0$. In this case $\bar{\mu} - \mu = \beta\hat{z}^\delta\{1 - 1/(1 + \delta)\} > 0$, leaving quality under-supplied (at the fixed $\hat{z}$ level) relative to the optimum.

Optimal Quantity and Quality. Up to this point only half the problem has been considered at any instant: quantity has been held fixed while quality was permitted to vary, and conversely. More generally, quantity and quality are determined simultaneously for a maximum of W, and they are determined simultaneously for a maximum of Π. When both quantity and quality are endogenous in this way, quality comparisons are complicated by the fact that the output level which is profit maximizing generally differs from that which is welfare maximizing. Our understanding of this complexity is aided somewhat by focusing first on the quality choice. To this end, let $z^0(\xi)$ give the profit-maximizing output as a function of ξ, and similarly let $z^*(\xi)$ give the optimal z

for each ξ. These are solutions of equations (6.6) and (6.5) respectively.

Using the Leibnitz rule for differentiation, the *optimum optimorium* of W is given by the stationarity condition

$$\frac{dW(z^*(\xi), \xi)}{d\xi} = p(z^*(\xi), \xi) \frac{dz^*(\xi)}{d\xi} + \int_0^{z^*} \frac{dp(s, \xi)}{\partial\xi} \, ds$$

$$- \frac{dc(z^*(\xi), \xi)}{dz^*} \frac{dz^*(\xi)}{d\xi} - \frac{dc(z^*(\xi), \xi)}{d\xi} = 0 \qquad (6.10a)$$

Grouping, factoring $dz^*/d\xi$, and using (6.5) reduces this to

$$z^*\{\bar{\mu}(z^*, \xi) - \kappa(z^*, \xi)\} = 0 \qquad (6.10b)$$

Alternatively, at the profit *optimum optimorium*,

$$\frac{d\Pi(z^0(\xi), \xi)}{d\xi} = \frac{dp(z^0(\xi), \xi)}{dz^0} \frac{dz^0(\xi)}{d\xi} + \frac{dp(z^0(\xi), \xi)}{d\xi}$$

$$+ \frac{dc(z^0(\xi), \xi)}{dz^0} \frac{dz^0(\xi)}{d\xi} - \frac{dc(z^0(\xi), \xi)}{d\xi} = 0 \qquad (6.11a)$$

Using (6.8a) this reduces to

$$z^0\{\mu(z^0, \xi) - \kappa(z^0, \xi)\} = 0 \qquad (6.11b)$$

From (6.10) aggregate surplus is increasing in quality when $\bar{\mu}(z^*, \xi) > \kappa(z^*, \xi)$ and, from (6.11), profit is increasing in quality when $\mu(z^0, \xi) > \kappa(z^0, \xi)$. The different output levels affect the μ, $\bar{\mu}$ and κ measures and further confound the comparison of optimal and equilibrium quality.[3]

E6.2 ──────────────────────────────────────

Resale Price Maintenance and Quality

Telser (1960) and Marvel and McCafferty (1984) have argued that resale price maintenance (RPM) is used by a manufacturer to increase the extent of nonprice competition among its retailer–dealers and specifically to assure that certain point-of-sale services are provided. Their analyses focus on products that cannot be marketed effectively by dealers without maintaining large inventories, highly trained and motivated salespeople, or other such costly presale services. Suppose that the manufacturer fixed a minimum dealer-to-customer price that exceeds the cost of reselling its product without any such services. In this circumstance the dealers will compete among themselves along nonprice lines

---

[3] While there is no general way to unconfound quantity and quality differences when comparing (6.10) with (6.11), one special case is partially helpful. Suppose that there are constant marginal costs c and a fixed cost F, giving total cost $c(z, \xi) = c(\xi)z + F$. Then, $\kappa(z^*, \xi) = \kappa(z^0, \xi)$. (Otherwise we might require z^* to be "close" to z^0 and κ to be a "nearly" constant function of z.) Comparing (6.10) and (6.11) in this case, we find that whether or not the monopolist over-supplies or under-supplies quality depends on the sign of $\bar{\mu}(z^*, \xi) - \mu(z^0, \xi)$. While there is no difficulty in principle in establishing this sign, in practice the calculation is complicated by the different outputs. More generally, both the conditions of demand and cost will determine whether quality is over- or under-supplied.

(point-of-sales services) to gain a market advantage. Telser maintained that this competition generally continues until the margin is reached where the dealers' reselling cost equals the manufacturer's fixed retail price. The competitive (homogeneous) dealers receive no profit and, by adjusting the retail price, the manufacturer can establish the level of point-of-sale services that will be offered with its product.

Telser further argued that alternatives to RPM are not viable as they would generally involve large transaction costs. Unrestricted competition on price encourages dealers to "free ride" on those dealers providing the higher-level services, since the manufacturer cannot (legally) provide compensation to just those cooperating dealers (say, by discrimination in wholesale price). RPM is said to be a welfare-increasing vertical restraint in these cases, for the firm will maintain that level of competitive retail price where the dealer services provided just equal their value to the marginal consumer.[4] Bork (1978, chs 1 and 4) and Posner (1976), for example, make this efficiency argument. From the above analysis of optimal quality provision the reader now knows that such welfare statements cannot be made on the basis only of the marginal valuation of services. Although the marginal consumer may benefit from RPM services, inframarginal consumers may be made worse off.

Comanor (1985) and Comanor and Kirkwood (1985) have specifically argued that *infra*marginal customers are likely to be knowledgeable in the sense that they would not benefit importantly from the point-of-sale services brought on by RPM, while the customers *at the margin* are likely to be less knowledgeable. Ignoring quantity and cost differences at the pre- and post-RPM levels, they in turn argue that $\bar{\mu}(z, \xi^0) < \mu(z, \xi^0)$, where ξ^0 is the RPM level of services, so that the services are over-supplied. That is a correct conclusion, given their full range of assumptions. However, admitting the pre- and post-RPM quantity and cost differences and using the equally plausible converse assumption concerning who is knowledgeable and who is not (as, for example, suggested by Salop and Stiglitz, 1977) might alternatively lead to the conclusion that RPM services are optimal or under-supplied.

Quality and Market Structure. It is important to note that the above results do *not* imply that the bias in product quality occurs only in the presence of monopoly output restrictions. Suppose that marginal costs are constant in output but increasing in product quality, $c(z, \xi) = c(\xi)z + F$, and let the industry

---

[4] Marvel and McCafferty (1984) use a complement to Telser's free-riding argument. They note (p. 348) that "Retailers are responsible for much more than mere warehousing. They serve as their customers' agents, selecting from a wide variety of available merchandise those items most likely to appeal to their clientele. By stocking a particular product on its shelves, the retailer attests that the quality and suitability of the items in question are consonant with the retailer's overall reputation. But this sort of dealer recommendation is subject to the same sort of free-riding as more tangible presale services. Consumers who are familiar with the reputation of a retailer as well as the branded items that retailer offers for sale will find such information useful even if they purchase the goods elsewhere. So long as branding ensures consistent quality of the good across dealers, high-quality dealers will be unable to capture a premium price for the certification they provide."

output be chosen at the socially optimal level by competitive price-taking firms $z^0 = z^*$. Quality is still under-supplied when $\mu(z^*, \xi)$ is decreasing in z despite the fact that there is a competitive equilibrium. Conversely, when $\mu(z^*, \xi)$ is increasing in z, the competitive equilibrium will over-supply quality. In fact, the monopoly restriction of output may result in a more nearly optimal supply of quality. To see this, suppose that the marginal value of quality falls with greater levels of output and the monopoly output is less than optimal ($z^0 < z^*$); then it may be that the average value $\bar{\mu}(z^*, \xi)$ (at the greater output z^*) will be closer to the marginal value $\mu(z^0, \xi)$ (at the lesser output z^0) than is the marginal value $\mu(z^*, \xi)$ (at z^*). This case is illustrated in figure 6.2. As drawn there, the monopolist over-supplies quality, but not to the extent that would be true if it were to produce the greater quantity z^*. In fact, if the monopolist were to further restrict output to the level $\bar{z}$, it would be supplying optimal quality. Do not be misled in this case: although *quality* is optimally supplied, this is clearly not the first-best situation as the *output* level is obviously not optimal.

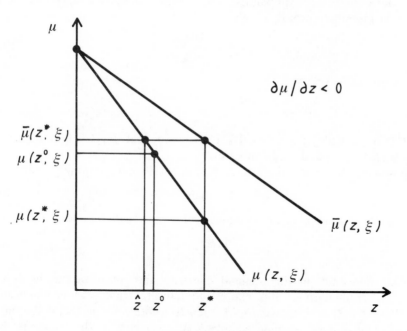

Figure 6.2
Equilibrium and optimal quality

The Lesson. The essential source of the quality bias lies not in the degree of competition (or monopoly), but more generally in the limited information content of price (provided that the firm is not discriminating in price). The profit-maximizing (nondiscriminatory) monopolist and competitive industry both reach their quality decision based on the price that will be paid for quality at the *margin*. In contrast, a quality increase is socially desirable if the *average* benefit $\bar{\mu}(z, \xi)$ exceeds the *average* cost $\kappa(z, \xi)$. The inefficiency arises because these social benefits imply an increase in firm profits only if the marginal "consumer" is also average, that is, if $\bar{\mu}(z, \xi) = \mu(z, \xi)$. There is, however, nothing which assures this constancy of the marginal "consumer"; in fact, that restriction seems rather unlikely in general.

E6.3

Quality Supply and Demand Elasticity

For the case where the elasticity of demand is independent of quantity, but may depend on quality, Spence (1976a) has developed a specific measure of quality bias. His analysis begins with the "partial" maxima defined with respect to quantity:

$$W^*(\xi) = \max_z W(z, \xi) \qquad (6.12a)$$

and

$$\Pi^0(\xi) = \max_z \Pi(z, \xi) \qquad (6.12b)$$

Let the ratio of these expressions, that is, the fraction of aggregate surplus captured as monopoly profits, be given by

$$\beta(\xi) \equiv \frac{\Pi^0(\xi)}{W^*(\xi)} \qquad (6.13)$$

Differentiating this yields

$$\beta'(\xi) \equiv \frac{d\beta(\xi)}{d\xi} = -\frac{dW^*(\xi)}{d\xi} \frac{\Pi^0}{(W^*)^2} \qquad (6.14)$$

For $\Pi^0 > 0$, $\text{sgn}\{\beta'(\xi)\} = -\text{sgn}\{dW^*(\xi)/d\xi\}$ so that $\beta'(\xi) < 0$ indicates that quality is under-supplied, and conversely.

Suppose now that demand elasticity $\eta(\xi)$ depends *only* on quality and

$$p(z, \xi) = f(\xi)z^{-1/\eta(\xi)} \qquad (6.15)$$

Some differentiation and rearranging using this specification yields

$$\beta(\xi) = \left\{1 - \frac{1}{\eta(\xi)}\right\}^{\eta(\xi)} \qquad (6.16)$$

which depends only on the demand elasticity and, in turn, on the level of quality. Differentiation of this expression indicates that $\beta(\xi)$ is increasing in $\eta(\xi)$. Thus, if $\eta(\xi)$ is decreasing in ξ, then so is $\beta(\xi)$. Using (6.14) this in turn indicates that quality is under-supplied. Conversely, if the elasticity is an increasing function of quality, then quality is over-supplied, and if η does not vary with quality, then the monopoly chooses the optimal level of quality (for its output).

6.2   Product Variety with Symmetric Substitutes

The product quality chosen by the monopolist is one aspect of product diversity in an economy. A second concern is with the rate of product innovation and the level of product variety in oligopolistic interactions. Since the underlying problem in the monopoly supply of quality is that price does not reflect marginal quality valuation, we suspect a similar market failure mechanism in the provision of product variety (brands): the profits of the marginal brand that would be sufficient to lead to its market appearance will not generally equal the brand's contribution to aggregate surplus.[5] A divergence therefore arises between the product variety that would be selected for production from a social standpoint and that occurring in an equilibrium of profit-maximizing firms. Does such a market failure mechanism also operate when firms are monopolistically competitive?

Demand. Suppose that there is a continuum of firms indexed by j. Each is assumed to produce (actually or potentially) a differentiated, imperfectly substitutable product. Let z_j be the output of the particular firm j, and let J be the set of firms producing at any stage of the industry development (sometimes called *active* firms). Aggregate utility is assumed to be quasi-linear and of the specific form

$$\hat{u}(z, y) = u\left(\int_{j \in J} v_j(z_j)) + z_0\right) \tag{6.17}$$

where y is income, $u(v)$ is an increasing concave function of $v \equiv \int_{j \in J} v_j(z_j)$, and each v_j is increasing and concave in z_j with $v_j(0) = 0$. This specification of utility is similar to that used in chapter 5, section 5.3, and the reader is referred there for full details.

Given the quasi-linearity of utility, the inverse demand for each j is simply

$$p_j(z_j) = u'(v)v_j'(z_j) \tag{6.18}$$

where the primes indicate the obvious partial derivatives. It is of particular note that $u'(v)$ is a proportionality factor common to the (inverse) demand of each firm. With the entry of a new firm to the market and, *ceteris paribus*, an increase in v, the inverse demand of each active firm falls by the same proportion (since marginal utility is decreasing in v). Being related in this way to the number of firms (products), v is thought of as an index of product variety in the sense that an increase in variety increases v and decreases $u'(v)$, which leads to a downward shift in demand for any brand.

Profits. For each active firms j assume that the total costs $c_j(z_j)$ are increasing and convex in output. In turn, profits can be written as

$$\pi_j(z_j) = u'(v)v_j'(z_j)z_j - c_j(z_j) \tag{6.19}$$

In this form, it is seen that the competitive interaction among firms occurs only through the aggregate product variety variable v and, more directly, the demand proportionality factor $u'(v)$. Using (6.19) with given v and $u'(v)$, we find that firm j will be profitable if and only if[6]

---

[5] Again, it is assumed that firms do not price discriminate.

[6] With perfect substitutes $v_j(z_j) = z_j$ and therefore $v_j' = 1$. In this case (6.20) reduces to the usual condition that price is greater than average cost.

$$u'(v) \geqslant \frac{c_j(z_j)}{z_j v_j'(z_j)} \tag{6.20}$$

E6.4 ——

Demand for Product Variety

Dixit and Stiglitz (1977) have provided an equilibrium solution to the above model using specific functional forms for utility and cost. To begin, they let $v_j(z_j) \equiv z_j^{\sigma}$, $0 < \sigma < 1$ and $v \equiv \int_{j \in J} v_j$, which gives (6.17) the form $U = u(v) + z_0$. Next, they use the cost function $c_j(z_j) = F + cz_j = F + cv_j^{1/\sigma}$ so that the profit function (6.19) has the specific form

$$\pi_j(v_j) = \rho v_j - (F + cv_j^{1/\sigma})$$

where $\rho = u'(v)\sigma$ is the price of the v-output. Conditions for a zero-profit Nash-in-v equilibrium are then

$$\rho(1 - \eta_j) = \frac{c}{\sigma} v_j^{1/\sigma - 1}$$

$$\rho v_j = F + cv_j^{1/\sigma}$$

where $\eta_j = \{(v/\rho)(\partial \rho / \partial v)\} v_j / v$ is the elasticity of the v-demand times firm j's v-market share. These two expressions correspond to the marginal revenue equality with marginal cost at the profit maximum and revenue equality with cost when there is free entry. In the large-numbers case v_j/v is small, and these two expressions reduce to the usual condition that price equals marginal cost equals average cost (the long-run competitive solution in the homogeneous v-output).

Excess Capacity and Optimal Variety. In the v-market each firm produces at the welfare optimum, minimum unit cost scale. The traditional excess capacity argument (recall chapter 4, section 4.2) based on the monopolistic competition equilibrium at the usual tangency point where the firm's downward-sloping demand equals average cost, is thus seen to be inappropriate as it fails to consider consumer's demand for variety. This, we should note, is consistent with Demsetz's (1959, 1964) early observations that Chamberlin's analysis fails to consider preference for variety and that, when such preferences are properly accounted for, the level of output in a monopolistic competition equilibrium is in fact socially optimal.

The optimality of output is not first best, however, as it is straightforward to show in this model that product variety is under-supplied. In figure 6.3 the long-run supply (LRS) schedule is indicated as the locus of minimum average costs for the succession of firms producing greater outputs. The v-product demand $\rho(v)$ and the industry equilibrium output v^0 are also indicated. In addition to $\rho(v)$ there is the marginal utility of the v-output $\partial U/\partial v = u'(v) = \rho(v)/\sigma$. Since $0 < \sigma < 1$, the marginal utility schedule lies everywhere (proportionately) above the v-demand as shown in the figure. In turn, the socially optimal level of variety (measured by v) is given at v^*, at the

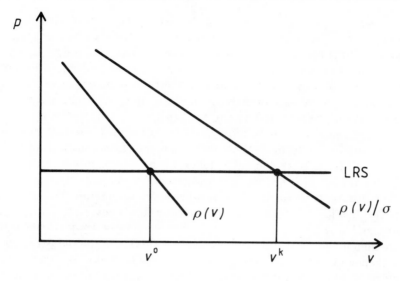

Figure 6.3
Under-supply of variety

intersection of the marginal utility and marginal cost of v. This particular equilibrium provides insufficient variety. It is important to note that this result is quite specific to the assumptions that have been made, as will be clear from developments later in this chapter.

6.2.1 Entry and Variety

Our immediate interest is in the extent of product variety in a large-numbers free-entry competitive industry. Chamberlin's monopolistic competition is the model commonly used in this regard, and it is used here with two modifications. First, with the entry of new firms the aggregate output (and variety) measured by v will be assumed to increase. Because of decreasing marginal utility, $u'(v)$ will then fall with the entry and each firm will have its demand "shifted in" proportionately, in the fashion of Chamberlin. With rising marginal cost this will in turn cause each inframarginal firm to restrict its output. While this will cause the sum of the $v_j(z_j)$ for the inframarginal firms to decrease, the marginal firm's contribution to v must more than offset that decrease. The second assumption is also tied to the nature of competition. While v is assumed to increase with entry, it is nonetheless assumed that each firm is a price-taker in the sense that it perceives that its output changes do not affect v and, in turn, the $u'(v)$ price proportionality factor. (This second assumption has already been used in E6.4.) We refer to these as the **modified monopolistic competition** (MMC) assumptions.

Entry Sequence. Suppose, for the moment, that all existing and potential firms are identical in both the products they offer and their cost. In this case, the ordering of firms for entry would be irrelevant – none could produce any level of z-product or v-product at lower cost than any other. When this strong degree of homogeneity does not obtain it seems clear that the specific identity of active and inactive firms becomes important, as is the sequence of entry. Less efficient firms, measured in terms of their greater cost to produce revenues for any level of $u'(v)$, would be expected to be inactive and the sequence of entry or exit as $u'(v)$ changes should be directly related to this efficiency. What specific differences should be admitted among the firms?

To begin, assume that firms differ in both the kind of product they produce and their cost of production. Whether or not any firm can be profitable with some given v depends on the value taken on by the right-hand side of (6.20). Specifically, the list of firms that can be sustained in the industry depends on the minimum firm-specific values of that right-hand side term. Those firms with $\min_{z_j}\{c_j(v_j)/z_jv_j'(z_j)\} < u'(v)$ will be profitable, and conversely. Moreover, as v increases and $u'(v)$ decreases, the collection of profitable firms (measured by these minimum values) will decrease. Thus, to survive in the industry firms must reduce their cost per dollar revenue to a minimum. Following Spence (1976a), this suggests that we catalog exit and entry opportunities according to a sequence index s^0 given for each firm j by[7]

$$s_j^{\,0} \equiv \min_{z_j} \left\{ \frac{c_j(z_j)}{z_jv_j'(z_j)} \right\} \tag{6.21}$$

To ease the notation somewhat renumber the firms such that for any two distinct firms m and n, $s_m^{\,0} > s_n^{\,0}$ implies $m > n$, and conversely. The ordering of firms by the s^0 index reveals the list of firms in the industry at each moment. For example, let J indicate the marginal firm which, for some given v, causes (6.20) to hold with equality. Then all firms $j \leqslant J$ will be profitable and active, and conversely all those $k > J$ will be unprofitable and remain outside the industry.

The specific output which minimizes (6.21) derives from the stationarity condition

$$\frac{c_j(z_j)}{z_jv_j'(z_j)} = c_j'(z_j)\{v_j'(z_j) + z_jv_j''(z_j)\} \tag{6.22}$$

Notice that the minimizing z_j does not depend on the aggregate product variety variable v, and therefore the ordering of firms by $s_j^{\,0}$ is unaffected by the number which are active. If firms were to enter the industry arbitrarily, it would generally be the case that firms arriving early-on incur negative profits with new entry, so that they would then have to exit. Such "mistakes" do not occur with entry by ascending s^0 values.

Equilibrium Variety. By reason of the aggregate utility specification (6.17) the rivalrous interaction among firms occurs only through the aggregate variable v. Despite this, the monopolistic competition assumption here is that firms perceive that their output decisions do not affect v. The equilibrium therefore takes on a quite simplified form. The first of the equilibrium conditions are those occurring

[7] Strictly, the revenues of firm j are $p_jz_j = (u'v')z_j$, but u' appears in the denominator of $s_j^{\,0}$ for each firm. As a result, the ordering of firm by $s_j^{\,0}$ is identical with the ordering of firms by cost per unit revenue.

with the profit maximization behavior $(\partial \pi_j / \partial z_j)_v = 0$, which yields

$$u'(v) = \frac{c_j'(z_j)}{v_j'(z_j) + v_j''(z_j)z_j} \tag{6.23}$$

In addition, the long-run equilibrium requires that the marginal firm J earns zero profits: $\pi_J = 0$. The conditions given by (6.22) and (6.23) jointly with $\pi_J = 0$ determine equilibrium outputs, aggregated variety v, and prices.

To develop some intuition about the equilibrium conditions it is helpful to think of the process by which they come to be satisfied. Suppose that entry is sequential. Each potential entrant calculates its profit opportunity *post*-entry, given the extant firms. Following the MMC assumptions, the entry causes v to increase and $u'(v)$ to fall. At the same time that the demand shifts in for each firm, caused by the smaller u', the s^0 index of the (new) marginal firm rises. At long-run equilibrium the marginal firm J just makes zero profits and $u' = s_J$. (Note also that $u' \geqslant s_J^0$ for all firms $j < J$ because s^0 ranks by profitability. The converse holds for inactive firms, none of which can be profitable at the equilibrium u'.) Figure 6.4 illustrates these results. There, because u' is strictly decreasing in the number of active firms and s^0 is strictly increasing, a uniform convergence to the unique equilibrium variety J^0 occurs.

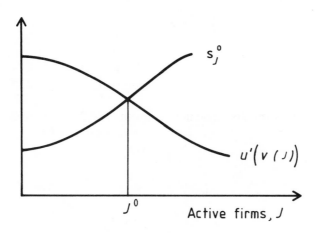

Figure 6.4
Equilibrium variety

E6.5

Equilibrium Variety: A Special Case

A numerical example is helpful here. Let the aggregate utility be given by $u(v) = v^\theta$ with $v = \int_j \alpha_j z_j$. Each firm's cost includes fixed and variable components $c_j(z_j) = \bar{c}_j z_j^2 + F_j$, where $\bar{c}_j$ is the constant unit cost and F_j is the fixed part. Firms enter the industry according to the s^0 ordering, which for each firm j is given by (6.22)

$$s_j^0 = \min_{z_j} \left(\frac{\bar{c}_j z_j^2 + F_j}{z_j v_j'(z_j)} \right) = \frac{2}{\alpha_j} (\bar{c}_j F_j)^{1/2}$$

The cost parameters $\bar{c}_j$ and F_j and the demand parameter α_j determine the order of entry. Roughly, firms with low cost parameters and high α_j have low s_j^0 and enter early; large cost parameters and low α_j bring late entry.

Each firm chooses a profit-maximizing output assuming that the aggregate v level is fixed, that is, each solves

$$\max_{z_j} (u'\alpha_j z_j - \bar{c}_j z_j^2 - F_j) \tag{6.24}$$

which has the stationarity condition (for producing firms)

$$u'\alpha_j = 2\bar{c}_j z_j$$

or

$$u' = \frac{2\bar{c}_j z_j}{\alpha_j} \tag{6.25}$$

Since u' is independent of j, the outputs must be chosen so that the right-hand side of (6.25) is equal for all producing firms. In addition, the last (marginal) firm J to enter must earn zero profits, which requires

$$u'v_j' = \bar{c}_j z_J - \frac{F_J}{z_J}$$

This solves for

$$u' = \frac{1}{\alpha_J} \left(\bar{c}_J z_J - \frac{F_J}{z_J} \right) \tag{6.26}$$

Since the marginal firm also maximizes profits, (6.25) and (6.26) must hold jointly and therefore

$$z_J = \left(\frac{F_J}{\bar{c}_J} \right)^{1/2} \tag{6.27}$$

Finally, using (6.25) u' is determined as

$$u' = \frac{2}{\alpha_J} (F_J \bar{c}_J)^{1/2} \tag{6.28}$$

and the quantity

$$z_J = \frac{\alpha_J}{2\bar{c}_j} u' = \frac{\alpha_j}{\bar{c}_j} \left(\frac{F_J \bar{c}_J}{\alpha_J^2} \right)^{1/2} \tag{6.29}$$

is produced by the inframarginal firms $j < J$.

6.2.2   Optimal Variety

In contrast with equilibrium conditions, the welfare optimum requires that the number of firms J and the output level of each be chosen to maximize the aggregate surplus

$$W(v, z) = u(v) - \int_{j \in J} c_j(z_j) \tag{6.30}$$

Again, $v = \int_{j \in J} v_j(z_j)$ depends on the number of producing firms, the associated v_j "technology" of each, and the output levels. Spence (1976a) has offered an instructive solution for the welfare maximum by addressing two nested problems, that is,

$$\max_{v} \left[u(v) - \min_{z,j} \left\{ \int_{j \in J} c_j(z_j) \text{ s.t. } \int_{j \in J} v_j(z_j) = v \right\} \right] \tag{6.31}$$

In this form, the solution procedure is to work the optimization stagewise, beginning with the "inner" problem

$$C(v) \equiv \left\{ \min_{z,J} \int_{j \in J} c_j(z_j) \text{ s.t. } \int_{j \in J} v_j(z_j) = v \right\} \tag{6.32}$$

$C(v)$ is the minimum cost as a function of the aggregate variety v defined by this inner solution. This function is then used in the "outer" maximizing problem to determine the overall solution

$$\max_{v} \{ u(v) - C(v) \} \tag{6.33}$$

Inner Minimization. In the cost minimization problem (6.32) both the number and the identity of producing firms are critical to the solution. To see this, suppose that there is a fixed number of producing firms, each of which chooses an output level to satisfy the (inner) constrained cost minimization. Each of these active firms chooses its z_j to solve

$$\frac{c_j'(z_j)}{v_j'(z_j)} = \lambda \tag{6.34}$$

where λ is the multiplier associated with the v constraint. This requires that the incremental cost associated with changes in v_j be equalized across producing firms. An infinite variety of output vectors satisfies this set of marginal conditions, depending on the specific collection of firms in the market. For example, if the cost minimization were accomplished using a collection of relatively high-cost firms, the minimum achieved would also be relatively high. Some procedure is therefore needed for selecting the producing firms in a way which minimizes the minimum cost for the given v. The obvious solution here is to identify and order firms by a "minimum cost per unit v" index s^* where for each firm j

$$s_j^* \equiv \min_{z_j} \left\{ \frac{c_j(z_j)}{v_j(z_j)} \right\} \tag{6.35a}$$

To keep the inner cost to a minimum (for the given v), all that is then necessary is to select J firms so that no inactive firm has a smaller s_j^* than any active firm. Let the output z_j^* solve (6.35a), that is,

$$\frac{c_j(z_j^*)}{v_j(z_j^*)} = \frac{c_j'(z_j^*)}{v_j'(z_j^*)} \tag{6.35b}$$

Finally, renumber firms by this index such that for two distinct firms m and n, $s_m^* > s_n^*$ implies $m > n$, and conversely.

How many firms should there be? What is the optimal J? For a given v, minimizing J solves

$$C(v) \equiv \min_J \left[\int_{j \in J} c_j(z_j^*) - \lambda \left\{ \int_{j \in J} v_j(z_j^*) - v \right\} \right] \qquad (6.36)$$

The stationarity condition associated with this minimum is

$$\lambda = \frac{c_J(z_J^*)}{v_J(z_J^*)} \qquad (6.37)$$

The reader will recognize this as the left-hand side of the necessary condition (6.35b) for c_j/v_j to be minimized. Thus there are the following relationships for the socially optimal marginal firm J:

$$\lambda = \frac{c_J}{v_J} = \frac{c_J'}{v_J'} = s_J^* \qquad (6.38)$$

For the socially optimal inframarginal firms $(j < J)$ the relationship (6.35b) obtains.

Outer Maximization. Suppose that the number and identity of firms and their output levels are determined in the above way. Aggregate surplus can then be written as a function of v: $u(v) - C(v)$. This has an interior maximum with respect to v given by $u'(v) = C'(v)$. From the envelope theorem applied to (6.36) note that $C'(v) = \lambda(v)$. Using these facts and (6.38) finally gives

$$u'(v) = C'(v) = \lambda(v) = s_J^* \qquad (6.39)$$

at the *optimum optimorium*. Substituting $u'(v)$ for λ in (6.34) it is seen that each producing firm chooses z_j such that $u'(v)v_j'(z_j) = c_j'(z_j)$. The left-hand side of this equality is simply price, so that the marginal cost pricing rule for the welfare optimum occurs as usual. This marginal condition *and* the sequencing of the product entries by (6.35) are the essential determinants of the welfare optimum.

These results are illustrated in figure 6.5. With s_J^* strictly increasing in J and

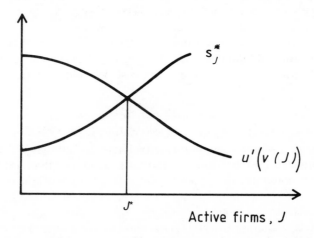

Figure 6.5
Optimal variety

$u'(v(J))$ strictly decreasing in J, there is uniform convergence to the unique optimal number of firms J^*. It is important for the reader to note that the $u'(v)$ schedule in figure 6.5 is based on the marginal cost equals price rule for determining z_j, $v_j(z_j)$, and in turn $v = \int_0^J v_j(z_j)$. In contrast, the $u'(v)$ schedule which is used in determining the equilibrium variety in figure 6.4 is based on the (generally different) marginal cost equals marginal revenue rule.

E6.6

Optimal Variety: A Special Case

Suppose that $c_j = \beta_j z_j + F_j$ and $v_j = \alpha_j \exp(z_j)$. This example derives the ordering of firms as they would optimally enter the industry, identifies the marginal firm, and derives the price and outputs of each at the social optimum.

The ordering for optimal entry is by the s^* index given by (6.35)

$$s_j^* = \min_{z_j} \left\{ \frac{\beta_j z_j + f_j}{\alpha_j \exp(z_j)} \right\} \tag{6.40}$$

which solves for

$$s_j^* = \frac{\beta_j}{\alpha_j \exp\{(\beta_j - F_j)/\beta_j\}} \tag{6.41}$$

Using (6.39) gives

$$u'(v) = \frac{\beta_J}{\alpha_J \exp\{(\beta_J - F_J)/\beta_J\}} \tag{6.42}$$

where J indicates the marginal firm at the optimum. Finally, there is, the price to prevail for each product

$$p_j = u'(v)v_j' = \alpha_j \exp(z_j^*)u'(v) \tag{6.43}$$

where z_j^* is given by (6.40) and $u'(v)$ by (6.42).

6.2.3 Equilibrium and Optimality

Equilibrium variety and output levels are generally not a welfare optimum. The first source of divergence arises from the different entry sequences of firms: profit-maximizing firms enter according to increasing values of $s_j{}^0$ (which is minimized cost per dollar revenue) and entry stops when the marginal firm earns zero profit, while welfare-maximizing firms enter according to increasing s_j^* (which is minimized cost per unit v) and entry stops when marginal surplus is zero. The second, and perhaps more fundamental, source of divergence between the equilibrium and optimum arises because profit-maximizing firms in the above "monopolistic competition" analysis simply do not compete in a way which leads to an equality of their price and marginal cost. Finally, the above analysis and its results are quite special because the firms' products are restricted to be symmetrically substitutable, that is, there is an aggregate utility function of the particular form (6.17). How sensitive is the equilibrium–welfare relationship in product variety to changes in these three things? We deal with the questions concerning the entry sequence and zero-profit stopping point in the remainder of this section. Using essentially the same symmetrical substitution model as in section 6.2.5 we then investigate the role of the MMC in producing the results that we have reached. Finally, in section 6.3 we consider the provision of variety in an essentially different model with asymmetric localized competition.

Alternative Specifications of $v_j(z_j)$. To see specifically how the sequence of entry and zero-profit equilibrium conditions affect optimality, consider the special case where $v_j(z_j) = \alpha_j z_j$. Differentiating, we have $v_j(z_j) = z_j v_j'(z_j)$. Using these expressions in (6.21) and (6.35) gives $s_J{}^0 = c_j/z_j v_j' = c_j/v = s_j^*$, so that the sequencing of firms by s^0 and s^* is the same for this case. This means that the market entry sequence of new product varieties will be socially optimal. That leaves us only to determine whether the equilibrium number of varieties is also optimal. At the market equilibrium the last firm to enter makes zero profits, which by (6.20) and (6.21) implies $u'(v^0) = s_j{}^0$,[8] and the social optimum conditions yield the same solution $u'(v') = s_j^*$ by (6.38). Given that the s-sequences are identical, then the J and v which solve these two equations will be the same and the market equilibrium will be socially optimal.

Suppose now, somewhat less restrictively, that $v_j(z_j) = \delta_j z_j{}^{\gamma_j}$ with $\delta_j > 0$ and $0 < \gamma_j < 1$. Each v_j is isoelastic in z_j, and γ_j is the elasticity number. For this specification

$$z_j v_j'(z_j) = \gamma_j \delta_j z_j{}^{\gamma_j} = \gamma_j v_j(z_j) \tag{6.44}$$

and the respective sequence conditions are related by $s_J{}^0 = s_j^*/\gamma_j$. In the special case where $\gamma_j = \gamma$ for all j (again, with $0 < \gamma < 1$), the sequencing of products by s^0 and s^* will be the same. Despite that, the market equilibrium condition $u'(v^0) = s_J{}^0 = s_j^*/\gamma$ and optimality condition $s_j^* = u'(v^*)$ are not the same. As a result, given $\gamma < 1$, the value of the marginal variety produced in equilibrium is greater than the value of the marginal variety produced optimally and the market supplies fewer product varieties than optimal.

The case where the γ_j differ in the cross-section of firms is somewhat more complicated. Since $s_j^* > s_j{}^0$, with the "size" of the inequality depending inversely on the size of γ_j, low γ_j products will be "undervalued" by firms and therefore late to enter relative to the preferences of the consumer. This statement can also be made in terms of the demand elasticity by noting from (6.18) that the inverse demand for this case is $p_j = u'(v)\delta_j\gamma_j z_j{}^{\gamma_j-1}$. As smaller γ_j implies a steeper inverse demand function and low price elasticity of demand, then products with low price elasticity will be relatively late to enter or will not be offered by profit-maximizing firms. The converse of these statements also holds.

For more general forms of $v_j(z_j)$ the intuition of the preceding case continues. The ratio $s_j{}^0/s_j^*$ continues to be given by $z_j v_j'(z_j)/v_j(z_j)$. For $z_j v_j'(z_j)/v_j(z_j)$ small and, in turn, $s_j{}^0/s_j^*$ small, the inverse demand will be steep (there will be small groups of high-value users) and product variety j will be late to enter or will not be offered at all. Finally, note that $u'(v)z_j v_j'(z_j)$ is firm j's revenues

---

[8] E6.3 develops the equilibrium conditions in this case. The reader can quickly prove the condition $u' = s_j{}^0$ for that example by comparing equations (6.26) and (6.30).

and, for v_j small relative to v, $u'(v)v_j(z_j)$ is product j's contribution to the consumer surplus portion of W. Thus,

$$\frac{u(v)z_j v_j'(z_j)}{u'(v)v_j(z_j)} = \frac{z_j v_j'(z_j)}{v_j(z_j)} \tag{6.45}$$

can be thought of as the ratio of product j's revenue to its incremental consumer surplus. When a product's revenues are small relative to its incremental surplus it will enter relatively late in the variety sequence, if it enters at all. As the size of the ratio $z_j v_j'(z_j)/v_j(z_j)$ depends directly on the product's demand elasticity we have the rule of thumb that varieties with low price elasticity will be relatively late to enter the market, if they enter at all.

The reader should not understand from the above discussion that the equilibrium variety is always less than the optimal. Consider, for example, the case with $v(z_j) = az_j - (b/2)z_j^2$ for all j. (For negatively sloped positive demands, it is also required that a, $b > 0$ and $a - bz_j > 0$.) This gives $s_j^0/s_j^* = \{az_j - (b/2)z_j^2\}/(az_j - bz_j^2) > 0$, which can be rewritten simply as $s_j^0 > \alpha s_j^0$ with $0 < \alpha < 1$ a constant for all j. While the sequencing of the varieties will be the same, the market equilibrium condition $u'(v^0) = s_j^0 = \alpha s_j^*$ and the optimality condition $s_j^* = u'(v^*)$ imply that the marginal value of equilibrium variety is less than the marginal value at the optimum: in this instance the market oversupplies product variety.

6.2.4 Product Variety with Imperfect Competition

To this point equilibrium levels of product variety have been derived from the MMC variant of monopolistic competition, where each firm uses the "price-taking" conjecture $dv/dz_j = 0$. A question of interest is whether alternative forms of market competition yield a qualitatively similar relationship between market equilibrium and optimal variety. As the industry equilibrium can change significantly with a change in rivalry, it is expected that the relationship will also change.

To hold complications to a minimum in answering this question, consider an aggregate utility function with the simple form

$$u\left(\int_j v_0(z_j)\right)$$

where z_j is firm j's output, $v_0(z_j)$ is increasing and concave with $v(0) = 0$, and $u(\cdot)$ is also increasing and strictly concave. Note that $v_0(\cdot)$ is the same function for each firm, which implies that the products of the firms are perfect substitutes when identical quantities are produced. The concavity of each $v(z_j)$ nonetheless means that consumers prefer some variety.[9]

---

[9] If the firms are identical, what meaning can be given to product variety? Here we can think of a quite specific situation with J otherwise identical restaurants. Because of "crowding" effects, consumers prefer the restaurant providing the fewest number of diners. When all restaurants are equally crowded (same z_j) consumers are indifferent to them, but not otherwise. Increased variety (number of restaurants) allows the crowding to be reduced and (other things equal) consumers made better off for a given number of meals served. However, the increasing convex cost functions do not permit one restaurant per customer. Along this line, Lamson (1970) found that "uncrowdedness" contributed importantly to movie theatre prices in large metropolitan areas.

Assume further that the firms have identical costs and therefore produce identical quantities in a zero-profit symmetric equilibrium. We continue to use the two general assumptions that new entry leads to an increase in the aggregate variety variable v and a reduction in output per firm. Other than these, no particular assumptions are made about the competition among the firms.

Let $z(J)$ indicate the equilibrium output per firm when there are J active firms and assume that $z(J)$ is a differentiable function of J. With J firms there is then an aggregate output of $Jz(J)$. Using this symmetry, we can write the aggregate surplus function simply as

$$W(J) = u(Jv_0(z(J)) - Jc(z(J)))$$ (6.46)

Using (6.18) we obtain the uniform price per unit output with J firms producing as $p(J) = u'(Jv_0(z(J)))v_0'(z(J))$, which implies per firm profits of

$$\pi(J) = p(J)z(J) - c(z(J))$$ (6.47)

Again, $W'(J^*) = 0$ gives the optimal variety J^* and $\pi(J^0) = 0$ yields the equilibrium variety for whatever form of competition occurs among the firms.

Briefly, the strategy for analyzing the supply of variety is to sign the derivative $\partial W(J^0)/\partial J$. If this is positive, then there are welfare gains to further expansion and variety is under-supplied at the equilibrium, and conversely, if it is negative, then there are welfare losses to further expansion and variety is over-supplied at the equilibrium.

First, differentiate $W(J)$. Adding and subtracting $u''v_0'z(J^0)$ to the result and rearranging gives (arguments to functions are generally omitted hereafter)

$$W'(J) - \pi(J) = J\{p(J) - c'\} \frac{\partial z(J)}{\partial J} + u'\{v_0 - v_0'z(J)\}$$ (6.48)

At the zero-profit equilibrium $\pi(J^0) = 0$ and therefore

$$W'(J^0) = \frac{1}{\eta}\left(\alpha + \frac{1-\alpha}{J^0}\right)J^0 \frac{\partial z(J^0)}{\partial J} + u'\{v_0 - v_0 z(J^0)\}$$ (6.49)

Here, we use the stationarity condition $(p - c')/p = \{\alpha + (1 - \alpha)H\}/\eta$, where η is the market demand elasticity, $H = 1/J$ in the symmetric equilibrium, and α is the proportionality constant of the quantity conjecture $dz_k^e/z_k = \alpha dz_j/z_j$.[10] Recall from SE3.3 that $\alpha = 1$ corresponds to the perfectly collusive outcome, $\alpha = 0$ gives Cournot–Nash competition, and $\alpha < 0$ leads to even more competitive outcomes.

Whether or not $W'(J^0)$ is positive or negative, and welfare is increasing or decreasing with additions to variety at the equilibrium, depends on the two effects given by the terms on the right-hand side of (6.49). The first of these terms relates to quantities and the second to varieties. Specifically, the second term is positive if $v_0'' < 0$, that is, consumers prefer variety. If this is the case, the second term measures the difference between the increment $u'v_0$ to gross surplus and the increment $u'v_0'z$ to revenues of a new variety. This is positive when new entrants (not price discriminating) do not capture the entire value that consumer's place on their variety.

---

[10] For a step-by-step derivation of this expression see chapter 12, section 12.1.

The first term on the right-hand side of (6.49) depends on two things: the effect of a new variety on aggregate output $J^0 \partial z(J^0)/\partial J$, which we have previously assumed to be negative,[11] and the form $[\alpha + \{(1 - \alpha)/J^0\}]$, which may be either positive or negative depending on the constant α. With Cournot–Nash competition ($\alpha = 0$) and J^0 small the first term on the right-hand side is negative, for less-competitive behavior ($\alpha > 0$) it is negative, and for greater competition ($\alpha < 0$) and J^0 large it is positive and goes to zero as α approaches $-1/(J^0 - 1)$.

Given that the first and second terms may have opposite signs (depending on the conjectures), it is not possible to state generally the direction of the bias on variety at the equilibrium. Although with less-competitive firms ($\alpha > 0$) there is the possibility of over-supply and for more-competitive firms ($\alpha \leqslant 0$) the tendency is for under-supply, other significant factors are also involved in the relationship.

E6.7

Equilibrium and Optimal Variety

Suppose that oligopolists produce identical products: $v_0(z_j) = z_j$. The exact difference between the equilibrium and optimal number of firms can be developed for the frequently used case of linear demand $p(z) = z - bz$, constant cost $c(z) = cz + F$, and Cournot–Nash competition at the market stage. For this case the reader can easily show that equilibrium output is given by

$$z(J) = \frac{1}{J + 1} \left(\frac{a - c}{b} \right) \tag{6.50}$$

Substituting this in the profit function and solving for J at zero profits gives (again ignoring the integer problem)

$$J^0 = \left\{ \frac{(a - c)^2}{b_\kappa} \right\}^{1/2} - 1 \tag{6.51}$$

The number of firms solving the optimality condition $\partial W(J)/\partial J = 0$ is, alternatively,

$$J^* = \left\{ \frac{(a - c)^2}{b_\kappa} \right\}^{3/2} - 1 \tag{6.52}$$

These last two conditions can be solved to yield $J^* = (J^0 + 1)^{2/3} - 1$. If, for example, the free-entry equilibrium number of firms is 7, the socially optimal number is just 3; similarly, if the equilibrium number is 26, the optimal number if 8. In this case excess entry is quite large.

Suppose, alternatively, that the firms in the industry are cartelized (say, by government fiat). In this case the monopoly aggregate output is $Jz(J) = (a - c)/2b$, which must hold for all J. Since this output is unaffected by

---

[11] Bulow, et al. (1985) and Mankiw and Whinston (1986) refer to this as "strategic substitutability" and "business stealing" respectively.

entry, the socially optimal number of firms is one, which would minimize the fixed set-up costs incurred. If the number of firms is not restricted by the cartel, firms will enter the industry to dissipate all profits: the rent-seeking turns the monopoly profits to a deadweight loss.

6.3   Product Variety with Localized Competition

The analysis of product variety above has been limited to products which are symmetric substitutes so that with the entry of each new variety the demand of all extant firms shifts in proportionately. Competition is symmetric and universal, not localized. This analysis leaves unanswered the question of optimal variety and its relationship with equilibrium variety when rivalry is localized. This issue can be addressed in the context of a model similar to that developed in chapter 5, section 5.2, and the usual spatial representation of utility

$$u = \mu - \tau(l)l \tag{6.53}$$

and surplus

$$v = \mu - \tau(l)l - p \tag{6.54}$$

Here the notation is standard: p is product price, $l \equiv |\theta - \theta^0|$ is the arc distance from the brand to the consumer's ideal product (location), $\tau(l) > 0$ is the disutility rate per unit l, and $\mu(\cdot)$ is an increasing strictly concave function. To be concrete, suppose that $\tau(l)l = \tau l^\delta$ where $\tau > 0$ and $\delta > 0$ are constants. For $\delta = 1$ there is the commonly used case where the disutility is linearly related to the consumer's arc distance from his ideal brand.

In the standard way let the set of feasible product and consumer locations be the unit circle and assume (a) that producing firms are located symmetrically about that circle and (b) that I consumers are located uniformly on the circle with density ω. Once more, each consumer takes at most one unit of the commodity and each firm produces a single product (brand) incurring an (identical) fixed set-up cost F and constant costs per unit c. Finally, it is convenient to scale physical units such that $c = 1$.

Suppose that there are J active firms and consider some particular firm setting price p. Further, suppose that this firm's rivals have a fixed and uniform price $\bar{p}$. As a result $\bar{v} = \mu - \bar{p} - \tau/J$ is the surplus received by a consumer exactly at a rival firm's location, and the consumer at distance l from the firm given by

$$l = \left(\frac{\mu - p - \bar{v}}{2\tau} \right)^{1/\delta} \tag{6.55}$$

would be just indifferent to the firm's brand and to that of its neighbor. If the "outside good" always yields less surplus, the firm's demand function is then

$$z = 2(\omega I)l \tag{6.56}$$

where the 2 accounts for the fact that l extends to both sides of the firm.

Optimal Variety. With J equally spaced brands, each attracting $1/2J$ consumers to its left and right, aggregate surplus has the form

$$W(J) = 2J(\omega I) \int_0^{1/2J} (\mu - \tau l^\delta - 1) \, dl - JF \qquad (6.57)$$

Integrating (6.57) gives

$$W(J) = 2J(\omega I) \left\{ \frac{\mu - 1}{2J} \frac{(1/2J)^{\delta+1}}{\delta + 1} \right\} - JF$$

so maximizing $W(J)$ with respect to J using the price-taking behavior usual in monopolistic competition gives the optimal variety

$$J^* = \frac{1}{2} \left\{ \frac{2\tau\delta(\omega I)}{(\delta + 1)F} \right\}^{1/(\delta+1)} \qquad (6.58)$$

The reader can see that J^* is increasing in the disutility rate as expected.

Equilibrium Variety. The two usual conditions for a symmetric market equilibrium are that firms maximize profits and that entry leads to zero profit. That is, J^0 must be such that

$$\pi = (p - 1)z - F = 0 \qquad (6.59a)$$

and simultaneously

$$\frac{\partial \pi}{\partial z} = 0 \qquad (6.59b)$$

From this last condition we obtain

$$p = 1 - z \frac{\partial p}{\partial z} = 1 + 2\tau\delta l^\delta \qquad (6.60)$$

where z is given by the demand function (6.56), $z = 2(\omega I)\{(u - p - \bar{v})/2\tau\}^{1/\delta}$, and $\partial p/\partial z$ is derived from this. Substituting (6.56) and (6.60) into the zero-profit condition (6.59a) yields

$$2\tau\delta l^\delta (2\omega Il) = F \qquad (6.61)$$

Since the equilibrium is symmetric, the spacing between firms is identical and is therefore given by $l^0 = 1/2J^0$. Substituting this distance in (6.61) and rearranging gives the equilibrium number of brands (variety) in terms of the model parameters:

$$J^0 = \frac{1}{2} \left\{ \frac{4\tau\delta(\omega I)}{F} \right\}^{1/\delta+1} \qquad (6.62)$$

Finally, using the ratio of (6.58) to (6.62) leads to the correspondence between J^0 and J^* as a function of the distance parameter δ:

$$J^0 = J^*\{2(\delta + 1)\}^{1/(\delta+1)} \qquad (6.63)$$

For the usual case where the disutility of a brand decreases linearly with the arc distance from the ideal, $\delta = 1$ and $J^0 = 2J^*$: the equilibrium produces twice the optimal variety. This was the result developed earlier in chapter 5, section 5.2.3. More generally, the ratio J^0/J^* is decreasing in δ and, although there is always an over-supply of variety in this model, the extent of the over-supply decreases in δ.

Summary. From the above results it is seen that the interplay of many specific assumptions exogenously placed on the model industry determines whether or not equilibrium product variety is excessive. However, these group into two broad effects. A firm offering a new product gives consideration to the net revenues that will be created, not the amount of consumer surplus. This tends to produce too little product variety. Against this, the firm gives no consideration to the external effect that its entry has on the demand for substitute products offered by existing firms, an effect which tends to produce too much variety.[12] The underlying details of the market, including levels of fixed cost, own- and cross-elasticities of demand, conjectural variations, etc., determine which of these two effects will dominate and whether there will be an over- or under-supply of variety.

Supplementary examples

SE6.1 Monopoly and Product Variety with Increasing Returns

Although the analysis in section 6.1 limits the monopolist's choice to a single variety (quality), Guasch and Sobel (1980) note that this is not a necessary restriction. Consider, for example, a monopolist who is able to produce two products ($j = 1, 2$). Suppose further that there are increasing returns and that the cost function $TC = F + c_j z_j$ obtains for each product.

Let there be a population of consumer types indexed by α and uniformly distributed on the $[1, 2]$ interval. We assume that each consumer of type α has a reservation price αv_j for each product j. Finally we make the usual assumption that each consumer purchases at most one unit of at most one of the products.

To keep things simple and concrete assume the specific parameter values $v_1 = 1$, $v_2 = 2$, $c_1 = 0$, and $c_2 = 1$. There are, of course, three possible product strategies for the firm: produce product 1 alone, produce product 2 alone, or produce both. Several rather straightforward calculations permit us to compare the market equilibrium product variety, profits, and aggregate surplus with these at the social optimum.

Product 1 Alone. The monopolist selects the lower bound on types α' to be served and price p to maximize its profits (recall that $c_1 = 0$):

$$\max \int_{\alpha'}^{2} p \, d\alpha - F \tag{6.64}$$

for $\alpha' \geq p$, $\alpha' \geq 1$. The optimal choices are $\alpha' = p = 1$, which gives profits depending on fixed costs $1 - F$.

Product 2 Alone. The profit maximization problem here is quite similar to the above case:

---

[12] Again, these two effects correspond to the two terms on the right-hand side of equation (6.49).

$$\max \int_{\alpha'}^{2} (p - 1)\, d\alpha - F \tag{6.65}$$

for $2\alpha' \geqslant p$ and $\alpha' \geqslant 1$. The optimal decisions are $\alpha' = 5/4$ and $p = 5/2$, which gives profits of $9/8 - F$. Notice that producing product 2 alone yields greater profits than producing product 1 alone for all values of fixed cost.

Both Products. Using the obvious notation, the monopolist must now solve

$$\max \int_{\alpha'}^{\alpha''} p_1\, d\alpha + \int_{\alpha'}^{2} (p_2 - 1)\, d\alpha - 2F \tag{6.66}$$

for $\alpha' \geqslant p_1$, $2\alpha'' - p_2 = \alpha' - p_1$, $2 \geqslant \alpha''$, and $\alpha' \geqslant 1$. The solution here is $\alpha' = p_1 = 1$, $\alpha'' = 3/2$, and $p_2 = 5/2$, which yields profits of $5/4 - 2F$.

For $F < 1/8$ it is most profitable for the monopolist to produce both goods. For $F > 1/8$ product 2 alone will be optimally produced. In the second case, consumer surplus will be zero for all types $1 \leqslant \alpha \leqslant 5/4$ and equal to $2\alpha - 5/2$ for all types $5/4 \leqslant \alpha \leqslant 2$. In the alternative case where both products are produced, consumer surplus is $\alpha - 1$ for types $1 \leqslant \alpha \leqslant 3/2$ and $2\alpha - 5/2$ for $3/2 \leqslant \alpha \leqslant 2$. Thus if $F < 1/8$ a little arithmetic indicates that requiring the monopolist to produce only product 2 would result in a reduction in aggregate surplus. Moreover, this example indicates that a monopolist *may* choose greater product variety to increase profits. Again, the general presumption that monopolists restrict variety is incorrect.

SE6.2 Monopoly Supply of Durable Quality

As will be shown in detail in chapter 8, product durability can be treated as a quality variable. Our purpose here is to show that, in a very simplified context, durability has a specific quality form which results in optimal supply by a monopolist. The symbols z, ξ, and p are as usual. In addition, let $s = \xi z$ be the total services offered by a quantity z of the good with durability ξ per unit, and let ϕ be the (unit quality) service price which implies $p = \phi\xi$ as the price per unit of the good of durability ξ. Suppose that costs are constant in the sense that $c(z, \xi) = c(\xi)z$; then the profit function for the monopolist is

$$\Pi(z, \xi) = \xi D(\xi z)z - c(\xi)z$$

$$= \xi z \left\{ D(\xi z) - \frac{c(\xi)}{\xi} \right\} \tag{6.67}$$

where $\xi D(\xi z)$ is the inverse demand for the durable good. Aggregate surplus is

$$W(z, \xi) = \xi \int_{0}^{z} D(\alpha\xi)\, d\alpha - c(\xi)z$$

$$= \xi z \left\{ \frac{1}{z} \int_{0}^{z} D(\alpha\xi)\, d\alpha - \frac{c(\xi)}{\xi} \right\} \tag{6.68}$$

Comparing (6.67) and (6.68), note that both π and W have maxima with respect to durability when the average durability cost $c(\xi)/\xi$ is minimized. More generally, the reader can see that in those situations in which the inverse demand is of the form $f(\xi)D\{f(\xi)z\}$, with $f(\xi)$ an increasing function of ξ, quality will be optimally supplied by the monopolist. This result should not, however, be understood to imply that the optimal and equilibrium quantities are the same. Complicating aspects of the monopoly supply of durable goods are considered in detail in chapter 8.

SE6.3   Monopoly and Dominant-product Varieties

A frequent question is whether or not a monopolist operating *without* fixed set-up costs for brands would offer product varieties satisfying every consumer's unique tastes. Early analyses concluded that market structure was irrelevant in this case (see, for example, Swan, 1970; Lancaster, 1975). The underlying argument was quite simple: were a monopolist not to supply every consumer with his most preferred variety, some profitable opportunity would be forgone.

A number of criticisms of this line of reasoning have recently appeared. Perhaps the most frequently cited of these notes that, in the absence of price discrimination, some varieties when sold at *monopoly prices* might be dominated on a price per unit quality basis by neighboring varieties. Consumers would switch their choices because of this dominance, reducing the number of varieties produced. In chapter 7 we will consider this possibility when certain methods of price discrimination are practiced. It is instructive for the moment, however, to consider the irrelevance argument and its critics in the absence of discriminatory pricing.

Consumers and Demand. We use the basic two-dimensional noncombinable-in-use characteristics model set out in chapter 4, section 4.3, and a graphical analysis following White (1977). In figure 6.6 the characteristics ζ_1 and ζ_2 define

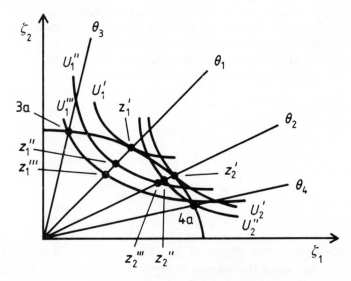

Figure 6.6
Variety and market structure

the varieties of available goods, with $\theta_j = (\zeta_2/\zeta_1) \geq 0$ indicating the particular variety j. Varieties θ_1, θ_2, θ_3, and θ_4 are shown specifically from among those which are possible. As is usual, movements outward along each ray θ_j indicate that greater quantities are supplied.

In the figure, RTS indicates the locus of (mutually exclusive) quantities of the different varieties that can be produced using some given quantity of factors. All points on RTS thus represent the same level of factor costs and, at a competitive equilibrium with free entry, all quantities of the varieties along that locus must sell for the same price. For completeness let us note the several technology assumptions underlying the properties assumed for the RTS locus: it is assumed to be a homothetic expansion (or contraction) of all other constant-factor-cost loci, returns to scale are constant, and it is strictly concave to the origin, implying diminishing characteristic rates of substitution in producing new varieties. Moreover, it is assumed in the figure that the units in which characteristics are measured have been scaled so that RTS, and all constant-factor-cost loci, are quarter-circles.

It is assumed that the characteristics ζ_1 and ζ_2 exhaust the consumption possibilities; then each consumer seeks the commodity which forms his optimal characteristic bundle. The indifference contours for individual i with utility functions $u_i(\zeta_1, \zeta_2)$ are indicated in the figure by u_i', u_i'', and so forth. Each utility is assumed to be increasing and strictly quasi-concave. Finally, for simplicity we will further assume that all consumers have the same income level and deal with two typical individuals, 1 and 2.

Equilibrium Variety. As a first case assume that the two consumers are served by competitive producers at long-run equilibrium, so that price is equal to unit cost, revenues equal total costs, and each consumer's income equals the revenues received on each product variety. Therefore RTS is also the budget constraint locus for each consumer. Consumer 1 optimally purchases variety θ_1 in quantity z_1' and consumer 2 optimally purchases variety θ_2 in quantity z_2'.

Now assume that some single firm is granted a government franchise carrying with it the exclusive right to produce all varieties between θ_3 and θ_4. Competitive producers still sell θ_3, along with all varieties to the "left" of it, and θ_4, along with all varieties to the "right" of it. For consumer 1 alone, the monopolist's best strategy is to continue offering variety θ_1, but to supply only the indicated quantity z_1''' (rather than quantity z_1') to take all the consumer's income. To do this, a price of z_1'/z_1''' times the competitive level is now charged for variety θ_1. In turn, the monopolist's profits are given by the distance $z_1' - z_1'''$ in the figure and the consumer's utility is reduced from u_1' to u_1'''.[13] The monopolist can do no better, for any further reduction in 1's utility would lead him to switch to the competitively supplied good at z_3'.

It would seem that the monopolist would pursue a similar strategy for individual 2. This would imply taking competitive revenues of z_2' but supplying only z_2'' units of θ_2 for a monopoly price equal to z_2'/z_2'' times for the

---

[13] In the figure utility functions are assumed to be homothetic so that the monopolist's price changes do not lead to the purchase of different varieties by consumers. This is only a simplifying assumption and our main points continue to hold for nonhomothetic functions.

competitive level. Any higher price would lead individual 2 to purchase variety θ_4 at z'_4. Using this strategy it would seem that the monopolist earns $z'_2 - z''_2$ when producing vareity 2.

For the above prices to be sustainable by the monopolist it would be necessary to prohibit individual 1 from purchasing variety θ_2. If that were not done, individual 1 could take θ_2 at the prevailing price and increase his utility from u''_1 to u'_2. This switch would have the effect of reducing the monopolist's anticipated profits by the amount $(z'_1 - z'''_1) - (z'_2 - z'''_2) \geqslant 0$. If the switching cannot be prevented and the monopolist cannot charge different consumers different prices for the same variety, then the monopolist has just two recourses: it can either raise the price of variety θ_2 beyond the z'_2/z''_2 level (then selling z''_2 to individual 2 and z'''_1 to individual 1) or it can reduce its price for variety θ_1 to z'_1/z''_1 (then selling z''_1 to individual 1 and z''_2 to individual 2). These changes would make the price–variety bundles "incentive compatible" in the sense that each consumer finds the bundle intended for him to be the one he prefers from among all of those offered. Note, however, that the incentive compatibility constraint reduces the monopolist's profits relative to the level which would be possible if the individuals could be costlessly forbidden from resale. The details of such discriminatory schemes are considered next in chapter 7.

7 Price Discrimination

It is usual in the analysis of markets to think of firms as selling their output at a single price to all comers. This is an unnecessary and inappropriate simplification, for firms will generally find it profitable to fashion their terms of sale to account for buyer differences. Price discrimination is pervasive. This fact is often missed as price discrimination is commonly analyzed in the context of, and therefore thought to be confined to, situations in which firms have a relatively large measure of monopoly power and sell homogeneous goods to fully informed consumers. None of these things are required and, as we will see, differentiated products and imperfectly informed consumers contribute significantly to the range of discriminatory selling policies that are possible.

The Usual Case. The standard textbook example of discrimination considers a monopolist selling a physically homogeneous product in two (independent) submarkets across which resale is impossible. In our usual notation, the firm's profits are revenues from both markets minus costs of total supply:

$$\pi(z_1, z_2) = p_1(z_1)z_1 + p_2(z_2)z_2 - c(z_1 + z_2)$$

The obvious stationarity conditions $MR_1 = MR_2 = MC$ obtain: the firm maximizes revenues from any given output by equating the marginal revenues from the two submarkets, and it maximizes profits by choosing the output level where that marginal revenue just equals marginal cost.[1] The equality of marginal revenues at the optimum implies

$$p_1\left(1 - \frac{1}{\eta_1}\right) = p_2\left(1 - \frac{1}{\eta_2}\right)$$

where $\eta_j \equiv -(\partial z_j/\partial p_j)(p_j/z_j)$ is the firm's demand elasticity in market j. Thus, when different prices can be sustained in the submarkets, the firm sets a lower price where the demand is more elastic. For example, movie theaters often set lower ticket prices for children, and airline passengers booking in advance generally pay lower fares than those booking for immediate departure.

---

[1] For each product j, $0 = \partial\pi/\partial z_j = p + p(\partial p_j\partial z_j)(z_j/p_j) - \partial c/\partial z_j$, where the second term on the right-hand side is marginal revenue.

Preconditions for Discrimination. It is apparent that several preconditions must exist for price discrimination to occur profitably. To begin with, the properties of the good and the conditions of sale must be such that it is not too costly for the firm to prohibit low-price buyers from reselling to those charged a higher price. Personal services generally fall in this category when they are not physically transferable and ordinary capital goods can be made nonresaleable when the manufacturer adopts a lease-only policy and installs covenants against subleasing. As will be made clear below, there are many rather standard selling strategies which make it costly for buyers to resell among themselves but impose only a small additional cost on the seller.

If it is assumed that resale is not a problem, a monopolist can extract each consumer's surplus provided that it is not too costly to know his demand price.[2] This gives rise to the second precondition for price discrimination: the identification (to some degree) of demand schedules. In most textbook treatments consumers are assumed to be sorted according to an observable index perfectly correlated with their demand prices. In practice, however, increasing costs of information and the large number of factors influencing demand means that the index will be observed with less than full accuracy (with "noise") and will be less than perfectly correlated with demand price. Thus the index employed will often lead to an imperfect level of price discrimination. For example, magazine subscriptions are sold at reduced rates to students and senior citizens, airlines give discounts during the winter months and raise their fares during holiday periods, and hotels let "kids stay free." These are not schema for distinguishing exactly by demand price. Rather, they are of an imperfect degree of precision, discriminating roughly, but are also relatively inexpensive to implement. The seller can resort to multiple indexes to more exactly divide consumers by their demand prices, but such means are also more costly to implement and further drain any surplus captured. The equality of marginal return (in consumer surplus captured) and marginal implementation cost define, in principle, an optimal discriminating scheme. When consumers are identified in this way, using an index more or less correlated with demand price, **index selection**, or **sorting by index**, is said to occur.

An alternative to sorting consumers according to an observable index is based on the notion that, in a properly designed selling policy, consumers voluntarily reveal their demand type by the purchases they make. Consider, for example, a firm which offers two different qualities of its product, with the higher-quality version bearing a higher price. Suppose that the combination of price and quality for the two products is such that those consumers placing a greater value on high quality select the higher-quality item and pay the higher price. There is price discrimination in this case when the difference in prices is less than the incremental cost of supplying the higher quality. More generally, when the seller adopts a product and pricing policy which provides incentives for consumers to reveal their demand price in actual purchases, **self-selection** is said to occur.

---

[2] The procedure for capturing this surplus is straightforward in principle. One possibility is that the seller first calculates that output level where, for each consumer, demand price equals marginal cost. Each consumer would then receive an all-or-nothing offer under which he could buy that quantity for a given amount (almost) equal to the maximum amount he would pay for that quantity (his consumer surplus).

7.1 Price Discrimination by Degree

Price discrimination is profitable for the firm simply because some consumers are willing to pay more for some commodity than others (*interpersonal* differences) and/or various consumers are willing to pay more for initial units than for subsequent one (*interunit* differences). On this fact, Pigou (1932) distinguished three degrees, or basic forms, of discrimination. It is a tribute to the clarity of his insight that his categorization is still in common usage.

Pigou's discussion on price discrimination begins with the following outline:

> ... A **first degree** would involve the charge of a different price against all the different units of commodity, in such wise that the price exacted for each was equal to the demand price for it, and no consumers' surplus was left to the buyers. A **second degree** would obtain if a monopolist were able to make *n* separate prices, in such wise that all units with a demand price greater than *x* were sold at a price *x*, all with a demand price less than *x* and greater than *y* at a price *y*, and so on. A **third degree** would obtain if the monopolist were able to distinguish among his customers *n* different groups, separated from one another more or less by some practicable mark, and could charge a separate monopoly price to the members of each group. This degree, it will be noticed, differs fundamentally from either of the preceding degrees, in that it may involve the refusal to satisfy, in one market, demands represented by demand prices in excess of some of those which, in another market, are satisfied. (Pigou, 1932, p. 279).

First Degree. With first-degree price discrimination the charge for the total number of units sold is the sum of the buyer's demand prices on each successive unit. Buyers are required to pay this sum and take the entire amount in an all-or-nothing offer. When using this price policy, the seller extends production and sales up to the point at which its marginal cost equals average revenue, since it can sell additional units at the successively lower prices without lowering its price on inframarginal units. In this case the seller provides the competitive level of output. Despite the fact that the distribution brought about with first-degree discrimination may seem inequitable from the consumer's viewpoint, the solution is allocatively efficient: on the last unit purchased by each consumer the firm charges marginal cost, and it is therefore impossible to increase aggregate surplus with an increase or decrease in output.

Second Degree. Second-degree price discrimination occurs when a seller employs a price policy based on a sequence of prices $p_1 > p_2 > \ldots > p_N$ in the following way: (a) all comers are sold all units for which they have reservation demand prices greater than or equal to p_1 at price p_1, (b) all comers are sold all units for which they have reservation demand prices less than p_1 but greater than or equal to p_2 at price p_2, and so forth through group and price p_N. While no buyer is excluded from the opportunity to trade in this case, not all surplus is extracted from every buyer. The local water company, for example, uses second-degree price discrimination when it charges a given rate (to all users) for the first 2,000 cubic feet of water per period, a somewhat lower rate for the next

1,000 cubic feet, and a still lower rate for all additional amounts (three groups). If a customer were to use, say, 3,500 cubic feet during the billing period, he would have total expenditures of $TE = 2000p_1 + 1000p_2 + 500p_3$, where $p_1 > p_2 > p_3$. In turn, his average price would be $TE/3500$, which would be greater than his marginal price p_3. Consumers demanding other quantities of water would be charged different average prices and, perhaps, different marginal prices.

Third Degree. With third-degree price discrimination buyers are again separated into groups and a single generally different price is established for each group. (As will be clear below, the constituents of each group need not be identifiable a priori.) In the usual case, some group members will have a demand price below that offered to their group (their demand price may be met in some other group), leaving those buyers excluded from the market. In addition, other buyers will generally receive surplus so that there is not full extraction. The usual multimarket examples of discrimination, as in the introductory paragraphs of this chapter, are of the third degree. The local electricity company, for instance, charges different rates for domestic and commercial users. While marginal revenue is equated for the two markets, and presumably also set equal to marginal cost, the commercial user is charged the lower rate since its demand for electricity is (usually) more elastic.

While first-degree price discrimination is efficient relative to the single-price monopoly case, the exclusion of buyers in third-degree discrimination raises the possibility that the same sort of relative efficiency will not obtain. Suppose, for example, that a firm which originally sold its output at a single price of $100 now separates its clientele into two groups, selling to one at $90 and the other at $110. While the lower price will increase demand for the product, the higher price to the second group will reduce surplus because those consumers with demand prices between $100 and $109.99 and placed in this second group (rather than in the $90 group) will withdraw their trade from this seller. Depending on the numbers of individuals in the two groups who gain surplus and lose surplus, welfare can be increased or decreased by the imperfection arising in the use of third-degree discrimination.

Welfare Bounds for Third-degree Discrimination. Robinson (1933, pp. 188–95), Samuelson (1967, pp. 42–5), and Schmalensee (1981) have shown that the exact welfare change brought about with third-degree discrimination depends on the convexity of the underlying demand. It is tedious to derive the exact measure, but Varian (1985) has developed some useful bounds.

Varian's analysis compares the aggregate surplus arising when a good is sold using a uniform (nondiscriminatory) price policy and when it is sold using a multimarket third-degree discriminatory policy. To set aside unnecessary complications assume away all income effects and let the good be produced with constant unit cost. We think of $n = 1, 2, \ldots, N$ markets with demand in each given by $z_n = z_n(p_n)$, where the location is as usual. Aggregate surplus with discriminatory prices is

$$W(\{p_n\}) = \sum_n CS_n(p_n) + \sum_n (p_n - c)z_n \qquad (7.1a)$$

where the first-term on the right-hand side is the total of consumer surplus and the second term is the associated profits. With a uniform price $\bar{p}$ charged in all markets the aggregate welfare is, similarly,

$$W(\bar{p}) = \sum_n CS_n(\bar{p}) + \sum_n (\bar{p} - c)\bar{z}_n \qquad (7.1b)$$

where $\bar{z}_n$ is the quantity sold in market k at price $\bar{p}$. The change is welfare associated with the move to discriminatory prices from uniform prices is

$$\Delta W = \sum_n \{CS_n(p_n) - CS_n(\bar{p})\} + \sum_n (p_n - c)z_n + \sum_n (\bar{p} - c)\bar{z}_n \qquad (7.2)$$

Several properties of the consumer surplus function permit bounds to be established for ΔW. Recall from chapter 1, section 1.4, and chapter 2, section 2.4 that (a) the derivative $\partial CS_n(p_n)/\partial p_n = -z_n(p_n)$ of the consumer surplus function with respect to price is equal to the negative of the ordinary demand, and consequently (b) $\partial^2 CS_n(p_n)/\partial p_n^2 = -\partial z_n(p_n)/\partial p_n > 0$ so that the consumer surplus function is convex when demand is negatively sloped. Since CS is convex, the mean value theorem at $\bar{p}$ gives

$$\frac{\partial CS_n(\bar{p})}{\partial p} (p_n - \bar{p}) \leqslant CS_n(p_n) - CS_n(\bar{p}) \qquad (7.3)$$

Using (a) for the derivative in this expression, substituting it in (7.2), and collecting terms yields

$$\Delta W \geqslant \sum_n (p_n - c)\Delta z_n \qquad (7.4)$$

where $\Delta z_n = z_n - \bar{z}_n$. Using the mean value theorem once more, at p_n, gives

$$\frac{\partial CS_n(p_n)}{\partial p} (\bar{p} - p_n) \leqslant CS_n(\bar{p}) - CS_n(p_n) \qquad (7.5)$$

Similar substitutions and rearrangements yield

$$\Delta W \leqslant (\bar{p} - c)\sum_n \Delta z_n \qquad (7.6)$$

Given $\bar{p} - c > 0$, a necessary condition for third-degree price discrimination to result in a gain in aggregate surplus is that is increase *total* output. Note that this says nothing about the welfare gain or loss of individual consumers, any one of which may be better or worse off with the discrimination.

Perfectly Discriminatory Prices. The shortcomings of second- and third-degree price discrimination underline the ideal properties of the first degree.

PD1: (extraction) no consumer captures any surplus from the commodity.
PD2: (exclusion) no consumer purchases the commodity if his reservation demand price is less than the seller's marginal cost.
PD3: (inclusion) every consumer purchases the commodity if his reservation demand price exceeds the seller's marginal cost.

From these properties it should be clear why first-degree price discrimination is usually said to be "perfect."

E7.1

Value of Service Pricing

Third-degree price discrimination under a "value of service" pricing label was for years a common practice of railroads. Friedman (1979) has analyzed a polar case of this practice based on the so-called long-haul–short-haul distinction. His analysis explains the seemingly incongruous observation that freight rates can be higher between two intermediate points on a service line than they are for carriage over the full line length (including the intermediate section).

Suppose that the railroad has a monopoly over some short haul, but competes with a group of competitive ocean shipping firms on the long haul. For example, the railroad line might run from point N (New York) to point S (San Francisco) via D (Denver), while the ships carry freight (only) between N and S. Because the ocean shipping industry is competitive, at equilibrium its price p^c equals its average and marginal cost. The railroad company's cost is made up of the usual fixed and variable components: the fixed cost is given by $F_{NS} = F_{ND} + F_{DS}$, which is the sum of the sectional costs, and the unit costs are assumed to be constants and also made up from sectional parts ($c_{NS} = c_{ND} + c_{DS}$). The demands for the various freight services are illustrated in figure 7.1, where D_{ND} is the demand for services from New York to Denver, and similarly for D_{NS} and D_{DS}.[3] To abstract from unnecessary details we will also assume that the freight services are identical by ship or railway and these demands pertain for services by either.

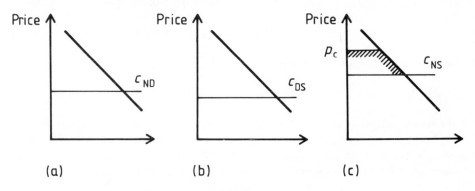

Figure 7.1
Price discrimination: (a) N to D; (b) D to S; (c) N to S

A discriminatory price policy is optimal for the railroad. The form of the policy is, however, somewhat complicated by the existence of the competitive shippers. For first-degree discrimination, the railroad should follow D_{ND} and D_{DS} down to the levels where they intersect the unit costs c_{ND} and c_{DS} respectively (see figure 7.1). For the long-haul freight services from New York

---

[3] Clearly, the New York to San Francisco demand is not simply the sum of that over the New York to Denver and Denver to San Francisco segments.

to San Francisco, the competitive price p^c establishes a bound above which the railway cannot price. However, surplus can be extracted from the long-haul user down D_{NS} below p^c and above c_{NS}. When the competitive price is lower than the intercept of either D_{ND} or D_{DS}, for some customers the price for the long haul will be lower than it is for the short haul and there is discrimination between the hauls.

7.2 Index Selection

The standard microeconomic theory text sets out its analysis of price discrimination in a passage linked to the single-seller monopoly offering a single physically uniform commodity. As we will see below, the most frequently observed and interesting cases of price discrimination occur in nearly opposite situations, with rival firms selling heterogeneous goods often under conditions of zero profit imposed by free entry. Even more in contrast, price discrimination may be a necessary selling tactic for firms if they are to survive in a rivalrous environment. In this regard Phlips (1983) suggests that we consider the restaurant business, where there are few monopolies (except in isolated locations), little evidence of collusion, generally intense rivalry, and a high degree of product heterogenity. Despite these "nonstandard" conditions, a variety of discrimination schemes are routinely employed: we see, for example, children's plates, early evening specials, senior citizen and trucker discounts, two-for-one coupons, and selections by complete dinners or *à la carte*.

Spatial Competition. The spatial variant of monopolistic competition is a useful framework in which to examine third-degree price discrimination by index selection. To this end, consider the model first set out in chapter 5, section 5.2, where each of $j = 1, 2, \ldots, J$ firms produces a differentiated product – a brand. The brands' characteristics and consumer preferences are assumed to differ along only one dimension, which is represented by a unit circumference circle,[4] consumers are assumed to be uniformly located about this circular market, and sellers (brands) are symmetrically located along the market separated by an arc distance of $1/J$. The location of each brand j along the circle is indicated by the parameter θ_j. To avoid the polar case where J becomes infinite and each consumer is served by his "own" brand, economies of scale are assumed to occur in the production of brands with each firm j having the total cost function

$$c_j = cz_j + F \tag{7.7}$$

---

[4] More exactly, suppose that there are two "fundamental characteristics" differentiating each brand. Relevant consumption choices, holding aside scale, are then summarized by the ratio of these two "fundamental characteristics." In turn, each brand can be identified by the (angle of the) single ray along which it lies in the two-dimensional "fundamental characteristics" plane. The *location* of brands and consumers refers to a specific ray angle, which is referred to as a *characteristic combination* and measured along the unit circumference circle. For details, recall chapter 4, section 4.3.

The notation is as usual: z_j is the output, $c > 0$ is the constant unit cost, and $F > 0$ is the fixed cost.

On the demand side the $i = 1, 2, \ldots, I$ consumers are distinguished according to three parameters. For individual i these are (a) the **location** θ_i of his most preferred characteristic combination, (b) a **demand price** v_i for that combination, and (c) a constant **strength of preference** τ_i measuring the "disutility" associated with moving a unit arc-distance away from θ_i. If each consumer is limited to the purchase of one unit of one brand or none, these specifications mean that the net surplus individual i receives from the choice of some brand j is

$$\text{CS}_i = (v_i - p_j) - \tau_i |\theta_i - \theta_j| \tag{7.8}$$

where p_j is j's price and $|\theta_i - \theta_j|$ denotes the arc distance between the characteristic combination of brand j and that preferred by i. Each consumer chooses that brand which maximizes his surplus.

To keep focused, in the sections immediately following two key seller costs are held aside: those associated with identifying relevant demand elasticities and those associated with prohibiting resale among consumers. Moreover, it is assumed that there are no legal prohibitions against price discrimination.

7.2.1 Sorting by Preference

To deal with the simplest case first, let $v_i = v$ and $\tau_i = \tau$ for all i, so that consumers differ only by their ideal product θ_i (that is, their location on the unit circle). This restriction leaves us with the model studied in chapter 5, section 5.2, There, attention was restricted to a uniform "delivered" pricing policy for the firm, where every consumer, regardless of location (preference), paid the same price for the brand. The Nash-in-price conjectures standard in models of monopolistic competition were used and a demand with three segments resulted. Figure 7.2 shows this demand for brand θ_j, assuming that all other brands have prices held fixed at level $\bar{p}$. When p_j is high relative to $\bar{p}$, only those consumers close to θ_j buy from j.[5] The particular consumers at a distance from θ_j, to both right and left, such that they receive exactly zero surplus from j define the extent of j's market area. When consumers just outside j's market area receive negative surplus from all other brands and purchase an "outside" good, gaps are formed between the market areas of the firms. These conditions are illustrated in figure 7.3(a) and describe the monopoly segment of j's demand curve shown in figure 7.2.

Firm j's demand function in this monopoly case is (these correspond to equations (5.27))

$$z_m{}^m(p_j; \bar{p}) = \frac{2I(v - p_j)}{\tau} \qquad \text{for } p_j < v \tag{7.9a}$$

$$= 0 \qquad \text{for } p_j \geq v \tag{7.9b}$$

As firm j raises or lowers its price in this demand segment, customers are lost to or gained from the outside good. In this sense j does not compete with other

---

[5] Any residual income is used to purchase the outside good.

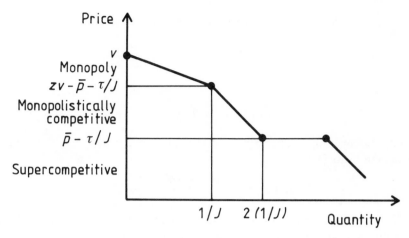

Figure 7.2
Demand segments

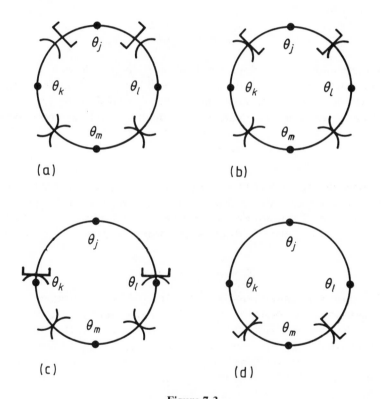

Figure 7.3
Market areas: (a) monopoly; (b) monopolistically competitive kink; (c) monopolistically competitive; (d) supercompetitive

brands in the industry, not even with the producers of the next-closest brands.

As p_j falls relative to $\bar{p}$ the gap between the market areas of firms j and k (on the left) and firms j and l (on the right) diminishes and, at some point, just becomes equal to zero. The price marking this "kink" is given by

$$\frac{v - p_j}{\tau} + \frac{v - \bar{p}}{\tau} = \frac{1}{J} \tag{7.10a}$$

or

$$p_j = 2v - \bar{p} - \frac{\tau}{J} \tag{7.10b}$$

As p_j falls below this level the monopolistically competitive region is entered and j's demand satisfies

$$z_j{}^c(p_j; \bar{p}) = \frac{I(\bar{p} + \tau/J - p_j)}{\tau} \tag{7.11}$$

This monopolistically competitive demand segment is indicated in figure 7.2 and the associated market areas are illustrated in figure 7.3(c).

Finally, there is the supercompetitive segment where j undercuts its neighboring brands. This is illustrated in figures 7.2 and 7.3(d). The mill prices which delineate this region are given by

$$p_j < \bar{p} - \frac{\tau}{J} \tag{7.12a}$$

(again, all these cases are developed in detail in chapter 5, section 5.2).

Here, consumers located exactly at and (relative to j) distant from neighboring brands receive greater surplus from j's brand because of its very low price. For completeness we note that j may also be undercut, and this occurs when

$$\bar{p} < p_j - \frac{\tau}{J} \tag{7.12b}$$

Price Discrimination. Rather than having firm j charge a single price, suppose instead that it charges each consumer a price which varies with location. Continuing with the Nash-in-price assumption, all other firms hold their price fixed at $\bar{p} > c$. Firm j would ideally sort customers according to their *gross* surplus

$$S_i = v - \tau|\theta_i - \theta_j| \tag{7.13}$$

For v and τ positive, common and known in the cross-section of individuals, S_i is decreasing in the arc distance $l_{ij} = |\theta_i - \theta_j|$ that consumers lie away from firm j's location. The consumer's location – this arc distance – is therefore an index perfectly correlated with the consumer's gross surplus. By observing the distances l_{ij}, S_i can be calculated under the conditions assumed for v and τ.

Setting $p_j{}^i = S_i$, firm j captures the full extent of each consumer's surplus. In this case the buyer at j's location pays the highest price v and the price falls at the rate τ for other consumers according to their arc distance from j. If competition from sellers of other brands is ignored, the left and right boundaries of firm j's market area will be determined at the point where its marginal cost just equals the consumer surplus captured. These boundaries are given by the locations θ_* (to its right and left) solving

$$c = S_* = v - \tau|\theta_* - \theta_j| \tag{7.14}$$

where c is the constant marginal cost of production. All consumers at θ_* and closer will be charged a price $p_j{}^i = S_i \geq c$.

Figure 7.4 illustrates this perfect discrimination solution. Quantity $\hat{z}_j$ is sold with nonuniform prices while $z_j{}^0$ is sold under the alternative uniform price policy. Using the index S_i to discriminate increases profit from $p_j{}^0 x \omega \hat{p}_j$ to $\upsilon xy \hat{p}_j$ as indicated in the figure.[6]

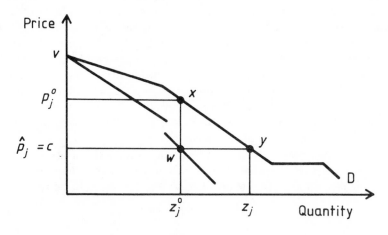

Figure 7.4
Index sorting by S_i

7.2.2 Sorting by Type

Suppose now that consumers differ not only in their ideal brand (location), but also in their demand price and strength of brand preference. With these extended differences, an index (or indexes) related to consumer surplus and serving as a basis for discriminatory prices would generally involve the three parameters θ_i, υ_i, and τ_i. Whatever the specific details of the index selection, the information that surplus-extracting sellers require concerning consumer preferences is increased.

It helps in thinking about methods of discrimination in this case to group individuals with the same pair of (υ_i, τ_i) values. We refer to such homogeneous groups as **types**. Following Shaked and Sutton (1983, 1984) and Borenstein (1985), suppose that the individuals in *each* type are located uniformly about the unit circle.[7] This means that the demand functions with monopoly and competitive segments developed in section 7.2.1 can be viewed as pertaining to a specific type. In turn, there are as many demand schedules of the form shown in figure 7.3 as there are consumer types. However, and this is the real complication, different types may be consuming in different segments of the demand schedule even when each firms sells at one price.

---

[6] The figure is illustrative in that it assumes the prices $p_j{}^0$ and $\hat{p}_j$ occur in the competitive segment of the demand. Other segments could be involved depending, among other things, on the level of $\bar{p}$ and c. It is always required that $p_j{}^0 \geq \hat{p}_j$, however.

[7] While each type is assumed to follow the uniform density in location, the total number of individuals of any given type may differ in the cross-section of types.

Following Borenstein (1985), figure 7.5 illustrates the manner in which the demand facing firm j is built up when it sets a price above that of all other brands: $p_j > p_k = \bar{p}$ for all firms $k \neq j$. Depending on type, every consumer falls into one of three categories relative to product j.

1   *Lost to competition* Rearranging (7.12b) gives the conditions for firm j to lose a customer to supercompetitive pricing: $\tau < J(p_j - \bar{p})$. For fixed prices and number of firms, whether or not an individual consumer is lost in this way depends only on the individual parameter τ. Types satisfying this inequality are indicated by T_4 in figure 7.5. They are characterized by weak strength of location preference and they choose brands largely on the basis of price differentials. For example, as j increases its price and the difference $p_j - \bar{p}$ becomes larger, consumers with larger values of τ will (supercompetitively) shift away from firm j. Conversely, there is a reduction in the types lost supercompetitively as p_j goes to $\bar{p}$ (or the number of firms decreases).

2   *Served* Types whose best brand is that offered by firm j and whose demand price is less than that firm's price will purchase from j. This specifically requires the values of parameters τ and v to be such that

$$\tau > J(p_j - \bar{p}) \tag{7.15a}$$

and

$$v > p_j \tag{7.15b}$$

There are, moreover, two ways in which this set of consumers can be served: monopolistically or in monopolistic competition. If conditions (7.15) obtain, (7.10a) provides the values of v and τ which defined the consumer types at the margin between these two segments:

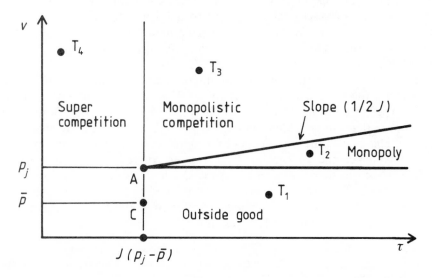

Figure 7.5
Demand segments and consumer types

$$v = \frac{p_j + \bar{p}}{2} + \frac{\tau}{2J}$$

which has a slope of $1/2J$ and a vertical intercept midway between the prices p_j and $\bar{p}$ (see figure 7.5). Types with v large relative to τ, represented by T_3 in the figure, are served competitively; types with τ large relative to v, represented by T_2, are served monopolistically. Notice also that an increase in the number of firms J "crowds" the product space and the size of j's monopoly region decreases.

3 *Lost to outside good* For $v = p_j$ only those consumers located at brand j's location will purchase from j (again, assuming $\tau \geqslant 0$). All other consumers, those with strong brand preferences, $\tau > J(p_j - \bar{p})$, and relatively low price, $v < p_j$, will be lost to firm j and the industry. These consumers purchase the outside good instead.

Aggregate Demand. If the prices of rival products are held fixed, the quantity to be sold by firm j at any price is the simple sum of the demand from those types falling in the monopoly and monopolistically competitive regions. In the continuous case we would integrate over these demand functions weighted by the population density obtaining in each region of the (v, τ) consumer space. For example, in the symmetric case where all firms charge the same price (and there is no supercompetition) the total demand z_j is given by[8]

$$z_j = 2I \int_0^x \int_{p_j}^{p_j + \tau/2J} \frac{v - p_j}{\tau} h(v, \tau) \, dv \, d\tau + \int_0^x \int_{p_j + \tau/2J}^x \frac{1}{J} h(v, \tau) \, dv \, d\tau \quad (7.16)$$

where the first and second set of integrals on the right-hand side give the monopoly and monopolistically competitive demands respectively and $h(v, \tau)$ is the density function of types. The difficulties in developing Nash equilibrium conditions are apparent from the complexity of this demand specification.[9] That is not of concern here, as our present interest is limited to some special aspects of price discrimination in this case.

Discrimination, Type and Demand. The surplus received by an individual depends on the location θ_i, strength of brand preference τ_i, and demand price v_i parameters as indicated on (7.14). These individual-specific parameters would be sufficient information for discrimination if the product were sold by a single isolated firm. The availability of substitutes and market competition, however, limits the extent of the surplus that can be captured by any firm. In this case the maximum that any one firm can charge any buyer is no longer the buyer's demand price, but the price (adjusted for any characteristic differences) being charged by the firm's lowest-price rival when that is below his demand price. How does the presence of substitute products affect the firm's ability to

---

[8] Also, as the proportion of the population with "low" τ decreases, the supercompetitive segment becomes quantitatively less important.

[9] See Borenstein (1985) for further indications of this complexity. The problem, in part, is that the aggregate demand function (aggregated across all consumer types) will have a large number of kinks. These kinks introduce many pathological solutions and the analysis fails to provide economic insights.

discriminate? And how specifically does that effect depend on whether or not the firm is selling competitively or monopolistically?

An answer to these questions can be developed in terms of the standard relationship between the consumer surplus and the price elasticity of demand. The firm's demand function, after all, embodies whatever prices rivals (are perceived to) charge. Given the state of competition, the demand function is the schedule of maximum prices that would be paid for the given commodity in comparison with all others. Answers to the above questions thus center on how these elasticities are related to the v and τ parameters. The demand equations (7.9) and (7.11) are the basis for developing these relationships. In the monopolistically competitive segment, equation (7.11) can be used to calculate the price elasticity of the quantity demanded as

$$\eta^c = \frac{-p_j}{p_j - \bar{p} - \tau/J} \tag{7.17}$$

And, in the monopoly segment, using (7.9) similarly gives

$$\eta^m = \frac{-p_j}{p_j - v} \tag{7.18}$$

The interesting feature of these elasticity measures is that they depend on different preference parameters. The elasticity of demand in the monopolistically competitive segment η^c depends on the consumer's strength of brand preference τ but not on the demand price v. Consumers who are served competitively by a firm cannot be sorted in elasticity using an index based on v, unless v is otherwise correlated with τ in the population. Conversely, η^m depends only on the demand price v and not at all on τ. Those consumers who are served monopolistically by the firm cannot be sorted in elasticity, again as a basis for third-degree discrimination, using an index based on τ unless that parameter happens to be correlated with v in the population of consumers. Finally, note that

$$\frac{d\eta^c}{d\tau} = \frac{-p_j}{J(p_j - \bar{p} - \tau/J)^2} < 0$$

so that τ is inversely related to η^c: when served competitively, consumers with greater strength of preference have more inelastic demands and would face higher discriminatory prices. Similarly,

$$\frac{d\eta^m}{dv} = \frac{-p_j}{(p_j - v)^2} < 0$$

and v is inversely related to η^m: when served monopolistically, consumers with greater demand prices have more inelastic demand and they would face higher discriminatory prices.

In summary, monopolistic competition among firms selling heterogeneous brands does not forestall price discrimination. It does, however, change the nature of index selection from that usual in the single-seller (single-product) monopoly. In this usual case, discrimination takes the standard form of "value-of-service" pricing, with the monopolist charging the greatest price to those consumers with the greatest demand price. This aspect is captured in equation (7.18) where v is the sole individual-specific parameter in the demand elasticity. With product differentiation, a second basis for index sorting consumers can arise. Buyers with high strength of brand preference τ can be profitably sorted from those with low strength in a discriminatory scheme (for example, by offering "branded" and "private label" versions of the product; see Frank, 1983). This aspect is captured in equation (7.17) where τ is part of the demand elasticity specification. Unfortunately, the strength of preference basis for discrimination is often overlooked, as it is not part of the standard monopoly model.

Costs of Index Sorting. Throughout the above discussion it has been assumed that there are prohibitive costs for consumers to arbitrage price differences by reselling. Under this assumption, whether a firm can profitably sort consumers by an index depends on two considerations: (a) the degree of competition and the heterogeneity of the consumer population, which jointly determine the gross gain possible from discrimination; (b) the cost of observing the distinguishing characteristics of consumers as a basis for index sorting them. More generally the firm must also incur costs to separate consumers, making it costly for them to arbitrage by reselling. For a given consumer population, sellers will reduce the precision with which they observe consumer characteristics as the cost of observation increases. Similarly, they will reduce their separation efforts as these costs become larger. Grouping consumers in somewhat coarse index ranges can reduce the observation and separation costs, but it also reduces the ability of the seller to extract consumer surplus. The obvious marginal conditions obtain.

E7.2

Base Point Pricing and Other Discriminatory Practices

The geographic separation of buyers often creates opportunities for profitable price discrimination. In such cases the buyer's location relative to the seller is the index used in selection. The systems of index selection are based on either "delivered" prices (the seller pays for transportation) or nonuniform free on board (fob) prices (the seller sets factory, or mill, prices and the buyer pays for transportation). Perhaps the most notorious, if not widespread, of the delivered price systems occurs when sales are made from a *basing point*. In this system the delivered price is equal to a base price plus the costs of freight to the place of delivery calculated from a pre-designated basing point, which need not be the location of the seller's factory.

When several such basing points are employed, each with different base prices, a *multiple basing point* system is obtained. In this case the delivered price is commonly calculated as the lowest combination of base price plus freight to the delivery site. When the actual cost of freight incurred from the seller's plant to the buyer is less than that calculated in the basing point price, *phantom freight* is said to be paid. When, alternatively, the actual freight cost is less, there is said to be *freight absorption*. Given that the production and basing points differ, either most buyers will pay phantom freight or there will be freight absorption. In cases where an otherwise identical product is sold to such buyers, the reader can readily see that price discrimination occurs when the delivered price less actual transportation cost (the mill price) differs across buyers. If the basing point happens to be the seller's plant, then the presence of either phantom freight or freight absorption directly indicates discrimination.

While geographic price discrimination (location index selection) is the form most frequently investigated under antitrust statutes, it is not the most frequently observed. Since Kessel (1958), the classic textbook example has been price discrimination in medicine based on an income index. Think also of how theaters discriminate in favor of senior citizens, students and children, of how telephone rates vary by time of day and week, of how residential and business rates differ for electricity prices and of how airline fares are established depending on length of stay, advance booking time, destination, and route taken. Students of economics know all too well how universities give tuition discounts (scholarships, fellowships) to better students (who are also sought by other universities and therefore have more elastic demands for a particular school). These are only a small sample of the many everyday instances of price discrimination by index selection.

Finally, the reader can take some comfort in the 1988 schedule of membership dues for the American Economic Association and subscription to the *American Economic Review* (*AER*), which might be considered as evidence that economists can (in fact) practice what they preach:

> $38.50 for members with annual income of $30,000 or less;
> $46.20 for members with annual income between $30,000 and $40,000;
> $53.90 for members with annual income above $40,000;
> $19.25 for junior members (registered students);
> $200.00 for subscriptions by libraries, institutions, or firms.

Liebowitz (1986) surmises that most photocopying of copyright protected material is done in libraries and involves academic journals. Since such institutions pay higher subscription rates, he argues that photocopying does not subtract much from the revenues of publishers. Instead, he maintains, photocopying reduces the price elasticity of demand for journals by institutions and increases it for individual subscribers. Erkkila (1986) is not fully impressed by the *AER* efforts at discrimination. He asks, for example, why there is no discrimination among institutions, for surely the *AER* is copied differently in municipal libraries than in academic or corporate libraries. Finally, it is of interest to note that Erkkila presents some evidence that (generally nonprofit) law journals are much less likely than economic journals to price discriminate.

7.3   Self-selection

When the costs and imprecision of index sorting significantly reduce profitability, the firm can alternatively structure its product line and terms of sale in a fashion which provides incentives for buyers to reveal their willingness to pay.

We ask here about the general restrictions that must be placed on product offerings, including terms and conditions of sale, to make self-selection effective as a means of price discrimination.

7.3.1 The Basic Model

Think of a monopoly seller who maximizes profits by tailoring **commodity bundles** ϕ_i, one for each of the i, $k = 1, 2, \ldots, I$ buyer types in the market. The bundles are specifically designed to solve

$$\max \pi(\phi_1, \phi_2, \ldots, \phi_I) \tag{7.19a}$$

subject to

$$U_i(\phi_i) \geq U_i(0) \qquad \text{for all } i \tag{7.19b}$$

$$U_i(\phi_i) \geq U_i(\phi_k) \qquad \text{for all } i \text{ and } k \tag{7.19c}$$

The commodity bundles can be described by various attributes (each ϕ_i is a vector), including those defining the relevant physical characteristics of the commodity and the conditions of sale (price, warranty, credit terms, delivery date, etc.). To maximize (7.19a) the bundles must be designed to extract as much consumer surplus as possible. The "as possible" qualification is given by the constraints: the bundle designed for any buyer type must lead to the sale of all units for which the type's demand price is greater than marginal cost *and* it must not permit the type to escape surplus extraction by purchasing a bundle for any other type. That is, the constraints are of two kinds.

1 **Outside good constraints:** the set of I restrictions given by (7.19b) requires that the seller offer bundles such that each type i finds one bundle yielding utility not less than the $U_i(0)$ value of the outside good.
2 **Incentive compatibility constraints:** the $I(I - 1)$ restrictions imposed by (7.19c) insure self-selection by requiring that there is only one bundle ϕ_i which is (weakly) preferred by type i in comparison with all other available bundles.

What Bundles Specifically? It is frequently observed that firms offer both branded and generic versions of their product. Otherwise identical versions of canned foods, ready to eat cereals, razor blades, paper products, tires, watches, and so on are sold with the brand name of the manufacturer *and* under the private labels of marketing agents. In almost all cases, the "unbranded" versions have lower prices and, although some consumers know generally that such private labeling occurs, most do not know clearly the branded to unbranded correspondences. One explanation of this phenomenon is that branding is just a bundling of quality information, more or less, with the product under consideration.[10]

---

[10] In *FTC v. Borden Co., 383 U.S. 637* (1966), the Supreme Court ruled that Borden had used unlawful price discrimination in selling its homogenized canned evaporated milk at a higher price when branded than for its private label version of "like grade and quality." On remand, however, an appelate court ruled that there was no injury to competition in such a practice if the price difference between the versions simply reflected "consumer preferences" for the branded item (see *Borden Co. v. FTC, 381 F.2d 175* (1967), p. 181 of the opinion).

To see briefly how such bundling works in a discriminatory way, suppose that buyer types differ in the strength of their preferences as in the spatial analog of monopolistic competition (recall section 7.2.2). In this case the seller discriminates by sorting the types with strong brand preferences (charging them the higher price) from those with weak strength of preference. Consumers will sort themselves when they are imperfectly informed (pre-purchased) and cannot identify the output of any given manufacturer without a brand name. Types with strong preferences for one manufacturer's product will self-select the higher-priced branded product (provided that the price differential is not too large) and those with weak preferences will buy the cheaper private label. In this case we think of the ϕ_i bundles as differing in price and information (brand name).

A wide range of bundle descriptions have been used in applications of the general problem (7.19).[11] While this suggests that we deal with the surplus extraction by self-selection in a general way, the details of the problem solution are easiest to understand in a specific context. The analysis to follow specifically deals with the price–quality bundles.

7.3.2 Self-selection with Price and Quality

Suppose that the commodity bundles of interest are those defined by price (p) and quality (ξ) pairs: $\phi_i = (p_i, \xi_i)$.[12] Further, let individual types differ only in a single way in their preference over ϕ as measured by the *taste* parameter t_i. In turn, write $U_i(\phi_i) = U(p_i, \xi_i, t_i)$ and order types by i such that $t_i > t_{i-1}$ for all i. At times it will be convenient to refer to types with greater t_i (or i) as having "higher taste."

Single-Crossing, Monotonicity, and Adjacency. The aspect of the general self-selection problem (7.19) that is perhaps the most difficult to deal with is the large (I^2) number of incentive compatibility constraints. In this regard, one helpful set of restrictions on types assumes that (a) $U(\cdot)$ is increasing in the quality index ξ and decreasing in price p, (b) $U(\cdot)$ is quasi-concave, and (c) $U_{pt}(p, \xi; t) \geqslant 0$ and $U_{\xi t}(p, \xi; t) > 0$. These restrictions imply that the rate of substitution between p and $\xi (-U_{\xi t}/U_{pt})$ is strictly increasing in the taste parameter t for all commodity bundles; that is, higher-taste types are willing to pay more for a given increment in quality at every quality level. The immediate and important consequence of this is that any two price–quality indifference contours for any two types (with different tastes) can cross at most once, as illustrated in figure 7.6. Cooper (1984) and Maskin and Riley (1984) refer to this as the **single-crossing property** of preferences. The key implication of such single crossing is that the incentive compatibility constraints (7.19c) for any ϕ_i can then be written simply in terms of the utility they provide for the immediately

[11] The general problem has been adapted by Mirrlees (1971, 1976) and Atkinson and Stiglitz (1976) to the choice of optimal tax policy, by Stiglitz (1977), where the firm seeks to sort customers by the probability of accident, by Mussa and Rosen (1978) and Spence (1980), where the monopolist designs a self-selection scheme using price–quality bundles, and by Chiang and Spatt (1982) and De Vane and Saving (1983), where sellers use different price–time bundles.

[12] Again, ξ may measure the single relevant characteristic of a product, or it may be a scalar-valued index of multiple characteristics as, for example, developed by Bresnahan (1982).

neighboring types $i - 1$ and $i + 1$. We work our way to this result in several steps, the first of which is to show a monotonicity property that derives directly from single crossing.

Let $t_i > t_k$, with i having higher taste than k. Further, consider three price–quality pairs $\phi = (p, \xi)$, $\hat{\phi} = (\hat{p}, \hat{\xi})$, and $\phi^* = (p^*, \xi^*)$. Suppose that $p \geq p^*$ and $\xi \geq \xi^*$ on the price–quality plane, which leaves ϕ northeast of ϕ^*. The single-crossing property of utilities implies that if type k prefers ϕ to ϕ^*, then so must type i. As a second case suppose that $p^* \geq \hat{p}$ and $\xi^* \geq \hat{\xi}$. Now, the single crossing implies that if type i prefers $\hat{\phi}$ to ϕ^*, then so must type k. These two taste-related aspects of interpersonal preferences are called the **monotonicity** result. Figure 7.6 illustrates this monotonicity using the single-crossing property and two types $t_i > t_k$. Of first note in the figure is the fact that the indifference level marked by U_i' indicates pairs preferred to those marked by U_i'' (since utility is decreasing in p and increasing in ξ). Consider the pair (p^*, ξ^*) where U_i'' crosses U_k'' and divide the price–quality plane into four quadrants about this point. Of particular interest is the northeast quadrant, where type k's preferred set is a subset of type i's preferred set. In this quadrant any bundle preferred by k must also be preferred by i. Conversely, in the southwest quadrant i's preferred set is a subset of that for type k, and any bundle preferred (relative, again, to ϕ^*) by i must also be preferred to k.[13]

The final implication of the single-crossing property (**adjacency**) is now easily understood: when type i prefers bundle (p_i, ξ_i) to adjacent bundles (p_k, ξ_k) for $k = i + 1$ and $k = i - 1$, this implies that i prefers (p_i, ξ_i) to (p_l, ξ_l) for *all*

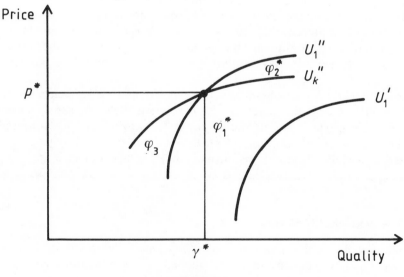

Figure 7.6
Single crossing

---

[13] It helps in understanding figure 7.6 to note that, relative to ϕ^*, (a) ϕ_2 is in i's preferred set but not in k's, (b) ϕ_3 is in k's preferred set but not in i's, and (c) ϕ_1 lies in the preferred set of both i and k.

bundles $l = 1, 2, \ldots$. Proof of this adjacency relation is by a straightforward iteration of the monotonicity property.

In short, the single-crossing property, through the implied monotonicity and adjacency, greatly reduces the complexity of the general problem (7.19) for it means that we need impose the self-selection constraints on any type i only for the immediately neighboring types $i + 1$ and $i - 1$.[14]

Profits. The final requirement to be placed on the model is critical, but less controversial. Specifically, it is assumed that the seller's profits are increasing in prices p_i and decreasing in quality ξ_i, and the isoprofit contours in (p, ξ) space are convex (π is quasi-concave).

E7.3

Price Discrimination with Ideal Index Selection

As a basis of comparison for self-selection results, it is useful to look first at the ideal index selection solution. Following Cooper (1984), assume for the moment that the taste-type parameter of each consumer can be precisely observed without cost and that reselling among consumers is prohibitively expensive. In this case (a) the incentive compatibility restrictions (7.19c) are irrelevant and (b) when the seller just captures the surplus of each consumer the constraints (7.19b) hold as strict equalities. Since the incentive compatibility restrictions are not necessary and reselling is assumed impossible, the (p, ξ) rate of substitution for each type t_i can be set equal to the rate of (isoprofit) transformation between p and ξ for the firm. Because types are precisely observed and surpluses are fully captured, this tangency occurs on iso-utilities where each type is just indifferent to consuming the good or not (note that the iso-utility contours are marked that way in the figure and that they pass through the origin).

Figure 7.7 illustrates the solution for two-types t_1 and t_2. It is clear from the figure that in this case the index selection solution does not satisfy incentive compatibility since type 2 prefers the bundle (p_1^*, ξ_1^*) to the one he is offered by the seller, that is, $U(p_1^*, \xi_1^*; t_2) > U(p_2^*, \xi_2^*; t_2)$. As reselling is "exogenously" prohibited with index selection, this incompatibility is no problem.

7.3.3   The Price–quality Result

If self-selection is to be employed successfully, the seller must offer incentive compatible bundles. For this to occur, the adjacency condition requires that

---

[14] When the firm has more than one, two decision variables or the number of parameters defining consumer preferences is greater than the adjacency condition generally will not follow. Some limited results have been obtained for such cases; see, for example, Spence (1980) for multiproduct pricing, Cooper and Hayes (1984) for multiperiod insurance, and Matthews and Moore (1984) for monopoly provision of warranties and quality.

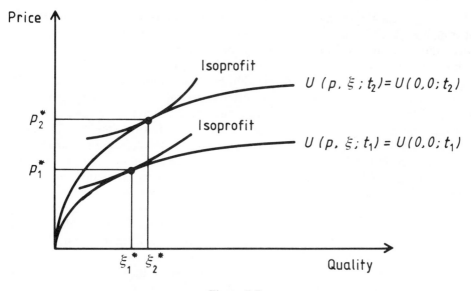

Figure 7.7
Index selection

every type i be offered a bundle preferred to that made available to neighbors. This requirement, plus the fact that the seller maximizes a profit function which is increasing in p and decreasing in ξ, means that the (p, ξ) bundles will follow a quite specific pattern. The following restatement of the general self-selection problem (7.19), and especially the form of the constraints, makes this pattern clear:

$$\max \pi(p_1, \xi_1; p_2, \xi_2; \ldots; p_I, \xi_I) \tag{7.20a}$$

subject to

$$U(p_1, \xi_1; t_1) = U(0, 0; t_1) \tag{7.20b}$$

$$U(p_i, \xi_i; t_i) > U(0, 0; t_i) \qquad i = 2, \ldots, I \tag{7.20b'}$$

$$U(p_i, \xi_i; t_i) = U(p_{i-1}, \xi_{i-1}; t_i) \qquad i = 2, \ldots, I \tag{7.20c}$$

$$U(p_i, \xi_i; t_i) > U(p_{i+1}, \xi_{i+1}; t_i) \qquad i = 1, 2, \ldots, I - 1 \tag{7.20'}$$

The outside-good constraint on the firm's profits is now written in two parts, for the equality can possibly hold only for the type with the lowest taste ($i = 1$). If $U(p_i, \xi_i; t_i) = U(0, 0; t_i)$ for $i > 1$, then the monotonicity condition (that price and quality both be nondecreasing in t) would imply $U(p_{i-1}, \xi_{i-1}; t_i) > U(p_i, \xi_i; t_i)$, which defeats self-selection. Thus, the constraint must hold with equality for the lowest-taste type. Otherwise, the seller could increase profits by raising p_1, and all other bundle prices, without violating the conditions for self-selection.

Incentive Compatibility. The incentive compatibility constraints also have two parts. These correspond to the two halves of the adjacency condition: each type must be indifferent to his bundle and the one offered to the next-lowest type

(7.20c), and each type must strictly prefer his bundle to that offered to the next-highest type (7.20c'). The logic of these adjacency conditions becomes clear when the purchase decisions are considered in sequence. To do this, refer to figure 7.8 where there are just three types ($I = 3$). It is easiest to begin with the highest type since there is no self-selection constraint imposed from above. As a result, whatever the bundle (p_2, ξ_2) offered to the second-highest type, the monopolist can adjust type 3's bundle along the indifference contour given by $U(p_2, \xi_2; t_2)$ to maximize profits. Thus type 3 is offered the bundle SS3 where the indifference contour $U(p_2, \xi_2; t_3)$ is just tangent to the seller's isoprofit π_3. For types below the highest, the situation is somewhat more complicated and the monopolist maximizes profits where (a) each type is just indifferent to its bundle and the one taken by the next-lowest type (condition (7.20c)) and (b) each type strictly prefers his bundle to the one taken by the next-highest type (condition (7.20c')). Type 2, for example, is offered bundle SS2 which is just incentive compatible with bundle SS3 but yields less profit than bundle E2 – if E2 were offered, however, it would be purchased by type 3. Similarly, type 1 is offered bundle SS1 which is just incentive compatible with bundles SS2 and SS3 but leads to less profits that bundle E1.[15] Again, if E1 were offered, types 2 and 3 would prefer that and foil the surplus extraction scheme. Note, finally, that the type 1 indifference contour through SS1 intersects the origin and indicates price–quality combinations which yield zero surplus to type 1.

All the above conditions arise from the underlying fact that the profit function is increasing in p and decreasing in ξ but utility has the opposite properties, decreasing in p and increasing in ξ. Thus, if the constraints do not follow the

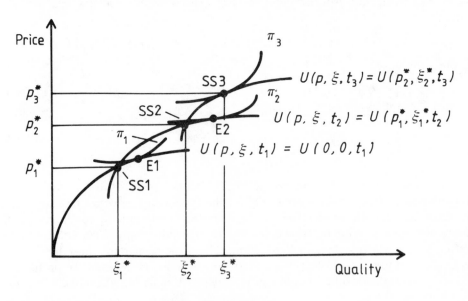

Figure 7.8
Sorting by self-selection

[15] The reader can see the importance of the single-crossing property here. Since $U(p_2^*, \xi_2^*, t_3)$ passes through SS2, it must then pass southeast of SS1.

indicated pattern, both the firm and any type *i* could gain in the neighborhood of the solution with increases in *both* price and quality.

Self-selection Solution. To extract consumer surplus in the fashion of index selection, the seller offers bundles to lower-taste types which would be preferred by higher-taste types (this gives rise to the usual exogenous prohibition against reselling). To make the discrimination self-selective, with buyers accurately revealing their type by their purchases, it is necessary that constraints be imposed on the feasible bundles so that types do not have an incentive to "cross over." This means that higher types must be offered some surplus to induce them away from the bundles designed for lower types. For the profit-maximizing seller, whose profits increase in the prices set for bundles, it is accordingly clear that (a) the outside good constraint (7.20b) will be binding for the lowest type and (b) the incentive compatibility constraints (7.20c) will be binding for all higher types.

The "biases" due to self-selection are evident in this sorting. The highest type *I* is always served efficiently in the sense that (for the achieved level of utility) producer surplus is maximized. If that were not so, the seller could move along *I*'s indifference contour and increase profits (without violating any incentive compatibility constraint, for there is no higher type). For any type below *I*, the utility–MRS and profit–MRS equality does not obtain (the allocative efficiency condition). As a result, with self-selection all taste types except *I* receive bundles of lower quality and price than they would under *costless* index selection.[16] If the incentive compatibility constraints were not imposed, both consumers and the producer would benefit from increasing both price and quality in the neighborhood of the self-selection bundle.

7.4 Nonlinear Prices

Product differences coupled with self-selection selling policies permit price discrimination even when it is costly to observe the relevant demand characteristics of consumers. In many cases, such as with electricity, the product is unyieldingly homogeneous so that the price–quality self-selection mechanism considered above is inapplicable. The underlying self-selection principle still applies, however, as price–*quantity* bundles can be profitably used.

Nonlinear Prices. Some standard terminology is helpful in setting out these ideas. A **linear pricing schedule** occurs when the firm adopts a *pure price policy*: a single price is set and all units are sold at this price. The linearity arises in the

---

[16] The interpretation of this self-selection "bias" varies depending on the context of the problem. For example, in Stiglitz (1977), where price and insurance coverage form the bundles, self-selection is said to produce "incomplete" insurance (see SE7.2 for details). Note, finally, that there may be occasions when the seller can extract more surplus from the high type if he constrains the low type to a zero purchase than if he allows the low type to purchase a strictly positive amount. For example, if the lowest type in the population is sufficiently small, then it will pay the seller to exclude them entirely. See Seade (1977) for such a corner solution in the context of an income tax problem.

consumer's **outlay schedule** $\omega(z) = pz$, where p is the constant price paid by the consumer for every unit purchased. Alternatively, the outlay is **nonlinear**, $\omega(z) = p(z)z$, when each unit's price differs with the number of units purchased. In this second case the derivative of the outlay schedule with respect to quantity is the *marginal* price and this differs from the *average* price $p(z)$.

Perhaps the most familiar example of a nonlinear schedule is the **two-part tariff**. This selling policy is generally recognized by the fixed entrance (membership, qualification, privilege) fee $F > 0$ and a (frequently constant) unit price p such that

$$\omega^t(z) = F + pz \qquad \text{for } z > 0$$
$$\qquad\quad = 0 \qquad\qquad \text{for } z = 0 \tag{7.21}$$

where $\omega^t(z)$ indicates the consumer's outlay at each quantity z. The superscript t denotes the two-part tariff. Note that the marginal price p is less than the average price $p_{avg}(z) = F/z + p$ for strictly positive quantities. For example, a franchise contract typically involves a fixed "up-front" fee and then a per unit price on some factor used in the franchisee's output (along with a contract stipulation that the franchisee take its requirements of this factor from the franchisor), telephone charges are typically made up of a fixed monthly fee and a constant price per message unit, and, for those who shave, shaving service is paid for with a fixed fee for the razor plus a price per unit blade.

A second familiar nonlinear pricing schedule is **block pricing**, where marginal price increases or decreases for successively greater units of demand. With two blocks this takes the form

$$\omega^b(z) = p_H z \qquad\qquad\qquad \text{for } 0 \leqslant z \leqslant z^*$$
$$\qquad\quad = p_L z + (p_H - p_L)z^* \qquad \text{for } z > z^* \tag{7.22}$$

where p_H is the (high) price for quantities in the initial block $[0, z^*]$ and p_L is the (low) price for the trailing block $[z^*, \infty)$. Telephone tariffs often have this form. For the first z_1 message units or less a lump sum F is paid, for message units from z_1 to z_2 the rate is p_1 per unit, and for more than z_2 units the rate is $p_2 < p_1$ per unit. The quantity discounts used in retailing are also examples of block pricing.

E7.4

Self-selection with Two-part Pricing

To establish a link with the self-selection theory of section 7.3, note that with two-part (block) tariffs consumers are free to choose the price–quantity pair which they want to purchase. A frequently used example of such tariffs, which emphasizes how they reveal the consumers' willingness to pay, has been developed by Telser (1965). The example is based on the trade practices of International Business Machines (IBM). For many years IBM would only lease its computing and tabulating machines to users; it would not sell them (see *IBM v. United States, 298 U.S. 131* 1986). The lease agreement was always stated as a fixed fee per shift per time period. Until the early 1950s, the lease also required that lessees buy their supply of data (punch) cards from IBM.[17]

In such a **tie-in sale**, sellers of one product require their customers to make all their purchases of a second complementary product from them. In the IBM case, let F be the unit rental rate for the computing machine and p the unit price of the cards. Further, let z_i indicate the number of cards used by consumer i per unit time. The price paid for the (bundled) computing *services* is therefore $p_i = F + z_i p$. As Telser observes, the card costs depend on the number of cards used and "reveal the intensity" of the consumer's demand for (the cost savings on using the) computing services. It is clear that p_i is a two-part tariff where F is the fixed fee and $z_i p$ is the variable part. By choosing the number of cards, each consumer chooses a particular price–quantity bundle. The tie-in thus enabled IBM to extract greater surplus from consumers valuing the computer service more.[18] Alternatively, IBM could have charged each consumer a different rental rate per time period and allowed them to purchase their card requirements freely. However, that would have presumed that IBM possessed the (index selection) information to discriminate in this way. The self-selection two-part tariff leaves consumers to reveal that information.

Feasibility. A nonlinear price schedule will be an effective method of price discrimination only when the product cannot be rebundled and resold by consumers. If the outlay schedule $\omega(z)$ is **subadditive**, $\omega(z^a) + \omega(z^b) > \omega(z^a + z^b)$, then several consumers could combine their purchase (say, using a buyer's cooperative) and defeat the nonlinear schedule. Alternatively, if $\omega(z)$ is **superadditive**, $\omega(z^a) + \omega(z^b) < \omega(z^a + z^b)$, then each consumer could divide his purchases into ever decreasing lots to foil the discrimination scheme. In the next sections the correspondence between these feasibility requirements and the incentive compatibility constraints of the general self-selection model are developed.

7.4.1 Price–quantity Bundles

Assume, as before, that there is a large but finite number of consumer types. Each type i has increasing and quasi-concave subutility $u(z_i, t_i)$ when purchasing quantity z_i of the good. $u(\cdot)$ is a subutility in that it arises from a quasi-linear

---

[17] If the machines had a mechanical failure and IBM repair technicians discovered that a lessee was using unauthorized cards, IBM imposed a penalty by charging (prohibitively) for its repairs.

[18] In addition to their role in price discrimination, tying arrangements may act as a way of information gathering in noncooperative games. Cummings and Ruther (1979) offer than explanation in the matter of *Northern Pacific Railway v. U.S., 356 U.S. 1* (1957). There, buyers of Northern Pacific's land were required to ship forest products developed from this land over the Northern Pacific Railway *unless* lower rates and/or better service were available from competing railways. Cummings and Ruther argue that the tying of railway services to the purchase of the land was not for surplus extraction, but to provide an incentive for buyers to disclose the lower rates and conditions of service offered by its rivals. The contracts did not include any obligation that the Northern Pacific meet the competition, and so there was no commitment to deter cheating.

utility, so that the marginal utility of income is constant and equal to unity. For reasons which should now be clear, suppose further that u follows the single-crossing property in the cross-section of types.

When faced with a nonlinear (quantity-dependent) price schedule, each type chooses a quantity and therewith a price and outlay. Consumer i clearly prefers the quantity–outlay bundle $\{z_i, \omega(z_i)\}$ to bundle $\{z_j, \omega(z_j)\}$ when

$$u(z_i, t_i) - \omega(z_i) \geq u(z_j; t_i) - \omega(z_j) \tag{7.23}$$

Suppose that the types are ordered such that, for all z, $u(z; t_i) < u(z; t_j)$ implies $t_j > t_i$ and $j > i$. Then an outlay schedule $\omega(z)$ will be consistent with the incentive compatibility conditions (7.20) when

$$\omega(z_1) = u(z_1; t_1) \tag{7.24}$$

$$\omega(z_2) = u(z_2; t_2) - u(z_1; t_2) - \omega(z_1)$$

$$\omega(z_3) = u(z_3; t_3) - u(z_2; t_3) - \omega(z_2)$$

$$\vdots$$

$$\omega(z_I) = u(z_I; t_I) - u(z_{I-1}; t_I) - \omega(z_{I-1})$$

Notice in this recursion that individuals of the lowest type 1 receive no surplus. For type 2, there is a surplus of $u(z_2; t_2) - \omega(z_2) = u(z_1; t_2) - \omega(z_1)$, which is the difference between the outlay for z_1 and the type 2 individual's demand price for that quantity (as an all-or-nothing offer). This pattern continues, with successively higher types receiving successively greater surplus. Recognizing the recursive structure, it is usual to write these incentive compatibility constraints more compactly in the form

$$\omega(z_i) = \sum_{k=1}^{i} \{u(z_k; t_k) - u(z_{k-1}; t_k)\} \geq 0 \qquad \text{for all } i \tag{7.25}$$

The firm's problem is to find the discriminatory outlay schedule $\omega(z)$ and the associated price schedule which maximizes profit subject (7.25). The reader can now see that this is a specific application of the general self-selection problem (7.20). Rather than going directly to the allocation results that were developed in that earlier section, it is instructive to follow a somewhat indirect analysis for the moment.

7.4.2 Nonlinear Pricing and Welfare

To distinguish between nonlinear pricing schedules which are profit maximizing and those which are socially optimal we follow Spence (1979) and focus on the total surplus maximization problem:[19]

$$\max(\lambda S + \pi) \tag{7.26}$$

where

$$S = \sum_i N_i \{u(z_i; t_i) - \omega(z_i)\}$$

[19] A similar formulation is used by Roberts (1979), Katz (1983), and Oren et al. (1983).

is the sum of individual consumer surpluses and

$$\pi = \sum_i N_i \omega(z_i) - c\left(\sum_i N_i z_i\right)$$

is the firm's profits (producers' surplus). In this problem we consider only incentive compatible outlay schedules. That is, the solutions to problem (7.26) are made subject to (7.25).

The parameter λ of (7.26) determines the general properties of the aggregate criterion. Choosing $\lambda = 1$ leads to the usual unconstrained welfare maximization. At the other pole, with $\lambda = 0$, there is pure profit maximization. There are also intermediate cases with $0 < \lambda < 1$: for example, λ might be set to establish some regulated positive (not necessarily maximizing) profit level $\pi \geq 0$.

Writing the total surplus out in full gives

$$\lambda S + \pi = \lambda \sum_i N_i u(z_i; t_i) - c\left(\sum_i N_i z_i\right) + (1 - \lambda)\sum_i N_i \omega(z_i) \qquad (7.27)$$

Substituting from the incentive compatibility constraints (7.25) for each $\omega(z_i)$ in turn yields

$$\lambda S + \pi = \lambda \sum_i N_i u(z_1; t_i) - c\left(\sum_i N_i z_i\right)$$
$$+ (1 - \lambda)\sum_i N_i \left\{\sum_{k=1}^{i} u(z_k; t_k) - u(z_{k-1}; t_k)\right\}$$

$$(7.28)$$

Since the right-hand side of this equation expresses welfare as a function of the z_i alone, it is used in the derivation of the stationarity conditions of $\lambda S + \pi$:

$$\frac{\partial u(z_i; t_i)}{\partial z_i} = \frac{N_i}{N_i + (1 - \lambda)\bar{N}_{i+1}}\left(\frac{\partial c}{\partial z_i}\right) + \frac{(1 - \lambda)\bar{N}_i}{N_i + (1 - \lambda)\bar{N}_{i+1}}\left(\frac{\partial u(z_i; t_{i+1})}{\partial z_i}\right) \qquad (7.29)$$

for each $i = 1, 2, \ldots, I$ and

$$\bar{N}_i \equiv \sum_{k=i}^{I} N_k \qquad (7.30)$$

which is the total number of individuals of type i and higher. Choose $\bar{N}_{I+1} \equiv 0$. Given that the utility is quasi-linear, type t_i individuals pay price $p_i = \partial u(z_i; t_i)/\partial z_i$ and equations (7.29) quickly determine the optimal nonlinear pricing schedule for both the welfare optimum ($\lambda = 1$) and the profit maximum ($\lambda = 0$).

Self-selection Results. For profit-maximizing sellers, the results derived in this way are analogous to those developed in section 7.3 with price–quality selection. Setting $\lambda = 0$ in (7.29) gives

$$p_i = \frac{N_i/(\partial c/\partial z_i) + \partial u(z_i; t_{i+1})/\partial z_i}{N_i + \bar{N}_{i+1}} \qquad (7.31)$$

The usual self-selection results follow from this condition. First, consumers of the highest type t_I purchase the good at marginal cost (since $\bar{N}_{I+1} \equiv 0$). Second, those of lower type purchase suboptimal quantities at a price above marginal cost, and specifically at a price which is a weighted average of marginal cost and the marginal value placed on the commodity by the next-highest type. Finally, surplus received is increasing in type with individuals of the lowest type purchasing at a price which just makes them indifferent to the considered good and the alternative "outside" good. Once again, these are the standard self-selection relations set out in section 7.3.

Welfare Optimum. To express the welfare criterion let $\lambda = 1$ in (7.29). The associated stationarity condition for each z_i is both simple to derive and quite usual:

$$p_i = \frac{\partial c}{\partial z_i} \tag{7.32}$$

For a homogeneous good we have once more the well-known result that it is optimal to have a uniform (nondiscriminatory) price equal to marginal cost. This is in contrast with the profit-maximizing self-selection conditions where only the highest type pays a price equal to marginal cost.

7.5   Price Discrimination Methods

The extent of price discrimination, as with all the firm's activities, is a decision made at the margin. The optimal extraction of consumer surplus must balance diminishing returns with increasing costs. When it is costly to observe individual demand characteristics directly, so that index selection is ineffective in capturing consumer surplus, the seller is likely to turn to indirect self-selection methods for discrimination. Commodity bundling, block booking, requirement contracts, and tie-in sales are frequently used by multiproduct firms in this way. For single-product firms, nonlinear price schedules designed as multipart tariffs, block tariffs, and quantity discounts are similarly used. A wide range of these methods are considered in the Supplementary Examples that follow. In chapter 8 we describe in detail how the durable-good monopolist's incentive to price discriminate in a time sequence of markets is foiled by consumers with rational expectations.

Supplementary examples

SE7.1   Price Discrimination in Competitive Retailing

Retailing is a generally competitive industry in which a variety of self-selection price discrimination schema have developed. To look briefly at one of these, let us assume that consumers can be divided into two types. Members of the first have high opportunity cost for their time and therefore find it uneconomical to follow prices closely and seek out many bargains. The second type finds such search activity much more cost effective. The implication of this difference in time opportunity cost is that the demand of the second type will be more elastic. We expect that sellers will attempt third-degree price discrimination if it is not too costly to identify the individual type members. How is this done?

One way is to let the consumers select whether or not to use coupons which provide a discount on certain merchandise. Clipping and handling the coupons is costly, however, as it requires considerable time and patience. Because of this, few buyers of the low-elasticity type will use the coupons, while many of the high-elasticity type will. The effect of the coupon is to lower the price to the desired type (Narasimham, 1984, and Villcassim and Wittnik, 1985, review the literature on coupons.) The reader can see that beverage container refunds and trading stamps operate in a similar way to price discriminate against customers with greater time opportunity costs.

Salop (1977), Shilony (1977), Rosenthal (1980), and Varian (1980) have also shown how periodic sales, discounts, and "specials" arise with a mixed-strategy equilibrium in price and discriminate against the same high-search-cost types. Png and Hirshleifer (1987) show how offers by one seller to match the price of others operate in a similar discriminatory way. To take a specific example, tourists in an area have high search costs whereas locals do not. Sellers sort these two classes by their offers to match any other retailer's price. Because of their high search costs, tourists generally do not know the prices of various sellers, but locals do and take advantage of the offers to match.

SE7.2 Price Discrimination in Insurance

Price discrimination by self-selection generally occurs when sellers have high costs in directly observing the detailed demand characteristics of buyers. The insurance market provides an interesting example in this respect, since it is difficult for insurance companies to accurately determine the accident probabilities of specific consumers at the time that the coverage contract is written (this example was developed by Stiglitz, 1977). Nonetheless the contract must specify the risks covered, the amount of insurance, and the policy premium.

Will a single contract be made available to all individuals? Alternatively, will the contracts differ, with higher-risk individuals paying higher premiums? Will the companies only insure high risks, or only low risks? The self-selection selling mechanism we use to answer these questions provides no surprises: high-risk individuals will receive full insurance coverage and average- to low-risk individuals will receive only partial coverage or none at all.

Buyers and Sellers. We assume that the insurance market is made up of a large number of heterogeneous buyers and a large number of identical competitive sellers. A competitive insurance equilibrium occurs when, with respect to any given contract, (a) firms are price-takers, (b) there is equality of demand and supply, and (c) two entry/exit conditions obtain – first the set of all insurance contracts offered must earn zero expected profits for the active firms, and second no insurance contract outside the equilibrium set can make positive expected profits.

Let the insurance buyers have end-of-period wealth W_s depending on the uncertain state s. It is easiest to restrict attention to two states: $s = 1$ indicates the "no loss" state and $s = 2$ indicates the "loss" state. With financial loss l, the expected utility from purchasing coverage k at a policy premium (price) p is given by

$$U = hu(W - l + k - p) + (1 - h)u(W - p) \qquad (7.33)$$

where the $u(\cdot)$ are elementary utilities exhibiting risk aversion, h is the probability of loss, and $W_1 = W - l + k - p > 0$ and $W_2 = W - p > 0$. For the moment we will assume that individuals are identical, and particularly that they have the same risk (probability of loss).

Pooling Equilibrium. The insurance companies are risk neutral and supply all contracts which yield them positive expected profits. At the zero-profit free-entry equilibrium each contract must be such that

$$\bar{\pi} = h(p - k) + (1 - h)p = 0 \qquad (7.34)$$

which implies a contract price of $p = hk$. Note that this result assumes that there are no fixed costs.

It is clear from (7.33) that individuals purchase insurance to shift wealth from their no loss state to their loss state. Since $\bar{\pi} = 0$ and $p = hk$, the rate of exchange is the constant $(1 - h)/h$: each unit of coverage is worth an additional $1 - h$ in state 2 wealth, but takes h from state 1 wealth. This follows from substituting $p = hk$ in the definitions for W_1 and W_2 to obtain

$$W_1 = W - hk$$

$$W_2 = W - l + (1 - h)k$$

and therefore

$$\frac{\mathrm{d}W_1}{\mathrm{d}W_2} = \frac{1 - h}{2h} \qquad (7.35)$$

as the coverage is changed.

The constant exchange opportunity locus is indicated by the line $\overline{W}E$ in figure 7.9. The implicit prices for claims to wealth in the states are in the ratio of the state probabilities. When the insurance contract prices yield zero profits they are said to be *actuarially fair* and the line $\overline{W}E$ is referred to as the *fair odds* line. In the figure, $\overline{W}$ represents the individuals' endowment point and E is the equilibrium point. E is reached by the usual constrained utility maximization logic, where the rate of market exchange just equals the rate of claims substitution. The rate of substitution between state claims to wealth occurs with constant expected utility, or where

$$\left(\frac{\mathrm{d}W_2}{\mathrm{d}W_1}\right)_U = \frac{-(1 - h)u'(W_1)}{hu'(W_2)} \qquad (7.36)$$

At the optimum (7.35) and (7.36) must be equal, so that $u'(W_1) = u'(W_2)$ and therefore $W_1 = W_2$. With risk aversion and actuarially fair prices there is full coverage in the sense that end-of-period wealth is equalized across states. (Equilibrium point E is on the 45° ray.)

Heterogeneous Individuals. Suppose now that individuals differ in their risk probabilities only and, because of prohibitively high observation costs, the insurance firms cannot identify who has what risk. To keep things simple, let

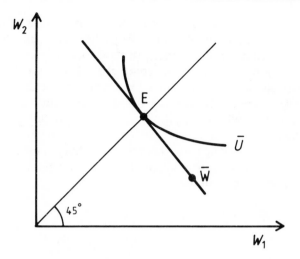

Figure 7.9
Pooling equilibrium: identical individuals

there be just two risk types: a fraction n of the population has a high probability of a given loss h_a and the remaining fraction $1 - n$ has a low loss probability $h_b < h_a$. Without individual specific information the insurers know, by experience, only the average probability of loss:

$$\bar{h} = nh_a + (1 - n)h_b \qquad (7.37)$$

Now the actuarially fair price is $p = \bar{h}k$ and the *market odds* line has slope $-(1 - \bar{h})/\bar{h}$. Because the individuals differ in expected utility, there are now two rates of state claims substitution. For the a types there is

$$\left(\frac{dW_2}{dW_1}\right)_{U_a} = \frac{-(1 - h_a)u'(W_{a1})}{h_a u'(W_{a2})} \qquad (7.38a)$$

and for the b types there is

$$\left(\frac{dW_2}{dW_1}\right)_{U_b} = \frac{-(1 - h_b)u'(W_{b1})}{h_b u'(W_{b2})} \qquad (7.38b)$$

At any given W_1 and W_2,

$$\left(\frac{dW_2}{dW_1}\right)_{U_a} = \frac{1 - h_a}{h_a} \frac{h_b}{1 - h_b} \left(\frac{dW_2}{dW_1}\right)_{U_b} \qquad (7.39)$$

The slope of the high-risk type a indifference curve is less than that of the low-risk type b indifference curve at every (W_1, W_2) pair. The U_a and U_b indifference curves can therefore only have one intersection, as illustrated in figure 7.10. Moreover, the market odds line that goes through that intersection, with slope $-(1 - \bar{h})/\bar{h}$, must lie between the slopes of the two indifference curves as indicated in the figure.

Point α in figure 7.10 denotes a single insurance contract (and with it an allocation of wealth across the two states) which might be made available to both individuals as a candidate for equilibrium. $\alpha \bar{W}$ is the market odds line along which the firms have zero expected profits as required for equilibrium. The problem with α as an equilibrium contract lies elsewhere. To see what is wrong, consider the contract at β. High-risk types prefer α and would purchase that, but the low-risk b types prefer the contract β. If β is sufficiently close to α, then the β contracts would give almost the same expected profit as the α contract if it were offered only to the less risky. As α produces zero expected profits when offered to all individuals, it must then provide positive expected profits when taken only by the low-risk individuals. A similar argument pertains for any single contract along the market odds line. Thus, if there is an equilibrium the individuals cannot be "pooled" into a single contract, but each must be offered a separate contract.

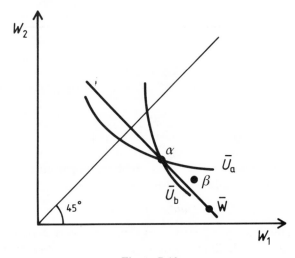

Figure 7.10
Heterogeneous individuals

Separating Equilibrium. The properties of the two contracts are illustrated in figure 7.11. Rather than just one market odds line, there are now two fair odds lines: $\overline{W}A$ for a types and $\overline{W}B$ for b types. Since $h_a > h_b$, $\overline{W}A$ has greater absolute slope than $\overline{W}B$. On the $\overline{W}A$ line the contract E_a is most preferred and gives the high-risk individuals complete coverage (equalized claims). The most preferred contract for the low-risk individuals is contract E'. Unfortunately, that contract is not incentive compatible for the high-risk a types would also purchase it if it were generally offered. Contracts along $\overline{W}B$ give zero expected profits only if restricted to the low-risk b types; if also adopted by the high-risk individuals they would provide negative expected profits. That is, E_a and E' cannot be an equilibrium set of contracts, for they are not incentive compatible when self-selected. The reader can quickly see from the analysis in section 7.3 that the equilibrium contract for low-risk types must keep the high-risk types at E_a, which means that E_a, E_b is the (separating) equilibrium pair.[20]

---

[20] Existence of a separating equilibrium in competitive markets is not generally guaranteed as Rothschild and Stiglitz (1976) show. The reader should compare the one-good (pooling) equilibrium and two-good (separating) equilibrium here with that developed in section 4.2.1.

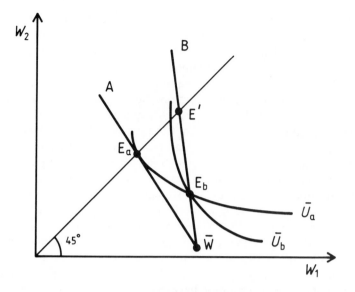

Figure 7.11
Separating equilibrium

SE7.3 Price Discrimination by Commodity Bundling

Why does the Los Angeles Symphony Orchestra offer annual subscriptions to its concert series while at the same time selling tickets for individual performances? Why do restaurants offer both complete meals and the same dishes *à la carte*? Why do Pepsi and Coca-Cola sell large 32 oz family bottles, at a family price, and also sell regular 12 oz bottles at a somewhat higher price per ounce? More generally, how do we explain the fact that multiproduct firms often sell their outputs both bundled and separately? Adams and Yellen (1976) have suggested a discriminatory pricing explanation of these practices and it is to a graphical analysis based on their study that we turn in this example.[21]

First let us be clear about two key qualifications of the model to be developed: (a) attention is limited to a single (monopoly) firm selling just two *demand-independent* goods $j = 1, 2$; (b) consumers exhibit *discrete choice* preferences – each has a postive demand price for the first unit of good and a zero demand price for all succeeding units of that good.

Bundling Strategies. The standard nondiscriminating monopoly of elementary price theory is based on what may be termed a **pure components** price policy: at announced market prices p_1 and p_2 the firm sells to all who would purchase its products 1 and 2 respectively at these prices. When sold separately, any

---

[21] There are several other explanations for a commodity bundling sales policy. Coase (1960), Demsetz (1968a), and Alchian and Demsetz (1972) have argued that bundling may be preferred by the seller (and buyer) when there are associated cost savings in production and/or exchange transactions. Complementarity in consumption may also explain some instances, as Bailey (1954) and Telser (1979) have noted.

individual buys good j only if his demand price v_j is equal to or greater than the good's market price p_j. On this approach, consumers are separated into four possibilities as indicated in figure 7.12(a). The group I consumers have $v_1 \geqslant p_1$ and $v_2 \geqslant p_2$ and purchase both commodities. Other consumers in the groups indicated by II and IV, who have demand prices in excess of market prices for only one of the commodities, buy commodities 1 and 2 respectively. The last group of consumers, group III, have $v_1 < p_1$ and $v_2 < p_2$ and therefore do not purchase either product. Note finally that the figure indicates constant unit costs c_1 and c_2 for the two products. These can be ignored for the moment, except to note that the goods are also assumed to be independent in supply in the sense that the production of one does not affect the cost of the other.

Figure 7.12(b) illustrates consumer groupings for an alternative **pure bundle** selling policy. In this case the monopolist offers *only* bundles of the goods for sell. Without loss of generality, we suppose that these bundles are made up of one unit of good 1 and one unit of good 2.[22] The products are *demand independent* in the sense that each consumer's demand price for the bundle is the simple sum $v_b = v_1 + v_2$. Let p_b indicate the bundle's market price. In the figure, individuals lying in group V have $v_b > p_b$ and purchase the bundle; all other individuals purchase nothing.[23]

Figure 7.12(c) illustrates the last of the three selling policies to be considered – **mixed bundling**. In this case the seller offers each commodity price separately *and* the pure bundle. For mixed bundling to be of interest, the market prices must be such that $p_b < p_1 + p_2$. Otherwise, it is not different from the pure components strategy, as no consumer would ever purchase the bundle from the seller when he can construct it for himself at a lower price. (In figure 7.12(c) this means that the $p_b p_b$ diagonal line must never have a point in area 3a.)

The overlay of figures 7.12(a) and 7.12(b) produces 7.12(c) and illustrates the way in which consumers are divided into four groups by mixed bundling. (These groups, it should be remarked, are different from the four obtained when the goods are priced as pure components.) The consumers lying in group 4 (excluding boundaries) have $v_2 < p_2$, $v_1 < p_1$, and $v_b < p_b$: they purchase nothing from the firm. Consumers lying in 1a have $v_1 > p_1$, $v_2 < p_2$, and $v_b < p_b$: they purchase commodity 1 alone. Those in 1b have $v_2 < p_2$, $v_1 \geqslant p_1$, and $v_b \geqslant p_b$, and purchase either commodity 1 alone or the bundle, depending on which gives the greater surplus. The surplus from commodity 1 is $v_1 - p_1$ in this case, and from the bundle it is $v_1 + v_2 - p_b$. Since $p_b < p_1 + p_2$, however, the surplus is greater from commodity 1 and that single commodity is purchased by the group 1b individuals.[24] By a similar line of argument, consumers in groups 2a and 2b purchase only commodity 2. Individuals in the final group 3 (made up of subparts 3a, 3b, 3c, and 3d) purchase only the bundle, since for

---

[22] Any combination of the commodities can be expressed as a one-to-one bundle by an appropriate scaling of the units of measure.

[23] Along the price line $p_b p_b$ the individuals are, of course, indifferent to purchasing.

[24] This result can be seen graphically. Choose any point (individual) in area 2a and draw a horizontal line beginning at that point to the p_1 price line. This horizontal line passes through the $p_b p_b$ diagonal. The distance from the individual's point to the intersection of the horizontal with $p_b p_b$ is $v_b - p_b$ and the greater distance from the individual's point to the intersection of the horizontal with the p_1 line is $v_1 - p_1$.

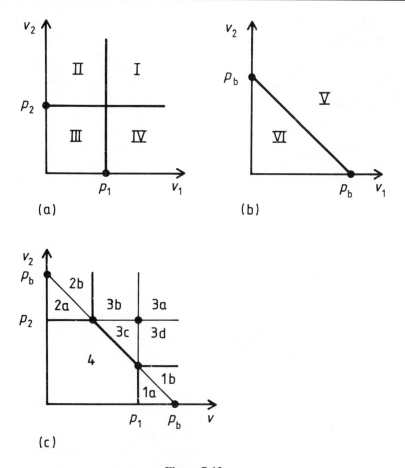

Figure 7.12
Commodity bundling with independent commodities: (a) pure components; (b) pure bundling; (c) mixed bundling

them $v_1 + v_2 \geqslant p_b$, $v_2 \geqslant p_b - p_1$, and $v_1 \geqslant p_b - p_2$. That is, group 3 individuals receive greater surplus from the bundle than from purchasing good 1 or good 2 separately.

Relative Profitability. What bundling policy will the seller adopt? That depends on the relative demands for the separate components and the bundle and, with that, the profits they might yield.[25] Some rules of thumb concerning the

[25] The precise calculation of profits requires detailed knowledge of the consumer distribution over the (v_1, v_2) plane. For example, in comparing figures 7.12(a) and 7.12(c) note that consumers in group 3c, those not purchasing when the commodities are sold separately, buy the bundle when it is offered. In addition, some of those consumers (in 3b and 3d) who purchased only one commodity with pure components buy both with mixed bundling. The result is that the output (of both goods) is generally increased with mixed bundling. Whether or not this is a profitable policy for the firm depends on the distribution of consumers on the (v_1, v_2) plane and costs of production, for against the gain in output there are those individuals in 3a who bought both goods under the pure components policy and continue to buy both with mixed bundling, but at a price less than the price of the separate components ($p_b < p_1 + p_2$).

relative profitability of the three selling methods can be developed by comparing them with perfectly discriminatory prices. Specifically, we ask about the extent to which the methods provide for surplus extraction, exclusion, and inclusion. The "more perfect" is the discrimination, the greater are the profits. The following variants on two illustrations by Adams and Yellen (1976, pp. 480–8) develop these ideas.

Illustration 1. For the first example, suppose that there are just four consumers (A, B, C, and D) whose reservation demand prices lie along a straight line with slope − 1 as shown and tabulated in figure 7.13. Each consumer values the

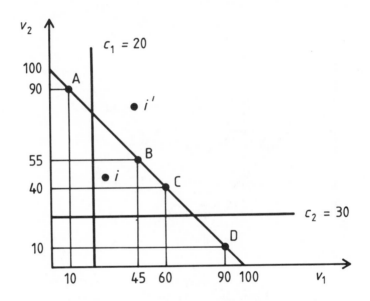

Strategy	p_1	p_2	p_b	π
PC	60	90	—	140
PB	—	—	100	200
MB	90^-	90^-	100	230

Strategy	v_1	v_2	b
A	10	90	100
B	45	55	100
C	60	40	100
D	90	10	100

Figure 7.13
Relative profits

bundle identically ($v_b = v_1 + v_2 = 100$), but the relative value of the component commodities differs. Under pure components (PC in the figure), profits are maximum (at 140) when $p_1 = 60$ and $p_2 = 90$. In this case, consumer D has a surplus of $90 - 60 = 30$, consumers A and B are excluded from purchasing product 1, and B, C, and D do not buy product 2.

If, alternatively, the seller used a pure bundling policy (PB in the figure) with $p_b = v_b = 100$, the extraction and inclusion conditions of perfect price discrimination could be met. The resulting profits are $\pi = (100) \times 4 - (20 + 30) \times 4 = 200$, which is an increase of 60 compared with the pure components policy. Note, however, that the pure bundling policy excludes buyers with reservation prices below cost, as consumer A purchases commodity 1 ($v_1 = 10$, $c_1 = 20$) and consumer D purchases commodity 4 ($v_2 = 10$, $c_2 = 30$).

Mixed bundling (case MB in the figure), which can move consumers into additional groups, is helpful in this regard. In this case the seller sets $p_1 = 90$ (selling to D), $p_2 = 90$ (selling to A), and $p_b = 100$ (selling to B and C). Profits increase to 230 (since no sales are now at valuations below cost), all surplus is extracted, and there is exclusion.[26] In this particular situation mixed bundling satisfies the extraction, inclusion, and exclusion properties of perfect price discrimination.

Illustration 2. Mixed bundling provides a second advantage over pure bundling. Consider, for example, the "negative correlation" situation depicted in figure 7.14: B and C place high value on both goods; A and D value only one highly. Notice that the bundle price of 120 extracts all the B and C surplus, while the separate prices of $p_1 = 90$ and $p_2 = 90$ extracts all the surplus of A and B respectively.

SE7.4 Commodity Bundling Complements and Substitutes

While the discussion of bundling in SE7.3 deals with products which are independent, it is not difficult to allow for either substitutes or complements. Following Demsetz (1973a) and Lewbel (1985), it is only necessary to recognize that the difference between each consumer's bundle demand price v_b and the prices $v_1 + v_2$ of the two components separately is an indication of his view of product interdependence. We let $\delta = v_b - (v_1 + v_2)$. Then there are three general cases to be considered: complements $\delta > 0$, substitutes $\delta < 0$, and the previously treated case of independent goods $\delta = 0$.[27] With this characterization, each consumer can be described by a triple (v_1, v_2, δ), where δ defines the degree of substitutability or complementarity. In turn, we think of the consuming population as being distributed in the corresponding three-space as shown in figure 7.15.

---

[26] To insure that D purchases good 1 and A purchases good 2 it may be necessary to set p_1 and p_2 slightly less than 90.

[27] Note that these are not the usual definitions of substitutes and complements based on cross-elasticities. The present definitions in terms of δ do, however, have the benefit of not involving any income effect, and δ is measured directly in terms of utility (and dollars given our assumption of quasi-linear utility).

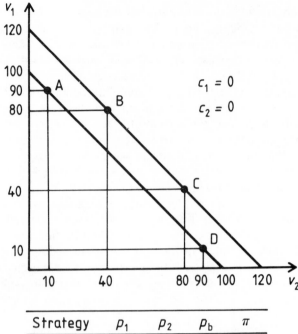

Strategy	p_1	p_2	p_b	π
PC	80	80	–	320
PB	–	–	100	400
MB	90^-	90^-	120	420

Figure 7.14
Mixed bundling advantage

Figure 7.15 indicates several (v_1, v_2) cross-sections, that is, planes on which δ is fixed. The two-space method of bundling analysis developed for independent goods can be repeated on any such cross-section. That is, for each such constant-δ cross-section we can partition the two-space of consumers (differentiated by v_1, v_2) according to their preferences for pure components and the bundle. The partition boundaries occur where there is indifference to good 1 alone $(p_1 = v_1)$, good 2 alone $(p_2 = v_2)$, and the bundle $(p_b - \delta = v_1 + v_2)$.[28] Lewbel (1985) has noted that there are two different cross-section types according to this partitioning of consumers, as illustrated in figure 7.16. The cross-section shown in figure 7.16(b) occurs when $\delta \geqslant p_b - p_1 - p_2$, while that shown in figure 7.16(a) occurs with the alternative $\delta < p_b - p_1 - p_2$. There is one cross-section for each value of δ, but every cross-section follows one of these two patterns.[29]

---

[28] This last plane derives from $p_b = v_b = \delta + v_1 + v_2$.
[29] For emphasis: $p_b < p_1 + p_2$ is required if the consumers are to purchase bundles at all. Thus $p_b + p_1 + p_2 < 0$ and the case with $\delta \geqslant p_b - p_1 - p_2$ shown in figure 7.16(a) deals only with strong substitutes, while the case with $\delta < p_b - p_1 - p_2$ shown in 7.16(b) deals with weak substitutes and all complements.

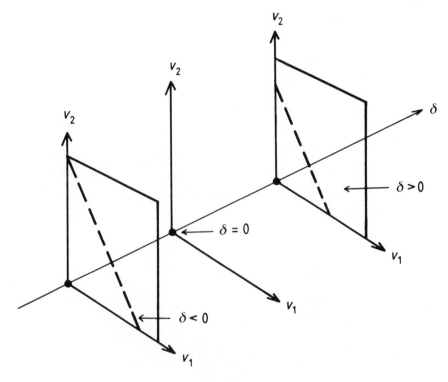

Figure 7.15
Consumer distribution

Consider first the group of individuals for whom the products are either weak substitutes or complements so that figure 7.16(a) is generally applicable. Using a comparison of market prices and demand prices, consumers are partitioned according to their purchase decisions in the usual way: those in areas labeled 2a and 2b purchase product 2 and, similarly, those in 1a and 1b purchase product 1. For example, in area 2b good 2 is purchased and not the bundle (which also has positive surplus). The easiest way to see this is to consider some typical consumer x in the 2b area of figure 7.16(a). The surplus offered to x by the bundle is given by the vertical distance xy (from x to the $p_b - \delta$ diagonal), while the surplus offered to x by good 2 is the greater distance xz (from x to the p_2 horizontal). The areas where the bundle is purchased, or where no purchase is made, are also indicated.

When products 1 and 2 are strong substitutes ($\delta \ll 0$) and the condition $\delta < p_b - p_1 - p_2$ holds, figure 7.16(b) is applicable and there is a similar analysis of surplus and purchase decisions. The length of the segment AB in the figure depends directly on the absolute value of δ. As δ varies across consumers the diagonal $p_b - \delta$ shifts up and down, but it must intersect along this segment and not "below" point A (where $\delta < p_b - p_1 - p_2$ would be violated) nor "above" point B (where $p_b < p_1 + p_2$ would be violated). In areas 1a and 1b only good 1 is purchased. The rationale for this purchase in 1a is that it is the only option giving positive surplus. In 1b surplus is positive for both good 1

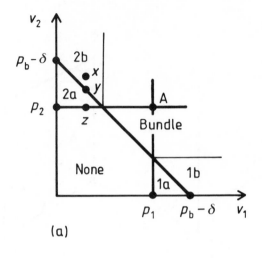

(a)

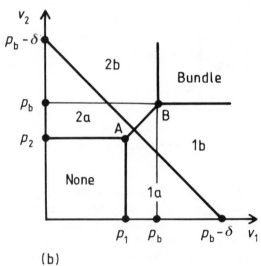

(b)

Figure 7.16
Complements and substitutes: (a) $\delta \geqslant p_b - p_1 - p_2$; (b) $\delta < p_b - p_1 - p_2$

alone and the bundle, but the good 1 surplus is greater.[30] A similar analysis pertains for the 2a and 2b areas. The bundle and no-purchase areas are arrived at in obvious ways.

Finally, note that figures 7.16(a) and 7.16(b) deal only with the case of mixed bundling, but they reduce to the case of pure components when it is further required that $p_b = p_1 + p_2$, and pure bundling occurs if p_1 and p_2 are each taken to be infinitely large.

Comparative statics analyses of prices (varied either separately or in specific proportions) can easily be developed using these diagrams. This involves nothing

---

[30] Take any point (individual) in 1b. The horizontal distance from that point to the diagonal is $v_b - p_b$ and the greater horizontal distance from the individual's point to the p_1 vertical is $v_1 - p_1$.

more than shifting the price lines and noting the effects on the resulting consumer partitions. This exercise is left to the reader.

SE7.5 Price Discrimination and Tying Arrangements

Bowman (1957) developed the classic rationale for tying contracts as a device for revealing the intensity (elasticity) of individual buyer demand. In his analysis the two products involved are complementary and the demand is continuous in the sense that the buyers are not restricted to take either one unit or none of the product.[31] Buyers with higher demand prices for the tying product (as one case, Bowman refers to a button fastener machine) demand more units of the tied product (the buttons) at each price. This positive (complementary) relationship between the demand for tying and tied products is used to the seller's advantage by pricing the tied product above its marginal cost. As a result, a greater surplus is captured from those buyers placing a greater value on the tied product (since that value is proportional to their usage of the tying product).

Price Discrimination, Tying and Vertical Integration. A second example of tying and price discrimination focuses on the intermediate market between an "upstream" monopolist and a "downstream" competitive industry. Suppose that the downstream firms produce according to a technology that combines inputs in variable proportions. This is the situation first analyzed by Vernon and Graham (1972) using a graphical analysis similar to that in figure 7.17. There the isoquant z^0 obtains for the competitive final good industry when using various quantities of the two factors x_1 and x_2. Suppose that the upstream monopolist produces x_2 and sells it using a pure price policy at a price in excess of marginal cost ($p_1 > c_1'$). In contrast, factor 2 is assumed to be supplied competitively at marginal cost ($p_2 = c_2'$). In the figure the isocost line A_2A_1 reflects the ratio of input prices p_1/c_2' and the factor expenditure level $E = p_1x_1 + c_2'x_2$. The vertical intercept A indicates the number of units of factor 2 that can be purchased with E if no factor 1 were purchased. That is, E can be measured in x_2 terms; for example, the factor combination indicated by point X can be said to cost A_2 (units of factor 2) to produce.

Consider next the isocost line B_2B_1 which would also produce output z^0 using the same X factor combination. B_2B_1, in contrast with A_2A_1, has a slope c_1'/c_2' which reflects competitive prices for both factors. At these prices the cost of factor combination X is B_2 (units of factor 2). If z^0 units are produced downstream in both cases, the monopolist earns profits of $A_2 - B_2$, which is the difference between what X costs when x_1 is priced competitively and when it is priced monopolistically.

Vertical Integration. At this point Vernon and Graham consider the implications of forward vertical integration, where the monopolist merges with all the downstream firms. It is immediately clear that the monopolist, if he were to continue producing z^0, could increase his profits by using the efficient factor combination X^* for which the isocost D_2D_1 is just tangent to the z^0 isoquant.

---

[31] This relaxes both key assumptions of the model in SE7.3.

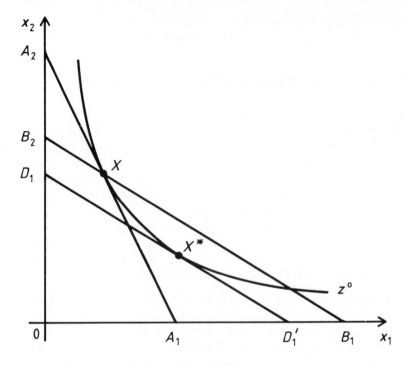

Figure 7.17
Factor substitution

(This requires that factor 1 has an internal transfer price between upstream and downstream divisions equal to its marginal cost.) Measured again in units of factor 2, the monopolist's profit would increase from $A_2 - B_2$ to $A_2 - D_2$ by this efficiency in production. Thus the sum $B_2 - D_2$ represents an incentive for forward integration (again, provided that quantity z^0 is produced both before and after integration).

Tying. The reason why the unintegrated monopolist cannot extract full monopoly benefits from the downstream firms is that, with a variable proportions technology, those firms substitute away from his factor as p_1 rises relative to p_2.[32] This suggests a second way, other than vertical integration, in which the full benefits of monopoly might be captured. Suppose that the monopolist purchases factor 2 on the market at the competitive price c'_2 and ties the purchase of that factor to the purchase of factor 1. Downstream firms would be entitled to purchase factor 1 from the monopolist only if they also bought their full requirements of factor 2 from him. Then, if the monopolist sold the tied and tying factors at prices p_1 and p_2 such that $p_1/p_2 = c'_1/c'_2$, the downstream producers would return to the efficient expansion path generated by competitive prices. However, to extract the full monopoly benefit, the factor prices must

---

[32] If the downstream production were subject to a fixed proportion technology involving factor 1, then this substitution would not be possible and the monopolist could extract the full benefits of a monopoly price.

exceed their marginal costs by just the amount which is sufficient to increase the downstream firms' average cost to the final product monopoly price.

Figure 7.18 illustrates the extraction of monopoly surplus by the tying arrangement. D is the final product (inverse) demand with associated marginal revenue MR. The schedules MC_1 and AC_1 indicate marginal cost and average cost respectively for the final product when both factors are priced at their marginal cost. The maximum profit for the monopolist requires that the monopoly price p_m obtains in the final good market (and the competitive firms earn zero profits). Using the tying arrangement, the factor prices are both raised proportionately to maintain $p_1/p_2 = c_1'/c_2'$, so that the downstream cost schedules shift from MC_1 and AC_1 to MC_2 and AC_2. With these costs the competitive downstream firms produce z_m at a price p_m and the upstream firm captures its full monopoly rents.[33,34]

Customer Services. Vertical restraints may also arise based on an externality argument. For example, as Telser (1960) shows, free-riding on the provision of costly *pre*-sales services without some such restraints reduces the aggregate demand for the manufacturer's product and reduces his profit. Minimum retail price maintenance or exclusive territories are suggested as solutions to the free-riding. Bolton and Bonano (1987) contrast this situation with the alternative where retailers provide *cum*-sales or *post*-sales services. In these later cases different levels of retailer service, providing products of different quality at retail, allow the manufacturer to offer different price–quality bundles in a way

---

[33] Burstein (1960a, b) and Blair and Kaserman (1978a) provide further details. Blair and Kaserman (1980) also show that the monopoly rents can be captured under various fixed fee and per unit output arrangements.

[34] Flath (1978) provides an alternative explanation for tying in his analysis of *U.S. v. American Can Co. 87 F. Supp 18* (N.D. Cal. 1949). American Can leased can-closing machines to canners at prices below cost, but required that canners take their requirement of cans from American over the same period as the machine lease. Using a market foreclosure rationale, the Court demanded that American limit the requirements contracts to one year and that it offer the closing machine for sale at attractive prices.

Flath suggests an efficiency explanation for the lease-requirements arrangement: two risks are shifted from packers to the can producer. The first is that of bearing the capital cost of an expensive can-closing machine in seasons of crop shortage, when it will see only slight usage. In crop-short years few cans are used and the payment for the machine is commensurately less. Presumably the payments are recouped in bumper crop years when the demand for cans is larger. The second risk shifted by the lease-requirements arrangement is due to the practice of packers of purchasing crops by forward contracts, that is, they agree to purchase the future output of certain growers at a specific price. Since the spot market price of cans is inversely related to the spot market price of the crops placed in the cans, any packer can hedge his forward contract to purchase crops using an offsetting forward contract to purchase cans. The variety of yields across growing regions and different crops makes such an "insurance" scheme natural for the can producers.

Flath has noted that two testable hypotheses follow from his analysis. First, the lease-requirements arrangement would not be used for those can users whose demand was more certain, such as to the beer industry, petroleum industry, etc. That was in fact the case; American did not use the lease-requirement contracts in these industries. Second, small canners, who would seem to be least able to manage the two forms of risk, would be harmed most by the Court's decree. That too was the case, as these marginal canners strenuously complained in a related action – *U.S. v. Continental Can Co., 128 F, Supp. 932* (N.D. Cal. 1955) – that the fully compensatory rentals mandated by the Court were driving them from the business.

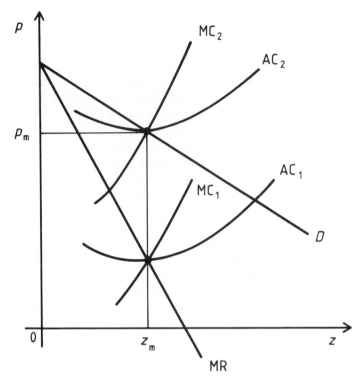

Figure 7.18
Final product prices and output

which facilitates price discrimination by self-selection.[35]

SE7.6   Price Discrimination, Market Division, and Resale Price Maintenance

In *Klor's Inc. v. Broadway-Hale Inc.*, *359 U.S. 207* (1959), a number of The Broadway's suppliers of household appliances refused to deal with Klor's, a discount outlet located not far from The Broadway in San Francisco. The refusal occurred at the request of The Broadway. Liebeler (1976) has shown that refusals to deals of the Klor's type generally have the same economic consequences as certain forms of price discrimination, types of market division, and resale price maintenance. He develops the parallel for a simplification of the

[35] Another form of so-called vertical restraint – closed territory distribution – where retailers are assigned exclusive rights to all consumers within a given territory (or with given characteristics) to diminish intraband competition, has also been frequently considered as enabling price discrimination. In *White Motor v. U.S.* (1963), for example, it was discovered that White used a closed territory distribution scheme in which all state and federal government accounts were reserved for itself – dealers were forbidden from approaching these customers. Assuming that the demand for these accounts was relatively elastic, White profited from selling to them at lower prices.

More generally, privately optimal vertical market restraints generally have ambiguous welfare effects when competition is imperfect either at the manufacturer (upstream) or retail (downstream) level, because the degree of competition (monopoly) expressed by the firms will generally depend on the nature of the restraint (see Rey and Tirole, 1986).

Klor's situation.

Consider a refrigerator manufacturer WE that decides to distribute its product through independent retailers. WE advertises its refrigerators nationally in several media. Still, it is important to supply information at the point of sale where consumers can closely scrutinize quality, have the salesperson explain certain aspects of operation, and generally "kick the tires." WE contracts with The Broadway along with other chain department stores to handle its refrigerators in this way. The Broadway trains its salespeople to properly represent the refrigerators, and it stocks and displays them. Its costs, including those of providing the desired level of point-of-sales services, leads to a price of say $1000.

This method of distribution is effective for a period, until Klor's opens a small discount store in the neighborhood. It offers no information services on the products it handles, carries no inventory, and displays no models. It simply has catalogs, which include the WE refrigerators. It discounts the generally prevailing retail prices by 20 percent. As things progress, The Broadway's sales of refrigerators fall off drastically, even though there appear to be as many potential customers as ever. However, Klor's is selling just in excess of the number of WE refrigerators that The Broadway had previously sold. Not lacking in business acumen, The Broadway detects the problem and informs WE that it cannot continue to offer the extensive point-of-sale service on the WE line under the prevailing conditions. Yet these point-of-sale services are the least-cost method available for demonstrating the high-quality features of the WE product and allow it to capture the price premium necessary to sustain that high quality level.

In response, WE might charge a 20 percent price premium to Klor's in an attempt to offset the cost that The Broadway has in providing point-of-sale services. There are two problems with such price discrimination: Klor's might be acquiring their supply of WE refrigerators on a "bootleg" basis,[36] and, more fatally, such discrimination would be illegal under the Robinson–Patman Act. Alternatively, WE might provide The Broadway with an exclusive territory in which it is the sole supplier of its refrigerators. If such a territory were assigned in a way which would prohibit Klor's free-ride on The Broadway's point-of-sale services, it is also likely that it would lead to a less than optimal number of retail outlets and that would adversely affect WE's overall sales. Liebeler notes at this point that the market division could achieve the same economic impact as discriminatory pricing, although neither is preferred in this case.[37]

Liebeler continues by showing how resale price maintenance, which would require that Klor's adopt the same $1,000 retail price as The Broadway, protects property rights in information and ends the free-ride that Klor's otherwise takes on The Broadway's point-of-sale services. Resale price maintenance is the preferred solution in this case, as it allows the large number of retail outlets necessary to cover the area effectively. Again, resale price maintenance produces the same price result as would market division or price discrimination.

---

[36] This was the critical problem faced by Sylvania and Schwinn, as noted in *Continental T.V. Inc. v. GTE Sylvania, 433 U.S. 36* (1977) and *U.S. v. Arnold Schwinn & Co., 388 U.S. 365* (1967) respectively.

[37] See *White Motor Co. v. U.S., 373 U.S. 253* (1963) where market division was used in this way.

SE7.7   Consumers may Benefit from Quantity Discounts

While a monopolist selling to identical consumers with known demand can use nonlinear prices to extract all consumer surplus, a duopoly equilibrium arrived at using nonlinear pricing may leave consumers better off than with linear prices. Following de Meza (1986), we prove this result in a two-stage game with duopolists selling substitute goods. At the first strategic (and nonmarket) stage each of the $j = 1, 2$ duopolists announces a two-part pricing schedule having a fixed fee F_j and a per unit price p_j.[38] At the second market stage the firms choose quantities to supply, given this pricing schedule. We will assume that quantities and prices are known with certainty by all and that there are no income effects associated with price changes.

Market Stage. The firms' decisions here are straightforward. The Nash-in-quantity equilibrium involves no rationing provided that the price adopted at the strategic stage is not below marginal cost. As we will see below this is the case.

Strategic Stage. Here the firms fashion pricing schedules, each specifying a fixed fee and a per unit price. The solution concept is Nash in these price and fee variables. Given the fixed and per unit charges of its competitor k, firm j is presented with a (residual) demand for its product and acts as a monopolist with respect to that demand. Thus firm j sets its per unit price equal to its marginal cost $(p_j = MC_j)$ and extracts all consumer surplus using the fixed fee, $F_j = CS(p_j)$.[39]

Equilibrium. Figure 7.19 illustrates the *symmetric* two-stage equilibrium in nonlinear price schedules using the demand functions usually associated with Chamberlinian analysis (recall chapter 4, section 4.2): DD' is the demand facing each firm when each sets the same price, dd' is the Nash-in-price perceived demand of each firm when its rival sets price p^1, and $p^n D'$ is the Nash-in-price demand of each firm when its rival sets a price of zero. The relevance of this last schedule is that we assume that marginal costs are zero (alternatively, think of each per unit price as the excess of some positive constant marginal cost). We have already established that the optimal nonlinear pricing policy of each firm is to set price per unit equal to marginal cost and the fixed fee to extract the *perceived* consumer surplus. As a result, in equilibrium the price per unit is zero and the fixed fee is equal to the area $0p^n D'$ for each firm.

While the firm using a fee equal to $p^n D$ thinks that it is extracting all the consumer surplus, that is not the case. Since the firms have equal price in a symmetric equilibrium, DD' is the relevant demand schedule for measuring that

---

[38] We will call the per unit charge the "price" and the fixed charge the "fee."

[39] Note that, given the two-part pricing policies and surplus extraction, the demand of each duopolist has a point of discontinuity. As firm j lowers its price relative to that of the rival firm k, k's demand shifts in and the size of any surplus obtained by consumers of good k falls. At some sufficiently low price p_j^i, the surplus obtained by consumers from k's product will just equal zero. Any further cut by firm j below p_j^i will abruptly shift all the trade from good k to good j. (Otherwise, with fixed p_k and F_k the consumers would have negative surplus.) Note, however, that this discontinuity does not alter the optimal strategy choice of the firms.

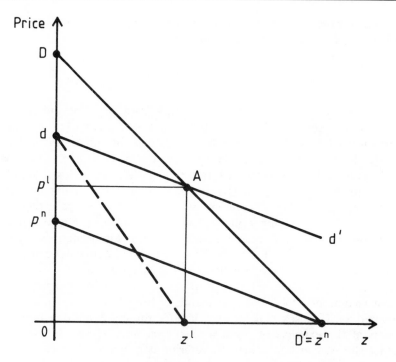

Figure 7.19
Equilibrium prices and surplus

surplus. Specifically, $0D'D$ less the fee $0p^nD'$ (this difference is the area $p^nD'D$) is the surplus retained by each firm's consumers. Thus, $2p^nD'D$ is the total uncaptured surplus in the symmetric nonlinear pricing equilibrium.

Equilibrium with Linear Prices. The above solution can be quickly compared with the usual Chamberlinian solution with (nondiscriminating) linear prices. Again, we use figure 7.19. In this case the symmetric equilibrium is given by the prices and outputs p^l and z^l, where each firm sets its marginal revenue equal to the zero marginal cost. In turn, total consumer surplus is twice the area p^lAD.

Although the figure illustrates the case where $p^nD'D > p^lAD$, so that consumers are better off under the two-part discriminatory scheme, this is not a general result. The reader should be able to see that when the firm demand is sufficiently elastic the inequality is reversed and the two-part discrimination leaves consumers worse off.

SE7.8 Two-part Tariffs Pareto Dominate Linear Prices

While a uniform price equal to marginal cost is Pareto optimal, such a pricing policy produces negative profits in the natural monopoly case where marginal cost is everywhere less than average cost. One solution to this problem is an "augmented" uniform price above marginal cost designed to bring the seller's profits to zero. Out intent here is to show that there generally exists a nonlinear

price schedule which Pareto dominates such an augmented linear schedule.
  Consider the two-part tariff set out earlier:

$$\omega^t(z) = \quad F + pz \qquad \text{for } z > 0 \tag{7.40}$$

$$\neq \quad 0 \qquad \text{for } z = 0$$

where F, $p \geqslant 0$. In figure 7.20(a) the outlay $\omega^0(z) = \bar{p}z$ is indicated by the
straight line through the origin with constant slope equal to $\bar{p} > \text{MC}$. The
two-part tariff $\omega^t(z)$ with "entrance fee" F defines the other straight line in the
figure. By choice of F and p in the specification of ω^t it is always possible to
partition consumers about some quantity z_1 such that the enclosed area between
ω^0 and ω^t to the right of z_1 is larger than the enclosed area to the left. (The
reader can verify that these "compensation areas" can also be established with
block pricing schemes.) Thus a move from a uniform price above marginal cost
to an appropriate nonlinear price schedule can be made desirable for consumers
in the aggregate: gainers (to the right of z_1 with large demands) can in principle
compensate losers (to the left) for the shift in pricing policy.
  Willig (1978) has observed that if there is a positive association between
consumer income and the level of demand for the good, then, while the shift to
the two-part tariff raises real income, it does this by benefiting higher-income
consumers at the expense of those with low income. This distributional effect,
he further shows, can be avoided by offering consumers a choice of linear and
two-part price schedules. This analysis is summarized in figure 7.20(b). Suppose
that consumers can choose either the uniform price $\bar{p}$ (with ω^0) or they can
choose to pay the fee $F = \alpha t(\alpha, t > 0$ are constants) for the right to purchase
their supplies at the lower price $p - t$. Let ω^t indicate this two-part schedule.
The linear and nonlinear outlay schedules intersect at the quantity z_2 where
$\bar{p}z_2 = \alpha t + (p - t)z_2$ or $z_2 = \alpha$. Clearly, consumers who demand less than z_2
will choose the uniform outlay ω^0, and those with demands greater than z_2 will
choose the two-part tariff. Thus the solid line, breaking at z_2, defines the
relevant outlay schedule as a two-block tariff policy. Consumers with demand
below z_2 are indifferent to the uniform price policy and the two-block policy,

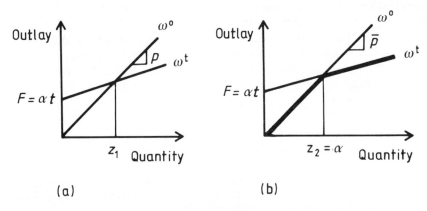

(a)   (b)

Figure 7.20
Linear and nonlinear price schedules: (a) optimality in aggregate; (b) optimality for
individuals

and those above are better-off. It is left to the reader to show that there is a choice of α and t parameters so that the seller's profits when offering the option in price schedules is equal to that with the uniform price $\bar{p}$.

SE7.9   Price Discrimination in Disneyland

One of the classics in discriminatory two-part tariffs is Oi's (1971) analysis of Disneyland's pricing policy. He begins with a question: ". . . If you were the owner of Disneyland, should you charge high lump sum admission fees and give rides away, or should you let people into the amusement park for nothing and stick them with monopolistic prices for the rides?" (Oi, 1971, p. 77).

Some notation is helpful in following Oi's answer to this question. Among other things, a two-part tariff imparts a discontinuity in the consumer's budget constraint, which takes the form

$$pz + F + z_0 = y \qquad z > 0$$
$$z_0 = y \qquad z > 0 \tag{7.41}$$

where z measures the Disneyland rides, p is the uniform price per ride, F is the lump-sum entrance fee to the park, z_0 is the outside good (numeraire), and y is income. Note for later use that

$$p \frac{\partial z}{\partial y} = 1 - \frac{\partial z_0}{\partial y} \tag{7.42}$$

along the budget constraint when $z > 0$. The demand for service depends on the price and the post-entry net income $y - F$, which we write as $z = z(p, y - F)$. Since y and F enter the demand in this fashion we have

$$\frac{\partial z}{\partial y} = - \frac{\partial z}{\partial F} \tag{7.43}$$

When the two-part pricing policy is used, Disneyland's profits depend on its choice of both p and F. These should provide a maximum for

$$\pi = pz(p, y - F) - F - c(z) \tag{7.44}$$

where $c(z)$ is the total variable cost. To keep things simple for the moment, suppose that all consumers are identical; this, as we will see, means that Disneyland can perfectly price discriminate with the choice of only one F and one p. Differentiating π with respect to F and substituting (7.42) and (7.43) gives

$$\frac{\partial \pi}{\partial F} = 1 - \left(p - \frac{\partial c}{\partial z} \right) \frac{\partial z}{\partial y} = \frac{\partial z_0}{\partial y} + \frac{\partial c}{\partial z} \frac{\partial z}{\partial y} \tag{7.45}$$

With positive income effects (normal goods) and rising marginal cost, this derivative is positive: increases in the entrance fee increase Disneyland's profits, as long as the individual decides to enter. At whatever price p that Disneyland sets, the optimal fixed fee is the one which captures all the consumer surplus. Let $F^*(p)$ indicate this full surplus-capturing function.

A fact of interest at this point is $dF^*(p)/dp = -z$. To establish this equality, think of $F^*(p)$ as the area above p and below the (constant utility) income-compensated demand. Then, for small decreases in p, F^* increases by $z\,\mathrm{d}p$ or $\mathrm{d}F^*(p)/\mathrm{d}p = -z$.

What level of p maximizes Disneyland's profits? That follows from the stationarity condition

$$\frac{\partial \pi}{\partial p} = 1 - \left(p - \frac{\partial c}{\partial z}\right)\frac{\partial z}{\partial p} + z + \frac{\partial F^*}{\partial p} = 0 \qquad (7.46)$$

The last two terms of this expression cancel, which gives the usual prescription of price equal to marginal cost. In short, Disneyland perfectly price discriminates to maximize profits by setting the price of a ride equal to its marginal costs and imposing an entrance fee F^* equal to the consumer surplus at that price. This is illustrated in figure 7.21, where the shaded area is F^*, D is the income-compensated demand, and z^* rides are sold.

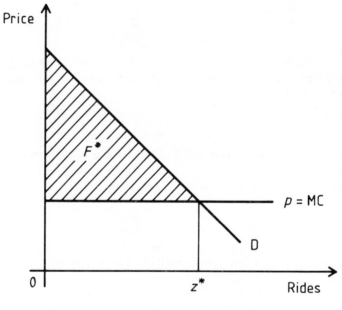

Figure 7.21
Two-part tariff

The assumption of identical individuals is important in reaching this simplified result. More generally, as Oi notes, the unit price of each ride is set equal to marginal cost, but different consumers must be charged different entry fees F_i^* equal to their individual surplus at that unit price. This scheme would still provide first-degree price discrimination. To be sure, such precision in setting the F_i^* would be prohibitively expensive, and Disneyland has resorted to a second-degree approximation. Standard entrance fees with a wide variety of reductions for children, senior citizens, military personnel, groups booking in advance, etc., form the second-degree blocks.

8 Markets for Durable Goods

Are there incentives for producers of a durable good to limit resale markets for used versions of the good? Do these incentives depend on the extent of monopoly power possessed by the producer? Why do monopoly producers often lease the durable rather than sell it outright? Why do monopoly sellers frequently adopt production technologies with high ratios of variable to fixed costs or produce goods with less durability than we would generally expect?

The twist in the analysis of durable goods, of course, comes from the fact that they are long lived. This complicates economic analysis because there are then important interrelationships existing between the markets for new and used versions of the good. The price that a durable-good seller can charge at any date depends not only on its current level of output, but also on the buyer's expectations about future stocks and output levels since these determine the implicit rental rate of the good's future service flow and, with discounting, the current demand price.

The manner in which current price and future price expectations are related is critical to the profits that can be earned by the durable-good producer. The relationship can be controlled in part by the producer's manufacturing and selling techniques, the rate at which the durable depreciates (its durability), the organization of future markets, and finally by the specific manner in which buyers form expectations about equilibrium conditions in those markets. In this chapter these various effects are investigated serially beginning with models having limited dynamics and moving to models in which the relationships among market demand, the firm's pricing policies, and consumer expectations over time are explicit and central to the analysis.

8.1 Durability and Monopoly

Wicksell (1934), Martin (1962), Kleiman and Ophir (1966), Levhari and Srinivasan (1969), and Schmalensee (1970) were early contributors to the literature on product quality, each arguing that monopolists offer goods of lower durability (quality) than those that would be produced under similar cost and demand conditions by a competitive industry. Drawing attention to several inconsistencies between the formal analysis and stated conclusions in these early studies, Swan (1970, 1971) showed there was no unambiguous link between monopoly power and reduced durability. His so-called "independence" result stood for only a short period, as a new variety of models was designed to reveal precisely what it was that yielded independence. Our intent in this section is to review these findings in general and the independence question in particular. This analysis is brief, as it is largely intended to serve as background for the expressly dynamic models of later sections.

8.1.1   The Independence Result

Perhaps the best place to begin any analysis of product durability is Hirshleifer's (1971) study of incentives for monopolists to withhold economically efficient inventions from the market (see also Kihlstrom and Levhari, 1977; Koutsoyiannis, 1979, p. 165; Saving, 1982; Liebowitz, 1982). This begins with a monopolist's having to choose between producing two different light bulbs: an original bulb with a one-year service life and an "improved" version with a two-year life *and* cost of production less than twice that of its less durable alternative. The key to this analysis is the representation of light bulbs of different durability (quality) by a single demand characteristic, *unit light services*.

Figure 8.1 will be the discussion focus. Of first note in the figure is the fact that the horizontal axis measures lighting *service* per period, not the quantity of light bulbs. In turn, D indicates the (inverse) demand for such service, with MR being the associated marginal revenue. For the moment we interpret the demand for service in such a way that consumers place no value on durability *per se*. That is, consumers consider two one-year bulbs as a perfect substitute for one two-year bulb. More generally, any combination of bulbs producing the same stream of services over time is assumed to be valued equally by consumers. To complete the model components, c_1 in the figure is the constant industry average (and marginal) cost of providing light services when producing bulbs with a one-year life and c_2 is the cost of providing comparable services when producing bulbs with a two-year life. c_2 lies below c_1 since it is assumed that the production cost of the two-year bulb is less than twice that of the one-year alternative. Further, the level of these costs is assumed to be unaffected by whether industry production is monopolized or perfectly competitive.

Given c_1 and c_2, it is straightforward to see how the independence result occurs. The profit-maximizing monopolist would choose to produce two-year bulbs at service level z_m; the rivalry among competitive firms leads to the same extended durability choice, but at service level z_c. More generally, when light service cost schedules can be ranked unambiguously because they do not cross at any quantity less than the competitive level, the monopolist will act just as the competitive industry in adopting the socially efficient minimum cost durability.

Stating the independence result in this way highlights a key sufficiency condition: the nonintersection of service cost schedules. To emphasize this fact consider an additional light bulb having a three-year life and declining industry cost of service schedule as shown by c_3 in the figure. In choosing among the three potential products the monopolist continues to produce two-year bulbs at service level z_m. Now, however, the competitive industry adopts the three-year bulbs and produces service z'_c. In this case monopoly power leads to products with reduced durability. This is not a general result, however. Suppose alternatively that the c_2 schedule in the figure indicates service costs for four-year bulbs. In this case the monopolist would choose to produce a more durable bulb than the competitive industry. (Note also that the extended durability would not be socially efficient.)

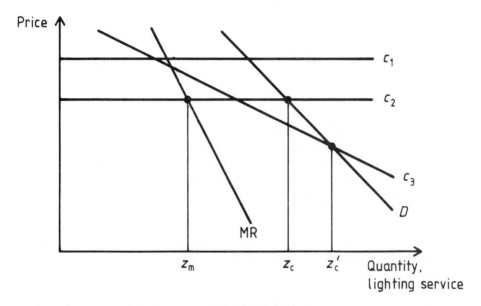

Figure 8.1
Monopoly and durability

Preferences for Durability. Underlying the analysis of figure 8.1 is the assumption that consumers place no value on durability *per se*. Otherwise it would be necessary to allow durability to be a demand parameter in addition to being a parameter of the unit service cost schedule, or equivalently it would be necessary to measure services on a value-adjusted basis, reflecting the value-in-use from increased durability by a reduction in the service cost schedule. If a positive value is assumed for durability, by this latter method the value-adjusted cost-of-service schedule for, say, two-year bulbs would decline relative to that for one-year bulbs. Thus, while the demand for durability *per se* does not in itself destroy the independence result, it does hold out the *possibility* that value-adjusted cost-of-service curves would, with different rates of decline, cross in ways that would cause the monopolist to choose a durability different from that chosen by competitive firms.[1]

---

[1] In a similar fashion, dropping the assumption of constant returns to scale is a helpful, although not sufficient, condition in producing cross-overs (see Kamien and Schwartz, 1974). Moreover, it is known that those assumptions which (multiplicatively or additively) separate the cost-of-service function into quantity and durability components are sufficient to assure against cross-overs. See, for example, Swan (1972) and Schmalensee (1979a).

The presence of depreciation and maintenance expense, the use of pricing policies designed to discriminate among purchasers, and the opportunity for one period's use to substitute for another have more recently been shown to affect the independence result. It is to these somewhat more complex issues that we turn in the following sections.

8.1.2 Durable-good Monopoly and Price Expectations

With durable goods the outstanding stock links consumer demand across the time sequence of markets and, in turn, links time-optimal prices. This produces special problems for the monopoly seller of a durable good. Perhaps the clearest way to introduce these problems is to follow an early illustration by Coase (1972, p. 143):

> Assume that a supplier owns the total stock of a completely durable good. At what price will he sell it? To take a concrete example, assume that one person owns all the land in the United States and, to simplify the analysis, that all land is of uniform quality. Assume also that the landowner is not able to work the land himself, that ownership of land yields no utility and that there are no costs involved in disposing of the land. If there were a large number of landowners and the price were competitively determined, the price would be that at which the amount demanded was equal to the amount of land in the United States. If we imagine this fixed supply of land to be various amounts either greater or smaller, and then discover what the competitively determined price would be, we can trace out the demand schedule for American land.

At this point in his analysis Coase asks what a monopolistic landowner would charge for a unit of land. The answer does not follow immediately from the usual marginal revenue and marginal cost equality of elementary price theory.[2] Rather, Coase finds that the monopolist landowner is effectively unable to exercise any monopoly power. His argument goes as follows. If the monopolist could, it would elect to sell the profit-maximizing quantity of land at some initial period and then retire from the trade. However, that would be a "time-inconsistent" or noncredible strategy in the sense that once some initial quantity of land is sold, the monopolist will find itself faced with a residual demand. Exploiting that residual by selling some additional quantity at a lower price would allow the monopolist to increase its profits. In fact, the possibility of exploiting the residual demand, after any given number of unit sales, exists as long as the total quantity sold falls short of the amount offered by competitive landowners. Price discriminating over time in this way, the monopolist landowner would seem to sell the same amount as his competitive counterparts and, with a positive interest rate, Coase argues that the monopolist will attempt to make these sales as rapidly as possible.

There is, of course, a problem with his line of reasoning. Rational consumers

---

[2] Marginal revenue equals marginal cost is, of course, always the profit-maximizing condition (given suitable continuity). At issue here is *what* demand and cost schedules are relevant.

will surely anticipate that the monopolist will eventually produce the competitive level of output and, if the time lags between periods are small, they will accordingly value all land immediately at the competitive price. Left in this way Coase's conclusions are quite unusual: the monopolist must sell at the competitive price and earn no more than the competitive firm. Note that the monopolist maximizes its profits at each date subject to the buyers' knowledge (rational expectation) that at each then-future date he will also choose the output which maximizes profits.[3]

Leasing and Other Commitments. At this point Coase argues that a lease-only policy may be designed by the durable-good monopolist to overcome the difficulties in receiving a monopoly price. The key difference between a short-term lessor and a seller is that when the lessor–manufacturer produces beyond the simple monopoly level it suffers the capital loss on all previously sold (inframarginal) units. That is, with a leasing policy the reduction in price and the capital losses that accompany any overproduction are incurred by the lessor. In contrast, when that durable-goods producer considers sales beyond the monopoly point the capital losses are borne by earlier purchasers in whose interest the seller has no immediate concern. Knowing these different possibilities for losses and gains, intelligent buyers will surely understand that associated production incentives, or lack of them, and adjust the price that they will pay accordingly.

There are other commitments beyond short-term leasing that the durable-goods monopolist may use to assure buyers that production beyond some limit will not occur. Lithographers, for example, often publicly destroy their plates after a pre-specified number of impressions. Repurchase agreements, obligating the seller to take back any unit at a previously negotiated price, may also be used, for these impose the costs of over-production on the seller and "self-enforce" a production limit. Price protection agreements, where any buyer may legally demand the lowest sales price to occur for a number of periods following his purchase, act in a similar way to make the seller liable for over-production capital losses.[4] Finally, the firm may adopt a production technology which permits only a limited number of units to be produced in any period without prohibitively increasing unit costs. Such capacity constraints, when conspicuous, also inform consumers that the monopolist will not over-produce.[5] In each of these cases the durable-good monopolist avoids the Coase competitive result by making (irrevocable) commitments which limit production. While the potential gains to such policies are clear, in the final analysis the feasibility and extent of such commitments will depend on their cost.

The differences between monopoly seller and lessor outputs when the seller does not make a commitment to limit production are developed in the next

---

[3] The developments of chapter 9 show that this assures a "subgame perfect" solution.

[4] For example, Sultan (1974) found this to be a standard provision in sales contracts for large steam turbine generator sets during the mid-1970s period.

[5] As a final possibility, not developed here, Ausubel and Denreckere (1987) observe that duopolists generally realize positive profits in a Cournot–Nash game. For this reason, they suggest that licensing a second-source supplier of the durable may also occur. See also Shepard (1985).

section. In the following section we investigate how commitments can be used advantageously by the monopoly seller.

8.2   Recursion and Rational Expectations

For the moment consider the simplest dynamic model based on two periods and a single perfectly durable (nondepreciating) perfectly divisible good.[6] Purchases are made in a competitive market with no buyer believing that it can have any effect on the market price of the good. Let $t = 0$ be the initial (or current) period and $t = 1$ the next (or future) period, with ρ the one-period discount factor. For added simplicity suppose that the inverse time-separable demand per period for durable-good service level S is $p = \alpha - \beta S$, where $\alpha, \beta > 0$ are constants. Here, the price p is the rental rate per period for a quantity of the good supplying service level S, and the demand is time separable in the sense that the prices and quantities in the demand relationship are of the same date. (If the price at some period t_0 affected the quantity demand at some different period t_1, then the demand would not have this separability.)

As a convenience, scale S such that one unit of the good provides one unit of service per period. This means that S can then be equivalently thought of as the stock of the good. Thus, when z_0 units are produced at period zero the rental rate for that initial period is $p_0 = \alpha - \beta z_0$. If z_1 new units are produced at $t = 1$, making $z_0 + z_1$ the stock or cumulative units in service (there is no depreciation), the rental rate at this next period is $p_1 = \alpha - \beta(z_0 + z_1)$.

E8.1

Durable-good Supply, Competitive Sellers, and Monopoly Lessor

A numerical example is helpful in clarifying the two-period interaction. Suppose that demand is linear, as above, and that all costs are variable and constant at the level c.

Competitive Sellers. When the (perfectly) durable good is produced by a competitive industry it is clear that

$$z_0^c = \frac{\alpha - c}{\beta} \tag{8.1}$$

units will be produced at $t = 0$ and none in the future period ($z_1^c = 0$). That is, the rental price is equal to marginal cost in both periods, and the industry profits are zero.

Monopoly Lessor. Suppose, alternatively, that the durable good is produced by a monopolist lessor.[7] When z_0 units are produced and leased at $t = 0$, the

---

[6] The basic model used in this section was developed by Bulow (1982); see also Stokey (1981) and Bond and Samuelson (1984).

[7] Leasing may be impossible for both legal and practical reasons. In classic antitrust cases involving United Shoe Machinery, IBM, and Xerox, who began their businesses by only renting their products, the firms were ordered by the courts to make sales at attractive rates also. Some commodities simply do not lend themselves to leasing. For example, DeBeers, the diamond monopolist, would find little demand for leased (uncut) diamonds.

monopolist earns $z_0(\alpha - \beta z_0) - cz_0$ in profits in that period. When an additional z_1 units are produced and leased at $t = 1$, then $p_1 = \alpha - \beta(z_0 + z_1)$ and the profits at that future period are $(z_0 + z_1)\{\alpha - \beta(z_0 + z_1)\} - cz_1$. The monopolist leasing to maximize the present value of its profit stream solves the problem

$$\max_z[z_0(\alpha - \beta z_0) - cz_0 + \rho\{(z_0 + z_1)\{\alpha - \beta(z_0 + z_1)\} - cz_1\}]$$

where ρ is the discount factor. The optimal (nonnegative) leasing plan is apparent in this case. All production occurs in the initial period:

$$z_0{}^1 = \frac{\alpha(1 + \rho) - c}{2\beta(1 + \rho)} \geq 0 \qquad (8.2a)$$

$$z_1{}^1 = 0 \qquad (8.2b)$$

and the same number of units are leased during both periods. Note for later use that an interest rate of zero ($\rho = 1$) yields $z_0{}^1 = (2\alpha - c)/4\beta \geq 0$ with accompanying positive profits of $(2\alpha - c)(2\alpha + 5c)/8\beta$.

Used-good Markets. A frictionless market for used, or secondhand, versions of the durable good is assumed to exist. This serves two purposes. First, it means that the monopoly seller will not be able to effectively price discriminate among the buyers at any instant. Second, it means that, even with a time-separable demand (as specified above), different individuals may be in the market at different dates: some consumer may choose the services of the durable good for only one period, knowing that he will be able to resell in the used-good market in the following period. In this way durable goods will be supplied even though any one individual uses their services for only some short period.

8.2.1 Monopoly Seller Solution

The monopoly lessor of a durable good faces a problem which is analytically similar to that it would face if the good were not durable and were sold outright. The monopolist who sells a durable outright faces a somewhat different problem. The origin and details of this difference are revealed when solving the seller's market problem recursively. Beginning at $t = 1$, suppose that the monopolist has previously produced and sold some amount z_0 at $t = 0$. Because of this, the residual demand it faces at $t = 1$ is $p_1 = \alpha - \beta z_0 - \beta z_1$ and, setting marginal revenue equal to the constant marginal cost c, its optimal output at the future period is

$$z_1^*(z_0) = \frac{\alpha - c - \beta z_0}{2\beta} \qquad (8.3)$$

Notice that this is an optimal production *rule*: z_1^* depends on the initial period production level z_0, the marginal cost, and the demand parameters. Regardless of the monopolist's decision at $t = 0$, (8.3) describes the optimal output choice for $t = 1$.[8]

---

[8] In the durable goods (and macroeconomics) literature the label "time consistency" is often used for this optimality property. It corresponds to the notion of subgame perfection to be developed in chapter 9, section 9.3.

When the monopolist produces and sells z_1^* units at $t = 1$, the rental price falls from $p_0(z_0)$ to $p_1(z_0 + z_1^*)$ as shown in figure 8.2. This, at first glance, seems to be unimportant to the monopolist seller, who has no direct interest in maintaining the rental price (and, in turn, the capital value) of the units sold at period zero.

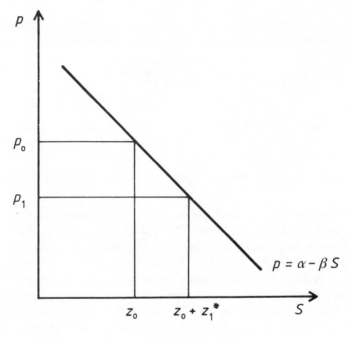

Figure 8.2
Monopoly seller

Consumers in the market at period zero, mindful of the incentives that the monopoly seller will have in the future, adjust the price that they will pay for the durable good to reflect its value in future periods. As a result, the $t = 0$ inverse demand will be made up of two parts: (a) the rental value of the durable good services at $t = 0$, and (b) the present value of $t = 1$ rental service based on the expectation that the monopolist will sell its optimal number of units in that future period. In the linear demand case considered here, the date zero price is given by

$$p(z_0; c) = \alpha - \beta z_0 + \rho[\alpha - \beta\{z_0 + z_1^*(z_0)\}]$$

$$= \alpha - \beta z_0 + \frac{\rho(\alpha + c - \beta z_0)}{2} \tag{8.4}$$

where we substitute for $z_1^*(z_0)$ using the optimal rule of equation (8.3). Notice that, unlike static analyses, this inverse demand depends on the level of the firm's (next period) *cost*. The importance of this fact for alternative business strategies will be clear later.

Faced with the price function (8.4), the monopolist's $t = 0$ problem is to solve

$$\max_{z_0{}^s}(\{p_1(z_0{}^s) - c\}z_0{}^s + \rho[\alpha - \beta\{z_0{}^s + z_1^*(z_0{}^s)\} - c]z_1^*(z_0{}^s)) \qquad (8.5)$$

where the superscript s is now used to indicate the monopoly *seller*. Substituting from (8.3) and (8.4), the stationarity value for $z_0{}^s$ can be found. In turn, the optimal $z_1{}^s$ is derived from (8.3).

Solution Cases. Four possible production cases occur for the monopoly seller (MS) depending on the relationship between cost and demand parameters. If there is no time preference ($\rho = 1$), the solution values for the cases are indicated as MS1–MS4 in table 8.1 (again, these results were first developed by Bulow, 1982). For comparison, the table also repeats (from E8.2) the optimal production plan of the monopoly lessor (ML) and competitive industry (C).

Table 8.1 Two-period Production ($\rho = 1$)

Case	z_0	z_1	Profits	Parameters
MS1	$\dfrac{2\alpha}{5\beta}$	$\dfrac{1}{2\beta}\left(\dfrac{3\alpha}{5} - c\right)$	$\dfrac{\alpha^2}{5\beta} + \dfrac{(\alpha - c)^2}{4}\beta$	$0 \leqslant c \leqslant \dfrac{3\alpha}{2}$
MS2	$\dfrac{\alpha - c}{\beta}$	0	0	$\dfrac{3\alpha}{5} \leqslant c \leqslant \dfrac{2\alpha}{3}$
MS3	$\dfrac{1}{2\beta}\left(\alpha - \dfrac{c}{2}\right)$	0	0	$\dfrac{2\alpha}{3} \leqslant c \leqslant 2\alpha$
MS4	0	0	0	$c \geqslant 2\alpha$
ML	$\dfrac{1}{2\beta}\left(\alpha - \dfrac{c}{2}\right)$	0	$\dfrac{(2\alpha - c)(2\alpha + 5c)}{8\beta}$	$0 \leqslant c \leqslant 2\alpha$
C	$\dfrac{\alpha - c}{\beta}$	0	0	$0 \leqslant c \leqslant \alpha$

The level of the monopolist's marginal cost relative to the demand parameter α determines which of the four MS cases will occur. In MS1 the marginal cost is lowest – so low in fact that the firm's period zero production level is independent of c. Production at time 1, however, does vary inversely with marginal cost. In MS2 the monopolist produces more than he would if he leased and had the same cost level. If the monopolist seller were to produce the lessor's period zero output, consumers here (and in the MS1 and MS3 cases) would realize that it would profit the seller to produce an additional amount in period 1 also. Because of this, it is in the seller's interest to produce somewhat more at the initial date and receive the benefit of reducing buyer expectations about the future output. In MS3, with even higher marginal costs, the seller finds it optimal to do exactly as the lessor and profits are maximized with $z_1 = 0$. In MS4 the costs are so high that the monopolist does not find it profitable to produce at all.

Seller and Lessor. The critical distinction between the seller and the lessor is that with leasing any capital losses to "over-production" are borne by the monopolist; that is, the costs are internalized. In contrast, the capital losses incurred with a seller's over-production are borne by the purchasers. Intelligent buyers will foresee this difference and the incentives for production it implies and accordingly adjust the price that they will pay for any unit at any date. With this foresight it is the monopolist rather than his customers who must pay for the lack of contracts internalizing the effects of over-production.

In minimizing the difficulties caused by the durability of its good, the monopolist may often find it in his interest to act in a significantly different way than either a lessor or a competitive firm. As one possibility, the monopoly seller may build a production facility which effectively limits its production. Changing production cycles and order lead–lag relationships may also help: by their very nature discrete time intervals between outputs impose a certain degree of commitment, as future production must be delayed for a minimum specified interval. As the interval goes to zero, this commitment disappears as we will see in section 8.3. Producing a less durable good can also act as a commitment as we will also see in section 8.3. Perhaps the most obvious commitment, and the one that we deal with first, is for the firm to establish a high marginal cost production operation with a capacity restriction.

8.2.2   Commitments

Suppose that the monopolist has a continuum of production technologies available. The distinguishing feature of these technologies that concerns us here is that each results in a different combination of (constant) marginal cost c and (period zero) fixed cost $F(c)$. The level of fixed cost is related to the choice of marginal cost and in particular it is assumed that $F(c)$ is decreasing and convex in c. To incorporate this added feature in the prior analysis only requires that $F(c)$ be subtracted from equation (8.5) (this analysis generally follows Bulow, 1982).

Giving the monopolist the choice of technology (that is, the choice of c) opens new strategies. For example, suppose that the monopolist chooses a greater level of marginal cost (smaller fixed cost) than that which would minimize the unit costs of producing any planned output. The a priori reasoning for such a choice is that higher marginal costs will act as a signal to consumers that lower levels of future output, and higher future prices, are forthcoming. This, in turn, shifts out the period zero demand and, when the proper balance is struck between incremental costs and revenues, provides greater overall profits. The analytics of such a balance are of present concern.

We limit our attention to the MS1 case of table 8.1 as the analysis of other cases proceeds in a similar way. Substituting the optimal values of z_0 and z_1 in the profit function (8.5) with fixed costs yields

$$\pi(c) = \frac{\alpha^2}{5\beta} + \frac{(\alpha - c)^2}{4\beta} - F(c) \tag{8.6}$$

The optimal choice of c then satisfies the stationarity condition

$$\frac{-(\alpha - c)}{2\beta} - F'(c) = 0 \tag{8.7}$$

At the optimum, the decrease in fixed cost, with increases in c, will be adjusted to equal $(\alpha - c)/2\beta$. Does this combination of fixed and marginal cost minimize the total cost of producing the optimal outputs?

The optimal production level of the monopoly seller (Table 8.1, case MS1) is

$$z_0 + z_1 = \frac{1}{2\beta}\left(\frac{7\alpha}{5} - c\right) \tag{8.8}$$

Thus at the optimum the decrease in marginal cost which increases fixed cost by $1 would be

$$\Delta c = \frac{(1/2\beta)(7\alpha/5 - c)}{(1/2\beta)(\alpha - c)} = \frac{7\alpha/5 - c}{\alpha - c} \tag{8.9}$$

which is greater than unity. For example, when $c = 0$, $\Delta c = \$7/5$, and when $c = 3\alpha/2$, $\Delta c = \$2$. The firm does not choose to minimize its cost of production at any given level of output, for a greater cost informs consumers that there will be reduced future output and this increases prices in both periods. This greater marginal cost, through the demand and revenue effect, maximizes profits.

E8.2

Commitment to a Technology

A concrete example helps in understanding the basis for the monopolist's choice of technology. Suppose that there are just two technologies available. Although the interpretation is somewhat strained, let the first technology give zero marginal cost and positive fixed costs $F(0) = 5\alpha^2/20\beta$, and let the second technology be polar to the first with constant marginal costs $c = 3\alpha/5$ and zero fixed cost $F(3\alpha/5) = 0$.

Suppose, as a first case, that the monopoly seller adopts the zero marginal cost technology. Continuing with the assumption of a zero interest rate, table 8.1 (MS1) indicates optimal sales $z_0 = 2\alpha/5\beta$ and $z_1 = 3\alpha/10\beta$. At these quantities equation (8.4) gives $p_0 = 9\alpha/10$ and $p_1 = \alpha - \beta(z_0 + z_1) = 3\alpha/10$. (The imputed rental price at period zero is therefore $6\alpha/10$.) In turn, total revenues are $9\alpha^2/20\beta_1$ and, with fixed cost of $5\alpha^2/20\beta$, the firm's profits are $\alpha^2/5\beta$.

If, alternatively, the firm adopts the second technology then, again from table 8.1 (MS1), optimal sales are $z_0 = 2\alpha/5\beta$ and $z_1 = 0$. In turn, $p_0 = 6\alpha/5$, $p_1 = 3\alpha/5$, total revenues are $12\alpha^2/25\beta$, and total costs are $(2\alpha/5\beta)(3\alpha/5) = 6\alpha^2/25\beta$. Profits are $6\alpha^2/25\beta$, which are greater than those with the first technology.

By adopting the zero fixed cost, high marginal cost technology the monopolist provides consumers with a commitment to produce less in the future period (than it would under the alternative technology). Although the total cost of production of this lesser output is greater than for the alternative technology, the higher cost nonetheless yields greater profits because the commitment signals consumers that the firm will restrict period 1 output.

8.3   Rational Expectations and Imperfect Durability

Holding aside the possibility of commitments, the incentive for the durable-good monopolist to exploit the future residual demand diminishes the current price it receives at every output level. When the good has less than perfect durability, this result is somewhat ameliorated. As will be seen, the replacement sales brought about by depreciation provide the monopoly seller with new market opportunities. Specifically, the seller will find it optimal to further limit its optimal production at any date, as undue expansion not only reduces current prices and profits but also reduces the profitability of future replacement sales. We consider this case in some detail in this section, again comparing competitive, monopoly lessor, and monopoly seller results.[9] The use of a capacity constraint (commitment) by a monopoly seller of an imperfectly durable good is then considered in a final section.

8.3.1   Imperfect Durability

Suppose that time varies continuously and consider an infinite horizon. Even though time is continuous, production and market exchanges are assumed to occur coincidentally and instantaneously at discrete dates, which we will call **market dates**. In turn, a **market interval** is the length of time between successive market dates, which is assumed to be uniform and denoted by τ. (There are, for example, t/τ market dates between calendar times zero and t.)

Since the good is not assumed to be perfectly durable, its stock depends on prior levels of production and now a constant and continuous rate of depreciation δ. If S_t is the stock of the durable good at some market date t, then at the next market date $t + \tau$ the stock is $S_{t+\tau} = S_t \exp(-\delta\tau) + z_{t+\tau}$, where $z_{t+\tau}$ is the amount produced at $t + \tau$. Note that large values of the depreciation rate δ imply a less durable good, and conversely.

We will assume that at each market date t the (stationary) demand for the services of the durable good is linear:

$$p(S_t) = \alpha - \beta S_t \tag{8.10}$$

where $\alpha, \beta > 0$ are the same constants for each t and $p(S_t)$ is the service price or rental rate at that instant.[10] The rental rate on any stock S_t, after a market interval τ, necessarily considers the rate of depreciation

$$p_t = D(S_t, \delta, \tau) = \int_0^\tau p[S_t \exp(-\delta\tau) \exp\{-(\tau + \delta)s\}]\, ds \tag{8.11}$$

$$= \alpha(\delta, \tau) - \beta(\delta, \tau)S_t$$

where

---

[9] Stokey (1981) develops the basic model for this case. Bond and Samuelson (1984) and Kahn (1986) provide additional details.

[10] Stokey (1981) and Bulow (1982) use a similar linear demand. Bond and Samuelson (1984, appendix A) analyze the general nonlinear case where the demand is required only to have a negative slope.

$$\alpha(\delta, \tau) \equiv \frac{\alpha[1 - \exp\{-(r + \delta)\tau\}]}{r + \delta}$$

$$\beta(\delta, \tau) \equiv \frac{\beta[1 - \exp\{-(r + \delta)\tau\}]}{r + 2\delta}$$

and r is the instantaneous discount rate.

Consistent Expectations. As in the two-period model, buyers form expectations of future stocks as a basis for calculating future rental rates and, discounting these, they calculate the price to be paid for units currently produced. The time t expectations about the stocks at $t_1 \geq t$ will be denoted by $S_{t_1}^e(S_t, \tau)$, where the notation indicates the dependence of the expectation on both the current stock S_t and the market interval τ. Of course, $S_t^e(S_t, \tau) = S_t$ since the current stock is assumed to be exactly observable. It is further required that expectations are **consistent** in the sense that

$$S_{t_2}^e(S_t, \tau) = S_{t_2}^e(S_{t_1}^e(S_t, \tau), \tau) \tag{8.12}$$

for all market dates $t \leq t_1 \leq t_2$. Consistency requires that, if the expectations at date t_1 are fulfilled, then expectations about the date t_2 stock will not be altered in moving from t to t_1.

The price that buyers would pay at market date t for a unit of the durable good is given by the present value of all future rental rates based on consistent expectations, that is,

$$p(S_t, \delta, \tau) = \sum_{n=0}^{\infty} \exp\{-(r + \delta)\tau_n\} D(S_{t+n}^e(S_t, \tau), \tau) \tag{8.13}$$

The monopolist uses this demand function and its marginal cost, which is again assumed to be constant (and stationary) at level c, to calculate its optimal output policy.

E8.3

Competitive and Monopoly Lessor Stocks

Competitive production of the durable good occurs at market date t when the price from (8.13) equals marginal cost: $p(S_t, \delta, \tau) = c$ at each market date t. With the stationarity of the underlying service demand (8.10) and marginal cost, the same durable-good stock then obtains at each market date (between these dates, exponential depreciation occurs). Let $S^c(\delta, \tau)$ indicate this stock. **Rational expectations**, requiring that the expected stock in fact obtain when the expectations are used, implies $S_{t_1}^e(S_t, \delta, \tau) = S^c$ for all market dates $t_1 \geq t$ when $S_t = S^c$ (the nature of rational expectations is discussed in greater detail in section 8.3.2).

Competitive Stock. Using this condition in (8.13) determines the competitive stock in terms of the parameters:

$$S^c(\delta, \tau) = \frac{\alpha(\delta, \tau) - [1 - \exp\{\tau + \delta)\tau\}]c}{\beta(\delta, \tau)} \tag{8.14}$$

Monopoly Lessor Stock. The durable-good stock of the monopolist who leases its output can be determined similarly. In this case, production is chosen to achieve a level of stock S^1 which maximizes the present value of lease payments:

$$\pi^1 = (\alpha(\delta, \tau) - \beta(\delta, \tau)S^1 - [1 - \exp\{-\tau + \delta)\tau\}]c)S \qquad (8.15)$$

where $[1 - \exp\{-(\tau + \delta)\tau\}]c$ is the cost of capital services per market interval (it is the payment per unit of services having present value equal to c). The stationarity point of π^1, using (8.14), yields

$$S^1(\delta, \tau) = \frac{S^c(\delta, \tau)}{2} \qquad (8.16)$$

That is, the monopoly lessor maintains a stock of just half the competitive level.

Monopoly Seller. With a good that depreciates there is a distinction to be made between sales which provide an increment to the stock of the good and those which are for replacement only (to offset depreciation). The importance of this distinction will be seen below when we look at equilibrium conditions. Here it is simply noted that the increments $S_t - S_{t-1}$ to the stock between two dates and the replacements $\{1 - \exp(-\delta\tau)\}S_{t-1}$ together have the expression

$$z_t = (S_t - S_{t-1}) + \{1 - \exp(-\delta\tau)\}$$
$$= S_t - S_{t-1}\exp(-\delta\tau) \qquad (8.17)$$

When the depreciation rate is exogenously given, it is evident from (8.17) that the monopoly seller can be thought of as choosing either a time sequence of production amounts at each date or, equivalently, a time sequence of the durable-good stock. We adopt the latter view, which gives the present value optimization problem

$$\max_{\{S_n\}s_{t_1=t+1}} \sum_{}^{\infty} \{S_{t_1} - S_{t_1-1} - \exp(-\delta\tau)\}\{p(S_t, \delta, \tau) - c\}\exp\{-r\tau(t_1 - t)\} \quad (8.18)$$

where S_t is the given beginning stock. Again, the maximum is to be found with respect to the *time sequence* of stocks.

8.3.2   Rational Expectations Equilibrium

Recall from (8.13) that the price function $p(\cdot)$ in the maximand (8.18) involves expectations about the future. This introduces the problem, usual in the multiperiod market context, of how expectations are formed and how they correspond to actual market occurrences as time unfolds. Stokey (1981) has investigated two solution concepts based on a form of rational expectations. In the first, a time sequence $\{S_t, S_{t+1}, \ldots\}$ is said to be a **rational expectations equilibrium** (REE) if it solves the maximum problem (8.18) for a consistent expectations function $S_{t_1}^e(S_t, \tau) = S_{t_1}$ at all $t_1 \geq t$. That is, the REE assumes that the buyer's expectations along the optimal stock sequence will be fulfilled. The second solution concept, termed the **perfect rational expectations equilib-**

rium (PREE), is an REE with the additional property that expectations would continue to be fulfilled if an unexpected exogenous shock were to perturb the durable-good stock at any date away from the equilibrium path. A PREE is therefore described by an expectation function $S_{t_1}{}^e(S_t, \tau)$ for all $t_1 \geq t$ satisfying the consistency condition (8.12) and having the added property

$$[S_t{}^e(S_t, \tau), S_{t+1}{}^e(S_t, \tau), S_{t+2}{}^e(S_t, \tau), \ldots] = \text{argmax } \pi(S_t, \tau) \qquad (8.19)$$

for a given beginning stock S_t.

A Special Case of Expectations. There are many possible ways in which expectations can be formed consistently and, in turn, provide REE and PREE. In the remainder of this chapter we follow Stokey (1981) and use an expectations function with two parameters $\bar{S}$ and κ:

$$S_{t_1}{}^e(S_t, \tau) = \bar{S} + \kappa^{(t_1-t)}(S_t - \bar{S}) \qquad (8.20)$$

where $\bar{S}$ is a limit stock and $\kappa \geq 0$ is a constant rate of adjustment. It is straightforward to show that, with this function, expectations are consistent in the sense of (8.12).

Using (8.20), the optimal stock sequence (given the beginning S_t) is simply described by the two values $\bar{S}$ and κ which solve the stationarity conditions associated with (8.18):

$$\left[\alpha(\delta, \tau) - [1 - \alpha \exp\{-(r + \delta)\tau\}] \, c - \beta(\delta, \tau)\bar{S}\left(1 + \frac{1 - \exp(-\delta\tau)}{1 - \kappa \exp\{-(r + \delta)\tau\}}\right) \right]$$

$$- \kappa^{t_1-t}\left[\beta(\delta, \tau)(S_t - \bar{S})\left(1 + \frac{\kappa - \exp(-\delta\tau)}{\kappa[1 - \exp\{r + \tau)\tau\}]}\right)\right]$$

$$= 0 \qquad (8.21)$$

for all $t_1 \geq t$. As this condition must hold at each market date and the second term is multiplied by κ^{t_1-t}, each of the two bracketed terms must be zero for a solution. The second of these terms solves for the optimal κ, in terms of the underlying parameters, as follows:

$$\kappa(\delta, \tau) = \frac{1 - [1 - \exp\{-(r + 2\delta)\tau\}]^{1/2}}{\exp\{-(r + \delta)\tau\}} < 1 \qquad (8.22a)$$

Substituting this into the first bracketed term of (8.21) then gives

$$\bar{S}(\delta, \tau) = \frac{S^c(\delta, \tau)}{\omega(\delta, \tau)} \qquad (8.22b)$$

where $\omega(\delta, \tau) = (1 + \{1 - \exp(-\delta\tau)\}[1 - \exp\{r + 2\delta)\tau\}])^{-1/2}$.

Limiting Solutions. Rearranging (8.22b) reveals that ω is the ratio of the competitive stock to the limit stock. As the market interval τ goes to zero (trading becomes continuous) and/or the depreciation rate δ goes to zero (the good becomes perfectly durable), $\omega = 1$ in the limit and the stock of the good produced by the monopoly seller becomes the competitive level $\bar{S}^c$. This corresponds to the situation discussed originally by Coase, for which it is usual to say that the market is *saturated* in the limit.[11] In the opposite limiting case where the good depreciates rapidly (it is perishable), there is also a simple solution: $\lim_{\delta \to \infty} \omega(\delta, \tau) = 2$ (for $\tau > 0$), which implies $\bar{S} = S^c/2$. Since $S^l = S^c/2$, from (8.16), the monopoly seller's limiting stock is the same as that established by the monopoly lessor.

Finally, in the more likely cases where τ and δ take on intermediate values (with $\omega > 0$), then $\bar{S} < S^c$ and the monopoly seller's price remains above the competitive level. In fact, for $\tau > 0$ it is easily shown that $\partial\omega(\delta, \tau)/\partial\delta > 0$, which means that as long as the good is less than perfectly durable the monopoly seller's stock will be less than the competitive level. This result differs from the perfectly durable case analyzed by Coase since replacement sales will be necessary even when the steady state stock is reached, and the monopoly seller then refrains from producing the competitive stock to increase the profitability of the long-lived stream of replacement sales.

8.3.3   Commitment Strategies

Not only does the PREE provide answers to key analytical questions, it also suggests several business strategies for the seller. First, the seller might effectively lengthen the market interval τ to increase its profits. Alternatively, the seller might influence consumers' expectations of future production by limiting its capacity to produce at any instant. These possibilities are of course related: they are both based on commitments that the firm makes about the level of future production. We can see the essential nature of such commitments by dealing with a usual case: the installation of a permanently fixed, restrictive manufacturing capacity. This situation differs from that described in section 8.2.2, for the imperfect durability of the good now means that the capacity constraint will generally have two effects. Not only can it restrict the *rate* at which the seller alters the stock of the good, it can also determine the *level* of the limiting stock.

Since the focus is to be on a manufacturing capacity constraint, it is convenient to assume that markets remain open continuously ($\tau = 0$). As was seen above, the absence of some sort of commitment to lower future production leads the seller to produce the competitive stock immediately and maintain it for all time. To avoid this, suppose that the firm installs its manufacturing operations in such a way that some specific quantity $\bar{z}$ is the maximum production rate. When it produces that rate at time t then

$$\dot{S}_t = \bar{z} - \delta S_t \tag{8.23}$$

is the associated rate of change in the durable-good stock. The time path of the durable good is then described by integrating (8.23) to obtain

$$S_t = \frac{\bar{z}}{\delta} \{1 - \exp(-\delta t)\} \tag{8.24}$$

---

[11] Coase's argument was that with continuous trading the durable-good monopolist is in fact in competition with himself. Buyers will view the goods of the monopolist sold tomorrow as perfect substitutes for those sold today only when there is no loss in waiting from today till tomorrow, which requires that these dates be infinitesimally close.

which assumes a zero initial stock (zero constant of integration). This integration also assumes that the limiting stock $\bar{z}/\delta = \bar{S}$ is not greater than the competitive stock S^c. This is reasonable, as S^c is produced when the durable-good price just equals marginal costs and stocks beyond that level will never be economic.

Optimal Capacity. What will the optimal level of the capacity be for the firm? To answer this question we need an expression for the firm's profits and, even more immediately, an expression for prices and expected stocks over time. If we continue to assume that the optimal choice for $\bar{z}$ is such that $\bar{z}/\delta \leqslant S^c$, then (8.16) provides the consumers' (rational) expectations of the stock to obtain at each date.[12] Substituting this in the price equation (8.13) and rearranging gives

$$p_t = \frac{\alpha}{r - \delta} - \frac{\beta(\bar{z}}{\delta} \left\{ \frac{1}{r + \delta} - \frac{\exp(-\delta t)}{r + 2\delta} \right\} \tag{8.25}$$

Substituting this price in the expression for the firm's present value gives

$$\pi_0(\bar{z}, \delta) = \int_0^\infty (p_t - c)\bar{z} \exp(-rt)\, dt$$

Further assuming $\bar{z}/\delta \leqslant S^c$ and integrating yields

$$\pi_0{}^s(\bar{z}, \delta) = \frac{\beta\bar{z}}{r(r + \delta)} \left(S^c - \frac{\bar{z}}{\delta} + \frac{r}{r + 2\delta}\frac{\bar{z}}{\delta} \right) \tag{8.26}$$

We now only require to find the $\bar{z}$ which maximizes this present value. The stationarity point of (8.26) with respect to $\bar{z}$ is

$$\frac{S^c}{2} - \frac{\bar{z}}{\delta} + \frac{r}{r + 2\delta}\frac{\bar{z}}{\delta} = 0 \tag{8.27a}$$

As we have required $\bar{z}/\delta \leqslant S^c$, this last equation holds only for $r \leqslant 2\delta$ (Bond and Samuelson, 1984, outline the solution when $r > 2r$). Solving for $\bar{z}/\delta$ gives

$$\frac{\bar{z}}{\delta} = S^c\left(\frac{r + 2\delta}{4\delta}\right) = S^c\left(\frac{r}{4\delta} + \frac{1}{2}\right) \tag{8.27b}$$

Note that $\bar{z}/\delta$ is decreasing in the depreciation rate δ (since this makes replacement sales consume a greater portion of output) and increasing in the discount rate r. Substituting (8.27b) in (8.26) and simplifying gives the optimal present value

$$\pi_0{}^s = \frac{\alpha^2}{2\beta}\frac{r + 2\delta}{4\delta r(r + \delta)} \tag{8.28}$$

Since all the parameters on the right-hand side of this expression are positive, $\pi_0{}^s$ is greater than zero.

How do the capacity-constrained monopoly seller's profits compare with the (unconstrained) lessor and competitive levels? Recall from equations (8.15) and (8.16) that the lessor's present value is $\pi_0{}^l = \alpha_2/4$. From equation (8.28) this further implies that $\{(r + 2\delta/2\delta r(r + \delta))\} \leqslant 1/3\delta^2$ when $r \leqslant 2\delta$, which was required. Since $\pi_0{}^c = 0$, we have $\pi_0{}^c < \pi_0{}^s < \pi_0{}^l$ as expected.

[12] For $\bar{z}/\delta < S^c$ the monopolist will, of course, produce at capacity, that is, it will choose $z_t = \bar{z}$ for each t.

Summary. The monopoly seller of an imperfectly durable good makes replacement sales even when the stock of the good is not growing. When such sales occur and the market interval is not zero, the limiting stock is below that produced in competition. As the market interval goes to zero the stock (and profits of the seller) approaches the competitive level. To restrict its sales the monopolist can install a manufacturing facility whose capacity is adjustable only at prohibitive cost. If this is done and markets are open continuously ($\tau = 0$), the firm optimally chooses a level of production which sustains a stock below the competitive level. With a linear demand function this reduced stock is optimal for the monopolist provided that the market rate of interest is less than half the rate at which the durable good depreciates.

Supplementary examples

SE8.1   Natural Monopoly and Irreversible Costs

Although not necessary, it is usual to think of the durable-good monopolist as having a *natural* monopoly. What we mean by that, and the circumstances in which such an equilibrium market structure will arise, are issues considered here. Consider a commodity (perhaps durable) measured by z with inverse demand $p(z)$ which is decreasing, bounded at zero output, and with some specific level $\hat{z}$ such that $p(\hat{z}) = 0$. To enter into production of this good, an irreversible cost F must be made; let the variable cost of production be constant at c. What is crucial about this specification is that average total costs are decreasing and the fixed component is sunk. Suppose, finally, that there are an arbitrarily large number of potential entrants and that this technology is freely available to all. (As usual, demand and cost conditions are assumed to be stationary over time.)

Think now of the industry at some starting time $t = 0$. The potential producers, it is assumed, make their investment and output decisions before $t = 0$ in an *exogenously given sequence*: each decides whether to enter and incur F in sunk costs and, if so, what (constant) flow of output to produce for ever. Number the firms such that firm 1 chooses first in this sequence, firm 2 chooses second, and so forth. Let all subsequent decision-makers know of the decisions of all prior decision-makers. Inventories are ignored and industry price is determined by aggregate production.

The entry decision of any firm j is straightforward: enter if $\{p(z) - c\}z_j > F$, where z_j is j's equilibrium output flow and z is the corresponding aggregate. If the "integer problem" is neglected, firm j's entry is deterred at the aggregate flow level $\bar{z}$ if $\{p(\bar{z} + \bar{z}_j) - c\}z_j(\bar{z}) = F$ where $z_j(\bar{z})$ is j's best reply. Figure 8.3 illustrates how $\bar{z}$ provides a residual demand which leaves firm j able to cover its fixed cost F. Note that $\bar{z}$ depends on the properties of the demand function, the variable costs, and the sunk cost. It also depends critically on the assumption that firms enter sequentially and with full information about their rivals' moves and intentions (further details are given in chapters 9, 10, and 11, and in SE9.4, SE10.2, SE10.5, and SE11.7 specifically).

With these things as background, it is now straightforward to show that the first firm (the "natural monopolist") deters all subsequent entry by its decision

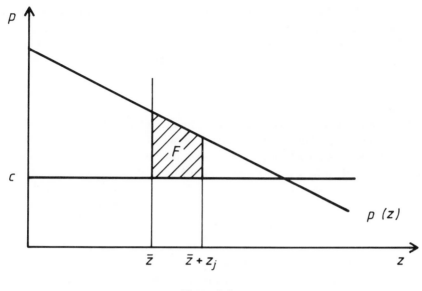

Figure 8.3
Natural monopoly

to enter. Entry is deterred if firm 1 chooses $\bar{z}$. Firm 1 understands that if it chooses any output flow less than $\bar{z}$ entry will take place until that aggregate output is reached. This, he further understands, will lead to an equilibrium price no greater than $p(\bar{z})$. Because of the uniformity of incremental costs, this means that firm 1 will be better off selling any additional output (up to $\bar{z}$) rather than having this done by another firm. A **natural monopoly** results.

SE8.2 Multiproduct Natural Monopoly

In the game set out in SE8.1 firms are active players while consumers are treated as passive agents whose behaviour is simply reflected by demand functions and the rules of the game. An alternative view of natural monopoly, suggested by Borch (1962), Faulhaber (1975), and Littlechild (1975), is based on a cooperative game where the firms are passive and consumers are the active players. The objective of consumers in this game is to convert their resources into a product; to do this, they will generally find it advantageous to form "buyer coalitions."

To see how the cooperative game is played consider the well-known "cost-sharing" case. Suppose that a durable-good monopolist is engaged in the production of m distinct commodities. For example, the monopolist might produce a homogeneous product, such as a computer, which is then sold in m different markets. Alternatively, the monopolist might produce a different computer for sale in each of its markets. Assume, however, that each market can be represented by a single aggregate buyer. The set of all buyers will then become the game players.

Let $M = [1\ 2\ \dots\ m]$ indicate the set of all buyers or markets and let S be a subset of M. Assume that the monopolist has fixed costs in providing service to each possible subset of buyers. Let this fixed cost be represented by the set function $F(S)$, with $F(\varnothing) = 0$ where $\varnothing$ is the empty set. We say that there is a **multiproduct natural monopoly** if $F(S)$ is *subadditive*, that is,

$$F(S) + F(S') \geqslant F(S + S') \tag{8.29}$$

whenever $S \cup S' = \varnothing$.

Suppose now that there is free entry into the manufacture of computers and that the competing firms can serve some or all of the monopolist's buyers. By free entry we mean that all firms in the industry have access to the same technology and therefore can produce according to the same cost function F.

The monopolist must determine prices for each of its buyers which satisfy a number of constraints. First, the prices must be high enough for revenues to be equal to total costs. If we let $p = [p_1 p_2 \ldots p_m]$ be a price vector, then

$$\sum_{i=1}^{m} p_i = F(M) \tag{8.30}$$

Moreover, to prevent coalitions of buyers from obtaining their machines from an alternative firm, the prices must also satisfy the constraints

$$\sum_{i \in S} p_i \leqslant F(S) \quad \text{for all } S \text{ in } M \tag{8.31}$$

Again, the above inequalities must hold for all S coalitions possible in M. Prices which satisfy conditions (8.30) and (8.31) jointly are said to be in the **core** of the game.

Whether a natural monopoly can be sustained depends on conditions (8.30) and (8.31) being met simultaneously. The analysis is formally identical with the problem of cross-subsidization. To determine whether subsidization occurs (or whether entry is possible) it is necessary to examine all possible groups of machines instead of individual machines by themselves. Second, and perhaps more important, there may be technological reasons why no prices may simultaneously provide revenues to cover costs and deter entry. That is, subadditivity of the cost function is not a sufficient condition for the existence of a sustainable monopoly (absence of cross-subsidization) in the cooperative game. Even with declining average costs, a natural monopoly may not be sustainable when there are multiple markets.

As one case in which a sustainable monopoly is impossible, consider a variant of an example discussed by Faulhaber (1975). Suppose that the computer manufacturer wishes to sell in three markets. Each market has a projected demand of X calculations (transactions) per period. In order to satisfy this demand, the monopolist can install one small computer at several locations, each of which can provide a maximum of $2X$ calculations per period, or it can install a single large computer which can provide $3X$ calculations. The cost of the small computers is $200 each, whereas a large computer costs $350. In each case, there are local implementation costs of $100 per market. If $M = [1, 2, 3]$, the total costs, including implementation, for the various alternatives are

$$F([1]) = F([2]) = F([3]) = \$300 \tag{8.32a}$$

$$F([1, 2]) = F([1, 3]) = F([2, 3]) = \$400 \qquad (8.32b)$$

$$F([1, 2, 3]) = \$650 \qquad (8.32c)$$

The cost function is subadditive: only one computer is needed to serve the three markets. However, to prevent entry by rivals, the monopolist's prices must satisfy $p_1 + p_2 \le \$400$, $p_1 + p_3 \le \$400$, and $p_2 + p_3 \le \$400$. These three conditions jointly imply $p_1 + p_2 + p_3 \le \$600$. From this we see that it is impossible for the monopolist to cover total costs of \$650 and at the same time deter the entry of rivals.

9 Theory of Games and Oligopoly

Classic economic theory is concerned with market equilibria where firms independently make value maximizing decisions. A long-standing and fundamental objection to such models is that their solutions are of interest only if each firm has control over every relevant variable in its environment. To be sure, some model variables may be directly controllable in this way, and others may be statistically controllable by the firm and therefore treated as an indifferent nature. However, yet other variables, on which a firm's value can critically depend, are generally under the control of other firms who wish to maximize value in a way which may conflict with or complement the efforts of the first firm.

The tradition of competitive industry analysis is to remove this interdependence by viewing the interaction among firms as a group of mutually determining problems in which a disinterested nature fixes some variables. When the decisions of rivals interact to determine each's payoff, competitive analysis is strained and a fundamentally different theory of the market is needed. Because the study of industrial economics deals routinely with such situations, it requires an understanding of such *interactions* – modes of behavior among firms whose actions are interdependent. Readers already familiar with games of strategy will have recognized this element in the discussion of oligopoly in chapter 3. The purpose of the present chapter is to provide a clearer foundation for the analysis of such interactions. This foundation is helpful not only in understanding classical oligopoly models; it is necessary in understanding modern developments in the theory of markets and particularly the dynamics of competition.

9.1 Games of Strategy

In contrast with the usual optimization model, game theory concerns the optimal choice of several decision-makers, each with potentially different and interdependent payoff criteria. In industrial economics these decision-makers (players) are generally firms and the payoffs are profits. The rivalry in an industry with $j = 1, 2, \ldots, J$ firms is described as a J-player game. If $J = 1$, then the game ("against nature") degenerates to the usual optimization problem. When participating firms can adopt only a finite number of strategies for play, the game is said to be finite; otherwise it is infinite. For the particular circumstance where the sum of the payoffs across firms is identically zero for all possible strategies, the game is said to have zero sum.

Two final distinctions are of particular importance in industrial economics. First, firms may act as a group, taking a concerted mutually beneficial action. This seems reasonable in many circumstances, as long as it is also recognized that there are generally incentives for each firm to promise to act in the group's interest and then, with all other firms acting in that cooperative way, to cheat on that promise to pursue its own best interest. Thus, the key aspect of a **cooperative game** is that the firms have the capacity to make binding commitments (to secure the common good). In contrast, a **noncooperative game**, where each firm acts unilaterally in its own best interest, occurs in situations where such binding agreements are too expensive to be negotiated and/or enforced. For example, the usual Cournot oligopoly illustrates a J-firm noncooperative game (when an effective regulatory agency is absent).

The second critical distinction is between static and dynamic games. The inclusion of multiple decision and payoff dates in games generally introduces important choices of strategy not found in static one-period models. For the moment these considerations are held aside and the games are static in the sense that they are restricted to just one decision and payoff date. Dynamic games are systematically considered from section 9.5 onwards.

Two complementary methods of characterizing noncooperative games, called normal and extensive forms, are generally employed. Roughly, these relate to describing the game either by a pairing of payoffs and strategies or by a more elementary and detailed move-by-move analysis. Because its structure appears to be less complex, it is usual to consider the normal form game first.

9.2   Games in Normal Form

A game in **normal form** has four parts to its specification:

1 the set of $j = 1, 2, \ldots, J$ **players** (firms);
2 the set of **profit payoffs** over which the firms have preference;[1]
3 the **strategy set or strategy space** (list of admissible decisions), one set for each firm;
4 the **payoff rule** which associates a profit outcome for each firm with each selection of strategies by the firms.

By use of the payoff rule the firms' preference for profits also induces a preference for strategies. As a result, a normal form game is equivalently (and more usually) defined by a set of firms, a collection of strategy sets, and

---

[1] It is assumed throughout that player firms have payoff (outcome) functions which are linear in profits. When payoffs are uncertain we assume that firms are risk neutral and maximize expected profits.

preferences of the firms expressed over the Cartesian product of the players' strategy sets. How are such games played and what solutions do they yield?

9.2.1   Strategies and Solutions

We begin by restricting attention to noncooperative games involving a finite number of firms (J) and finite strategy sets. Let $S_j = [s_j{}^1, s_j{}^2, \ldots, s_j{}^N]$ be j's **strategy set**, where each $s_j{}^n$ indicates a distinct admissible **strategy** to be played by j. The across-firm collection of such sets – the (Cartesian) product $S = S_1 \times S_2 \times \ldots \times S_J$ – represents every possible combination of strategies that can be played by the firms. Each **strategy combination**, each $s \in S$, is an ordered set containing one strategy selection for each of the J firms. A strategy combination defines a "play of the game." For each such play the profits of firm j are represented by $\pi_j(s)$; for any two strategy combinations s, $s' \in S$, firm j prefers s to s' iff $\pi_j(s) \geq \pi_j(s')$.

A two-firm game with finite strategy sets is commonly referred to as a **bimatrix game**, as it is conveniently represented by a pair of payoff matrices (Π^j, Π^k) with individual elements $\pi_j(s_j{}^n, s_k{}^m)$ and $\pi_k(s_j{}^n, s_k{}^m)$ respectively for the two firms j and k. Usually these two matrices are condensed into one array by pairing the payoffs. For example, the profit payoff bimatrix of table 9.1 indicates a two-firm bimatrix game in which firm j's strategies correspond to the rows of the array and firm k's strategies to the columns. Each ordered pair (cell) in the array indicates the payoff associated with the indicated choice of strategies, with firm j's profits listed first and k's listed second. If firm j were to play strategy 1 ($s_j{}^1$) and firm k were to play strategy 2 ($s_k{}^2$), then the payoffs are $(0, 0)$, that is, both firms receive zero profits. How do the firms behave? In view of the indicated payoffs it seems natural that $s_j{}^1$ and $s_k{}^1$ would be chosen.

Table 9.1   Strategies and Payoffs

	$s_k{}^1$	$s_k{}^2$
$s_j{}^1$	(1, 1)	(0, 0)
$s_j{}^2$	(0, 0)	(−1, −1)

9.3   Nash Solution Concept

Let $s = [s_1 s_2 \ldots s_J] \in S$ be a particular strategy combination in a game played by J firms. Further, let $(s^0 : s_j)$ indicate a combination in S obtained when firm j's strategy $s_j{}^0$ is replaced by an alternative s_j. Then, $s^0 \in S$ is defined to be a **(Nash) equilibrium** of the game when, for every admissible strategy $s_j \in S_j$, the profit payoff of every firm j is such that $\pi_j(s^0) \geq \pi_j(s^0 : s_j)$.

The definition is at times stated using a slightly different terminology: a strategy choice s_j^* by firm j is termed a **best response** to s if, for every $s_j \in S_j$, $\pi_j(s : s_j^*) \geq \pi_j(s : s_j)$. A Nash equilibrium point is then found where every firm's strategy is a best response to the given strategies of the remaining firms. This second terminology makes it clear that every Nash equilibrium point corresponds to a self-enforcing choice in the sense that no firm can *unilaterally* (that is, given the others' strategy choices) increase its profit by changing its strategy choice.

There is a final point about the Nash equilibria that requires early note. The equilibria can be defined by a set of quantity strategies, or price strategies, or any other decision variables of the firms involved. The nature of the product, the production technology, and the features of the market will be important considerations in determining which strategy variables are relevant in any given case. As we will make quite clear, the choice of strategy variable will critically affect the nature of the resulting equilibria and must be made with appropriate care (recall also the discussion in section 3.2).

9.3.1 Why Nash Equilibria?

From a normative perspective we can think of the firms as entering into a discussion of play until they reach a *nonbinding* agreement to use certain strategies. After this agreement has been reached, the firms separate and all subsequent communication among them is prohibited. Each firm then adopts a strategy, its actual strategy, without knowledge of the actual choice of the other player firms. Each firm may select the strategy specified in the nonbinding agreement, or it may ignore that agreement. When the strategies agreed upon constitute a Nash equilibrium, the agreement will be *self-enforcing* in the sense that, assuming that every other firm follows the agreement, it is optimal for each firm to abide by the agreement.[2]

Despite this desirable feature, there are several problems with the Nash solution concept as the following two examples suggest.[3]

E9.1

Existence and Uniqueness

Consider two profit-maximizing firms who must choose either to enter $(s_j{}^1, s_k{}^1)$ or not to enter $(s_j{}^2, s_k{}^2)$ a natural monopoly market. There are four possible outcomes. If both enter, each loses L; if neither enters, each earns zero; if just one of the firms enters it earns M while the other earns B. Let $0 < B < M$. The outcomes are given in the bimatrix game of table 9.2(a) where it is seen that the

---

[2] Only a very few solution concepts to noncooperative games have found widespread use in economics. The Nash concept, with refinements to be noted later, must be the most popular; in fact, when an equilibrium is spoken of without qualification in some economics context it is understood that a Nash equilibrium is being considered. In some (small number of) interesting situations the Nash equilibrium is found to be dominated by an alternative strategy combination (in the sense that all players are better off with this alternative). For such situations a "dominant strategy equilibrium" is often suggested as being the appropriate solution concept (see Moulin, 1982, and section 9.3.2 below).

[3] It is also frequently noted that the Nash equilibrium solution for noncooperative zero-sum games is consistent with the minmax solution concept (see SE9.6). That is, for zero-sum games Nash equilibria are just game-theoretic saddle points.

Table 9.2 (a) Multiple Equilibria; (b) No Equilibrium; (c) Dominant Equilibrium

(a)	s_k^1	s_k^2
s_j^1	$(-L, -L)$	(M, B)
s_j^2	(B, M)	$(0, 0)$

(b)	s_k^1	s_k^2
s_j^1	$(1, -1)$	$(0, 0)$
s_j^2	$(0, 0)$	$(1, -1)$

(c)	s_k^1	s_k^2
s_j^1	$(5, 5)$	$(0, 10)$
s_j^2	$(10, 0)$	$(1, 1)$

strategies (s_j^1, s_k^2) and (s_j^2, s_k^1) are *both* Nash equilibrium points. Moreover, the profit outcomes are distinct: firm j prefers the first point and firm k prefers the latter. What industry equilibrium will result? Not only are there multiple equilibria, the equilibrium pairs are not entirely "stable." An argument could be made, for example, that firm j will insist on using s_j^1, hoping to induce k to shift to s_k^1, and conversely for firm k.

In addition to multiple solutions, there is the potential for no Nash solution to exist.[4] For example, consider the bimatrix game of table 9.2(b). Given s_j^1, k's best response is s_k^2; given s_k^2, j's best response is s_j^2; in turn, given s_j^2, k's best response is s_k^1; coming full circle, given s_k^1, j's best response is s_j^1. It is quickly, and uncomfortably, seen that none of the four indicated strategy pairs is a Nash equilibrium for the game.

Even when there is a *single* Nash equilibrium point, it is not always clear that it makes full sense.

E9.2

Dominance

Consider two firms producing substitute products. Each considers upgrading the quality of its product. The firms may either choose high quality (the first strategy s^1) or the original quality (the second strategy s^2). The profit payoffs for the four possible game outcomes are as table 9.2(c). Note that if both choose high quality (s_j^2, s_k^2) the cost of producing that high quality (without any redistribution of market share and few new customers) leads to low profits for both firms.

In this game, strategy s_j^2 is j's best response and s_k^2 is k's best response giving (s_j^2, s_k^2) as the unique equilibrium pair with profits $(1, 1)$. However, if both firms play "wrong" – they do not adopt the Nash best response – the profit outcome is $(5, 5)$, which is better for both. The trouble with the dominant-strategy pair (s_j^1, s_k^1) is that each firm can gain at the expense of the other in moving either to (s_j^2, s_k^1) or to (s_j^1, s_k^2). If arrangements for prohibiting such "double-crosses" are not unduly expensive then (s_j^1, s_k^1) makes sense as an equilibrium.

---

[4] Here we restrict attention to pure strategies. A mixed strategy Nash equilibrium does exist for this game.

Prisoners' Dilemma and Dominant Strategies. A game of the form set out in E9.2 is generally referred to as a **prisoners' dilemma**. The name arises from the specific context in which these games were first discussed. Suppose that j and k are prisoners being separately interrogated concerning a crime. The strategies and payoffs in this context are based on the following scenario: if both confess they are both sentenced to ten years in jail; if both remain silent both are sentenced to two years in jail; if one confesses while the other does not, the confessor is released but the other is sentenced to 15 years in jail. The Nash equilibrium occurs when both prisoners confess, but remaining silent is the dominant strategy. Remaining silent, however, leaves the fear of being "double-crossed."[5] (Dominant-strategy solutions to prisoners' dilemma games are considered in section 9.3.2.)

Pareto Optimality and Nash Equilibrium. The Nash equilibrium, where no player can do better than the Nash strategy given that others are playing Nash strategies, is a much less stringent equilibrium concept than that which would have players choose dominant equilibria (when they exist) or, more generally, choose equilibria that serve any mutual interest. For this reason our intuition is that Nash equilibria are not generally Pareto optimal. We can quickly see that this intuition is correct.

At an interior Pareto optimum it is required to maximize

$$\sum_j \alpha_j \frac{\partial \pi_j}{\partial s_k} \quad \text{for all } k = 1, 2, \ldots, J \quad (9.1)$$

where the $\alpha_j > 0$ are weights of the index $\sum_j \alpha_j \pi_j$. Let the solution to (9.1) be given by $s^* = [s_1^* s_2^* \ldots s_J^*]$. Suppose now that at s^* the firms' interests generally conflict in the sense that if one firm were to increase its s_j^* this would increase its profits but lower those of all other firms, that is

$$\frac{\partial \pi_j(s^*)}{\partial s_j} \geq 0 \qquad \frac{\partial \pi_k(s^*)}{\partial s_j} < 0 \quad (9.2)$$

for all $j, k = 1, 2, \ldots, J$ and $j \neq k$. This is a sufficient condition for the profit-possibility frontier of the firms to have a negative slope. Given (9.2), then (9.1) implies that $\partial \pi_j(s^*)/\partial s_j > 0$ at a Pareto optimum.[6] The interior Nash equilibrium s^0 alternatively requires $\partial \pi_j(s^0)/\partial s_j = 0$, and for this case the Nash equilibrium is not Pareto optimal. Rather, there are alternative strategies which, if played, would make some firms better off. Despite this, by the Nash solution concept it is not in any firm's unilateral interest to act otherwise.

While the solution concept has positive aspects, the preceding examples reveal that it also has difficulties: Nash equilibria may not exist, they may be dominated, or they may not be unique when they do exist. The existence and uniqueness problems hold the potential for being especially aggravating. That potential is not borne out, however, because the existence and uniqueness of a

---

[5] Lave (1962) found that in (experimental) repetitions of prisoner's dilemma games isolated subjects were able to cooperate without communication. For a detailed review of Lave's work and other such experiments see Plott (1982).

[6] The strict inequality here results from the strict inequality for all other firms in (9.2). If $\partial \pi_k/\partial s_j \leq 0$ in (9.2), then there is the possibility that the Nash equilibrium would be Pareto optimal.

Nash equilibrium (in nonrandomized strategies) is guaranteed under commonly assumed conditions which are not unduly restrictive.

Existence and Uniqueness. The usual proof of existence of a Nash equilibrum relies on one of several fixed-point theorems of functions. Roughly, in the proofs a mapping is defined on the set of all *J*-tuples of strategies, with each *J*-tuple being mapped into another in such a way that every firm's strategy in the second *J*-tuple is a perturbation of its original strategy in the direction of a best response to the rival firms' strategies in the first *J*-tuple. Being each firm's best response to the strategies of its rivals, the conditions under which there exists a *J*-tuple which maps into itself, are also the conditions assuring the existence of an equilibrium point. As long as the number of players is finite, the relevant strategy sets are strictly convex and compact (in finite-dimensional Euclidean space), and the (scalar-valued) profit functions are continuous and strictly quasi-concave, such a mapping, and a Nash equilibrium point, will exist.[7] The strictness of the convexity and quasi-concavity assures uniqueness.

Nash Equilibrium and Strategy Variables. While the assumption of the Nash solution concept that other players do not change their strategies may seem restrictive, it is not. Rather, if one firm anticipates a nonzero reaction by a rival in terms of some strategic variable, then it is only necessary to describe its strategy (by a different choice of strategic variable) in such a way that this reaction is part of the description. The reader is here reminded of chapter 3, section 3.2, where the details of such strategy definitions were discussed and methods were set out for finding the Nash strategy variable corresponding to any representative nonzero conjecture. In short, the appropriate consideration is not whether the Nash solution concept is reasonable, but what strategy sets are available and relevant to the firms.

9.3.2 Dominant-strategy Equilibria

As the prisoners' dilemma game of E9.2 made clear, the Nash equilibrium concept is sometimes counter-intuitive as there may be alternative strategies which make all players better off. In such situations a dominant-strategy solution concept has frequently been invoked (see for example Moulin, 1982, and Pearce, 1984). While the sense of this concept and its several variations are easily understood, some additional terminology is helpful in setting these out exactly.

Suppose that the rivals of some firm j play the strategy combination $\bar{s}_j \equiv [s_1 s_2 \ldots s_{j-1} s_{j+1} \ldots s_J]$. Then firm j's **strongly best response** to $\bar{s}_j$ is the strategy s_j^{**} giving it the greatest payoff $\pi_j(s_j^{**}, \bar{s}_j) > \pi_j(s_j, \bar{s}_j)$ for all admissible $s_j \neq s_j^{**}$. The strongly best response exists only if no other strategies are equally good or better as a reaction to the given strategies of the rivals. In turn, a

---

[7] This is a consequence of the observations that (a) a continuous function attains its maximum on a compact set (thus the best-response correspondence of each firm is nonempty valued and is upper semicontinuous in the strategies of other players); (b) the set of values attaining the maximum of a quasi-concave function on a convex set is convex (so that the best-response correspondence of each player is convex); and (c) an upper semicontinuous, nonempty, and convex-valued correspondence (the Cartesian product of the firm's best responses) has a fixed point (Nash equilibrium).

strategy s_j^{**} is said to be a **dominant strategy** for firm j if it is j's strongly best response to *all* responses by its rivals: $\pi_j(s_j^{**}, \bar{s}_j) > \pi_j(s_j, \bar{s}_j)$ for all $\bar{s}_j$ and all admissible $s_j \neq s_j^{**}$. A **dominant-strategy equilibrium** is a combination of strategies each of which is dominant. One characteristic of prisoners' dilemma games is that they have dominant-strategy equilibria.

Most games, however, do not have dominant-strategy equilibria or even dominant strategies for single players. This gives rise to the less restrictive concept of weak dominance: a **weakly dominant strategy** s_j^* for some firm j is its best response to all responses of its rivals in the sense $\pi_j(s_j^*, \bar{s}_j) \geqslant \pi_j(s_j, \bar{s}_j)$ for all $\bar{s}_j$ and all admissible $s_j \neq s_j^*$. A dominant strategy (when it exists) is a subset (perhaps proper, perhaps null) of weakly dominant strategies. Strategies which are *not* weakly dominant are said to be **dominated**. Finally, an **iterated dominant-strategy equilibrium** (when it exists) results from the following algorithm: (a) for some original game delete one dominated strategy from the strategy set of some player; (b) for the reduced game determine dominated strategies, and delete one if one exists; (c) repeat step (b) until only one strategy remains for each player or a dominant-strategy equilibrium obtains.[8]

E9.3

Iterated Dominant-strategy Equilibria

Consider a simple market entry game involving a single entrant k and an incumbent firm j. Assume that, on entry, the firms simultaneously choose one of two marketing strategies. We indicate these by s_j^1, s_j^1 for firm j and similarly for firm k. The profit outcomes corresponding to the strategy selections are given in table 9.3. Although the entrant firm k suffers a loss at every turn of the game, it nonetheless values entry because a presence in this market (independent of the strategy it chooses) greatly enhances its profits in a complementary market. In this case the entrant's concern is with minimizing its loss. The reader should note that the game has zero sum in the sense that, with each strategy combination, the payoffs sum to zero.

Table 9.3 Zero-sum Payoffs

	s_k^1	s_k^2
s_j^1	$(10, -10)$	$(10, -10)$
s_j^2	$(5, -5)$	$(15, -15)$

Inspection of the table reveals that neither firm has a dominant strategy. The entrant firm k does have a weakly dominant strategy, however: s_k^1 is weakly dominant since its payoff is not less than the choice of s_k^2. Suppose that the

---

[8] In addition to the following example, E9.8 and SE9.3 illustrate iterated dominant-strategy solutions. A variation of this solution concept is frequently used in eliminating certain strategies in repeated games with incomplete information (see section 9.7.2).

incumbent firm j recognizes this and deletes $s_k{}^2$ as a possibility. This leaves a reduced game made up of only the first column of the table. For this reduced game the incumbent j has a dominant strategy $s_j{}^1$, and the combination $(s_j{}^1, s_k{}^1)$ stands as the iterated dominant-strategy equilibrium.

9.4   Games in Extensive Form

A critical limitation of the normal form description is that it gives few details about the way that the game is played. The order of the moves making up strategies, information available to the firms at different decision stages, and the evolution of the game are not apparent in this form. In contrast, the **extensive game form**, usually expressed in decision tree structure, is explicit about all these things.

Figure 9.1 illustrates a game in extensive form for duopolists j and k. Firm j has a single move (action) in play against both nature and firm k. Firm j's move is indicated by the node (vertex) of the tree labeled j. When it is j's turn to make a decision as the game unfolds, it may choose an action represented by any of the lines (branches) emanating from that node. For example, if j chooses the line leading to node N, it will then be nature's turn. Nature is a "chance" player who, in its turn, takes certain actions with specified probabilities. In the case illustrated in figure 9.1, nature has two "choices": it ends the game with probability $\frac{1}{4}$ by moving along the line from N labeled in that way; alternatively, with probability $\frac{3}{4}$ it will move to node kC, where firm k will then have the opportunity to move. Notice that the game tree specifies not only the actions available to each firm, but also the order of play.

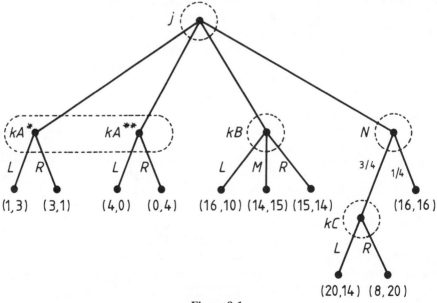

Figure 9.1
Game in extensive form

If node kC occurs, firm k would surely choose action R leading to the terminal node at which the profit outcome is $(8, 20)$, that is, where firm j receives a payoff of 8 and firm k receives a payoff of 20. This is preferred to the move L at node kC, where firm k only receives 14. As we assume that the firms act noncooperatively, the fact that firm j receives profits of 8 with k's play of R, where it would receive 20 otherwise, is of no concern to firm k. If, alternatively, firm j chooses the line leading to kB at the onset, then firm k's choices of profits for itself would be 10, 15, and 14. In this case, k would choose move M, which maximizes its profits at 15 and leaves firm j with profits of 14.

More generally, a game tree has the following component parts.

1 **Nodes:** each node is a point in the game where some player makes a move. Nodes are distinguished as follows: a *successor* to some node A is a node occurring after A in the game (in figure 9.1 kC is a successor to N, but it is not a successor to kB); a *predecessor* to some node A is a node that occurs before A; the *beginning* of the game is defined as the node which has no predecessors; the *ending* node (or nodes) of a game is that (are those) with no successors.

2 **Branches:** each branch (or line) emanating from a node indicates a specific action by some player.

3 **Payoffs:** payoff for each player is associated with each ending node.

4 **Game path:** each sequence of moves (collection of branches) leading from the beginning node to an ending node is termed a game path.

9.4.1 Information Structure

In figure 9.1 firm j moves first. After observing j's decision, firm k moves. Suppose now that firm k's observation of j's move is imperfect: while it knows exactly if j moves along the branches to nodes N or kB, it cannot differentiate between j's moves to either kA^* or kA^{**}. In this case we say that nodes kA^* and kA^{**} comprise a single information set, labeled kA and indicated by the dotted line enclosing them. More exactly, an **information set** for any firm k is a collection of nodes belonging to k along different game paths in a game tree that might be k's actual node at some moment, but among which it cannot then distinguish. In the present case this delineation, or restriction, informs us that firm k does not know if it is at kA^* or kA^{**}, and so it will not have perfect information concerning the profit that will result from its choices at the moment. The uncertainty obviously complicates firm k's decision. If it is at kA^*, then move L is preferred and leads to profits of 3. Alternatively, if it is at kA^{**}, R is preferred with profits of 4. Firm k would clearly be better off if it had perfect information and knew whether firm j adopted either move kA^* or move kA^{**} (exclusively). Finally, when some information set contains only a single node, it is said to be a **singleton**. For example, k's information set at kB is a singleton.

Consider for the moment the "restricted" game in which firm j can only choose either kA^* or kA^{**}. The situation arising with this game has two interpretations. First, and as the figure seems to suggest, the game can be played with firm j moving ahead in time of firm k and concealed so that j's move is not observable by k. Alternatively, the game can be interpreted as if both firms choose *simultaneously* so that k cannot know j's move. Whichever interpretation is used, the normal form "restricted" game of table 9.4 applies. Note that a Nash equilibrium does not obtain for this portion of the game.

Table 9.4 "Restricted" game Payoffs

	L	R
kA^*	(1, 3)	(3, 1)
kA^{**}	(4, 0)	(0, 4)

The critical role of information is further stressed by the two games set out in figure 9.2, where the strategies available to firm j are L and R, and firm k has L, M, and R available. In figure 9.2(a) the two possible decision nodes for firm k constitute a single information set, which means that k does not know j's action. This may reflect either the situation where both firms act simultaneously (without observing the other) or a two-stage decision sequence where j acts earlier and is perfectly secretive about its move. Figure 9.2(b) displays a "similar" game. Although it differs only in information structure from that in figure 9.2(a), that difference is critical to the solution. Observe that each node of firm k in this new game constitutes a separate information set, which we take here to mean that firm j moves first and k exactly observes j's action before its own move.

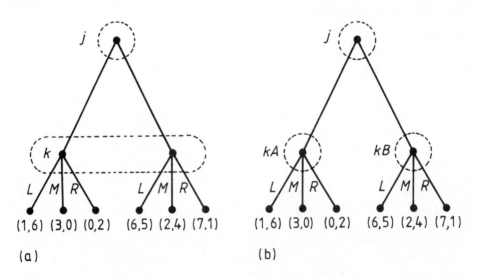

Figure 9.2
Two games differing only in information structure

Pure Strategies and Information Structure. For the moment, assume that each firm forms a plan of action prior to the start of the game and then follows that plan throughout the play. The plan, called a **pure strategy**, is a mapping from each firm's information sets to its strategies such that each information set is assigned to a particular one of these strategies. For example, in the game in figure 9.2(a), firm k has one information set with three moves or 3^1 pure strategies. In the game in figure 9.2(b) firm k has two information sets and three moves in each for a total of $3^2 = 9$ pure strategies.

Rules of the Game. It should now be clear that the conditions under which the game is played are critical to the equilibrium reached. Because of this, it is helpful to clearly set out what are called the **rules of the game:**

1 a set of J firms (players);
2 a finite game tree, like that in figure 9.1, whose nodes represent action opportunities and whose emanating lines indicate the alternative actions available (there is also a distinguished node indicating a first move);
3 a partitioning of nodes into a set of chance nodes and a set of nodes for each firm indicating its moves;
4 a probability distribution on the lines leaving each chance node;
5 a partition of each firm's set of nodes into subsets of moves, called information sets, within which the nodes cannot be distinguished from one another because of imperfect information;
6 an identification of corresponding lines for all moves in each information set;
7 a J-vector of profit payoffs at each terminal node of the tree.

It is also usual to assume that all rules of the games are **common knowledge:** not only does each firm know the rules of the game, but he also knows that all others know the rules and that all others know that he knows the rules, etc.

9.4.2 Cournot and Stackelberg Games

Recall the detailed description of the Cournot and Stackelberg oligopolies in chapter 3. Both games employ the Nash solution concept and both use output as the strategy variable. The essential, and critical, distinguishing feature of these games lies in their information structure. Figure 9.3 illustrates the extensive game form and the information structure differences for the duopoly case.

In figure 9.3(a) the rules of play for the Cournot duopolists can be envisaged as having one of two forms: (a) the firms choose outputs simultaneously, or (b) firm 2 moves after 1, but without knowledge of 1's output decision.[9] These possibilites are indicated by the fact that 2's decision nodes are fully enclosed in a single information set. The Stackelberg game of figure 9.3(b) is similar to the Cournot game, except that firm 2 now moves after firm 1 and, moreover, knows firm 1's earlier output decision exactly. In the Stackelberg case all information sets are singletons. The usually significant differences in equilibria which arise with this change in information structure were noted in chapter 3, section 3.3. Here, it is emphasized that in these games the solution concept is Nash; only the information structures differ.

---

[9] The figure illustrates the decisions of the firms using the decision z_1 or z_2 along one branch, and a second branch which represents all other possible decisions at the node.

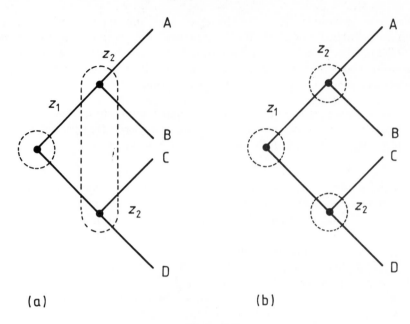

Figure 9.3
(a) Cournot and (b) Stackelberg duopoly

9.4.3 Equilibria in Pure Strategies

A game is said to have **perfect information** if each information set contains exactly one node; otherwise the game is one of **imperfect information**. For example, the game in figure 9.2(b) has perfect information, whereas those in figures 9.1 and 9.2(a) do not. Cournot and Bertrand oligopolies are games of imperfect information; the Stackelberg oligopoly game has perfect information. In games with perfect information there can be no simultaneous moves and all players must observe nature's moves exactly, so that each player knows precisely his node in the game tree at each moment.

An important aspect of games with perfect information is that they have at least one equilibrium point in pure strategies. This property is easily shown by backward induction using the principle of optimality in the fashion of dynamic programming.[10] Consider a variant of the game given in figure 9.1 wherein nodes kA^* and kA^{**} are separate information sets (so that the game becomes one of perfect information). We begin with node kA^*, which can be replaced by the terminal payoff vector $(1, 3)$ since that would be firm k's choice at that node. Similarly, kA^{**} can be replaced by $(0, 4)$, kB by $(14, 15)$, and kC by

---

[10] The classic proofs of the theorem have been given by Zermelo (1912) and, more rigorously, by Kuhn (1953). The solution principle here is straightforward: in a multistage system it is unnecessary to consider, at any point, solutions which are nonoptimal. Stated conversely, this is Bellman's (1957) "principle of optimality": "An optimal policy has the property that whatever the initial (wealth) state and (consumption and investment) decisions are, the remaining decisions must constitute an optimal policy with regard to the state resulting from the first decision." Proof of the principle is by contradiction. Simply, if the remaining decisions are not optimal then the entire policy could not be optimal.

(8, 20). Nature's chance play at node N can in turn be replaced by the expected value $\frac{1}{4}(16, 16) + \frac{3}{4}(8, 20) = (10, 19)$.[11] With these values, firm j's decision involves a choice of $(1, 3)$, $(0, 4)$, $(14, 15)$, and $(10, 19)$, which are now associated with the tree branches going to kA^*, kA^{**}, kB, and N respectively. Thus, node j can be labeled with $(14, 15)$, reflecting the fact that firm j's optimal strategy is to select the action leading to node kB. Firm k's choice is stated contingently: choose L if at kA^*, R if at kA^{**}, M if at kB, and R again if at kC. It is easily shown that the above pair of pure strategies, which we label $\{kB, (L, R, M, R)\}$, is a Nash equilibrium for the game since each strategy is optimal given the other.

9.4.4 Equilibria in Mixed Strategies

While it may seem nonsensical at first glance, there are circumstances in which it is optimal for firms to select their course of play at random from among the available strategies. Recall, for example, the bimatrix game from E9.1, shown in table 9.2(b). Again, since s_j^1, k's best response is s_k^2; given s_k^2, j's best response is s_j^2; in turn, given s_j^2, k's best response is s_k^1; coming full circle, given s_k^1, j's best response is s_j^1 none of the four pure strategy pairs is a Nash equilibrium for the game. As an alternative method of play suppose that firm j randomly chooses a strategy where the randomization leaves the firm indifferent in value to the two alternatives. Straightforward calculations show that this randomization yields an expected profit of $\frac{1}{2}$ to j, regardless of firm k's action.

The above example suggests that in some circumstances it might pay to choose a strategy using a randomization which leaves the player indifferent (in value) to the pure strategies. This is the essential logic leading to the concept of a mixed strategy. When a firm has only a finite number N of pure strategies, a **mixed strategy** for firm j is an N-vector of probabilities $h_j = (h_j^1, h_j^2, \ldots, h_j^N)$,[12] where each pure strategy n is to be chosen with probability h_j^n. That is, we think of the firm as choosing only the probabilities by which it will play from the list of pure strategies. A game played with mixed strategies is referred to as the **mixed extension** of the pure strategy game.[13]

Entry and Natural Monopoly

Consider two firms contemplating entry to a new market. Each has strictly decreasing unit cost, the usual condition leading to a natural monopoly.[14] The

---

[11] Again, firms are assumed to be risk neutral and therefore maximizers of expected profits.

[12] These probabilities satisfy the usual conditions $h_j^n \geq 0$ and $\Sigma_h^N h_j^n = 1$.

[13] For the new game to make sense, each firm must act to maximize expected profits in situations with uncertainty. This has a basis in unanimous shareholder support for firm decisions, where individual shareholders satisfy conditions sufficient for expected utility maximization and there is aggregation of preferences (see Krouse, 1986, ch. 8).

[14] For alternative and detailed descriptions of the conditions giving rise to natural monopoly, recall chapter 8, SE8.1 and SE8.2.

strategy choices of the firms are *enter* (s^1) and *not enter* (s^2), and these result in the (present value) payoffs shown in table 9.5. If neither firm enters, the game has a value of unity to both firms as the consumers will substitute the goods currently being produced by the firms. If both firms enter the new market, output is shared at a competitive price and both firms lose -2. If only one firm enters while the other does not, then the entrant captures monopoly rents of 4 while the firm remaining outside obtains nothing.

Table 9.5 Firm Payoffs

	$s_k{}^1$	$s_k{}^2$
$s_j{}^1$	$(-2, -2)$	$(4, 0)$
$s_j{}^2$	$(0, 4)$	$(1, 1)$

Pure Strategy Equilibria. The entry game has two Nash equilibria in pure strategies: $(s_j{}^1, s_k{}^2)$ and $(s_j{}^2, s_k{}^1)$ – one firm enters while the other does not. The difficulty with these solutions is that they are asymmetric: identical firms will deal with the situation in radically different ways depending on which equilibrium is chosen. The mixed extension of the game provides a more "satisfying" symmetry to the equilibrium and so we consider that.

Mixed Strategy Equilibrium. Because of the symmetry of the payoffs, it is only necessary to calculate the mixing probabilities of one firm, knowing that they will be the same for its rival. At a mixed strategy equilibrium firm j must be indifferent to entering or not entering. Then the indifference requires

$$E\pi_j(s_j{}^1) = h(-2) + (1 - h)4 \tag{9.3}$$
$$= h(0) + (1 - h)1 = E\pi_j(s_j{}^2)$$

where h indicates the probability that k chooses entry. The indifference requires $h = 0.6$. That is, the symmetric mixed strategy equilibrium has the firms choose to enter with probability 0.6 and not enter with probability 0.4. If these strategies are played there is a 0.36 chance of both entering, a 0.16 chance that neither will enter, and a 0.24 chance that only one will enter. Some simple calculations give the equilibrium expected payoff: $E\pi_j = E\pi_k = 0.4$. A repeated version of this game is developed in chapter 10, SE10.5.

It is often thought that mixed strategies are counter-intuitive, since "real" firms do not undertake decisions at random. That is not generally true either explicitly or implicitly. As we saw in chapter 7, for example, firms may price discriminate by posting prices randomly, knowing that individuals with low search costs will seek out low prices and individuals with high search costs will not. On the implicit level, it should be noted that all that we generally ask of our models is that they describe firm behavior, and the strategies that are adopted may be *as if* they are chosen randomly even when the competing firms are always certain about their decisions. (E9.7 and SE9.4 below provide examples of this *as if* choice.) In any case, the reader should reserve judgment about the practicality of mixed strategies until their applications are further developed.

Analytically, the importance of games in mixed extension is due to the fact that every finite game, with or without perfect information, has a Nash equilibrium in mixed strategies. Nash's original existence proof of this theorem follows the sketch given in section 9.3.3, with the role of the mixed strategy being to (*ex ante*) "convexify" the strategy sets and in turn assure that the firm profits functions are continuous in the strategies.[15]

9.5 Dynamic Games

Look back now at the game illustrated in figure 9.1 (section 9.4.2). Using the principle of optimality, we derived the *single* strategy pair $\{kB, (L, R, M, R)\}$ as the equilibrium solution for the perfect information variant of that game. On reflection, it becomes apparent that all strategy pairs of the form $\{kB, (\cdot, \cdot, M, R)\}$ are also Nash equilibria of the game.[16] This is one instance of the more general fact that games in extensive form may have equilibria not found by recursion using the principle of optimality.

9.5.1 Perfect Equilibria and Credible Threats

To understand why the principle of optimality does not necessarily generate all Nash equilibria, consider some singleton node X in an extensive game tree and delete from the tree all nodes and lines except X, its successor nodes, and the paths joining X and these successors. The graph produced in this way is called a **subtree** (of the original tree). Let Γ indicate the overall (original) game and Γ_x this specific subtree. When every information set of Γ is either completely contained in Γ_x or is disjoint from that subtree, then the subtree Γ_x constitutes a game in itself. In this case Γ_x, the subtree with X as the "beginning" move, is called a **subgame**. When we use backward recursion, and the principle of optimality in particular, a Nash equilibrium is produced for the subgame with this X origin and (more generally) for *every* subgame of the original game. In this way, the recursion procedure only yields solutions which are in equilibrium for the game as a whole *as well as for every subgame*.

For example, in the perfect information variant on the game in figure 9.1, the recursion procedure does not produce the strategy $\{kB, (L, R, M, R)\}$. While this is a Nash equilibrium for the game as a whole, the recursion procedure

---

[15] It is well known, for example, that the Bertrand model does not have an equilibrium in pure strategies when the firms' marginal costs are everywhere increasing. Allen and Hellwig (1986) derive a mixed strategy solution for this case, showing that (independent of the number of firms) there is always a positive probability that some firms will adopt a price close to the monopoly level. See also SE9.1.

[16] For firm j, kB is the best response to firm k when it uses any strategy of the form $(\cdot, \cdot, M, R)$, and conversely.

using the principle of optimality does not identify it as a Nash equilibrium because that strategy is *not* optimal for the subgame originating at node kA^{**}. To distinguish these solution concepts, a set of strategies for a noncooperative game is said to be (subgame) **perfect** iff the strategies yield a Nash equilibrium for every subgame of the considered game.[17] More exactly, a strategy s^0 of the game Γ is said to yield a (subgame) perfect equilibrium of Γ if, for *every* subgame Γ_x of Γ, the restriction $s_x{}^0$ of s^0 constitutes a Nash equilibrium of Γ_x. In turn, perfect strategies yield **perfect Nash equilibria**. Clearly, perfectness imposes stronger solution conditions than the unrestricted Nash equilibrium concept.[18]

Notice that all decisions in the recursion procedure employing the principle of optimality are best given the node, or state, of the game. That is, decisions are state contingent, taking the form of decision rules. It is usual to say that strategies formed in this state contingent fashion are **closed loop** as, in each case, they map the then relevant history of the game into an action. What we have shown above is that such closed-loop strategies lead to perfect equilibria. Perfectness is thus the natural result of applying the principle of optimality recursively in the solution of multistage (dynamic) games: in this way all subgames of the original game are dealt with optimally (whether along the a priori equilibrium path or not) and this assures that an equilibrium results in every subgame.

Perfect Equilibria in Research and Development Licensing

Gallini (1984), Katz and Shapiro (1985), and Kamien and Tauman (1986) have developed perfect Nash equilibria for games involving patent licensing. We consider a simple variant of their analyses in which there is a single patent-holder who charges a fixed license fee to any of the J firms in an industry who would use the patent.[19] The maximum fee that any firm would pay for a license depends on the increment in profits that can be expected from using the patent. The game interaction arises from the fact that the innovation-induced in-cremental profits of any firm are generally decreasing in the number of firms adopting the license, and the patent-holder–licensor's profits derive from the sum of license fees collected.

To keep the model as simple as possible, suppose that the $j = 1, 2, \ldots, J$ potential licensees are identical (at the onset): each produces a homogeneous product with cost cz_j, where c is a constant marginal cost and z_j is output.

---

[17] See Selten (1975), who was the originator of this "refinement" to the Nash equilibrium solution concept.

[18] While subgame perfection may appear to greatly restrict the admissible equilibria, in games of imperfect information that generally will not be the case. A subgame must have its beginning node as a singleton and never divide any information set of the original game. As a result, in games with extensive information set linkages across nodes the only subgame will often be the game as a whole.

[19] The alternative considered by Katz and Shapiro and by Kamien and Tauman is to use a combination of fixed license fee and royalty.

Denote the inverse industry demand function by $p(z)$, with z the aggregate output. Firm 0 holds the patent to an innovation which lowers the marginal cost of any user from c to $c^* < c$.

Decision Sequence. In the development of the industry, the licensor has the only move at the first stage. It chooses a fixed fee ϕ_j to charge each potential licensee j. Let $\phi = [\phi_1\phi_2 \ldots \phi_J]$ denote the fees set in this way. At the second stage the producing firms, each observing the schedule ϕ, simultaneously and independently choose whether or not to license. As a result of these decisions the J producing firms are divided into two parts: a set L who have agreed to license and a complementary set N who have chosen to produce without the license at the original higher marginal cost. Knowing L, of course, means that we also know N. Denote the specific licensing decision of firm j by $l_j(\phi)$, which takes on the value of unity when the firm agrees to license and zero when there is no agreement. At the third stage, with both ϕ and L observed by all firms, the firms simultaneously and independently choose output levels. Each firm j's output choice $z_j(\phi, L) \geq 0$ is a function of both the fee schedule ϕ and the set L of licensing firms. The game made up of these three stages is described by player strategy and payoff sets.

Strategy Sets. A strategy for the patent-holder–licensor is a fee schedule $\phi \geq 0$. A strategy for the jth potential licensee is a pair $\{l_j(\phi), z_j(\phi, L)\}$. It is of particular note that the strategies of the J firms are decision *rules* based on what is known at the appropriate decision stage. A $(J + 1)$-tuple $s = [\phi, \{l_j(\phi), z_j(\phi, L)\}]$ is a strategy combination for all firms and defines the development of the industry.

Payoff Sets. If there are no transaction costs in implementing the licenses, the profit payoff for the patent-holder is simply the sum of the fixed fees collected from those firms in the license set L:

$$\pi_0(s) = \sum_{j \in L} \phi_j$$

The profit payoff of the jth producing firm depends on the specific decisions made by it and its rivals. The licensing decision is one important part of this and separates the otherwise identical firms into two payoff groups:

$$\pi_j(s) = \{p(z) - c^*\}z_j - \phi_j \qquad \text{for } j \in L$$
$$= \{p(z) - c\}z_j \qquad \text{for } j \in N$$

Equilibrium Concept. When we restrict attention to pure strategies, a combination $s^0 = \{\phi^0, [l_j^0, z_j^0]\}$ is a (subgame) perfect Nash equilibrium of the three-stage game if the following hold:

1 ϕ^0 is the patent-holder's best response for the $\{l_j^0, z_j^0\}$ strategy choices of the J producing firms;
2 for every feasible license schedule ϕ, $l_j^0(\phi)$ is the best response of firm j given the $l_k^0(\phi)$ licensing decisions of all rivals $k \neq j$;

3 for every feasible license schedule ϕ and every feasible partitioning of firms L, $z_j{}^0(\phi, L)$ is the best response of firm j given the output decisions $z_k{}^0(\phi, L)$ of all rivals $k \neq j$.

The difference between a perfect Nash equilibrium and the (general) Nash equilibrium is evident in the above specification: in the perfect equilibrium (2) holds for every feasible ϕ, and not just ϕ^0, and (3) holds for every feasible ϕ and L, and not just ϕ^0 and L^0.

The reader is referred to Gallini (1984), Katz and Shapiro (1985), and Kamien and Tauman (1986) for solution details.

Credible Threats. As E9.5 and figure 9.1 suggest, the concept of perfectness is meant to deal with the fact that out-of-equilibrium behavior is irrational in nonperfect strategies. Selten (1975) has argued that virtually all game paths are reachable whenever an a priori equilibrium strategy is played because of the probability of a firm mistake – he called it a "tremble." Each firm should, as a result, incorporate this out-of-equilibrium possibility in its strategy choice and therefore make a rational choice at *every* information set. A subgame perfect equilibrium has this property: it is every firm's best response to follow its equilibrium strategy whatever move has *actually* been played in previous periods by other firms. This contrasts with a nonperfect equilibrium, where it is in every firm's interest to follow its equilibrium strategy provided that all other firms followed equilibrium strategies in prior play.

The requirement of perfect equilibria limits the choice of strategies by firms. For example, firms cannot then use threats to influence a rival's decision unless the threats are credible, that is, optimal for the then ensuing subgame. There is also the converse: for example, an incumbent's strategy to prey on an entrant by reducing price below average and marginal cost if entry occurs is not credible as it generally does not maximize post-entry profits. While this strategy is ruled out by the perfectness refinement, Nash equilibria without that refinement permit subgame nonoptimality and, with that, empty threats.

E9.6

Credible Threats and Market Entry

The relationship between credible threats and subgame perfect equilibria is clarified using an example suggested by Dixit (1982). Consider an entry game with a monopolist (firm m) who can charge one of two prices, say high or low, and an entrant (firm k) who can choose to enter the monopolist's market or not. Suppose that the entrant makes its choice first; the monopolist observes this and then makes its pricing choice. The extensive form of such a game is illustrated in figure 9.4.

In the figure, L and H indicate the low and high prices chosen by the monopolist. Entry (E) and no entry (NE) decisions of the entrant are also marked. The profit payoffs associated with each of the strategies are indicated at the terminal nodes with the monopoly firm m's profits listed first. Notice that the game is one of perfect information, which insures that an equilibrium obtains in pure strategies.

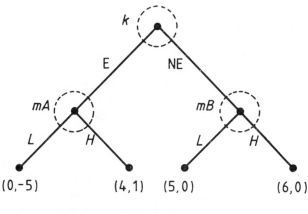

Figure 9.4
Entry game

If the would-be entrant remains out of the market, then the monopolist optimally chooses the high-price strategy and its profits are 6 (and, of course, there are no profits for the entrant). If firm k enters then the optimal choice for the monopolist is to collude with the entrant to set high prices, which gives profits $(4, 1)$, respectively. Obviously, entry with collusion $\{E, (H, H)\}$ is the equilibrium strategy produced by backward recursion. It is therefore a perfect equilibrium. Note, in contrast, that $\{NE, (L, H)\}$, where firm k does not enter and m adopts the rule imposing L if he does and H if he does not, is also a Nash equilibrium as it is a best response for each to its rival's choice. However, this second equilibrium strategy is not perfect as it calls, unreasonably, for the monopolist to price low when firm k enters. In contrast, the subgame beginning at node mB has the monopolist optimally playing the collusive high price strategy. The low price occurring in the nonperfect (full) game equilibrium would be irrationally played at mA, so that this reaction to entry must be seen as a noncredible threat.

Suppose now that, by some prior decision, the monopolist is able to make a prior binding contract (say, with a third party) which would require the forfeiture of $5 in all circumstances in which it prices H. Having made such a commitment, the monopolist will always find it optimal to price L in the event of entry (for if it priced H at mA it receives $4 - 5 = -1$, which is less than the zero for pricing L). A prospective entrant knowing of this contract will remain out of the market. In turn, the monopolist will choose L, earning a payoff of 5. In this case the binding contract commitment makes the monopolist's threat to price L on entry credible, and entry is successfully deterred. Notice finally that, since it is always optimal for the monopolist to price L, the $5 forfeiture is never made to the third party. This suggests a counter-strategy for the entrant.

He need only call this fact to the attention of the third party and, in turn, offer to pay a small sure amount in return for voiding the contract. That would again leave the monopolist without a credible threat (see Easterbrook 1981b, for a range of such counter-strategies).

9.5.2   The Chain Store Paradox

Suppose that the entry game of E9.6 is repeated in a sequence of markets. At each repetition the moves available to the firms remain the same as in the underlying *one-time*, or *one-shot*, game. Despite this, each firm's choice of an optimal strategy is now potentially different as it may now condition its move at any repetition on the prior history of moves. Does history matter in a way that the repeated game solution differs from its one-shot counterpart?

We know that perfect equilibrium strategies can be produced in dynamic games by backward recursion using the principle of optimality, and that is the basis of Selten's (1978) analysis of repeated market (multimarket) play. He specifically considers a "chain store" variant of the model in E9.6. At each stage $k = 1, 2, \ldots, \kappa$ in his analysis, a new firm considers entry into the kth market of the chain store monopolist. If some firm chooses to enter then the incumbent monopolist i must decide whether to price low (predatory, ϕ) or high (accommodating, a). When a low price is used by the incumbent against some entrant e, entry is unprofitable ($\pi_e{}^\phi < 0$) and e exits after one period. When a high price is used the monopolist shares the market with the entrant, both are profitable ($\pi_i{}^a = \pi_e{}^a > 0$), and the duopoly continues forever. While on a *one-market* basis the incumbent prefers the high, accommodating, price in response to entry, the best of all cases is the monopoly profit with no entry at all: $\pi_i{}^m > \pi_i{}^a > \pi_i{}^\phi$. These profit–payoff relationships are as in the one-period model except that now the profits of the incumbent are the sum of those earned in the κ separate markets.

Chain Store Paradox. History would seem to be important in determining the multimarket repeated play. Our expectation, more specifically, is that the established monopolist will set low prices in response to early-on entry in an effort to build a reputation for toughness, which then deters entry in all subsequent markets. Notwithstanding this intuition, Selten shows that with entry the monopolist always prices high: the perfect equilibrium of the repeated game has every market shared.

Selten proceeds by backward recursion using the principle of optimality to this "unraveling" result. Should entry occur in the last-stage market, he reasons, the monopolist's best response is to accommodate and price high. Thus, there is no credible threat and entry occurs. Since the entry in this final market is completely determined and all firms have this as common knowledge, there is then no possibility of influencing the entry decision (in this last market) by threats or actions in the next-to-last market. Thus entry in the next-to-last market can be expected to lead to the same accommodating response by the incumbent, and all firms know this also. Proceeding by induction the result follows. Every move, at each stage, is made just as in the one-shot game.

Despite the fact that players can condition their behavior at any stage on the observed prior behavior of rival players, equilibria which are more profitable for all players than any of the one-shot games do not emerge. This provides what Selten has called the **chain store paradox:** the behavior which is intuitively expected of repeated games is in fact contrary to perfect equilibrium behavior. [20]

Kreps and Wilson (1982a, b), Milgrom and Roberts (1982a, b), and others have subsequently observed that Selten's recursion argument is undermined, and an entry deterrence equilibrium obtains in the repeated game when either of the following two conditions obtain: (a) there is an infinite (or indefinite) repetition of the entry game (and future payoffs are not discounted too highly) and/or (b) there is lack of common knowledge. The first of these conditions in what is generally termed a **reputations** model is considered in section 9.6; a class of **signaling** models based on an entry game in which entrants have "incomplete" information is then considered in section 9.7.

9.6 Repeated Games: The Reputations Model

Consider an oligopoly game $N(J, S, \pi)$ with J firms, finite strategy set S, and payoffs $\pi = [\pi_1, \pi_2, \ldots, \pi_J]$. The rules of this game call for one repetition of play, and so we refer to it as the *one-shot*, or *constituent*, game. Now, suppose that some superset of rules calls for the repetition of N at each of the dates $t = 1, 2, \ldots, T$, where the terminal date T may be finite or infinite. Further, suppose that in the repeated game the firms' concern is with the present value of profits:

$$v_j = \sum_t \rho_{jt} \pi_{jt}(s_t) \tag{9.4}$$

where $0 \leq \rho_{jt} \leq 1$ are discount factors, $s_t = [s_{1t} s_{2t} \ldots s_{Jt}]$ is the strategy combination of the J firms at repetition t, and the π_{jt} are the associated profits of firm j at t. We indicate a **repeated game** built up in this way from an underlying one-shot game by the notation $\Gamma\{N(J, S, \pi), \rho, T\}$.

Let s^0 be an equilibrium strategy combination for the one-shot game $N(\cdot)$. When the firms accumulate no information in the repeated play of the one-shot game, playing s^0 at each date of the repeated games is also an equilibrium strategy of $\Gamma(N, \rho, T)$. That is, for a repeated game made up of independent plays of a one-shot game in which firms do not have any recall of their prior moves, the sequence of play is no different from a sequence of play of the isolated one-shot games. This leads us to consider the more interesting case in which firms have memories and accumulate information about prior play.

Perfect Recall. Except where noted explicitly, we restrict attention to games with **perfect recall:** at every point where a firm has a decision to make, it is assumed that it knows what it has previously known and what decisions it has previously made. [21] That is, each firm knows which information sets were

---

[20] Luce and Raiffa (1966) had previously described similar results for repeated prisoners' dilemma games, and Radner (1985) later reached exactly the same result in a constant-cost Cournot oligopoly with linear demand.

[21] E9.8 provides an example where the firms have limited recall and employ "Markov strategies."

previously reached and what decisions it made at each. The importance of such perfect recall in dynamic games is that it enables attention to be focused on so-called **behavioral** strategies – those in which the move at every date depends on the then current information.

Open- and Closed-Loop Strategies. With perfect recall any player can adopt a strategy in the date t subgame as a function of the state of the system (history, accumulated information) of the game up to that date. If Ω_t indicates this state at date t, then the function $s_{jt}(\Omega_t)$ is a decision function which specifies firm j's strategy choice at t (provided that it is admissible in the one-shot game) and $s_j = [s_{j1}(\Omega_1)s_{j2}(\Omega_2) \ldots s_{jT}(\Omega_T)]$ is a **closed-loop** strategy for the repeated game.[22]

Closed-loop strategies in general depend on information which becomes available after the beginning of the game, as the game evolves. In contrast, there are **open-loop**, or **pre-commitment**, strategies under which the decision by a firm at each t does not depend on any information that becomes available with the play of the game. As we will later stress, when there is no randomness in the game, the players are rational, predictable, and mistake free, and firms have unlimited powers of calculation, then open- and closed-loop equilibrium strategies will be identical. When these conditions do not obtain, then with recall the closed-loop strategy seems a more reasonable assumption about firm strategy selection.

9.6.1 Reputation and Entry Deterrence

The paradox in the chain store game arises essentially from the unraveling that occurs with the backward solution logic. Milgrom and Roberts (1982a) break this unraveling process by having no last stage at which entry is always optimal; that is, they use an infinite (or indefinite) repetition of the game. In this case entry-deterring equilibrium strategies for incumbent and entrant arise based on a reputation that the incumbent maintains for preying on entrants.

Reputation Strategies. Suppose that there is an infinite horizon. Again, the incumbent may price low (prey) or price high (accommodate) in response to entry. When predation is chosen the entrant is unprofitable and exits at the end of the period. The high, or accommodating, price results in a shared market with positive profits for both firms. With this short background, consider the following entry-deterring strategies.

> *Incumbent:* (a) price low if entry occurs and an accommodating response has not previously been used; (b) price high if entry occurs and an accommodating response has ever been adopted in prior play; (c) use the monopoly price if entry is not attempted.

---

[22] There is some possibility for confusion here. An *action* is a decision by a firm at some node of an extensive game. A collection of such actions, one for each node, which extends over the entire play of the game is a *strategy*. In a repeated game, strategies in the one-shot (sub)game are actions in the repeated game.

Entrant: if any prior entry has been accommodated, then enter; otherwise, do not enter.

Under rather general conditions, noted below, these strategies lead to an entry deterrence equilibrium. Roughly, the potential entrant for the first market anticipates that it will be preyed upon and therefore does not enter, and that same logic applies to potential entrants in all following markets.

Rationality of the Equilibrium Strategies. Again, let π_i^ϕ and π_i^α respectively be the incumbent's per period profits in any market in which it preys on (ϕ) or accommodates (α) entry. When, alternatively, entry is not attempted, the incumbent remains a monopoly and earns π_i^m per period. We assume, quite naturally, that $\pi_i^m > \pi_i^\alpha > \pi_i^\phi$. Suppose now that entry occurs in some market and, using the above strategies, the incumbent preys, so that the entrant exits after one period. The incumbent's present value of this course of events is $\pi_i^\phi + \rho\pi_i^m/(1 - \rho)$, assuming that cash flows occur at the beginning of each period. If, alternatively, the incumbent meets some entrant with accommodation, and therefore shares that market forever, it has present value $\pi_i^\alpha/(1 - \rho)$. The predatory response is optimal when it yields a greater present value, or when

$$\pi_i^\phi + \frac{\rho\pi_i^m}{1 - \rho} > \frac{\pi_i^\alpha}{1 - \rho}$$

which rearranges to

$$\rho > \frac{\pi_i^\alpha - \pi_i^\phi}{\pi_i^m - \pi_i^\phi} \tag{9.5}$$

The one-shot cost of predatory pricing must be less than the present value of the gains to monopoly compared with market sharing. Since $\pi_i^m > \pi_i^\alpha > \pi_i^\phi$, the inequality will hold for ρ sufficiently close to unity (discount *rate* close to zero). In this case, a reputation equilibrium is established in which the incumbent, regardless of its single-market best response, preys on entrants to develop and sustain a reputation for being a predator.

Reputation as a Self-fulfilling Expectation. The rationality of the entry deterrence equilibrium is based on a somewhat circular argument. The reputation for preying on entrants deters entry only because potential entrants believe it will. If they did not have this belief, but instead believed that regardless of the incumbent's prior actions it would accommodate entry, then the incumbent would have no incentive to create or sustain a reputation, and again the entrants' expectations would be fulfilled. Notice the circularity in these cases: it is optimal for the incumbent to act in the way in which entrants expect it to act, and each entrant's expectations are rational because the incumbent acts in that way. That is, the incumbent's reputation for preying on entrants (or not) is built on a **self-fulfilling expectation**.

Multiplicity of Equilibria. While it has some intuitive appeal, the deterrence equilibrium of the repeated entry game is only one of many possible equilibria.

As we noted above, the "opposite strategy" with accommodation and entry at every stage is also a (self-fulfilling) reputations equilibrium, as is the equal-sharing strategy where the incumbent alternates with accommodation and predation while the potential entrants correspondingly choose to enter or remain outside. The entry deterrence equilibrium does, however, provide the greatest present value for the incumbent and this may be appropriate when it is the first mover.

Discounting. The *rate* at which any firm discounts its future profits in a multiperiod game generally depends on three things: the period length, time preferences, and the probability that the game might end at any date. Given the latter two things, the discount rate is decreasing with a shorter period length. In the discrete time models we generally deal with, there are no moves within periods and, *ceteris paribus*, the discount rate then measures the length of this inactive time.

If it is assumed that the period length is fixed, the role of time preferences is usual but the role of the probability that the game ends, that is there is **indefinite repetition**, is not. While the *expected* length of the market game is finite with indefinite repetition, it is still proper to model it as one of infinite duration whenever there is *some* chance of it continuing forever. Suppose, for example, that the probability of the game ending in any period is given by a geometric distribution. Because of this there is a constant probability h that the game will end in any period, given that it has lasted that long. If r is the constant rate of time preferences, then in this case the firm will have a discount factor of $\rho = (1 - h)/(1 + r)$, $0 \leqslant \rho \leqslant 1$, between any two periods in an infinite horizon model. There is indifference between \$1 now and \$$1/(1 + r)$ at the next date if the sum is paid for sure, and, with a probability of $1 - h$ that the game continues and the payment is made, there is then indifference between \$1 now and \$$\rho$ dollars then when the firm is risk neutral. For a small ρ all that is necessary is that the *product* of $1 - h$ and $1/(1 + r)$ be small, which may come from large h, large r, or both.

9.7   Incomplete Information: The Signaling Model

As we noted earlier, there are two alternatives for incorporating history into extensive games and thereby disrupting the recursion which eliminates dynamic coordination and produces the chain store paradox. In addition to infinite (or indefinite) repetition of the underlying one-shot game, incomplete information can also disrupt the backward recursion scheme. What specifically is meant by incomplete information?

9.7.1   Player Types

In the analysis of noncooperative games it is frequently assumed, as we have to this point, that all "rules" of the game are common knowledge. In contrast, there are games of **incomplete information** where the firms are uncertain about some key aspect of the game situation, including payoff functions, the strategies available to specific firms, and/or the information other firms have about the game. The analytical difficulty that arises with such incomplete information is one of infinite regress. Consider, for example, a simple duopoly game in which neither player knows the profit–payoff of the other (but each knows its own). In this case, firm j's strategy choice depends in part on what strategy it expects firm k to pursue, which depends of course on the payoffs that firm k can obtain from various choices. This expectation by j about k can be thought of as a first-order expectation. Firm j's choice of strategy will also depend on what it thinks that firm k's first-order expectation about his own payoffs will be, which we can think of as a second-order expectation. In turn, there is the question about what j thinks that k thinks that j thinks about k's profit–payoffs – a third-order expectation. These thoughts about thoughts about thoughts of course go on without end, and they similarly obtain for firm k.

Harsanyi (1967, 1968a, 1968b) has developed an approach to this problem which simply constructs a more usual and tractable game of imperfect information *equivalent* to the one with incomplete information. Before describing his approach it is important to distinguish between **incomplete** and **imperfect** information. Recall that in a game of **imperfect** information some (or many) player(s) at some stage of the game has (have) an information set comprising more than one node. While every player knows the extensive game form – the rules of the game are common knowledge – not all players always know where they are in the game tree. In contrast, a game of **incomplete** information occurs when strategy and/or payoff sets are not common knowledge but only known probabilistically. That is, with incomplete information not all players know exactly which of many games they are in fact playing.[23]

With this as background, we think again of a duopoly where the firms can be of different **types**. The type of any given firm is determined by a (possibly) large number of attributes: its costs, demand conditions, financial characteristics, product features, managerial psychology, etc. The type description includes everything that is significant in determining the strategy selection behavior of the firm. One often-used form of incomplete information can be reflected by the fact that firm j knows it own type t_j exactly, but knows the type t_k of its rival only probabilistically.

Following Harsanyi, suppose that each t_j is drawn from a **type population** T_j with the joint distribution $R(t_j, t_k)$ governing the selection of types. Next, consider a normal form game augmented such that, at the onset of play, there is a chance move in which types t_j and t_k are determined by a draw from R. At this juncture, firm j discovers its own type with certainty, and similarly for firm k. Given this revelation and the distribution R, firm j also forms a conditional probability distribution $R_j(t_k|t_j)$ governing the likelihood that firm k is of any type and that k similarly forms a conditional distribution $R_k(t_j|t_k)$. By this procedure the game with incomplete information becomes a game of complete, but imperfect information. The latter game is amenable to our usual solution concepts, where the expected profit–payoffs of the firms which are the relevant

---

[23] In addition to information completeness and perfection categories, games are sometimes categorized by their certainty. A game is said to be **certain** if after the first player moves there are no chance moves by nature. Games which do not have this property are conversely said to be **uncertain**.

basis for strategy choices (at each date) are those based on the (updated) conditional probabilities then obtaining.

Formally, the reconstruction of the game with **incomplete information** consists of the following five elements:

1 a set of $j = 1, 2, \ldots, J$ players;
2 sets of actions Ω_j available to players;
3 sets T_j of player "types";
4 a joint probability distribution $R(t_1, t_2, \ldots, t_J)$ on types;
5 payoffs $\pi_j(s, t)$ associated with each choice of strategies $s = (s_1, s_2, \ldots, s_J)$ and types $t = (t_1, t_2, \ldots, t_J)$.

Briefly, the play of the (one-shot) game goes as follows: chance chooses t from the set $T_1 \times T_2 \times \ldots \times T_J$ according to the probabilities given by R; in turn each player is informed of his own type (but not necessarily that of others) and selects strategy s_j. The payoff is $\pi_j(s; t)$.

E9.7

Bayesian Equilibrium in Cournot Duopoly

Suppose that there are two rivals j and k playing quantity strategies with continuous payoff functions[24]

$$\pi_j = (a_j - b_j z_k - z_j)z_j \tag{9.6a}$$

$$\pi_k = (a_k - b_k z_j - z_k)z_k \tag{9.6b}$$

The positive parameters a_j, b_j, and b_k are common knowledge. The parameter $a_k > 0$ is known by firm k (it knows its own profit type), but the game is of incomplete information in that firm j only knows a_k probabilistically. Suppose further that k can be one of two types and that is known by firm j. With prior probability h firm j believes that k is of type a_{k_1} and with probability $1 - h$ it believes that it is of type a_{k_2}. Let $a_{k_1} > a_{k_2} > 0$.

A **Bayesian equilibrium** for this (static) game is a set of best response quantity strategies for the duopolists which are conditional on the player types. The strategies are best response in the sense that each firm maximizes its expected profits knowing its own type and taking the type-conditional strategies of its rival as given. In short, the Bayesian equilibrium is a Nash equilibrium for the game where firms maximize expected profits and strategies are chosen from larger type-conditional sets.

As firm k has complete information as it is easiest to deal with its problem first. Taking z_j as given, firm k solves the problem

$$\pi_k^*(z_1) = \max_{z_k} \left(a_k z_k - b_k z_j z_k - z_k^2 \right) \tag{9.7}$$

---

[24] This example is adapted from game theory class notes by J. Cave and S. Salant, University of California, Santa Barbara, 1984.

which yields the reaction function

$$z_k^* = \frac{a_k - b_k z_j}{2} \tag{9.8}$$

In a game of complete information each player deals exactly with the known reaction function of its rival. Here, however, firm j only knows k's a type probabilistically and therefore is uncertain whether to use $z_k^{*1} = (a_{k_1} - b_k z_j)/2$ or $z_k^{*2} = (a_{k_2} - b_k z_j)/2$. For a Bayesian equilibrium, j treats these alternatives using its (prior) probabilities to maximize expected profits:

$$E\pi_j^* = \max_{z_j}\left[h\left\{a_j z_j - \frac{b_j z_j(a_{k_1} - b_k z_j)}{2} - z_j^2\right\}\right. \tag{9.9}$$
$$\left. + (1 - h)\left\{a_j z_j - \frac{b_j z_j(a_{k_2} - b_k z_j)}{2} - z_j^2\right\}\right]$$

which solves for

$$z_j^* = \frac{b_j \bar{a}_k - 2a_j}{2(b_j b_k - 2)} \tag{9.10}$$

with $\bar{a}_k = ha_{k_1} + (1 - h)a_{k_2}$. Notice that the greater is the expected a_k the greater is firm j's output. Thus, among other things, the equilibrium depends on j's beliefs.

Figure 9.5(a) illustrates these results. Because firm k has full knowledge, it has the single reaction function r_k^c shown in the figure. In contrast, firm j's incomplete information leaves it with two reaction functions to consider. With complete information the equilibrium would be either at point C_1 or point C_2 depending on whether a_{k_1} or a_{k_2} and, in turn, $r_k^c(z_k; a_{k_1})$ or $r_k^c(z_k; a_{k_2})$ obtains. With the asymmetric, incomplete information the equilbrium is at point $\bar{C}$ based on the "averaged" reaction function $r_j(z_k; \bar{a}_k)$ and $r_k(z_j)$.

Given the type probability h and the various parameters, the strategies $\{z_j^*, z_k^{*1}, z_k^{*2}\}$ constitute the Bayesian equilibrium for the static game. After firm j calculates the type-conditional strategies z_k^{*1} and z_k^{*2} it acts *as if* it were facing a rival playing a mixed strategy (with mixing probability h). Firm k, with full knowledge, simply plays $z_k^* = (a_k - b_k z_j^*)/2$.

Price Competition. The duality between Cournot and Bertrand solutions set out in chapter 3, section 3.3 (recall also SE3.5) allows us to quickly recast the above game as one in which firms compete in price. All that is necessary is to exchange prices for quantities and complements for substitutes. This leads to profit functions in prices, corresponding to (9.6a) and (9.6b), given by

$$\pi_j = (\alpha_j - \beta_j p_k - \gamma_j p_j)p_j \tag{9.6c}$$
$$\pi_k = (\alpha_k - \beta_k p_j - \gamma_k p_k)p_k \tag{9.6d}$$

where $\beta_j = 1/(b_j b_k - 1)$, $\alpha_j = (a_k b_j - a_j)\beta_j$, and $\gamma_j = b_j \beta_j$. Corresponding to (9.8) and (9.10) there are then the stationarity conditions

$$p_k^* = \frac{\alpha_k - \beta_k p_j}{2\gamma_k}\gamma_k \tag{9.8'}$$
$$p_j^* = \frac{\beta_j \alpha_k - \alpha_j}{2(\beta_j \beta_k - \gamma_j \gamma_k)} \tag{9.10'}$$

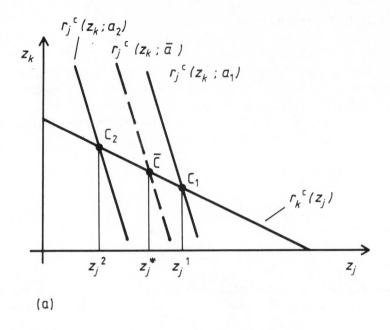

(a)

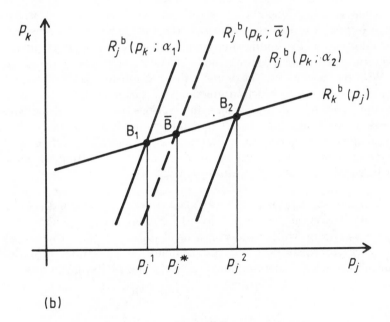

(b)

Figure 9.5
Bayesian equilibria for static games: (a) Cournot duopolists; (b) Bertrand duopolists

Two key facts about this Bertrand solution are of interest. First, for $\beta_j < 0$ the equilibrium price p_j^* is negatively related to the expected value of α_k. Second, for $\beta_k < 0$ firm k's equilibrium price moves directly with that of firm j. For example, when the probability h becomes larger, then $\bar{\alpha}_k$ also becomes larger and the prices of both firms fall. Because of this it is often said that the products of the firms are **strategic complements**. Using R_j^b and R_k^b to indicate reaction functions in price, figure 9.5(b) indicates the complete information α_{k_1} equilibrium at point B_1 and similarly for α_{k_2} and point B_2. The asymmetric incomplete information equilibrium occurs with the averaged reaction function at point $\bar{B}$.

9.7.2 Perfect Bayesian Equilibria

In contrast with the static game of E9.7, the repeated play of games with incomplete information, with a single chance draw of types at the onset, introduces several new and interesting solution aspects. These arise because players can make use of the information content in its rival's early moves to revise its probability estimate of that rival's type in all subsequent plays of the game. It is important at the outset to stress that the manner in which players update their beliefs will affect the equilibrium that occurs.

Beliefs as a State Variable. A vector of state variables which collects past information on each rival's type is central to the analysis of market games with incomplete information: as the game progresses over time, each firm j carries a state variable describing its current probability estimate of every other firm's type. The probability distribution for each k is at times called k's **reputation** (as held by j), or more usually the holder's perspective is adopted and it is called j's **belief** (about k). In the extensive incomplete information game, the beliefs correspond to the probability estimates that the players assign to the nodes in any information set. In practice, the number of state variables is kept to a minimum, and the solution procedure for such models made tractable, by assuming only a few possible types and a symmetry in beliefs among firms.

Equilibrium Concept. In a game of incomplete information each firm updates its beliefs about the type of its rivals by deduction from observed market actions. Along an equilibrium path this updating assumes that rivals are playing equilibrium strategies. The condition which is now new and important is that the strategies adopted by any firm depend on the particular beliefs it holds for rival types. As a result, an equilibrium cannot be specified in terms of strategies alone, but must also include a specification of beliefs at each date and how they evolve over time depending on the game history. More exactly, an equilibrium is specified by a strategy combination *and* a rule for updating beliefs such that the strategies are Nash best responses.

As the beliefs are probabilities, the obvious and commonly used updating method is Bayes' rule. That leads us to define a **perfect Bayesian equilibrium** for a finite J-firm game Γ with perfect recall as a strategy combination s and a system of beliefs h such that, for every node of Γ, (a) the strategies for the remaining game are optimal given the beliefs and strategies of rivals and (b) the beliefs of each firm at each information set are consistent with the history of the game in the sense that each firm's beliefs are updated by Bayes' rule provided that the equilibrium path is being followed and there is some rule for updating beliefs not inconsistent with Bayes' rule when out-of-equilibrium behavior is observed. The fact that beliefs follow Bayes' rule along the perfect Bayes equilibrium path does *not* significantly restrict the interpretation that firms will give to out-of-equilibrium occurrences. As such occurrences obtain with zero probability according to the firm's prior beliefs, there are no hard-and-fast rules about how the firm should respond. Perhaps the most straightforward and commonly used rule is the so-called *passive conjecture*, which gives such occurrences zero weight so that they bring about no change in probability beliefs.[25]

Sequential Equilibria. One especially interesting variant of the Bayesian equilibrium concept has been suggested by Kreps and Wilson (1982a). It involves not only strategies, which, given probability beliefs, have the Nash equilibrium best-response property at each decision node of the extensive game, but also a rule for firms to update their assessment of the probability associated with its rival's type at each period. The rule is consistent with Bayesian revision and, unlike the perfect Bayesian equilibrium concept, includes a particular method for probability revision when a zero-probability event is observed. More exactly, out-of-equilibrium occurrences result in probability beliefs which are updated in a way which assures "trembling hand" perfection. The reader is referred to Selten (1975), Kreps and Wilson (1982a), Van Damme (1983, chapter 6), and Grossman and Perry (1986) for specific details.

9.7.3   Signaling: Entry with Asymmetric, Incomplete Information

Think back now to the "chain store paradox" posed in Selten's repeated entry game. In addition to the earlier assumptions, suppose now that the potential entrants are uncertain of the established monopolist's profit function (type), and particularly whether the monopolist would find it profitable to use low or high prices given that entry occurs in some market. Adopting low prices has two possible effects. First, and as before, it has an effect on the monopolist's short-run profits. Second (this is new, and is due to the repeated asymmetric incomplete information game), the pricing may also revise other potential entrant's probabilities that the monopolist is of a type that prices low with entry. One, or several, episodes of low pricing with entry may give the monopolist the reputation of being of a type which, in fact, it is not.

Limit-entry Pricing. Recall Selten's chain store paradox dealing with an incumbent monopolist who sells in J different markets. To the incumbent's consternation, there are also J would-be producers, one per market, who consider entry. These entry decisions are assumed to occur in sequence, over J periods, with any jth potential entrant knowing the actions in all prior entry

---

[25] There is also the *intuitive criterion* suggested by Cho and Kreps (1987), where if some firm were of a type that could not benefit from out-of-equilibrium behavior no matter what beliefs were specified for it, then the beliefs for that firm type would be set to zero. Roughly, the criterion eliminates out-of-equilibrium strategies that are weakly dominated by any proposed equilibrium strategies. See also Banks and Sobel (1987).

subgames. If entry does occur in some market, the incumbent can use one of two strategies in response: either it can be predatory by using low prices, which results in negative profits for the entrant, or it can use high prices and accommodate the entrant, with the result that both earn positive profits.

Again, we let subscripts i and e denote the incumbent and the entrant respectively and superscripts ϕ and a denote the predatory and accommodation behavior. There are three profit pairs to be considered at each stage of the entry game: (π_i^ϕ, π_e^ϕ) and (π_i^a, π_e^a) occur with entry depending on the strategy employed by the incumbent, and if entry does not occur $\pi_e^0 = 0$ will be the entrant's alternative payoff while the incumbent earns monopoly profits $\pi_i^m > 0$.

Suppose that $\pi_i^\phi > \pi_i^a$ so that the incumbent firm perfers predation to accommodation when entry occurs. With all things common knowledge and $\pi_e^\phi < 0$, the unique perfect equilibrium is for each entrant to remain outside the market. This is quite clear. The contrasting point made by Kreps and Wilson (1982a, b) and Milgrom and Roberts (1982a, b) is that incomplete information, even based on a small amount of uncertainty, can greatly alter the economics of this situation and result in entry.

Types and Beliefs. Some additional (and usual) terminology is helpful in the analysis of the asymmetric incomplete information situation. When $\pi_i^\phi > \pi_i^a$ we will think of the incumbent as low cost, and when $\pi_i^a > \pi_i^\phi$ we will think of it as high cost. The asymmetry in information arises because the entrant does not know exactly the cost type of the incumbent, but only has an a priori probability estimate $h > 0$ that the incumbent is low cost. In contrast the incumbent knows exactly its type and that of every possible entrant. It should be emphasized that the entrants' incomplete information about the cost type of the incumbent is the only source of uncertainty in the model: all other things remain common knowledge.

Signaling. Other things being equal, the incumbent prefers to retain a monopoly in each market. It would therefore like to signal potential entrants to its markets that they will face low prices. If the signal is convincing, entry will be deterred regardless of the incumbent's costs. The problem for the incumbent is how to signal. As suggested above, using low prices in early markets may provide the incumbent with a reputation among potential entrants that it is low cost (even when it is not). When the incumbent uses low prices to build such a reputation, it attempts to balance the profits lost in early markets with the monopoly profits gained from deterring entry in later markets. This procedure becomes rather complicated at this point, for rational entrants will surely understand the incumbent's incentives to deceive them and will not necessarily use low initial prices to infer that the incumbent is low cost. Further, the incumbent will know that the potential entrants know that it will attempt to deceive them and take advantage of that, and so on. This infinite regress is resolved in the perfect Bayesian equilibrium solution.

Equilibrium Categories. There are three general kinds of equilibria for this entry game: **pooling**, in which the incumbent's first-period market price is independent of its cost level (and therefore it does not reveal its type);

separating, in which the incumbent chooses different prices depending on whether it is high or low cost (and therefore it reveals its type); **mixed** or **semi-separating**, in which the incumbent uses a mixed strategy. Here, attention is given to the mixed strategy equilibrium; the pure strategy cases are considered in chapter 10, section 10.5, and the phasing of the three equilibria over time in a T-period model are considered in chapter 14, section 14.4.

Two-Period Mixed Strategy Equilibrium. As a first step in the analysis of the chain store model, suppose that there are just two markets (potential entrants). Further, let the parameters be such that the expected profits from entry are positive: $(1 - h)\pi_e^a + h\pi_e^\phi > 0$. In this case it is clear that the entrant would enter a one-market one-period model. For the two-period case, Ordover and Saloner (1987) have developed a variant of the more general Kreps and Wilson (1982a) mixed strategy equilibrium. If some technical details are ignored, that strategy has the following parts:

1 there is entry in the first period (market);
2 (a) there is entry in the second period *if* the entry in the second market did not bring forth a predatory response or (b) the second potential entrant uses a mixed strategy in deciding to enter or not *if* the entry in the first market resulted in predation;
3 the low-cost incumbent always preys on entrants;
4 the high-cost incumbent uses a mixed strategy in the first market;
5 the high-cost incumbent always accommodates entry in the second period.

It is of particular note in this solution that a low-cost ploy is used: when it is high cost, the incumbent uses a mix of predatory and accommodation responses in an effort to lead the entrant into thinking it has low cost. This behavior is designed to signal low cost and thereby deter entry in the future market.

A perfect Bayesian equilibrium requires that these five strategy elements are optimal under conditions where they would be employed, given the rival's strategy. The low-cost incumbent, by definition, preys on each entrant, and the high-cost incumbent will always accommodate an entrant in the second (last) period. Thus elements 3 and 5 of the equilibrium strategy are optimal. Moreover, 2(a) is optimal since only the high-cost incumbent would respond with accommodation. That leaves us to consider parts 1, 2(b), and 4. As 2(b) and 4 involve mixing pure strategies, some additional notation helps in this regard. Let $\text{pr}(A|t)$ be the probability that response A is taken by the incumbent given it is of type t; for example, $\text{pr}(\phi|L)$ is the probability that the incumbent will prey on the entrant given it is low cost and similarly $\text{pr}(\alpha|H)$ is the probability that accommodation is used when high cost.

To begin, consider the optimality of part 2(b). Suppose that the second potential entrant has observed entry in the first market with a rivalrous response by the incumbent. Entrant 2 then uses Bayes rule to update its prior probability h that the incumbent is low cost:

$$\text{pr}(L|\phi) = \frac{\text{pr}(\phi|L)h}{\text{pr}(\phi|L)h + \text{pr}(\phi|H)(1 - h)}$$

Since $pr(\phi|L) = 1$, this simplifies to

$$pr(L|\phi) = \frac{h}{h + pr(\phi|H)(1 - h)} \tag{9.11}$$

For the entrant at the second period to choose a mixed strategy it must be indifferent to entering or not entering; that is, $pr(L|\phi)\pi_e^\phi + \{1 - pr(L|\phi)\}\pi_e^\alpha = 0$. This solves for $pr(L|\phi) = \pi_e^\alpha/(\pi_e^\alpha - \pi_e^\phi)$, which when substituted in (9.11) gives

$$pr(\phi|H) = - \frac{h\pi_e^\phi}{(1 - h)\pi_e^a} > 0 \tag{9.12}$$

When a high-cost incumbent meets entry with predation in the first market with this probability, the entrant in the second market will have a Bayes updated probability estimate which is just enough higher than its prior estimate to make it indifferent between entering and not entering the market. As a result it will stand ready to randomize its entry decision and part 2(b) is optimal.

We next examine the optimality of part 4: that the high-cost incumbent's choice of a mixed strategy is optimal under certain conditions. For the high-cost incumbent to be indifferent to using either a predation or an accommodation response to entry requires that $pr(entry|\phi)\pi_i^a + \{1 - pr(entry|\phi)\}\pi_i^m = \pi_i^a(1 + h)/h$, which on rearranging solves for

$$pr(entry|\phi) = 1 - \frac{(\pi_i^a - \pi_i^\phi)}{h(\pi_i^m - \pi_i^a)} \tag{9.13}$$

If entry occurs in the second market and the incumbent has preyed on the entrant in the first market, the high-cost incumbent will be indifferent between a predation and accommodation response in the second market. Thus the mixed strategy of part 4 is optimal under these conditions.

Finally, consider the optimality of part 1, that there will be entry in the first market. This is optimal when the parameters of the game are such that the entrant's expected profits (using the prior probabilities h) are positive:

$$h\pi_e^\phi + (1 - h)[pr(\phi|H)\pi_e^\phi + \{1 - pr(\phi|H)\}\pi_e^a] \geqslant 0 \tag{9.14}$$

As the incumbent randomizes its response to the entrant if it is high cost, the term in square brackets is the expected profit of the entrant given that the incumbent is high cost.

Summary: Mixed Strategy Equilibrium. If the potential entrants have the prior probability h that the incumbent is low cost, then in equilibrium entry will be dealt a predatory response in the first market with a probability greater than h. This occurs because not only does the low-cost incumbent always prey, but there is some positive probability that the high-cost incumbent will also respond in that way as part of its attempt at deception. If the high-cost incumbent fails to respond with predation in the first market, it reveals its high-cost type and there will surely be entry in the second market. By responding with predation, however, the incumbent leaves the entrant in the second period unsure about the incumbent's type and this may forestall that entry.

Multimarket Solution. In the case of many markets, as with the original chainstore model, the asymmetric information perfect Bayesian equilibrium gains additional properties. In the early-on markets the predatory response is used with probability unity and there is no entry, except by mistake. The high-cost incumbent uses the low-cost ploy: it preys to signal low cost. As the number of remaining markets decreases and the value of the ploy to the high-cost firm becomes less, it begins to play a mixed strategy with strictly positive probability for both predation and accommodation, and some entry occurs. As the number of remaining periods becomes even smaller, the value of the ploy to the high-cost incumbent become even less, it plays accommodation with increasing frequency, and more entry occurs. Finally, the ploy has no value and the high-cost incumbent always accommodates.[26]

9.8   Implicit Collusion in Repeated Games

Consider a prisoners' dilemma game with firms j and k, each with two strategies and having the specific payoffs given in the bimatrix of table 9.6. The combination of actions (a_{j_1}, a_{k_1}) provides the cooperative solution to the one-shot game and (a_{j_2}, a_{k_2}) is the noncooperative Nash equilibrium combination.

Table 9.6 Prisoners' Dilemma

	a_{k_1}	a_{k_2}
a_{j_1}	$(3, 3)$	$(-3, 5)$
a_{j_2}	$(5, -3)$	$(1, 1)$

Suppose now that the game is repeated infinitely with firm k adopting the **tit-for-tat strategy:** (a) choose a_{k_1} in the first period and (b) at each subsequent period make the move adopted by rival firm j one period earlier. Note that tit-for-tat is a first-order **Markov strategy** in the sense that firm k conditions its play at any date not on the entire history of the game, but only on the immediately preceding action of its rival. Aumann (1981) and Axelrod (1987) has shown that in the class of Markov strategies the unique iterated dominant-strategy equilibrium of the repeated prisoners' dilemma game has both players adopt tit-for-tat.

If at the first period and thereafter firm j chooses a_{j_1}, it receives the cooperative payoff 3, but if it chooses to free ride by playing a_{j_2} to capture payoff 5, firm k's use of tit-for-tat will force firm j to also play tit-for-tat as a best response and thus limit it to payoffs of -3 and 5 in an alternating sequence forever. Firm j's average payoff in this penalty phase is $(-3 + 5)/2 = 1$ per

---

[26] Using product quality supply as a context, the asymmetric information perfect Bayesian equilibria for a T-period horizon in chapter 14, section 14.4. The time sequence of pooling, semi-separating, and separating equilibrium stages is developed there in detail.

repetition, which is lower than if it had not chosen to free ride. When future profits are not discounted too heavily, the "penalty" embedded in the infinitely repeated tit-for-tat play overwhelms any one-time gain to free riding at any finite date and therefore allows the cooperative one-shot actions (a_{j_i}, a_{k_i}) to be employed as stationary long-run equilibrium strategies. This is the repeated game story of **implicit collusion** or **conscious parallelism**. The role of the infinite horizon in the repeated game is clear: it assures that there are always enough periods in the future, no matter what date is then current, to cause the then-present cost of the penalty to offset the one-period gain from free riding.

Recall from section 9.6.1 that the discount factor ρ may reflect both the market's time rate of preference (the discount rate r) and the constant probability h that the game, if not actually infinite, will end with any repetition (indefinite repetition). Specifically, $\rho = (1 - h)/(1 + r)$. In the tit-for-tat game with greater discounting (smaller ρ) the short-run profit from free riding is weighted more heavily relative to the stream of reduced profits in the penalty phase. In the extreme where the discount rate is very large and/or the probability of the game ending at any date is very large, ρ would be very small and the game could take on the properties of the one-shot game in which short-run payoffs supersede those of the long run and free riding is optimal. The implicitly collusive solution more generally occurs in the opposite case: low r, high h, and ρ sufficiently close to unity.

E9.8

Trigger Prices and Implicit Collusion

Suppose that J identical firms with constant unit cost c play price strategies in an infinitely repeated game. When all firms play a price p^* greater than the one-shot Bertrand equilibrium price and less than or equal to the monopoly price, each receives one-shot profits $\pi_j^* = (p^* - c)D(p^*)/J > 0$. If all firms play p^* in the repeated game then each has a present value $v_j^* = (1 + \rho + \rho^2 + \ldots)\pi_j^* > 0$, where ρ is again the discount factor.

Free Riding and Cartel Enforcement. Suppose that the firms are playing p^* in repetitions of the game and that some firm k considers shading its price while all others adhere to p^*. If it takes the adhering firms just one market period to detect this free riding (by observing that they sell nothing at that market date), then k's short-run gain is $\pi_j^* J$ (approximately, since its price is just below p^*). Suppose further that the adherents react to the free riding by reverting to the one-shot Bertrand prices p^b forever after. Given that these firms choose p^b, the firm k's best response is also to choose p^b so that all firms earn zero profits forever after.

When not to Free Ride. Rational firms contemplating the one-period gain to free riding will balance the gains and losses to the strategy. Specifically, free riding will not be optimal for firm j when (note that $1 + \rho + \rho^2 + \ldots = 1/(1 - \rho)$)

$$\pi_j^*(1 + \rho + \rho^2 + \ldots) \geq \pi_j^* J$$

or

$$\rho \geq \frac{J - 1}{J} \qquad (9.15)$$

That is, when the discount factor is greater than or equal to $(J - 1)/J$, the price p^* will be sustained as an equilibrium for no firm will find it optimal to free ride. Notice that as J increases the discount factor necessary to sustain the cooperative prices approaches unity. In the duopoly case $\rho \geq 1/2$ is required.

Detection Lags and Free Riding. As a variant on the above analysis, suppose that the adherent firms, because of detection lags or a lag in their ability to change prices, do not react to the free riding for two periods. This increases the short-run gain to free riding to $\pi_j^*(1 + \rho)$, and free riding will be ill-advised when

$$\pi_j^*(1 + \rho + \rho^2 + \ldots) \geq \pi_j^* J(1 + \rho)$$

or

$$\rho \geq \left(\frac{J - 1}{J}\right)^{1/2} \qquad (9.16)$$

For any given J the discount factor which sustains the cooperative equilibrium is larger than that which will be necessary with one-period detection, but this difference becomes smaller as the number of firms becomes larger. For example, with a duopolist the difference in ρ is between 0.5 and 0.72 respectively, whereas with 10 firms it is between 0.9 and 0.95.

9.8.1   Repeated Games and the Folk Theorem

The tit-for-tat and trigger pricing equilibria outlined above indicate that the rivalry that occurs in a repeated game can be different from that in the underlying one-shot game. When firms condition their behavior on their past actions and the past actions of rivals, strategies which are not in any one firm's short-run interest may be optimal in the long run as attempts to capture the short-run profits may cause rivals to punish this "deviant" behavior. The oldest systematic statement of this idea is the so-called **Folk theorem**. This theorem informs us that the payoffs to Nash equilibrium strategies in the infinitely repeated game $\Gamma\{N(J, S, \pi), \rho, \infty\}$ are the feasible individually rational payoffs in the one-shot game $N(J, S, \pi)$ provided that there is sufficiently little discounting of the future. A vector of profits $\pi^*(s^*) = [\pi_1^*(s^*)\pi_2^*(s^*) \ldots \pi_J^*(s^*)]$ is **feasible** in the one-shot game N if it is a convex combination of pure strategy J-tuples, and π^* is **individually rational** if it Pareto dominates the **minimax** outcome π_j^{mm} for each j, that is, if

$$\pi_j^*(s^*) \geq \pi_j^{\text{mm}} \equiv \min_{\bar{s}_j} \max_{s_j} \pi_j(s) \qquad (9.17)$$

where $\bar{s}_j$ is a feasible set of strategies chosen by j's rivals. As the name suggests, the minimax profit $\pi_j{}^{mm}$ is that level below which firm j cannot be forced by its rivals.[27] Note that the individually rational strategies s^* giving rise to π^* are not restricted to be Nash equilibria for the one-shot game N, but generally are a *larger* set of outcomes. In a nutshell, and as we will clarify in the following discussion, the Folk theorem informs us that virtually any set of payoffs can be obtained as a perfect equilibrium if the game horizon is long enough and the discount factor is sufficiently close to unity.

One of the first written proofs of the Folk theorem is that of Aumann and Shapley (1976). It is instructive to sketch it here. To keep the development simple, let $J = 2$ and assume that $\pi^* = [\pi_1^*\pi_2^*]$ is a feasible and individually rational payoff combination in N. Write $\pi^* = \Sigma_l \alpha^l \pi^l$ where each π^l is a payoff pair corresponding to a pure strategy pair of the one-shot game and the α^l are positive weights. We can in turn write $\alpha^l = \beta^l/\beta$ where the $\beta^l > 0$ are integers and β is their sum.[28] Thus the payoffs π^* can be thought of as arising from the repeated game Γ as an average payoff from choosing those strategies which yield the profit vector π^1 for β^1 periods, π^2 for β^2 periods, etc. After β periods this sequence is then repeated, and so on.

In addition to the above scheme, a repeated game strategy must indicate each firm's responses to its rival when the rival deviates from the course of play described above. Such deviations will be called **free riding** here, as the deviant's attempt to capture a short-term gain comes at the expense of its nondeviant rivals. It is at this point that the individual rationality of π^* becomes important. Because π^* has this property, the profits of each firm are at least equal to its minimax level: $\pi_j^* \geq \pi_j{}^{mm}$. Let $s_k{}^{mm}$ be the minimax mixed strategy of each firm k required to hold firm j to $\pi_j{}^{mm}$ and consider the following play in the repeated game. At the onset the firms play, as above, to obtain average profits π^*. If firm j chooses to free ride at some date t, then at the very next date each rival firm k plays the minimax strategy $s_k{}^{mm}$ and continues to do so forever. This punishes firm j by forcing its profits down to the minimax level $\pi_j{}^{mm} \leq \pi_j^*$. Since the game is infinitely long and the discounting is sufficiently small, the loss of profits $\pi_j^* - \pi_j{}^{mm}$ per repetition from this punishment can be made to have a present value which offsets any one period gain to free riding. Since this punishment consequence is known, the free riding will not occur in the first place *if* the threat to punish is credible. (This "if" is discussed further below.) Infinitely repeated games are special in this regard, for at any period of the game (and with any history) the remainder of the game is still infinitely long and small per period punishments can be made large in present value relative to the free-riding gain (with sufficiently small discounting).

Two important aspects of the folk theorem are evident from the above discussion. First, it brings about what we think of as a "cooperative" outcome of the one-shot game N by noncooperative play in the infinitely repeated game Γ. The per period profit π^* is not based on any outside enforcement contract; it is a noncooperative outcome of Γ.[29] The repetition of the game, with its

---

[27] The minimax strategies need not be unique, and they may be mixed strategies.

[28] The assumption here is that the α^l- are rational numbers. See Aumann and Shapley (1976) for the alternative case.

[29] Once more, π^* is a noncooperative solution of the repeated game Γ. While it is also usual to emphasize that π^* is a cooperative solution to the one-shot game N, that has no importance as the relevant game here is the repeated one.

possibilities for punishment of free-riding behavior, is in a sense the enforcement mechanism (recall E9.8). Second, the Folk theorem is important because it informs us that in an infinitely repeated game the set of equilibrium outcomes are generally much greater than those of the underlying one-shot game. As the sketch of the proof makes clear, any collection of individually rational outcomes can be an equilibrium path of Γ.

The Folk Theorem with Perfection. Rubinstein (1979) has observed that the strategies implied by the Folk theorem are not in general (subgame) perfect for, given that one firm free rides, it may not be in its rival's best interest to respond with the minimax strategy forever.[30] That is, the threat to use such a minimax punishment might not be credible and therefore not adequate to deter free riding. This is an interesting possibility, as the concept of subgame perfection was introduced earlier, in the finite extensive form game, to eliminate Nash equilibria which occur as noncredible threats made on an out-of-equilibrium path. Perhaps the requirement of perfection in the repeated game Γ can also reduce the number of equilibria admitted by the Folk theorem. Rubinstein's results are a qualified negative in this regard, as he shows that the Folk theorem extends from simple Nash equilibrium to perfect Nash equilibrium (in Γ) provided that there is no discounting. No reduction in the number of equilibria occurs with this addition of perfection to the Nash solution concept.

More recently, Fudenberg and Maskin (1986) have extended the Folk theorem to include both subgame perfection and discounting. They also leave us with a negative result: provided that the discounting is sufficiently small (the discount factor ρ is sufficiently close to unity) and a dimensionality condition (to be outlined below) obtains, then the set of perfect equilibrium outcomes to the repeated game $\Gamma(N, \rho, \infty)$ converge to the individually rational set of outcomes for the one-shot game N. Perfection with discounting does not reduce the multiplicity of repeated game equilibria.

The essential idea underlying the Fudenberg and Maskin proof of the "perfect Folk theorem" is as in the original version: when a firm free rides, it is met by a minimax response from its rivals. In their version, however, the punishment phase is limited to a length of time which just dissipates any gain to the free riding. Perfectness is assured by an incentive to those firms not free riding in the form of a small increment to their average profitability. It is possible for this incentive to be offered, the equilibrium made perfect, and the threat to punish made credible provided that the payoff set meets a full dimensionality condition. This condition requires that the set of payoffs that strictly Pareto dominate the minimax payoff combination in the one-shot game have dimension J, so that there then exists an *average* payoff vector $\bar{\pi}$ interior to the feasible payoff region where the incentive payoffs $[(\bar{\pi}_1 + \varepsilon) \ldots (\bar{\pi}_{j-1} + \varepsilon)\bar{\pi}_j(\bar{\pi}_{j+1} + \varepsilon) \ldots (\bar{\pi}_J + \varepsilon)]$ are feasible. For those firms not free riding, a reward of $\varepsilon > 0$ in average profits can be made when punishing any free rider. This condition is trivially met when there are just two firms involved in the repeated game. It is satisfied for three or more firms when, for each firm, there is some payoff combination in which its

---

[30] Note that the statement of the theorem specified only that the repeated game equilibrium is Nash, not (subgame) perfect Nash.

profit is (a) greater than its minimax profit and (b) different from the profits of every other firm.

For any infinitely (indefinitely) repeated game a combination of individually rational strategies s^*, credible punishment strategies and discount factors are said to be **incentive compatible** when they assure that free riding will not occur and thus leave the strategies s^* to be played along the equilibrium path.

9.8.2   Trigger Strategies

The early statements of the Folk theorem by Friedman (1971, 1983) and Telser (1972) focused on trigger strategies sustaining the one-shot game collusive outcome as a noncooperative perfect Nash equilibrium of the repeated game. Roughly, **trigger strategies** are those occurring when the observation by any firm of deviant play by one of its rivals triggers a punishment equilibrium strategy in *all* subsequent repetitions of the game.

Consider a homogeneous-good J-firm oligopoly immune from entry and suppose that the firms cannot observe the outputs chosen by their rival but only the industry aggregate. Let $\pi^* = [\pi_2(z^*)\pi_2(z^*) \dots \pi_J(z^*)]$ indicate individually rational profits in a one-shot game when the firms produce outputs $z^* = [z_1^* z_2^* \dots z_J^*]$. Denote the Cournot–Nash equilibrium profits by $\pi^c = [\pi_1(z^c)\pi_2(z^c) \dots \pi_J(z^c)]$ with outputs $z^c = [z_1{}^c z_2{}^c \dots z_J{}^c]$. The z^* solution is such that $\pi_j(z^c) \leqslant \pi_j(z^*)$ for each j. Finally, the profit of some firm j who free rides, but is not detected, is $\pi_j(z^* : z_j{}^0) = \max_{z_j}(z^* : z_j)$, where $(z^* : z_j)$ is z^* with z_j replacing z_j^* and $z_j{}^0$ is the optimal free-riding output.

Suppose that individually rational strategies z^* are played as above. In the one-shot game each firm j has an incentive to free ride since it then receives profits $\pi_j(z^* : z_j{}^0)$ which are generally preferred to $\pi_j(z^*)$. In the infinitely repeated oligopoly game trigger strategies are an enforcement mechanism (threat) made by all firms that, in the event free riding is detected, each will change its one-shot collusive behavior to some one-shot noncooperative equilibrium behavior – here the Cournot–Nash play. Specifically, each firm j chooses outputs according to the following **trigger output** rules.

1   As long as the industry output is observed to be $\Sigma_j z_j^*$ continue to choose z_j^*.
2   If at any market date some firm is found to free ride and industry output is greater than $\Sigma_j z_j^*$ continue to choose z_j^*, and then permanently revert to the one-shot Cournot–Nash equilibrium output $z_j{}^c$:

The two key aspects of the trigger strategy are that the threat to revert to the punishment phase is credible (because it is Nash equilibrium behavior) and that no firm can free ride on the trigger strategy and increase its average profits, given that other firms hold to their trigger strategies (that is, the trigger strategy is a Nash equilibrium for the repeated game).

More specifically, Friedman (1971) proves the following theorem. Let $\Gamma(N, z, \pi)$ be a repeated oligopoly game and let z^c be the Cournot–Nash equilibrium of the underlying one-shot game N. Then the trigger strategy pair (z^c, z^*) is a subgame perfect equilibrium of Γ if the (constant) discount factor is such that

$$\rho_j > \frac{\pi_j(z^* : z_j{}^0) - \pi_j(z^*)}{\pi_j(z^* : z_j{}^0) - \pi_j(z^c)} \tag{9.18}$$

for all j.[31] The combination (z^c, z^*, ρ) is incentive compatible when (9.18) holds and the outputs z^* are sustained along the equilibrium path.

The proof of incentive compatibility first shows that (z^c, z^*) is an equilibrium point and then it is subgame perfect. We can sketch the proof by first supposing that all firms except j adopt the trigger strategies. Firm j plays the trigger strategy until some market date t, and then free rides by choosing $z_j{}^0$ to immediately receive profits $\pi_j(z^c : z_j{}^0)$. One date later the free riding is detected, the cartel dissolves, and all firms play Cournot strategies. This results in a stream of profits for j made up of three parts as follows:

$$(1 + \rho_j + \ldots + \rho_j{}^{t-1})\pi_j(z^*) + \rho_j{}^t\pi_j(z^* : z_j{}^0) + (\rho_j{}^{t+1} + \rho_j{}^{t+2} \ldots)\pi_j(z^c)$$

$$= \frac{1 - \rho_j{}^t}{1 - \rho_j} \pi_j(z^*) + \rho_j{}^t\pi_j(z^* : z_j{}^0) + \frac{\rho_j{}^{t+1}}{1 - \rho_j} \pi_j(z^c) \tag{9.19}$$

If firm j's present value of profits when not free riding is greater than the amount given by (9.19), then the trigger strategy of firm j is a best response to the trigger strategy of all others. This inequality is just the condition (9.18), which establishes (z^c, z^*) as an equilibrium strategy. Subgame perfection is straightforward to argue and is left to the reader.

9.8.3 Implicit Collusion or Not?

The essential concept of repeated rivalry among oligopolistic firms with perfect recall is as old as Cournot's original analysis. While not making it part of his formal model, Cournot clearly recognized that the output change of one duopolist will in general provoke retaliation and thus provide an incentive for some sort of accommodation. In the dynamic models developed above we have seen how firms can reach the one-shot cooperative payoff without an explicit binding contract. In repeated play, the "implicit contract" which enforces the one-shot cooperative payoff as the equilibrium is the credible threat of the firms to react to (punish) any free rider. This is the game-theoretic description of implicit collusion. Do not be misled: the collusive aspect of these outcomes are those occurring in the (irrelevant) one-shot game; in the relevant repeated game the play is in fact noncooperative – it is neither cooperative nor collusive. Despite this possible confusion, it is common to use the term **implicitly collusive** to mark individually rational outcomes occurring as the result of the Folk theorem in repeated games. With this warning we use that terminology also.

An unfortunate difficulty with the repeated game approach to oligopoly is that it produces its implicit collusion much too abundantly. As the Folk theorem informs us, every individually rational strategy is a perfect equilibrium outcome in an infinitely repeated game, including those which produce payoffs just slightly greater than the minimax levels. Thus there is little comfort and little

---

[31] Note the similarity of this condition to that supporting the reputation equilibrium in (9.5).

practical real-world success when the economist claims that some particular strategy arises as a perfect equilibrium in an infinitely repeated game.[32]

Finally, the implicit collusion produced in infinitely repeated games, like the reputations equilibrium, is based on a circularity in logic that is also disconcerting. The problem is that history matters only in the most indirect way in such models. Each firm's profits at any given repetition depend only on the strategies adopted by its rivals at that repetition, which means that each firm's strategy at any repetition depends on the past history of the game (industry) only because all other firms' strategies do. These self-fulfilling expectations, labeled *bootstrapping* by Fudenberg and Tirole (1986a), unfortunately seem to be too abstract a basis for conduct in real-world industries. In contrast, we think of history, and particularly learning through experience, as playing a much more direct and pervasive role in explaining what real firms do.

9.9   Game Theory and Industrial Economics

Perhaps the most active area of research in industrial economics has been the use of noncooperative games to analyze market competition. One of the key benefits of this research has been the discipline it has imposed on the economist, for a model of market competition constructed in this way requires an explicit, detailed statement of the game in its extensive form: strategic variables must be specified, the precise times at which decisions are made and payoffs realized must be noted, information structures must be identified, and solution concepts must be stated clearly. More specifically, all the rules of the game noted in section 9.4.1 must be set out systematically. Having models which are explicit about these things has been important to recent progress.[33] As subsequent chapters unfold, the reader will see that often as much is learned about the economics of industry in the careful statement of such models as is learned from their solution.

Anyone who has been to the ballpark knows that you ". . . can't tell the players without a scorecard." We therefore offer the following catalog (scorecard) of the dynamic oligopoly games developed in the preceding pages.

DYNAMIC OLIGOPOLY
A REPEATED GAMES

1 Reputation model (section 9.6)
   (a) Complete information
   (b) Infinite (or indefinite) repetition
   (c) Incentive compatibility
   (d) Multiplicity of self-fulfilling equilibria

---

[32] In chapter 12 this criticism is avoided to some extent by focusing on nondominated outcomes, (see section 12.3 on cartels and price wars specifically).

[33] One old problem seems to become more acute with the insight provided by game theory. Since the systematic use of game-theoretic analyses identifies rules of the game which can produce desired results, the economist must be careful not to "design" theories for policy use in a way which simply substantiates a preconceived advocacy position.

2 Signaling model (section 9.7)
   (a) Incomplete information
   (b) Finite horizon
   (c) Perfect Bayesian equilibria
       (i)   Pooling
       (ii) Separating
       (iii) Semi-separating

3 Implicit collusion model (section 9.8)
   (a) Complete information
   (b) Infinite (or indefinite) repetition
   (c) Incentive compatibility
   (d) Multiplicity of self-fulfilling equilibria

B   MULTISTAGE GAMES (chapters 10 and 11)

The scorecard informs us that there are two major categories of dynamic oligopoly models, those based on repeated games and those based on nonrepeated, or multistage, games. In turn, there are three basic repeated game models: reputation, signaling, and implicit collusion. The very brief notes on the key features of these models call attention to differences and similarities (compare reputation and implicit collusion models and contrast these with the signaling model). While the application of the reputation and signaling models has been to questions of entry, the essential analytical structure extends itself naturally to issues concerning industry exit, provision of product quality, capacity expansion, etc., as set out in the following chapters. The implicit collusion model also extends to new applications when further developed to deal with finite horizons, limited punishment intervals, and random demand and/or cost shocks, as will be clear in chapter 12. We are only left to explain what the scorecard means by multistage games: this is the subject of chapters 10 and 11.

Supplementary examples

SE9.1   Capacity Restrictions and Bertrand Equilibrium

In a variation on the Bertrand Nash-in-price solution, Edgeworth (1897) argued that, at least for short-run analyses, the competing firms should be constrained in their production capacity. This avoids the paradox Edgeworth saw in the fact that Nash-in-price play among homogeneous-good firms always yields the competitive solution, even with two firms. Here we show that his variation does not generally have an equilibrium in pure strategies, but an equilibrium may exist in its mixed extension. The mixed prices are such that the average price lies somewhere between the competitive and monopoly levels, with probabilities for both extremes.

To keep complications to a minimum, we consider duopolists 1 and 2 with outputs z_1 and z_2 respectively, and let the market demand be linear and scaled such that

$$z = a - p \tag{9.20}$$

where $z = z_1 + z_2$ and $a \geq 0$ is the "market size" demand parameter. Further, we assume that production costs are zero. A useful basis of comparison will be the Cournot equilibrium which, ignoring the capacity constraints for the moment, is uniquely given by $z_1 = z_2 = a/3$, $p = a/3$, and $\pi_1 = \pi_2 = (a/3)^2$ using the obvious notation. The Bertrand equilibrium, also without the capacity constraints, is as usual the competitive solution where price equals marginal cost: $z_1 = z_2 = a/2$, $p = 0$, and $\pi_1 = \pi_2 = 0$.

Capacity Constraints. To be of interest the capacity levels κ_1 and κ_2 of each firm must be less than the size of the market; $\kappa_j \leq a$. For convenience, further assume that $\kappa_1 = \kappa_2 = \kappa$. The role of the capacity restrictions are evident if we suppose that one firm, say j, sets $p_j = 0$ at some first market date and therefore cannot supply the entire demand at that price. The manner in which firm j rations its output to buyers will determine the *contingent*, or *residual*, demand faced by its rival firm k at that market date. However that rationing occurs, firm k will then act as a monopolist when facing that contingent demand schedule. Using an informal dynamic analysis, Edgeworth proposed that, at a second market date, firm j would raise its price to be just less than the previous monopoly price levied by its rival, and a time sequence of markets would follow during which the firms would adjust and readjust price. The range over which price was to fluctuate during this sequence was noted by Edgeworth to depend on the capacity constraint κ. It is also important to note that this range depends on the nature of the first firm's rationing rule and, in turn, the contingent demand left to its rival.

Bertrand with Capacity Constraints is Cournot. For the moment assume that buyers have equal access to firms and that the individual firm demand schedules are given by

$$
\begin{aligned}
z_j &= a - p_j & &\text{if } p_j < p_k \\
&= (a - p_j)/2 & &\text{if } p_j = p_k \\
&= a - \kappa - p_j & &\text{if } p_j > p_k
\end{aligned}
\tag{9.21}
$$

Of immediate interest are the upper and lower bounds on prices defining Edgeworth's range of fluctuations with this demand specification. These are derived as follows. When one firm sets a price arbitrarily close to the lower bound, the rival has the choice of meeting that low price or adopting the highest possible price. At equilibrium, the rival must be indifferent to these two possibilities, so that

$$\kappa \underline{p} = (a - \kappa - \bar{p})\bar{p}$$

where $\underline{p}$ and $\bar{p}$ are the lower and upper price bounds respectively. The high-price firm's demand is, however, given by its price and the capacity constraint. That is,

$$\bar{p} = \frac{a - \kappa}{2} \tag{9.22}$$

In turn,

$$\underline{p} = \frac{1}{\kappa}\left(\frac{a - \kappa}{2}\right)^2 \tag{9.23}$$

What is especially interesting about this result is that as κ becomes smaller and approaches $a/3$, then $\underline{p} = \bar{p} = a/3$, which is exactly the Cournot solution. That is, as the capacity parameter approaches one-third of the market size, Edgeworth's range of price fluctuations collapses to a single point and a pure strategy noncooperative (Cournot) equilibrium appears in this Bertrand game.[34]

Price Dispersion: The Mixed Strategy Equilibrium. Although the convergence of Bertrand duopoly with capacity constraints to the Cournot solution is interesting, we assume alternatively that $a/3 \leqslant \kappa \leqslant a$ and look for an equilibrium in mixed strategies. The mixed strategy in this duopoly is a pair of probability distributions on prices with the property that, for each firm, any price chosen with positive probability must be (*ex ante*) optimal against its rival's probability mixture. For a problem of similar analytical structure, Griesmer et al. (1967) have shown that the portion of the strategy space having positive probability density is a single interval and that no price in this interval, except possibly the upper bound, has a lumping of probabilities. Let $[p_*, p^*]$ indicate that interval. In this case the probability that $p_j = p_k$ is zero, and the demand facing each firm is made up of just two segments:

$$
\begin{aligned}
z_j &= \min\,(\kappa,\, a - p_j) & \text{if } p_j < p_k \\
&= \max\{0,\, \min(\kappa,\, a - \kappa - p_j)\} & \text{if } p_j > p_k
\end{aligned}
\tag{9.24}
$$

If we let $h_k(p)$ be the cumulative density function of k's price when a mixed strategy is employed, then the expected profit of firm j is

$$
\pi_j = p_j E(z_j)
\tag{9.25a}
$$

where the expected quantity demanded is

$$
\begin{aligned}
E(z_j) &= \{1 - h_k(p_j)\}\{\min(\kappa,\, a - p_j)\} \\
&\quad + h_k(p_j)\max\{0,\, \min(\kappa,\, a - \kappa - p_j)\}
\end{aligned}
\tag{9.25b}
$$

Two facts are useful in reducing the complexity of this expression. First, $\bar{p} < a - \kappa$.[35] Secondly, no firm will set a price less than $\underline{p} = (1/4\kappa)(a - \kappa)^2 \geqslant a - \kappa$, as shown earlier in equation (9.23). When these facts are used in (9.25), it simplifies to

$$
\pi_j(p) = p[\{1 - h_k(p)\}p + h_k(p)(a - \kappa - p)]
\tag{9.26}
$$

With some simple algebra this solves for the density function:

$$
h_k(p) = \frac{\kappa - (\pi_j/p)}{p + 2\kappa - a}
\tag{9.27}
$$

---

[34] Kreps and Scheinkman (1983) consider a two-stage oligopoly model in which each firm irreversibly selects plant capacity (at an initial stage) before engaging in Bertrand-like price competition (at a second stage). They show that, with concave demand and other mild restrictions, the unique equilibrium of this two-stage Bertrand game is equivalent to the Cournot outcome. This suggests that the Cournot equilibrium can be viewed as the result of price competition among capacity-constrained rivals. In this sense they refer to the Cournot equilibrium as optimal.

[35] If the opposite assumption is made, then $\pi_j(\bar{p}) = \bar{p}\{(1 - h_k(\bar{p}))(a - \bar{p})$ which is equal to zero unless $h_k(\bar{p}) > 0$. However, both firms cannot sell κ at $a - \kappa$ so that this case is not feasible.

At equilibrium $\pi_j(\kappa)$ takes on a constant value for all choices of p in the interval $[p_*, \bar{p}]$, and therefore this last equation gives the mixed strategy equilibrium once π_j is evaluated. To do this, first note that the greatest price must be $\bar{p} = (a - \kappa)/2$, for when the greatest price is set the firm knows that it will be undercut by its rival (in this case any price other than $(a - \kappa)/2$ will not be optimal). Using $\bar{p}$ to evaluate $\pi_j(\kappa)$ and substituting in (9.27) gives the equilibrium cumulative density

$$h_k(p) = \frac{\kappa p - (a - \kappa)^2}{4p(p + 2\kappa - a)} \qquad (9.28)$$

and similarly for firm j. The reader can verify that as κ approaches a the capacity constraint becomes binding and this density collapses giving the Cournot solution $p = a/3$.

Capacity Constraints and Implicit Collusion in Repeated Play. Brock and Scheinkman (1985) consider an infinitely repeated version of Edgeworth's game. In their analysis each of J firms produces a homogeneous product with identical marginal cost c and plant capacity κ. Also, as above, consumers have full information and purchase only from the lowest-priced firm, which gives the demand $z(\min_j p_j)$. We are informed from the preceding analysis that the static (one-shot) play of the price-setting game yields (a) an equilibrium price such that demand is $J\kappa$ if κ is small, (b) an equilibrium price equal to marginal cost c if κ is sufficiently large (not binding), and (c) a mixed strategy equilibrium for medium κ. Using an extension of the analysis developed above, Brock and Scheinkman further show that the per firm profit $\pi_j^c(\kappa, J)$ in this static game is decreasing with the number of firms J. Let $p^c(\kappa, J)$ indicate the associated equilibrium price.

In their repeated game firms use an individually rational price $p^*(\kappa, J)$ (to be admissible, $z(p^*) \leq J\kappa$) until some firm free rides, at which time the firms revert forever to their static (one-shot) equilibrium strategies. The per repetition loss during this punishment phase is $\{z(p^*)/J\}(p^* - c) - \{z(p^c)/J\}(p^c - c)$. The price p^* will sustain an implicit collusion equilibrium when the short-run gain from free riding does not exceed the loss during the resulting punishment. The short-run gain comes from the opportunity for some firm to shade its price below p^* and then sell to its full capacity constraint. Thus the gain to free riding is (approximately)

$$(p^* - c)\left\{\kappa - \frac{z(p^*)}{J}\right\}$$

and for p^* to sustain the implicit collusion it is required that

$$\frac{\rho}{1 - \rho}\left\{\frac{z(p^*)}{J}(p^* - c) - \frac{z(p^c)}{J}(p^c - c)\right\} \geq (p^* - c)\left\{\kappa - \frac{z(p^*)}{J}\right\} \qquad (9.29)$$

Using a linear demand function $z(\cdot)$, Brock and Scheinkman derive the implicitly collusive price p^* and profits as a function of exogenously given values for capacity κ and the number of firms. Interestingly, in this case they show that increases in J, with given κ, increase the gain to free riding and decrease the one-shot profits π_j^c. The two offsetting effects balance for mid-range values of J, where the greatest profits occur for implicit collusion.

SE9.2   Rationing Rules, Demand, and Oligopoly Outcomes

Despite their frequent use, neither the Cournot nor the Bertrand models of oligopoly are without problems. The requirement for an auctioneer to establish price in the Cournot quantity model is generally thought to be an objection and, as we saw in SE9.1, the Bertrand model is paradoxical unless there are capacity constraints. The usual way to link these models and reduce the objections is to think of firms as adjusting their capacity at some first stage of analysis and then later choosing price with the given capacity. Although this appears to be an interesting possibility. it does not yield unambiguous results, for the manner in which the unobserved residual demand (remaining after capacity-constrained production) is rationed is critical in determining the properties of the equilibrium. We investigate this issue here.

The Model and Some Background. Consider a homogeneous-good duopoly protected from entry and producing its output at zero cost. For the moment, suppose that κ_1 and κ_2 represent plant capacity investments for firms j and k respectively. Let the technology of the firms be fixed proportion so that κ_1 and κ_2 can be scaled in units of output. We continue to think of these investments as being chosen at some strategic stage and, in this example, focus only on the market-stage output decisions. As was shown in SE9.1, for such a situation the Nash-in-price equilibria occurs only in mixed strategies, with the firms generally charging different prices. This example also showed that, when the lower-priced duopolist could not meet the entire market demand (because of its capacity constraint), its rival's (residual) demand depended on the specific manner in which demand was rationed by the low-price seller. Our specific interest here lies in showing that different policies of rationing result in different market-stage equilibria.

Kreps and Scheinkman (1983) develop a two-stage oligopoly model in which firms choose plant capacities at an early stage and then, at a later market stage, reach a Bertrand Nash-in-price equilibrium. What is important about their analysis is that, when demand is concave and the rationing rule is *pro rata* (as described below), the (unique) perfect equilibrium output levels of their game are equivalent to those that would result in a one-stage Cournot equilibrium. They conclude that Cournot equilibria can be thought of as implying price competition among firms who choose the scale of their plant at a (prior) strategic stage or, as they state, ". . . quantity precommitment and Bertrand competition yield Cournot outcomes."

In many real-world markets manufacturing and distribution capacities are in fact developed long before the firms' pricing decisions are made. In these cases, the results obtained by Kreps and Scheinkman would seem to be quite important. As we have suggested, however, the nature of the market-stage equilibrium depends on the rationing rule employed by the lower-priced firm. What rationing rule was adopted by Kreps and Scheinkman, and is their equivalence result robust under reasonable alternatives?

Pro Rata Rationing. Suppose that the negatively sloped market demand $z(p)$ arises in an economy of identical consumers, so that each consumer has the same demand schedule. Let duopolist 1 set a lower price than duopolist 2 ($p_1 < p_2$). Suppose further that $z(p_1) > \kappa_1$, so that firm 1 cannot supply all that is demanded at its chosen price. In this situation, Kreps and Scheinkman assume that firm 1 rations its output by restricting the quantity purchased by each consumer to a *pro rata* portion $\kappa_1/z(p)$ of the amount that consumers would otherwise take. This produces a residual demand for firm 2 given by $z(p_2) - \kappa_1$, which is simply a "left shift" in the market demand by κ_1 as shown in figure 9.6(a).[36]

Proportional Rationing. An alternative rationing rule was suggested by Beckman (1965) in a similar two-stage duopoly with capacity constraints (this Beckman rule was used in E9.7). Beckman also viewed the market demand as arising from identical consumers. However, he thought of the low-price firm 1 as selling its production on a first-come first-served basis and presumed that customers arrived randomly at the sellers. Consumers who came to firm 1 after it had sold out received nothing. In this case the residual demand facing firm 2 is $z(p_2)\{1 - \kappa_1/z(p_1)\}$ for $p_2 > p_1$ and is illustrated in figure 9.6(b). The Beckman rationing rule seems reasonable as it treats all consumers symmetrically. The Kreps–Scheinkman rule does not have this symmetry, but instead assumes that (somehow) sellers identify buyers by their reservation prices and sell only to those who place the highest value on the product.

Rationing Rules and Size of the Residual Demand. Davidson and Deneckere (1986) have shown that the Kreps–Scheinkman and Beckman residual demand schedules are in fact extremals for rationing rules of the general form where each consumer is limited to $z^*(p_1)$ units with service on a first-come first-served basis. Moreover, they show that (a) increases in the limit $z^*(p_1)$ lead to a greater residual demand, (b) when the $z^*(p_1)$ limit is chosen in a profit-maximizing manner by firm 1, the Beckman residual demand is obtained (that is, $z^*(p_1)$ is chosen to be nonbinding), and (c) with a rationing rule of a general form and $z^*(p_1)$ chosen to be profit maximizing, a Cournot equilibrium cannot be reached in the market-stage game. To quickly prove (b) and (c), suppose that κ_1 and κ_2 have been chosen at some prior stage and that firm 1 chooses some particular $z^*(p_1)$ for use at the market stage. Greater values of this limit lead to a more favorable residual demand for firm 2, leading firm 2 to set a higher price p_2. These higher prices for p_2 in turn benefit firm 1, since it will then be lower priced for higher prices p_1. Thus firm 1 increases its own profits by increasing its rationing limit $z^*(p_1)$ and, as this holds uniformly, no limit will be placed on individual purchases.

---

[36] We can produce the same residual demand by assuming that the market demand is made up of heterogeneous individuals each of which purchases just one unit of the good provided that the price is below their reservation price. In this case the low-price firm satisfies only those individuals whose reservation price is greater than or equal to p_1. In this case the rationing is efficient in the sense that it maximizes consumer surplus: with costless reselling (a strong assumption) every unit has the same marginal valuation (price) and this equals the marginal cost of the owning consumer's supply.

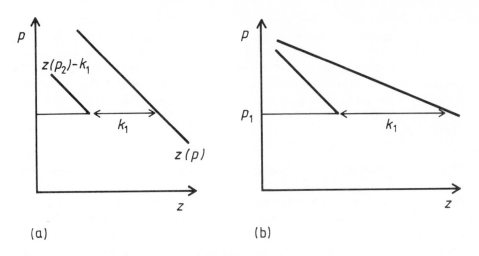

Figure 9.6
Residual demand: (a) Kreps–Scheinkman; (b) Beckman

SE9.3   Corporate Raids and Tender Offers

Suppose that a firm is poorly managed and that a prospective buyer (a corporate raider) can improve the management. Specifically, let the firm's per share value under the extant poor management be $p > 0$ and let the per share value with the new management be $p + \phi$, where ϕ are the rents provided by the new management.

The raider extends a tender offer of p^* per share for any share conditional on obtaining a majority interest.[37] While any tender price $p < p^* < p + \phi$ will leave both the raider and the current shareholders better off, this is not an equilibrium result. Rather, some shareholders will hold out in anticipation of a subsequent higher tender price. The iteration of this offer and re-offer process stops when the raider receives zero payoff. If the tendering process is costly, the raider then makes a loss if it bids. To see this result note that (a) all bids $p^* > p + \phi$ are dominated strategies, as they yield sure losses for the raider, (b) for all bids $p^* < p + \phi$ any (small) shareholder who expects the raid to succeed with certainty will not tender, as tendering under such circumstances is dominated by holding out for the greater value $p + \phi$, and so the raid fails, and therefore, (c) the only equilibria are no raiding or, provided that raiding costs are zero, $p^* = p + \phi$.

The Dilution Strategy. Holding-out seems to invalidate the common argument that an ill-managed and low-priced firm can be raided by skilled managers and its value thereby increased. The hold-out problem can be defeated, however. Grossman and Hart (1980) suggest a "dilution" strategy: the shareholders adopt charter provisions which allow a successful raider to sell the acquired firm's

[37] We assume that the expense of removing the current management by a shareholder proxy fight is prohibitive.

assets to a second firm owned by the raiders on terms which are disadvantageous to the first firm. In this way the raider receives more from the raid than just its share of the raided firm's profits, and the shareholders who do not tender suffer a loss.

SE9.4 Supply Coordination: Sequential or Simultaneous Entry?

When a pool of identical firms consider entry to an industry, how many will in fact enter? The usual view, based on a fixed demand and economies of scale in early levels of production, is that just enough enter so that the last earns nonnegative profits but if any other firm entered those profits would be negative. This is the standard and unique perfect equilibrium answer when the firms enter sequentially. It is also the Nash equilibrium answer when firms make their entry decisions simultaneously. It is usual to argue that the simultaneous solution is unconvincing, as it would generally involve an unreasonably large degree of coordination among the firms.

Alternatively, consider an entry model based on a symmetric mixed strategy equilibrium of a game in which firms can revise their entry decision if insufficient or excessive numbers of firms choose entry. The supply coordination that we otherwise find unreasonable is then achieved in the long run as a reaction to short-run errors. The analysis, of course, applies only in situations where sunk costs of entry/exit are insignificant.

A simplified model indicates the method of analysis and results. We consider just two firms and think of some stage of the game where the firms, having previously made their entry decisions, are faced with their choice of market strategy that is, choice of price or output. The bimatrix of payoffs of table 9.7 is assumed to obtain. When both firms enter, each loses $-\pi$, when just one enters, it earns the monopoly profits π^m while the other firm (possibly in a complementary-good industry) earns $0 \leq \pi^0 < \pi^m$; when neither enters, zero profits are earned.

The entry game has three Nash equilibria: (enter, out), (out, enter), and the symmetric mixed strategy in which the probability h of entry makes each rival indifferent to entry or out:

$$h(-\pi) + (1 - h)\pi^m = h\pi^0 \tag{9.30}$$

which gives

$$h = \frac{\pi^m}{\pi^m + \pi^0 + \pi} \leq 1 \tag{9.31}$$

Table 9.7 Entry Payoffs

	2 enters	*2 out*
1 enters	$(-\pi, -\pi)$	(π^m, π^0)
1 out	(π^m, π^0)	$(0, 0)$

Despite the fact that they are Nash best-response equilibria, the two pure strategies are somewhat unreasonable solutions. First, they are in fact significantly different solutions with significantly different rewards for the firms. Second, they imply a high degree of coordination among the firms. More likely, we would find a supply coordination problem.[38] Each firm's investment choice requires that it forecast its competitor's plan: will the competitor enter or not, and when? Uncertainty and *ex post* errors in the forecasts are surely the norm in such situations. As a result, the mixed strategy equilibrium of the above game is more likely to be descriptive of actual entry processes, at least on an a priori basis. Sometimes both enter, and sometimes only one enters. Notice finally that the probability that the firms fail to "coordinate" – both enter or both do not enter – is $h^2 + (1 - h)^2$ which has its largest values at zero and unity where monopoly profits would be near zero or very large respectively. Joint entry is most likely with mid-values of h where π^m and π^0 are not too different. A detailed discussion of entry in this and similar models is the subject of chapters 10 and 11.

[38] Smith (1982) notes the parallel between supply and demand coordination problems: ". . . This [supply coordination] is essentially a problem in information failure and there is an exact analogy for demand coordination. An example would be a movie theatre. Prospective viewers of a movie may know the supply of seats available with certainty, but (even if the ticket price is correctly set to maximize profit give expected demand) there is no mechanism to insure that the correct number of people will arrive for any given screening. To assure themselves seats, some people will arrive too early – wasting time. Others may arrive too late – wasting the trip if the show sells out. The problem arises not because the price is wrong *ex ante*, but because the behavior of individual demanders cannot be perfectly predicted. Demanders of the movie make incorrect forecasts about the actions of other demanders and the result is demand coordination failure. The obvious solution in this case is strategic (preemptive) purchases of tickets, i.e., reservations."

10 Entry with First-mover Advantages

The study of entry and exit generally begins with a distinction between incumbent and entering firms and centers on the observation that some actions affecting future entry, and an eventual industry equilibrium, are uniquely available to an incumbent. When firms move simultaneously in a static economic setting, more options are preferred to less. In multistage games of strategy that principle is inapplicable, for it may be optimal for an incumbent to restrict its options in early play to affect the solutions possible in the future.[1] In particular, early-on investments by an incumbent may favorably affect reaction functions, and the game equilibrium, in a subsequent market period. Multistage games in which actions are taken to determine outcomes in a later (sub)game are said to involve a **strategic** interaction. The possibility that is the center of attention in this chapter is that the strategic moves of an incumbent may alter a potential rival's profit opportunities enough to make entry unattractive. The symmetry between entry deterrence and exit-inducing strategic behavior is also developed.

10.1 Barriers to Entry

Analyses concerned with an incumbent bent on entry deterrence have had a long, if not always clearly articulated and analytically sound, history in market theory. The early literature of industrial economics generally dealt with these issues by using one of two behavioral models. The first of these is based on the so-called **Sylos hypothesis**, where potential entrants believe that an established firm will offer and maintain its (high pre-entry) level of output in the face of entry whether or not it is profitable for it to do so (see Bain, 1956; Modigliani, 1958; Sylos-Lambini, 1962). That is, the entrants are assumed to act as though the incumbent is irrevocably committed to a particular output policy. Models alternatively founded on the **excess capital hypothesis** permit the incumbent to

---

[1] Recall chapter 9, sections 9.5–9.7. This line of analysis was first developed by Schelling (1960), who concluded that "... narrowly irrational decisions may be rational within an extended framework."

vary its output, but instead assume that (a) the entrant bases its entry decision on the *captial* employed by the incumbent and (b) the incumbent adopts a capital level which leads to future production above the entry-deterring level.[2] Again, these policies are to be implemented whether or not they are profit maximizing. With respect to the Sylos hypothesis, we must ask about the optimal market decisions of the incumbent should entry occur. With respect to the excess capacity hypothesis, we must ask about the optimal level of capital to be adopted given the rules of play at the post-entry market stage.

Rational Deterrence. Since Spence's (1977a) analysis of excess capacity as an entry deterrent, these questions have been a focal point in industrial economics. In a reply to Spence's proof that "excess" investments in plant capacity could be used by an incumbent firm to deter entry *if* the entrant believed that the incumbent would use its full capacity to produce post-entry, Dixit (1980) asked whether or not this was a credible belief. His answer was based on two requirements: (a) the entrant should act rationally, and (b) once the entrant has entered, and also committed itself to some given level of investment, the incumbent should also respond in a rational manner. As we will see, in an equilibrium based on these rationality requirements the incumbent will not generally act according to either the Sylos or excess capacity hypothesis, but will accommodate entry instead.

Barriers, and More Barriers. The conditions of entry are critical to an industry's overall performance. Entry limits the ability of monopolies to exploit their power and, when sellers have differential efficiencies, entry assures that early-arriving less efficient firms are replaced by more efficient entrants. For this reason, entry conditions and potential competition are often as important as actual competition to industry analyses. In the literature it has been usual to summarize the conditions of entry in an industry by listing "barriers to entry". Presumably, if the list is long and the items are significant, then potential entry is not an important constraint on incumbent firms.

Barriers to entry arose as a serious issue in industrial economics during the 1950s as part of the attempts to explain some evidence of high rates of return in structurally concentrated industries.[3] Despite the fact that the idea of a barrier is intuitive – we all know one when we see it – a precise, widely-held definition of the concept did not arise in the static setting then used. Bain (1956), who was among the first to rely on the concept, was quite loose on the subject. He simply noted that the "height" of an entry barrier was positively related to the extent to which established firms were able to sustain their price above minimum average cost without inducing entry. As examples of barriers he listed

---

[2] See, for example, Pashigian (1968), Wenders (1971), and Spence (1977a) for applications of this hypothesis.

[3] The first systematic evidence was that developed by Bain (1951). Using eight-firm concentration ratios (CR 8) for a 1936–40 sample of 42 US four-digit industries, he found that the after-tax profits as a percentage of equity averaged 11.8 percent for those industries with CR 8 greater than 70 percent compared with 7.5 percent for those industries with lesser concentration. Whether these rates of return were in fact persistently high for the same industries and whether the results extend to a larger sample has been questioned by Brozen (1974). See also Clarkson (1977).

four possibilities: economies of scale, absolute cost advantages, large capital requirements, and product differentiation. Neither the list nor Bain's underlying definition have been generally accepted. Two alternative definitions of the period were those of Ferguson (1974) and Stigler (1968). To the Bain desiderata, Ferguson added a measure of inefficiency – that prices be greater than marginal cost. In contrast, Stigler (1968, p. 76) defined barriers from a fundamentally different viewpoint: ". . . as a cost of producing (at some or every rate of output) which must be borne by a firm which seeks to enter an industry but is not borne by firms already in the industry."

The differences between these definitions are substantial. For example, while adopting either the Bain or Ferguson view leads to the conclusion that economies of scale are a barrier to entry, by Stigler's definition they are not (only differences in cost *schedules* are). Both advertising and large capital requirements are barriers to Bain because, in his interpretation of the facts, they appear to be systematically related to higher than average rates of return; in contrast, these are not barriers for Ferguson unless they also give rise to scale economies, and Stigler would require that there be asymmetrical access to advertising technology and/or capital markets for the presence of such entry barriers.

Not only are there problems created by differences among these popular definitions, but von Weizsacker (1980a, b) and Demsetz (1982a) stress more fundamental problems common to the three. Demsetz comments on these with a clear example:

> . . . A requirement that an official medallion must be owned by operators of taxis is a barrier to entry if the number of medallions available is less than the number of taxis that would operate without such a requirement or if the medallion is costly to obtain. Suppose it were true that such licenses, which may be resold subsequently, also must be purchased from the city *at market-determined prices*. Insiders and outsiders (to the industry) face the same cost, the medallion price plus automotive costs, so Stigler's definition fails to identify the barrier, and, since the price of the medallion must dissipate profit, so do Bain's and Ferguson's. (Demsetz, 1982a, p. 50).

More generally, Demsetz's argument is that a barrier to entry is any obstacle to efficient contracting between consumers and a would-be entrant. Thus, barriers are generally inherent in any assignment (or occurrence) of property rights.[4] His corollary is that the problem of defining rights is no different from that of creating properly scaled legal barriers to entry. As an illustration of the complications (and misinterpretations in efficiency analysis) he notes:

> . . . The barrier to entry literature obscures the important issue raised by the phenomenon of firms facing negatively sloped demand curves. . . . [there must] be a barrier to the production of some mix of output if the demand curves facing existing firms (and, possibly, entrants) are negatively sloped, and this must be true whatever the relationship between price and

---

[4] Grossman (1981) and Fisher et al. (1983, pp. 168–9) also define barriers to entry in this way.

unit cost. The demand facing a producer is negatively sloped because there are "natural" or "legal" obstacles (such as trademark protection) to *perfect* imitation (meaning an imposter who duplicates product contents, name, and packaging). Trademark privileges may reduce the quantities sold of an *existing* product, but they may also increase the number of new products enjoyed by customers and even make some products profitable to produce that would be unprofitable in the absence of such legal protection. Elimination of such legal protection is likely to reduce prices and increase sales of products already produced, but it also reduces incentives to develop new ones. Whether these legal barriers to entry are desirable cannot be judged without explicit or implicit comparison of the values of alternative mixes of outcomes. (Demsetz, 1982a, p. 51)

Whereas Demsetz would argue that a licensing requirement (say, the taxi cab medallions) is a barrier to entry even if licenses were available to all firms at competitive prices, Bain would not find a barrier since no firm would earn economic profits in such a situation. This highlights the fact that Bain's definition, being based on a market equilibrium *result*, introduces not only exogenous market conditions but also firm conduct.[5]

10.2   Entry and Strategy

If would-be entrants behave rationally, entry is deterred (and there are entry barriers in the Bain sense) when positive profits are earned by incumbent firms and negative profits are earned by the entrant *post*-entry. That is, the decision to enter requires that consideration be given to the nature of the rivalry and the industry equilibrium following entry. Some aspects of this prospective equilibrium may or may not be signaled by the pre-entry behavior of the incumbents. For that reason it is generally necessary to consider several decision stages in the analysis of entry.

E10.1 ───

Multistage Decisions: Brand Loyalty and "Lock-in"

The basic components of a multistage decision system are illustrated in figure 10.1. At each stage there are the following.

1   An initial *state variable* κ_{t-1} that gives all relevant information about the economic system at the onset of stage t analysis (state variables may be vector valued).
2   An *output state variable* κ_t that gives all relevant information about the economic system at the end of stage t.

───

[5] Recall from chapter 3, E3.8 and E3.9, the different prospects for entry depending on whether firms are engaged in price or quantity competition (conduct).

3 *Decision variables* d_t that control the operation of the stage t economic system.

4 A *stage return*, which is a scalar variable that measures the payoff as a function of states and decisions: $r_t = r_t(d_t, \kappa_t; \kappa_{t-1})$.

5 A *stage transformation* f, expressing each component of the output state as a function of the initial state and decisions: $\kappa_t = f(d_t, \kappa_{t-1})$. If f has an inverse function then $\kappa_{t-1} = f^{-1}(d_t, \kappa_t)$, which is the basis for analysis by backward recursion.

The same factors occur with the state transition from κ_t to κ_{t+1} and the choice of d_{t+1} at stage $t + 1$. Multistage optimization problems that can be solved in a stage-by-stage fashion are said to be decomposable. Let $g\{r_T(\kappa_T, d_T), r_{T-1}(\kappa_{T-1}, d_{T-1}), \ldots, r_1(\kappa_1, d_1)\}$ be the overall multistage return and suppose that the state variables are linked over time. A sufficient condition for a stage-by-stage solution by recursion (decomposition in the fashion of dynamic programming) is that g be additive and increasing in the individual stage returns r_t and that there exist a stage transformation function f or f^{-1} (see Mitten, 1964). Such conditions are usually assumed.

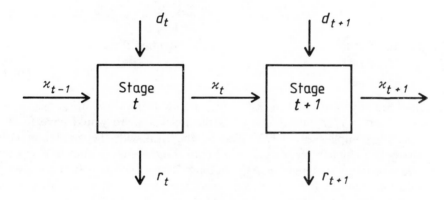

Figure 10.1
Multistage model

Brand Loyalty: The Lock-in Effect. Firms frequently think of market share as a state variable. The argument is that buyers display "brand loyalty" and therefore do not all instantly move when a (quality-adjusted) price difference appears between brands. A variety of reasons are offered for such inertia. For example, it is often said that buyers are "locked-in" by some specific capital investment in using one seller's brand.[6]

When market shares in some current period depend on previous market shares and on current prices, do sellers find it profitable to exploit the buyers' inertia by setting so high a price that it will sacrifice most of its market share?

[6] von Weizsacker (1984) and Klemperer (1987a, b) give detailed discussions of this and other models of consumer brand loyalty. See also chapter 12, SE12.5, in which consumer switching costs in an overlapping generations model are analyzed.

To answer this question, consider a simple two-stage model with two firms $j = 1, 2$. The prior decisions of these firms, we suppose, leave them with market shares m^0 and $1 - m^0$ respectively at the beginning of the period $t = 1$ under consideration. The firms set price noncooperatively, with p_j being firm j's price. Assume that firm 1's market share, arising from its price decision at $t = 1$, is given by the differentiable function[7]

$$m^1 = m^1(m^0, p_1 - p_2) \qquad (10.1)$$

which is such that $m^1 > m^0$ iff $p_1 < p_2$, that is, $\partial m^1/\partial p_1 < 0$. Market share is the state variable here and (10.1) is the state transition equation.

Following Farrell (1986a), assume that the total number z of buyers remains fixed for the two firms. Then firm 1's profit function can be written $\pi_1 = p_1(m^1 z) - c(m^1 z)$, where c is the constant unit production cost and $m^1 z$ is firm 1's period 1 sales. Given the initial state m^0, the Nash-in-price equilibrium conditions for firm 1 are

$$m^1 + (p_1 - c)\frac{\partial m^1}{\partial p_1} = 0 \qquad (10.2a)$$

Similarly, for firm 2,

$$1 - m^1 + (p_2 - c)\frac{\partial m^1}{\partial p_1} = 0 \qquad (10.2b)$$

which uses the fact that $\partial m^1/\partial p_2 = -\partial m^1/\partial p_1$. Dividing these conditions gives

$$\frac{p_1 - c}{p_2 - c} = \frac{m^1}{1 - m^1} \qquad (10.3)$$

From this equality note that if $m^1 > 1/2$, then at the equilibrium $p_1 > p_2$. Suppose that $m^0 > 1/2$, then if $m^1 < 1/2$ the market share would have to rise because $p_1 > p_2$ implies $m^1 > 1/2$. That is, the firm with the greater market share charges a higher price than its rival *and* remains the larger firm nonetheless. Moreover, this implies greater profits for the large firm. It should be stressed that this result arises directly from the inertia properties *assumed* of the state transition in (10.1).

10.2.1   State Space Representation of Two-stage Entry

We distinguish two decision stages. At the **pre-entry** or **strategic** stage ($t = 0$) the incumbent firm is assumed to have a choice of output level and a **state variable** κ. The state variable imposes *irreversible initial conditions* on the **post-entry** or **market** stage ($t = 1$) where price and/or output decisions are made. While it would normally be expected that the state variable is vector valued, it is usual to avoid the technical problems associated with large state space dimensionality and focus on one, or at most two, state variables.[8] The

---

[7] It is also assumed that the total number of buyers remains constant. Thus there may be switching among brands but no buyer drops from the market with price changes.

[8] See Kreps and Spence (1984) and Fudenberg and Tirole (1986b) for reviews of one-state-variable representations.

capital stock specialized to the firm is frequently used in this regard. As will be seen below, this abstraction from all aspects of industry history except the current level of one variable is a rewarding analytical device, albeit one that requires the exercise of caution in interpretation of results.

On viewing the incumbent's choice of κ, each potential entrant forms *expectations* about the nature of the industry equilibrium at the market stage should it choose to enter. The value that the would-be producer assigns to entry is the expected value of its post-entry equilibrium profits, again conditional on κ. Entry will occur when this value is positive so that an incumbent firm seeking to deter entry may use its choice of κ in a way which makes that value nonpositive.

10.2.2 Credible Deterrence

To follow this behavior more specifically, suppose for the moment that there is just one potential entrant (firm 2) and one incumbent (firm 1). The incumbent chooses κ at the initial stage $t = 0$ as outlined above. The rivalry at the following stage then produces an equilibrium in the market subgame with strategies $s^* = [s_1^{1*}(\kappa) s_2^{1*}(\kappa)]$, and this yields profit payoffs $\pi_j^1(s_1^{1*}(\kappa), s_2^{1*}(\kappa))$ for each firm $j = 1, 2$. Again, when deciding whether to enter or not, the entrant presumes that it enters and looks specifically to its equilibrium profits. In addition to the usual demand and cost conditions, the equilibrium and those profits depend on two things. First, and clearly visible in the notation, there is a dependence on the state variable κ fixed by the incumbent's earlier choice at $t = 0$. Second, the equilibrium depends on the specific rules of play (indicated by the asterisk) in the market subgame: the specific strategy variables adopted, the sequence of moves, and the information available to the firms.

Given the detailed rules of the market subgame, the incumbent's choice of κ is said to be a **credible entry deterrent** if $\pi_2^1(s_1^{1*}(\kappa), s_2^{1*}(\kappa)) \leq 0$. That is, entry is deterred if, at the market equilibrium when entry is assumed, firm 2 expects to earn at most zero profits. It is critical to recognize in all this that it is the *beliefs* of the entrant about the market equilibrium which are (or are not) credible.

Some terminology is helpful here. Schelling (1960) makes a distinction between threats and commitments. Both are of the same form: "If you take action α, I will take action β, which will cause you to regret your decision α." A **threat**, however, is such that the firm has no rational incentive to carryout action β; the distinguishing aspect of the **commitment** is that, given α has occurred, then it is the second firm's *best* response to choose β. It is in this sense that commitments are credible and threats are not. To stress this fact we use the redundancy "credible commitment" at times.

Irreversibility. On a moment's reflection it is obvious that the state variable must be irreversible, and not *costlessly* changeable at the market stage, if it is to act as a *credible* entry deterrent. For example, suppose that the state variable represents the firm's capital investment. Then the irreversibility occurs in the sense that the capital has zero (alternative use) market value once installed by the firm. (Golden arches at a fast-food restaurant are one possibility.) If the capital stock undergoes physical depreciation with use then this cost is reflected in the variable cost function. In turn, the irreversible investment equals the investment cost of the capital less this depreciation.

If the firm's investments were reversible, its prevailing level could not serve as an initial condition in the market-stage subgame. It is also clear that the degree of irreversibility (cost of revision) of the incumbent's $t = 0$ decision is not an inherent property of that decision, but more generally is a matter of design. For example, assume that an incumbent firm incurs a large sunk cost by investing in long-lived *firm-specific* capital.[9] Its future short-run cost function is then, we further assume, shifted down, making its marginal cost of production lower at high output levels. In this case it is reasonable to assume that such an investment alters the expectations of potential entrants, increasing their appraisal of the incumbent's post-entry output level and thereby reducing the attractiveness of entry. It thus may be (strategically) optimal for the incumbent to "over-invest" relative to the optimal level, given that entry is otherwise impossible, and thereby deter entry.[10] If, however, the incumbent's investment is not in firm-specific assets, but in assets whose market value equals their investment cost, there is little reason for any rival's expectations to be influenced by the then reversible investment level.

The list of firm-specific capital investments which can act as commitments in this way is limited largely by our imagination. Product-specific advertising might work when it forms a substantial stock of information to be distributed over time.[11] Location (when there are significant costs of moving), investments in learning, inventory (when production rates are fixed), labor costs which have a quasi-sunk nature, and certain research and development investments also belong to this list.

10.3 Capacity Expansion with Quantity Competition

We seek the Cournot–Nash equilibrium conditions for the two-stage model, not just that obtaining in the post-entry competition. Attention is more specifically restricted to perfect equilibria, which requires best replies on every possible subgame. If both the firms have κ as common knowledge at $t = 1$, then a perfect equilibrium requires that both firms fashion optimal $t = 1$ decision rules which are best responses for any given κ.[12]

---

[9] Firm specific means that the capital has zero (or low) alternative market value once it is put in place by the firm.

[10] Here, as is usual in the literature, we assume that the incumbent is a single-firm monopolist or cartel. Most real industries, in contrast, seem to have several noncolluding incumbents. In this case effects external to any given firm could lead the incumbent oligopolists to under-invest in capital.

[11] Spence (1977a, b, 1980) and Cubbin (1981), using variants on the Sylos postulate with its neglect of commitment credibility, have developed models of advertising entry deterrence. Baldani and Masson (1981) have constructed a model where the effects of advertising are perfectly durable, fixed costs imply economies of scale in advertising, post-entry behavior is noncooperative, pre-entry expectations are rational, and advertising is used strategically in reaching a perfect equilibrium which is entry deterring. For contrary results see Schmalensee (1983).

[12] The incumbent's choice of capital κ would not have strategic importance if κ were unobservable

Some notation is helpful in filling out the details of the two-stage interaction. Let $z^t = [z_1{}^t, z_2{}^t]$ be the outputs of firms 1 and 2 at each date t. As entry cannot occur until $t = 1$, it is required that $z_2{}^0 = 0$. Each firm must allocate part of its costs to (firm-specific) capital prior to production. We continue to use the incumbent–entrant dichotomy and the asymmetric timing of capital investments: the incumbent firm takes the first move, making its capital decision at the strategic stage; entrants, in contrast, cannot move in any fashion until the final market stage. Moreover, the incumbent's investment in capital is assumed to be irreversible in any part, although it would only complicate matters in a bookkeeping way to permit partial irreversibility.

The asymmetric play means that at the market stage the incumbent will have a cost advantage over the entrant, who must then incur the full cost of producing any given output level. Other things being equal, this advantage leaves the incumbent with a larger equilibrium market share. But, is this advantage sufficient to permit it to deter entry: to be profitable should entry occur while the entrant would not be profitable? As we will shortly see, that depends on certain conditions of demand and cost and the rules of play at the strategic and market stages.

Capital and Costs. Let $\kappa_j{}^t > 0$ indicate the capital decision of firm j at each stage t. The incumbent and entrant use $\kappa_1{}^0 + \kappa_1{}^1$ and $\kappa_2{}^1$ respectively in total capital to produce their $t = 1$ output.[13] (Again, $\kappa_2{}^0 \equiv 0$ as the entrant cannot move at $t = 0$). Since the market-stage capital choices $\kappa_2{}^1$ and $\kappa_1{}^1$ are incidental to the following analysis (with just two stages), it is convenient to hold these decisions fixed, and aside, and use $\kappa \equiv \kappa_1{}^0$ to indicate the single explicit capital decision of the model. It is assumed that all capital is purchased in competitive factor markets at a constant ϕ dollars per unit. Finally, to simplify the discussion we refer to the capital choice of the incumbent, but the reader should more exactly understand that this means the choice of *irreversible* capital.

At the market stage the short-run cost functions $c(z_1, \kappa)$ and $c(z_2)$ obtain for firms 1 and 2 respectively. These functions depend on the firm's output and the previously installed capital and are assumed to be differentiable and to satisfy the following marginal conditions:

$$\frac{\partial c}{\partial z_j}, \frac{\partial^2 c}{\partial z_j{}^2}, \frac{\partial^2 c}{\partial \kappa_j{}^2} > 0$$

$$\frac{\partial c}{\partial \kappa_j}, \frac{\partial^2 c}{\partial \kappa_j \partial z_j} < 0$$

Demand. For each firm j there is the inverse demand function $p_j(z_j, z_k)$ which is differentiable and decreasing in own-quantity: $\partial p_j / \partial z_j < 0$. It is also assumed

---

to the entrant, for in this case the entrant's decision rule could not be based on that prior capital decision. Similarly, if by some special contract the entrant pre-commits (at $t = 0$) to an output level in the market subgame, then its choice would again be independent of κ and the capital choice of the incumbent would again have no strategic role.

[13] The κ are required to be positive, eliminating the possibility of capital reversibility from period to period.

that a finite "choke" price exists where the quantity demanded is zero.

The sequential decision process is summarized in figure 10.2. Unlabeled branches represent (all) other values which can be taken on by the decision indicated at each node. Note that the entrant's decision nodes at the market stage constitute a single information set, which is consistent with Cournot–Nash play at that stage.

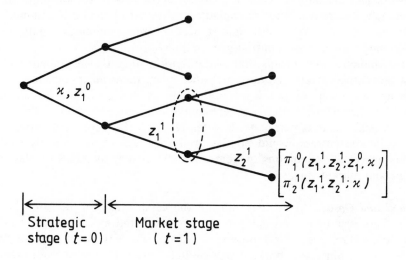

Figure 10.2
Two-stage entry game

Market Subgame. The quantity solution in the market subgame is based on the profits of the incumbent

$$\pi_1{}^1 = p_1{}^1(z^1)z_1{}^1 - c(z_1{}^1, \kappa) \tag{10.4a}$$

and the entrant

$$\pi_2{}^1 = p_2{}^1(z^1)z_2{}^1 - c(z_2{}^1) \tag{10.4b}$$

(Again, superscripts indicate the time period: for example, $z_2{}^1$ is the period 1 output decision of firm 2.) A key aspect of the game is the *asymmetry* in cost functions, which occurs because of the incumbent's prior choice of capital.

Given κ, the best replies in outputs for the market subgame are derived from the usual (static) marginal revenue – marginal cost equality rules

$$p_1{}^1(z^1) + z_1{}^1 \frac{\partial p_1{}^1(z^1)}{\partial z_1{}^1} = \frac{\partial c(z_1{}^1, \kappa)}{\partial z_1{}^1} \tag{10.5a}$$

$$p_2{}^1(z^1) + z_2{}^1 \frac{\partial p_2{}^1(z^1)}{\partial z_2{}^1} = \frac{\partial c(z_2{}^1)}{\partial z_2{}^1} \tag{10.5b}$$

10.3.1 Market Equilibrium

The reaction functions $r_1{}^c(z_2{}^1, \kappa)$ and $r_2{}^c(z_1{}^1)$ are associated with the Cournot–Nash stationarity conditions (10.5). The subgame equilibrium is illustrated by the (unique) intersection of these reaction functions at point C in figure 10.3.[14] Of particular interest here is the fact that the equilibrium output pair $\{z_1^{1c}(\kappa), z_2^{1c}(\kappa)\}$ depends on the incumbent's previously chosen capital κ, which affects its cost schedule and in turn its reaction function. When incumbent and entrant compete at the market stage, the resulting equilibrium point then depends on κ. For the demand and cost conditions given above and the specification of Cournot play with substitute goods, the following properties hold (see chapter 3, section 3.1.7):

C1 z_1^{1c} and z_2^{1c} are continuous and differentiable in κ;
C2 the reaction function r_1^{1c} is increasing in κ;
C3 equilibrium outputs are such that $\partial z_1^{1c}/\partial \kappa > 0$ and $\partial z_2^{1c}/\partial \kappa \leqslant 0$.

Larger values of κ increase the incumbent's market-stage equilibrium output and decrease that of the entrant. For example, if the incumbent (optimally, at $t = 0$) chooses the specific capital level κ^* indicated by figure 10.3, then the entrant's best response is not to enter the industry.

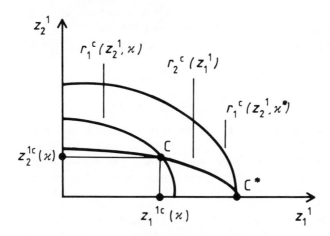

Figure 10.3
Market subgame Cournot equilibria

10.3.2   Strategic Effect

Substituting the equilibrium outputs in the profit function (10.4) gives the incumbent's market-stage (indirect) profits in terms of the state variable κ:

$$\pi_1^{1c}(\kappa) = p_1^{1}(z^{1c}(\kappa))z_1^{1c}(\kappa) - c(z_1^{1c}(\kappa), \kappa) \qquad (10.6)$$

---

[14] Note that the profit of each firm is generally a function of both outputs. When the associated Hessian matrix of these functions (with respect to outputs) is negative definite, a unique Cournot equilibrium exists (sufficiency). This condition obtains in the usual example where the market demand is linear and the marginal cost functions are nondecreasing. Recall chapter 3, section 3.1, and chapter 9, section 9.2. (The negative definiteness is also the stability condition (3.7) for the standard adjustment mechansim.)

For later use note that the marginal value of κ to the incumbent is[15]

$$
d\pi_1^{lc} = \left\{ p_1^{1}(z^{lc}) + z_1^{lc} \frac{\partial p_1^{1}(z^{lc})}{\partial z_1^{1}} - \frac{\partial c(z_1^{lc}, \kappa)}{\partial z_1^{1}} \right\} \frac{\partial z_1^{lc}}{\partial \kappa} \, d\kappa \qquad (10.7)
$$

$$
- \frac{\partial c(z_1^{lc}, \kappa)}{\partial \kappa} \, d\kappa + z_1^{lc} \frac{\partial p_1^{1}(z^{lc})}{\partial z_2^{lc}} \frac{\partial z_2^{lc}}{\partial \kappa} \, d\kappa
$$

The first term on the right-hand side is as expected and, from the stationarity condition (10.5), is zero. The second term at the right-hand side, which measures the *direct effect* of κ on the cost of production, is also as expected. Since increases in κ are assumed to reduce the short-run (variable) cost, this direct-effect term is (sign included) positive. The final term on the right-hand side, involving $dz_2^{lc}/d\kappa$, is new: it measures the marginal value to the incumbent of κ-induced changes in the *entrant's* stage 1 output. It is usual to call this marginal value the **strategic effect** (SE) of κ.[16] This effect is strategic in the sense that it links the $t = 0$ decision of one firm to the equilibrium decision of its rival at the later period $t = 1$. By definition, static games do not allow strategic effects.

What is the sign of the strategic effect? With substitute goods $\partial p_1 / \partial z_2 < 0$. With Cournot play $dz_2^{lc}/d\kappa \leqslant 0$ from result C3 above. Together, these imply that the strategic effect is positive when entry occurs ($z_2^{lc} > 0$) and (10.9) is zero otherwise.

It is helpful to rewrite (10.9) symbolically as

$$
d\pi_1^{lc} = \left(-\frac{\partial c}{\partial \kappa} + \text{SE} \right) d\kappa \qquad (10.7')
$$

From this it is apparent that the choice of investment brings with it two effects. First is the direct effect: it is positive (under our above assumptions) and occurs whether the incumbent anticipates entry or not. The second effect is strategic: it is also positive (again, under the above assumptions), but occurs only when the incumbent anticipates entry.

Strategic Effect and Costs. As the level of κ will be chosen in view of the two effects indicated in (10.7'), the strategic effect will generally have implications for the firm's cost structure. In this regard, note first that to minimize the present value of costs for any given sequence of outputs z_1^{0*} and z_1^{1*}, as the incumbent would if entry were unanticipated or impossible, κ is chosen to satisfy

$$
\min_{\kappa} \left\{ c(z_1^{0*}, \kappa) + \phi\kappa + \rho c(z_1^{1*}, \kappa) \right\}
$$

where ρ is the discount factor between periods. The associated solution condition is

$$
\phi = - \frac{\partial c(z_1^{0*}, \kappa)}{\partial \kappa} - \rho \frac{\partial c(z_1^{1*}, \kappa)}{\partial \kappa} \qquad (10.8a)
$$

In the conventional way the cost of capital ϕ is equal to its present marginal value in reducing production costs.

[15] It is assumed here that demand and cost functions and reaction functions are such that $\pi_1^{lc}(\kappa)$ is a suitably differentiable function of κ.

[16] Dixit (1986) calls this the "indirect effect."

Alternatively, in a two-stage interaction the incumbent foresees the effect that its early decisions can have on later equilibria and then κ is chosen to solve the long-run problem

$$\max_{\kappa} \{p_1^0 z_1^{0*} - c(z_1^{0*}, \kappa) - \phi\kappa + \rho\pi_1^{1*}(\kappa; z_1^{1*})\}$$

The solution condition for κ is now somewhat different:

$$\phi = -\frac{\partial c(z_1^{0*}, \kappa)}{\partial \kappa} - \rho\frac{\partial c(z_1^{1*}, \kappa)}{\partial \kappa} + \rho z_1^{1*}\frac{\partial p_1^1(z_1^{1*})}{\partial z_2^1}\frac{\partial z_2^1}{\partial \kappa} \qquad (10.8b)$$

The first two terms in the right-hand side are as in the static case. The last term on the right-hand side is the strategic effect arising with the two-stage decision process and measures the impact of the early capital decision by firm j on its rival's later output decision. Compare (10.8b) with (10.8a): since the strategic effect is positive and c is decreasing in κ, investment in the two-stage perfect equilibrium is carried beyond the level which would otherwise give the short-run, simultaneous decision, minimum-cost schedule at the market stage.

10.3.3 Strategic Over-investment

At the initial stage of the two-stage interaction the incumbent chooses both capital and output to maximize its profit stream, that is,

$$\max_{\kappa, z_1^0} \{p(z_1^0)z_1^0 - c(z_1^0, \kappa) - \phi\kappa + \rho\pi_1^{1*}(\kappa)\} \qquad (10.9a)$$

is solved. Stationarity conditions for this solution are twofold:

$$\frac{\partial p(z_1^0)z_1^0}{\partial z_1^0} - \frac{\partial c(z_1^0, \kappa)}{\partial z_1^0} = 0 \qquad (10.9b)$$

$$\phi + \frac{\partial c(z_1^0, \kappa)}{\partial \kappa} = \rho\frac{\partial \pi_1^{1*}(\kappa)}{\partial \kappa} \qquad (10.9c)$$

The first of these expressions is the usual static marginal revenue and marginal cost equality. The second expression follows (10.8b) and arises from the two-stage interaction: the $t = 0$ marginal cost of capital is equated with the present value of its future marginal profits. This marginal profit, the reader will recall, is given by the two final terms of (10.7) and (10.8b) and specifically includes the strategic effect.

The presence of this strategic effect in the stage zero solution conditions means two things: (a) with respect to investment in capital, the incumbent will choose a κ greater than that when entry is impossible (or not anticipated); (b) with respect to both stage zero and stage 1 outputs, because κ is greater in the sense of (a) and marginal costs are lower, the incumbent will have a greater output (and lower price) at both stages.[17] In passing, it is of note that these

---

[17] As will be made clear in section 10.6, this over-investment leads to a **limit-pricing** outcome when the pre-entry price is less than the monopoly price which would obtain if entry were not anticipated (see also Milgrom and Roberts, 1982a; Saloner, 1982; Matthews and Mirman, 1982). These results are in contrast with the early theories of limit pricing due to Zeuthen (1930), Kaldor (1935), and Bain (1949), which were developed in essentially static settings. Friedman (1983, section 9.1) develops in detail the inconsistencies and irrational firm behavior which are generally part of these static analyses. His comments also apply to the *ad hoc* dynamic limit pricing models of Gaskins (1971) and Lee (1975).

results are consistent *in sign* with the traditional "excess capital" and "Sylos postulate" behavioral assumptions. However, the over-investment and greater output level need not be of the magnitude which actually deters entry, as these traditional analyses assert, but may only limit the entrant's output and profits. When will deterrence in fact occur? That is our next subject.

E10.2

Over-investment: Quantity Competition with Discrete Capital

A specific example and graphical analysis will help our intuition at this point. To begin, hold aside the $t = 0$ decisions of the incumbent. Let the firms produce a homogeneous good with aggregate output $z = z_1 + z_2$. Suppose further that demand is linear ($p = a - bz$) and the firms' cost functions are linear in part and separable as follows:

$$c_1 = F_1 + \phi\kappa + \omega z_1 \qquad\qquad z_1 \leqslant \kappa \qquad\qquad (10.10a)$$

$$c_1 = F_1 + (\phi + \omega)z_1 \qquad\qquad z_1 > \kappa \qquad\qquad (10.10b)$$

$$c_2 = F_2 + (\phi + \omega)z_2 \qquad\qquad\qquad\qquad (10.10c)$$

where ϕ, $\omega > 0$ are constant units costs of capital and variable factors in output, and F_1, $F_2 > 0$ are fixed components of cost. (Here, κ is specifically measured in *output service units*.) The production technology is fixed proportions and capital is limitational: if the incumbent has installed capital $\bar{\kappa}$ at $t = 0$ and it produces $z_1^1 \leqslant \bar{\kappa}$, then its marginal costs of production are simply ω; for $z_1^1 > \bar{\kappa}$ these marginal costs increase to $\phi + \omega$. The linear demand and cost means that the market-stage Cournot reaction functions are also linear.

Reaction Functions. Figure 10.4 illustrates the range of reactions possible for firm 1 as a function of the relative sizes of κ and the firm's output.[18] Two extreme cases help to establish this range. First is the curve labeled $\bar{r}_1^c$, which applies when equation (10.10b) determines production cost (with marginal cost $\omega + \phi$). The second curve $\underline{r}_1^c$ obtains when $\kappa \geqslant (a - \omega - \phi)/3b$, the cost function is given by (10.10a), and marginal costs are therefore equal to ω alone. For intermediate values of κ the line AED indicates the incumbent's reaction. As the jump in the reaction function occurs at $z_1 = \kappa$, by the choice of κ the incumbent has some discretion in designing the conditions under which it will play the market subgame.

The Cournot reaction function for firm 2 is the ordinary one, and indicated by the r_2^c schedule in the figure. As the entrant has no installed capital at the onset of the market subgame, its marginal costs are constant for all output levels (see (10.10c)) and only one such schedule obtains independent of κ. The

---

[18] In the figure it is assumed that $(a - \omega)/2 > \phi$ to assure that the Cournot–Nash equilibrium exists.

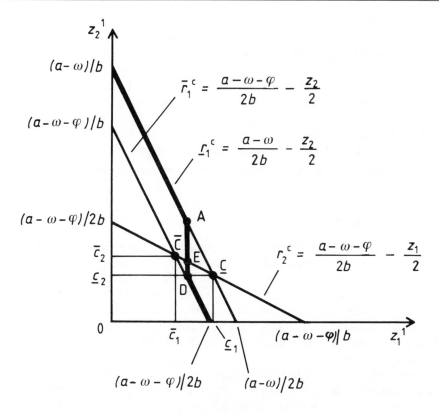

Figure 10.4
Cournot reaction functions: capital given

essential asymmetry between incumbent and entrant is that the former has some ability to choose its reaction function in the market subgame, but the entrant does not.

Market Equilibrium. The market-stage equilibrium is found in the standard way by the intersection of reaction functions. In the usual static case the reaction functions depend simply on exogenous parameters of demand and cost. In the present two-stage case, however, the choice of κ shifts the incumbent's reaction function and alters the equilibrium position of the subgame. As the incumbent chooses κ, its reaction functions ranges from r_1^c to $\bar{r}_1^c$ and the equilibrium (intersection) point moves along r_2^c from $\underline{C} = (\underline{c}_1, \underline{c}_2)$ to $\bar{C} = (\bar{c}_1, \bar{c}_2)$,[19] which are the Cournot–Nash solutions with $\bar{r}_1^c$ and $\underline{r}_1^c$, respectively. The point $\bar{C}$ is a symmetric equilibrium point in the sense that it has both duopolists enter the market-stage game with capital equal to zero, so that equal outputs are produced ($\bar{c}_2 = \bar{c}_1$). In contrast, the solution $\underline{C}$ is asymmetric.

Note that these two end points are independent of the incumbent's actual

---

[19] For the specific situation illustrated in figure 10.4, E is the equilibrium point between $\underline{C}$ and $\bar{C}$.

choice of κ. When the jump in the incumbent firm's reaction function occurs to the left of $\bar{c}_1$, $\bar{C}$ remains as the intersection point of the reaction functions. Similarly, when the jump in the incumbent firm's reaction function occurs to the right of $\underline{c}_1$, $\underline{C}$ remains as the intersection. Thus, even for choices of $\kappa \leqslant \bar{c}_1$, the equilibrium point will be $\bar{C}$ and for choices of $\kappa \geqslant \underline{c}_1$ the equilibrium will be at $\underline{C}$. $\bar{C}\underline{C}$ represents the range of Cournot–Nash equilibria for the market subgame. Note finally that, because optimal choices of κ lie in a definite range with a specific upper bound, the incumbent's choice of an arbitrarily large capital level to deter entry will not generally be an optimal strategy.

10.3.4 Entry Deterrence

Because the incumbent's capital and output decisions are separated in time with the two-stage game, the incumbent does not give consideration to the (sunk) capital cost of its stage zero choice when making its market-stage production decision. The potential entrant, in contrast, does not have a similar time separation: rather, when contemplating entry at the market stage the entrant must simultaneously incur both variable and capital (sunk) costs. Entry is deterred when the revenues anticipated by the entrant in this way do not cover the *sum* of these costs.

An entry deterrence equilibrium requires a $z_2{}^{lc} = 0$ corner solution to the market subgame. Such a solution will occur when the incumbent assigns a positive value to incremental capital at this point. The incumbent finds that increasing its κ, and its output, also increases its profit. Using superscript minus to indicate the (left-hand) derivative as κ increases and, similarly, the superscript plus to indicate the (right-hand) derivative as κ decreases, at $z_2{}^{lc} = 0$ we obtain

$$\left(\frac{\partial \pi_1{}^{lc}}{\partial \kappa}\right)^{-} = -\frac{\partial c(z_1{}^{lc}, \kappa)}{\partial \kappa} + z_1{}^{lc} \frac{\partial p(z^{lc})}{\partial z_2{}^{l}} \left(\frac{dz_2{}^{lc}}{d\kappa}\right)^{-} > -\frac{\partial c(z_1{}^{lc}, \kappa)}{\partial \kappa}$$

$$+ z_1{}^{lc} \frac{\partial p(z^{lc})}{\partial z_2{}^{l}} \left(\frac{dz_2{}^{lc}}{d\kappa}\right)^{+} = -\frac{\partial c(z_1{}^{lc}, \kappa)}{\partial \kappa} = \left(\frac{\partial \pi_1{}^{lc}}{\partial \kappa}\right)^{+} \qquad (10.11)$$

Given that $z_1{}^{lc}$ is positive and demand is negatively sloped, the inequality is based on the fact that the left-hand derivative $(dz_2{}^{lc}/d\kappa)^{-}$ is negative at this corner. In turn, the incumbent's stage zero optimal choice of κ involves a pair of inequalities:

$$-\phi - \frac{\partial c(z_1{}^{0}, \kappa)}{\partial \kappa} + \rho \left(\frac{\partial \pi_1{}^{lc}}{\partial \kappa}\right)^{-} \geqslant 0 \qquad (10.12a)$$

$$-\phi - \frac{\partial c(z_1{}^{0}, \kappa)}{\partial \kappa} + \rho \left(\frac{\partial \pi_1{}^{lc}}{\partial \kappa}\right)^{+} \leqslant 0 \qquad (10.12b)$$

When (10.12b) holds as a strict equality there is an entry deterrence equilibrium. Increases in κ beyond the level that would occur if entry were impossible (or unanticipated) deter the entrant from market-stage participation.

E10.3

Entry Deterrence with Quantity Competition

A numerical example illustrates the strategic use of capital to limit the entrant's output at the final market stage and suggests conditions under which strategic entry deterrence might occur. For simplicity, a linear (time-invariant) demand is assumed:

$$z_1 = 2 - 2p_1 + p_2 \tag{10.13a}$$

$$z_2 = 2 - 2p_2 + p_1 \tag{10.13b}$$

with associated inverse demands

$$p_1 = 2 - \frac{2z_1}{3} - \frac{z_2}{3} \tag{10.14a}$$

$$p_2 = 2 - \frac{2z_2}{3} - \frac{z_1}{3} \tag{10.14b}$$

The (time-invariant) cost functions admit a cost-decreasing capital variable for the incumbent firm 1:

$$c_1 = (2z_1 - \kappa)z_1 \qquad \text{for } \kappa_1 < 2z_1 \tag{10.15a}$$

$$c_2 = z_2^2 \tag{10.15b}$$

Market Subgame Equilibrium. Using the demand and cost specifications gives the profit functions at the market stage:

$$\pi_1^1(z^1, \kappa) = \left(2 - \frac{2z_1^1}{3} - \frac{z_2^1}{3}\right)z_1^1 - (2z_1^1 - \kappa)z_1^1 \tag{10.16a}$$

$$\pi_2^1(z^1) = \left(2 - \frac{2z_2^1}{3} - \frac{z_1^1}{3}\right)z_2^1 - (z_2^1)^2 \tag{10.16b}$$

In the usual way the Cournot stationarity conditions associated with these profit functions yield reaction functions as follows:

$$r_1^{1c}(z_2^1, \kappa) = \frac{3}{8} - \frac{z_2^1}{16} + \frac{3\kappa}{16} \tag{10.17a}$$

$$r_2^{1c}(z_1^1) = \frac{3}{5} - \frac{z_1^1}{10} \tag{10.17b}$$

Note that these reaction functions are both negatively sloped, with r_1^{1c} having a larger (absolute) constant slope than r_2^{1c}. As a result, there exists a unique and stable equilibrium point given by the intersection of these equations:

$$z_1^{1c}(\kappa) = 0.34 + 0.188\kappa \tag{10.18a}$$

$$z_2^{1c}(\kappa) = 0.566 - 0.018\kappa \tag{10.18b}$$

Substituting these output functions in (10.14a) gives the equilibrium price functions

$$p_1^{1c}(\kappa) = 1.59 - 0.119\kappa \tag{10.19a}$$

$$p_2^{1c}(\kappa) = 1.51 - 0.052\kappa \tag{10.19b}$$

It is of note that the solution equations (10.17) and (10.18) are consistent with the general principles that (a) r_1^c shifts out with greater κ (r_2^c remaining constant) and (b) the resulting equilibrium has z_1^{lc} increasing in κ and, conversely, z_2^{lc} decreasing in κ.

Substituting from (10.18) into the profit functions for firm 1 and simplifying gives the "indirect" profits

$$\pi_1^{lc}(\kappa) = p_1^{lc} z_1^{lc}(\kappa) - \{2z_1^{lc}(\kappa) - \kappa\} z_1^{lc}(\kappa) \tag{10.20}$$

$$= 0.35 + 0.35\kappa + 0.1\kappa^2$$

From this the marginal profitability of capital is calculated as

$$\frac{\partial \pi_1^{lc}}{\partial \kappa} = 0.35 + 0.2\kappa \tag{10.21}$$

which is positive and increasing in κ.

Perfect Two-stage Equilibrium. At stage zero the incumbent solves the present value of maximization problem given by (10.9). Here the present value of firm 1's profits have the specific form

$$\pi_1^0(z_1^0, \kappa) = p_1^0 z_1^0 - (2z_1^0 - \kappa)z_1^0 - \phi\kappa + \rho\pi_1^{lc}(\kappa)$$

$$= \left(2 - \frac{2z_1^0}{3}\right)z_1^0 - (2z_1^0 - \kappa)z_1^0 - \kappa$$

$$+ (0.35 + 0.35\kappa + 0.1\kappa^2) \tag{10.22}$$

where $\phi = \rho = 1$ is chosen for simplicity. The associated stationarity conditions are

$$\frac{\partial \pi_1^0}{\partial z_1^0} = 2 - \frac{4z_1^0}{3} - (4z_1^0 - \kappa) = 0 \tag{10.23a}$$

$$\frac{\partial \pi_1^0}{\partial \kappa} = z_1^0 - 1 + 0.35 + 0.2\kappa = 0 \tag{10.23b}$$

These solve for the optimal capital $\kappa = 0.71$ and the optimal period zero output $z_1^0 = 0.51$. In turn, this level of κ determines exactly the Cournot equilibrium point in the $t = 1$ market-stage play: $z_1^{lc} = 0.47$ and $z_2^{lc} = 0.55$ ($p_1^{lc} = 1.51$, $p_2^{lc} = 1.47$).

A Static Game. Suppose, alternatively, that the incumbent firm does not anticipate entry at $t = 1$. In this nonstrategic case it would simultaneously choose κ, z_1^0, and z_1^1 (for later implementation) to maximize

$$\pi_1^0(z, \kappa) = p_1^0 z_1^0 - (2z_1^0 - \kappa)z_1^0 - \kappa + p_1^1 z_1^1 - (2z_1^1 - \kappa)z_1^1 \tag{10.24}$$

(again, with $\phi = \rho = 1$). The stationarity conditions of this problem are

$$\frac{\partial \pi_1^0}{\partial z_1^0} = 2 - \frac{4z_1^0}{3} - 4z_1^0 + \kappa = 0 \tag{10.25a}$$

$$\frac{\partial \pi_1^0}{\partial z_1^1} = 2 - \frac{4z_1^1}{3} - 4z_1^1 + \kappa = 0 \tag{10.25b}$$

$$\frac{\partial \pi_1^0}{\partial \kappa} = -1 + z_1^0 + z_1^1 = 0 \qquad (10.25c)$$

Because of the zero discount rate ($\rho = 1$), output at both stages is planned to be identical as indicated by (10.25a) and (10.25b). The final equation requires in turn that $z_1^0 = z_1^1 = 0.5$ with accompanying prices $p_1^0 = p_1^1 = 1.67$ and optimal capital level $\kappa = 0.67$. At date zero the incumbent, not anticipating entry, chooses $z_1^0 = 0.5$ and $\kappa = 0.67$ and *expects* to choose $z_1^1 = 0.5$ at the next period. However, firm 2 enters and from (10.18) a Cournot equilibrium results with[20]

$$z_1^{1c}(0.67) = 0.34 + 0.188(0.67) = 0.465 \qquad (10.26a)$$

$$z_2^{1c}(0.67) = 0.566 - 0.018(0.67) = 0.554 \qquad (10.26b)$$

Notice that, when recognizing the threat of entry, the incumbent firm acts strategically to increase its capital level from 0.67 to 0.71. This in turn increases the incumbent's output from 0.465 to 0.47 and reduces the entrant's output from 0.554 to 0.55.

10.3.5. Dynamic Competition

Having set out the nuts and bolts of the two-stage interaction, it is useful to step back somewhat to be sure that it is understood just exactly what kind of model has been developed and specifically how it differs from static analyses. The reader should note the following.

1. The oligopolists are rational; they foresee the present and future implication of their decisions and maximize the present value of profits.
2. The model focuses on two key strategy variables, capital and output. Other, possibly important, variables are held aside and profits as a function of the two strategies are exogenously specified.[21]
3. The entry decision of each firm is endogenous.
4. The analysis is based on the perfect Nash equilibrium concept in the strategy variables. This means that the process of competition among the firms is dynamic: as time and the state of the industry evolves, firms recognize this and act on that information.

10.4 Capacity Expansion with Price Competition

The Cournot two-stage interaction can easily be reformulated to reflect a wide variety of strategies in the market subgame. The most frequently used alternative is Bertrand play. It is worth noting in advance that the interest in this alternative interaction arises from the fact that the Nash-in-price market stage

---

[20] The reader can quickly check that the (following) equilibrium output and price for firm 2 give it positive profits.

[21] Fudenberg and Tirole (1986b) refer to this as the "black-box" property of such models.

generally leads to an *under*-investment of irreversible assets, in contrast with the *over*-investment in the Nash-in-quantity interaction and equilibrium.

10.4.1 Price, or Bertrand, Market Competition

The mechanics of Nash-in-price play at the market stage is a straightforward variation of the Nash-in-quantity model. We use the usual Bertrand situation: the goods can be either substitutes or complements, but on the price plane the reaction functions $R_j{}^b(p_k)$ are upward sloping and intersect just once.[22] Further, let firm 1's reaction function be steeper than that of firm 2 as indicated in figure 10.5. Because of this, there exists a unique stable Nash-in-price equilibrium at the market stage (recall chapter 3, section 3.1.7). We continue to assume that the incumbent has a first-mover advantage by its choice of cost-decreasing investment at $t = 0$, $\partial c(z_1, \kappa)/\partial \kappa < 0$. The market-stage solution depends on that prior choice, and this is indicated by the *equilibrium* prices $p^{1b} = \{p_1{}^{1b}(\kappa), p_2{}^{1b}(\kappa)\}$. For these demand and cost conditions the following facts obtain (see the comparative statics analysis of chapter 3, section 3.1.7, for proof).

B1 $p_1{}^{1b}$ and $p_2{}^{1b}$ are continuous and differentiable in κ;
B2 the reaction function $R_1{}^{1b}(p_2{}^1, \kappa)$ is decreasing in κ;
B3 equilibrium prices are such that $\partial p_1{}^{1b}/\partial \kappa < 0$ and $\partial p_2{}^{1b}/\partial \kappa < 0$.

A positive slope for the reaction functions on the price plane and **B2** implies **B3**.[23]

Figure 10.5 illustrates two different Bertrand equilibria at points B and $\bar{\text{B}}$. The difference between these arises from the different capital levels κ and $\bar{\kappa}$ respectively used by the firm in the two situations (note that $\bar{\kappa} > \kappa$). Following **B2** above, increases in κ "shift in" in $R_1{}^{1b}$. What specific level of capital will be chosen by the firm?

Strategic Effect. Associated with the Bertrand market solution is the indirect profit function for the incumbent

$$\pi_1{}^{1b}(\kappa) = p_1{}^{1b}(\kappa)z_1(p^{1b}(\kappa)) - c(z_1(p^{1b}(\kappa)), \kappa) \tag{10.27}$$

In turn, the marginal value of κ at equilibrium is given by

$$d\pi_1{}^{1b} = \left(z_1{}^1 + p_1{}^{1b}\frac{\partial z_1{}^1}{\partial p_1{}^1} - c_1'\frac{\partial z_1{}^1}{\partial p_1{}^1}\right)\frac{\partial p_1{}^{1b}}{\partial \kappa}\,d\kappa - \frac{\partial c_1}{\partial \kappa}\,d\kappa \tag{10.28}$$

$$+ (p_1{}^{1b} - c_1')\frac{\partial z_1{}^1}{\partial p_2{}^1}\frac{\partial p_2{}^{1b}}{\partial \kappa}\,d\kappa$$

The first term on the right-hand side is the usual incremental revenue–incremental cost equality for static profit maximization when choosing price.

---

[22] The $R_j{}^b$ can be negatively sloped and still produce a unique Nash-in-price equilibrium. In this alternative, the following results will be reversed relative to the standard case.

[23] Because greater κ reduces the equilibrium prices of both goods, it is usual to say that the goods are **strategic complements** (although they remain substitutes in the usual sense).

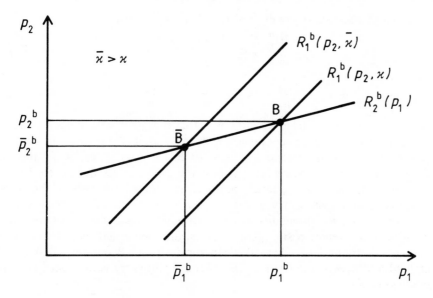

Figure 10.5
Bertrand equilibria

This is zero from the stationarity condition. The second term is also as expected and reflects the *direct effect* of κ on the firm's cost. The final term on the right-hand side is new to the two-stage interaction: this *strategic effect* measures the impact of κ on firm j's profit through its impact on the equilibrium price of firm 2. With substitutes $\partial z_1/\partial p_2 > 0$, and $p_1{}^{1b} - c_1' > 0$ from the stationarity condition. These sign conditions along with B3 mean that increases in κ decrease $p_2{}^{1b}$ so that $\partial p_2{}^{1b}/\partial \kappa < 0$. Taking these conditions together, the result is that the Bertrand strategic effect is *negative*.

As in the Cournot market case it is helpful to write (10.28) symbolically as

$$d\pi_1{}^{1b} = \left(-\frac{\partial c}{\partial \kappa} + SE\right) d\kappa \qquad (10.28')$$

Since it is negative, the strategic effect of κ at equilibrium is to diminish firm 1's profits. The reader should note that this is the opposite of the positive strategic effect (in outputs) with Cournot quantity competition.[24]

10.4.2 Strategic Under-investment

The incumbent's problem at the strategic stage is to maximize the present value of its profit stream:

$$\max_{\kappa, z_1{}^0} \{p_1{}^0 z_1{}^0 - c(z_1{}^0, \kappa) - \phi\kappa + \rho\pi_1{}^{1b}(\kappa)\} \qquad (10.29a)$$

---

[24] Again, the reader is reminded that this is the result with the *standard* Bertrand (strategic complements) assumptions by which the reaction functions are positively sloped on the price plane. When, alternatively, these reaction functions are negatively sloped, the strategic effect will be positive just as in Cournot market play.

The associated stationarity conditions in $z_1{}^0$ and κ are respectively

$$\frac{\partial p_1{}^0 z_1{}^0}{\partial z_1{}^0} - \frac{\partial c(z_1{}^0, \kappa)}{\partial z_1{}^0} = 0 \tag{10.29b}$$

$$\phi + \frac{\partial c(z_1{}^0, \kappa)}{\partial \kappa} = \rho \frac{\partial \pi_1{}^{1b}(\kappa)}{\partial \kappa} = \rho \left(SE - \frac{\partial c}{\partial \kappa} \right) \tag{10.29c}$$

Equation (10.29b) is the usual requirement that marginal revenue equal marginal cost. Equation (10.29c) is concerned with the marginal properties of capital at the optimum: the rightmost equality uses (10.28') and indicates, again, the roles for direct and strategic effects. Recall that the direct effect of κ is to decrease costs. Thus, relative to the (static simultaneous choice) case where the incumbent does not anticipate entry and SE is zero, Bertrand play *with* a negative strategic effect and the possibility of entry causes the incumbent to *under*-invest in κ and to have greater costs, greater prices, and decreased output. This result is illustrated in figure 10.5 where the equilibrium point $\bar{B}$ obtains when entry is anticipated and occurs; alternatively B obtains when entry is *not* anticipated but nonetheless occurs.

Summary. Consider duopolists producing substitute goods. An irreversible investment that lowers the incumbent's marginal cost shifts out its reaction function and causes its rival's output to shrink with Cournot quantity competition at the market stage. With Bertrand price competition, however, irreversible investments which lower the incumbent's marginal cost result in a lower price for the incumbent and its rival (and there are accompanying increases in outputs). An investment that, for example, re-allocates some variable to fixed cost *may* hurt the Bertrand duopolist, since the result is greater output and lower prices for him and his rival.

E10.4

Under-investment with Price Competition

The two-stage interaction with Bertrand market play can be illustrated with the demand and cost conditions used earlier in E10.3. For reference they are repeated here:

$$z_1 = 2 - 2p_1 + p_2$$
$$z_2 = 2 - 2p_2 + p_1$$
$$c_1 = (2z_1 - \kappa)z_1$$
$$c_2 = (z_2)^2$$

The notation is as earlier and it is noted that these functions are stationary (pertain to each period).

The market-stage ($t = 1$) profits of the firms, as a function of prices, are

$$\pi_1{}^1(p^1) = \{p_1{}^1 - 2(2 - 2p_1{}^1 + p_2{}^1) + \kappa\}(2 - 2p_1{}^1 + p_2{}^1) \tag{10.30a}$$

$$\pi_2{}^1(p^1) = \{p_2{}^1 - (2 - 2p_2{}^1 + p_1{}^1)\}(2 - 2p_2{}^1 + p_1{}^1) \tag{10.30b}$$

When the usual calculations are used, the Bertrand market-stage game results in the reaction functions

$$R_1{}^{1b}(p_2{}^1, \kappa) = \frac{18 + 9p_2{}^1 - 2\kappa}{20} \qquad (10.31a)$$

$$R_2{}^{1b}(p_1{}^1) = \frac{10 + 5p_1{}^1}{12} \qquad (10.31b)$$

These functions are positively sloped on the price plane, with $R_1{}^{1b}$ having a greater slope than $R_2{}^{1b}$. In addition, it is of interest that a greater capital level lowers the intercept of $R_1{}^{1b}$, shifting it "in." Solving these reaction functions simultaneously yields the equilibrium prices

$$p_1{}^{1b} = 1.57 - 0.123\kappa \qquad (10.32a)$$

$$p_2{}^{1b} = 1.49 - 0.05\kappa \qquad (10.32b)$$

Because the reaction functions are positively sloped and $R_1{}^{1b}$ is shifted in with greater κ, both equilibrium prices fall with greater κ. Substituting these values in expression (10.31a) for firm 1 profits and simplifying gives

$$\pi_1{}^{1b}(\kappa) = 0.30 + 0.34\kappa + 0.095\kappa^2 \qquad (10.33)$$

Strategic Stage. At the strategic stage the incumbent is alone in the market. It chooses an initial level of output $z_1{}^0$ and makes a commitment to capital to solve the discounted profit problem, where $z_1 = 3 - (3p/2)$ for $z_2 = 0$:

$$\pi_1{}^0 = p_1{}^0(3 - \tfrac{3}{2}p_1{}^0) - \{2(3 - \tfrac{3}{2}p_1{}^0) - \kappa\}(3 - \tfrac{3}{2}p_1{}^0) - \phi\kappa + \rho\pi_1{}^{1b}(\kappa) \quad (10.34)$$

The stationarity conditions follow in the usual way. If we again assume that $\phi = \rho = 1$, these computations give $\kappa = 0.75$, $p_1{}^0 = 1.66$, and $z_1{}^0 = 0.61$. With this level of capital chosen strategically, the post-entry market-stage equilibrium is $p_1{}^{1b} = 1.48$ and $p_2{}^{1b} = 1.45$ from equations (10.28). Finally, the post-entry equilibrium outputs and profits are $z_1{}^{1b} = 0.5$, $\pi_1{}^{1b} = 0.35$, $z_2{}^{1b} = 0.55$, and $\pi_2{}^{1b} = 0.42$.

The reader can show that the incumbent here strategically under-invests relative to the case where entry is impossible or unanticipated.

10.5 Perfectly Contestable Markets

Irreversibility in investments lies at the center of any strategic effect. Our understanding of this concept is improved by looking at the opposite case, where every investment of every firm if perfectly reversible, sunk costs are identically zero, and there is no incentive for strategic choice. This brings us back to the classical case where the industry structure and equilibrium are determined by demand conditions and production technologies, without strategic considerations.

Baumol et al. (1982) explore the perfect reversibility analysis in two steps. For a given industry and all possible output plans they first describe the structure of the industry giving rise to minimum cost. They then describe a market entry and exit process which allows such a structure to result. More formally, their equilibrium industry configuration is reached by several successively nested conditions:

1 An industry structure or configuration is said to be **feasible** if each of the firms active in the industry selects a nonnegligible output that permits its production costs to be covered at market clearing prices.
2 An industry structure or configuration is said to be **sustainable** if it is feasible and provides no profitable opportunities for would-be entrants who conjecture that the incumbents' prices will be fixed for a period long enough for them to produce, at minimum costs, any desired output.
3 Markets are said to be **perfectly contestable** when sustainability is a necessary condition for market equilibrium.

The obvious example of a sustainable market structure is that obtaining in a long-run competitive equilibrium, which makes a perfectly competitive market perfectly contestable.

E10.5

Monopoly as a Sustainable Market Structure

A less obvious example of a perfectly contestable market occurs when all existing and would-be entrants have the same cost schedules and the only intersection of industry demand and any firm's average cost occurs in the range of increasing returns. In this case the single producer selling at the intersection point is a sustainable industry structure, but this natural monopoly clearly does not produce the competitive output level.

The monopoly result can be made somewhat more specific. Let the common cost function be $c(z) = F + cz$ and $c(0) = 0$, where F is the fixed cost and c is the constant marginal cost. Further, let $\pi^m = \max_z \{p(z)z - cz\}$ indicate the net revenues of the monopolist. Suppose that $F < \pi^m$. Then the unique sustainable price p^m solves $(p^m - c)z(p^m) = F$, where $z(p)$ is the demand function. Any price less than p^m gives negative profits and any greater price will be undercut by rivals. For this example, perfect contestability implies: (a) there is a unique producer and therefore technical inefficiency; (b) the producer earns zero profits; (c) average cost pricing obtains.[25]

It is possible and instructive to view contestability from a game-theoretic perspective. For example, in E10.5 the price p^m is the Nash equilibrium outcome of a game in which each would-be producer chooses price first and

---

[25] This case was first considered by Demsetz (1968b). He also notes that average cost pricing is socially efficient *given* that taxes and subsidies are prohibitively costly to implement. For a similar analysis using quantity strategies see Grossman (1981) and recall chapter 3, E3.8.

then, on viewing the announced prices of all rivals, each firm decides whether or not to produce. If the incumbent's price is greater than p^m, a would-be producer enters at some lower price and makes a profit before the incumbent can lower its price in response. After the incumbent responds, the entrant exits. As will be seen below the timing sequence of the model, where entrants can "adjust quantity" faster than the incumbent can adjust price, implies near perfect reversibility of all investments. This timing, termed "hit-and-run tactics," is critical to the perfect contestability result.

10.5.1 Price Contracts and the Contract Period

Our principle interest here is in demonstrating that without irreversible invest-ments and sunk costs only *sustainable* industry structures can deter entry. Some notation is helpful in proceeding to this result. Let there be $j = 1, 2, \ldots, J$ active and inactive firms and let time pass continuously. For simplicity, assume that at some beginning (reference) date $t = 0$ there is a single incumbent firm (a monopolist) $j = 1$. Using capital stock k_1^0, this firm produces the output (flow) level z_1^0 and incurs variable costs $c(z_1^0, k_1^0)$. The remaining inactive firms (potential entrants) are treated symmetrically: they have access to the same technologies as the incumbent and can purchase capital at the same market price ϕ per unit as does the incumbent.

Suppose that would-be entrants offer *price contracts* in competition for the market.[26] Specifically, think of a (representative) entrant $j = 2$ who quotes a price p_2. If that price is not matched or bettered by the incumbent, firm 2 enters into a supply contract with consumers. This contract specifies delivery of the (flow) output z_2 at price p_2 over a fixed **contract period** of length τ. Letting $Z(p)$ be the market demand at price p, it is of course required that $z_2 \leq Z(p)$. The incumbent can deter 2's entry only by matching or bettering price p_2, in which case firm 2 simply remains inactive with zero capital and cost.

10.5.2 Entry, Equilibrium, and Reversibility

When firm 2 enters into a price contract with some set of consumers, it employs a level of capital k_2^0 and concomitantly incurs capital cost ϕk_2^0. It will be useful to parameterize the portion of that capital cost which is sunk and, at a later point, investigate the changes in the market equilibrium which occur as the sunk cost (the parameter) goes to zero. Suppose that at the end of the contract period the entrant sells its capital for a salvage price of ϕ^* per unit, with $0 \leq \phi^* \leq \phi$. ϕ^* is our parameter: if $\phi^* = 0$, for example, all capital costs are sunk, while at the other extreme with $\phi^* = \phi$ the capital investment is perfectly reversible at τ (no sunk costs obtain).[27]

Suppose that firm 2 enters, adopting an optimal level of capital given its variable cost function, the factor costs ϕ and ϕ^*, and the price p_2 it has quoted. Given the rules of play for all market dates after τ, the present value of the then future profit stream to both the entrant and the incumbent can be written as a

---

[26] This follows the assumption of Baumol et al. (1982); see chapter 3, section 3.2.1 for details.

[27] Physical depreciation of the capital stock, when it occurs, is part of the variable cost function.

function of the state variables k_1^0 and k_2^0. Let $v_1^\tau(k_1^0, k_2^0)$ and $v_2^\tau(k_1^0, k_2^0)$ indicate these present value functions at time τ. The specific forms of v_1^τ and v_2^τ will depend in the details of the future rivalry. While that indeterminacy seems problematic, since each firm has the option of selling its capital for salvage at τ, lower bounds on values to be taken on by these functions are known:

$$v_1^\tau(k_1^0, k_2^0) \geqslant \phi^* k_1^0 \tag{10.35a}$$

$$v_2^\tau(k_1^0, k_2^0) \geqslant \phi^* k_2^0 \tag{10.35b}$$

This, as will be made clear below is sufficient information on the post-τ future to reach interesting conclusions about entry at $t = 0$.

In deciding whether or not to enter at $t = 0$, firm 2 looks to the present value of its profit stream

$$v_2^0 = \rho_\tau(p_2 z_2 - c(z_2, k_2^0))\} - \phi k_2^0 + \exp(-r\tau) v_2^\tau \tag{10.36}$$

where r is the instantaneous discount rate and ρ_τ is the present-value annuity factor over the $[0, \tau]$ contract period. The would-be entrant seeks a price-stipulating contract with $p_2 < p_1^0$, a flow of output $z_2 \leqslant Z(p_2)$, and an optimal level of capital k_2^0 which will maximize v_2^0. If this maximum is greater than zero, then firm 2 will in fact enter the industry for at least the initial contract period. Using the lower bound (10.35b), we find that such entry requires

$$v_2^0 \geqslant \rho_\tau\{p_2 z_2 - c(z_2, k_2^0)\} - \frac{\phi - \phi^* \exp(-r\tau)}{\rho_\tau} k_2^0 \tag{10.37}$$

To simplify the notation and at the same time more clearly reveal a key aspect of the above inequality, let

$$\delta \equiv \frac{\phi - \phi^* \exp(-r\tau)}{\rho_\tau} = r\phi + r\left\{\frac{\phi - \phi^* \exp(-r\tau)}{1 - \exp(-r\tau)}\right\} \tag{10.38}$$

From (10.37), δ can be interpreted as the (instantaneous) *implicit rental rate* on a unit of capital. Note that when $\phi = \phi^*$, so that the investment is perfectly reversible, $\delta = r\phi$. For irreversible investments $\phi - \phi^* \geqslant 0$ and $\delta > r\phi$ – the implicit rental rate exceeds that obtained with perfect reversibility. The operative concept is that the rate δ depends positively on the irreversibility of the capital employed.

We now return to firm 2's entry decision. Whatever the manner in which entry is undertaken, the entrant will choose its capital to minimize its total cost. Let this minimized cost be given by

$$c^*(z_2, \delta) \equiv \min_{k_z^0} \{c(z_2, k_2^0) - \delta k_2^0\} \tag{10.39}$$

In turn, the inequality (10.37) bounding the firm's value becomes

$$v_2^0 \geqslant \rho_\tau\{p_2 z_2 - c^*(z_2, \delta)\} \tag{10.40}$$

The term in braces represents the instantaneous profit flow during the contract period; in this term δ, through its effect on c^*, accounts for the salvage value of the capital involved.

The key aspect of this last inequality is the link that it establishes between the would-be entrant's overall profit possibilities and its profit flow in the initial contract period $[0, \tau]$. As a result, a necessary condition for entry to be unprofitable, and therefore not attempted by firm 2, can be written in terms only of that initial period: entry will not occur if

$$p_2 z_2 - c^*(z_2, \delta) \leq 0 \qquad (10.41)$$

for all admissible prices and output. In addition to the implicit rental rate, only prices and outputs of the initial contract period are involved in this entry criterion.

It is critical that the entry criterion is based on the cost c^*, which is a function of δ. The earlier definition of a sustainable industry structure, in contrast, requires a lack of profitable opportunities for entrants based not on c^* and δ, but on the cost function c where full unit costs of capital ϕr are applied. From (10.38) we have already noted that $\delta = r\phi$ when the capital is perfectly reversible ($\phi = \phi^*$). Additionally, note that $\lim_{r \to \infty} \delta = r\phi$; that is, as the contract period becomes arbitrarily long the implicit rental rate per unit also becomes equal to that with full investment cost imputation. Therefore, under either of the two conditions providing for $\delta = r\phi$, the incumbents are shielded from entry only if the prevailing structure of the industry is sustainable. Since entry can be attempted at every instant, in the *absence* of irreversibility entry deterrence requires that the industry structure be sustainable at every instant.

Incumbent Profits. The above results are also helpful in establishing an upper bound on the level of profits that any incumbent firm may sustain. In figure 10.6 the greatest price that an incumbent can set without providing entry is given by p_1^0, where the market demand $Z(p)$ intersects the entrant's average cost $c^*(z_2, \delta)/z_2$. The incumbent's average cost is similarly given by $c(z_1, r\phi)/z_1$ and, since the incumbent can just meet the would-be entrant's prices without provoking entry, the shaded area indicates the maximum sustainable profits.

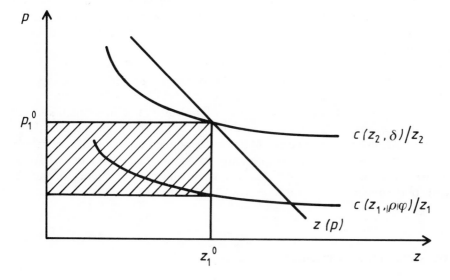

Figure 10.6
Sustainable incumbent profits

Again, this profit is proportional to the difference between δ and $r\phi$, which is given by the second term on the right-hand side of (10.38) and dependent on the reversibility of the capital investment and the length of the contract period.

Suppose that the contract period is nonzero. Then, as the degree to which capital investments are irreversible (measured by the difference $\phi - \phi^*$) goes to zero so does the upper bound on monopoly profits. This means that any small departure from reversibility leads only to similarly small increases in equilibrium prices and monopoly profits.

Perfectly Contestable Markets. An equilibrium in a perfectly contestable market must be a sustainable configuration of firms. Otherwise, it would be profitable for some new firm to enter (without cost) and make profits. This would change the configuration.

Baumol et al. (1982) stress two aspects of the contestable market equilibrium. The first is based on the sustainability property: the industry's total costs must be minimized at the equilibrium output. Neither a change in the number of firms nor changes in the distribution of production among existing firms can lower average cost. The proof of this proceeds by contradiction, roughly as follows. In the equilibrium configuration of firms none earns profits. Thus an alternative configuration with lower costs at the same output and prices would earn positive profits. That is, at least one firm in the alternative configuration would earn positive profits. This firm (or firms) could therefore adopt the same profitable operation within the equilibrium configuration, leaving us with the contradiction that the original equilibrium was not sustainable. The second aspect of the equilibrium is that, if there are two or more firms, every good will be sold where price equals its marginal cost. If price were less than marginal cost, then by producing one less unit (eliminating the marginal nonprofitable unit) profits could be increased, making the candidate equilibrium nonsustainable. If price were greater than marginal cost, then in the obvious way entry would occur. (The presence of a second firm is necessary in this second case to assure that the entrant can sell more than the offending firm without an appreciable drop in price.)

Brock (1983) has questioned the application of contestability models to industry, arguing that it is unlikely that firms can adjust production capacities faster than prices can adjust. In this regard it is usual to refer to the railroad industry, where capacity expansion requires time-consuming investments in land and tracklaying. However, Bailey and Panzar (1981) argue convincingly that in the airline industry new city-pair routes can be opened and closed very rapidly. As will all theories, great care is necessary to assure that the model desiderata are consistent with industry facts. Unfortunately, there is no theory of industry which is both universal and useful.

10.6   Limit-entry Pricing

In the entry situations developed so far in this chapter entrants and incumbents have enjoyed complete information. At each decision stage each firm has been assumed to know its own demand and cost and those of all rivals, both in the present period and in all future periods. Given this prescience, the focus has been on the link between the incumbent's decisions at an early period and the best responses that potential entrants make at subsequent market periods. While the resulting strategic interaction is of interest and importance, it is usual to note that firms do not have the complete information presumed in such analyses. More generally, firms do not precisely know demand and/or cost conditions at any date, and even less is known about future dates. Analyses of entry, it is thus argued, must be fashioned as games of incomplete information.

Some important steps have been made in this direction. One class of these models is concerned with situations in which the incumbent has perfect information but entrants do not. This seems to be a natural case for analysis, for it recognizes that the incumbent's experience counts for something. The information asymmetry may arise from the entrant's lack of fundamental knowledge concerning the incumbent's demand, product characteristics, or cost. While the focus is on the incumbent's cost in this regard, that is a convenience and the crucial fact is that entrants only have imperfect information concerning the incumbent's payoff function. (The strategy sets of both firms are common knowledge.)

As was seen in chapter 9, section 9.7, a key feature of incomplete asymmetrical information arrangements is that the history of market moves can be used by the disadvantaged firm to update information about its rivals. Here, the potential entrants can specifically review prior attempts at entry and the incumbent's reaction to these to extract information about the incumbent's cost type. The incumbent knows this and attempts to use its pricing strategy to deceive the potential entrants. In turn, the entrants know that such deceptions are being played and use that information to condition their entry decisions and the incumbent knows this, and so forth in infinite regress. In such dynamic games the relevant solution concept is the perfect Bayesian equilibrium, as the reader will recall from chapter 9, section 9.6.

Types of Equilibrium. The reader should now recall the specific analysis of entry using the asymmetric incomplete information (signaling) model of chapter 9, section 9.7. There, it was noted that signaling models generally have three categories of equilibria: *pooling* (*nonrevealing*), in which the incumbent's price in anticipation of entry is independent of its cost type so as not to convey information, *separating* (*revealing*), in which the incumbent's price depends on its type, and *semi-separating*, where the incumbent deals with potential entry using a mix of revealing and nonrevealing strategies and thus reveals its type not surely, but only with some probability.[28]

In chapter 9, section 9.7.3, we restricted attention to two market periods and an incumbent which may be of (only) a high- or a low-cost type and developed details of a mixed strategy equilibrium with the following results. If a potential entrant has the prior probability h that the incumbent is low cost, then in

---

[28] In the context of product quality supply, the T-period asymmetric information and perfect Bayesian equilibrium are constructed in chapter 14, section 14.4, and the development over time of pooling, semi-separating, and separating equilibrium phases is demonstrated.

equilibrium entry will be dealt a rivalrous response in a first market with a probability greater than h. This occurs because not only does the low-cost incumbent always react rivalrously, but there is some positive probability that the high-cost incumbent will also respond in that way as part of its attempt at deception. If the high-cost incumbent fails to respond rivalrously in the first market, it reveals its high-cost type and there is entry in the second market. By responding rivalrously, however, the incumbent leaves the entrant in the second period unsure about the incumbent's type and this may forestall that entry.

In solving for the semi-separating equilibrium it was first presumed that the incumbent used mixed strategies and then the entrant's beliefs and optimal strategies were calculated for each of the two incumbent types assuming that the incumbent always acts optimally. A similar method is used here to derive conditions for pooling and separating equilibria.

Notation and Model Details. The pure strategy pooling and separating equilibria can be investigated most directly by dealing with a single entrant and a single market opening at two periods. This simplifies the notation relative to what would be necessary for the chain store situation of chapter 9, section 9.7.3.

There is an incumbent firm whose payoff function is unknown to the entrant (but known to the incumbent itself). The entrant believes with prior probability h that the incumbent is high cost and *accommodating* (a), and with probability $1 - h$ that it is low cost and *predatory* (ϕ). The entrant (e) observes the price set by the monopolist incumbent in the first market period and, using what it learns from that, chooses whether to enter that market in the second market period. Other than this asymmetrical incomplete information about the incumbent's type, all other aspects of the game are common knowledge.

Let π_e indicate the profit function of the entrant and suppose that after entry (if it occurs) the incumbent's type is made known to the entrant. The incumbent is revealed to have either the accommodating payoff function π_a or the predatory function π_ϕ. Let these profit functions be concave in price. If there is entry at period 2, a duopoly equilibrium is reached with payoffs $\{\pi_a(p_2{}^{a*}), \pi_e(p_2{}^{a*})\}$ or $\{\pi_\phi(p_2{}^{\phi*}), \pi_e(p_2{}^{\phi*})\}$, where $p_2{}^a$ and $p_2{}^{\phi*}$ are respectively the equilibrium prices with the accommodating and predatory types. If there is no entry at period 2, then $\pi_e = 0$ and the incumbent sets a monopoly price to earn either $\pi_a(p_2{}^{am})$ or $\pi_\phi(p_2{}^{\phi m})$, depending on its type.

For the entry question to be of interest it is assumed that $\pi_e(p_2{}^{\phi*}) < 0 < \pi_e(p_2{}^{a*})$: if the incumbent is predatory the entrant takes a loss with entry (and thus exits after the one-period experience), but if the incumbent is accommodating then the entrant–duopolist earns positive profits (and remains thereafter). The entrant would have to know the incumbent's type to not enter mistakenly into competition with the predatory incumbent and could enter profitably when the incumbent is accommodating.

To have the following equilibria differ from that which would occur with complete information the accommodating incumbent must undertake some form of deception in choosing its period 1 price. The incentive for the deception must be that "two monopolies are worth more than a monopoly and a duopoly," that is,

$$\pi_a(p_1{}^{am}) + \rho\pi_a(p_2{}^{am}) > \pi_a(p_1{}^{am}) + \rho\pi_a(p_2{}^{a*}) \tag{10.42}$$

As the focus is on limit-entry pricing strategies in the following analyses, it is assumed that this inequality holds.

10.6.1 Pooling (Nonrevealing) Equilibrium

In this case the incumbent's period 1 price is independent of its type and thus is not revealing. As a result, the prior probability h that the potential entrant attaches to the incumbent's being accommodating remains as its posterior probability. If the potential entrant is assumed to be risk neutral, it will enter at period 2 if its expected profits are positive and it will not enter if they are negative. Thus a necessary condition for the deception to work is that the cost and demand conditions, and probability beliefs, are such that[29]

$$E\pi_e^* = h\pi_e(p_2^{a*}) + (1 - h)\pi_e(p_2^{\phi*}) < 0 \qquad (10.43)$$

Necessary Conditions. Given that (10.43) obtains, what limit-entry price is optimal for the incumbent to employ at period 1? While this price cannot depend on the type, the motives of the accommodating and predatory types will establish bounds for the price. To see this, suppose first that the incumbent is predatory. If such an incumbent were to use the period 1 monopoly price $p_1^{\phi m}$, it would at worst be mistaken for an accommodating type and entry would take place. In this case the predatory incumbent's present value would be $\pi_\phi(p_1^{\phi m}) + \rho\pi_\phi(p_2^{\phi m})$. To use a limit price p_1^l and assure entry deterrence, the predatory incumbent takes a reduced period 1 profit in return for the period 2 monopoly gain giving a present value $\pi_\phi(p_1^l) + \rho\pi_\phi(p_2^{\phi m})$. For the nonrevealing limit price p_1^l to be adopted by the predatory type thus requires it to be more profitable:

$$\pi_\phi(p_1^{\phi m}) - \pi_\phi(p_1^l) \leqslant \rho\{\pi_\phi(p_2^{\phi m}) - \pi_\phi(p_2^{\phi*})\} \qquad (10.44a)$$

The present value of the gain to period 2 monopolization must outweigh the value of the loss from limit-entry pricing, otherwise the predatory incumbent will not attempt deception. A parallel argument is made when the incumbent is accommodating, in which case the limit-entry price must satisfy

$$\pi_a(p_1^{am}) - \pi_a(p_1^l) \leqslant \rho\{\pi_a(p_2^{am}) - \pi_a(p_2^{a*})\} \qquad (10.44b)$$

The inequalities (10.44a) and (10.44b) describe a range of prices which are necessary for a pooling equilibrium.[30] From the concavity of the profit function and (10.42), Milgrom and Roberts (1982b) derive this range as a function of cost and demand function parameters, showing that it includes $p_1^{\phi m}$ but not p_1^{am}.

---

[29] Suppose that $E\pi_e^* > 0$ and that entry occurs at period 2. In this circumstance there is no reason for the incumbent to disguise itself in early play. Instead, it would optimally choose its type-dependent monopoly price at the first period and reveal its type. Therefore (10.43) is a necessary condition for a pooling equilibrium.

[30] These are also sufficient conditions. To see this, suppose that the incumbent selects a period 1 price outside the range. This would lead the potential entrant to infer that the incumbent is accommodating, and entry would then occur. Given the entry, the incumbent would be better off playing its period 1 monopoly price. That is, there is no incentive for the incumbent to adopt a price outside the limit-entry range defined by inequalities (10.44).

In the pooling equilibrium both incumbent types choose the same price. While this price is always less than the accommodating monopoly price it may equal the monopoly price of the predatory incumbent. In any case, the pooling equilibrium occurs with the limit-entry price fully deterring entry. Whether or not the limit-entry price is socially preferred to the complete information equilibrium (where entry occurs with the accommodating type only) depends on, among other things, the exact limit price chosen: while $p_1{}^l < p_1{}^{am}$, which increases welfare, the absence of entry with the accommodating type raises prices in the second period.

10.6.2 Separating (Revealing) Equilibrium

In the separating equilibrium the incumbent chooses a price which depends on its type and is thus fully revealing. As a result, necessary conditions for an equilibrium are that the accommodating incumbent does not choose the equilibrium price of the predatory type and, conversely, that the predatory incumbent does not choose the accommodating type's equilibrium price. Given that (a) types are to be revealed by the equilibrium prices, (b) period 2 entry will occur once the accommodating incumbent is revealed, and (c) $p_1{}^{am}$ has the same period 2 profit consequence for the accommodating type as any other revealing type and maximizes period 1 profits, then the accommodating incumbent will choose $p_1{}^{am}$ and earn $\pi_a(p_1{}^{am}) + \rho\pi_a(p_2{}^{a*})$. For the separating equilibrium to occur in the first place, the accommodating incumbent must not have an incentive to adopt the price of the predatory firm $p_1{}^l$. That is, it is necessary that

$$\pi_a(p_1{}^{am}) + \rho\pi_a(p_2{}^{a*}) \geq \pi_a(p_1{}^l) + \rho\pi_a(p_2{}^{am})$$

or, stated in a fashion which weighs period 1 results against period 2 results,

$$\pi_a(p_1{}^{am}) - \pi_a(p_1{}^l) \geq \rho\{\pi_a(p_2{}^{am}) - \pi_a(p_2{}^{a*})\} \qquad (10.45a)$$

In a parallel way, the predatory incumbent's choice of the nonrevealing price $p_1{}^l$ must be such that it prefers the deception to using its monopoly price and (at most) inducing entry:

$$\pi_\phi(p_1{}^{\phi m}) - \pi_\phi(p_1{}^l) \leq \rho\{\pi_\phi(p_2{}^{\phi m}) - \pi_\phi(p_2{}^{\phi*})\} \qquad (10.45b)$$

Given that the accommodating incumbent uses its monopoly price, the inequalities (10.45) jointly define necessary conditions on the predatory type's limit price $p_1{}^l$ for a separating equilibrium.[31]

The inequalities (10.45) define a range on the limit price. A natural question is why does the predatory type not simply use its monopoly price $p_1{}^{\phi m}$ and deter entry to its market? If it were to do so, then the accommodating incumbent would choose not to reveal itself by also using $p_1{}^{\phi m}$. Thus, when a separating equilibrium occurs, the predatory type must choose $p_1{}^l < p_1{}^{\phi m}$ and this establishes an upper bound on the limit-entry price.

---

[31] Following note 30 concerning the pooling equilibrium, these necessary conditions can also be shown to be sufficient by choosing out-of-equilibrium beliefs and noting how these lead the accommodating and predatory incumbent back to equilibrium prices.

Do not misunderstand the predatory incumbent's deception in this case: it does not work. The potential entrant knows the difference between $p_1{}^{am}$ and $p_1{}^1$, learns the type of the incumbent exactly, and enters only when that type is accommodating (just as with complete information). The predatory firm uses the deception $p_1{}^1 < p_1{}^{\phi m}$ to distinguish itself from an accommodating type (which would also use $p_1{}^{\phi m}$ if the predatory type used that price). While this causes a reduction in the period 1 profits of the predatory type, that is offset by the loss that would occur if the predatory type were mistaken for being accommodating and entry induced. The interesting aspect of this deception is that, relative to the complete information case, (a) the period 2 results are identical with separation and complete information, and (b) $p_1{}^1 < p_1{}^{\phi m}$ means that the limit price results in a welfare gain.

10.7 Reputation, Strategic Effects, and Signals

The theoretical literature of industrial economics provides three scenarios of entry deterrence based on the *reputations* which can be created in repetition of an underlying (one-shot) game (chapter 9, section 9.6.1), *multistage strategic interaction* effects (sections 10.2 and 10.3), and asymmetric incomplete information with *signaling* (section 10.5). The underlying and unifying feature of these models is that each is a dynamic game in which what happens at one point in time has implications for what is optimal in the future. Our focus on what may be optimal in the future has been the entry question: in view of prior moves and the prospects for the future calculated from them, will a potential entrant find it optimal to enter? Entry deterrence, or a barrier to entry to use the usual terminology, is not explained in a static one-shot context.

Reputation as an Entry Deterrent. Perhaps the least satisfactory dynamic story of entry deterrence is that built on the reputation for predation created by the incumbent in an infinite repetition of the one-shot entry game. The reader will recall from chapter 9, section 9.6.1, that the equilibrium reputation strategies which deter entry absolutely in the inifinite-horizon repeated-game setting are only one of many such perfect equilibria. Others include the polar case in which entry occurs and is accommodated at every repetition. No aspect of the formal model tells us which of these self-fulfilling equilibria is appropriate in any given situation. Moreover, the reputation equilibrium does not admit mistakes, deviations, or observation noise as that absolutely destroys reputations and deterrence. The incumbent's reputation is created out of nothing at the beginning of play; it is not earned or based on prior judgment. If the incumbent fails to act rivalrously to entry at any repetition, it loses its reputation completely and irrevocably. These aspects of the reputations equilibria do not appear realistic.

Strategic Deterrence in Multistage Games. Entry deterrence is less precariously balanced in the multistage (nonrepeated) games of sections 10.2 and 10.3. There, strategic effects arise naturally in situations where firm-specific assets enhance productivity and firms maximize long-run profits. In these cases the

incumbent takes into consideration the future implications of its current investments, with certain knowledge that the future will evolve optimally. Depending
on the strategy variable, the first mover may over- or under-invest to gain or
give up market share to its rival. In some exceptional circumstances the over- or
under-investment may deter rivals from entering the industry (or exist may be
induced) rather than simply reducing their positive profit opportunities.

Information and Signaling Deterrence. The principal discomfort with the
strategic interaction story of entry deterrence is the complete information
setting. We all know that history matters in industrial economics, not only
because it fixes some clearly observable facts, but also because it reveals, more
or less, previously unknown aspects of rivals and markets. In the limit-entry
pricing models potential entrants take advantage of the information latent in the
incumbent's actions in early periods and incumbents prey on the lack of
information of the would-be rivals and manipulate what new information is
supplied by their behavior. While at first glance the variety of equilibria that can
result in such situations, and their rich implications for entry deterrence, appear
to be a strong basis for a positive theory, this requires careful handling. The
central role of probability beliefs in these models more generally means that it is
unlikely that we will be able to predict which equilibrium is appropriate in a
given industry. The corollary to this is that we will generally be able to fit the
entry characteristics of every industry to some set of beliefs. For example, a
complete information game with a *non*credible threat to deter entry can be
made into a perfect Bayesian equilibrium strategy with some specification of
information completeness. The critical question in such models is who has what
kind of information. As always, this demands much of the economist's art, not
simply his or her science.

Supplementary examples

SE10.1   Strategies and Counterstrategies in Entry Deterrence

Pyatt (1971), Wenders (1971), Spence (1977a), and Dixit (1979, 1980), among
others, have considered the case where the firm-specific investment takes the
form of plant capacity. Easterbrook (1981b) has raised several objections to the
practical importance of this theory. He first notes:

> . . . The strategy works, if it works at all, only for established firms. It
> depends on the assumption that the predator's plant costs are "sunk" while
> the entrant's are yet to be incurred. Only that combination allows the
> predator to ignore its fixed costs and make production decisions based on
> marginal cost alone, for only then is it as cheap to produce at the point
> where marginal cost equals price as it is not to produce at all. A predator
> could not plan to drive out an established rival by building a big plant with
> the ability to produce at low marginal cost, for then the rival's costs are
> sunk and the predator's higher costs are yet to be incurred. The predator
> must then make its production decisions on the basis of total costs, while

its rival can turn the tables and look only to its marginal costs. This restriction on the scope of the theory obviates concern about many potential predatory strategies. And it is a substantial restriction – it means not only that an upstart firm cannot predate against an established rival, but also that a predator cannot hold its monopoly if demand is growing. Each increment of demand can be seen as a new "market," for which the established firm must compete on the same basis as the rival. It means, too, that the monopoly cannot last longer than some fraction of the useful life of the predator's first plant. Once it comes time to rebuild, the predator and the potential entrant stand on the same footing, and whichever firm builds the plant with the lower average cost will claim the market. (Easterbrook, 1981b, p. 291)

A second problem with the strategic capacity selection theory is that entrants can enter into long-term contracts to ensure that the low-marginal-cost predator does not use any excess capacity that it may have. Since the predator's customers are paying a monopoly price, the entrant can offer the customers a more profitable deal in an alternative long-term contract at the entrant's marginal cost. Once the entrant has committed itself to long-term contracts for the entire output of an efficiently sized plant, it is invulnerable to retaliatory price cuts by the predator. In fact, the predator's only rational response is to reduce its production and monopolize the residual portion of demand. In a similar way, this process can be repeated by other entrants, leaving the predator to sell only the output of one efficiently sized plant. In this case the predator would sell at the competitive price (its rivals' marginal cost). A potential predator with foresight would, of course, not build the large inefficient plant to begin with.

Product- and Firm-specific Capital. The role played by the specificity of investments is critical to strategic capacity selection. In this regard, Archibald et al. (1986) stress that it is the *firm* specificity of capital which is important and that *product*-specific capital becomes firm specific only when it is indivisible. A variant of the fixed-proportions homogeneous duopoly case of E10.2 can be used to make their point.

Recall figure 10.4 illustrating the solution to the model in E10.2. The locus of possible market-stage Nash-in-quantity equilibria is indicated by the segment $\bar{C}\underline{C}$ along r_2^c in that figure. The exact equilibrium point depends on firm 1's choice of capital κ at the earlier strategic stage. Suppose that firm 1 chooses capacity $\kappa = \underline{c}_1$, which gives the duopoly equilibrium $\underline{C}$ (recall that, for the fixed-proportions technology outputs, we have scaled so that one unit of capital produces one unit of output). To see that product-specific capital is not generally a basis for credible commitment if it is divisible, consider what happens if firm 2 attempts to purchase some of firm 1's capital.

In our analysis of this possibility we assume that firm 1's capital at the asymmetric equilibrium $\underline{C}$ is less than the total capital that would be employed at the symmetric equilibrium $\bar{C}$, that is $\underline{c}_1 < \bar{c}_1 + \bar{c}_2 = 2\bar{c}_1$. If firm 2 were to purchase $\underline{c}_1 - \bar{c}_1$ units of firm 1's (divisible) capital and $2\bar{c}_1 - \underline{c}_1$ additional units outside, it would impose the equilibrium at the symmetric point $\bar{C}$. Will firm 1 be better off with this arrangement?

Joint profits are maximized at the symmetric point $\bar{C}$ and thus are greater than those at $\underline{C}$. With the purchase arrangement firm 1 receives half the profits at the symmetric solution plus some fraction of firm 2's profit, which is determined by the price that 2 pays for the capital purchased from firm 1. The exact price paid depends on the bilateral bargaining solution, but if firm 1 enters into a contract with 2 to sell some of its capital it must be better off at $\bar{C}$. However that works out, firm 1's "commitment" to capital in an attempt to force the asymmetric solution is unsuccessful since the divisibility means that the decision is not reversible.

SE10.2 Entry Deterrence with Sequential Market Play

In the two-stage interaction with Stackelberg market-stage play some analytical interest (which is probably not of much empirical importance) has been expressed in the case where the firms have fixed-proportions production technologies as in E10.2 and the entrant is the Stackelberg leader.[32] In this case the entrant selects a point on the incumbent's market-stage reaction function to maximize its own profits. While the incumbent forfeits the market-stage prerogatives of the leader, it nonetheless retains the advantage of making the strategic-stage capital commitment and, in this way, fixing the specific reaction function which the entrant must face in the market subgame.

A graphical analysis of this case suggested by Ware (1984) is instructive. The linear reaction functions $\underline{r}_1{}^c$, and $r_2{}^c$ resulting from using the demand and cost functions given in E10.2 are illustrated in figure 10.7. (These are defined in the same way as the reaction functions in figure 10.4.) As in E10.2, the incumbent's overall reaction function depends on its prior strategic choice of capital and again has a jump at the capital level which is adopted. The isoprofit contours of the entrant–leader are also shown. These decrease on moving "outward" from the simple monopoly point $z_2{}^{1m}$ for the entrant. The Stackelberg equilibrium at the market stage depends on the incumbent's choice of κ. There are four cases to consider.

1. Figure 10.7(a) illustrates the usual tangency equilibrium at point $A = (a_1, a_2)$ when κ is "small." The bold line moving first along $\underline{r}_1{}^c$ and then jumping to $\bar{r}_1{}^c$ represents the incumbent's overall (Cournot) reaction function. Point A maximizes the entrant–leader's profits given that function. For all values of κ less than a_1, the jump in 1's reaction function is to the left of a_1, but the entrant's profits are still maximized at the same tangency A.

2. When the incumbent chooses capital in the interval $a_1 < \kappa < \bar{c}_1$, the profit maximum for the entrant–leader will not occur at a tangency point, but instead at the kink illustrated by point B in figure 10.7(b).

[32] See Salop's (1978) argument for the entrant quantity leadership role. Dixit (1980) also considers this case.

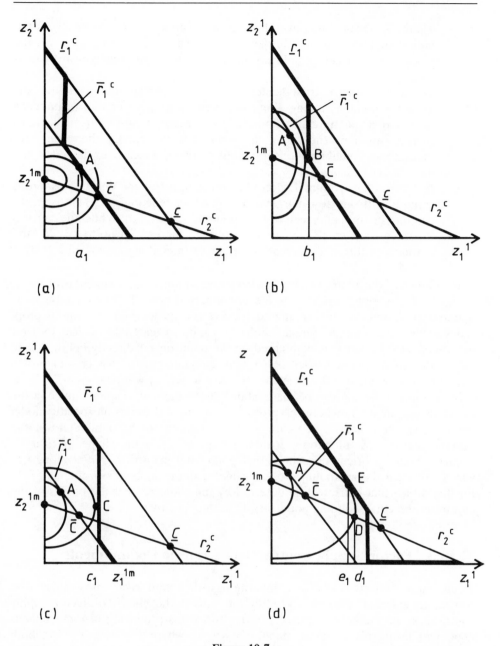

Figure 10.7

Stackelberg equilibria: (a) tangency equilibrium $(0 \leqslant \kappa \leqslant a_1)$; (b) corner equilibrium $(a_1 < \kappa < \bar{c}_1)$; (c) tangency equilibrium $(\bar{c}_1 < \kappa \leqslant d_1)$; (d) tangency equilibrium $(\kappa < d_1)$

There the incumbent's overall reaction function just meets $\bar{r}_1{}^c$.[33] As the initial conditions for the market subgame vary with κ from a_1 to $\bar{c}_1$, the Stackelberg market equilibrium points along the $A\bar{C}$ segment are generated.

3 For $\kappa > \bar{c}_1$ the entrant–leader will first maximize its profits at the tangency point occurring along the vertical segment of the incumbent's overall reaction function. Point $C = (c_1, c_2)$ of figure 10.7(c) illustrates such a situation. Increasing the level of κ beyond $\bar{C}_1$ then generates Stackelberg equilibria along $r_2{}^c$ until point D, which is explained in the next case, is reached.

4 In figure 10.7(d) point E occurs at the tangent of the entrant's isoprofit contour with the low-marginal-cost reaction function $\underline{r}_1{}^c$. This isoprofit contour in turn intersects $r_2{}^c$ at point $D = (d_1, d_2)$. While the vertical tangency provides the maximum profits to the entrant up to $\kappa = d_1$, the entrant's profits will be greater at point D than along $r_2{}^c$ for all $\kappa > d_1$.

In summary, the market-stage Stackelberg equilibria (as a function of κ) lie along the line segment $A\bar{C}D$ plus the disconnected point E. Fortunately, some of these equilibria can be eliminated by giving consideration to general properties of the incumbent's strategic choice of capital. Clearly, from firm 1's view the disconnected point E is dominated by the point on $r_2{}^c$ directly below it, and so $\kappa \leq d_1$ will always be chosen. Also, firm 1 unambiguously has greater profits at $\bar{C}$ than at any point in the segment $A\bar{C}$, and so $\kappa \geq \bar{c}_1$ will be chosen.

No a priori statement can be made about the incumbent's capital choice in the remaining segment $\bar{C}D$ where the profit-maximizing κ depends on specific model parameters. For example, in figure 10.7(c) variations in the parameters of the demand and/or cost function can alter the point $z_1{}^{1m}$, the shape of firm 1's isoprofit contours originating about that point, and in turn the point along $\bar{C}D$ which will yield the maximum present value of the incumbent's profits at $t = 0$. Finally, notice that entry will be deterred by the choice of κ if the profits of the entrant at the corresponding point on $\bar{C}D$ are nonpositive.

SE10.3 Factor Supply Contracts as Strategic Commitments

Firms can act strategically in competition with extant rivals as well as with respect to entrants. Maksimovic (1984) has used the choice of factor supply contracts in an example of this. Consider two firms producing a homogeneous good and facing the linear demand $p = a - z$, where $z = z_1 + z_2$. Let both firms produce with the same constant marginal cost c. The profit of each firm j is then

$$\pi_j = (a - z)z_j - cz_j \tag{10.46}$$

The usual calculations yield the Cournot–Nash reaction functions

---

[33] Recall from E10.2 that $\bar{C} = (\bar{c}_1, \bar{c}_2)$ is the Cournot equilibrium point when the high marginal cost function $\bar{r}_1{}^c$ is applicable.

$$r_j{}^c(z_k) = \frac{a - c - z_k}{2} \tag{10.47}$$

which are identical because of the symmetry of the firms in demand, cost, and rules of play. Figure 10.8 illustrates the Cournot–Nash solution at point C where

$$z_j{}^c = \frac{a - c}{3} \tag{10.48}$$

for both firms. Substituting these outputs in (10.46) gives the equilibrium profits $\pi_j{}^c = (a - c)^2/9$. Level contours of profits, as combinations of z_1 and z_2, are also indicated in the figure. (For later use, note in the figure the direction in which the profits for the firms increase and that profits are at a maximum for each firm when each produces the monopoly level and its rival's production is zero.)

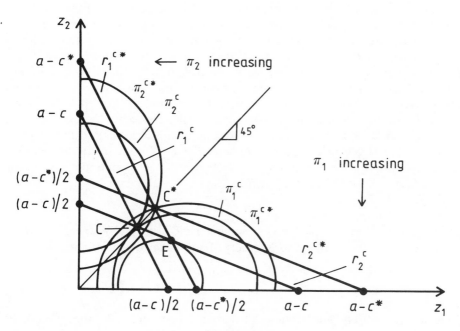

Figure 10.8
Strategic and nonstrategic variable cost

The Ploy. Suppose, for the moment, that firm 2 does not know firm 1's cost. That is, the game is of asymmetric incomplete information (recall chapter 9, section 9.7.3). Firm 1 sees an opportunity in this and boasts that it has (constant) marginal costs of $c^* < c$. Suppose further, and also for the moment, that firm 2 believes 1's boast and, so that it does not reveal its true cost conditions, firm 1 acts as though c^* were its marginal cost. Following (10.47) the reaction function of firm 1 then becomes

$$r_1{}^{c*} = \frac{a - c^* - z_2}{2} \tag{10.49}$$

while that of firm 2 is unaltered. Assume that $c^* < c$; this shifts the reaction of firm 1 "up" as shown in figure 10.8. Under these conditions, the new Cournot–Nash equilibrium is at E with outputs $(z_1{}^c, z_2{}^c)$. The lack of exact information on costs, firm 1's boast of cost c^*, firm 2's belief of this boast, and firm 1's actions consistent with the charade produces value for firm 1: it now has profits $\pi_1{}^e > \pi_1{}^c$ as indicated. Firm 2, however, is worse off with $\pi_2{}^e < \pi_2{}^c$.

When the true unit cost of firm 1 is common knowledge, E cannot be a perfect equilibrium. In this case $r_1{}^c$ is not credible as firm 1's best response, for it implies a lower cost than 1 actually possesses and that is (assumed to be) known.

Credibility. In a game of complete information reaction $r_1{}^c$ will be credible if firm 1 can in fact lower its marginal cost (irreversibly) to a level which makes $(z_1{}^c, z_2{}^c)$ a point on the reaction function. This suggests that firm 1 actually transforms some of its variable cost to a fixed cost. Suppose, for example, that firm 1 approaches its factor supplier with a two-part payment contract offering to pay a fixed fee F (irrevocably, in advance) and per unit factor costs of c^* per unit. (Here we assume that there is only one composite factor of production and units are scaled such that its marginal physical product is unity.) If the factor supplier has the same common knowledge as firm 1 and has the same computational skills, then the factor supplier will foresee the industry equilibrium at E and be indifferent between charging firm 1 according to the two-part scheme or the single price c provided that $F + c^* z_1{}^c = c z_1{}^c$. If the two-part scheme is used, $r_1{}^c$ becomes credible, E becomes the equilibrium point, and firm 1 is better off at the expense of firm 2.

Firm 2 Reacts. Firm 2 will surely not be passive in this. Rather, we would expect that both firms will act strategically. To consider this possibility, let

$$c_1^* = \alpha_1 c$$

$$c_2^* = \alpha_2 c$$

where α_1, $\alpha_2 > 0$ are the fractions of marginal cost chosen by the firms to be variable in their input supply contracts. Now think of each firm j as choosing α_j in a Nash-in-α game to maximize

$$\pi_j = (a - z^c) z_j{}^c - \alpha_j c z_j{}^c \tag{10.50}$$

where the outputs z^c are to be chosen subsequently in a Cournot–Nash market game. From (10.49) it is known that the market equilibrium output is a function of marginal cost and therefore the (symmetric) strategic problem for each firm is

$$\max_{\alpha_j} \left\{ \left(a - 2 \frac{a - \alpha_j c}{3} \right) \frac{a - \alpha_j c}{3} - \alpha_j c \frac{a - \alpha_j c}{3} \right\} \tag{10.51}$$

The usual stationarity gives $\alpha_j = a/2c$. Thus both firms choose $\alpha_j c = a/2$ as variable cost. Using (10.49) again, we obtain the market solution

$$z_j{}^{c*} = \frac{a - a/2}{2} - \frac{z_k{}^{c*}}{2} \tag{10.52}$$

or $z_j{}^{*c} = a/6$, which compares with $z_j{}^c = (a - c)/3$ from (10.48) in the non-strategic case.

The market Nash equilibrium for the strategic case is illustrated as point C^* in figure 10.8. Note from the profit level contours that nonstrategic behavior is dominant and we might at first expect the firms to jointly agree not to pursue such behavior.[34] The problem is that there are gains to be made by cheating on this agreement. That choice lies in a prisoners' dilemma game, and its resolution requires additional considerations.

SE10.4   Exit: Signaling as a Strategic Advantage

The strategic concept that firms take actions at one stage to influence their rivals' play in a subsequent game applies equally well to industries in which one firm attempts to induce others to exit. This example focuses on an exit game in which asymmetric information plays a pivotal role. This quantity-setting model has the same analytical structure as the limit-entry pricing game of entry deterrence discussed in section 10.6 (for similar exit models see Saloner, 1987, and Gal-Or, 1987).

Information Structure. Consider homogeneous-good duopolists. Looking forward to monopoly profits, firm 1 would like to force firm 2 to exit the industry. The advantage that 1 has in this regard is that its costs of production are known only imperfectly by its rival firm 2. To deal with the simplest case, assume that 1's costs can be of just two levels (and that this is known by firm 2) and firm 2 has the prior probability $1 - h$ that firm 1's (constant) marginal costs are high and it is accommodating (c_{a1}) and probability h that they are low and it is predatory ($c_{\phi1}$). All other facts about the industry and firm rivalry are common knowledge, including the probability h.

Ploys and Signals. Consider a noncooperative game with two market periods. In both periods the firms play Cournot strategies which result in equilibrium profits $\pi_j{}^c(c_j, c_k)$. Either firm, and especially firm 2, can exit at the end of either period. Suppose that $\pi_2{}^c(c_{\phi1}, c_2) < 0 < \pi_2{}^c(c_{a1}, c_2)$: in this case firm 2 exits if it knows (with certainty) that firm 1 is predatory; otherwise it prefers to remain.[35] Firm 1, knowing this situation for firm 2, has an incentive to *signal*

---

[34] Restricting attention to $\alpha_j < 1$ (and $F > 0$), it is required that the parameters satisfy $a/2 < c$. In this case $z_j{}^c > z_j{}^{c*}$ and a comparison of strategic and nonstrategic profits shows $\pi_j{}^c > \pi_j{}^{c*}$: the strategic behavior results in smaller profits and increased output (see again figure 10.8). The reader can quickly show that, conversely, strategic behavior with $f < 0$ and $\alpha_j > 1$ (when $a/2 > c$) would reduce outputs and increase profits.

[35] In a model that runs parallel to this, Roberts (1986) assumed that the incomplete information of firm 2 is about the level of demand (and not firm 1's cost). Specifically, firm 2 observes only the industry price with firm 1's output *not* common knowledge. As a result, firm 2 is uncertain whether the demand level is "high" or "low" and tries to deduce this from the market price. A low price signals firm 2 that the demand level is also low and induces exit.

that it is predatory (even if it is not) for this would induce exit and leave it with monopoly profits $\pi_1{}^m$ which are greater than its duopoly profits. Firm 1 signals that it is predatory by producing the output level that a predatory firm would. When firm 1 is accommodating and it signals that it is predatory we say that it is using a *ploy*.

The key aspects of exit-inducing behavior can be brought to focus most easily with a linear demand $p = a - z$, where $z = z_1 + z_2$ and output units are scaled so that the slope coefficient is unity. In a game with incomplete information firm 2, using Cournot conjectures, would calculate its best response to a known level of output for firm 1 consistent with 1's known marginal cost. However, in the present game firm 1's marginal cost is known only probabilistically and this in turn leaves firm 2 with only probabilistic information about 1's output level: it may be z_{a1} with probability $1 - h$ or $z_{\phi 1}$ with probability h. The accommodating output z_{a1} derives from firm 1's Cournot best response to the problem to maximize $\{a - (z_1 + z_2) - c_{a1}\}z_1$ which, with z_2 fixed, yields

$$z_{a1} = \frac{a - z_2 - c_{a1}}{2} \tag{10.53}$$

and similarly for the predatory firm 1. Firm 2 operates rather differently. Given its incomplete information, suppose that it maximizes *expected* profits:

$$\bar{\pi}_2 = h\{a - (z_{\phi 1} + z_2) - c_2\}z_2 + (1 - h)\{a - (z_{a1} + z_2) - c_2\}z_2 \tag{10.54}$$

The Cournot reaction function associated with (10.51) is easily derived: $z_2 = \{a - c_2 - (hz_{\phi 1} + (1 - h)z_{a1})\}/2$, which depends on the *expected* output of firm 1.[36]

Separating Equilibrium. For firm 2 to remain in the market and a two-good separating equilibrium to occur, firm 1's predatory output $z_{\phi 1}$ must be large enough so that, if it were accommodating, it would be better off revealing itself (producing the accommodating output) rather than using a predatory ploy (and causing firm 2 to exit). This would require cost and demand parameter values such that

$$\{a - (z_{a1} + z_2) - c_{a1}\}z_{a1} + \rho\pi_1{}^c(z_{a1}, z_2)$$
$$> \{a - (z_{\phi 1} + z_2) - c_{a1}\}z_{\phi 1} + \rho\pi_1{}^m(z_{a1}) \tag{10.55}$$

where ρ is the discount factor between periods and $\pi_1{}^m(z_{a1})$ is the second-period monopoly profit for the accommodating firm 1. When the inequality does not hold, firm 2 exits and there is a pooling one-good equilibrium.

When firm 2 decides to remain in the market, the accommodating firm 1 chooses its output to satisfy (10.53) subject to (10.55). Similarly, the predatory firm 1 would choose $z_{\phi 1} = (a - z_2 - c_{\phi 1})/2$ subject also to (10.55). When (10.55) holds as an equality, (10.51), (10.53) and (10.55) are solved simultaneously to produce the two-firm equilibrium. The solution $z_{a1}{}^c$ will generally be greater than that in the static one-period game since the predatory firm 1 will

---

[36] If the firms were to move sequentially with the incumbent being the first mover, firm 2 could use the information in firm 1's output choice to revise its prior probability. In this case, the posterior updated probability $h(z_1)$ would appear in (10.51) and the following arguments.

produce somewhat more (compared with the static game) to signal its type. This implies, in turn, that firm 2 will generally produce less for given z_{a1} – since, from (10.51), z_2 is decreasing in z_{a1}. Moreover, as (10.53) informs us that z_{a1} is increasing in z_2, this also implies that the accommodating firm 1 will produce rather more than in the static game.

While they are both signaling models, the separating equilibrium in the present model produces results different from those in the limit-entry pricing model of section 10.5. There, the accommodating firm adopts its monopoly price and leaves the predatory firm to distinguish itself by using a limit price below its monopoly price. In the present exit model both types of firm 1 produce above their monopoly output levels in the first period, while the rival firm 2 produces a smaller quantity. Firm 2, fearful that it faces a predatory firm 1 that would expand output to signal that fact, does away with the need for such signaling by reducing its own output.

SE10.5   Exit from Natural Monopoly

Consider a discrete-time repeated-game version of E9.4 (chapter 9) in which the two identical firms j and k, again with decreasing unit cost, compete in an industry in which the demand only permits one firm to be profitable. When both firms remain in the industry each earns negative profits $-\pi^*$ per period. We assume here that implicit collusion is impossible. When one firm exits, to earn zero profits thereafter, the remaining firm earns monopoly profits $\pi^m > 0$.[37]

Riley (1980) and Milgrom and Weber (1982) have shown that there is a continuum of Nash equilibrium strategies for this game.[38] One obvious equilibrium strategy combination is for firm j to exit immediately and for firm k to remain as the monopolist. Because the firms are identical, these exit and monopolist roles may also be reversed. These pure strategies have significantly different implications for the firms involved and thus do not seem to be reasonable characterizations of the exit problem. The mixed extension of the game, in contrast, produces a symmetric solution which seems to be much more descriptive of what occurs in real industries.

Mixed Strategy Equilibrium. Let h be the constant (over time) probability that either firm (we will use j) chooses to exit given that its rival still remains. Let $Ev_j{}^r$ be the expected discounted present value of j's profits if it remains; conversely, $Ev_j{}^e = 0$ is the value of immediate exit. At any date the present value of these two pure strategies will be equal in the mixed strategy equilibrium. With discount factor ρ the equilibrium condition is therefore

$$Ev_j{}^r = h\pi^m + (1 - h)(-\pi^* + \rho Ev_j{}^r) = 0 = Ev_j{}^e \qquad (10.56)$$

which solves for

---

[37] If implicit collusion were reached in this game the firms would both earn positive period profits when remaining and there would be little incentive for exit. Such a situation would be socially suboptimal as the decreasing cost schedules imply that any level of industry output is produced at lower cost by just one firm.

[38] This is essentially a game form called "war of attrition."

$$h = \frac{\pi^*}{p^* + \pi^m} \qquad (10.57)$$

as the mixing probability (recall that $\pi^* > 0$).

The two firms remain in the industry for a random number of periods.[39] Each firm exits the industry with probability depending directly on its losses from remaining in the duopoly and inversely on the level of profits obtainable if it survives as the monopolist. The mixing probability is such that the gain from staying any longer just dissipates the gain from being the surviving monopolist.

Ghemawat and Nalebuff (1985) have considered an asymmetrical variant of the above model, arguing that large firms are more inefficient, have large π^* and smaller π^m, and are therefore more likely to exit sooner. Whinston (1986) contests the large-firm inefficiency assertion, as does the empirical evidence of Demsetz (1973b).

---

[39] The socially optimal solution is of course for only one firm to produce a given level of output. Thus a smaller h from a greater π^* and/or a smaller π^m are (other things being equal) socially preferred.

11 Symmetry in Competition: Research and Development

Analyses of entry and industry equilibria in general, and the models of chapter 10 in particular, are based on an asymmetrical rivalry in which an incumbent first mover commits itself to an investment policy to narrow the range of replies open to would-be entrants.[1] The market advantage which is created by the investment is typically one of lower variable cost in subsequent play, where the entrant must incur the full costs of production on entry. Not only does this cost asymmetry generally lead the incumbent to a greater equilibrium share of the post-entry market, but under certain conditions it provides an advantage sufficient to forestall entry.

The choice of capacity is the usual specific example of strategic behavior and illustrates well the nature of the first-mover advantage. It also illustrates the arguments of those who find this asymmetry unduly restrictive in a wide variety of applied work. This second line of reasoning goes somewhat as follows. If capacity is an irreversible investment at the moment production decisions are made, as it must be if it is to have any strategic role, then the entrant's capacity should be equally sunk and should also be committed before production. The market-stage equilibrium should not therefore be developed with the entrant incurring both variable and sunk cost and the incumbent only incurring variable costs. This implies too great an asymmetry in favor of the incumbent and produces obviously unbalanced results. It seems more realistic with respect to many situations that the market-stage equilibrium should result from both firms incurring only variable costs conditional on their sunk capacity.

On this rationale, in the analysis to follow we consider several two-stage games in which all competitors make investment decisions at the early strategic stage. We ask whether this added equality in play in the market subgame then means that strategic behavior is moot.

---

[1] It is worth emphasizing here that some types of games give the follower, not the first mover, the advantage (see Baldwin and Childs, 1969). The most interesting of these cases occur when first movement creates a nonexclusionary public good for subsequent movers. Think, for example, of the consumer-good innovator who must incur the information costs associated with developing the demand for a new product while follow-on imitators need only establish an identity as a seller. A particular instance of this is described by Krouse (1984).

Allowing the firms to choose capital simultaneously at the strategic stage leads to an analysis most appropriately applied to industries where firms stand on equal footing with respect to product innovation or new increments in demand. For example, in industries where technical advances are widespread or existing markets are growing, each new market increment provides more or less symmetrical opportunities for firms. To remind us of this situation (compared with those modeled in chapter 10) we focus here on the firm-specific investments in research and development (R&D). This also provides us with the opportunity to develop some insight into an important area of industrial economics.

Two-Stage Interaction. For the most part in this chapter we rely on the simplicity of a duopoly. The firms make their second-stage market decisions taking as given their prior commitment to R&D investments. In section 11.1 the market-stage subgame is assumed to be Nash-in-output and the equilibrium is first described as a pair of best-response rules where each firm's output is a function of the R&D previously undertaken. In the usual way these best-response rules define an indirect profit function for each firm in terms of R&D capital. These, in turn, are the payoff functions at the initial (strategic) stage where the firms play a Nash-in-R&D game. The resulting equilibrium capital levels, through the use of the best-response rules, determine the perfect equilibrium outputs at the market stage. This Nash-in-R&D – Nash-in-output interaction will be indicated by $\Gamma(\kappa, z)$. In section 11.2 the interaction is revised to have Bertrand price competition at the market stage while the strategic play remains Nash-in-R&D. This capital–price interaction is indicated by $\Gamma(\kappa, p)$. The chapter concludes with an analysis of incentives and methods for firms to license new technologies.

11.1   Research and Development with Quantity Competition

Again, the interaction has two stages: the first, **strategic**, play of the game is Nash-in-R&D; the second, **market**, play is Nash-in-output.

Information and Decisions. Unless noted otherwise, the usual conditions are common knowledge: each firm knows the market demand schedule, the cost function, and the rules of play at both stages. As to the specific decisions made by the firms, recall that in chapter 10 markets opened at both periods, so that the incumbent first mover made both output and capital investment decisions in the $t = 0$ initial period. In this chapter it is alternatively assumed that output markets open only at the second date $t = 1$. This simplification does not materially affect the results, and it does permit the two-stage interaction and an alternative single-stage (static) formulation of the problem to be compared more directly.

Demand. The output of the firms j, $k = 1$, 2 with $j \neq k$ can be heterogeneous; it is only required that the goods be *substitutes* in the sense that increasing the output of good j (measured by z_j) reduces the total and marginal revenue of firm k. That is, if $R_j(z) = p_j(z)z_j$ is firm j's revenue function, it is required that

$$\frac{\partial R_k}{\partial z_j} < 0 \qquad \frac{\partial^2 R_k}{\partial z_k \partial z_j} < 0 \qquad (11.1)$$

Costs. Each firm j's total *long-run* costs of production are given by $c(z_j, \kappa_j) + \phi\kappa_j$, where ϕ is the unit cost of κ. The *short-run* cost function $c(z_j, \kappa_j)$, which applies at the market stage, is determined for each firm j by the output level z_j *and* the previously adopted (and irreversible) R&D investment κ_j.[2] Using subscripts to indicate partial derivatives, let $c(\cdot)$ be suitably differentiable with $c_z \geq 0$, $c_{zz} < 0$, and $c_\kappa < 0$: marginal cost is increasing at a decreasing rate and R&D expenditures are cost reducing. Finally, to assure an interior solution it is required that production involve some R&D capital.

11.1.1 Solution Concept and Equilibrium

Under the assumptions on demand and costs adopted above, there exists a unique Cournot equilibrium in the market subgame. $z_1^c(\kappa)$ and $z_2^c(\kappa)$ are output functions of the installed R&D capital, where the superscript c indicates Cournot solution values. Substituting these in the $\pi_j(z)$, we obtain the associated indirect profit functions $\pi_j^c(\kappa) = \pi_j(z_j^c(\kappa), z_k^c(\kappa))$ and, in turn, the *long-run* profit functions applicable at the strategic stage:

$$\pi_1^0(\kappa) = \pi_1^c(\kappa) - \phi\kappa_1 \qquad (11.2a)$$

$$\pi_2^0(\kappa) = \pi_2^c(\kappa) - \phi\kappa_2 \qquad (11.2b)$$

Each firm j maximizes $\pi_j^0(\kappa)$ in a Nash-in-κ game. The resulting R&D equilibrium values $\kappa^c \equiv (\kappa_1^c, \kappa_2^c)$ simultaneously solve

$$\frac{\partial \pi_j^0}{\partial \kappa_j} = 0 \qquad \text{for each } j \qquad (11.3)$$

The perfect two-stage Nash equilibrium is given by these κ^c investments *and* the associated market-stage outputs $z_j^c(\kappa^c)$ for each j.

Strategic Solution. The equilibrium point of the strategic stage derives from the stationarity of π_j^0 with respect to κ_j:

$$\frac{\partial \pi_j^0}{\partial \kappa_j} = -\phi + \frac{\partial \pi_j^c}{\partial z_j}\frac{\partial z_j^c}{\partial \kappa_j} + \frac{\partial \pi_j^c}{\partial z_k}\frac{\partial z_k^c}{\partial \kappa_j} = 0 \qquad (11.4)$$

which reduces to

$$\frac{\partial \pi_j^c}{\partial z_k}\frac{\partial z_k}{\partial \kappa_j} - \phi = 0 \qquad (11.5)$$

since $\partial \pi_j^c/\partial z_j = 0$ from the stationarity conditions at the market stage.[3] Some rearrangement of this last expression gives

$$\frac{\partial c}{\partial \kappa_j} + \phi = \frac{\partial R_j^c}{\partial z_k^c}\frac{\partial z_k^c}{\partial \kappa_j} > 0 \qquad (11.6)$$

---

[2] That is, the choice of κ_j is equivalent to adopting a specific *short-run* cost function and, in this limited sense, costs are endogenous to the two-stage analysis.

[3] The second-order sufficiency condition is usual: $\partial^2\pi_j^0/\partial\kappa_j^2 < 0$. Following chapter 3, section 3.1.2, the R&D game is stable if $D \equiv (\partial^2\pi_1^0/\partial\kappa_1^2)(\partial^2\pi_2^0/\partial\kappa_2^2) + (\partial^2\pi_1^0/\partial\kappa_1\partial\kappa_2)(\partial^2\pi_2^0/\partial\kappa_2\partial\kappa_1) > 0$.

where the right-hand side is the **strategic effect**. The sign inequality follows from the fact that the goods are substitutes – recall the definition given in (11.1) – and from the comparative statics result developed in chapter 3, section 3.1.7, where increased usage of cost-reducing capital by firm j reduces the Cournot equilibrium output of firm k.

What is the impact of the strategic effect? Note first that, for each j, total costs are $c(z_j{}^c, \kappa_j) + \phi\kappa_j$ and these are minimized with respect to κ_j when $\partial c/\partial \kappa_j + \phi = 0$. This, along with the cost restriction $\partial^2 c/(\partial \kappa_j)^2 > 0$, means that (11.6) implies that R&D is "over-used" relative to the cost-minimizing level. The reader can see that this result is *qualitatively* similar to the asymmetric interaction of chapter 10, section 10.2.

Static Solution. For comparison, suppose instead that the firms make their R&D and output decisions in a static (nonstrategic) way by choosing R&D and output levels *simultaneously* at a single point in time. In this case a Nash equilibrium is reached where the following conditions hold jointly for both firms j:

$$\frac{\partial \pi_j{}^0}{\partial z_j} = \frac{\partial R_j{}^c}{\partial z_j} - \frac{\partial c(z_j, \kappa_j)}{\partial z_j} = 0 \tag{11.7a}$$

$$\frac{\partial \pi_j{}^0}{\partial \kappa_j} = -\frac{\partial c(z_j, \kappa_j)}{\partial \kappa_j} - \phi = 0 \tag{11.7b}$$

Equation (11.7a) is identical with that at the market stage of the two-stage strategic model and, treating κ parametrically, gives the same equilibrium output *functions* of κ, that is $z_j{}^c(\kappa)$. Comparison of equation (11.7b) with (11.6) shows the difference between strategic and nonstrategic behavior: whereas in the static case the firms choose κ to minimize their cost of producing any output, firms in the two-stage $\Gamma(\kappa, z)$ interaction use R&D investments beyond this cost-minimizing level as they also give consideration to the impact that their R&D has on their rivals' subsequent output choices.

E11.1

Research and Development and Patent Races

The model of R&D competition analyzed above has two critical features. First, it is assumed that there are an infinite number of research strategies, indexed by κ, available to each firm. If it is assumed further that each firm's research results in a (different) patentable idea, the models imply that a continuum of possible patents is available. Second, the R&D payoff functions of the firms are all continuous in κ: if a firm changes its strategy slightly, its payoff only changes slightly.

Since the work of Barzel (1968), R&D competition within an industry is often modeled as having mutually exclusive results: a single patent is issued which precludes a payoff to any firm other than that acquiring the patent. Those firms losing the patent race have zero (gross) payoff regardless of their R&D effort. Such R&D games are in the form of a **tournament**, or **contest**, where performance is rewarded on the basis of the firm's rank within the set of all realized performances.[4] As E9.2 demonstrated, the discontinuous nature of the payoff to R&D caused by the use of patents generally means that a Nash-in-R&D equilibrium will not exist. The following example avoids this sort of discontinuity by first allowing the winner to be determined probabilistically and then assuming that each firm's payoff is the *expectation* of the various discrete possibilities. The expected payoff function is continuous in the firm's strategies.

Consider two firms competing for a single payoff (prize) R. The contest nature of the game is displayed when firm 1 wins the prize, for then firm 2 necessarily loses, and conversely. The firms compete for the contest prize using R&D expenditures κ_1 and κ_2 respectively. Associated with any expenditure pair is the probability $h(\kappa_1, \kappa_2)$ that firm 1 wins the payoff; firm 2's probability of winning is therefore $1 - h(\kappa_1, \kappa_2)$. In turn, the *expected* payoffs to the firms are

$$\bar{\pi}_1 = Rh(\kappa_1, \kappa_2) - \kappa_1 \tag{11.8a}$$

$$\bar{\pi}_2 = R\{1 - h(\kappa_1, \kappa_2)\} - \kappa_2 \tag{11.8b}$$

Neglecting the argument to the probability function, suppose that $h_1 > 0$, $h_2 < 0$, and $h_{11} < 0$, $h_{22} > 0$, where subscripts indicate the obvious differentiation by the κ_1 and κ_2 arguments. The inequalities impose a positive but diminishing marginal effect of each firm's cost on its own probability of success and assure a unique equilibrium solution to the game described below.

Static Solution. The stationarity conditions for a Nash-in-κ equilibrium of the static (simultaneous choice) R&D contest are usual:

$$\frac{\partial \bar{\pi}_1}{\partial \kappa_1} = Rh_1 - 1 = 0 \tag{11.9a}$$

$$\frac{\partial \bar{\pi}_2}{\partial \kappa_2} = -Rh_2 - 1 = 0 \tag{11.9b}$$

Dynamic Game with Commitment. Suppose alternatively that firm 1 can irrevocably commit to its level of R&D prior to firm 2's choice (the order of play is Stackelberg). Then the total derivative

$$\frac{d\bar{\pi}_1}{d\kappa_1} = \frac{\partial \bar{\pi}_1}{\partial \kappa_1} + \frac{\partial \bar{\pi}_1}{\partial \kappa_2} \frac{d\kappa_2}{d\kappa_1} \tag{11.10}$$

determines firm 1's profit rate – here $d\kappa_2/d\kappa_1$ is the slope of firm 2's reaction function. As the partial derivative $\partial \bar{\pi}_1/\partial \kappa_1$ is zero at the Nash equilibrium, then along the stationarity condition (11.9a)

$$\frac{d\kappa_2}{d\kappa_1} = \frac{\partial^2 \bar{\pi}_2/\partial \kappa_1 \partial \kappa_2}{\partial^2 \bar{\pi}_2/\partial \kappa_2{}^2}$$

$$= \frac{Rh_{12}}{\partial^2 \bar{\pi}_2/\partial \kappa_2{}^2} \tag{11.11}$$

The denominator of this expression is negative by the second-order conditions.

[4] Green and Stokey (1983) and Nalebuff and Stiglitz (1983a) provided detailed properties for tournaments and contests.

Substituting this in (11.10) gives the differential effect of κ on expected profits:

$$\frac{d\bar{\pi}_1}{d\kappa_1} = \frac{\partial\bar{\pi}_1}{\partial\kappa_2}\left(\frac{Rh_{12}}{\partial^2\bar{\pi}_2/\partial\kappa_2{}^2}\right) \tag{11.12}$$

Since $\partial\bar{\pi}_1/\partial\kappa_2 = Rh_2 < 0$, $\text{sgn}(d\bar{\pi}_1/d\kappa_1) = \text{sgn}(h_{12})$: firm 1 will over commit to R&D (relative to the static profit maximizing level) if and only if $h_{12} > 0$.

A similar analysis for firm 2 leads to

$$\frac{d\bar{\pi}_2}{d\kappa_2} = \frac{\partial\bar{\pi}_2}{\partial\kappa_1}\left(\frac{Rh_{12}}{\partial^2\bar{\pi}_2/\partial\kappa_2{}^2}\right)^{-1} \tag{11.13}$$

With $\text{sgn}(d\bar{\pi}_2/d\kappa_2) = -\text{sgn}(h_{12})$, firm 2 over-commits to R&D when $h_{12} < 0$. Note finally that the contest is played without a strategic effect when the R&D decisions of the firms cannot affect their rival's probability of success, that is when $h_{12} = 0$. Reinganum (1983) and Dixit (1987) provide further details.

11.2 Research and Development with Price Competition

The above analysis need not be limited to the specific rules of the $\Gamma(\kappa, z)$ interaction. The obvious alternative is Bertrand price competition at the market stage instead of the quantity competition assumed above. Just as with the asymmetric models developed in chapter 10, the important feature of the Bertrand market in the symmetric case is that the accompanying strategic effect generally induces *under*-investment in R&D rather than the over-investment typical with Cournot market-stage play.

11.2.1 Perfect Equilibrium

An analysis of the $\Gamma(\kappa, p)$ interaction can be quickly set out, as it is only a small variation on the Cournot case. Each firm's revenue function and long-run cost function $c(z_j, \kappa_j) = \phi\kappa_j$ continue to apply as described in section 11.1.1. Let $R_j(p) = z_j(p)p_j$ be the associated revenue as a function of the pride and write the long-run profit function, also with price,

$$\pi_j{}^0(p, \kappa_j) = R_j(p) - c(z_j(p), \kappa_j) - \phi\kappa_j \tag{11.14}$$

$$= \pi_j(p, \kappa_j) - \phi\kappa_j$$

where π_j is the profit function pertaining to the choice of market prices for given κ_j – the "short-run" profit function.

Static Game. In the *static* simultaneous Nash-in-(p, κ) game, the equilibrium conditions (assuming existence) are given by the κ and p stationarity of (11.14):

$$\frac{\partial\pi_j(p, \kappa)}{\partial p_j} = 0 \tag{11.15}$$

$$\frac{\partial\pi_j(p, \kappa)}{\partial\kappa_j} = \phi \tag{11.16}$$

for $j = 1, 2$. These four equations solve simultaneously for the price and R&D values at the equilibrium.

Strategic Interaction and Perfect Equilibrium. In the two-stage game the Bertrand play at the market stage is described by the equilibrium price functions $p_1^{1b}(\kappa)$ and $p_2^{1b}(\kappa)$ which result from equation (11.15). Rather than expressing the strategic stage profits as a function of κ by directly substituting these price functions in π_j^0 – our usual procedure – it is instructive to follow Lee (1986) and treat the market-stage subgame solution as a constraint on the strategic stage choice. That is, at the strategic stage we think of each firm j as choosing its R&D to maximize π_j^0 subject to the Bertrand market-stage equilibrium conditions (11.15). The two-stage problem for firm j is therefore given by

$$\max_{k_j, p} \left\{ \pi_j(p, \kappa_j) - \phi \kappa_j + \lambda_j \frac{\partial \pi_j(p, \kappa_j)}{\partial p_j} + \lambda_k \frac{\partial \pi_k(p, \kappa_k)}{\partial p_k} \right\} \quad (11.17)$$

where λ_j, λ_k are multipliers for the constraints. It is the presence of the two constraint terms in the above maximand which assures that the solution is subgame perfect.

Assuming the existence of a solution, the equilibrium is given by (11.15), the stationarity by multipliers λ_j and λ_k, and the stationarity by the primary decision variables p_j, p_k, and κ_j respectively:

$$\frac{\partial \pi_j}{\partial p_j} + \lambda_j \frac{\partial^2 \pi_j}{(\partial p_j)^2} + \lambda_k \frac{\partial^2 \pi_k}{\partial p_k \partial p_j} = 0 \quad (11.18a)$$

$$\frac{\partial \pi_j}{\partial p_k} + \lambda_j \frac{\partial^2 \pi_j}{\partial p_j \partial p_k} + \lambda_k \frac{\partial^2 \pi_k}{(\partial p_k)^2} = 0 \quad (11.18b)$$

$$\frac{\partial \pi_j}{\partial \kappa_j} - \phi + \lambda_j \frac{\partial^2 \pi_j}{\partial p_j \partial \kappa_j} = 0 \quad (11.18c)$$

Eliminating the λ multipliers by repeated substitution and using (11.16) gives

$$\frac{\partial \pi_j}{\partial \kappa_j} = \phi - \frac{1}{D^*} \left(\frac{\partial \pi_j^2}{\partial p_j \partial \kappa_j} \frac{\partial \pi_j}{\partial p_k} \frac{\partial \pi_j^2}{\partial p_k \partial p_j} \right) \quad (11.19)$$

where $D^* = (\partial^2 \pi_j / \partial p_j^2)(\partial^2 \pi_k / \partial p_k^2) - (\partial^2 \pi_j / \partial p_j \partial p_k)(\partial^2 \pi_k / \partial p_k \partial p_j)$.[5] Equations (11.15) and (11.19) jointly describe the perfect equilibrium condition with $\Gamma(\kappa, p)$ play.

Strategic and Static Comparison. The difference between the static and two-stage analysis again centers on the condition defining the marginal profitability of the R&D decision: compare conditions (11.16) and (11.19). From prior analyses the reader immediately recognizes the term in parentheses on the right-hand side of (11.19) as the *strategic effect*. Once more, whether or not the firm over- or under-invests in R&D relative to the static game depends on the sign of the strategic effect. If the usual stability condition $D^* > 0$ is assumed, that sign depends on the product of the three derivatives of π_j. To sign these, it

---

[5] The reader immediately recognizes that $D^* > 0$ is the stability condition for the market-stage Bertrand game (recall chapter 3, section 3.1.3).

is helpful to express π_j in terms of the underlying demand and cost functions. This gives

$$\frac{\partial \pi_j{}^2}{\partial p_j \partial \kappa_j} = -\left\{ \frac{\partial^2 c(z_j, \kappa_j)}{\partial z_j \partial \kappa_j} + \frac{\partial c(z_j, \kappa_j)}{\partial \kappa_j} \right\} \frac{\partial z_j}{\partial p_j} \leq 0 \qquad (11.20a)$$

$$\frac{\partial \pi_j}{\partial p_k} = \left\{ p_j - \frac{\partial c(z_j, \kappa_j)}{\partial z_j} \right\} \frac{\partial z_j}{\partial p_k} \geq 0 \qquad (11.20b)$$

and

$$\frac{\partial \pi_j{}^2}{\partial p_k \partial p_j} = \left\{ p_k - \frac{\partial c(z_k, \kappa_k)}{\partial z_k} \right\} \frac{\partial^2 z_k}{\partial p_j \partial p_k} - \frac{\partial z_k}{\partial p_j} \geq 0 \qquad (11.20c)$$

The sign of (11.20a) is negative when the own-demand is negatively sloped and both cost and marginal cost decrease with increasing R&D. The sign of (11.20b) is positive when the goods are substitutes. This leaves us only to verify the sign of (11.20c). In this regard, first note that if the demand functions are separable in p_j and p_k then $\partial \pi_j / \partial p_k \partial p_j = 0$, giving the identical solutions for the static and two-stage games. Since this is not generally the case, it seems reasonable to assume $\partial^2 z_k / \partial p_j \partial p_k < 0$, which is consistent with the earlier assumption (11.1) concerning the inverse demand. This in turn means that, with substitute goods, $\partial^2 \pi_j / \partial p_k \partial p_j \geq 0$ as indicated in (11.20c). The overall result of the signs in (11.20) is to yield a negative strategic effect. In contrast with quantity competition, price competition (may) lead to less R&D than in the static game (where costs are minimized).

Given the "under-investment", the $\Gamma(\kappa, p)$ perfect equilibrium implies smaller outputs, greater prices, and greater profits than occur in the static game. Following Lee (1986), figure 11.1 indicates how these results are derived. In the figure the various graphs are identified by the specific equation that they

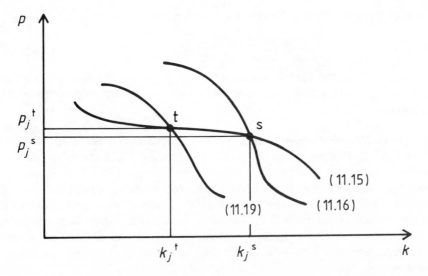

Figure 11.1
Static and perfect equilibria

represent. The graph of equation (11.15) is negatively sloped from the second-order condition for the profit maximum at the market stage, the graph of (11.16) is negatively sloped from (11.20a), the graph of (11.15) intersects the graph of (11.16) from below because of the stability condition $D^* > 0$, and, since the right-hand side of (11.19) is positive, the graph of (11.19) must be negatively sloped. Point t and superscript t identify the perfect two-stage equilibrium, which occurs at the intersection of (11.15) and (11.19); point s and superscript s identify the static equilibrium which occurs at the intersection of (11.15) and (11.16).

E11.2

Empirical Regularities in Research and Development

The cornerstone of empirical studies relating industry and firm economics to R&D activity on the one hand and that activity to economic progress on the other hand has been the "Schumpeterian conjectures" (see Schumpeter, 1939, 1976). Because Schumpeter dealt with these topics using a broad brush, his followers have taken considerable liberty in the design of empirical tests of these conjectures. Nonetheless, from the many studies three general empirical hypotheses have developed: (a) monopoly, measured by a concentrated market structure and/or greater industry profits, fosters technological innovation; (b) large firms are more effective in R&D than are their smaller counterparts; (c) diversified firms are better prepared to exploit new technologies than are narrowly based firms, and therefore these diversified firms are more likely to be innovators.

The result of the body of statistical research along these lines has been a modest collection of empirical regularities. These have surely not acquired the status of "laws," or even "facts," as most of the test results come with qualifications owing to the data available to create an index of R&D *activity*. Not surprisingly, both input and output measures have been used as activity indexes. Firm R&D expenditures and some count of scientific and engineering personnel, typically adjusted for sales, assets, or total employment, have been employed on the input side. Patents (or major patents) granted, patent renewals, and licenses of trade secrets have been employed separately and jointly as R&D output measures.[6]

Research and Development Inputs and Outputs: Scale Economies. Industry cross-section studies generally find a positive correlation between R&D inputs, measured by both expenditures and number of research personnel, and the rate of innovation, measured by patents acquired (see Scherer, 1965; Schmookler, 1966; Mansfield, 1968; McLean and Round, 1978). Using nonlinear regression model forms of the "innovative production function" (linking R&D inputs to outputs) and industry cross-section data, Grabowski (1968), Bailey (1972) and

---

[6] There has been a recent addition to the output measures. In a canvas of technology, engineering and trade journals, the US Small Business Administration collected information on roughly 8,000 innovations introduced in 1982. The innovations are classified by four digit SIC industry and large or small firm size. See Acs and Audretsch (1988) for details.

Kohn and Scott (1978) report that scale economies, if they exist at all, are minimal.[7] Bound et al. (1984) provide a useful summary.

Demand and Research and Development. The rate of growth in demand for the products of an industry is generally found to be positively related to its level of R&D activity (see Scherer, 1982). This "demand pull" property was first noted by Schmookler (1966) who specifically argued that the larger the potential market the more R&D activity would be directed to it because (a) the profitability of innovation increases with market size, and (b) random encounters between inventive talent and problems requiring solution are more likely the more production activity is directed to meeting demand. Mowery and Rosenberg (1979) give a critique of Schmookler and this literature.

Research and Development, Firm Size and Market Structure. The stimulus for empirical analyses of links between R&D and firm size is loosely provided by Schumpeter's conjecture that economies of scale in R&D imply a greater rate of innovation in large firms. Empirical studies generally find that R&D employment and expenditures appear to increase proportionately, or slightly less than proportionately, for manufacturing firms with more than 999 employees (see Horowitz, 1962; Mansfield, 1963; Scherer, 1965; Acs and Audretsch, 1988). However, in several studies with more disaggregated firm size measures it has been found that very small firms employ proportionately more R&D personnel than their medium and large counterparts (see Loeb and Lin, 1977; Schrieves, 1976; Link, 1980).

The literature generally reports an ambiguous relationship between industry concentration and various measures of R&D inputs and outputs: see Horowitz (1962), Hamberg (1966), Scherer (1967), Kelly (1970), and Rosenberg (1976) who used input measures, and Williamson (1965), Allen (1969), and Levin and Reiss (1984) who used output measures. Using patent activity, Lunn (1986) presents some evidence of a positive relationship for small concentration levels and a negative relationship for large levels. More recently, Acs and Audretsch (1988) report an "unequivocal" negative relationship between innovation output and concentration.

Scientific Base and Specific Innovations. While Schumpeter generally saw "demand-push" as the dominant factor in innovation, others have argued for a "technological push" based on the concept that fundamental scientific knowledge provides the key opportunities for innovation. Scherer (1965), Kelly (1970), and Rosenberg (1976) report evidence of a significant role for technological opportunity; Phillips (1971) and Schmookler (1966) find the role of little significance.

Learning Effects. It is frequently maintained that, because learning involves costs, successful firms have an advantage over their less successful rivals. This "success breeds success" hypothesis is supported by Grabowski's (1968) study of

---

[7] Mansfield (1968) does, however, report such scale economies for the chemical industry, and Acs and Audretsch (1988) find that the number of innovations (measured as indicated in note 6) increased with R&D expenditures, but at a decreasing rate. Fisher and Temin (1973) and Kohn and Scott (1982) provide precise theoretical foundations for Schumpeter's postulate concerning the link between R&D and scale economies. Both argue that existing empirical tests are generally ill formed.

R&D in the chemical, drug, and pertroleum industries, and Phillips's (1971) study of the commercial aircraft market.

Research and Development and Market Value. Pakes (1984, 1985) has reported a significant positive relationship between stock market values and patented inventions.

Research and Development and Unionization. It has been argued that unions capture rents from intangible investments in general and from R&D investments in particular. Connolly et al. (1986), Hirsh and Link (1987), and Acs and Audretsch (1988) report negative correlations between R&D activity and unionization and interpret these results as indicating restricted R&D because of the lack of full appropriability by firm owners.

11.3 Licensing and the Diffusion of Innovation

There are three usual ways by which the innovations resulting from R&D activity diffuse through an industry: *ex ante* licensing, *ex post* licensing, and imitation. Licensing of either form is a voluntary contractual assignment of rights to the use of an innovation which permits the innovator to capture some or all of the gains from widespread application of its technology. *Ex ante* licensing offers the licensee advance rights to the technological findings from a specific R&D activity, whatever that may be. In contrast, *ex post* licensing, which occurs after R&D is complete and its results are known, offers rights to quite specific technologies. In both cases the rights to the technology are exchanged according to some payment schedule and generally with restrictions on the use of the technology. It is usually thought that an *ex ante* licensee relies on the R&D activity of the licensor and terminates its own independent search for new technology. The *ex post* licensee, in contrast, continues its own R&D activity, but finds the innovation of the licensor superior to its own development.

Imitation differs fundamentally from licensing in that imitators unilaterally take, without compensation to the innovator, some of the benefits of an innovation. Mansfield et al. (1981) found in a study of 48 product innovations in the chemical, drug, electronic, and machinery industries that roughly 60 percent of those innovations bearing patents were successfully imitated (avoiding patent infringement) within four years. (The patents, however, were estimated to increase the cost of imitation by about 11 percent.)[8] Imitation occurs when the

---

[8] In a second study involving 100 firms and 13 industries, Mansfield (1985) found that information concerning competitive R&D decisions and outputs is generally available. This is to be expected, he notes, as there is a wide variety of information channels among firms competing in R&D: ". . . In some industries there is considerable movement of personnel from one firm to another, and there are informal communications among scientists and engineers working at various firms, as well as profession meetings at which information is exchanged. In other industries, input suppliers and customers are important channels (since they pass on a great deal of information), patent applications are scrutinized very carefully, and reverse engineering is carried out." (Mansfield, 1985, p. 221.)

costs of patent application and enforcement or otherwise securing trade secrets, are significant and the costs of delay associated with the imitation process are small.[9]

Incentives to License. Tandon (1983) compares the private and social incentives for licensing, and its effect on R&D, for the case of perfectly competitive product markets (see also McGee, 1966). With a single cost-reducing innovation Tandon finds that licensing at the profit-maximising fee is equivalent to producing as a monopolist and therefore concludes that licensing does not affect R&D activity. Salant (1984) (see also SE11.3) has found to the contrary: he argues that *ex post* licensing can alter the R&D decisions in asymmetrical oligopoly when the expectations of returns from future licenses encourages greater research by high-cost firms. Gallini (1984) and Gallini and Winter (1985) draw the distinction between *ex ante* and *ex post* licenses in this regard and argue that the importance of *ex ante* licensing lies in deterring entry and limiting the independent research capabilities of rivals. Given enough asymmetry in firms, then, licensing is likely to have an impact on the underlying R&D decisions.

In view of the potential impact, we ask what incentives exist for patent licensing. A patent-holder will generally find it profitable to license an innovation that is used in a commodity produced under diminishing returns, as the licensing will lower unit costs and expand the market.[10] The value of the increased output at lower cost must then be captured by the licensor in fees so that low transaction costs and an implementable two-part fee schedule are also desiderata. While these two conditions would seem to be fairly common, the incidence of licensing is rather spotty in the US economy. Why?

Following Arrow's (1962) early lead, Shapiro (1985) emphasizes three information problems that may limit the ability of an innovator to capture the full value of his innovation. First, there may be asymmetric information concerning the innovation's value, with the innovator holding a higher valuation and not compromising it with the potential licensee's valuation.[11] Second, the innovator may believe that innovation will not only better its rival's immediate production and products, but also provide information allowing the rival to be a more

---

[9] Baldwin and Childs (1969) find evidence that innovation in the US steel industry has been slowed by ease of imitation. Nelson and Winter (1982) provide simulation results that suggest that imitators are better off than innovators under a wide variety of reasonable conditions.

[10] There are other incentives also. Braun and MacDonald (1982) and Shepard (1987) argue that the second source created when a technology is licensed induces quality competition (reliability of delivery for example) and allows the supplying firms to commit to a quality level that would not be credible for a single supplier. When consumers value quality this increases demand. Shepard gives conditions where this increase in demand might be expected to leave the licensor better off from dual production even when there are increasing returns. It has also been suggested that licensing agreements may be collusion facilitating practices as they can include covenants which (a) restrict the licensee to specific territories or customer classes, (b) establish a price ceiling or floor on the final product price, or (c) limit production quantities. Concerning the legality of such license restrictions see Priest (1977).

[11] Depending on the relative bargaining power of the parties, some fractional sharing in value might arise. Taylor and Silberston (1973) and Caves et al. (1983 both report that on average roughly 40 percent of an innovation's (*ex post*) value is captured by the licensor.

capable innovator. This last source of value is difficult to capture in a license.[12] Third, the innovator may not be able to observe the potential licensee's output and thus not be able to use a per unit royalty as part of the license contract. We will hold these problems aside for the moment and, in their absence, consider the incentives to license using both fixed fees and royalty payments.

11.3.1 Optimal Fixed Fees and Royalties in Licensing

The revenues received by an innovator from any license agreement must be weighed against the fact that the technology exchanged makes licensees more effective competitors. In general, if the licensing increases *industry* profits, then the innovator should not hold the innovation exclusively but instead should license and, through a fee schedule, extract the increment in value that the innovation otherwise provides to licensees.

Quantity Competition and Ex Post *Licensing.* Some notation and model detail are helpful in analyzing the incentive. We consider duopolists j and k in quantity competition. Suppose that, on the basis of prior R&D, firm j holds a patent on a cost-reducing technology. Firms j and k respectively have costs $c_j{}^0$ and $c_k{}^0$ without the innovative technology and lower costs c_j^* and c_k^* with it. We also use superscript zero to indicate reaction functions *prior* to the innovation. These are illustrated as $r_j{}^0(z_k)$ and $r_k{}^0(z_j)$ in figure 11.2(a) and in the usual way provide the pre-innovation industry equilibrium point at E^{00}.

Drastic Innovations. When firm j innovates and uses the low-cost technology exclusively its costs fall from $c_j{}^0$ to c_j^*. This alters its reaction function, shifting it out to say $r_j^*(z_k)$ as shown in figure 11.2(a). Because k does not have access to the technology its costs remain unchanged and its reactions continue to lie along $r_k{}^0(z_j)$. The equilibrium arising in this circumstance is at E^{*0}, where j produces the entire industry output, as a monopolist, and firm k withdraws from the industry (since the prevailing price with j's monopoly production is less than k's marginal cost). In this case it is said that the innovation is **drastic**. There is no licensing in this situation, as the innovator directly captures the maximum profits (at the lowest cost) that can be obtained in the industry.

Nondrastic Innovations. The more common situation is illustrated in figure 11.2(b). Again, the pre-innovation reaction functions yield the equilibrium point E^{00} with the firms earning profits $\pi_j{}^{00}$ and $\pi_k{}^{00}$. Suppose once more that firm j innovates and does not license to firm k. This produces the equilibrium at the intersection of r_j^* and $r_k{}^0$, as k's reaction function does not change. Under standard assumptions the profits π_j^{*0} captured by firm j in this equilibrium are greater than its pre-innovation level: $\pi_j^{*0} > \pi_j{}^{00}$. Note that firm j's post-innovation cost advantage is not sufficient to yield it a market monopoly, in

---

[12] In a survey of innovations and licensing Caves et al (1983) note that about 43 percent of licensees contain a "technology flowback" provision which required the licensee to share all advances or improvements in the licensed technology with the licensor. While the effectiveness of such provisions in practice is not generally known, Yu (1981) describes several successful cases.

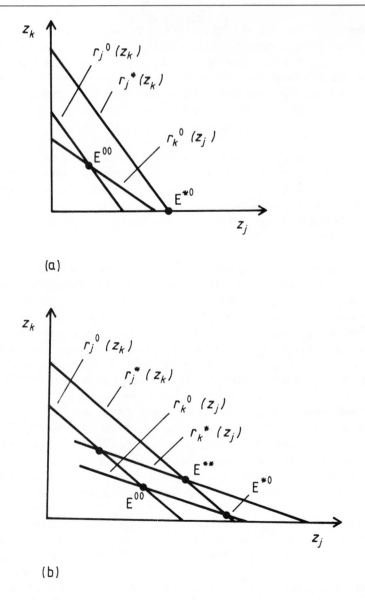

Figure 11.2
Incentives to license: (a) drastic innovation; (b) nondrastic innovation

contrast with that depicted in figure 11.2(a). The "relatively small" cost reduction which simply makes j better off and disadvantages k in this case, without driving it from the market, is generally referred to as a **nondrastic** innovation.

The question before firm j is whether to license its innovation or not. This clearly turns on whether it can increase its profits beyond π_j^{*0} in doing so. If j were to give the rights of its innovation for firm k without compensation, then k's lower cost c_k^* would lead to the reaction function r_k^* and an industry equilibrium at E^{**}. As a result, the gift leads to a decrease in j's profits and an increase in k's profits relative to the equilibrium at E^{*0}. The gift will not be made.

Suppose instead the firm j exchanges its innovative technology for a per unit royalty just less than the cost savings $c_k^* - c_k{}^0$. When firm k accepts the license, it lowers its direct per unit cost of production but leaves unchanged its total per unit cost (including royalty). As a result, the licensing with royalty equilibrium is at E^{*0} as before. Now, however, firm j earns π_j^{*0} from its own production *and* captures k's value of producing at lower unit cost. Given that firm k produces a positive amount at E^{*0} under the license, then it makes royalty payments and increases firm j's profits relative to the no-license solution.

Fixed-fee Per Unit Licenses. When it is costly for the innovator to monitor the output of its licensee rivals royalties cannot be used reliably and the license contract instead specifies a fixed fee. The difficulty with the fixed fee alone is that it does not alter the licensee's per unit cost and therefore leaves the industry equilibrium at E^{**} where firm j's profits (without license fees) are reduced relative to the no-licensing equilibrium at E^{*0}. If the license with fixed fees increases industry profits, if $\pi_j^{**} + \pi_k^{**} \geq \pi_j^{*0} + \pi_k^{*0}$, then a fixed fee just less than $\pi_k^{**} - \pi_k^{*0}$ would provide an incentive to license. Thus the question of whether to license with a fixed fee turns simply on the impact of the licensing on *industry* profits.

In an analysis of this situation Katz and Shapiro (1985) show that both drastic and nearly drastic innovations will be held for the innovator's exclusive use, for the same reasons as noted above. However, for small nondrastic innovations by one of the two *equally* efficient firms, licensing will occur when the marginal revenue associated with the industry demand has negative slope at the pre-licensing equilibrium output. This condition always holds for linear demand, for example, and so small innovations will be licensed using only fixed fees (again, assuming that per unit royalties are impractical) in this case.

Price Competition. The analysis of licensing incentives with price competition and heterogeneous goods proceeds in parallel with the quantity competition analysis. A license using fixed fees and per unit royalties will be offered by the innovator if and only if it raises industry profits (in which case the value of the innovation to the license is fully captured by the licensor). Again, drastic innovations will not be licensed and nondrastic innovations will. However, under price competition it is more likely that even smaller cost reductions will be drastic. The critical twist in price competition comes with homogeneous goods and equally efficient firms (pre-innovation), for then every innovation is drastic. The innovator has $c_j^* < c_k{}^0$; it thus sets a price just below $c_k{}^0$ and drives its rival from the market.

11.3.2 External Licensing

An alternative to the above licensing situation occurs when the innovation arises from an R&D laboratory which is separate (independent) from any producing firm and without the resources, or inclination, to enter production. To keep our analysis focused, suppose that the innovation can be used only in one industry. In this case, the problem facing the innovator is to choose the optimal number of oligopolists to be licensed in that industry. The problem is not trivial as the value of the innovation to any given licensee (and thus the amount that can be captured in a license fee) depends on the number of firms which are licensed. The interdependence arises because the innovative technology reduces the marginal costs of the licensees, in turn alters their reaction functions, and finally determines a different equilibrium for the industry. The equilibrium profits of licensees clearly depend on the number of reaction functions which are altered in this way.

Kamien and Tauman (1986) study this interdependence in derived demand for licenses using a symmetric oligopoly in quantity competition with linear demand and constant unit costs.[13] As above, they find that the optimal per unit royalty is equal to the cost savings. The innovator offers this contract to all oligopolists and they all accept. Since their total marginal costs (production and royalty) are unaffected by the license, the original reaction functions and equilibrium are continued and the potential demand interdependences do not appear.

Despite the rewards to royalty licensing, Kamien and Tauman show that a license contract using only a fixed fee is more valuable. Roughly, the reason is that the fixed fee leaves the licensees' reaction functions to reflect the lower marginal cost of the new technology and the resulting interdependences in demand can be used to create monopoly power and increase industry profits. These greater profits are then extracted using the fixed fee.

Supplementary examples

SE11.1   Research and Development: Indivisibilities, Uncertainty, and Appropriability

Since Arrow (1962), the conventional wisdom has been that an economy made up of monopolies will under-invest in innovative activity in the sense that technical progress will be less rapid than under socially optimal conditions or in a competitive economy. Arrow argued that three of the classic reasons for allocative efficiency also apply to R&D invention: indivisibilities, uncertainty, and the fact that firms typically cannot appropriate the full social returns to R&D.[14] A review of the key steps in Arrow's analysis is instructive here. We begin with a positive, but negatively sloped, industry demand $p(z)$. As the first

---

[13] Katz and Shapiro (1985) consider a somewhat more general model than this. They analyze licenses sold using a pure price policy (a price is set and all who would license at this price can) and a pure quantity policy (a fixed number of licenses are announced for sale and the highest bidders above a minimum win these). The pure price policy is shown to be inferior as it fails to exploit the interdependencies among the oligopolists, each of whom makes its license purchase decisions taking as given the number of others who would purchase.

[14] It must be emphasized that it is the *scale* of R&D investment that is of concern here. In addition to Arrow's interest in the limited appropriability, Leung (1983) and Spence (1984) have noted that the spillover of knowledge from one firm to another acts to cause under-investment relative to socially optimal levels. This second form of appropriability is the key rationale for a patent system with a "winner take all" characterized as in E11.1. Loury (1979) and Dasgupta and

case consider a single-seller monopoly with constant marginal cost c_0. If we let $R(z) = p(z)z$ be revenues, then the optimal output for the monopolist occurs where $R'(z) = c_0$. This yields maximum profits as a function of marginal cost given by

$$\pi^m(c_0) = \max_z \{R(z) - c_0 z\} \qquad (11.21)$$

Following Arrow's analysis, think of a discrete stand-alone R&D project which, when successful, leads to a lower marginal cost c_1, that is, $c_1 < c_0$. The innovation is unique in the sense that there are no similar or competing innovations. With the above notation, the project has (private) present value to the monopolist given by

$$v^m = \frac{\pi^m(c_1) - \pi^m(c_0)}{r} \qquad (11.22)$$

where r is the appropriate discount rate. (The profit flows are assumed to obtain in perpetuity). In figure 11.3 the flow $\pi^m(c_1) - \pi^m(c_0)$ is indicated by the area $c_1 E A c_0$ made up of the increment $c_1 D A c_0$ to profits at the original quantity $z_0{}^m$ and the profits ADE from the increase in output from $z_0{}^m$ to $z_1{}^m$. The monopolist will adopt the cost-saving innovation if its expected present value is greater than its present cost: $h v^m > \kappa$, where h is the probability that the cost reduction will occur with an R&D investment of κ.

Socially Optimal Innovation. How does the monopoly solution compare with that which is socially optimal? The optimality requires that price equals marginal cost both before and after the innovation: $p_0^* = c_0$ and $p_1^* = c_1$. In turn, the social value of the innovation v^* is the difference between consumer surplus (CS) before and after (the social discount rate is also assumed to be r):

$$v^* = \frac{CS(p_1^*) - CS(p_0^*)}{r} = \frac{CS(c_1) - CS(c_0)}{r} \qquad (11.23)$$

In figure 11.3 the flow $r v^* = CS(p_1^*) - CS(p_0^*)$ is given by the area $c_1 G B c_0$. It is clear from the geometry in this case that $r v^* > r v^m$; that is, the monopolist will not adopt all socially beneficial innovations.

The incentive for innovation by competitive firms follows similar steps. At the pre-innovation competitive equilibrium, price equals the marginal cost c_0. The innovating firm protected by patent can then charge some price ε less than c_0 or it can charge the price where its marginal revenue equals c_1. If it is assumed that c_0 constrains the monopoly price, the innovation has the value

$$v^c = \frac{\{(c_0 - \varepsilon) - c_1\} z_0{}^c}{r} \qquad (11.24)$$

Stiglitz (1980a) find that the patent mechanism generally leads to over-investment since rivalrous innovators care about who wins the patent race whereas society's concern is only with having someone succeed. Katz (1986) has argued that in many interesting cases the appropriability problem can be solved without the distortions of the patent system by cooperative R&D ventures. Finally, Reinganum (1981a, b) has modeled technological diffusion as the result of strategic behavior by firms who understand that knowledge spills over as time passes. In her model the firms, knowing of the spillover, choose to be either imitators or innovators. For the specific assumptions she makes, innovation turns out to be the preferred role.

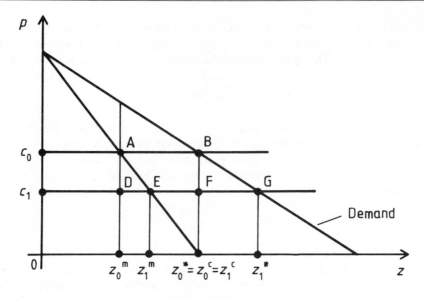

Figure 11.3
Innovation and market structure

Figure 11.3 indicates the profit flow (approximately) by the area c_1FBc_0. The geometry of the figure clearly shows that the present-value relationships are $v^* > v^c > v^m$. The monopolist engages in less innovation than the competitive industry and less than is socially optimal.

Some Reservations. Demsetz (1969) has argued that the monopolist in the above analysis begins with a somewhat smaller output than the competitive industry and this biases the results (see also Yamey, 1970 and Ng 1971). What happens if the monopoly and competitive industries are compared at the same pre-innovation output? This can be done in figure 11.3 by making the demand curve of the competitive industry the marginal revenue curve of the monopolist.[15] Then, at least for the linear demands, it is straightforward for Demsetz to show that the value of the innovation to the monopolist is greater than that to the competitive industry. The intuition for this result is that the incentive to take the innovation promising a (per unit) cost saving is less for the monopolist simply because its output is less. When this output difference between the markets is held aside, then Arrow's difference in incentive to innovate disappears.

Dasgupta and Stiglitz (1980a, b) have emphasized several other serious limitations to Arrow's analysis: the innovation is discrete, and so the analysis tells us nothing about marginal incentives for cost reduction; partial equilibrium analysis does not answer the question of whether there will be more innovation in an economy completely composed of monopolies compared with an otherwise identical economy with all competitive industries; the analysis ignores the

---

[15] That is, we think of figure 11.3 as depicting two situations: a monopoly and a competitive industry facing exactly one half the quantity demanded at any price as the monopoly.

distortions which would be produced in order for the government to finance the subsidies to support the socially optimal innovation; finally, the analysis does not consider that competition and monopoly affect the risks associated with R&D differently.[16] The reader is referred to Dasgupta and Stiglitz for detailed comments on these issues.

SE11.2   Sequential Research and Development

In this example the model of section 11.2 is amended to consider the implications of sequential R&D moves at the strategic stage along with quantity competition at the market stage. To begin, recall the notation of that section. Because of the sequential play in R&D, it is helpful to number firms: $j = 1$ will be the first to choose its R&D investment, $j = 2$ is second, and so forth. When $\kappa_j > 0$ is chosen, then firm j is said to enter the industry. Formally, entry involves payment of the cost ϕ per unit of R&D capital and in this way investing $\phi \kappa_j > 0$.

The R&D game is Stackelberg-like in that each firm j observes the R&D choice (and therefore the market-stage short-run cost function) of all prior entrants and, in turn, understands that all firms $k > j$ will know his choice. After all firms have been permitted their R&D decision and these are common knowledge, the market stage commences. Unlike the R&D decisions, active firms (those that chose entry) make their output decisions (simultaneously) in Cournot fashion.

Let $\kappa = (\kappa_1, \kappa_2)$ indicate the strategic choices of R&D by firms 1 and 2. By observing κ at the beginning of the market stage, both firms can compute the Cournot equilibrium outputs $z_1{}^c(\kappa)$ and $z_2{}^c(\kappa)$. The output rules then form the basis for the choice of κ at the strategic stage.

Research and Development Selection. At the strategic stage, firm 2 observes κ_1 and in choosing its optimal κ_2 calculates the equilibrium point of the market stage play.[17] The optimal κ_2 is thus a function of κ_1, which we write as $\kappa_2{}^s = \kappa_2{}^s(\kappa_1)$ where the superscript s indicates that the optimal point occurs in sequential Stackelberg-like play. Knowing that this policy is optimal for firm 2, firm 1 in its prior move (rationally) calculates the dependence of the market-stage equilibrium on its own R&D decision, choosing κ_1 to

$$\max_{\kappa_1} \pi_1{}^0(\kappa_1, \kappa_2{}^s(\kappa_1))$$

Suppose that a solution to this problem exists and is unique; call it $\kappa_1{}^s$. Then (a) $\kappa_1{}^s$ determines $\kappa_2{}^s$ and (b) $\kappa_1{}^s$ and $\kappa_2{}^s$ jointly determine the equilibrium point

---

[16] Dasgupta and Stiglitz view R&D as a process of random sampling. With R&D expenditure κ, their inventions derive from a Poisson process with parameter $\lambda(\kappa)$ where $\lambda'(\kappa) > 0$ and $\lambda''(\kappa) < 0$. Thus pr[invention at t] $= \lambda(\kappa) \exp[-\lambda(\kappa)t]$ and pr[invention before t] $= 1 - \lambda(\kappa) \exp\{-\lambda(\kappa)t\}$. The present value v_0 of the firm is given by $v_0 = \pi_0 - \kappa + \lambda(v^* - v^0)/r$. where π_0 is the current profit flow and v^* is the post-invention value. This is the sum of the present value of the current profit flow plus the expected capital gain. This solves for $v_0 = \{\lambda v^* + (\pi_0 - \kappa)\}/(\lambda + r)$. This last expression is commonly used in the R&D literature.

[17] Again, we assume the firms do not produce at the strategic stage.

$z_1{}^c(\kappa_1{}^s, \kappa_2{}^s)$, $z_2{}^c(\kappa_1{}^s, \kappa_2{}^s)$. These R&D and output pairs constitute a perfect Nash solution to the two-stage game.

Entry Deterrence. Firm 1, the first mover at the strategic stage, reduces firm 2's market-stage output by choosing a high level of R&D. For deterrence to occur, the R&D level of firm 1 provides it with a low short-run marginal cost schedule and therewith a high Cournot equilibrium output. This high output leaves a low residual demand for firm 2, reducing its output and maximum profits. Firm 2's entry is deterred when this maximum is at best zero.

The potential for rational entry deterrence need not always be present. There are, in fact, cost and demand specifications following the general requirements set out in section 11.1 such that firm 2's Cournot equilibrium output would be strictly positive even if the leader firm 1 used an arbitrarily large R&D level.

The proof of this last statement is instructive. Let $\bar{z}_1$ be the output level for firm 1 which leaves a residual demand so that firm 2 can, at best, just earn zero profits, that is, z_1 is entry deterring. Let z_1^* be that output level where the marginal revenue associated with the industry demand is just zero. By the prior cost assumptions, even if firm 1 adopted an arbitrarily high R&D level, its marginal cost would be everywhere nonnegative. Therefore, for any level of R&D the most that firm 1 would produce is z_1^*. Since firm 1's monopoly output is simply its Cournot output when $z_2 \equiv 0$ and this Cournot reaction is decreasing in z_2, then it will produce less than z_1^* if firm 2 produces anything at all. This makes the residual demand facing 2 (if it enters) at least $p_2(z_1^*, z_2)$. As $p_2(\bar{z}_1, z_2)$ is the residual demand that just deters entry, a sufficient condition for entry deterrence is that $z_1^* < \bar{z}_1$.

Many Entrants. Suppose that conditions are such that firm 1 cannot keep firm 2 from entering. That is, a (high) entry-deterring output is not 1's best (Cournot) reply to any z_2, and thus is not credible. Nonetheless, it is quite clear that, for the cost, and demand conditions we have imposed, there will be some number J of independent firms whose Cournot equilibrium best replies imply an aggregate output z such that the residual demand available to the $(J + 1)$th firm does not permit that last firm strictly positive profits and therefore deters its entry.

Comparing Sequential and Simultaneous Research and Development Equilibria. We want to show first that $\kappa_1{}^s > \kappa_1{}^c$ and, conversely, $\kappa_2{}^s < \kappa_2{}^c$. The incumbent uses relatively more R&D and the second firm relatively less in comparison with the corresponding simultaneous Nash-in-R&D game. From this result the relative equilibria outputs for the two interactions can be compared.

Because both simultaneous and sequential models have identical market-stage play (albeit with different R&D levels), the profit payoff *functions* $\pi_j{}^0(\kappa)$ at the strategic stage are identical in these interactions. Figure 11.4 illustrates the equilibrium R&D decisions under the assumption that a unique equilibrium occurs in the strategic play. When the incumbent firm 1 is leader it exploits firm 2's known Cournot response. By moving to point S, the incumbent selects the R&D level that maximizes its profit while keeping firm 2 on its reaction function $r_2{}^c(\kappa_1)$. Comparing S and the usual Cournot equilibrium at C, we have

$\kappa_1{}^s > \kappa_1{}^c$ and $\kappa_2{}^s < \kappa_2{}^c$ as expected.

The implications of the differing R&D levels for the market stage equilibrium are evident in figure 11.5. The reader will recall from chapter 3, section 3.1.5, that (under the cost and demand conditions imposed there and here) the effect of a lower level of cost-saving investment shifts in the reaction function, and

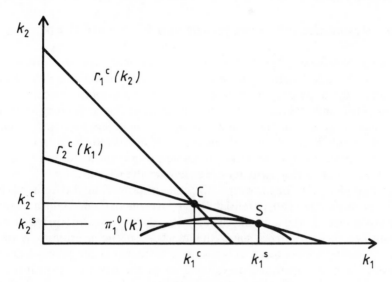

Figure 11.4
Research and development equilibria

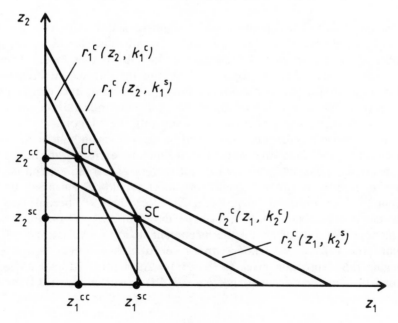

Figure 11.5
Market-stage equilibria

conversely. With the indicated differences in R&D from the strategic stage, the SC interaction results in a smaller output for the R&D follower firm 2 and a larger output for the incumbent R&D leader relative to the $\Gamma(\kappa, z)$ interaction. The reader can quickly show that the profit implications of these results are $\pi_1^{sc} > \pi_1^{cc}$ and $\pi_2^{sc} < \pi_2^{cc}$.

SE11.3   Research and Development and Monopoly Persistence

Gilbert and Newberry (1982) analyzed the possible strategic effects of an incumbent firm's R&D activity when the invention resulting from the R&D can be protected by a patent. The equilibrium in their model occurs with the incumbent firm undertaking all research and acquiring a sleeping patent (the research success is not implemented). It has been noted that this "monopoly persistence" result is overturned when research outcomes are uncertain or the firms are permitted to contract either to share production or research. Here, we consider the impact of *ex post* patent licensing on their result.

Gilbert and Newberry begin with an incumbent possessing a patent monopoly, but there is the recognized potential R&D investments can yield a patentable substitute product. If the entrant/rival makes the investment first and patents the substitute, the two firms share the market on the presumption that the products are perfect substitutes. If we assume further that the post-R&D market stage results in noncooperative play, the sum of the duopolists' profits will be less than that with a full monopoly. Gilbert and Newberry find that the incumbent monopolist would have an incentive to "throw money at the R&D problem" so as to beat even more efficient rivals in the patent race.

Pre-emptive R&D. The equilibrium for Gilbert and Newberry's two-stage game can be developed in a straightforward way with some notation. Let π^d be the profits of each firm should a duopoly follow the patent race, π^m be the post-race profits should a monopoly follow for the incumbent, Δc be the additional cost an inefficient incumbent must pay to beat the more efficient entrant in the patent race, and $\Delta\pi \equiv \pi^m - 2\pi^d > 0$ indicate the difference between industry profits with the monopoly and with the duopoly.

Gilbert and Newberry explain the incentive for the incumbent to use R&D pre-emptively in the following way. The incumbent earns π^d if the duopoly occurs, as does the entrant. This means that the entrant would expend up to π^d to win the race with other (equally efficient) would-be entrants. For the incumbent to deter entry, it must spend Δc more than π^d, because we have assumed this disadvantage. That is, an expenditure of $\Delta c + \pi^d$ on R&D would secure monopoly profits of π^m for the incumbent. If $\pi^m - (\Delta c + \pi^d) > \pi^d$, then the incumbent will indeed choose the level of R&D which deters entry. Rearranging this expression gives $(\pi^m - 2\pi^d) - \Delta c = \Delta\pi - \Delta c > 0$: as long as the incumbent's inefficiency does not exceed $\Delta\pi$, it will choose R&D to deter entry.

Post-Innovation Licensing. Salant (1984) and Cave (1985) have argued that the possibility of post-innovation bargaining and licensing undermines the

Gilbert anad Newberry deterrence results (see also Gallini, 1984; Gallini and Winter, 1985; Grossman and Shapiro, 1987). When transaction costs are not prohibitive, they specifically find that the efficient entrant will undertake the R&D and develop the invention with either the incumbent or the entrant then taking a patent license from the other to produce as a monopoly seller. Briefly, their argument goes as follows. First, with bargaining and licensing of patent rights, either the entrant or the incumbent will acquire both patents (for the original and new product) on some mutually agreeable terms. In this case there will be a single monopoly seller with total profits of π^m. Suppose that the entrant wins the patent race and enters into a contract with the incumbent either to sell full rights to its technology for that price or to purchase the incumbent's technology for $\pi^m - \pi^*$. In the second case the entrant would then produce as a monopolist. In both cases, the incumbent earns $\pi^m - \pi^*$ if it loses the patent race. Alternatively, to deter entry the incumbent is forced to spend $\pi^* + \Delta c$, in which case it earns $\pi^m - (\pi^* + \Delta c)$. Such deterrence is then rational if and only if $\pi^m - (\pi^* + \Delta c) > \pi^m - \pi^*$. Since this inequality cannot hold for $\Delta c > 0$, the incumbent never uses deterrence. Rather, the bargaining and licensing solution always occurs (ignoring transaction costs).

SE11.4   Risky Research and Development and Monopoly Persistence

A slightly more complex model with uncertainty about research outcomes, and without licensing, also avoids the Gilbert and Newberry "monopoly persistence" result. Again, consider an incumbent firm 1 and an entrant firm 2 choosing research expenditures κ_1 and κ_2 respectively. The expenditure yields research levels $\alpha(\kappa_1)$ and $\alpha(\kappa_2)$ within the two firms, with increasing but diminishing returns $\alpha' > 0$ and $\alpha'' < 0$. At given research levels the probability that the incumbent has success, and subsequently patents, is given by $h\{\alpha(\kappa_1) - \alpha(\kappa_2)\}$ where $h' > 0$, $h(0) = 0.5$, and of course $0 \leq h \leq 1$. In turn, $1 - h$ is the probability that the entrant is successful. Whichever firm wins, there is a subsequent decision: either leave the patent sleeping or develop the innovation for the market at an additional cost δ. The patent when developed yields net revenues R^*; if it is not developed by the entrant then the entrant earns zero, and if the incumbent does not develop it, then it earns R^0. The payoffs are summarized in table 11.1.[18] When these payoffs are used, the *expected* profit functions for the two firms become

$$\bar{\pi}_1 = (1 - h)(-\kappa_1) + h[\max\{(R^* - \kappa_1 - \delta), (R^0 - \kappa_1)\}] \qquad (11.25a)$$

$$\bar{\pi}_2 = (1 - h)(R^* - \kappa_2 - \delta) + h(-\kappa_2) \qquad (11.25b)$$

where the argument of the probability function $h(\cdot)$ is omitted for notational convenience.

The Nash-in-κ equilibrium for this game occurs at the joint stationarity point.

---

[18] The entrant's strategy of patenting without implementation is strongly dominated and not listed.

Table 11.1 Firm Payoffs

Developer	1's payoff	2's payoff
2	$-\kappa_1$	$R^* - \kappa_2 - \delta$
1	$R^* - \kappa_1 - \delta$	$-\kappa_2$
Neither	$R^0 - \kappa_1$	$-\kappa_2$

Partially differentiating the expected profit functions, equating them, and simplifying gives the equilibrium condition

$$\frac{\partial\alpha(\kappa_1)/\partial\kappa_1}{\partial\alpha(\kappa_2)/\partial\kappa_2} = \frac{R^* - \delta}{\max\{(R^* - \delta), R^0\}} \tag{11.26}$$

Depending on whether $R^0 \geq R^* - \delta$ or $R^0 < R^* - \delta$, either of two equilibria can result. If the net value of the invention is large, $R^* - \delta \geq 0$, then the right-hand side of (11.26) equals unity, which implies that the firms will undertake an equal amount of research ($\kappa_1 = \kappa_2$). Alternatively, when the invention has relatively low value, $R^0 < R^* - \delta$, the right-hand side of (11.26) is less than unity, the incumbent outspends the entrant on research ($\kappa_2 > \kappa_1$), and the patent is sleeping ($\delta = 0$).

SE11.5   Pre-emptive Research and Development and Scale Advantages

Dasgupta (1983) has studied the conditions under which an extant monopolist will find it profitable to pre-empt all potential innovations. Roughly, such pre-emption is not chosen by the monopolist unless there are increasing returns from the acquisition of patents.

A simple model can be used to develop the above results. Suppose again that there is an incumbent firm 1 and a single rival firm 2 competing for N patents. Suppose further that the innovations are identical, each yielding the same value to its patentee. Let the payoff to the incumbent when it wins n patents ($0 \leq n \leq N$) be given by $\pi_1(n)$. Similarly, when the rival wins n patents its payoff is $\pi_2(n)$. The patents are valued in the sense that (for $j = 1, 2$) more are preferred to less:

$$\pi_j(n + 1) > \pi_j(n) > 0 \qquad 0 \leq n \leq N - 1 \tag{11.27a}$$

It is also assumed that the incumbent firm has an advantage when an equal number of patents are taken:

$$\pi_1(n) > \pi_2(n) \qquad 0 \leq n \leq N \tag{11.27b}$$

and the uncommitted rival earns nothing $\pi_2(0) = 0$.

The final and critical assumption is that the rival's payoff is superadditive in the sense that

$$\frac{\pi_2(n)}{n} \geq \frac{\pi_2(n')}{n'} \qquad \text{for } n' < n \tag{11.28}$$

That is, the rival's average payoff (per patent) is nondecreasing in the number of patents held.

The importance of the superadditivity assumption is that it establishes the maximum bid price for any number of patents. For example, if the incumbent were to win exactly n patents when facing such a rival, he would do so by bidding nothing for the first $N - n$ and then the amount

$$\pi^*(n) = \frac{\pi_2(N) - \pi_2(N - n)}{n} \tag{11.29}$$

for each of the remainder. Since the rival's payoff is superadditive, it would not better this bid. This leaves a payoff to the incumbent in holding the n patents of

$$\pi_1(N) + n\pi^*(n) = \pi_1(N) + \pi_2(N) - \pi_2(N - n) \tag{11.30}$$

How should n be chosen by the incumbent to maximize its profits? That is left as an exercise for the reader. Our immediate interest is with the conditions for pre-emption. A sufficient condition for the incumbent to pre-empt every innovation is that the incumbent's payoff given by (11.30) be strictly increasing in n and such that

$$\pi_1(n + 1) - \pi_1(n) \geq \pi_2(N - n) - \pi_2(N - (n + 1)) \tag{11.31}$$

for all n. This condition is intuitive, as it simply requires that the total industry profits (the sum of those of the two firms) increase with the number of patents held by the incumbent. Will the profit-maximizing incumbent find it optimal to completely pre-empt? That would further require that the incumbent have returns increasing at an increasing rate, that is,

$$\pi_1(n + 1) - \pi_1(n) > \pi_1(n) - \pi_1(n - 1) \qquad \text{for } n \geq 1 \tag{11.32a}$$

and have the first patent advantage

$$\pi_1(1) - \pi_1(0) \geq \pi_2(N) - \pi_2(N - 1) \tag{11.32b}$$

SE11.6 Innovation, Patent Races, and Strategies

If an innovation, once discovered, were costlessly available to all who would use it, private entrepreneurs would not be able to appropriate the value of their R&D investments. This lack of ownership would discourage innovation and impose an inefficiency loss on the economy. Several solutions to the problem have been proposed. The first is to give innovators monopoly rights to their R&D successes by patent and copyright.[19] The second solution is to have government be the primary source of R&D, financing its efforts out of general revenues and permitting all who would use its innovations to do so without cost. The third solution is to foster private innovation by subsidizing private R&D, as with subsidies to universities.

---

[19] Patents, when used, are not always as effective as might be thought. Braun and MacDonald (1982), for example, found that semiconductor firms relied more on secrecy to protect their innovations from rivals because patents were too costly to effectively implement and enforce.

Appropriation of Gain with Bertrand Play. Those who concern themselves with the appropriability question as regards R&D and the design of the above solutions, roughly have in mind a game in which (two) identical competitors produce with constant unit costs and reach a Nash-in-price market equilibrium. In this case the firm's choice of whether to be an innovator, and incur R&D fixed costs F, or an imitator (without R&D costs) has the standard prisoners' dilemma format given in the bimatrix of table 11.2. The Nash equilibrium is for both firms to shun R&D, for innovation is a dominated strategy.

Table 11.2 The Prisoners' Dilemma

	k innovate	k imitate
j innovate	$(-F, -F)$	$(-F, 0)$
j imitate	$(0, -F)$	$(0, 0)$

The price competition, identical firms, and constant costs are critical to this equilibrium result (and, possibly, to the need for an appropriability solution, say by patent). Suppose, alternatively, that the (again identical) firms reach a Nash-in-quantity market equilibrium changing the profit entries in the above table. In this case the innovating firm would receive half the industry profits $\pi/2$ while incurring the fixed R&D cost F. If one firm (say j) could then make a binding commitment not to be the innovator and communicate this to its rival (for example, by selling its research capability), then the game would have an equilibrium R&D solution with firm j imitating its rival's innovation when $\pi/2 > F$. Or, lacking such a commitment, the game has a Nash equilibrium in the mixed extension with each firm playing innovation with a probability of 0.5.[20]

The Patent Race. Dasgupta and Stiglitz (1980a) set out the basic model of competitive R&D where the innovator's success is protected by a patent. A simplified version of their analysis is instructive here. We begin, as they do, with identical firms. If one of these firms makes an R&D expenditure of κ at date $t = 0$ it will succeed in the sought-after invention at date $T(\kappa) > 0$. Let $T'(\kappa) < 0$ and $T''(\kappa) > 0$, so that there are diminishing returns. While all firms have the same technological opportunities, the R&D competition is designed as a *race*, or *tournament*, in the sense that the firm achieving the invention first (the "winner") patents the invention and takes all R&D payoffs. All other contestant firms receive zero payoff from the patent race, despite their investment. The research period is endogenous, concluding with the discovery. Let π indicate the winner's payoff with $v = \rho^{T(\kappa)}\pi - \kappa$ being its present value with discount factor ρ.

Dasgupta and Stiglitz model the R&D competition as a one-stage game, looking for the Nash-in-κ equilibrium. To describe that equilibrium, they first

---

[20] This Nash-in-quality result does not imply that the imposition of a (costless) patent system would not be welfare enhancing.

argue as follows that no more than one firm will undertake R&D (that is, has $\kappa > 0$). Any firm that does not win has negative present value ($v < 0$) and is thus not value maximizing (given that it could also choose $\kappa = 0$ and with that $v = 0$). Suppose, alternatively, that several firms tie for the date of invention and share the prize equally. On the Nash-in-κ assumption any of these firms could then increase its R&D marginally, complete its invention marginally earlier, and assure that it alone is the winner. Thus, when the equilibrium exists, it must have one winner who is the only firm making an R&D expenditure and the κ^* level of that expenditure must be such that it yields zero present value for the firm.[21] (If $v > 0$, some firm could choose a marginally greater κ and assure itself of being a winner with $v > 0$.)

Despite first appearances, if *all* firms play Nash-in-κ then the *single* winner choosing κ^* cannot be an equilibrium, for the proposed winner will find that (on the assumption that all others hold $\kappa = 0$) it could increase its present value by reducing its R&D expenditure below κ^*. In short, an equilibrium in pure strategies does not exist for this game. It is apparent that the underlying reason for the failure of a pure strategy to produce an equilibrium is that the firms' payoffs are discontinuous in the strategy variables: small differences in research expenditures can cause large jumps in payoffs in the tournament setting.

Mixed Strategy Solution. Despite the discontinuities, a mixed strategy equilibrium does exist for the game. To show this we use the notation introduced above but now limit attention to just three firms. Let J indicate one such firm, with k and l its rivals.

In a mixed strategy equilibrium each firm will be indifferent to the pure strategies used in its mixed play. We know from above that each firm j receives zero payoff when playing either $\kappa_j = 0$ or $\kappa_j = \kappa^*$ as pure strategies. Thus, when j randomizes its R&D expenditure over the interval $[0, \kappa^*]$, its expected payoff must also be zero. That is, for each firm j,

$$\kappa^* \operatorname{pr}(\kappa_j \geq \hat{\kappa}_k \text{ and } \kappa_j \geq \hat{\kappa}_l) - \kappa_j = 0 \tag{11.33}$$

where κ is the pure strategy and $\hat{\kappa}$ is its randomization.[22] Given that the firms choose their mixed strategies independently, this reduces to

$$\kappa^* \operatorname{pr}(\kappa_j \geq \hat{\kappa}_k) \operatorname{pr}(\kappa_j \geq \hat{\kappa}_l) - \kappa_j = 0 \tag{11.34}$$

If we let $F_j(\kappa)$ be the cumulative density with which each firm j adopts R&D expenditure κ, this last equation can be arranged to yield

$$F_k(\kappa_j) F_l(\kappa_j) = \frac{\kappa_j}{\kappa^*} \tag{11.35}$$

At a symmetric equilibrium each firm chooses the same randomization, and therefore

$$F(\kappa) = \left(\frac{\kappa}{\kappa^*}\right)^{1/2} \tag{11.36}$$

solves for the R&D expenditure of each firm when $0 \leq \kappa \leq \kappa^*$. It is of interest

---

[21] κ^* solves $v = \rho^{T(\kappa^*)} \pi - \kappa^* = 0$.

[22] For $\kappa_j < \hat{\kappa}_k$ and $\kappa_j < \hat{\kappa}_l$ firm j receives nothing.

in this solution that the R&D rivalry for the patent produces zero expected profit for each firm. That is, competition for the patent monopoly dissipates any (*ex ante*) monopoly gain.[23]

SE11.7   Winner Take All with Price Competition

Technological competition at an early stage and then price competition in final-good markets leads to a "winner take all" result similar to that occurring in patent races. To see how this develops, consider a homogeneous-good Bertrand duopoly where both firms initially have constant marginal costs c_0 and at equilibrium each earns zero profits (recall chapter 3, section 3.1.4). Suppose that a single discrete innovation becomes available which, when adopted by either firm, lowers unit cost to $c_1 < c_0$.[24] If it is assumed that all costs and revenues are flows obtaining in perpetuity, the present value of the unit cost savings is $v = (c_0 - c_1)/r$, where r is the appropriate discount rate. When only one of the duopolists adopts the project it can price its output to earn $v = (c_0 - c_1)z_0/r$, where z_0 is the quantity demanded assuming that c_0 does not exceed the monopoly price at cost c_1.[25]

Let $C(t)$ indicate the known present value of investments (a sunk cost) associated with adopting the innovation at date t. The equilibrium time of adoption t^* for one of the duopolists is the solution of $v = C(t^*)\exp(rt^*)$. Given that one firm has adopted the innovation, the second will never invest, since the Bertrand competition with identical and constant unit cost will yield a post-innovation profit flow of zero (and therefore a loss of $C(t)$ to the rival adopting at date $t > t^*$). Note that if one firm planned to adopt after t^*, then the second could adopt slightly earlier. That is, any planned adoption after t^* by firm 1 would allow firm 2 to pre-empt it. This "winner take all" feature of this Nash-in-price game is similar to that occurring in a patent race (recall E11.1).

Strong Invariance to Market Structure. Sah and Stiglitz (1987) have developed an alternative model of R&D competition where innovation is uncertain and, if more than one firm succeeds with innovation, they compete in price in the final-goods market. Further, the firms may fund many discrete R&D projects to enhance their probability of success. Sah and Stiglitz's key result is termed "strong invariance": the number of R&D projects adopted in the industry, as well as the expenditures on all possible projects, is independent of the number of firms in the industry. A little extra notation allows us to follow their analysis. Suppose that all R&D projects are discrete and have either a successsful or an unsuccessful result. Let κ be the R&D expenditure on some project and $h(\kappa)$ the probability of its success, where $h_\kappa \equiv \partial h(\kappa)/\partial \kappa > 0$ and $1 > h > 0$ for positive finite expenditures. Each of the $j = 1, 2, \ldots, J$ firms can undertake as

---

[23] The efficiency of this and other forms of *rent-seeking* behavior are considered in chapter 2, section 2.4.

[24] Note that this is in contrast with the models generally set out in the text, where a continuum of investments indexed by κ are available.

[25] Recall section 11.3. Innovations which satisfy this relationship of monopoly price to new cost level are often called *nondrastic*. Otherwise, they are said to be *drastic*.

many projects as it chooses, but each one is directed toward the same specific invention (mutual exclusivity). If firm j spends κ_{jn} on project n and if it takes $n = 1, 2, \ldots, N_j$ projects, each of which have independent outcomes, then the probability that j will have at least one success is $H_j = 1 - \Pi_{n=1}^{N_j} \{1 - h(\kappa_{jn})\}$.

If it is assumed that the firms are Bertrand market competitors, then (a) positive rents R are received by any given firm if it innovates but no other firm does, and (b) zero rents are received if two or more firms innovate (the benefits of the innovation are captured by consumers with Bertrand competition). Let $\bar{H}_j \equiv \Pi_{k \neq j} \Pi_{n=1}^{N_k} \{1 - h(\kappa_{kn})\}$ indicate the probability that all firms except j will be unsuccessful in their R&D projects. In turn,

$$\bar{\pi}_j = RH_j\bar{H}_j - \sum_{n=1}^{N_j} (\kappa_{jn} + F) \tag{11.37}$$

is firm j's expected profits when incurring F in fixed project costs.

In a symmetric equilibrium where all projects are undertaken with the same expenditure κ, each has the same probability of success $h(\kappa)$, and each firm adopts the same number of projects N,

$$H = 1 - \{1 - h(\kappa)\}^N \tag{11.38}$$

is the probability than any firm is successful and

$$\bar{H} = \{1 - h(\kappa)\}^{JN-N} \tag{11.39}$$

is the probability that its competitors will be unsuccessful. On substituting these probabilities in the expected profit function, the stationarity conditions for maximum profits (with respect to both κ and N) and the symmetric equilibrium are given by

$$R(1 - h)^{JN-1}h_k = 1 \tag{11.40a}$$

$$R(1 - h)^{JN-1}h = \kappa + F \tag{11.40b}$$

These are two equations in the expenditure level per project κ and the number of projects per firm N.

Note that JN is the total number of projects undertaken by the industry; J and N appear only in this product in expressions (11.40) and therefore the product can be thought of as a single variable. This is the basis of Sah and Stiglitz's "strong invariance" result: a change in the number of firms J simply changes N and leaves the product JN and therefore the optimal κ unaltered. Thus the only effect of an increase (decrease) in the number of Bertrand competitors is to decrease (increase) the number of projects adopted by each. For example, with a triopoly each firm would undertake two-thirds the number of projects as a duopoly.[26]

---

[26] Sah and Stiglitz show further that, because the research outcomes are uncertain, it is socially desirable to have duplicate research efforts directed toward the same invention. Roughly, this results because the *ex ante* probability of overall success is enhanced by the duplication. In a similar mode, Tandon (1983) shows that Bertrand competition *may* lead to an excessive amount of duplication depending on the size of cost savings brought about by the invention.

12 Competition with Monopoly Outcomes

The tradition in industrial economics is to consider the static single-seller monopoly and large-numbers perfect-competition solutions as polar cases and to characterize industry solutions that lie between these poles as expressing some degree of monopoly power (say, as measured by the excess of price over marginal cost). It is also traditional to think of monopoly as resulting from cooperation among firms and, conversely, to equate the competitive solution with noncooperative behavior. Oligopoly solutions which express some degree of monopoly power are then thought to involve some degree of cooperation (see, for example, Scherer, 1980, chs 5 and 7, Shepard, 1985). Our intent in this chapter is to show that the traditional equivalence drawn between monopoly solutions and cooperation on the other hand and the competitive solution and noncooperative behavior on the other hand is misleading. There are more rules to the oligopoly game than are captured by simply specifying cooperative or noncooperative play.

Consider for example, and more generally as a benchmark, the perfectly competitive equilibrium with a homogeneous good. The usual rules of play for this game include noncooperative Nash-in-price strategies, one market period with simultaneous decision-making, and complete information. Holding to the noncooperative rule, variations in (a) the strategy variable, (b) the number of market periods and the sequence of decisions, and (c) available information about rivals and the way that is updated over time are important to the final industry equilibrium. While these variations can produce wide divergences from the perfectly competitive equilibrium – differences in monopoly power – each solution is based on *noncooperative* play.

In this chapter we are concerned with the manner in which variations in these rules determine the extent of monopoly power expressed by an industry. Section 12.1 retains the static complete-information noncooperative rules and asks what equilibrium effects are brought about by changes in the firms' strategy variables (represented by conjectural variations). This analysis carries some interest, as a key weighting factor in the relationship turns out to be a measure of the size distribution of firms in the industry. Thus it provides one way of characterizing the voluminous empirical literature relating profits (as a surrogate for monopoly power) and market concentration. In the remaining sections of the chapter a variety of explicitly dynamic oligopoly models, with and without incomplete information, are investigated. Along with other aspects of the equilibria, the implications of the various specifications on the degree of monopoly power are outlined.

In each model, and this is generally true throughout this book, the concern is with noncooperative solutions. There are no binding commitments among the firms and at every point in the game each acts unilaterally in its own best interest. We are thus left with the conclusion that other rules of play, rather than any relaxation in the noncooperative behavior of the industry constituents, lead to expressions of monopoly. Industry dynamics in which the history of play matters, in which information about rivals and market conditions is incomplete, and where the nature of the product and market institutions permit a range of strategy variables are all critical determinants of the oligopoly solution, each affecting the industry's expression of monopoly.

Two Warnings. It is usual in the literature to label oligopoly solutions which express some degree of monopoly power as "tacitly collusive" or "implicitly collusive." This is acceptable, if it is also understood that the reference to collusion does not imply any cooperation (binding commitments) among the firms.[1] Secondly, the literature frequently refers to noncooperative behavior as "competitive." That is also acceptable, if it is also understood that competitive behavior is only one ingredient used to reach the standard perfectly competitive industry solution. When, for example, it is stated that there is competition among some small number of Cournot–Nash oligopolists (static model with complete information) it should then be recognized that the competition results in a degree of monopoly at the equilibrium.

Finally, it should be noted that much of what is set out in this chapter has been developed earlier in chapters 3, 9, and 10. The reader is encouraged to review those chapters before beginning here, as there is considerable cross-referencing.

12.1 Structure, Conduct, and Performance

Beginning with Mason (1939) and then continuing perforce with Bain (1959) into the early 1970s, industrial organization economics turned from the standard microeconomic theory framework to an alternative structure–conduct–performance (SCP) paradigm. Although it is now strongly qualified in academic work, the SCP paradigm continues to be used with less qualification in survey and policy-setting analyses. Based on the concept that the available principles of microeconomics are inadequate to deal with the complex problems of "modern"

---

[1] Posner commented on this matter at an early stage: ". . . in some circumstances competing sellers might be able to coordinate their pricing without conspiring in the usual sense of the term – that is, without any overt or detectable acts of communication. This is the phenomenon that lawyers call conscious parallelism and some economists call oligopolistic interdependence, but I perfer to call implicit collusion in contrast to the explicit collusion of the formal cartel or its underground counterpart." (Posner, 1976, p. 40.)

business, the paradigm relies instead on casual observation of industries, institutional descriptions, and metaphor (see, for example, Bain, 1959, pp. 36–8, 295–301, 310–15). These analytical procedures are generally organized about maintained hypotheses linking the industry's structural characteristics broadly to the conduct patterns of its constituent firms and, in turn, to the industry's economic performance (deadweight loss). While the links among the paradigm's three elements are often said to "flow in all directions," firm conduct variables are frequently considered to follow from *industry* structure, and that structure is then directly and causally linked to performance (see, for example, Caves, 1982, ch. 2).

The link between industry structure and performance, in the form of concentration–profit studies, was the centerpiece of industrial economics in the period 1950–75.[2] The fundamental hypothesis maintained in those studies was the intuitive one that persistently concentrated industries result in greater monopoly power and profits.[3] Despite the time spent on variations of model specifications in these empirical studies, adherents to the SCP paradigm generally side stepped the development of any systematic theoretical basis for the hypothesized link between structure and performance. Rather, they simply posited the "apparent" tendency for implicit and overt collusion to be more prevalent in industries where concentration is high.[4]

In the last decade or so several theoretical links have been established between the size distribution of firms (industry concentration) and the industry's average profit level. In this section these links are studied in a static model using the conjectural variation representation of the Nash solution concept. This follows the developments by Rader (1972), Cowling (1976), Cowling and Waterson (1976) and Clarke and Davies (1983).

12.1.1 Structural Analysis

Consider an industry with $j = 1, 2, \ldots, J$ firms. When a homogeneous good is produced, each firm has a (potentially unique) cost schedule $c_j(z_j)$. On the demand side there is the usual notation: z_j denotes firm j's output level, $z = \Sigma_j z_j$ is the aggregate industry output, and the market price is inversely related to z in the function $p(z)$.

Each firm maximizes its profits $\pi_j(z) = p(z)z_j - c_j(z_j)$ by choosing z_j from the stationarity condition

$$p\left\{1 - \frac{1}{\eta}\frac{z_j}{z}(1 + \gamma_j)\right\} = c_j' \tag{12.1}$$

---

[2] Weiss (1974) reviews over 50 such studies in the manufacturing sector, while apologizing for not reviewing many others and omitting altogether the large literature on profits and concentration in banking.

[3] For some comments on the empirical test of this hypothesis see section 12.1.4.

[4] This is an appropriate place to note Sawyer's (1981, ch. 10) criticism of SCP analysis for its misplaced emphasis. In the SCP paradigm the conduct of firms is strongly conditioned by the industry structure. This means that the paradigm places emphasis on the industry rather than on the nature of the firms in the industry. The result, Sawyer argues, is that rivalry and competitive processes among firms are frequently overlooked or minimized.

where

$$\eta = -\frac{p}{z}\frac{dz}{dp}$$

and

$$\gamma_j = \frac{d(\Sigma_{k \neq j} z_k)}{dz_j}$$

are respectively the market demand elasticity and the quantity conjectural variations of firm j relative to the aggregate response of rivals and c'_j is the marginal cost.[5] For the moment, consider the Cournot–Nash solution, so that $\gamma_j = 0$ and (12.1) reduces to

$$p\left(1 - \frac{1}{\eta}\frac{z_j}{z}\right) = c'_j \tag{12.2}$$

Following Rader (1972, pp. 271–2) it is usual to multiply this expression by z_j and sum over all firms to give

$$L \equiv \sum_j L_j s_j \equiv \sum_j \left(\frac{p - c'_j}{p}\right) s_j = \frac{H}{\eta} \tag{12.3}$$

where $s_j \equiv z_j/z$ is firm j's market share, $L_j = (p - c'_j)/p$ is the price–cost margin for firm j, L is the **industry price–cost margin** (the market-share-weighted price–cost margins of constituent firms), and the sum of squared market shares $H \equiv \Sigma_j (s_j)^2$ is termed the **Herfindahl index** of industry concentration.[6] Notice that it is the *marginal cost* c'_j which is paired with price in the price–cost margin.

E12.1

Measuring Concentration

For any distribution of firm sizes (market shares) in an industry, the variance about the mean is given by $\text{var} = \Sigma_j (z_j - z/J)^2$. Completing the square and rearranging gives $H = (v^2 + 1)/J$, where v is the coefficient of variation in outputs, which is the ratio of the standard deviation to the distribution mean. As the firms tend toward equal shares, v goes to zero and $H = 1/J$. That is, the reciprocal of H, called the **numbers equivalent**, is the number of equal-sized firms which would generate that measure. Moreover, it is evident that

---

[5] Recall the interpretation of nonzero conjectural variations in static models given in chapter 3, section 3.1.1. Here, the conjectural equilibria parameterized by γ_j are to be viewed as representations of Nash equilibria with different strategy variables. As will be evident later, this representation is analytically convenient and leads to results which are relatively easy to interpret.

[6] We might alternatively use a definition of industry price–cost margin as the geometric mean of the L_j. In this case we have $L^* \equiv \Pi_j (L_j^{s_j}) = \Pi_j (s_j/\eta^{s_j}) = \exp(E)/\eta$, where $E \equiv \Sigma_j s_j \ln(s_j)$ is the entropy measure of concentration. Note that $L^*/\exp(E) = L/H$. See Encaoua and Jacquemin (1980) for the properties of the entropy measure. Hannah and Kay (1975), Davies (1979b), Geroski (1983), and Kwoka (1984) provide derivations for other concentration measures and comment on their applicability.

$0 < H \leqslant 1$, depending on the value of J ($\infty > J \geqslant 1$).[7]

In the United States concentration measures are usually based on the US Bureau of Census Standard Industry Classification (SIC), most often at the four-digit level. Concentration *ratios*, which reflect the percentage of a Census industry's value of shipments for the four largest firms (CR4) or eight largest firms (CR8) are generally employed. Ornstein (1976), using data from 1947 and 1956, reports a high degree of correlation between CR4 and the Herfindahl index for four-digit SIC industries.[8] As CR4 requires data on only four firms plus the industry aggregate and is highly correlated with H, it is the standard in empirical studies.

Table 12.1 gives weighted CR4 measures (using relative value of shipments as weights) for several years at the four-digit level. Notice that, on this basis, aggregate US concentration increased from 35 to 39 percent over the 15 years from 1947 to 1972. For cross-sectional comparison, Table 12.2 tabulates CR4, 50-firm H indices, and the numbers equivalent $(1/H)$ for selected four-digit industries in the census year 1982.[9]

Table 12.1 CR4 Trend

Year	CR4
1947	35
1958	37
1966	39
1972	39

Table 12.2 CR4 Cross-section

Industry	CR4	H	1/H
Meat packing	29	325	31
Pharmaceuticals	26	318	31
Soaps/detergents	60	1306	8
Petroleum refining	28	380	26
Tires/tubes	66	1591	6
Glass containers	50	966	10
Primary aluminum	64	1704	6
Metal cans	50	790	13
Computers	43	793	13
Radios/TVs	49	751	13

[7] Further properties of the Herfindahl index can be found in Hannah and Kay (1975). Kamerschen and Lam (1975) and Marfels (1975) compare H with other concentration indices. Schmalensee (1977b) and Benston (1985) examine the difficulties in deriving estimates of H from published data.

[8] UCLA Research Program in Competition and Business Policy, unpublished research. The rank correlation between CR4 and H using 1947 data on 110 industries is 0.99; using 1956 data on 107 industries it is 0.98. The rank correlation between changes in CR4 and changes in H over these two dates, based on 97 industries, is 0.92.

[9] Derived from *1982 Census of Manufacturers, Concentration Ratios in Manufacturing*, US Bureau of Census, Washington, DC, 1986.

Structural Model. The manner in which market shares are aggregated by the Herfindhal index makes it a useful measure of concentration: larger values of H occur when a few firms produce a larger portion of the industry output, and conversely. What about the proportional deviation (mark-up) L of market price over marginal cost? On the intuition that the greater the excess of market price over marginal cost the greater the extent of monopoly, Lerner (1934) defined L as the index of **monopoly power** expressed by the industry. Greater values of L imply greater monopoly power, and conversely: in the perfectly competitive case $L = 0$ so that there is no monopoly power, and with a single seller, or perfect cartel, L reaches its maximum (other things being equal).

Using these interpretations, Cowling and Waterson (1976) and others have suggested that the relationship given by (12.3) provides a theoretical justification for the long-standing hypothesis that industry concentration leads to poor industry performance (greater monopoly power, high price–cost margins). More generally equation (12.3) is referred to as the **structural model** and given the following interpretation. Industry *structure* (the concentration measure H and elasticity of demand η), working through *conduct* (profit maximization and the Cournot response of rivals), determines industry *performance* (the percentage mark-up L of price over cost). Analyses based on this specific model, where particular levels of concentration are interpreted as establishing acceptable and unacceptable monopoly power levels, have taken a prominent place in US antitrust policy (see the Department of Justice *Merger Guidelines 1984* and, more generally, Posner, 1976, and Liebeler, 1978).

Again, the structural model of equation (12.3) does not rely on any explicit form of collusive behavior. Rather, the monopoly power arises from the exogenous assumption of Cournot–Nash play and the restriction on entry (the model fixes the number of firms at J): these conditions assure that the equilibrium market price is above the industry-averaged marginal cost in what Cubbin (1975b, 1983) interprets as an "apparently collusive" arrangement. Again, do not be misled: the equilibrium here arises with best-reply responses in *noncooperative* Cournot–Nash competition.

Price–Cost Margin. While the Herfindahl index has many features which recommend it as a summary measure of industry structure (in a homogeneous-good industry), the price–cost margin is poorly suited as a measure of the deadweight loss arising from a monopoly restriction of output M_zL.[10] To see this simply, consider a quadratic approximation to the monopoly demand

$$z = b_0 + b_1 p + b_2 p^2 \tag{12.4}$$

where b_0, b_1, and b_2 are appropriate parameters assuring that, for positive prices and quantities, lower price leads to a demand for greater quantities. Redefine units so that the (constant) marginal cost is unity. Then, ignoring income effects, the monopoly deadweight loss is

$$M_zL = \int_1^{p^m} z(p)\,dp - (p^m - 1)z^m \tag{12.5}$$

where z^m and p^m are the monopoly output and price levels respectively.

---

[10] See chapter 2, section 2.4 for a full development of M_zL.

Performing the integration and making the obvious substitutions yields

$$M_zL = -\left(\frac{L}{1-L}\right)^2 \left\{\frac{b_1}{2} + \frac{b_2}{3}\left(\frac{3-L}{1-L}\right)\right\} \qquad (12.6)$$

M_zL is a nonlinear function of L with, as the reader can readily show, direct *and* inverse relationships both being possible depending on the sign and relative magnitudes of the parameters b_1 and b_2.

Even if attention were limited to regions where M_zL and L are positively related, in a cross-section of industries with different b_1 and b_2 the ordering of industries by L and M_zL would generally differ depending on the relative sizes of b_1 and b_2 across the industries. This is seen most clearly and simply for the linear demand case where (with $b_2 = 0$)

$$M_zL = -\frac{b_1}{2}\left(\frac{L}{1-L}\right)^2 \qquad (12.7)$$

Although M_zL is increasing in L here,[11] an industry with small L may have a relatively large M_zL (because b_1 is relatively large in absolute value), and conversely.[12]

E12.2 _____

Price–Cost Margins and Monopoly Deadweight Loss

Let the demand function facing the monopolist have the constant elasticity form

$$z = \alpha p^{-\beta} \qquad \alpha > 0, \beta > 1$$

where β is the elasticity and α is a "scale" parameter. In turn, the inverse demand is $p = \alpha^{1/\beta} z^{-1/\beta}$, and conditions for maximum profit with constant marginal cost c are simply

$$p^m = \frac{c}{1 - 1/\beta}$$

With some minor rearrangement we have the well-known result that the price–cost margin is constant for all levels of output, and is equal to the inverse of the demand elasticity: $L = \pi/p^m z^m = 1/\beta$. For later use, also note that the demand scale parameter α has no effect on p^m, L, or the monopoly profit rate $\pi/p^m z^m$.

The monopoly loss can be calculated in a straightforward way:

$$M_zL = \int_{z^m}^{z^c} \alpha^{1/\beta} z^{-1/\beta}\, dz - c(z^c - z^m)$$

---

[11] Note that, for this linear demand case, $dM_zL/dL = -b_1\{L/(1-L)\}\{(1-L+L)/(1-L)^2\} = -b_1 L/(1-L)^3$. Since monopolists operate in the "elastic" portion of demand where $\eta > 1$, $1 - L > 0$. As a result L and M_zL will be positively related.

[12] With some substitutions (12.7) can be written as $M_zL = (p^m z^m)L^2 \eta/2 = (p^m z^m)L/2$. (Caution: this expression is valid only for the single-seller monopoly.) Thus, the monopolist's revenue scales L to "produce" the total deadweight loss. That is, monopolies with small revenues will have small M_zL even when they exhibit a large degree of monopoly power.

where z^c is the competitive output level. The usual monopoly and competitive outputs can easily be expressed in terms of parameters

$$z^m = \alpha(c\beta^*)^{-\beta}$$

$$z^c = \alpha c^{-\beta}$$

Substituting these in the expression for M_zL gives, after some simplification,

$$M_zL = \alpha[\beta^*\{c^{1-\beta} - (c\beta^*)^{1-\beta}\} - c\{c^{-\beta} - (c\beta^*)^{-\beta}\}]$$

where $\beta^* = 1/(1 - 1/\beta)$. The term in square brackets is positive, so that the monopoly loss is necessarily positive. An increase in the demand parameter α therefore increases M_zL. However, as shown above α does not affect either L or $\pi/p^m z^m$. Variations in α can produce different values of the M_zL and these can be associated with any given price–cost margin (which is independent of α).

As a numerical example, consider the specific parameters $\alpha = 100$, $\beta = 1.8$, and $c = 0.5$, which give $L = \pi/p^m z^m = 0.56$ and $M_zL = 53.2$. For some second monopolist suppose that $\alpha' = 200$, $\beta' = 2.0$, and $c = 0.5$, which give $L' = (\pi/p^m z^m)' = 0.50$ and $M_zL' = 100$. In contrast with the usual result the monopolist with the greater price–cost margin and greater profit rate has the lower M_zL.

Monopoly Power and Profitability. Ignore for the moment the deficiencies that L has as a measure of M_zL. Further, assume that the marginal cost of each firm is constant (but not necessarily the same constant in the cross-section of firms). Multiplying L_j by z_j/z_j then gives

$$L_j = \frac{p_j z_j - c'_j z_j}{p_j z_j} = \frac{\pi_j}{R_j}$$

where π_j is firm j's profits and R_j is dollar sales. Under these assumptions, L_j is identical with the firm's *profitability* measured by the profit-to-sales ratio and L is the associated industry profitability measure. This equivalence generally lies behind the extensive literature using profit-to-sales ratios in market structure–monopoly power empirical studies. For example, in one study Long and Ravenscraft (1984, p. 7) comment (emphasis added):

> . . In recent years several contributions have been made which expand on the conceptual framework for the profit–concentration empirical work. Cowling and Waterson (1976), Gollop and Roberts (1979), Dansby and Willig (1980), Long (1982) and Martin (1983) have demonstrated that the Lerner Index, price minus *average* cost divided by price, is a measure of monopoly power which may be derived from an optimization exercise in long-run equilibrium models that include conjectural variables. This conceptual work provides additional support for the profit–concentration literature, particularly the studies which have used profit/sales as a dependent variable.

It is again stressed that the monopoly power index L_j is in the first instance the percentage excess of price over *marginal* cost, and it equals the profit-to-sales ratio only if average cost is assumed to be, or actually is, constant. Secondly, while monopoly power is often thought of in terms of excess profitability, this is a fallacy if monopoly power is intended to be a measure of welfare loss. As we have demonstrated above, the deadweight loss to monopoly can be associated with any degree of profitability.

Accounting and Economic Profits. While considering profit–concentration studies it should also be noted that accounting profit is generally an imperfect surrogate for economic profit. There are many, possibly large, errors in such a substitution. As Demsetz (1982b) has noted, monopoly profits will often be capitalized in the accounting value of the firm's assets (in, for example, goodwill, patents, or trademarks). A related problem occurs with rent-seeking, which may dissipate monopoly profits (recall chaper 2, section 2.4). Yet another problem arises when profits are based on accounting depreciation schedules or methods of expensing (R&D, advertising, etc.) which reflect tax considerations more than economic depreciation.

The underlying analytical problem in measuring economic profitability is to relate income flows to the specific investments (in time) which produce those flows. The key difficulty is that the *accounting* rate of return (ARR) associates current profit flow with a wide spectrum of prior investments, while *economic* rates of return (ERR) must associate specific future flows with current investments. One frequently mentioned case in which these "staging" problems are immaterial, and the ARR and ERR are equal, is when economic and accounting profit exhibit the same constant exponential rate of growth.[13] For a comprehensive analysis of the interaction between accounting measurement biases (relative to economic values) and measures of performance, the reader is referred to Stauffer (1971).

E12.3

Bain on Accounting and Economic Profits

In his early work on the concentration–profits relationship Bain (1951) was quite explicit about the differences between economic and accounting measures of profits. Bain's ideal (theoretical) measure of profitability was the ratio of excess profits to sales. He defined excess profits as ". . . a return in excess of all costs, including the interest cost of capital" (Bain 1951, p. 294). Bain's preferred surrogate for this measure was the ratio of accounting profits to equity, as data for that measure were generally available and, in a test suite, he found that this ratio was "highly correlated" with his excess profits-to-sales ratio. As the quotation from Long and Ravenscraft (1984) indicates, it is now common to use the excess profits-to-sales ratio directly by adopting the following technique. Note, to begin, that

[13] Furthermore, if the ARR exceeds this exponential growth rate g, then ARR > ERR > g, and conversely. Detailed analyses of these issues are provided by Solomon (1970), Stauffer (1971), Clarkson (1977), and Fisher and McGowen (1983).

$$\pi^a = \pi + c^*$$

where π^a is accounting profits, π is economic profits, and c^* is the opportunity cost of the firm's net investments κ. We can express these costs as $r^*\kappa$, where r^* is an appropriate risk-adjusted average discount rate. Next, note the identities

$$\frac{\pi}{R} = \frac{\pi^a - r^*\kappa}{R} = \frac{\kappa}{R}\left(\frac{\pi^a}{\kappa} - r^*\right)$$

Either the middle expression or that on the right-hand side (especially in logarithmic form) can be used as a proxy for economic profitability. In both cases, however, π^a/R is deficient as a surrogate for π/R as it ignores the quantity $r^*(\kappa/R)$.[14]

12.1.2 Causality and the Structure–Conduct–Performance Paradigm

Although (12.3) informs us that L and H are positively related, some care must be exercised to distinguish between this relationship and the causality usually expressed by those using the SCP analysis, that concentrated industry structure leads to poor welfare performance. The difficulty does not come from using L as a surrogate for M_zL, nor does it come from using an inappropriate concentration index. Rather, the difficulty arises from not distinguishing between exogenous and endogenous variables in the model. To see specifically what is at issue here, rewrite (12.2) as

$$\frac{z_j}{z} = \eta\left(1 - \frac{c_j'}{p}\right) \tag{12.8}$$

Summing over the industry and rearranging gives the market price as a function of parameters:

$$p = \frac{\eta\Sigma_j c_j'}{1 - \eta J} \tag{12.9}$$

Squaring both sides of (12.8), substituting this expression for p in (12.9), and again summing over the J firms yields an expression for the Herfindahl index of concentration as a function of the *exogenous* parameters J, η and the coefficient of variation v_c in costs (in the cross-section of firms):[15]

$$H = \frac{\Sigma_j z_j^2}{z^2} = -\eta^2 J + 2\eta + (1 - J\eta)^2\left(\frac{1 + v_c^2}{J}\right) \tag{12.10}$$

$$= \frac{1}{J} + \frac{(1 - \eta J)^2 v_c^2}{J}$$

---

[14] Further details are given by Liebowitz (1986) and Fisher (1987). In profit–concentration regression models with π^a/R as the dependent variable, the capital-to-sales ratio κ/R is used as one independent variable, making its estimated coefficient an estimate of the rental rate r^*. Collins and Preston (1969), using Bureau of Census data for 417 four-digit industries, estimated r^* at 13 percent for producer-good industries and 10 percent for consumer-good industries.

[15] Note that $\Sigma_j (c_j')^2/(\Sigma_j c_j')^2 = (1 + \theta_c^2/\bar{c}^2)/J = (1 + v_c^2)/J$ where θ_c is the standard deviation of c_j' in the cross-section of firms.

The amount by which H exceeds its lower bound $1/J$ is given by the second term in the last expression. This excess depends on the market demand elasticity and the cross-sectional variation in cost. Some manipulation of (12.10) shows that H is greater (a) the greater is the coefficient of variation (that is, the more disparity there is between firms in costs, and generally, the greater is the cost advantage of "leading firms") and (b) the greater is the market demand elasticity.[16] The effect of the number of firms on H is indeterminate, however. If it is assumed that v_c is independent of J, then

$$\mathrm{sgn}\!\left(\frac{\mathrm{d}H}{\mathrm{d}J}\right) = \mathrm{sgn}\!\left(\eta^2 J^2 - \frac{1 - v_c{}^2}{v_c{}^2}\right)$$

which can be positive or negative.[17]

A useful alternative expression for the price–cost margin (in terms of parameters only) comes from substituting (12.10) in (12.3) and rearranging to give

$$L = \frac{1}{J\eta} + \left\{\frac{(1 - \eta J)^2}{J\eta}\right\} v_c{}^2 \tag{12.11}$$

This result can be thought of, in a way analogous to (12.3), as a basis for measuring industry performance in terms of the fundamental demand and cost conditions given by the (exogenous) parameters η, J, and v_c. It should also be stressed that (12.10) and (12.11) are based on the assumption of Cournot–Nash play.

While the basic structural model implies a positive relationship between industry structure and industry performance, it is important to note from (12.10) and (12.11) that both H and L are determined at equilibrium by underlying cost and demand parameters. The usual SCP interpretation, which maintains that a causal link occurs between concentration and performance, goes beyond what in fact the simple structural model supports. To be sure H and L are positively related, but the most that can be said is that these (endogenous) variables are jointly determined by the same set of (exogenous) parameters.[18] While the usual SCP hypothesis of a causal relationship from H to L is not supported by the present model, it is of note that the model is consistent with the efficient structure arguments of McGee (1971) and Demsetz (1972, 1973b). Their hypothesis, that large firms gain their size (and concentrate markets) because of superior efficiency rather than collusive behavior, is consistent with (12.10) and (12.11) since both H and L are increasing in v_c.

[16] Substitute the expression for p from (12.9) in (12.10) and differentiate, giving $\mathrm{d}(z_j/z)/\mathrm{d}\eta = (1 - c_j'/\bar{c})$ where $\bar{c}$ is the industry mean marginal cost. Thus, if the firm's marginal cost is less than the average marginal cost in the industry, its market share will increase with a rise in η and conversely. Note also from (12.10) that high-cost firms have relatively low market shares and that these decrease as η increases.

[17] Suppose that $J = 10$ and $\eta = 1$, then concentration increases with the number of firms ($\mathrm{d}H/\mathrm{d}J > 0$) if $(1 - v_c{}^2)/v_c{}^2 < 100$ or $v_c > 0.01$ (approximately).

[18] See Geroski (1982a, b), Clarke and Davies (1983), and Domsimoni et al. (1984). It is occasionally noted that the causal interpretation nonetheless obtains since prior capacity decisions of the firms determine the market shares of the firms (industry structure H) and therefore (12.3) implies that structure is an "exogenous" determinant of the price–cost margin L. This is, of course, not correct, as making capacity exogenous (coming from a "prior period" in the static model) simply makes all things, both H and L, simultaneously depend on this exogenous parameter.

E12.4

Firm-level Profit–Concentration Analyses

The structural model has implications for profitability at the firm level as well as at the industry level. Multiplying (12.2) by z_j, rearranging terms, and dividing by pz_j yields

$$L_j = \frac{1}{\eta} \frac{z_j}{z}$$

Each firm's price–cost margin depends on the market elasticity of demand and its market share, but not directly on the concentration level H. The market share z_j/z, like H at the industry level, is an endogenous variable:

$$\frac{z_j}{z} = \eta - \left(\eta - \frac{1}{J}\right)\frac{c_j'}{\bar{c}}$$

which is derived by substituting p from (12.9) in (12.8).

From this expression we note that erroneously including H along with z_j/z to explain L_j in a firm-level (cross-sectional) regression may lead to unusual results, for at equilibrium H also depends on η. That is, since L_j is inversely related to η, while H increases with η, L_j and H may appear to be negatively related.

12.1.3   Market Structure and Price–Cost Margins

The implications of the structural model depends acutely on the choice of strategy variable (or the conjectural variation). For those inclined to believe that firms and an industry express monopoly power, a specification of Bertrand price competition and homogeneous goods would not seem appropriate. One of the more popular specifications is not much removed from that, however, as seen in the following example.

E12.5

Price–Cost Margins with Price Leadership

Following earlier work on the subject by Saving (1970), Landes and Posner (1981) developed the profits–concentration relationship for an industry characterized by Nash-in-price Stackelberg play. The reader will remember this as the model generally referred to as dominant-firm price leadership.[19] In this case a group of "dominant" firms choose price in their own interest, constrained only by a "fringe" of small firms who act as price-takers. The fringe supply function can be written as $z_f = z_f(p)$, where the subscript f indicates the fringe group. In turn, the demand facing the dominant group is $z_d = z(p) - z_f(p)$,

---

19   Recall chapter 3, section 3.3.2, for the basic model; see also Ordover et al. (1982).

where $z(p)$ is industry demand and the subscript d indicates the dominant group.

When the dominant group acts as a monopolist, its stationarity conditions for a profit maximum are

$$L_d \equiv \frac{p - c'_d}{p} = \frac{1}{\eta_d} \tag{12.12}$$

where c'_d is the marginal cost and η_d is the elasticity of $z_d(p)$. This elasticity can also be written as

$$\eta_d = \frac{\eta}{s_d} + \frac{s_f}{\eta_d} \eta_f \tag{12.13}$$

Here, $s_d = z_d/z$ is the dominant group's market share, $s_f = 1 - s_d$ is the fringe market share, η is the elasticity of $z(p)$, and n_f is the elasticity of the fringe supply. Thus the Lerner index (12.12) for the dominant group can be rewritten as

$$L_d = \frac{s_d}{\eta + s_f \eta_f} \tag{12.14}$$

We are informed by this expression that the market power of the dominant group varies directly with its market share and indirectly with the industry elasticity of demand, the market share of the fringe, and the elasticity of the fringe supply. That is, the *market shares* of the leader and fringe firms, *and not H*, are the appropriate concentration measures, in this version of the structural model.

Extensions of the structural model to Nash equilibria in other strategy variables can be represented by alternative specifications of the conjectural variations in (12.1). A "parameterization" of the equilibrium solution is helpful in interpreting any results, and we restrict the range of quantity conjectures in the cross-section of firms to those which are of the same constant proportionality in output, that is, firm j's conjecture about k is given by $dz_k^e/z_k = \alpha(dz_j/z_j)$, where $\alpha < 1$ is a constant for all firm pairs $j \neq k$. With this specification, more negative values of α imply greater monopoly power and, conversely, more positive values imply less monopoly power. In the specific case where $\alpha = 0$ the Cournot conjectures are repeated, and with $\alpha = 1$ the perfect cartel (single-firm monopoly) output occurs. As will be seen below one of the key advantages of this parameterization of oligopoly solutions is that the equilibrium conditions provide a basis for empirical measurement of the degree of monopoly by an estimation of α.

Stationarity. With $\gamma_j = \alpha(z/z_j) - \alpha$, the stationarity condition (12.1) becomes

$$p\left(1 - \frac{z_j/z - \alpha z_j/z + \alpha}{\eta}\right) = c'_j \tag{12.15}$$

Again, multiplying by z_j, summing, and rearranging gives

$$L = \frac{\alpha + (1 - \alpha)H}{\eta} \tag{12.16}$$

which relates the industry price–cost margin to the concentration measure H. When $\alpha = 1$, the cartel solution obtains and $L = 1/\eta$ – the "single firm" sets its price–cost margin equal to the inverse of the *market* elasticity of demand. When $\alpha = 0$, $L = H/\eta$ as in the Cournot form of the structural model.

H and L are Endogenous. The reader is now well aware of the difficulties in interpreting (12.16) as a causal link from H to L, as both of these (endogenous) variables derive more fundamentally from the model parameters. The expression for H begins by rewriting (12.15) as

$$\frac{z_j}{z} = \frac{\eta(1 - c_j'/p) - \alpha}{1 - \alpha} \tag{12.17}$$

Then summing this over the firms and solving for p gives

$$p = \frac{\eta \Sigma_j \, c_j'}{J(\eta - \alpha) - (1 - \alpha)} \tag{12.18}$$

Finally substituting this in (12.17), squaring, and summing again yields

$$H = \frac{1}{J} + \frac{\{1 - J(\eta - \alpha)/(1 - \alpha)\}^2 v_c^2}{J} \tag{12.19}$$

In accordance with our intuition, H is decreasing in J and η, and increasing in v_c. Note also that H approaches $1/J$ as α approaches the cartel solution of unity. In this limiting case the monopoly power of the cartel depends solely on the elasticity of demand, with very demand elastic goods not yielding much monopoly.

Just as earlier, the reader can substitute expression (12.19) for H in (12.16) to write the industry price–cost margin in terms of the fundamental parameters α, v_c, J, and η only. Finally, it should be emphasized that α has been assumed to be exogenous and not to vary across the firms in the industry.[20]

12.1.4　Profits and Concentration: The Empirical Link

Empirical tests concerned with the link between market performance and concentration have been based generally on the cross-section regression[21]

---

[20] It is noted on occasion that the present model does yield a causal relationship between structure H and price–cost margin L when the conduct parameter α is "endogenous." Roughly, the argument is that the conduct described by α at any date is determined by the structure of the industry in prior periods and therefore by (12.16) determines the price–cost margin performance. This line of argument is incorrect, however: if structure at some prior date affects the current α then that exogenous structure, through α, simultaneously determines both the current H and L.

[21] Roughly, the empirical research has had three stages of development. The first studies were designed as simple equality tests of group profit means across high- and low-concentration samples, as in the work of Bain (1951), Mann (1966), and Brozen (1971). The second stage used single-equation multiple-factor regression models designed to hold all other variables constant: Weiss (1974) reviews these studies in detail. More recently, simultaneous equations have been used in recognition that profits, concentration, and other factors (for example advertising) are jointly determined in a multimarket equilibrium (see Strickland and Weiss, 1976; Martin, 1979; Pagoulatas and Sorenson, 1980; Geroski, 1982b). In reviewing these, Ornstein's (1987) conclusion is that the studies using simultaneous equation are generally consistent with the single-equation results. Finally, we note that critical concentration ratios, below which $\beta = 0$ and above which $\beta > 0$, have also been suggested and reported by Bain (1951), White (1976), and Bradburd and Over (1982).

$$\pi_k = a_k + \beta C_k \qquad (12.20)$$

where k indexes the industries, π_k measures the average profitability of an industry, C_k measures industry concentration, and a_k includes other differences across industries.[22] The estimate of β, which describes any link between profits and concentration, is the focus of the regression.

Three Interpretations of the Facts. As model (12.20) is *ad hoc*, it can be found to be consistent with a wide variety of industry conditions and theoretical explanations. The **traditional SCP** interpretation has been that greater market concentration leads to a greater degree of collusion among the firms and that collusion in turn yields greater industry average profit. This causal interpretation is said to be verified by a significantly positive estimate of β. The more recent **revised SCP** interpretation is, less restrictively, based on the equilibrium condition (12.16), in which β then reflects the average value of $(1 - \alpha)/\eta$ for the cross-section of industries. After correcting for the industry demand elasticity, an estimate of α is derived; *ceteris paribus* (greater) implicit collusion is associated with (larger) positive β.

The final **efficient structure** interpretation of (12.20) is that of McGee (1971) and Demsetz (1972, 1974). Their concept of an empirical link between concentration and profits begins with the view that concentration results from competition in which the most efficient firms simultaneously gain both large size and large efficiency rents. As these firms weigh the most in industry average size and profits, their efficiency and size accounts for any finding of positive β.

Testing the Interpretations. Attempts to empirically disentangle the SCP and efficient structure explanations for $\beta > 0$ have followed two tacks.[23] The first is that originally used by Demsetz (1972). He assumes that collusion is a public good which, when present, yields high profitability for both large and small firms within an industry. He contrasts this with industry situations where some firms possess superior efficiency relative to others and only the large (superior) firms then gain high profitability. Demsetz (1972, 1973a, b), Caves and Pugel (1980), Clarke et al. (1984), Smirlock et al. (1984), and Schmalensee (1987) have reported empirical work along this line.[24] Salinger (1984) offers the second

---

[22] Bain (1956) specifically argued that persistently high concentration required barriers to the entry of new firms. He further distinguished four such barriers as potentially important: product differentiation, capital requirements, absolute cost advantages, and economies of scale. Therefore in statistical studies of the profits–concentration link it has been common to include some measure of barriers, as an independent variable, along with concentration. Bain (1956) and Mann (1971) subjectively determined high, medium, and low barriers for various industries and represented these by categorical variables (see also Shepard, 1972; Smirlock et al. 1984). Comanor and Wilson (1967), in contrast, used continuous rather than categorical variables to measure the "height" of various barriers: advertising-to-sales ratios are proxies for product differentiation, capital-to-output ratios as proxies for capital requirements, cost differences between large and small firms in an industry as proxies for absolute cost advantages, and various indices of average firm or plant size as proxies for economies of scale.

[23] This does not mean that there is unambiguous empirical evidence that $\beta > 0$. Roughly, the number of studies reporting no relationship between profitability and concentration is equal to that reporting a significant positive relationship (see Benston, 1985; Ornstein, 1987).

[24] The study by Smirlock et al differs from the others cited in this list in that it uses Tobin's Q as the measure of rents. Shepard (1985) has expressed several concerns regarding Tobin's Q in these regressions. See SE12.2 for further comments on this measure.

tack for disentangling the hypotheses, which is to associate high entry barriers and $\beta > 0$ with the presence of collusion and not efficiency. While it would be comforting to report decisive findings from these studies, they offer ambiguous results.

There are a variety of problems hindering empirical attempts to distinguish clearly between the explanations underlying the *ad hoc* profit–concentration model (12.20). At their core, the problems stem from (a) the arbitrary nature of accounting data and its inconsistency with economic concepts[25] and (b) the nature of inter-industry cross-sectional analysis which masks data variations and leaves parameter estimates lacking in precision and unbiasedness.[26] Because of the complexity of these problems, alternatives to the profit–concentration model have recently found favor. These empirical studies proceed by first positing a specific noncooperative industry equilibrium and then by confirming (or denying) its specific details from observed prices, costs, outputs, etc. Typically, these studies used pooled time series and cross-section data at the *firm* level.

The first and most direct applications of this approach have been by Rosse (1970) and Appelbaum (1979). Both assumed homogeneous industry goods and a particular specification of conjectures as a basis for their estimation of demand and cost (production) functions. Bresnahan (1981a) extended these studies to the heterogeneous US automobile industry by imposing a scalar measure of product differentiation, a "spatial" demand structure (similar to that set out in chapter 5, section 5.2) and a Nash-in-price oligopoly equilibrium.[27]

The most recent variation on this approach is suggested by the stationarity conditions (12.15), where it is explicit that the conjectural variations parameterize the specific industry solution. Each oligopoly solution corresponds to a specific conjectural variation – a specific α in (12.16). By including the conjecture α among the parameters to be estimated in a regression model based on the stationarity conditions, it is possible to infer the extent of monopoly power expressed by the industry from the value taken on by the conjecture.[28] The initial research along this line was the two-step analysis of Iwata (1974): first he derived (extraneous) estimates of cost and demand functions for the Japanese flat glass industry, and then he used these estimates in stationarity

---

[25] Specifically, accounting profits are systematically biased estimates of economic profits and there are no reliable complete methods for correction. Industry definitions used as a basis for data collection typically ignore critical demand interdependencies, ignore foreign competition, and ignore the local character of many markets.

[26] Cross-section studies can identify differences between long-run equilibria provided that the deviations from the equilibria are large enough (with limited data points) and not related to the set of independent variables. Neither condition seems to be generally the case. Not only do industry-level data average out such deviations, but observable industry-level data derive from the firm's decisions and are thus endogenous. The lack of identification means that more than one reasonable interpretation of estimated parameters will always exist.

[27] A variation on these studies has been to allow more flexibility in the equilibrium concept and, in turn, more flexible forms for firm demand and cost functions. With the increased dimensionality these studies attempt to draw inferences about firm demand and cost parameters, and apparent collusion, from the equilibrium comparative static properties of exogenous shocks to the industry (taxes, technical change, etc.). Just and Chern (1980), Sumner (1981), Bulow and Pfeiderer (1983), Baker and Bresnahan (1984), and Sullivan (1985) provide notable examples of this approach.

[28] Note here that we take the conjecture to express monopoly power (equilibrium industry price in excess of marginal cost) and not define the degree of "cooperation" among the firms.

conditions defining a conjectural equilibrium (assuming a symmetry of conjectures among firms) to calculate the implied values for the conjectural variation. In the usual way the conjecture, and demand and cost function parameters, were then used to infer the L measure of monopoly power expressed by the industry. Gollop and Roberts (1979) subsequently attempted to estimate a conjecture *function* to describe the different conjectures of firms in the asymmetric US coffee roasting industry. Their results, while open to some questions, indicated that Nash-in-quantity and Nash-in-price equilibria could be ruled out, and that some form of dominant-firm price-leadership solution was most likely. Similar results using similar methodologies have been reported by Geroski (1982b), Roberts (1984), Spiller and Favaro (1984), Slade (1987), and Roberts and Samuelson (1988). Details of the study by Spiller and Favaro are set out in SE12.4.[29]

12.2   Cartelization

A turning point in industrial economics occurred when Stigler (1964) systematically set out a "theory of oligopoly" based on the incentives for firms to correlate their pricing.[30] At the center of his theory is the argument that both the gains and costs of such a pricing arrangement are related to the variance in cross-firm market shares within an industry. Stigler's demonstration that this variance is related to industry concentration under certain conditions provides the first theoretical basis for the link between structure and performance.

Stigler's theory begins with the proposition that firms seek cartelization. This position makes sense in a non-cooperative setting if we think of cartels in the way that Stigler did, as including all mechanisms leading to correlated pricing in a dynamic setting. His simple yet profound idea is that, whether explicit or implicit, the decision to price in a parallel way is made by balancing the long-run potential gains to such a policy against its costs (including the expected value of any antitrust punishment costs). The gains to cartelization are greater the less elastic the *industry* demand and the greater the costs of (or the slower the rate of) new entry into the industry.

In Stigler's model firms compete in prices, not quantities. However, they do not observe their rivals' prices at any market date, but only observe their own output quantity (or market share). On this basis Stigler identified two broad costs of cartelization (holding aside antitrust punishment costs). The first is associated with establishing the cartel rules, including the sellers' costs of arriving at a price and allocating the outputs among firms in such a way that the price is maintained. The second is that associated with detecting deviations from the agreement and, when the necessary, enforcing it.

---

[29] A similar study of the UK automobile industry was performed by Cubbin (1975a).

[30] Beginning with Kalecki's (1939) formula $(p - mc)/p = 1/\eta$ relating price and marginal cost to industry elasticity of demand, Stigler's theory of oligopoly is based on the variant $(p - mc)/p = f(H)/\eta$ where $f(H)$ is an index of the effectiveness of collusion based on the concentration of the industry measured by H. The industry is said to be more collusive the greater its percentage excess of price over marginal cost. One close variant of the Stigler theory is developed in section 12.3. SE11.5 (chapter 11) is a somewhat more distant variant.

Stigler's analysis pivots on the fact that cartels are vulnerable to **free riders**, that is members using secret price cutting and nonmembers pricing slightly below the cartel. After the participants reach the price and other conditions which increase industry profits, each has an incentive to sell at a slightly lower effective price (either by lowering the explicit price or, less obviously, enhancing the terms and conditions of sale or product quality) since its profits will be higher at the much larger sales than the slightly lower price will bring. The cartel is unstable and will collapse as the sellers repeatedly free ride in this way.[31] Moreover, the cartel is particularly unstable and will collapse sooner when effective price reductions are easier to conceal. When entry to the industry is easy, interlopers will take advantage of the cartel's high price.

Concentration and Profits. For a world in which information costs are increasing and buyers and sellers generally have incomplete knowledge, Stigler specifically examined the way in which incentives to secretly cut price are affected by the size and number of buyers, the number of sellers, and the probability that a buyer who trades with some seller in one period will return to that same seller in the next in the absence of price cutting. Stigler, and more generally economists following the SCP paradigm, note that the concentration of sellers has a twofold significance in this regard. High seller concentration aids the initial cartel implementation by reducing the costs of reaching the original rules of play. Concentration also aids in the maintenance of the cartel by reducing the costs of detecting free riding by participants. Stigler was quite clear, however, that there is nothing about his theory to suggest that if an industry is made up of a few major sellers this will inevitably lead to cartel behavior.[32]

E12.6

Cartel Enforcement: Market Share Maintenance

Stigler's key point is that incentives for free riding must be controlled if a cartel is to survive. Osborne (1976) has proposed a market share maintenance rule as a strategy which can (under some conditions) act as such a control. The rule goes into effect in a repeated market game when some output expanding free rider is detected. The rule requires that cartel members adhering to the agreement retaliate by increasing their output in such a way that the cartel's original market shares are maintained. The rule works by forcing the free rider to share in the loss in cartel profits arising from its deviation in output. When detection is rapid and low cost, the rule then nullifies any expected gain from free riding. For the case of identical firms, the adherent members can credibly threaten to invoke the punishment rule,[33] which should forestall free riding in the first place.

---

[31] Osborne (1976), Holahan (1978), and Ulen (1983) provide specific descriptions of negotiation and enforcement problems in cartel stability.

[32] In fact, it is interesting to note that the cartels which have been successfully prosecuted under the antitrust laws have generally had rather large numbers of firms involved (Armentano, 1972).

[33] In the case where the firms are not identical, Holahan (1978) shows that the market share maintenance rule is not generally a credible threat.

Figure 12.1 illustrates the operation of the market share maintenance rule. The outputs of one adherent cartel member are given on the vertical axis and the free rider's outputs are on the horizontal axis. Because the firms are identical, the cartel solution occurs at point M on the 45° ray where the firms have equal shares and the isoprofit contours are tangent. (The subscript a refers to the adherent firm and f refers to the free rider.) This gives cartel output $z_{am} = z_{fm}$ for the firms.

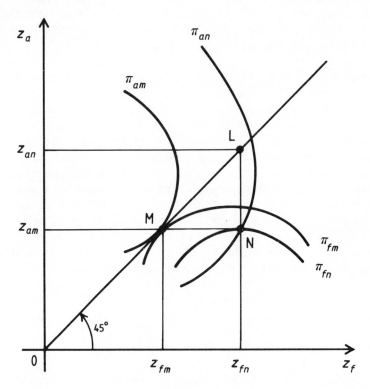

Figure 12.1
Market share maintenance rule

Suppose now that the free rider does just that and increases its output so that the point N is reached. Everything seems to work out well for the free rider: its profits increase from π_{fm} to π_{fn}. The adherent's profits, however, decrease from π_{am} to π_{an}. In response to this state of affairs, suppose that the adherent invokes the market share maintenance rule, moving the equilibrium back to the point L on the 45° ray.

Note that prior to free riding any one firm's threat to punish in this way is credible for the case illustrated, because the adherent's after free riding profits increase as it increases its output from z_{am} to z_{an} according to the rule. Both firms are worse off after the free riding and punishment than they were prior to the free riding. Thus, when it knows that it will be detected quickly and the cartel's threat of punishment is understood, the free rider would be better off not cheating in the first place. (More complex rules of punishment for free riding are considered below.)

12.2.1 Cartel Stability

The static, dominant-firm price-leadership model is frequently used in the analysis of cartel behavior.[34] In this model the dominant "firm" is taken to be a cartel of firms and the competitive fringe is made up of the outside free riders. The usual Stackelberg leader–follower roles are imposed on the two groups. Given these arrangements, the question that arises is that of an equilibrium level of free riding: is there a specific number of firms in the cartel and fringe which destroy incentives for cartel members to free ride or outsiders to join the cartel. This equilibrium division of firms between groups is said to result in a stable cartel arrangement. Of particular interest in this regard is a proposition by d'Aspremont et al. (1983) that there is always some sustainable cartel of firms acting as a dominant firm when the set of firms is finite. The main features of their analysis are as follows.

Suppose that there is a fixed number $J > 1$ of identical firms in a homogeneous oligopoly and let $\bar{J} \geq 1$ of these firms act as a cartel. The cartel maximizes profits on the assumption that the $J - \bar{J}$ excluded firms are takers of the price announced by the cartel. Since each of the J firms sets the same price, the firms are identical, and the firms in the fringe choose their output without any constraint,

$$\pi_f(\bar{J}) \geq \pi_d(\bar{J}) \tag{12.21}$$

where $\pi_f(\bar{J})$ denotes the per firm profit of fringe firms when there are $\bar{J}$ cartel members and $\pi_d(\bar{J})$ similarly is the per firm profit of the cartel members.

There are two aspects of cartel stability: (a) a cartel of $J \geq 1$ firms is said to be **internally stable** when $\pi_f(\bar{J} - 1) \leq \pi_d(\bar{J})$, and no cartel member can switch to the competitive fringe and increase its profits; (b) a cartel of $1 \leq \bar{J} \leq J - 1$ firms is said to be **externally stable** when $\pi_d(\bar{J} + 1) \leq \pi_f(\bar{J})$, and no fringe firm can increase its profits by joining the cartel. The cartel is said to be **stable** when both internal and external stability obtain.

A recursive argument is the basis of the proof that such a stable cartel exists in a dominant-firm price-leadership model. To begin, assume that the no cartel case ($\bar{J} = 0$) is externally stable and the one-member cartel ($\bar{J} = 1$) is internally stable. Then, if $\bar{J} = 1$ is externally stable, the solution is found; alternatively, $\bar{J} = 2$ must have internal stability (otherwise $\bar{J} = 1$ would have been stable) and if it is also externally stable, then the solution is found; alternatively, $\bar{J} = 3$ must have internal stability and if it also is externally stable, then the solution is found, and so forth until $\bar{J} = J$. If no stable cartel has been found to this point, then the J-member cartel has internal stability and it must also have external stability as all the firms in the industry are involved.

---

[34] Recall chapter 3, section 3.4, and E12.5; see also SE12.4.

E12.7

Internal and External Cartel Stability

A specific example developed by d'Aspremont et al. (1983) further clarifies the concept of stability and how it is related to incentives for firms to switch from their group. The example is based on an industry with $J = 5$ firms, with each identical firm having cost function $c(z) = z^2/2$ and aggregate demand $z(p) = J(1 - p)$. The cartel chooses the price p to maximize joint profits given the quantity $S(p)$ supplied by the competitive fringe. The residual demand faced by the cartel is therefore

$$z_d(p) = z(p) - (J - \bar{J})S(p) = J - (2J - \bar{J})p \tag{12.22}$$

since $S(p) = p$. Thus the profits (per firm) of the cartel members are

$$\pi_d(p, \bar{J}) = \frac{p\{J - (2J - \bar{J})p\}}{\bar{J}} - \frac{1}{2}\left\{\frac{J - (2J - \bar{J})p}{J}\right\}^2 \tag{12.23}$$

The profit-maximizing price is calculated in the usual way from the stationarity condition as

$$p^* = \frac{2}{4 - (\bar{J}/J)^2} \tag{12.24}$$

Substituting this in (12.23) gives the cartel profits (per firm) as

$$\pi_d(\bar{J}) = \frac{1}{8 - 2(\bar{J}/J)^2} \tag{12.25a}$$

and, in turn, the fringe profits (per firm) are

$$\pi_f(\bar{J}) = \frac{2}{\{4 - (\bar{J}/J)^2\}^2} \tag{12.25b}$$

Table 12.3 gives the cartel profits and fringe profits (both on a per firm basis) for all values of $\bar{J}$. In the table $\pi_f(2) < \pi_d(3)$ and $\pi_f(3) > \pi_d(4)$, making the cartel with $\bar{J} = 3$ stable. While the stability in this case is independent of the total number of firms, this will not generally obtain when demand is not linear and not multiplicative in J.

Table 12.3 Profits and Stability

J	0	1	2	3	4	5
$\pi_d(\bar{J})$	—	0.126	0.130	0.137	0.149	0.161
$\pi_f(\bar{J})$	0.125	0.128	0.136	0.151	0.177	—

Stability and Solution Concept. While the concepts of internal and external stability are important it must be understood that the existence results of d'Aspremont et al. (1983) and the specific results of E12.7 depend on the particular Stackelberg price leader and follower behavior attributed to the firms. More generally, there is good reason to believe that firms do not have an inherent preference for cooperative behavior (as assumed for the dominant-group firms), but instead adhere to a given policy because of the advantages offered relative to any other in *noncooperative dynamic* play. This second view of the industry, and the one implicit in Stigler's analysis, is the subject of the remaining sections in this chapter.

12.3 Implicitly Collusive Equilibria

Even though the strategies and payoffs of oligopolists are interdependent, it is rare that they are perfectly correlated. The industry joint profit maximum, for example, does not usually coincide with any single firm's short-run best interest and therefore is not a Nash equilibrium in the one-shot oligopoly game. The received theory of 1950–80 industrial economics, but not the intuition of many economists, was that the strong incentives for individual firms to free ride on cartel rules meant that monopoly outcomes were extremely unlikely (in this regard see McGee, 1971; Demsetz, 1974; Posner, 1976).

This idea has been tempered somewhat with the more recent knowledge that the relevant equilibria in repeated games fundamentally differ from those in the underlying one-shot game. As demonstrated in chapter 9, section 9.8, in dynamic oligopoly firms may condition their actions at any stage on the observed history of the industry. This means that an oligopolist may act in a way that is not in its short-run interest because an attempt to realize short-run gains may lead to future long-run losses if rivals retaliate. That was the case, for example, with the repeated game oligopoly equilibrium based on the simple market share maintenance rule set out in E12.6. There, a repeated game equilibrium based on incentive compatible rules which punished free riding was more profitable for *all* oligopolists than any equilibrium of the underlying one-shot game. While it is usual to term these more profitable repeated game equilibria as **implicitly collusive** outcomes, it is emphasized again that this is a reference to their character in the one-shot game; in the actual repeated game they are truly noncooperative solutions.

12.3.1 Cartel Enforcement

Two general methods for detecting and acting against free riders in implicitly collusive arrangements have received close attention: **trigger** and **random verification** strategies. When free riding is detected by either method it is assumed that some form of penalty is invoked as the firms revert to alternative noncooperative strategies. Recall from chapter 9, section 9.8, that with trigger pricing the cartel dissolves into a price war for some specified period, as if a free rider exists, when the observed market price is found to be below some previously agreed upon minimum. The punishment strategy corresponds to a noncooperative equilibrium of the one-shot game in which the associated payoffs of every firm – free riders and adherents – are worse with the implicitly collusive payoff.[35] As was also seen in chapter 9, section 9.8, the critical features of the trigger strategy equilibrium are as follows: (a) since the strategy constitutes a Nash equilibrium, no single firm can deviate from the strategy and gain; and (b) the threat to play the punishment phase of the trigger strategy on observing a free-riding outcome is credible.

With random output verification, the output of the firms is observed at random (and at a cost). When there are no random elements in demand or cost, the cartel knows exactly that a cheater exists because industry production beyond the aggregate quota is observed. Knowing the cheater's identity is of no specific importance in this case, as exclusion from the cartel only permits the cheater to free ride further. The only reaction to cheating here is the same as with a trigger strategy: dissolution of the cartel for a period of punishment.

E12.8

Trigger Quantities and Output Verification

When each firm can costlessly observe the decision made by its rivals, the trigger strategy and output verification rules lead to identical results. To see this specifically, think of a homogeneous-good duopoly ($j = 1, 2$) where at each discrete decision date t of an infinitely repeated game the firms choose quantities z_{jt} to produce and sell. Let the industry demand at date t be $p(z_t)$ where $z_t = z_{1t} + z_{2t}$ is the aggregate industry output. If a constant (and common) unit cost c is assumed, firm j's profits at t are

$$\pi_{jt} = \{p(z_t) - c\} z_{jt} \tag{12.26}$$

Given that a unique Cournot–Nash equilibrium is reached at each date, each of the (identical) firms supplies the (steady state) quantity z^c solving

$$p(2z^c) + z^c \frac{\partial p(2z^c)}{\partial z^c} = c \tag{12.27}$$

Let π^c indicate the flow profit of each firm at this equilibrium.

If the firms were to act as a monopoly and share the profits equally, then the output produced would be the solution of

$$p(2z^m) + 2z^m \frac{\partial p(2z^m)}{\partial (2z^m)} = c \tag{12.28}$$

where z^m is the output of each firm and $2z^m$ is the industry total. Let π^m indicate the flow profits of each firm at this monopoly equilibrium. In the following analysis we will restrict attention to the usual case where $z^m < z^c$ and $\pi^m > \pi^c$.

Repeated Play. Suppose that duopolist 1 adopts the following **grim strategy** for the repeated game: (a) produce z^m as long as firm 2 does the same; (b) if at

---

[35] In a well-documented example, Porter (1983b) and Ulen (1983) suggest that the price wars of 1880–6 occurring in the US railroad industry should be viewed as punishment phases designed to maintain the Joint Executive Committee cartel.

date t firm 2 does not produce z^m, then at the next date and all following dates produce the Cournot quantity z^c. (The strategy is grim because the punishment phase once begun, continues forever.) It is assumed that each firm can exactly observe the output of its rival and any quantity greater than z^m triggers the punishment phase.

Duopolist 2's optimal response to 1's grim strategy involves several considerations. First, if 2 produces z^m in each period it will earn flow π^m with present value π^m/r (r is the discount *rate*). If, alternatively, it produces the greater quantity z^0 at some date t, its profits at that (single) date will be $\pi^0 = z^0\{p(z^0 + z^m) - c\}$, and thereafter it will earn the Cournot profit rate π^c. Firm 2 will choose to cheat, and produce z^0 at some period, if

$$\pi^0 + \frac{1}{1+r}\left(\frac{\pi^c}{r}\right) > \frac{\pi^m}{r} \tag{12.29}$$

Since $\pi^m > \pi^c$, then with r sufficiently small the optimal response of firm 2 is to not to cheat but always to produce z^m. Moreover, if firm 2 adopts the same strategy rules (a) and (b) as firm 1, the equal-share monopoly outcome arises as the *noncooperative* equilibrium to the repeated game.

The monopoly solution is reached in this infinitely repeated game when the one-period gain to cheating is outweighed by the difference between the discounted losses from obtaining flow π^c, which is less than flow π^m.[36] Note, however, that as the discount rate becomes larger the repeated game develops the characteristics of the static game. For example, if r were 10^{10}, then the present value of payoffs one period hence and thereafter would be small and not likely to affect any firm's current move.

12.3.2 Trigger Price Strategies

It is helpful to recall the notation and results from chapter 9, section 9.8, at this point. Let $N(J, p, \pi)$ represent a one-shot normal form game with J firms, associated price strategy combinations p, and payoffs π related to the strategy combinations. Further, let $\Gamma(N, \rho, \infty)$ be the infinitely repeated game based on N and the date-to-date discount factor ρ. In the one-shot game the best reply payoff for each firm j relative to the strategy combination $p^* = [p_1^* p_2^* \ldots p_J^*]$ will be denoted by

$$\pi_j^0(p^*) = \max_{p_j} \pi_j(p^* : p_j) \tag{12.30}$$

where $(p^* : p_j)$ is the price vector p^* with p_j replacing p_j^*. If p^* is an individually rational price expressing some monopoly power in the one-shot game, then $p_j^0(p^*) = \text{argmax}\,\pi_j(p_j, p^*)$ is the optimal free-riding price and $\pi_j^0(p^*)$ is the optimal free-riding profit. In the repeated game, the present value of firm j's profits is given by

---

[36] The same solution can be produced with a finite horizon when decisions are made continuously and with instantaneous responses. Fudenberg and Tirole (1982) use this timing structure to produce a "cooperative" result in a repeated capacity investment game.

$$\sum_{t=0}^{\infty} \rho_j{}^t \pi_j(p_t) \tag{12.31}$$

when the price strategy combination $p_t = [p_{1t}p_{2t}\ldots p_{Jt}]$ is played at each date t.

A *stationary* trigger pricing equilibrium is a pair (p^*, p^b) such that $\pi_j(p^*) > \pi_j(p^b)$ where (a) p_j^* is firm j's play at $t = 0$ and (b) its play at date t is also p_j^* if $p_\tau = p^*$ for all $\tau < t$, otherwise the punishment strategy $p_j{}^b$ is played at t and henceforth.[37] As shown in chapter 9, section 9.8, the pair (p^*, p^b) is a subgame perfect Nash equilibrium point of the repeated game Γ when the one-period gain from cheating $\pi_j{}^0(p^*) - \pi_j(p^*)$ is greater than the discounted value of the profits forgone from adhering to the implicitly collusive prices $\rho_j\{\pi_j{}^0(p^*) - \pi_j(p^b)\}$, that is, when (this repeats equation (9.18))

$$\rho_j > \frac{\pi_j{}^0(p^*) - \pi_j(p^*)}{\pi_j{}^0(p^*) - \pi_j(p^b)} \tag{12.32}$$

E12.9

Cartel Enforcement with Trigger Pricing

As a numerical example of the trigger pricing equilibrium (E12.8 was based on trigger *quantities*), consider a variant of an infinitely repeated game developed by Telser (1972) and Friedman (1986). Suppose that there are three firms, each with zero costs and each facing the symmetric demand function

$$z_j = 60 - 3p_j + \sum_{k \neq j} p_k \tag{12.33}$$

The profits of each firm in the one-shot game are then

$$\pi_j(p) = 60p_j - 3p_j{}^2 + p_j \sum_{k \neq j} p_k \tag{12.34}$$

Because of the symmetry in cost and demand, the one-shot game equilibrium will have prices, outputs, and profits equal for the firms. With Nash-in-price (Bertrand) play this equilibrium is easily shown to be given by $p_j{}^b = 15$, $z_j{}^b = 45$ and $\pi_j{}^b = 675$.

Suppose that the implicitly collusive prices are those maximizing joint profits – the full monopoly prices. The one-shot equilibrium giving these prices is also symmetric and straightforward to derive: $p_j{}^m = 30$, $z_j{}^m = 30$, and $\pi_j{}^m = 900$. If (only) firm j free rides, then j's individual price, output, and profits are $p_j{}^0 = 20$, $z_j{}^0 = 60$ and $\pi_j{}^0 = 1200$. Using these results in the equilibrium condition (12.32) gives

$$\rho_j > \frac{1200 - 900}{1200 - 675} = 0.57 \tag{12.35}$$

The trigger pricing strategy is an equilibrium point for the game provided that

---

[37] The asterisk may indicate the full monopoly outcome, but that is not necessary. The superscript b may indicate the Bertrand outcome, but that is not necessary either. Recall chapter 9, section 9.8.1.

the firms have discount factors greater than 0.57 (or discount rates less than 75 percent). When this condition holds, the threatened punishment is credible because the firms revert to the Bertrand prices of the one-shot game.

Given that there is no uncertainty – no random components – in the above industry, attempts at free riding are easily detected. Each firm knows the market outcome when the implicitly collusive strategies are followed by all. Any observed deviation from this indicates a free rider and invokes the punishment phase. Thus any firm thinking about a price cut below the implicit collusion level would face a simple tradeoff. There is an increase in *short-run* profits by free riding, but against that the firm must permanently give up the difference between the implicitly collusive and punishment phase profits after its rivals react. The length of time that it takes rivals to detect the free riding and respond with the punishment strategy along with the rate at which future profits are discounted thus becomes important. When the response time of rivals is not too long and the firm does not weigh future profits too lightly, the threat of rivals to punish will be adequate to assure that free riding is not a unilateral best response.[38] For a large enough discount factor (small discount rate), the implicit collusion outcome will be an equilibrium, for it is then not in any firm's best interest to free ride.

12.3.3 Uncertainty, Cartel Cheating, and Price Wars

Suppose now that there is an exogenous source of demand uncertainty and, because of high costs of observation, firms do not exactly know their rivals' decisions. In this case output and market shares are a random function of prices and firms face an inference problem. When some firm has a smaller output or garners a smaller market share than anticipated, the cause may be either an adverse demand shock or a free rider attempting a secret move. While the source of the deviation cannot be resolved, provided that the exogenous demand variability is not too large a somewhat revised trigger strategy can support the implicitly collusive outcome.

The revision has two parts. First, instead of having the punishment phase (price war) triggered by *any* deviation from the market shares anticipated by the firms, suppose that the trigger level is set to allow a pre-specified percentage deviation. Porter (1983a) suggests the following rule: sum the square of the deviations in market share across the firms and when the sum equals a given fraction of the square of total industry demand, start the punishment phase. The second revision, to deal with uncertainty in the market, is to use a punishment phase of (possibly) finite length rather than the permanent phase employed

---

[38] Recall the discussion of the discount factor in chapter 9, section 9.8. A firm will discount the future depending on its rate of time preference *and* its estimate of the length of time remaining until the game is over. When firm j holds a constant probability h_j that the game will end at any date t (given that it has lasted until $t - 1$), then $\rho_j = (1 - h_j)/(1 + r_j)$ where r_j is the time preference rate. Each dollar at t is worth ρ_j dollars at $t - 1$. The implicit collusion equilibrium requires that h_j and r_j are not too large. Recall also the effect of detection lags from E9.8.

under certainty. This "forgiving" punishment allows for the possibility that the trigger price level was in fact a random demand event rather than the result of free riding.

A *Quantity-setting Game*. Porter (1983a) and Green and Porter (1984) developed the details of a trigger strategy for the repeated game when the market demand is subject to random shocks over time. They considered J identical firms producing a homogeneous good in an infinitely repeated market game. Each firm j chooses its output z_{jt} at each date t and this leads to the market price

$$p_t = p(z_t)\varepsilon \qquad (12.36)$$

where $z_t = \Sigma_j z_{jt}$ is the industry output, $p(\cdot)$ is the negatively sloped inverse demand function, and ε is an independent and identically distributed shock. Following a market event, the firms observe p_t, not the individual z_{jt}, and therefore are never certain whether a small observed price is due to a (correspondingly) small realization of ε or some free rider's exaggerated output.

Because outcomes are uncertain in this way, the firms are assumed to use expected profits as a payoff criterion. Let $\bar{\pi}_j(z^c) = E_\varepsilon[\{p(z^c)\varepsilon - c\}z_j{}^c]$ be the expected one-period profit of firm j when the Nash-in-quantity (Cournot) outputs $z^c = [z_1{}^c, z_2{}^c, \ldots, z_j{}^c]$ are chosen. Although more severe punishments exist, we follow Green and Porter and restrict attention to Cournot outcome in that phase. Next, let $z_j^* = z^*/J < z_j{}^c$ be some individually rational (implicitly collusive) output level for each firm j, where z^* is the output for the industry.[39] A trigger price equilibrium is then described by an output level z^*, a trigger price p^*, and a punishment period T.[40]

At the onset of the repeated game each oligopolist presumably chooses z_j^*. This output is maintained until the first instance where it is observed that $p_t < p^*$, at which time each firm j switches to $z_j{}^c$ for T periods. Once such a punishment period is under way, its length is fixed by the market conditions which triggered it in the first place and not by the firm's behavior during the punishment. After this punishment period, the oligopolists return to the implicitly collusive outputs z^*.

Given that the game is in the implicitly collusive phase, the expected present value of v_j of the payoff to each firm has two parts given by

$$V_j(z^*, p^*, T) = \frac{\pi_j(z^c)}{1 - \rho} + \frac{\pi_j(z^*) - \pi_j(z^c)}{1 - \rho + \rho(1 - \rho^T)h(z^*)} \qquad (12.37)$$

Here, $h(z^*) = \text{prob}\{p^* > p(z^*)\varepsilon\}$ is the probability that a price war will begin at any date given that the firms are choosing collusive quantities z^* and ρ is again the discount factor. (Note that h is a function of z^* and, although not expressed, the disturbance term ε.) The first term on the right-hand side is the expected present value of the Cournot output in perpetuity. To this is added the increase in expected present value that arises from the implicitly collusive outcome occurring in the nonpunishment phases. For the limiting case where

---

[39] It is not asserted that z^* is the joint profit-maximizing output.

[40] At least one such equilibrium exists for we can choose the one-shot solution $z^* = z^c$ and a trigger price and punishment period of zero.

$h = 0$, $V_j = \pi_j(z^*)/(1 - \rho)$; with zero probability of deviation the value of the firm is just the present value of the implicit collusion profit stream. Note also that increases in the length of the punishment period T decrease V_j. Thus, while the punishment must be long enough to deter cheating, it should not be any longer than necessary for that purpose.

Equilibrium. A quantity z^*, price p^*, and punishment period T form an implicit collusion equilibrium provided that two incentive compatibility best-response conditions are met: (a) there is no incentive for the firms to deviate from the quantities z^c during the punishment period, and similarly (b) there is no incentive for deviation from the quantities z^* during the implicitly collusive period. Condition (a) is satisfied immediately since play in each punishment phase is self-enforcing: the $z_j{}^c$ are the one-shot Nash-in-output responses. Condition (b) requires that $\partial V_j/\partial z_j = 0$ for all j, or on calculation

$$\frac{\partial \pi_j(z^*)}{\partial z_j} = \rho(1 - \rho^T) \frac{\partial h_j(z^*)}{\partial z_j} \left\{ \frac{\pi_j(z^*) - \pi_j(z^c)}{1 - \rho + \rho(1 - \rho^T)h(z^*)} \right\} \qquad (12.38)$$

Optimal Cartel Policies. Although many prices, quantities, and punishment periods may satisfy conditions (a) *and* (b), the *optimal* cartel chooses those strategies which solve, for all j, $\max_{(z^*,p^*,T)} V_j$ subject to (12.38) and Cournot play during the punishment. Porter (1983a) derives these optimal strategies. Here, it is sufficient to note that the solution implies (a) that the aggregate output z^* is greater than the one-shot (expected) joint-profit-maximizing level z^m and converges to z^m as the variance of ε goes to zero, (b) that the punishment period T may be finite or infinite, and (c) that the trigger price is lower than the expectation of $p(z^*)\varepsilon$ by an amount which varies directly with the variance of ε (greater forebearance occurs with greater uncertainty). Overall, if the noise level is not too large, there is some T such that the monopoly price can be sustained by discount factors close to unity. Porter (1983b) summarizes the implications of these results as follows:

> . . . One conclusion which emerges is that, when there is uncertainty, the prices charged in cooperative periods will not be as high as those which would maximize joint profits in a single period. In equilibrium, the marginal gains from cheating in cooperative periods must be exactly offset by the marginal losses implicit in the increased probability of a reversion to competitive behavior. The gains from cheating increase as prices in cooperative periods increase towards perfectly collusive levels, so expected losses must be increased by decreasing the market share deviations necessary to trigger a price war, or by increasing the length of reversionary episodes. . . . Furthermore, the greater the number of symmetric firms or the greater the degree of demand uncertainty, the closer the cooperative price is to competitive levels. If there are too many firms, or if demand uncertainty is too large, the only equilibrium will be that of competitive prices. . . . It is difficult to predict how the frequency and duration of competitive reversions will be affected by changes in market structure without specifying how the joint distribution of market share shocks is affected. However, Stigler's (1964) intuition that collusion is more difficult

the greater the number of firms seems reasonable, so that the frequency of reversions might be expected to increase with the number of firms.

It is worth emphasizing that the terms "cooperative" and "competitive" in the above comment are references to solutions of the one-shot game, and that all play in the repeated game is noncooperative. Moreover, the "competitive" solution will be characterized by the usual price equality with marginal cost if the good is homogeneous and the solution concept is Nash-in-price; more generally, however, the "competitive" solution will have price in excess of marginal cost by an amount which depends on the one-shot rules of play and the conditions of demand and cost.

Price or Quantity Competition? The above model uses quantities as strategic variables. If, instead, prices were the basis of competition, two key aspects of the analysis would be affected. First, when some single firm considers free riding with quantity competition, it presumes that its rivals in implicit collusion will hold their outputs fixed. This means that the (residual) demand faced by the potential free rider is the industry demand less the combined fixed outputs of these rivals (recall chapter 3, E3.8). In contrast with price competition and homogeneous products, the residual demand facing the free rider looking to cut price is the entire industry demand (recall chapter 3, E3.9). On this basis alone, price competition with homogeneous goods provides a greater incentive to free ride. Second, in the punishment phase the firms revert to Cournot equilibrium strategies when quantities are played, while when prices are played the punishment leads to Bertrand equilibrium strategies. As Cournot equilibria generally lead to positive profits and Bertrand equilibria do not (recall chapter 3, section 3.3), the punishment phase is more severe, and a greater deterrent to free riding, with price strategies. Specific details of the industry demand and cost conditions will determine whether this second effect offsets, in part or as a whole, the advantage of free riding with prices caused by the greater residual demand (relative to the quantity case).

E12.10

Trigger Pricing with Uncertain Demand

Consider the cartelization problem originally described by Stigler (1964): price-setting firms produce a standard product in an industry closed to new entry. This differs from the analysis given immediately above in that price, not quantity, is the strategy variable and it differs from E12.9 in that demand is uncertain, products are homogeneous, and the period of punishment is to be chosen as short as will support the collusion.

At the center of the analysis here is the fact that no firm can directly observe the prices set by rivals. This is not a problem in an implicitly collusive arrangement when there is complete information, for price cutting can then be detected immediately. Firms know their market share when rivals adhere to the collusive prices so that any deviation unambiguously signals a free rider. Things change markedly when there is an exogenous source of demand uncertainty. As above, this creates an inference problem: a market share different from that which was anticipated can result either from free riding or an adverse demand shock. As far as the implicit collusion arrangement is concerned, however, the inference problem is resolved in essentially the same way as with quantity-setting firms: when some firm's market objectives fall below an expected level, regardless of cause, a period of austerity begins.

To see how this goes with price-setting firms consider identical duopolists j and k faced with a stationary linear demand $z(p_j, p_k; \alpha) = \alpha - \min(p_j, p_k)$ and constant unit costs c. Let α be a random variable for both firms. To deal with the simplest case, suppose further that α can take on only one of two values: α_1 which occurs with probabililty $1 - h$ and α_2 which occurs with probability h. Let $0 \leqslant \alpha_2 \leqslant \alpha_1$, so that α_1 is the high-demand case. All properties other than α are common knowledge, including the probability h.

To reduce the number of things to be derived in this example, we will simply use the prices which maximize industry one-shot profits in the high-demand situation as the implicitly collusive prices: $p^m = p_j{}^m = p_k{}^m = (\alpha_1 - c)/2$. Let $\alpha_1 > c$ so that with p^m profits are positive in the high-demand state. To allow the low-demand state to be confused with free riding, let $\alpha_2 = p^m$ and therefore $z(p^m; \alpha_2) = 0$. This means that when the firms charge p^m in an implicitly collusive arrangement it will not be known by a firm experiencing zero demand whether this is the result of a free-riding rival or simply a low-demand state. In either case, the firms revert to the one-shot Bertrand play, set price $p^b = p_j{}^b = p_k{}^b = c$, and earn zero profits in the following high- and low-demand periods.

Having fixed the collusive and punishment price strategies, we are only left to determine the optimal punishment period. This optimal value will maximize each firm's expected present value at the beginning of the game, at the onset of a implicitly collusive period, subject to the constraint that T provides no incentive to deviate from the prices p^m during the collusive period.[41]

Incentive Compatability. The game begins in implicit collusion with each firm earning per period profits $\pi_j(p^m) = \pi_k(p^m)$. If firm j were to shade its price in this situation, it would capture one-period profits equal to (approximately) $2\pi_j(p^m)$, but then earn nothing for T periods of punishment. It will choose not to free ride if the one-period *increase* in profits $\pi_j(p^m)$ is less than the present value of the difference between (a) the expected value v_j, when in implicit collusion at the beginning of the next period and (b) the expected value $\rho^T v_j$ when in the punishment phase at the beginning of the next period which is a stream of zero profits for T periods plus the discounted value of beginning a new implicit collusion phase post-punishment. Thus incentive compatibility requires

$$\pi_j(p^m) \leqslant \rho(v_j - \rho^T v_j) \tag{12.39}$$

---

[41] Once more the p^b are best-response prices in the punishment period so that only the incentive compatibility of the p^m prices is at issue.

We can specify v_j in more detail. At the beginning of implicit collusion each firm has its value v_j determined by first-period and second-period components. From the first period it obtains $\pi_j(p^m)$ with probability $1 - h$ and zero with probability h, depending on the level of demand; from the second period, it obtains the present value of being either in the collusive state v_j with probability $1 - h$, since that occurs when demand is high, or the punishment state $\rho^T v_j$ with probability h, since the low-cost demand triggers punishment. That is,[42]

$$v_j = \{(1 - h)\pi_j(p^m) + h(0)\} + \rho\{(1 - h)v_j + h(\rho^T v_j)\} \qquad (12.40)$$

which solves for (cf. 12.37)

$$v_j = \frac{(1 - h)\pi_j(p^m)}{1 - \rho + \rho(1 - \rho^T)h} \qquad (12.41)$$

Substituting this in (12.39) and rearranging gives the incentive compatibility condition in terms of model parameters:

$$1 - 2h \geq \frac{1 - \rho}{\rho(1 - \rho^T)} \qquad (12.42)$$

where $\rho < 1$ and $T \geq 1$. It is of interest in the simple model here that this constraint involves no parameters of the firms' demand or cost. Only three parameters appear: the beliefs h, the discount factor ρ, and the punishment period T which is to be determined.

Optimal Punishment Length. The optimal T, which is established in the interest of the identical firms, must solve

$$\max_T v_j(T; p^m, p^b) \text{ s.t. } (12.42) \qquad (12.43)$$

From (12.41) note that v_j is decreasing in T, which means that the optimal T will be the smallest value solving the incentive compatibility constraint (12.42).

With respect to this constraint, observe first that for $\rho < 1$ the right-hand side of (12.42) is strictly positive, but the left-hand side is strictly positive only for $h < 1/2$. Therefore, if the probability of a low-demand period is greater than or equal to a half, there is no punishment period that will be consistent with the p^m and p^b price strategies. (When h is large the present value of *expected* gains to collusion is too low.) Assume $h < 1/2$, and note further that the right-hand side of (12.42) decreases with T. In this case the smallest T solving (12.42) gives the optimal punishment length. Specifically,

$$T^* = \ln\left\{1 - \rho - \frac{1 - \rho}{\rho(2h - 1)}\right\} \qquad (12.44)$$

12.3.4   Once More, the Implicit Collusion Story

Oligopolists in infinitely (or indefinitely) repeated games are frequently able to reach and support equilibrium outcomes which on a per period basis strictly

---

[42] The recursion equation occurs in this simple form because the demand and cost functions are stationary, the collusive and punishment strategies are stationary, and the horizon is infinite.

dominate those in the underlying one-shot game. These implicitly collusive outcomes do not arise from binding contracts among the firms. Because they result from unilateral noncooperative play instead, a requirement of the equilibrium is that it is based on a method for punishing free riders who would expand output or cut price. The method that is usual in this regard is that first set out in the Folk theorem: detected free riding is immediately punished by adopting new rules of play which lead the free rider to a stream of profits whose present value is less than the short-term free-riding gain. Further, for the implicitly collusive equilibrium to be sequentially rational, the noncheating firms must find it optimal to punish. In this regard it is usual to restrict punishments to occurring when some single trigger point is reached and to have the firms adopt the equilibrium strategies of the one-shot game during the punishment period. When the present value of the firms' profit streams are decreasing in the length of punishment, there is also an incentive to adopt a punishment period which is long enough to offset the gain to any free ride, but not any longer. That, in a nutshell, is the dynamic game story of implicit collusion.

This story will, of course, be much more complicated when additional real-world concerns are involved. Consider, for example, the implications of asymmetries in the firms' costs of production. In this case cartel profitability requires that lower-cost firms produce greater shares of the market so that each firm's costs are equal at the margin. This allocation of output would yield proportionately larger profits for the low-cost firms. Without some scheme for side payments, that would seem to be problematical: why should one group of firms sacrifice to serve the interest of another? Similarly, asymmetries in products, in methods of product distribution, in terms and conditions of sale, in methods of advertising and quality assurance, and, more generally, asymmetries of any kind complicate the implicit collusion story and leave us with a decision about which of the multiplicity of equilibria is applicable. This does not mean that implicitly collusive equilibria are not feasible in cases when firms have these asymmetries. Rather, the problem is that the implicit collusion story as it stands is not detailed enough to tell us which of many equilibrium strategies will be used and what payoffs will result.

The multiplicity of equilibria with or without asymmetries might be reduced by relying on "standard" industry practices. In this regard Schelling's (1960) concept of focal point equilibria has frequently been suggested to single out equilibria with special distinguishing characteristics. Scherer (1980, pp. 190–3), for example, describes several situations in the pricing of antibiotics and tobacco leaf where price focal points arising out of industry experience played central roles in determining implicitly collusive outcomes.[43] In experimental studies Roth and Schoumaker (1981) have reported on noncooperative bargaining games, with characteristics of the implicit collusion situation, in which the game experiences of the participants were critical determinants of the "cooperative" outcome. What we learn from all this is that institutional details and industry

---

[43] Farrell (1987) has also suggested that firms may use "cheap talk" – public announcements which have no direct cost or benefit – to describe strategies which, if played, would constitute a Nash equilibrium for the industry. Such an equilibrium becomes focal: if everyone expects the announced strategies to be followed then "cheap talk" can be a coordinating mechanism.

history are important aspects of determining what set of industry equilibria will be reached in the future. In this sense industrial economics at once becomes more theoretical *and* more descriptive.

E12.11

The Oligopoly Problem in Antitrust Law

Early court interpretations of the Sherman Act, section 1, emphasized the impact of collusion on market price and required only that there be a logical inference that the challenged behavior raised price beyond competitive levels. The courts generally based such inferences on economic factors, usually a concentrated market structure and/or specific pricing and exclusionary episodes.[44] With more recent cases this criterion has changed so that a conspiracy to fix prices, whether effective or not, has become a violation.[45] This *per se* illegality has meant that it is not necessary to develop economic evidence on prices or other market conditions of the market; it is only required to demonstrate an actual agreement among the firms. Moreover, such an agreement need not be worked out in "smoked-filled rooms," but can be inferred from circumstantial evidence, a so-called *meeting of minds*.

Market evidence of such a "meeting" has generally come from the collection and exchange of statistics concerning price, output, inventories, etc. (for example, by a trade association) or public announcements of intentions to act in specific ways in the future (commonly to raise prices). Whether a conspiracy in the sense of a genuine "meeting of minds" exists, finally, relies on the interpretation of facts. Nonetheless, the courts have been quite clear that implicit collusion in the sense that we have developed this concept – unilateral behavior which yields monopoly outcomes – does *not* involve conspiracy. As a result, implicit collusion, referred to as *tacit* collusion or *conscious parallelism* by the Courts and in legal writing, has drifted beyond the reach of the Sherman Act, section 1.[46] This so-called **oligopoly problem** has been troubling to many economists, lawyers, and courts, who feel that some remedy is desirable.

In an influential analysis, Turner (1962) concludes that a definition of agreement under the Sherman Act which covers implicit collusion is not possible. To do so, he argues, would dictate myopia and irrational behavior to oligopolistic firms and generally lead to welfare losses. In contrast, Posner (1969) adopts the view that section 1 can be useful in dealing with implicitly

---

[44] See, for example, *U.S. v. Trans-Missouri Freight Assn.*, 166 U.S. 290 (1897), and *U.S. v. Joint-Traffic Assn.*, 171 U.S. 505 (1898).

[45] *U.S. v. Trenton Potteries Co.*, 273 U.S. 392 (1927) and *U.S. v. Socony-Vacuum, Inc.*, 310 U.S. 150 (1940), are particularly decisive in this development.

[46] Repeated attempts to find implicit collusion in violation of the law under section 1 have been attempted, but have never been found sufficient in and of themselves. In cases where the allegation has been made, successful prosecution depended on other circumstances. See, for example, *U.S. v. Masonite Corp.*, 316 U.S. 265 (1942), *U.S. v. Paramount Pictures, Inc.*, 334 U.S. 131 (1948), *U.S. v. U.S. Gypsum*, 333 U.S. 364 (1948) and *U.S. v. Chas. Pfizer & Co.*, 367 F. Supp. 91 (S.D.N.Y. 1973). In addition, there have been several recent abortive attempts to find implicitly collusive behavior illegal under the Federal Trade Commision Act, section 5, using a theory of "shared" monopoly. See, for example, *In re Kellogg et al.*, Docket No, 8883 FTC (1981), and *In re Exxon Corp. et al.*, Docket No. 8934 FTC (1983).

collusive arrangements. Roughly, Posner argues that any implicitly collusive arrangement involves costs of detecting and enforcing a specific monopoly outcome and the Sherman Act can be seen as a device for increasing the costs involved in such coordination maintenance processes. Since implicit collusion is voluntary behavior, he continues, appropriate punishments will deter the "colluders." Such punishment should be imposed when certain economic evidence of implicit collusion is offered. For example, Posner would find some combination of the following evidence to be remediable: systematic price discrimination, persistent levels of excess capacity, infrequent price changes, sustained abnormal profits, refusals to offer discounts in the face of excess capacity, early announcement of price intentions, and public statements about "fair" prices for the industry's product. [47]

12.4   Coordination-facilitating Practices

The implicit collusion story would be more convincing, and appear less abstract, if facilitating practices in reaching agreements and reducing incentives for free riding were known and were known to be used. Salop (1986) and Holt and Scheffman (1987) have described several such possibilities generally revolving about contractual commitments which have the effect of "linking" firm reaction functions more closely. For example, provisions in a sales contract which guarantees that a firm will meet any rival's price decrease alters its reaction function and that of its rival. Other examples include firm commitments to factor supply contracts, which change their mixture of fixed and marginal costs (recall chapter 10, SE10.3), base-point pricing schemes, which alter the rival's price reaction functions at various geographic locations, and interfirm licensing contracts which involve per unit royalties and alter marginal costs (and, again, reaction functions). While there are some differences among these practices, the essential, common feature is revealed by an analysis of the meeting competition clause (MCC).

12.4.1   Meeting Competition Clauses

The MCC in a (time-limited) sales contract obliges the issuing seller to rebate to any buyer the difference between its purchase price and that received by any other purchaser of that product. The following example suggests how this "price protection" works in a stylized case.

E12.12

Meeting Competition: Transformed Payoffs

Consider a heterogeneous duopoly (firms 1 and 2) where the strategy sets high or low prices p_h or p_l at each date of a finite horizon (this example follows

---

[47] See McGee (1971) and Markovits (1974, 1975) for critiques of the Posner proposal.

Salop, 1986). The payoffs of the associated one-shot game are given in table 12.4. (The table entries list firm 1's payoffs first and firm 2's second.) The game has the prisoners' dilemma form: while the cooperative strategy (p_h, p_h) dominates all others, the Nash equilibrium is (p_1, p_1) and off-diagonal play results in a loss to the high-priced firm and a significant gain to the low-priced firm.

Table 12.4 Prisoners' Dilemma Payoffs

		p_h	Firm 2 p_1
Firm 1	p_h	(10, 10)	(−2, 15)
	p_1	(15, −2)	(5, 5)

As shown in chapter 9, section 9.6, the finite repetition of the (complete information) one-shot prisoners' dilemma game yields the one-shot Nash equilibrium (p_1, p_1) with payoffs $(5, 5)$. Our interest here is with credible selling policies capable of transforming the payoff matrix in such a way that the one-shot cooperative strategy (p_h, p_h) with payoffs (10, 10) becomes a Nash equilibrium for the repeated game. As one possibility, suppose that each firm adopts an MCC in its sales contract which requires a payment to subsequent buyers of \$6 if the firm charges any given buyer a price below p_h and its rival does not follow this decrease. The effect of the contractual penalty in repeated play is to transform the off-diagonal payoff slightly, but significantly, to that given in table 12.4. Now, the repeated game has two Nash equilibria, both along the main diagonal, and the implicitly collusive (p_h, p_h) strategy is dominant.[48] Again, the (p_h, p_h) strategy is a noncooperative outcome of the game in table 12.5, and there are incentives for the firms to independently adopt the price protection which gives rise to this second form of the game.

Table 12.5 Transformed Payoffs

		p_h	Firm 2 p_1
Firm 1	p_h	(10, 10)	(−2, 9)
	p_1	(9, −2)	(5, 5)

MCCs, while not frequently observed, are not uncommon either. Scherer (1980) and Hay (1982) give several specific examples, including the so-called Price Protection Policy adopted in 1965 by General Electric and systematically

---

[48] While the buyers individually accept the clause in the purchase contract, there is obviously an external cost to all buyers.

offered to all buyers of large steam turbine generator sets and offered selectively by its major rival Westinghouse (see also Sultan, 1972). Perhaps the most widely analyzed case is the FTC Ethyl litigation in which the Federal Trade Commission found that producers of lead-based gasoline additives employed both advanced notification of list price increases and MCCs to, it was alleged, enable implicit collusion.[49] More commonly, advertisements which promise rebates to buyers if better prices can be found can often be seen in local retail markets (and particularly in local "cutthroat" consumer electric goods markets).

Incentives for Meeting Competition Clauses. At first glance it would seem that, lacking some explicit (binding) agreement with its rival, any firm would be unwilling to offer the price protection of an MCC as that restricts its future pricing options and seemingly creates a competitive disadvantage. That that first glance can be wrong is shown by the following analysis.

The Meeting Competition Clause Model. Consider homogeneous-good duopolists j and k using price strategies in an infinitely repeated game. Let $\pi_j(p_j, p_k)$ indicate the strictly concave one-shot profit function of j at prices p_j and p_k. Further, assume that the reaction functions for the firms are positively sloped on the price plane with a unique intersection at $p^b = (p_j{}^b, p_k{}^b)$.[50] Label the firms such that $p_j{}^b \leq p_k{}^b$. Then there is always some MCC that can be offered by firm j with an individually rational price $p_k^* > p_j{}^b$, and responded to by firm k with price $p_j^* > p_k{}^b$, which yields an implicitly collusive equilibrium in which both firms earn greater profits than playing p^b. The proof of this proposition follows essentially from the positively sloped reaction functions, the strict concavity of the profit functions, and the credible commitment not to cut the price firm j placed on itself with the MCC.

The graphical analysis of the MCC in figure 12.2 helps our intuition concerning the proposition (this follows Cooper, 1984). In the figure $R_j{}^b(p_k)$ and $R_k{}^b(p_j)$ indicate the one-shot reaction functions of firms j and k respectively on the price plane with the one-shot solution prices p^b at point B. Suppose now that at some initial period firm j offers the MCC with price p_j^*. If that price increase were adopted *without* the MCC, then at a second period firm j would continue with p_j^* only if firm k has used p_k^{**}. Firm k, however, replies with $p_k^* = R_k{}^b(p_j^*)$. Let z_j^* be j's unit sales at the first period play (p_j^*, p_k^{**}). Given that the MCC was adopted, however, at the second period firm j must condition its best price response not only on k's price but also on the cost of any rebates that it would have to incur if it were to lower its price below p_j^*. The rebate cost is equal to the difference between prices times the z_j^* units. This cost is reflected in the second-period reaction function $R_j{}^{bb}(p_k)$ firm j with the MCC.[51]

---

[49] *In re Ethyl Corp., et al.* 101 FTC 243 (1983), Docket No. 9128, and dismissed *E.I. DuPont De Nemours and Co. v. FTC.* 729 F. 2d 128 (2nd. Cir. 1984). See Holt and Scheffman (1985) for details.

[50] Recall from chapter 3 that the existence and uniqueness requires $\partial^2\pi_j/\partial p_j\partial p_k + \partial^2\pi_j/\partial p_j^2 < 0$ and $\partial^2\pi_j/\partial p_j\partial p_k > 0$ for both firms j.

[51] The vertical distance between $R_j{}^b(p_k)$ and $R_j{}^{bb}(p_k)$ is thus proportional to z_j^*.

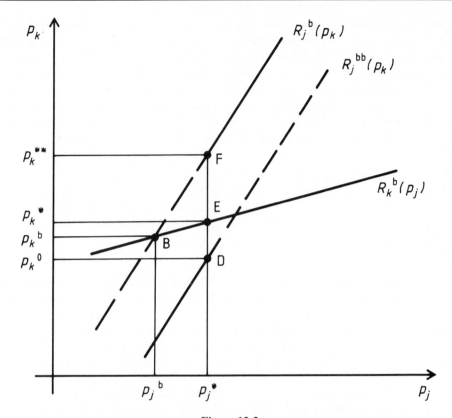

Figure 12.2
Meeting competition clause and implicit collusion

When firm k prices slightly below p_k^{**} and j has offered the MCC, j will not respond in price because the rebate costs will exceed the net revenues from any increase in sales. As shown in the figure, firm k would have to lower its price below p_k^0 for it to be profitable for firm j to lower its price (in view of the rebated costs involved). Firm k's best response is, however, at point E in the figure, along its reaction function. It is evident in the figure that the follower firm k gains more from the MCC sales policy than does the leading firm j (see Belton, 1987, for a detailed proof).

Finally, notice the gist of the above analysis. Firm j sets a higher price (along with the MCC) and firm k reacts to it by moving along its reaction function; that is, the MCC leads to Stackelberg play, with firm j acting as price leader and firm k as price follower.

12.4.2   Cross-licensing to Facilitate Collusion

Consider a single firm j licensing a patented cost-reducing innovation to its market rival, firm k. The license involves both a fixed-charge and a royalty (per unit) fee as a two-part tariff. Using the tariff, firm j controls firm k's reaction function in the market competition – recall from chapter 11, section 3, that the royalty fee can be used to shift the licensee's marginal cost schedule. For an innovation of sufficient value and a sufficiently high royalty rate, k's reaction function can be altered to intersect j's reaction function at the monopoly outcome for the industry. Note that this result (a) does not depend on whether the firms compete in price or quantity in the market and (b) gives the full monopoly value of the innovation to the patentholder, firm j.

A practice of some interest in antitrust law is **sham cross-licensing**.[52] Firms j and k, for example, might implement a cross-license for "innovations" along with per unit royalties. In this case the innovations are generally of minimal worth, but the royalties do not reflect this. Instead the royalties are designed to serve two purposes: (a) to alter the firms' marginal costs and reaction functions in a way that they will lead to the monopoly output; and (b) to allocate the monopoly profits between the firms according to a negotiated sharing rule.[53]

12.5 Competition for Monopoly

In contrast with strategies designed to facilitate collusion, either implicit or overt, sellers often use strategies intended to disadvantage rivals in *competition for monopoly*. Such competition may be legal or illegal under US antitrust statutes. Many economists, and some lawyers, would have this distinction in legality depend on whether or not the competition is likely to increase social welfare. Others hold to a more populist notion and condemn all practices which would diminish the number and variety of competitors (almost) regardless of their relative efficiency.

With respect to the matter of welfare-reducing practices, unfortunately nearly all methods of competition for monopoly have two sides. Depending on specific conditions on demand, cost, product design, market information, etc., most methods of competition can be either welfare increasing or welfare decreasing. Williamson (1968), in his paper "Economics as an antitrust defense: the welfare tradeoffs," makes the earliest systematic attempt at recognizing and reconciling these opposing effects. More recently, Demsetz (1974, 1982b), Liebeler (1976, 1978), Easterbrook (1981a) and Sidak (1983) have developed the efficiency-creating aspects of specific vertical and horizontal market practices which, from time to time, have been condemned by the courts. They suggest plaintively that much of what has passed for antitrust policy has been simply an attempt to force firms to act myopically, not in their unilateral long-run best interest, and that has commensurately harmed social welfare.[54]

---

[52] The classic here is *Hartford-Empire Co. et al. v. U.S.*, 272 U.S. 476. The Hartford-Empire and its codefendants were accused of cross-licensing more than 800 patents among themselves. These involved many market restrictions and elaborate royalty fee schedules.

[53] It is frequently argued that the allocation is achieved by restricting the use of the licensed-produced goods to specific territories or consumer classes; see, for example, Holt and Scheffman (1987).

[54] The explicit requirement that a firm act myopically was central to the plaintiffs' case in *Telex Corp. v. International Business Machines Corp.*, 510 F. 2d 894 (10th Cir. 1975), *cert. dismissed*, 423 U.S. 802 (1975), *ILC Peripherals Leasing Corp. (Memorex) v. International Business Machines Corp.*, 458 F. Supp. 423, 433 (N.D. Cal 1978), and *Berkey Photo, Inc. v. Eastman Kodak Co.*, 603 F.2d 263 (2nd Cir. 1979), *cert. denied*, 100th S. Ct. 1061 (1980).

The result is that there is some question as to whether it is generally possible to separate instances where competition for monopoly is welfare increasing from those where it is welfare decreasing. Rigid *per se* rules are surely much too naive given the complexity of modern market practices and what we know from economic theory. Rule of reason analyses may not be much, if any, better when consideration is given to the significant costs of adversarial litigation. While this is an important and interesting line of inquiry, it is by its own complexity and scope a problem within a problem and beyond our immediate purview.[55] Rather, we limit ourselves here to comments on several predatory practices that have received primary antitrust attention. The intent is simply to reveal the complexity of the issues and note the possibility of error in naive solutions.

12.5.1 Predatory Pricing

Allegations of unfairly underselling a rival – predatory pricing – have played a vivid role in antitrust folklore and filled a considerable portion of the courts' antitrust calendar. In the economic history of the United States, the classic case is the old *Standard Oil Trust*.[56] There, and more generally, the folklore imagines a large, unscrupulous, and powerful industrial giant which slashes price below cost to discourage entry and drive innocent rivals from the market. The giant finances its predatory forays using past profits and profits from distant markets. Competitors fall to bankruptcy and the monopoly spreads.

While that vision of predatory pricing is clear, in actual practice it is generally difficult to separate such "price dampening" from the routine give-and-take price competition that is so highly valued in producing market efficiency. How are low prices which are predatory separated from those which routinely have the effect of forcing less efficient rivals from the market and forestalling less efficient entrants?

Here we follow the generally accepted definition: **predation** occurs when a firm (or group of firms) (a) sacrifices short-run profits by acting in a way designed (b) either to force a rival from the market or to forestall a potential rival's entry with (c) the expectation of increased long-run profits because of the market absence of the rival.[57] The critical aspect of the definition is that the elimination of the rival occurs only because of the profit-sacrificing behavior, and would not occur otherwise. Thus predation is strategic behavior, but it is

---

[55] For further discussion see Areeda and Turner (1975, 1976), Scherer (1976), Easterbrook (1984), Demsetz (1982a), and Ordover and Saloner (1987).

[56] *Standard Oil Company of New Jersey v. U.S.* 221 U.S. 1 (1911). While that is the beginning, the allegations have continued prominently and recently with *FTC v. Anheuser Busch, Inc.*, 363 U.S. 536 (1960), *Utah Pie v. Continental Baking Co.*, 386 U.S. 685 (1967), *In re Realemon*, 92 FTC 669 (1978), *Pacific Engineering & Production Co. of Nevada v. Kerr McGee Corp.*, 551 F.2d 790 (10th Cir. 1977), and *Northeastern Telephone Co. v. American Telephone and Telegraph* 651 F.2d (2nd Cir. 1981).

[57] Areeda and Turner (1975), Williamson (1977), Bork (1978) and Ordover and Willig (1981), among others, use this definition. Scherer (1976) objects and would have us further restrict the predation label to the subset of cases in which the profit-sacrifice exit-inducing behavior *actually* results in a loss of social welfare. Easterbrook (1981a) argues convincingly that the analysis required to measure welfare effects directly, as Scherer would have us do, would be prohibitive in antitrust proceedings.

not *all* strategic behavior. For example, it does not (usually) extend to behavior which simply disadvantages a rival but does not force it from the industry. Nor does it extend to behavior which increases a firm's profits and, at the same time, forces a rival from the industry (as would a cost-reducing innovation).

Predation by an Advantaged Firm. Let us first note that the analysis and implications of limit-entry pricing run parallel to those of exit-inducing predatory pricing. The key difference between the two concepts is that the potential entrant must bear a cost on entering that has already been incurred by incumbents. When there are no sunk costs involved in entry, the analysis and implications of predatory pricing exactly parallel that of limit-entry pricing. Secondly, the focus in much of what follows is on predatory pricing. While the underlying logic is essentially the same as predation by other strategy variables there are important and subtle differences. [58]

McGee (1958) has emphasized that the cost of a predatory pricing episode to the predator is greater than that to the prey if the predator is larger; more generally, he shows that the losses are directly related to the market shares of the firms. [59] When the predator has an advantage over its prey, say in cost of production or distribution or product design, predation will be a successful strategy for monopolization, although it might not be optimal for the firm to acquire that monopoly. [60] That is generally clear from the analysis of oligopoly in chapters 3, 10, and 12. In the case of a significant advantage for the predator, predation will involve short-run losses that can be offset by the present value of a future monopoly (assuming that further entry, or re-entry by the once bankrupt prey, is easy to forestall).

Rationality of Predatory Pricing. Although market conditions and the advantage of the predator might be sufficient to make predatory pricing profitable, McGee has cogently argued that is only a necessary condition for the practice to be rational. Rationality requires not only that a positive balance be struck between the gains and costs of predation, but also that predatory pricing be superior to all other methods of eliminating rivalry. On this basis McGee concluded that predatory pricing is irrational, because it is generally more profitable to *acquire* rather than *undersell* a competitor. Although profound, the argument he offered for this conclusion is quite simple.

Think of two firms producing a single good in a market somehow protected from entry. Let one of the firms have an advantage in cost or product technology, whatever, and suppose that this advantage is sufficient to allow it to prey on and drive out its rival, knowing that the monopoly profit that would

---

[58] Nonprice predation practices that have frequently been mentioned include the installation of excess capacity (recall chapter 10), rapid product innovation or research and development (recall chapter 11), a variety of vertical restraints (recall chapter 7, SE7.5 and SE7.6), and product pre-announcements to "lock-in" consumers (recall chapter 11, SE11.3 and SE11.4, and see SE12.5).

[59] The short-term losses to a below-cost predatory pricing scheme will vary directiy with the rate of the firms' output. This is not the case with predatory advertising, research and development, and other strategies which involve fixed expenditure since then the cost of predation on a per unit basis would vary inversely with the firm's output rate.

[60] This may be true even if entry to the industry is forestalled without cost.

accrue post-exit will more than compensate for the losses during the predatory period. As an alternative to predation, consider with McGee the possibility of merger. How do the profits of such a merged firm compare with the profits of the predator and rival under the predatory scheme? Consider the two possibilities side by side on a time scale. Suppose that the merged firm can only do as well as the predator after it forces the rival from the market. Then the merger is preferred as it earns monopoly profits during the pre-exit period when the predatory pricing is taking place. Given rational firms and sufficient information, the firms will both understand this and a merger under some mutually agreeable terms will result. McGee concludes that predation is irrational.

Posner (1976, pp. 184–5) has argued that the literature has been "excessively influenced" by McGee's merger analysis. Following Yamey (1972), he notes that predatory pricing, while illegal, is more difficult to detect than a merger, and mergers are often contested under section 7 of the Clayton Act (amended by the Celler–Kefauver Act) as being anticompetitive. Second, when the predator operates in several markets, predation (but not merger) may be used to create a reputation for toughness that will discourage entry in other markets. Finally, he argues that a round of predatory pricing may be effective in reducing the market value of the prey's assets and thereby minimize the costs of later acquisition.[61] Nonetheless, he concludes

> . . . To be sure, this analysis does not establish that [predatory pricing] is an effective method of monopolization. To impose costs on a competitor by imposing the same or greater costs on oneself does not seem a very promising method of excluding a competitor. (Posner, 1976, p. 185)

Predation and Merger. Saloner (1987) has argued that the terms of any acquisition in anticipation of predation must depend on the actions that the potential predator can credibly threaten should the merger negotiations be unsuccessful. When future outcomes are asymmetrically uncertain, predatory behavior may be rational because mutually agreeable merger terms cannot be reached.

Saloner's analysis is based on two firms, 1 and 2, and a three-stage game. Stages one and three are market events, where the active firms choose quantities in Cournot–Nash competition. Stage two is an intervening date where firm 1 makes a take it or leave it offer to acquire firm 2. The game is one of incomplete asymmetric information: while firm 1 knows all things, firm 2 is uncertain of firm 1's costs which may be either "high" or "low." As is usual in such games, a perfect Bayesian equilibrium is sought and that derives from a backward recursion solution sequence.

1 *Final market stage* At this stage of the game either firm 1 has acquired firm 2 and a monopoly equilibrium is reached, or the acquisition did not

[61] Burns (1986) analyzed 43 acquisitions of the American Tobacco Company around the turn of the century and concluded that predatory price cutting did indeed reduce American's acquisition costs. McGee (1958) provides similar but less systematic evidence of Standard Oil's acquisitions of petroleum refining firms, and Elzinga (1970) also reports on such acquisitions by the old Gunpowder Trust.

occur and a duopoly equilibrium is reached. The duopoly solution reflects the (possibly) incomplete information of firm 2 much like the one-period Bayes equilibrium developed in E9.7.

2 *Intermediate, acquisition stage* In anticipation of the final market play, and using whatever information arises from the first-stage market outcome, firm 1 makes an offer to purchase firm 2. Whether that offer is accepted or not depends on firm 2's belief concerning firm 1's type, for that will determine both the expected value of the difference between the monopoly and duopoly outcome (the maximum acquisition price that will be offered) and the expected value of the duopoly profits for firm 2 (the minimum acquisition price that will be accepted). Given that the monopoly profits are greater than those in the duopoly equilibrium and firm 1 has complete information, the offer to acquire will always be accepted. A merger of assets is thus inevitable.[62]

Two interesting aspects of the dynamic competition are reflected in the takeover offer. First, if the high-cost firm 1 makes a different offer from that the low-cost firm 1 type, that will reveal its type and this information could then be used to the advantage of firm 2 in the following market game. In turn, that would affect the mutually acceptable offer conditions. Because of this, and restricting attention to the case where the merger is more valuable to the low-cost-type firm 1 (compared with the high-cost type), Saloner shows that the takeover offers will not differ between the firm 1 types.[63] Second, while the takeover offer is itself nonrevealing, can firm 2 use the strategy selection by firm 1 in the first game to infer firm 1's type?

3 *First market stage* As is usual with repeated games having incomplete asymmetric information, there are three possible equilibria: pooling, separating, and semi-separating. A low-cost firm 1 has an incentive to separate itself from a high-cost firm, as an acceptable takeover offer will be lower if firm 2 knows for sure that firm 1 is low cost. A high-cost firm has an incentive to use a low-cost ploy for the same reason. Just as in the limit-pricing analysis of chapter 9, section 9.7.3, and chapter 10, section 10.6, the adoption of the pure pooling or separating strategies or the mixed semi-separating strategy depends on the prior beliefs of firm 2 concerning types and the specific conditions of demand and cost (including the discount rate between stages).

[62] In a variant on this model, Saloner allows new entry to the industry at stage three *if* the takeover occurs in stage two. This reduces the value of the takeover to firm 1. Depending on the new entrant's belief concerning firm 1's type, the entry could produce a stage three equilibrium which left the merged firm worse off than it would have been if it had reached a duopoly equilibrium with the old rival firm 2.

[63] The intuition for the nonrevelation is by a contradiction. Let π_2^h be the stage three profits of firm 2 if firm 1 is high cost. If firm 1 is high cost it makes a takeover offer just slightly greater than π_2^h. If firm 1 is low cost it will not offer less than this level, for that would be matched by the high-cost type in a signaling ploy. Moreover, the low-cost type would not offer more than π_2^h. The only remaining case for revelation is for the low-cost firm 1 to make an offer less than π_2^h that is found to be unacceptable, but that can only occur if the acquisition is more valuable to the high-cost type, contrary to our assumption.

One difference between limit-pricing models and the present model is that the firm with incomplete information is now an *actual* rival. That introduces a twist in the analysis since firm 2's production depends on its belief of firm 1's type and production level which, coming full circle, depends on what firm 2 believes *and* produces. In the separating equilibrium this causes the low-cost firm 1 to produce a greater level than it otherwise would to distinguish itself. This leads the high-cost firm 1 to produce more than it would have done in the absence of such an expanded low-cost output, even though it is not attempting to pool. The final result of the expanded firm 1 outputs for both types is to *reduce* the equilibrium output for firm 2, and therefore reduce the minimum acceptable takeover offer. Saloner further shows that, under reasonable conditions, these offsetting outputs will lead to a greater industry output, a lower price, and a greater welfare than otherwise.

Entry for Buyout. As a complication to the strategy of acquisition in lieu of predation, Rasmusen (1988) notes that the possibility of takeover introduces a new sort of credible threat: a potential entrant might threaten an incumbent with entry knowing that the resulting duopoly equilibrium will reduce the incumbent's profit. Moreover, the threat is credible when the duopoly equilibrium leads to positive profits (above *fixed* entry costs) for the entrant. Some split of the excess of the incumbent's monopoly profits over its duopoly profits would be negotiated after the "entry for buyout." In summary Rasmusen notes:

> . . . If buyout is introduced, the same range of possibilities exists, but entry deterrence is less often possible or profitable. The fixed cost has two offsetting effects. Entry is more difficult, because unless the entrant's Cournot revenues cover his fixed cost of production (as distinct from his sunk entry cost), he cannot credibly threaten to remain in the market. If the fixed cost is large, however, the surplus from moving to monopoly from duopoly is greater, which increases the buyout price. . . . The equilibrium depends on the size of the fixed cost. (Rasmusen, 1988, p. 291)

12.5.2 The Long Purse and Predation

Telser's (1966b) analysis of "cutthroat competition and the long purse" holds aside the question of merger to focus on a second requirement of successful predation. Not only must the post-exit monopoly rents received by the predator be sufficient to offset its losses during an underselling period, but the predator must have a longer purse, a greater ability to finance the underselling losses, before it can bankrupt the prey. Simply, if it does not have this financial resource advantage then the prey can wait out any price war. Predation would not be a successful strategy in this case and, with rational expectations, it would not be attempted in the first place. Conversely, if the predator had a sufficiently long purse, its threat to outlast the prey in a price war would be credible and, once made, would cause a rational prey to exit immediately to avoid the otherwise inevitable losses. In either case, Telser argued that predation will not occur generally, but will only be seen when there is incomplete information or miscalculation.

Unraveling Proof. Telser's result is an application of the perfect equilibrium concept, and its proof proceeds by the same unraveling agrument that yielded the chain store paradox (recall chapter 9, section 9.5.2). Briefly, consider some last period when the prey has come to the end of its financial capacity; one more period of the price war will drive it into bankruptcy. In this case the predator will persist in underselling and force the prey out, since it will find the post-exit monopoly rents greater than relenting and sharing the market in the future. Given that all of this is common knowledge, the rational prey will choose to exit and avoid the last-period loss. A similar analysis follows for the next to last period and, by induction, for all periods. In this complete-information finite game the unraveling leads the prey to exit at the onset, when the first predatory threat is made, as a perfect equilibrium.

Thinking of the predation with long purse story in the same way as we did the chain store paradox suggests the two standard ways of avoiding unraveling and its implications for a general absence of predation. First, there is the option of an infinite (indefinite repetition) horizon game with a reputation (self-fulfilling expectations) equilibrium. In this case the infinite horizon would not make much sense for a price war that was being waged between two incumbent firms, but it might realistically pertain to infinitely (or indefinitely) repeated predation threats against potential entrants in an ongoing market. That was the specific situation analyzed in chapter 9, section 9.6, and the reader is referred there, now adding a long purse (greater financial resources) to the list of things which cause entrants to believe in the first place that the incumbent will prey on their entry. Along the self-fulfilling expectations, entry deterrence equilibrium path there can be mistaken entry only (trembles) and that is dealt with by predation.

The second usual option for avoiding unraveling, and here produce predatory episodes, is to limit common knowledge. It is after all unlikely that each firm will know exactly what financial resources the other will have and in turn know how long they might survive a price war. If we again couch the predation in an entry situation and assume that the incumbent has superior knowledge, it seems reasonable (as a first approximation) to let the information be asymmetric: because of its industry experience the incumbent knows all things, but the inexperienced entrant does not know the extent of the financial resources possessed by the incumbent – more exactly the entrant does not know the incumbent's cost of capital and thus how long it will force a price war. If the incumbent has a low cost of capital relative to the entrant, then it will have greater staying power. This is now exactly the situation analyzed in chapter 9, section 9.7 (in mixed strategies), and chapter 10, section 10.6 (with pooling and separating strategies), in which, because of the incomplete information, entry occurs and is variously dealt with by predation either as a single by the high-capital-cost incumbent or as a reaction of a low-capital-cost (long-purse) incumbent.[64] The uncomfortable aspect of this incomplete asymmetric informa-

---

[64] Benoit (1984) develops a model similar to this in which the role of the financial constraint is made explicit.

tion approach to predation is that the source of the differences in financing is left unexplained. How is it that the incumbent secures a low cost of capital relative to the entrant? Two possibilities have been suggested.

Cost of Capital and the Age of the Firm. Diamond (1984, 1985) has offered a combined adverse selection and moral hazard explanation that the likelihood of default on debt, and therefore the risk-adjusted cost of capital, is inversely related to the age of the firm. This age discrimination is therefore capable of producing the differences in capital costs necessary for the long-purse predatory argument.

His analysis revolves about three types of firms distinguished by their risk tolerance. There are risk-intolerant firms S which undertake only safe projects, strongly risk-tolerant firms R that take only risky projects, and firms M which are middling in risk and which, from time to time, adopt risky or safe projects depending on their relative returns. The firms finance their projects in a competitive capital market which, because of prohibitive costs of information, cannot separate the firms by type.

For simplicity we will assume here that risky projects have negative expected values and safe projects have relatively small positive present values. However, risky projects that are "successful" have *ex post* payoffs greater than .the safe project. All projects, safe or risky, have the same service life. Finally, we assume that valuations are according to risk-neutral rules (see Krouse, 1986, ch, 9).

The timing of the model is straightforward. Firms come on the scene in cohorts and periodically. Each cohort has a specific combination of S, R, and M firms. At the onset of each period each firm turns to the capital market for project financing. The capital lenders do not know the firm's type, only its cohort (or age). Loans are made with interest rates possibly differing by cohort, but not by type within a cohort. At the end of the project's life each firm pays off its loan if it can; firms with unsuccessful risky projects cannot repay, their assets are confiscated, and the firm disappears. With this structure Diamond derives the perfect Bayesian equilibrium path for the industry. For each cohort there are three phases having different interest rate characteristics.

1 Because they have accumulated few assets (retained earnings), so that little can be lost, and because the high-return tail of the profit distribution can be gained, at the onset type M firms adopt risky projects only. R and S firms choose projects as their polar risk tolerances require. As time proceeds a number of R and M firms will have unsuccessful outcomes and disappear from the market. Because of this the average risk of the cohort will fall and the competitive capital market will adjust by offering lower lending rates. At this lower rate the safe projects become more attractive to the M firms since the long-lived future cash flows they provide are then discounted less. The shorter expected horizon (more exactly the duration) of the risky cash flows means that they will increase proportionately less with the change in the discount rate.

2 At some time the reduced number of risky projects being undertaken

will result in a lending rate such that safe projects will become preferred by M firms. They will (all) switch to safe projects leaving only the few successful R firms to choose risky projects. This switch brings with it a sharp fall in the risk-adjusted lending rate. Thus "older" firms – those firms in phase 2 as compared with those in phase 1 – have lower interest rates. The market imperfection giving rise to this difference lies in the capital market's high cost of determining the type of projects adopted by firms within a cohort (age group). When firms are expected to be ongoing, with infinite life, this second phase continues.

3 If the industries involved have a limited life, then as the terminal date is approached the present value of the safe cash flow becomes less. This has the effect of making risky projects more appealing to the M firms – the duration of the risky and riskless cash flow streams is closer. In this case it will not be optimal for the M firms to abruptly shift to risky projects as that will have the effect of increasing the discount rate which will reduce the present value of their profits (and a fortiori make risky projects preferred). Rather, Diamond shows that it is optimal for the M firms to mix their choice of risky and safe projects over the final phase, with the mixing probability increasing so that only risky projects are selected as the terminal date is reached.

The key aspect of this analysis is that when the capital market possesses incomplete information concerning the type of projects adopted by individual firms the age of the firm can be a useful device for cost-of-capital discrimination. More specifically, new entrants (young firms) will have high costs of capital relative to old incumbents. The problem with this line of reasoning is that it ignores the incentives of firms who take safer projects to distinguish themselves, and it ignores the incentives for competitive lenders to gain trade by determining firms with safer projects to undercut the otherwise average market lending rate. There is a large information-seeking industry (security analysts, industry analysts) whose sole purpose is to uncover such information and reduce the cost of its disemination. Moreover, there should be unraveling as firms with lower than average risk have a strong incentive to cooperate by supplying discriminating information. Thus it is an open question whether the extent of the incomplete information will be sufficient to produce the results that Diamond suggests.

In a related explanation of cost-of-capital differences, Fudenberg and Tirole (1986a) have suggested that the likelihood of bankruptcy depends on the firm's retained earnings (assets). When there are significant costs of bankruptcy, these *expected* costs are greater for firms having less assets than for those with more. A competitively determined lending rate must then reflect this expected cost (of bankruptcy), with the effect that incumbents with greater assets have lower costs of capital than smaller-sized entrants. There are two problems with this explanation. First, the evidence of Baxter (1967) and Warner (1977) is that bankruptcy costs are too small to be important in this way. Second, even if these costs are not small, there is the argument of Haugen and Senbet (1978) that, with a capital market where security trading costs are small, investors will choose reorganization to avoid formal bankruptcy costs.

E12.13 ━━

Legal Standards for Predation

As neither law nor economics provides a clear theory of predatory behavior there has been a division in viewpoints toward antitrust policy relating to many business practices. On the one hand there are those who argue that the gains to vigorous competition are important, the likelihood of predation is small, and the costs of separating predatory and nonpredatory acts are great, and, as an implication of these things, little antitrust effort should be given to the matter. In contrast there are those who not only believe predation more prevalent and malevolent but also think that effective ways of discerning the behavior are available.[65] The case of predatory pricing has received particular attention in this regard, perhaps because of the widely discussed analysis by Areeda and Turner (1975) and their specific proposal that prices at or above marginal costs should be presumed lawful and those below marginal costs should be treated conversely.[66]

While the Areeda–Turner rule has greatly influenced US legal standards concerning predatory pricing, it has seldom been applied exactly.[67] Rather, the rule is commonly used as a starting point, with exceptions attempting to reflect various deficiencies. The first and most durable application of a qualified Areeda–Turner role occurred in *Hanson v. Shell Co.*,[68] which also has been interpreted as establishing an "entry barriers exception."[69] There, a two-stage test for the presence of predatory pricing was adopted:

1 pricing below marginal (or average variable) costs;
2 (a) pricing above marginal or average variable costs, but below average total cost when (b) entry barriers are high.

The ambiguity of accounting cost measurements, especially in multiproduct and

[65] These opposing views are seen, for example, in the recent industrial organization textbooks by McGee (1988) and Martin (1988).

[66] The first suggestion of cost-based standard for the detection of predatory pricing was by McGee (1958), who continues (McGee, 1980) to support such a rule. Kohler (1971) also proposed such tests. Areeda and Turner (1975) made the first systematic proposal relating product price to costs as a basis for antitrust policy. The earliest explicit acceptance of a cost-based rule by the courts occurred in *Utah Pie v. Continental Baking Co.*, 386 U.S. 685 (1967) where pricing below average total cost was part of the evidence taken to indicate predation. The error in using average total cost has meant that *Utah Pie* is not commonly used as a controlling precedent. One notable exception to this is *O. Hommel Co. v. Ferro Corp.*, 472 F.Supp 793 (W.D.Pa. 1979).

[67] *Janich Bros. Inc. v. American Distilling Co.*, 570 F. 2d 848 (9th Cir. 1977), *cert. denied*, 439 U.S. 829 (1978) and *Northeastern Telephone Co. v. American Telephone & Telegraph Co. et al*, 651 F2.d (2nd Cir. 1981) would seem to come the closest to unqualified acceptance of the rule. (However, the court's strict reliance on a cost-based test in *Janich* may have resulted from Janich's failure to build any part of its case around entry conditions or industry structure). Those who argue for an exact application of the Areeda–Turner rule maintain that, among its variants, it is the least likely to injure competition and is administratively practical (see McGee, 1980, p. 304).

[68] 541 F.2d 1352 (1976). See also *International Air Industries v. American Excelsior Co.*, 517 F.2d 714 (1975) for qualifications similar to those in *Hanson*.

[69] This interpretation of *Hanson* is explicit in *Murphy Tugboat v. Crowley*, 454 F.Supp. 847 (N.D. Cal 1978).

multimarket firms, has meant that the dual test 2(a) and 2(b) is generally invoked.[70] Thus, when an action involves predatory pricing the decision often turns on the question of high entry barriers.

Supplementary examples

SE12.1 Heterogeneous Oligopoly and Profits–Concentration

Cubbin (1974) extends the basic profits–concentration relationship to an oligopoly with heterogeneous products. In this case we write the jth firm's profits as

$$\pi_j(p) = p_j z_j(p) - c_j(z_j(p)) \tag{12.45}$$

where $p = [p_1 p_2 \ldots p_J]$ is the price vector. Stationarity conditions for a profit maximum are, in turn,

$$\frac{d\pi_j}{dp_j} = z_j + \left(\frac{\partial z_j}{\partial p_j} + \sum_{k \neq j} \frac{\partial z_j}{\partial p_k} \frac{dp_k^e}{dp_j}\right)(p_j - c_j') = 0 \tag{12.46}$$

In this expression the dp_k^e/dp_j are price conjectural variations. Suppose that the conjectural variations are constant for all j and k and denoted by γ_{jk}^*. Also, let

$$\gamma_j^* = \sum_{k \neq j} \gamma_{kj}^* \left(\frac{\partial z_j}{\partial p_k} \bigg/ \sum_{k \neq j} \frac{\partial z_j}{\partial p_k}\right) \tag{12.47}$$

be the indicated weighted average of these γ_{jk}^*. Using this definition, the stationarity conditions are rewritten

$$z_j + \left\{\frac{\partial z_j}{\partial p_j} + \gamma_j^* \sum_{k \neq j} \frac{\partial z_j}{\partial p_k}\right\}(p_j - c_j') = 0 \tag{12.48}$$

Appropriately multiplying and dividing by $-p_j/z_j$ and then rearranging gives

$$1 - \left(\frac{p_j}{z_j} \frac{\partial z_j}{\partial p_j} + \gamma_j^* \sum_{k \neq j} \frac{p_j}{z_j} \frac{\partial z_j}{\partial p_k}\right)L_j = 0 \tag{12.49}$$

It is instructive to develop the term in parentheses somewhat further. To begin, note that

$$\frac{dz_j}{dp_j} = \frac{\partial z_j}{\partial p_j} + \sum_{k \neq j} \frac{\partial z_j}{\partial p_k}\left(\frac{dp_k^e}{dp_j}\right)$$

Multiplying and dividing this expression by $-p_j/z_j$, and assuming uniform conjectures ($dp_k^e/dp_j = 1$) we obtain

$$\eta_j^1 = \eta_j^0 - \frac{p_j}{z_j} \sum_{k \neq j} \frac{\partial z_j}{\partial p_k} \tag{12.50}$$

Here, η_j^1 is j's demand elasticity assuming the price conjectural variations of unity and η_j^0 is the demand elasticity assuming price conjectural variations of zero. We can finally use (12.50) to write the price–cost margin L_j as

---

[70] Joskow and Klevorick (1979) have offered a list of characteristics for firms, products, and markets that is often used, not without criticism, to determine the height of barriers to entry in such situations.

$$L_j = \frac{1}{\gamma_j^* \eta_j^{\,1} + (1 - \gamma_j^*) \eta_j^{\,0}} \tag{12.51}$$

As $L_j = 1/\eta_j$ holds generally, where η_j is the elasticity of firm j's demand, (12.51) informs us that this actual elasticity can be thought of as a weighted average of the polar case elasticities $\eta_j^{\,0}$ and $\eta_j^{\,1}$. That the weights involve the conjectural variations is another expression of the importance of a more exact determination of these terms.

SE12.2   Tobin's Q and Monopoly Power

The ratio of the capital market value of the firm to the replacement value of its assets is termed Tobin's Q measure. It is frequently used as an index of monopoly power (see Tobin, 1957; Lindenberg and Ross, 1981; Smirlock et al., 1984). The intuition for this usage is that the monopoly profits of the firm (and rents to firm-specific factors) are captured in the firm's capital market value, while the asset replacement costs more generally reflect competitive rental rates. The exact way in which Q serves as an index of monopoly, when demand is stochastic, can be developed in a simple two-period model.

Suppose that at some initial period $t = 0$ the firm in question hires κ units of capital and L units of labor to produce z units of output at the next period $t = 1$. If this output is sold at an uncertain price p, then the firm's cash flow is given by the random variable

$$R = pz - \omega L - \phi\kappa \tag{12.52}$$

where ω and ϕ are respectively the wage rate and the unit cost of capital. To keep things simple it is further assumed that these factor prices are known at $t = 0$, and the factors are paid at $t = 1$.

Given the conditions underlying the standard capital asset pricing model, the $t = 0$ capital market value of the firm is[71]

$$V = \frac{\bar{R} + \{(\bar{R}_m - r_f V_m)/\sigma_m^2\}\, \text{cov}(R, R_m)}{r_f} \tag{12.53a}$$

where $\bar{R}$ is the expected value of R (using $t = 0$ probabilities), R_m is the random cash flow associated with the *market portfolio* ($\bar{R}_m$ and σ_m^2 are respectively the $t = 0$ mean and variance of the market portfolio), and r_f is the (one plus) riskless rate of return. It is usual to rewrite this expression as

$$V = \frac{R - \lambda\beta V}{r_f} \tag{12.53b}$$

where $\lambda \equiv \bar{r}_m - r_f$ is the so-called *market price of risk*, $\bar{r}_m \equiv \bar{R}_m/V_m$ is the expected market rate of return, and $\beta \equiv V_m \text{cov}(R, R_m)/V\sigma_m^2$ is the *systematic risk* of the cash flow R. This last expression is in a certainty-equivalent form, as $\lambda\beta V$ can be interpreted as the amount to be subtracted from the expected cash flow to exactly compensate for the cash flow risk. The difference in the numerator is the certainty-equivalent cash flow, which is then properly dis-

---

[71] Krouse (1986, chs 6 and 7) develops this model in detail.

counted to $t = 0$ by the riskless rate. Alternatively, (12.53b) can be solved for V to give

$$V = \frac{\bar{R}}{r_f + \beta\lambda} \tag{12.53c}$$

which is in a risk-adjusted discount rate form. Here the expected cash flow is discounted at a rate which reflects the cash flow risk (with $\beta\lambda$ being the risk premium above the riskless rate).

For each of expressions (12.53) note that maximizing V is different from maximizing $\bar{R}$ since β is also generally a function of the chosen output level. To see this effect, specifically let the stochastic properties of the firm's cash flow arise from demand uncertainty (alone) in the multiplicative form

$$p = p(z)(1 + \varepsilon) \tag{12.54}$$

where ε is mean-zero noise. Under this demand specification $\bar{p} = p(z)$, and

$$\beta = \frac{p(z)z \operatorname{cov}(\varepsilon, R_m)V_m}{V\sigma_m{}^2} \tag{12.55}$$

In turn, the stationarity point of V with respect to z is given by

$$(p'z + p)\left\{1 - \frac{V_m(\bar{r}_m - r_f)\operatorname{cov}(\varepsilon, R_m)}{\sigma_m{}^2}\right\} = MC$$

where MC is the marginal cost of z. If we let $\bar{\eta} = -(p'z/p)^{-1}$ indicate the elasticity of *expected* demand, the firm's price–cost margin can be written as

$$\frac{p - MC}{p} = \frac{1}{\bar{\eta}} + \frac{\bar{\eta} - 1}{\bar{\eta}}\left\{\frac{V_m(\bar{r}_m - r_f)\operatorname{cov}(\varepsilon, R_m)}{\sigma_m{}^2}\right\} \tag{12.56}$$

In the case where the firm's production exhibits constant returns to scale, the expected cash flow, using (12.49), is

$$\bar{R} = \frac{pz(\bar{\eta} - 1)V_m(\bar{r}_m - r_f)\operatorname{cov}(\varepsilon, R_m)}{\bar{\eta}\sigma_m{}^2} + \frac{1}{\bar{\eta}} \tag{12.57}$$

Substituting this in (12.53c) and rearranging finally gives

$$V = \frac{pz}{\bar{\eta}r_f + \beta} \tag{12.58}$$

This equation expresses the value of the firm as a function of its revenues, its expected demand elasticity, and its systematic risk.

Tobin's Q, again, is the ratio of the market value of the firm to the replacement value of its assets. If we let $\phi = r_f - 1$, then

$$Q = 1 + \frac{pz/\kappa}{\bar{\eta}r_f + \beta} \tag{12.59}$$

It is seen that β and $\bar{\eta}$ affect Q in the same way. For fixed β and pz/κ, Q is inversely related to $\bar{\eta}$ and therefore related to monopoly power. However, (a) more efficient firms will have a greater pz/κ ratio and a larger Q, and (b) less risky firms, with lower β will also have a larger Q. Thus using Q as a measure of monopoly power can potentially confuse monopoly power, efficiency, and risk effects.

SE12.3   Dominant-firm Price Leadership and Monopoly Power

In an analysis of the dominant-firm price-leadership model (recall chapter 3, section 3.4.3, and E12.5), Landes and Posner (1981) showed that the market elasticity of demand, the elasticity of supply, and market share of the competitive fringe constrain the ability of the dominant firm to increase price above marginal cost. Ordover et al. (1982) amend that analysis to allow for a group of "dominant" firms and a competitive fringe. We follow their variation on the homogeneous-good oligopoly and derive the Lerner index for one of the "dominant" firms.

To begin, let the market demand be $z(p)$ and suppose that there are $j = 1, 2,$ ..., N non-price-taking firms, each producing quantity z_j with associated market share m_j. Let η be the market demand elasticity, and let m_f and ε_f be the corresponding market share and supply elasticity for the price-taking fringe. At equilibrium we have

$$z(p) = z_f(p) + \sum_j^N z_j \tag{12.60}$$

where $z_f(p)$ is the supply of the fringe at price p. Differentiating (12.60) with respect to z_j and rearranging to form the elasticity of j's demand gives

$$-\frac{\partial p}{\partial z_j} \frac{z_j}{p} = \frac{m_j(1 + \lambda_j)}{\eta + m_f \varepsilon_f} \tag{12.61}$$

where $\lambda_j = \sum_{j \neq k}^N \partial z_k / \partial z_j$ is firm j's conjectural variation concerning the total output response of other non-price-taking firms. At firm j's profit maximum we also have

$$p(z_j) + z_j \frac{\partial p}{\partial z_j} - c_j = 0 \tag{12.62}$$

where c_j is the marginal cost. This solves for

$$L_j = \frac{p - c_j}{p} = -\frac{\partial p}{\partial z_j} \frac{z_j}{p} \tag{12.63}$$

The right-hand side of this last expression is the same as the left-hand side of (12.61). We conclude that j's monopoly power (Lerner index) is increased by its market share m_j and its conjecture λ_j, and is decreased by the market elasticity of demand η, the fringe supply m_f, and the elasticity ε_f of the fringe supply.

SE12.4   Estimating Monopoly Power

As noted in section 12.1.4, efforts have recently been made to estimate conjectural variations directly from market data. To set up the details of one such case, consider a homogeneous-good oligopoly with (inverse) market demand $p = p(z)$, where $z = \sum_j z_j$ is the aggregate industry output of the $j = 1, 2, \ldots, J$ firms. For this case the profit-maximum stationarity conditions become

$$p - c_j' + z_j \left\{ \frac{\partial p(z)}{\partial z_j} + \sum_{k \neq j} \frac{\partial p(z)}{\partial z_k} \frac{dz_k^e(z_j)}{dz_j} \right\} = 0 \tag{12.64}$$

This rearranges to give

$$p - c_j' + z_j \frac{\partial p}{\partial z} \left\{ 1 + \sum_{k \neq j} \frac{dz_k{}^c(z_j)}{dz_j} \right\} = 0 \tag{12.65}$$

where we use $dz/dz_j = 1$ and $dz_k{}^c(z_j)/dz_j$ is j's conjectural variation with respect to each rival firm k.

Suppose that the conjectures are in terms of quantities and are given by the following proportionality rule:

$$\frac{dz_k{}^c/z_k}{dz_j/z_j} = \alpha_{kj} + \beta_{kj} m_j \tag{12.66}$$

where $m_j = z_j/z$ is firm j's market share and α_{kj}, β_{kj} are constants. The percentage change in k's output perceived by j as a reaction to a given percentage change in its ouput is a linear function of its market share m_j. Substituting this conjecture in (12.65) and rearranging gives

$$\frac{c_j'}{p} = 1 + \frac{1}{\eta} \left\{ m_j + \sum_{k \neq j} (\alpha_{kj} m_k - \beta_{kj} m_j m_k) \right\} \tag{12.67}$$

Note that these J equations have only the market demand elasticity η as a common parameter.

Suppose next that there are just two groups of firms: call them D for dominant and F for fringe. Further assume that each firm characterizes its rivals' reactions based only on the group to which the rival belongs and let there be homogeneity of expectations across firms in the same group. Thus, for dominant firms (12.67) becomes

$$\frac{c_j'}{p} = 1 + \frac{1}{\eta} \{ m_j + \alpha_{DD}(m_D - m_j) + \beta_{DD} m_j (m_D - m_j)$$
$$+ \alpha_{FD}(1 - m_D) + \beta_{FD} m_j (1 - m_D) \} \tag{12.68}$$

for each $j \in D$ and m_D is the total market share of the dominant group of firms. A similar equation obtains for firms in the fringe group. It is of note that each such equation has five parameters (η, the αs, and the βs) and five independent variables.

Spiller and Favaro (1984) estimate the parameters for equations in this form using 1970 data from the Uruguayan banking sector. Their hypotheses included the following:

1 output matching behavior among dominant firms and by dominant firms relative to the fringe firms

$$\alpha_{DD} + \beta_{DD} m_j > 0 \tag{12.69}$$

$$\alpha_{DF} + \beta_{DF} m_j > 0 \tag{12.70}$$

2 dominant firms believe that fringe firms would behave competitively towards them

$$\alpha_{FD} + \beta_{FD} m_j > 0 \tag{12.71}$$

3 the fringe firms would have Cournot conjectures toward each other

$$\alpha_{FF} + \beta_{FF} m_j = 0 \tag{12.72}$$

These hypotheses were confirmed prior to a regulatory change relaxing entry barriers, but were not found after the change.

SE12.5　Clientele, or Lock-in, Effects

It is often asserted that a firm's monopoly power derives from the clientele base it has established with early-on investments. The usual reply to such a claim notes that the monopoly value of this clientele is zero, since higher monopoly prices will surely and swiftly drive the firm's trade to competitors. In chapters 13 and 14 we shall argue that imperfect market information may keep consumers from switching in this abrupt way (and therefore the cost of information will be the underlying source of monopoly). An alternative explanation, and the one investigated here, is the possibility that monopoly may arise in such situations when there are in-use costs to brand switching, say, because consumers make brand-specific investments in complementary assets.

The Clientele. Farrell and Shapiro (1988) use an overlapping generations model with young and old cohorts to explore the degree of monopoly that brand-switching costs may permit. In any given generational time period both cohorts exist; in the next such period the previously old cohort passes on, the previously young cohort becomes old, and a new young cohort arises. This exchange of cohort status goes on for infinitely many periods. The consumers are served by two firms selling products which are identical except with respect to a switching cost described below. Buyers and sellers have zero information costs and thus all information about prices, products, and conditions of trade is known.

Switching Cost. At each generational period the firms choose new (nondiscriminatory) prices for their products and, in turn, the cohorts choose the firm to patronize. The essential dynamics of the model comes from the imposition of a cost when using a new brand: consumers in the older cohort incur a cost on switching to a brand different from that which they used when young, and the young cohort faces that cost when first adopting one of the brands. The switching cost means that the firm which serves a young cohort in one period has an advantage relative to its rival in serving that cohort when it becomes old in the subsequent period. To keep these firms apart over time, the firm serving the old cohort without the switching cost in any period is called the *advantaged* firm and its rival is said to be *disadvantaged*.

The notation and complications can be held to a minimum by assuming that the number of consumers in the young and old cohorts are equal at each period and over periods. Moreover, scale the numbers in each cohort to equal unity, so that the *total* number of individuals at each period is 2, and let each consumer buy one unit of the good from either one firm or the other. On the supply side assume that the costs of production are zero, which makes each firm's profit simply equal to its price times the number of consumers served. Thus, at each period t the profits of the advantaged (a) and disadvantaged (d) firms are (j = a, d)

$$\pi_{jt} = 0 \qquad \text{if no trade}$$

$$= p_{jt} \qquad \text{if one cohort (young or old) is served} \quad (12.73)$$

$$= 2p_{jt} \qquad \text{if both cohorts are served}$$

Consumers choose the specific firm with which to trade on the basis of surplus received. If v is the consumer reservation price (for individuals of both cohorts), p_{jt} is the price set by firm j at period t, c is the initial brand adoption cost, and c^* is the brand switching cost, then the surpluses S_{ot} and S_{yt} for older and younger individuals respectively are

$$S_{ot} = v - p_{at} \qquad \text{with a firm trade}$$
$$\qquad\qquad\qquad\qquad\qquad\qquad\qquad (12.74a)$$
$$= v - p_{dt} - c^* \qquad \text{with d firm trade}$$

$$S_{yt} = v - p_{at} - c \qquad \text{with a firm trade}$$
$$\qquad\qquad\qquad\qquad\qquad\qquad\qquad (12.74b)$$
$$= v - p_{dt} - c \qquad \text{with d firm trade}$$

We will assume $c^* < c$ based on the assumption that some brand-specific capital is transferable.

Markov Alternating Equilibrium. Farrell and Shapiro restrict the firms to strategies where each firm can condition its action at any period only on the actions of the prior period (which determines whether it is currently an advantaged or a disadvantaged firm) and not the entire game history. Such strategies are commonly called (first-order) **Markov**, as are the resulting perfect equilibria. With this restriction, first note that at any period the advantaged firm earns positive profits for any $p_{at} > 0$ when it serves only the old cohort. This means that the disadvantaged firm would have to set a negative price less than the switching cost ($p_{dt} < -c^*$) if it is to compete with the advantaged firm for the trade of both cohorts. This is not a reasonable strategy to create an advantaged position in the subsequent period, for if it were its rival would then pursue a similar strategy in the subsequent period and being advantaged would then have no value. In short, when $c^* > 0$ it will not be profitable for the disadvantaged firm to sell to the old cohort. What can be said about the competition for the young cohort and with that the advantaged position at the next period?

Since prices cannot be discriminatory, the advantaged firm must reduce its price to the "captive" old cohort when competing for the young cohort. This means that the greatest price at which the disadvantaged firm can sell to the young cohort is (an ε below) the level where the advantaged firm is indifferent to selling to both cohorts or just the old cohort. If there is a positive price where the disadvantaged firm can offer to sell to the young cohort and it is optimal for the advantaged firm not to sacrifice the $p_{dt} + c^*$ rents from the old cohort in return for the $p_{dt} - \varepsilon$ revenues from the young cohort, then the firms will trade positions as advantaged and disadvantaged and take turns extracting the rents arising because of the switching cost.

When there are alternating positions for the firms, the optimal price strategy can be derived by looking at a typical period t in the infinite horizon of the model. At t, the maximum present value of the disadvantaged firm is

$$\pi_{dt}^* = p_{dt} + \rho\pi_{a(t+1)}^* \tag{12.75a}$$

where $\rho > 0$ is the one-period discount factor, $\pi_{a(t+1)}^*$ is the maximized value of the firm at period $t + 1$ given that the now-disadvantaged firm is then advantaged, and p_{dt} is the current price (profit) received from selling to the young cohort.[72] Similarly, the maximum present value of the advantaged firm is

$$\pi_{at}^* = p_{at} + \rho\pi_{d(t+1)}^* \tag{12.75b}$$

Note that $(p_{dt} - \varepsilon) + c^* = p_{at}$ allows the disadvantaged firm to capture the young cohort. These two valuation functions contain three unknowns π_{at}^*, π_{dt}^*, and p_{dt}. The final relationship which permits us to solve for these is that noted earlier: the disadvantaged firm chooses that price which just makes the advantaged firm slightly prefer serving only the older cohort, that is,

$$p_{dt} = p_{at} = 2(p_{at} - \varepsilon) \tag{12.75c}$$

Again, with ε small, we use equations (12.75) to solve for

$$\pi_{at}^* = \frac{2c^*}{1 - \rho} \tag{12.76a}$$

$$\pi_{dt}^* = \frac{2c^*}{1 - \rho} \tag{12.76b}$$

$$p_{at} = p_{dt} = 2c^* \tag{12.76c}$$

Note that (12.76c) implies positive prices and therefore the alternating position equilibrium is feasible.

The comparative statics of the switching cost and discount factor in this solution are exactly as expected: greater switching costs increase the price level and extractable monopoly rents, and a smaller discount factor increases price and decreases the present value of profits.

SE12.6   Signal Jamming: Information and Quality Competition

When oligopolists engage in a repeated game with incomplete information they can use the results at an early stage to update their information at subsequent stages. Riordan (1985) has developed a model of symmetric duopoly with quantity competition in which the symmetry allows the duopolists' first-period actions to reveal an unknown demand parameter and thereby allow all subsequent play to occur with complete information. The complication in such dynamic games is that each firm realizes that its actions are revealing informa-

---

[72] $\pi_{a(t+1)}^*$ is the present value of *all* then-future profits given that the firm is advantaged at $t + 1$. In dynamic programming terminology, this present value is called the optimal return function (of the current price decision) and equation (12.75a) is the basis for a two-period "equivalent" optimization problem for the firm. Krouse (1986, ch. 9) gives details of the dynamic programming technique applied to a similar consumption–investment problem.

tion to its rival and it would be better off acting in a way which provided false signals to disadvantage its rival. What is the resulting "signal jamming" equilibrium?

The Model. Consider the linear-demand constant-cost (quadratic profits) symmetrical duopoly. For each duopolist j profits are written as

$$\pi_j(z_j, z_k) = (a - z_k - z_j)z_j \tag{12.77}$$

The parameter $a > 0$ is the difference between the inverse demand and the firms' common constant cost. To keep our discussion simple, assume that costs are zero and that a is simply the demand parameter. While it is common to assume that some demand information is known to one firm but not the other, it is assumed here that the parameter a is unknown to either duopolist: there is *symmetric* incomplete information.

Static Play. Suppose, to begin, that the duopolists play Nash-in-quantity strategies, moving simultaneously in a one-shot (static) game. Firm j maximizes expected profits:

$$\max_{z_j} E(az_j - z_k z_j - z_j^2) \tag{12.78}$$

The solution for j is as usual:

$$z_j = \frac{\bar{a} - z_k}{2} \tag{12.79}$$

where $\bar{a}$ is the expected value of a based on firm j's prior probability estimate. Because of the symmetry we have

$$z_j{}^c = z_k{}^c = \bar{a}/3 \tag{12.80}$$

The Dynamic Game. When the above game is played in two successive periods, the firms can use the results of the first-stage play to update their probability estimates of a (a is assumed to be stationary over time and that fact is common knowledge). Specifically, each firm's ability to observe its market price after the first period, and its knowledge that its rival is identical with it, allows it to discover exactly the value of a. Since each firm j observes the first-period price $p_{j1}(z_{j1}^*, z_{k1}^*)$ and z_{k1}^* is known by symmetry, then[73]

$$a = p_{j1}(z_{j1}^*, z_{k1}^*) + 2z_{j1}^* \tag{12.81}$$

Firm j's price and its output choice seem to reveal a precisely. *If* this is so, then the second market period would be a game with complete information and each firm would then produce $z_{j2}{}^c = z_{k2}{}^c = a/3$.

False Signals. Suppose for the moment that (only) firm k really understands the above information and, rather than choosing z_{k1}^* at the first period, it

---

[73] Because the game now has two periods, the first-period decision will generally not be the simple $z_j{}^c$ quantity of the one-shot quantity-setting game.

actually chooses $z_{k1}{}^a$. Firm j, not understanding that this deception is taking place, calculates an erroneous demand intercept $\hat{a}$ from the first-period results:

$$\hat{a} = p_{j1}(z_{j1}^*, z_{k1}{}^a) + 2z_{j1}^* = a + z_{k1}^* - z_{k1}{}^a \neq a \tag{12.82}$$

Firm j's deception (measured by $z_{k1}^* - z_{k1}{}^a$) is generally referred to as **signal jamming** as it is an attempt to thwart a rival's ability to correctly infer the parameter a from market data. The uninformed firm j plays the second market game as though it knew a exactly. Using symmetry it thus optimally chooses the (one-shot, complete-information Cournot equilibrium) quantity

$$z_{j2}{}^c = \frac{\hat{a}}{3} = \frac{a + z_{k1}^* - z_{k1}{}^a}{3} \tag{12.83}$$

A key aspect of this expression is that it shows the links in rival's decisions over time. Note specifically that $dz_{j2}{}^c/dz_{k1}{}^a = -1/3$. Firm j's period-2 output responds inversely to firm k's actual first-period output choice.[74]

The signal jammer, firm k, is of course aware that its price in the first period is based on its quantity deception. It can therefore calculate the demand parameter correctly: $a = p_{k1} + \bar{a}/3 + z_{k1}{}^a$.[75] As a result its period-two decision is made under complete information:

$$\max_{z_{k2}} \left\{ \left(a - \frac{\hat{a}}{3} - z_{k2} \right) z_{k2} \right\} \tag{12.84}$$

which solves for

$$z_{k2} = \frac{a - \hat{a}/3}{2} = \frac{a}{3} - \frac{z_{k1}^* - z_{k1}{}^a}{6} \tag{12.85}$$

No One is Really Deceived. All of the above is, of course, dependent on the presumption that firm k understands and exploits the opportunities for signal jamming, but firm j does not. That is one possibility and it may be appropriate in some market situations. Rather than complete the analysis for that case, let us alternatively assume the more symmetrical situation where the firms are truly identical and each firm uses signal jamming against the other. Because of the symmetry, the two-stage game for this case can be solved by backward recursion for just one firm and the symmetry conditions can then be imposed on that solution to describe the equilibrium. Let us use firm k.

Substituting (12.85) in (12.84), using (12.82), and rearranging gives k's indirect profit function

$$\pi_{k2}^* = \left(\frac{a}{2} - \frac{\hat{a}}{6} \right)^2 = \left(\frac{a}{3} - \frac{z_{k1}^* - z_{k1}{}^a}{6} \right)^2 \tag{12.86}$$

In turn, k's first-period problem is to maximize the expected present value:

$$\max_{z_{k1}{}^a} E \left\{ (a - z_{j1} - z_{k1}{}^a) z_{k1}{}^a + \rho \left(\frac{a}{3} - \frac{z_{k1}^* - z_{k1}{}^a}{6} \right)^2 \right\} \tag{12.87}$$

---

[74] Riordan (1985) refers to this derivative as a "dynamic conjectural variation."
[75] Here, p_{k1} is observed, $\bar{a}$ is calculated, and $z_{k1}{}^a$ is the decision.

where once more the expectation is based on the prior probabilities over a. This problem yields the stationarity condition

$$\bar{a} - z_{j1} - 2z_{k1}{}^a + \rho\left(\frac{1}{3}\right)\left(\frac{\bar{a}}{3} - \frac{z_{k1}^* - z_{k1}{}^a}{6}\right) = 0 \qquad (12.88)$$

In equilibrium $z_{j1} = z_{k1}^* = z_{k1}{}^a$ so that

$$z_{k1}{}^a = z_{j1}{}^a = \left(\frac{\bar{a}}{3}\right)\left(1 + \frac{\rho}{9}\right) \qquad (12.89)$$

As a result of the attempt to deceive its rival, in equilibrium each firm chooses the first-period output $(\bar{a}/3)(1 + \rho/9)$, which is greater (more competitive) than the one-shot Cournot output $\bar{a}/3$ of the incomplete information game or than that which would obtain on average without any attempt to jam the signal.

SE12.7   Price Wars in Boom and Bust

One strong tradition in industrial economics has been to relate price wars to recessionary periods. Scherer (1980, ch 6–8) provides a long list of such examples in both manufacturing and service industries. In some interesting specific studies of automobiles by Bresnahan (1981a) and of railroads by Ulen (1983) and Porter (1983a, b), price wars have been found to occur oppositely, in periods of high demand. Rotemberg and Saloner (1986) have developed a model of implicit collusion which offers some explanation of these cases. At the center of their analysis is a random variable which may exogenously impose high or low levels of demand on the industry. They then show that an implicitly collusive firm has a greater incentive to free ride in the high demand period and this leads to price wars as the firms react by reversion to punishment-level prices. This incentive results from greater gains to free riding during high demand, as there is then a greater demand to be captured *and* the punishment to be imposed is less severe since that phase will average over cycles of demand. With two key differences, the details of their analysis are followed here. We will use price as a strategy variable where Rotemberg and Saloner use quantity competition, and we will think of the uncertain demand as having just two possible states boom (B) or bust (b).

The Basics. Consider $j = 1, 2, \ldots, J$ identical firms selling a homogeneous product in an infinite succession of markets. While the firms observe and know the industry demand level in the current market, they are (individually and collectively) uncertain about its future level, which may be boom with probability h or bust with probability $1 - h$. The probability h is identical and independent over time.

Suppose that the firms implicitly collude, setting price p_{B}^* or p_{b}^* in the current period depending on whether demand is at the boom or bust level. When these prices are used, the associated one-period profits for the industry are

$\pi_B^* > \pi_b^* > 0.$[76] If the implicit collusion is sustained, each firm has expected per period profits of

$$\bar{\pi}^* = h\pi_B^* + (1 - h)\pi_b^* \tag{12.90}$$

This is to be divided equally among the J identical firms. If the implicit collusion is maintained over all time, then the present value of each firm would be

$$v_j^* = \frac{\rho\bar{\pi}^*}{J(1 - \rho)} \tag{12.91}$$

where ρ is once more the one period discount *factor*.

Free Riding and Incentive Compatability. Suppose that free riders are detected at the end of the period in which they cheat, and that the firms attempt to enforce their implicit collusion arrangement by immediately and forever reverting to the one-shot Bertrand prices on detection. Since the free rider will cut price only slightly, given the homogeneous-good and price competition, the one-period gain to free riding if demand level $l = B, b$ occurs is (approximately)

$$\pi_l^0 = \pi_l^* - \frac{\pi_l^*}{J} = \frac{J - 1}{J}\pi_l^* \tag{12.92}$$

Recall that firms do not make their current pricing decisions until after the current level of demand is observed. Since $\pi_B^* > \pi_b^*$ the gain to free riding will be greater if a boom occurs. In the Bertrand play after free riding is detected, the firms earn zero profits. This leaves them without an incentive to free ride if and only if the one-period gain derived in (12.92) plus the succession of zero profits forever after is less than the expected present value of the firm's implicit collusion profit stream, that is,

$$\pi_B^0 \equiv \frac{(J - 1)\pi_B^*}{J} \le v_j^* = \frac{\rho\bar{\pi}^*}{J(1 - \rho)}$$

or

$$(J - 1)\frac{\pi_B^*}{\bar{\pi}^*} \le \frac{\rho}{1 - \rho} \tag{12.93}$$

Finally, let $\delta \equiv \pi_b^*/\pi_B^*$ in the above expression and rearrange to give

$$\rho \ge \rho_f \equiv \frac{J - 1}{\delta + J - 1 + h(1 - \delta)} \tag{12.94}$$

Notice that the *floor* discount factor ρ_f which is required to sustain p^* as an implicitly collusive equilibrium price depends on the number of (identical) firms, the ratio of bust to boom profits, and the probability h. The comparative statics of these parameters on ρ_f are as expected. The greater is J, the higher is the floor and thus the less likely will be the implicit collusion, just as in the certain

---

[76] One possibility for p_B^* is the one-shot monopoly price, and similarly for p_b^*. This is not necessary, however, and in turn neither is the $\pi_B^* > \pi_b^*$ ordering. The individually rational prices in the boom period may be small relative to the monopoly level and in the bust period they may be large relative to that level. Despite this, the ordering that we have assumed seems to be more reasonable.

demand situation. The smaller is the ratio of bust to boom profits (smaller δ), the higher is the floor and the less likely will be the implicit collusion. The intuition here is that the smaller is this ratio the smaller is the expected value of the foregone profit stream when free riding. Finally, the greater is the probability that boom demand occurs the lower is the floor and, again, the more likely will be the implicit collusion. This also accords with our intuition. The thing which makes the implicit collusion less likely with demand uncertainty is that the free rider can take its one-shot gain in a boom period and only suffer the present value of the *expected* collusion losses with boom and bust. When that loss is weighted more heavily by boom profits, then it is less likely that free riding will be profitable.

Optimal Collusive Price. Up to this point it has been assumed that implicitly collusive prices p_B^* and p_b^*, which are greater than unit costs, have been used by the firms. Provided that the incentive compatability constraint obtains, these prices yield an equilibrium path with implicit collusion. Our concern here, as in the analysis of implicit collusion and price wars under uncertain demand in section 12.3.3, is for the *optimal* cartel policy – the set of collusive prices which are not dominated in the sense that there are no other collusion-sustaining prices which give greater profits to the firms.[77] The twist in this analysis is that we must give freedom to the collusive prices and not constrain them by some a priori specification of relative π_B^* and π_b^* profit levels.[78] This means that incentive compatability constraints for both boom and bust periods must be imposed:

$$\pi_B \leq \frac{\rho}{(1 - \rho)(J - 1)} \bar{\pi}^* \tag{12.95a}$$

$$\pi_b \leq \frac{\rho}{(1 - \rho)(J - 1)} \bar{\pi}^* \tag{12.95b}$$

Using (12.90) and rearranging gives

$$\pi_B^* \leq \frac{\rho(1 - h)}{(1 - \rho)(J - 1) - \rho h} \pi_b^* \tag{12.96a}$$

$$\pi_b^* \leq \frac{\rho h}{(1 - \rho)(J - 1) - \rho(1 - h)} \pi_B^* \tag{12.96b}$$

The firms' expected profits are greater the closer p_B^* and p_b^* are to the one-shot monopoly prices $p_B{}^m$ and $p_b{}^m$ respectively. Thus, the boom constraint (12.95a) or (12.96a) will become binding before the corresponding bust constraint. In turn, by choosing the bust price at the monopoly level $p_b^* = p_b{}^m$, the firms' bust profits can be increased (to their maximum) and, using (12.96a), the boom constraint can, at the same time, be made less binding. Having chosen p_b^* in this way, then we are simply left to choose the boom price p_B^* at the maximum of that which causes (12.96a) to be binding or $p_B{}^m$. Whether or not p_B^* will also be

---

[77] More generally we could extend this optimality to determining the length of the punishment period, as was specifically done in E12.10. Here, that complication is not considered and the punishment continues to last forever.

[78] Above we *assumed* $\pi_B^* > \pi_b^*$; here we derive optimal collusive prices which, in turn, determine that inequality.

p_B^* will also be at the monopoly level depends on the parameters on the right-hand side of (12.96a). While it is generally expected that boom prices will be greater than the corresponding bust prices. This need not be the case. As Rotemberg and Saloner conclude, the implicit collusion prices may move either cyclically or counter-cyclically. In support of this second possibility they offer some empirical evidence from the cement industry using yearly data from 1947 to 1981.[79]

---

[79] The implicitly collusive scheme outlined above presumably obtained in that oligopoly.

13 Information and Advertising

This chapter is concerned with the relationships between consumer demand for and seller supply of product information and the properties of market equilibrium, with the effect of information cost and product characteristics on competition, the level of prices, and the extent of product variety on the one hand, and with the implications of these results for allocative efficiency on the other. These developments parallel those in chapters 4 and 5, except that here the nonnegligible increasing costs of supplying and acquiring information mean that consumers will act with imperfect knowledge. This is a critically important fact: it affects what consumers think is best and cheapest and, in turn, redefines market exchange opportunities and the strategies that will be used in buying and selling.

While it is now common to view advertising as a method of supplying product information, that has not always been the case. Based in part on the work of Robinson (1933) and Chamberlin (1933), in the period 1940–70 it was usual to condemn advertising as manipulative and intrinsically anticompetitive. Kaldor (1950) championed this view, emphasizing the adverse effects that advertising creates by altering relative market shares within an industry. His analysis was developed in two steps. First, he argued that advertising would almost surely increase industry concentration. Then, assuming implicitly a positive link between concentration and monopoly power, he reasoned that advertising was the basis for a substantial portion of the welfare loss associated with monopoly.[1]

It helps our understanding to separate Kaldor's several arguments linking advertising to increased concentration. His first, and fundamental, proposition was that the greater were the firm's advertising expenditures, the greater was its "pulling power" (advertising elasticity of demand). He also referred to this as "increasing returns to advertising scale." Assuming that advertising expenditures were maintained at a constant fraction of sales, Kaldor made the second point that these increasing returns coupled with capital market imperfections disadvantaged smaller firms. As a result, firms that were initially successful in advertising

---

[1] While Kaldor on occasion asserted that advertising leads directly to a resource misallocation (as the advertising of one firm "cancels" that of another), he primarily linked advertising to inefficiency through its effect on concentration and, in turn, diminished competition.

would increase their market shares by re-investing profits in still greater levels of advertising.[2] In conjunction with this mechanism Kaldor also argued that advertising creates "product differentiation," which in turn produces "brand loyalty" (smaller price elasticity of demand) and this also reduces the level of market competition.

Bain (1956) and his students generally adopted Kaldor's theory as a basis for a series of empirical studies.[3] Their interpretation of Kaldor's position was the "psychological premise" that advertising acts fundamentally by altering consumer preferences or by re-affirming extant preferences to a degree that makes consumer brand switching extremely difficult. Advertising in this *persuasion* view induces consumers to purchase the advertised brand by appealing to snobbery, bandwagon effects, vague associations of the product with desirable situations, etc. While Robinson's early comments predate much of this work it nonetheless provides us with its essence (emphasis added) ". . . the consumer will be influenced by advertising, which plays upon his mind with studied skill, and *makes him prefer* the goods of one producer to those of another because they are brought to his notice in a more pleasing or forceful manner" (Robinson, 1933, p. 30).

Advertising and Information. A market for a commodity is described by all those arrangements which facilitate the exchange of contracts and the physical transfer of the commodity. While a market is an improvement over a barter system, it generally does not bring about costless exchange of the commodity, for it is not an arrangement which automatically and costlessly provides perfect information on price, quality, location, etc. (despite the usual description of competitive markets). Rather, each market must develop specific methods to facilitate exchange with minimum information and transaction cost.

Rejecting the persuasion view, Telser (1964), Nelson (1970, 1974), Demsetz (1979), and others have argued that advertising is best understood as such an exchange-facilitating method: specifically, advertising creates a stock of information which lowers the consumer's cost of making discriminating product choices within the framework of a *fixed set of preferences.* If all the characteristics of a commodity are measurable and costlessly observable, then they would be known by consumers. Why then should advertising increase the consumer's marginal utility as Kaldor's asserts? The answer, Telser concluded, must lie in advertising's ability to reduce information costs and, in turn, leave consumers with greater equilibrium levels of product information. In contrast with the Kaldor tradition, the key implication of this alternative is that advertising information generally allows market prices to better equalize differences (or nondifferences) in products. To think of advertising as a device for altering the consumer's preferences, as a "taste" parameter of the utility function, he argued, cannot be an acceptable basis for an economic theory of choice, for changing preferences is

---

[2] The returns to advertising scale were not presumed to go on without end, but to level off and diminish after some point. This point defined an extant degree of concentration, which Kaldor thought varied in the cross-section of industries and generally implied oligopoly rather than pure monopoly market structures.

[3] See, for example, Mann et al. (1976) and Comanor and Wilson (1979). Galbraith (1967) adopts the same ideas. For introductory comments on the theory and its empirical tests see SE13.5.

an *ad hoc* exercise which explains too much after the fact and very little before.[4]

Except for section 13.3, where we look more closely at advertising as a taste-altering device, we will generally think of advertising as a method by which sellers supply information about their product's price and other characteristics. As buyers and sellers are not matched efficiently when there is ignorance about product price and quality, then the value of advertising, to both sellers and buyers, is that it enables a better matching of buyer and seller.

What is Advertising? The most common definition of advertising refers to paid-for advertisements in printed media (newspapers, magazines, handbills, etc.), in broadcast media (television and radio), on billboards, through direct mail, etc. This, however, is the narrowest of definitions.[5] Firms convey product information by much broader means: public relation staffs obtain "free" news coverage for the firm and its product, trained salespeople demonstrate products at point of sale, and different ways of packaging and labeling a product inform consumers of relevant facts. As we deal with advertising as information, throughout this chapter the reader can most generally think of advertising as the collection of all these things. In business firms this broad definition of advertising is commonly referred to as *promotional expenditure* and at times in the economics literature it is called *demand-increasing costs*. Here we follow the tradition of Braithwaite (1928) and Chamberlin (1933) and simply call it advertising.

The Demand and Supply of Advertising. Since it is generally less expensive to collect advertising fees from advertisers than from members of the buying audience, advertising is often said to be "bundled in" with the product. Despite some claims, this does not mean that there is joint supply in any usual sense, since advertising and the physical product typically result from distinct technical processes. Moreover, the amount of advertising received by an individual need not be directly related to his purchase quantity.

Not only is it usual to argue in this way that the supply of advertising and the advertised product are disparate, it is also argued that the respective demands are quite distinct. The line of reasoning is that the demand for advertising on any given brand arises more exactly from the individual's interest in purchasing one brand from within a product class, and, it is noted, the frequency with which this information is demanded is quite different from the frequency with which the product is purchased.

Those who have studied and specified aggregate (interindustry) advertising demand and supply functions apart from the demand and supply of the specific products to which they pertain point to the above distinctions (see, for example, Comanor and Wilson, 1974, chapter 2, Ornstein, 1977, chapters 1 and 2). The following analyses are not concerned with aggregate advertising in this isolated

---

[4] For further discussion of this issue see section 13.3 and, more generally, Fisher and McGowan (1979), Shapiro (1980), and Dixit and Norman (1978, 1979).

[5] While narrow, it is not significant. In 1981 broadcast media advertising in the United States was approximately $61 billion, or about 2.1 percent of gross national product and 3.3 percent of personal consumption expenditures (see Coen, 1982).

fashion. Instead, they focus more exactly on the market situations in which there is (initially) asymmetric information – where firms know the characteristics of their products, but consumers do not. In these situations the sellers choose price, product characteristics, and, to inform consumers of these, advertising levels; consumers choose those brands (using the information supplied by sellers) which have the perceived combination of price and characteristics maximizing their expected surplus. The interest here lies in the (jointly determined) equilibrium levels of product variety, price and advertising: how they relate to the underlying cost and demand conditions for the industry and to the technology and costs of information supply, and how they compare with socially optimal levels.

To deal progressively with the various problems of information, in this chapter we restrict attention to advertising which is truthful. In chapter 14 we deal with the complications caused by the possibility of untruthful or misleading representations.

E13.1

Some Limited Evidence on Advertising as Information

Those who stress the manipulative aspect of advertising and assert that it is generally anticompetitive often point to markets for liquid bleach, concentrated and bottled lemon juice, and other highly advertised products. The critical fact, they note, is that the most heavily advertised brands bear price premia over their "nearly identical" alternatives. Bayer and brand X aspirins come immediately to mind. Scherer (1980, pp. 381–3) and Shepard (1982) suggest other examples and summarize this view.

Those who stress the informative role, and argue that advertising is pro-competitive, point to neglected aspects of the products and product services when measuring the size of price premia (see Demsetz 1973a; Boyer, 1974; Brozen, 1974; Leffler, 1981; Krouse, 1984). There is some systematic evidence to support this information view. Benham (1972) is almost always mentioned first in this regard. Benham compared markets for eyeglasses in those states which completely restricted advertising by suppliers with those in states where there were few or no such restrictions. Using 1963 data, Benham found that where advertising was banned the price of eyeglasses averaged $37.48, and where there were not advertising restrictions the price averaged $17.98. A study of US toy manufacturer television advertising by Steiner (1973) also provides evidence that advertising reduces "inertia and ignorance" and, in turn, prices. Finally, Maurizi (1972) in an analysis of local laws prohibiting advertising of retail gas prices, Muris and McChesney (1979) in a study of advertising effects on attorney fees and quality of service, and Leffler's (1981) review of prescription drug advertising report similar pro-competitive information effects.

Buyer Screening. While we will generally focus on market situations where sellers are active in supplying information to uninformed buyers, there is the complementary analysis where the buyers are the active agents attempting to make informed product choices on the basis of market observable data. Such analyses have proceeded in the literature under the general head of "screening by buyers." Salop provides the following characterization:

> . . . Two types of screening devices may be distinguished. *Indices* are rules of thumb that sort on the basis of observable variables that directly bear on values. On average, former taxi-cabs have high depreciation rates; dealers named Nixon are thought to be unethical RATS (rational economic men). On the other hand, *self-selection* devices sort on the basis of evidence revealed by the seller's own decision. King Solomon's threat to cut the baby in half caused each mother-claimant to reveal her true identity. A red sportscar is avoided not because red sportscars are inherently of lower value; rather the personality-type who prefers a red sportscar is thought to be the type who engages in reckless driving and performs insufficient maintenance. The decision to purchase a red sport-scar reveals information regarding the owner and, hence, the quality of the car. (Salop, 1986, p. 6)

Salop continues by noting that when sellers become aware that buyers use such screening rules they will then have an incentive to use the consumer's reliance on the rules to misrepresent their product. For example, in the market for physician services consumers might use working hours as a screening device, with physicians working the longest hours thought to provide the highest quality (a demand effect). This would then allow incompetent physicians to mask their lack of skills by feigning long hours and thereby develop a reputation for competence. Bad physicians working long hours will thus attract patients from lazy but good physicians. The result is a "rat race," where every physician works harder (at the margin) in an effort to exploit the consumer's screen.[6]

13.1   Asymmetric Information and Adverse Selection

With the complete absence of brand-specific information consumers make their consumption choices randomly. The result is that different products carry the same price in a competitive equilibrium, and that price is equal to the marginal value of quality supplied on average in a competitive equilibrium. If it is assumed that sellers know and control their brand's quality and production costs are positively related to product quality, bad products then "drive out" good products: if buyers cannot distinguish quality until after the purchase has been made, there is no incentive for sellers to provide good quality and average quality falls. This is called the **adverse selection** problem. For the case of used cars, an example developed by Akerlof (1970) in the first systematic discussion of this phenomenon, owners who discover they have a "lemon" attempt to sell it to an unsuspecting buyer. In contrast, owners of high-quality cars do not offer

---

[6] Salop (1986, p. 7) notes that rat race dynamics may or may not have a stable upper bound on exploitation.

their cars for sale, since they are indistinguishable from the lemons and thus must sell at the average-quality price.

Such adverse selection, or "lemons," equilibria may be unstable when they leave unexploited gains (net of search cost) to those who identify products of greater quality. For example, if by private research some risk-averse (and atomistic) individual identifies a particular product which supplies at least the average level of the otherwise unknown quality, he is able to better himself by the utility difference between the known quality of the given brand and the average taken with risk, less an allowance for his cost of search. If quality determination costs are not prohibitive, there are incentives for each customer to search in this way for brand-specific information.

Generally, there will be economies of scale or specialization in the provision of quality information so that sellers are found to offer this information in a public manner. It is in the interest of any firm with a quality level equal to or above the market average to provide evidence of this fact and thereby improve the consumers' purchase decisions relative to a random choice among brands. Consumers in competition then bid up the price of this preferred brand from the price based on the industry average. Similarly, each firm which supplies a product equal or superior to those remaining undifferentiated has an incentive to provide brand-specific quality information and distinguish itself. Such an "unraveling" process continues until the brand with the next-lowest quality level is differentiated from that with the lowest quality.

Some details of the lemons equilibrium and methods of unraveling are set out in the following sections.

13.1.1 Lemons Equilibria

For the moment it is instructive to preserve the limited information structure originally used by Akerlof (1970) and assume that no method of information acquisition or supply is economical. As a result the quality information is persistently asymmetrical: each seller knows the quality of his own brand, but buyers have no brand-specific quality information. This means that potential buyers make their purchase decision based on only the *average* brand quality experienced in prior trials and choose randomly among brands when they do decide to buy. (If there is a large number of such trials, the sample average will be nearly equal to the true average quality of the brands.)

Let ξ be a measure of the actual quality level of products and assume that, in the cross-section of firms, ξ is uniformly distributed on the unit interval $[0, 1]$. It is also convenient to scale outputs so that each firm supplies one unit (in quantity) at its chosen quality level, that is $z(\xi) = 1$. (This requires Akerlof's fixed-output assumption.) By this scaling ξ can also be interpreted as the fraction of industry output which has quality level ξ or less. Finally, Akerlof assumes that the firm's (opportunity) cost $c(\xi)$ of supplying quality is increasing, so that

$$c'(\xi) \equiv \frac{dc(\xi)}{d\xi} > 0 \qquad (13.1)$$

and we make this assumption also.

Equilibrium Conditions. Depending on the prevailing price and costs of production and distribution, each firm chooses whether or not to market a given product. Suppose, for the moment, that those firms having specific product quality ξ_a or less are *active*, while (potential) sellers with products of quality greater than ξ_a (and with higher costs) do not produce at the prevailing price. For different levels of ξ_a the market *supply* price is given by marginal cost:

$$p_s(\xi_a) = c(\xi_a) \tag{13.2}$$

Since $c(\xi)$ is increasing in ξ, this meets with our restriction: suppliers with $\xi \leq \xi_a$ offer their product while those with $\xi > \xi_a$ do not. $z(\xi_a) = \xi_a$ is, in turn, the fraction of the potential (total) supply that is forthcoming at price $p_s(\xi_a)$ and, because quality is uniformly distributed across firms, $\bar{\xi} \equiv \xi_a/2$ is the average market quality.

In the absence of brand-specific quality information, the market *demand* price p_d depends on this average quality and the quantity supplied:

$$p_d(\xi_a) = f(z(\xi_a), \bar{\xi}) = f\left(\xi_a, \frac{\xi_a}{2}\right) \tag{13.3}$$

for which we make the usual demand slope and shift assumptions

$$\frac{\partial f}{\partial z} \leq 0 \tag{13.4a}$$

$$\frac{\partial f}{\partial \xi} > 0 \tag{13.4b}$$

An equilibrium occurs when the maximum quality obtaining in the market is such that demand and supply prices are equal. The quality level, price, and aggregate output determined in this way define an **adverse selection**, or **lemons, equilibrium**. Using (13.2) and (13.3), it is seen that at such an equilibrium the (maximum) quality ξ^l satisfies[7]

$$c(\xi^l) = f\left(\xi^l, \frac{\xi^l}{2}\right) \tag{13.5}$$

Optimal Quality. We now require to know how the lemons equilibrium quality level compares with the socially optimal level. The socially optimal quality level ξ_a maximizes aggregate surplus

$$W = \int_0^{z(\xi_a)} f(s, \bar{\xi}) \, ds - \int_0^{\xi_a} c(s) \, ds \tag{13.6}$$

When the revenues paid by consumers are offset with those received by firms, W is simply the value consumers attach to z units of average quality less the opportunity cost of producing those units. The stationarity point of W with respect to the (maximum) level of quality supplied is

$$\frac{dW}{d\xi_a} = \frac{1}{2} \int_0^{\xi_a} \frac{\partial f(s, \bar{\xi})}{\partial \xi} \, ds + \{f(z(\xi_a), \bar{\xi}) - c(\xi_a)\} = 0 \tag{13.7}$$

---

[7] A stable equilibrium also requires that the demand schedule intersect the supply schedule from above. See Stiglitz and Weiss (1981) for detailed conditions under which such an equilibrium (intersection) exists.

Let ξ^0 be the ξ_a solution of this condition. At the lemons equilibrium the rightmost term in the above expression is zero (see (13.5)), and as the integral's value is increasing in ξ_a,

$$\frac{dW(\xi^1)}{d\xi_a} > 0 \tag{13.8}$$

That is, quality is *under-supplied* at the lemons equilibrium relative to the level $\xi^1 \leqslant \xi^0$ which maximizes W.

E13.2

Quality in a Lemons Equilibrium

An example given by Leland (1979) illustrates the key properties of the lemons equilibrium. Suppose that the following linear demand and quadratic cost schedules pertain:

$$f(z, \xi) = \alpha + \beta\xi - \gamma z$$

$$c(\xi_a) = \delta(\xi_a)^2$$

where α, β, γ, and δ are constants. At the lemons equilibrium corresponding to (13.5) we then have

$$\delta(\xi^1)^2 = \alpha + \left(\frac{\beta}{2} - \gamma\right)\xi^1$$

Solving for the equilibrium quality gives

$$\xi^1 = \max\left(\min\left[\frac{(\beta/2 - \gamma) + \{(\beta/2 - \gamma)^2 + 4\alpha\delta\}^{1/2}}{2\delta}, 1\right], 0\right)$$

As a numerical example suppose that $\alpha = \beta = \gamma = \delta = 1$ and therefore $\xi^1 = 0.78$. In turn, $z(\xi^1) = 0.78$, $\bar{\xi} = 0.39$, and $p\{(z/\xi^1), \bar{\xi}\} = 0.61$.

Figure 13.1 illustrates the social optimum and lemons equilibrium solutions for

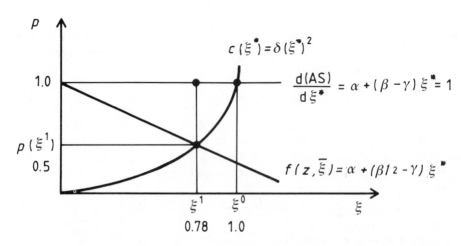

Figure 13.1
Comparative quality levels

the indicated parameter value and functional forms. Note from (13.7) that $dW/d\xi_a = \alpha + (\beta - \gamma)\xi_a \equiv 1$, which is independent of ξ_a as shown in the figure. The social optimum occurs when $dW/d\xi_a = c(\xi_a)$, or $\xi^0 = 1.0$, which is also indicated. In contrast, the lemons equilibrium occurs at the smaller quantity $\xi^l = 0.78$ calculated above. The shaded area between ξ^l and ξ^0, above $c(\xi_a)$ and below $dW/d\xi_a$ is the incremental aggregate surplus achieved when quality is expanded from the lemons equilibrium to the social optimum.

Note finally that the lemons equilibrium leads to a complete degradation of quality and the markets close ($\xi^l = z(\xi^l) = 0$), when the parameter values $\alpha = 0$ and $\beta/2 - \alpha \leq 0$ obtain. However, when $\alpha = 0$, $\xi^0 = 0$ only if $\beta - \gamma \leq 0$, which means that it is socially optimal for markets to be open when (in a lemons equilibrium) they are in fact closed only for the particular case where $\beta > \gamma \geq \beta/2$.

13.1.2 Unraveling: an Example

The lemons equilibrium arises with asymmetric information and is generally providing an inefficient level of quality. It therefore comes with some relief that the equilibrium is likely to be unstable, as there are incentives for sellers to inform buyers and for buyers to be informed. Product labeling, media advertising, and direct selling are a few of the methods used by sellers to reduce or eliminate the informational asymmetries. What is perhaps most important, buyers exchange information by word of mouth. The economics of these possbilities are set out in some detail in section 13.2 and chapter 14. As background for these developements we first consider a simple case in which product certification acts as an unraveling device.

Certification. It is some help to think of firms as selling a particular product, say concentrated and bottled lemon juice. Suppose further that there are seven such firms, each selling a single and unique brand of this juice. Because of management and technology differences, the products are produced under different quality control conditions. Each of the $j = 1, 2, \ldots, 7$ firms can be characterized by a probability h_j that any given unit of its output will be off-taste because of inappropriate control of its critical preservative ingredient. To simplify the following discussion, let these probabilities be given by the rule $h_j = (8 - j)/10$. This leaves firm 7 with the lowest probability of being off-taste, and firm 1 with the highest probability. Accordingly, we say that firm 7's product is of highest quality and, following through, firm 1's product is of lowest quality. We finally assume that quality information is asymmetrical at the onset: each firm knows its true h_j, but buyers without brand-specific information only know the overall distribution of probabilities. Because of this information different buyers assess the probability of product failure for each brand as being the industry average $\bar{h}$, which is 0.4 under the specific conditions assumed.

To obtain numerical results in this example assume further that (a) buyers are identical and place a monetary value of $+2$ on concentrated lemon juice which is not off-taste, (b) buyers place a value of -0.5 on an off-taste trial (the juice concentrate wastes other ingredients with which it is used in combination), (c) consumers are risk-neutral and maximize expected payoff, (d) product prices are competitively established, and (e) each consumer places a monetary value of 0.2 on the "outside good."

In a lemons equilibrium it is the average quality of goods that determines the (single) market price. In the absence of information transfers and given the above conditions, that price satisfies the inequality

$$(1 - \bar{h})(2) + \bar{h}(-0.5) - \bar{p} \geqslant 0.2$$

or, with $\bar{h} = 0.4$,

$$\bar{p} \leqslant 0.8$$

Firms producing a lemon concentrate with above average quality (and higher costs) will not find this price based on average quality attractive. However, if they could inform buyers of their brand's true quality, they could realize a higher price and, depending on the relative size of the price increase to the costs of information supply, this may be profitable. In this regard, assume that each firm can, for a fee, submit its product to a testing agency that will certify the true probability h_j for its product and make this information public. In this case the firm with the most to gain is firm 7, which can raise its post-certification price to satisfy

$$(1 - h_7)(2) + h_7(-0.5) - p_7 \geqslant 0.2$$

or, with $h_7 = 0.1$,

$$p_7 \leqslant 1.55$$

Thus, firm 7 would invest in quality certification as long as the fee is less than $1.55 - 0.8 = 0.75$. Suppose that the firm makes such an investment.

With firm 7's quality known, the average quality of the remaining six brands falls and $\bar{h}$ increases to 0.45. There is still an incentive for firms 6, 5, and 4 (who have quality above this new average) to submit to certification. Firm 6 has the greatest incentive: it will pay up to $p_6 - \bar{p}$, or $1.39 - 0.65 = 0.64$, in fees. In the now obvious way, the unraveling process continues until the certification fee exceeds the benefits to any of the remaining firms of revealing their brand-specific quality.

If we think of the certification fee as an advertising expenditure, with greater fees indicating greater levels of advertising, then Telser's early observations are also a summary of these results:

> . . . the prices of the more advertised goods might be greater than the prices of less advertised goods because of the higher average quality of the advertised goods. Second, even if the average quality were the same for both classes, it may be that the advertised goods vary less in quality. Thus the higher price of the more advertised goods may be explained by the stricter quality control exercised over these goods. If one were to choose at random an item from the class of non-advertised goods, the risk of unsatisfactory performance would be greater than if the choice were restricted to a random selection from the class of advertised goods. (Telser, 1964, p. 542)

Trademarks. In any unraveling process the tie-in between a seller's product and information specific to it by the use of a trademark is an important device to prevent other firms from "free riding" on one firm's supply of information. The rights established by the trademark make investments in brand name, and in brand quality, more fully appropriable. The result is that a firm which creates and sustains a consumer-valued stock of information (by advertising, certification, or whatever) does so to allow its product's quality to command the premium in exchange required to assure that this (higher-cost) quality level can be supplied.

13.2 Prices, Advertising, and Welfare

As a background to more complex models of advertising it is instructive to set out some key issues in their simplest form. Concrete examples also help and so we deal with laundry detergents, treating all other goods as a composite commodity. Suppose that detergents have just two relevant characteristics in consumption, say gentleness and washing power. Let $0 \leqslant \theta \leqslant 1$ indicate the (scaled) ratio of these characteristics in any brand, with a large θ indicating a high proportion of washing power to gentleness and conversely (recall chapter 4, section 4.2.3). Suppose further that consumers are spread uniformly in preference over the θ range and let the technology of consumption be such that the brands are not combinable in use; that is, intermediate values of θ cannot be produced by consumers when mixing brands with high and low values of θ.

Information. The usual full (or perfect) information assumption means that each consumer knows his own preferences, the θ of each detergent brand and the θ equivalent quality of the composite good, and the price of each brand (relative to the composite commodity which is taken as numeraire). Suppose that just two brands of detergents are marketed, one with high θ and the other in the lower part of that scale. Further, assume that the two brands have prices and locations in the market so that, with fully informed consumers, the market is served by the brand with high θ and half is served by the brands with low θ.

What happens when consumers are imperfectly informed, except that they know that two brands exist? In this case each brand is thought to be located at any point on the market line with equal probability and therefore each commands the same price. Given this state of affairs, consumers will make their product selection randomly, which leads to equal sales for the two brands just as with full information. Moreover, in this case there is no incentive for the firms to use costly advertisements to inform consumers of product characteristics, for with the uniformly spread preferences consumers are as likely to be buying any brand for the wrong reason as for the right reason.

While the market shares of the firms are unaltered in the shift from full information to complete ignorance, other aspects of the market allocation differ. For example, with complete ignorance half the consumers choosing the high-θ brand would be better-off having chosen the low-θ alternative, and conversely. Thus, by simply reassigning these consumers so that each is better matched to the brands, social welfare could be increased (assuming minimal reassignment costs). This provides a social incentive for informative advertising even though, in this case, there is no private incentive.

Relaxing some of the restrictive assumptions of the model would, of course, alter the equilibrium results. For example, firms faced with the choice of product design θ will generally choose different specifications depending on the state of consumer information, especially when consumers are not uniformly spread in preferences. In these more realistic cases, private incentives for informative advertising will arise, but there will still be the question of whether the equilibrium level will be socially optimal *given* the costs of advertising. It is to such complicating issues that we turn in the following sections.

13.2.1   An Equilibrium Model of Advertising as Information

The anticipated return from advertising depends on the nature of the buyers' information. Advertising is used to provide potential buyers with information concerning the identity of sellers, the characteristics of products that are being offered, and the terms and conditions under which they are sold. When buyers are completely informed about these things, advertising cannot affect purchasing behavior and therefore is not a profitable activity for the firm. The firm's return to advertising thus depends on the amount of information consumers have at any moment and on the amount of information a given number of advertising messages, each undertaken with a cost, provides to buyers. This, in turn, is determined by a variety of conditions in the market and by the specific nature of the firm's product.

The most completely specified and tractable models of informative advertising that develop these market conditions and product characteristics are those set in a spatial economy, where products and consumers have locations in a characteristics space. To follow that line of analysis we begin with the basic model given in chapter 5, section 5.2, and amend its "information structure." In this model we considered a continuum of buyers and a finite number of single-product sellers (brands) spread uniformly around a unit circle – the product characteristic space. Buyers express an interest in at most one unit of the product. When a brand is not located exactly at the buyer's location, some disutility is incurred with the purchase of a distant substitute. This disutility is assumed to be in direct proportion to the arc distance between the buyer's location (ideal brand) and the location of the brand selected. In the case that the brands poorly serve the consumer's interest – because of high prices or distant locations – the consumer allocates all his income to the purchase of the outside good.

Assume now, in contrast with chapter 5, section 5.2, that buyers are completely ignorant of the sellers' prices and locations (product characteristics). Using a particular informative advertising technology, to be specified below, sellers provide price and location information to buyers. Because of diminishing returns not every consumer has full price and quality information on every product. Using the available information, consumers nonetheless make (constrained) best-buy decisions. The properties of the resulting symmetric Nash equilibrium in price *and* advertising strategy are of interest.

Preferences and Demand. On the demand side the concepts and specific notations are those used in chapter 5, section 5.2, and can be recalled briefly. To begin, there are $j = 1, 2, \ldots, J$ brands of choice differentiated by price p_j and the parameter $0 \leqslant \theta_j \leqslant 1$ which, using the spatial analogy, identifies the location of each brand j on the unit circumference market. The number J of brands is endogenous and will be determined as an equilibrium condition. There are I consumers, identical except for the parameter $0 \leqslant \theta^0 \leqslant 1$ which defines each consumer's location (ideal characteristic combination). The utility of any brand is derived from the consumer's ideal and deviations from it: $U(\theta_j, \theta^0) - \mu^0 - \tau|\theta_j - \theta^0|$, where μ^0 is the dollar value that the individual places on the ideal brand, $|\theta_j - \theta^0|$ is the arc distance from θ^0 to θ_j, and τ is the constant rate of disutility per unit arc distance. We let μ be the equivalent dollar value of the (composite commodity) outside good; then each individual chooses that brand which maximizes the **net surplus**:

$$\max_j(v - \tau l_j - p_j) \geqslant 0 \tag{13.9}$$

where $v \equiv \mu^0 - \mu > 0$ and $l_j \equiv |\theta_j - \theta^0|$ simplify the notation.

To avoid the one-brand one-consumer solution we employ a simple cost structure with increasing returns based on a fixed cost $F > 0$ and a constant marginal cost $c > 0$. Moreover, we ignore considerations of economies of scope and assume that each firm sells just one brand, so that j indexes both firms and brands unambiguously.

Information and Advertising Technology. Initially it is assumed that buyers are ignorant of prices and characteristics. This may mean either that buyers know the catalog of price and characteristics available, but cannot link these with specific sellers, or that the catalog is not known. Either of these cases can be imagined: all that is important is that each buyer's search cost is large relative to the surplus supplied by any product, so that the advertising messages supplied by the sellers are the sole source of consumer information.[8]

Sellers, we will assume, are subject to a version of the advertising technology described by Butters (1977) when sending buyers information about both price and location (see also Balcer, 1981). A key aspect of this technology is its "shotgun" property: while advertising expenditure can be increased to expose a greater proportion of consumers to the firm's information message, this exposure is random and is not capable of being focused on, say, those nearby consumers who are more inclined to purchase its brand. Specifically, if $0 \leqslant \omega \leqslant 1$ is the **exposure level** chosen by the firm, then ωI consumers at random receive the firm's advertising. The "shotgun" aspect of the advertising means that any given consumer, regardless of his location relative to the firm, receives a message with probability ω.

The per capita cost of supplying information to these ωI consumers is given by the function $A(\omega)$, for which we assume $dA/d\omega > 0$ and $d^2A/d\omega^2 > 0$: not only does it cost more to increase the probability that any given consumer receives a message, it is also increasingly expensive to achieve that additional

---

[8] It is also assumed that dissemination of information by word of mouth is not used.

exposure.[9] To avoid uninteresting complications further assume that advertising is without its own fixed costs so that $A(0) = 0$. It must be stressed that $A(\omega)$ is not the cost of an advertising message in the usual sense, where every consumer receives and uses every message. Rather, $A(\omega)$ is simply the cost of advertising in a way that any consumer will receive a message with probability ω. Finally, we think of advertising exposure as being decisive, producing consumers with perfect recall. Once an advertising message is received by some consumer its content is always remembered.

E13.3

Advertising Cost Function

The specific form taken by $A(\omega)$ depends on the technology of advertising. Suppose, in contrast with our above assumption, that the firm must invest a fixed sunk cost F to prepare some printed medium and have it distributed in newspapers. Let R be the reach of the advertisement, which is equal to the circulation of the paper times the number of issues in which the advertisment appears. Following Butters (1977) and Balcer (1981), suppose also that the advertisement is randomly read by potential buyers and that the newspaper fee is a constant cost per unit circulation. Buyers who read the advertisement one or more times (in successive issues) know of the product and its advertised characteristics, and those who do not read the advertisement are totally uninformed about the product.

Consider the exponential demand function $a \exp\{-d(\phi + \tau l)\}$ where l is the distance from the consumer to the nearest retailer, τ is the cost per unit l, ϕ is the mill price, and a and d are parameters. Choose $a = d = 1$ as a normalization. Using this specification, Butters (1977, p. 468) shows that, if the advertising reach and the number of potential buyers are both large, then the fraction of buyers informed will be approximately $\omega = \{1 - \exp(-R/I)\}$. If we set α equal to I times the per unit newspaper cost, then

$$A(\omega) = \frac{F - \alpha \ln(1 - \omega)}{I} \tag{13.10a}$$

is the per capita advertising (fixed and variable) cost function.

Grossman and Shapiro (1984) have proposed an alternative form for $A(\omega)$ based on the availability of several media advertising forms and no fixed cost. Each medium is assumed to provide the advertiser with messages to the same constant fraction γ of consumers, so that γI consumers receive any given

---

[9] Advertising is supplied by the sellers of products. The greater is the quantity of advertising supplied (the greater ω) the greater are their costs. Whether or not the associated marginal cost increases with the level of advertising is an empirical question about which there is no definitive information. In contrast with the specification here, it has been suggested by some that average advertising costs $A(\omega)/\omega$ may be decreasing and that marginal costs are decreasing and below average. In this case the supply curve of ω would be negatively sloped and, because of advertising, there would be the likelihood of a natural monopoly, provided that production costs do not rise sufficiently. See section 13.4 for futher details.

advertisement. To simplify matters they additionally assume that the probability that any given consumer receives one from any medium is independent of the probability that he receives an advertisement from any other medium. This means that an advertiser using κ different media will have probability $\omega = 1 - (1 - \gamma)^{\kappa}$ that any given consumer receives an advertisement regardless of location. Inverting this gives the media requirements function $\kappa = \ln(1 - \omega)/\ln(1 - \gamma)$. If it is finally assumed that media advertisements have a constant cost α per consumer reached, then $\alpha\gamma I$ is the advertising expenditure for one medium and $(\alpha\gamma I)\kappa$ is the expenditure for κ media. In turn,

$$A(\omega) = \alpha\gamma \frac{\ln(1 - \omega)}{\ln(1 - \gamma)} \qquad (13.10b)$$

is the per capita cost of achieving an exposure level ω using κ different media.

The reader can quickly verify that for both specifications (13.10a) and (13.10b) $A(\omega)$ has the required marginal properties in ω.

Firm Demand. Each firm has two decision variables, price p and advertising (stipulated by the choice of ω). We will generally follow Grossman and Shapiro (1984) here and study only static symmetric Nash equilibria in these variables.[10] This means that the demand relevant to the *firm* is that in which own-price and own-advertising vary, but the price and advertising of the $J - 1$ rivals is held constant at, say, $\bar{p}$ and $\bar{\omega}$ respectively. Let $j = 0$ indicate the specific firm and brand under study.

The construction of firm 0's demand schedule is somewhat complicated by the fact that consumer information is imperfect and the advertising technology has a "shotgun" property. In particular, it is not possible to simply add up quantities demanded in a continuous region of the market (at a given price) since competition among firms is *not* localized. The nonlocalization occurs because (a) consumers may buy from a far-removed seller if they do not receive an advertisement from an intervening one, and (b) advertising is such that the probability of any consumer receiving a seller's advertisement is independent of either's location. This is an important difference from the full information spatial models, as developed in chapter 5, section 5.2, where competition is localized.

The nature of the nonlocalized competition implies firm demand functions of the general form

$$z(p, \omega; \bar{p}, \bar{\omega}) = \sum_n h_n(\omega, \bar{\omega})I_n(p, \bar{p}) \qquad (13.11)$$

where $n = 1, 2, \ldots, J$ indexes groups of consumers ranking brand 0 as nth highest in net surplus,[11] I_n is the number of consumers in the nth group, and h_n

---

[10] Perfect equilibria in a two-stage model in which the incumbent firm chooses advertising at an initial stage and that affects Bertrand play in a second market stage are considered in SE13.4. There the advertising commitment derives from a captive market effect.

[11] Again, the net surplus received from any brand is given by $(v - p) - \tau l$, where l is the distance from the consumer to the brand.

is the probability that consumers in that group will not receive an advertisement from a firm ranked higher in net surplus. The probability that any seller's advertisement results in a sale depends only on the particular group to which the consumer receiving it belongs. This probability multiplied by the number of group members and, in turn, the addition of these products across groups determines the total demand for brand 0.

Recall chapter 5, SE5.1, where expressions for the I_n were developed as follows: [12]

$$I_1 = I\left(\frac{\bar{p} - p}{\tau} + \frac{1}{J}\right) \tag{13.12a}$$

$$I_n = \frac{I}{J} \qquad n = 2, 3, \ldots, (N - 1) \tag{13.12b}$$

$$I_N = I\left(\frac{I}{J} - \frac{\bar{p} - p}{\tau}\right) + I - \sum_{k=1}^{N-1} I_k \tag{13.12c}$$

These quantities can be substituted directly in the demand function (13.11) for the respective groups.

Expressions for the probabilities h_n of the demand function are straightforward since each is independent of all others. First note that individuals in group $n = 1$ purchase brand 0 if they receive an advertisement from that firm. Thus $h_1 = \omega$. Individuals in group $n = 2$ purchase brand 0 if they receive an advertisement from firm 0 (probability ω) *and* they do not receive an advertisement from the firm producing the brand with the greatest net surplus for these individuals (probability $1 - \bar{\omega}$). This means that $\omega_2 = \omega(1 - \bar{\omega})$. If the net surplus of every brand is positive for every consumer (at prevailing prices), then by induction we arrive at the general expression

$$\omega_n = \omega(1 - \bar{\omega})^{n-1} \qquad n = 1, 2, \ldots, J \tag{13.13}$$

Note that as the individuals become more remote from the firm and the group index n becomes larger, the probability ω_n that the brand will be purchased by any individual in that group becomes smaller.

Substituting the probabilities (13.13) in the general expression (13.11) for demand gives

$$z(p, \omega) = \omega \sum_n (\omega - \bar{\omega})^{n-1} I_n(p, \bar{p}) \tag{13.14}$$

It is interesting that the advertising technology adopted here, while seemingly complex, results in a demand which is simply in direct proportion to the exposure level chosen. As a consequence of this proportionality the exposure elasticity of demand η_ω is identically unity:

$$\eta_\omega \equiv \frac{\omega}{z} \frac{\partial z}{\partial \omega} = 1 \tag{13.15}$$

In turn, the more usual advertising (expenditure) elasticity is

$$\eta_A \equiv \frac{A}{z} \frac{\partial z}{\partial A} = \frac{A}{\omega} \frac{\partial \omega}{\partial A} \tag{13.16}$$

[12] See equations (5.76b), (5.78b), and (5.79c) respectively.

which depends only on the properties of the underlying cost function $A(\omega)$.

Substituting the three expressions for I_n from (13.12) in (13.14) and summing yields the demand function

$$z(p, \omega) = \frac{I\omega(\bar{p} - p)}{\tau} \{1 - (1 - \bar{\omega})^{J-1}\} + \frac{I\omega}{J\bar{\omega}} \{1 - (1 - \bar{\omega})^J\} \quad (13.17)$$

This function is difficult to interpret in this form but Grossman and Shapiro (1984) note that, for large J, $(1 - \bar{\omega})^J$ and $(1 - \bar{\omega})^{J-1}$ will be close to zero and (13.17) can be approximated by

$$z(p, \omega) = I\omega \left(\frac{\bar{p} - p}{\tau} + \frac{1}{J\bar{\omega}} \right) \quad (13.17')$$

In this large-numbers form the demand is as expected: z is directly related to the firm's advertising exposure ω and its price advantage $\bar{p} - p$, and is inversely related to the advertising level of other firms $\bar{\omega}$ and consumers' strength of brand preference τ.

In contrast with the advertising elasticity, the usual price elasticity of demand for the general form (13.17) is rather more complicated, but in the large-numbers case it can also be simplified:

$$\eta_p \equiv \frac{p}{z} \frac{\partial z}{\partial p} = \frac{p\bar{J}\omega}{\bar{J}\omega(\bar{p} - p) + \tau} \quad (13.18)$$

Because ω enters demand in the simple multiplicative way, it does not affect the price elasticity. Rather, the "general" level of brand information $\bar{\omega}$, is a key factor in η_p. Note that

$$\frac{\partial \eta_p}{\partial \bar{\omega}} = \frac{p\bar{J}\tau}{\{\bar{J}\omega(\bar{p} - p) + \tau\}^2} > 0$$

as each term in this expression is positive. This accords well with our intuition on the role of information: increases in the general level of brand information increase the demand elasticity and concomitantly reduce optimal prices. Monopoly power is reduced with better information. Finally, when the perfect information condition $\bar{\omega} = 1$ holds and $p = \bar{p}$, then $\eta_p = pJ/\tau$. This is just the result developed in chapter 5, section 5.2.3, and implies (unbounded) increasing demand elasticity with increasing numbers of firms.

E13.4

Advertising and Consumer Surplus

Because of the uniformity of buyers and sellers, a case of interest is that where firms locate symmetrically about the market, all set the same price p and the same exposure level ω. It is instructive to calculate the aggregate consumer surplus (CS) in this case. The special form of the individual utility function makes this a straightforward task. There are two parts to the surplus:

$$CS = (v - p)I\{1 - (1 - \omega)^J\} - D \quad (13.19)$$

The first term represents the surplus that would be received by consumers if each could purchase his ideal characteristic combination – the quantity $1 - (1 - \omega)^J$ is the fraction of the total population consuming the product. In turn, D represents the disutility incurred by consumers in having to select products some distance from their ideal (location). The task remaining is to write D in terms of model parameters, price, and the advertising exposure level. This calculation requires that we know exactly what brand each consumer in fact purchases, and, as the following steps indicate, this is somewhat complicated by the fact that competition is not localized.

The firms, being located symmetrically, are each a distance $1/J$ along the market circle. Consumers receiving an advertisement from their nearest brand incur *average* disutility $d_1 = \tau/4J$ (since consumers are uniformly spread up to a maximum distance $1/2J$ from the brand purchased). Consumers who do not receive an advertisement from their nearest brand, but receive one from the next nearest incur average disutility $d_2 = 3\tau/4J$ (in this case consumers are spread uniformly over a distance from 0 to $3/2J$). By induction it is quickly seen that the average disutility incurred by consumers taking the nth closest brand is $d_n = (2n - 1)\tau/4J$. Since the number of consumers in each of these $n = 1, 2, \ldots, J$ groups is $\omega_n I_n$, the aggregate disutility becomes

$$D = \sum_n d_n(\omega_n I_n) \tag{13.20}$$

Substituting for ω_n from (13.13) and I_n from (13.12) gives

$$D = \frac{\tau I}{4J\omega} \left[(\omega - \omega) + (1 - \omega)^J \{\omega - 2(1 + \omega J)\} \right] \tag{13.21}$$

after summing and some rearrangement.[13] In the large-numbers case, where $(1 - \omega)^J$ is small the approximation

$$D = \frac{\tau I}{4J} \left(\frac{2 - \omega}{\omega} \right) \tag{13.21'}$$

can be used. Because of the uniformity of prices, the aggregate disutility is independent of price and depends only on the advertising exposure level.

13.2.2   Equilibrium and Welfare

By using the above demand and cost functions, firm 0's profits can be written as

$$\pi(p, \omega) = (p - c)z(p, \omega) - A(\omega)I - F \tag{13.22}$$

In the large-numbers case, where the demand has the simplified form given by (13.17'), the stationarity of profits in p yields

$$p = \frac{1}{2} \left(\bar{p} + c + \frac{\tau}{J\omega} \right) \tag{13.23a}$$

From the stationarity in ω we have

---

[13] This expression relies on the derivative $\Sigma(1 + n)(1 - \omega)^n = \mathrm{d}\{\Sigma(1 - \omega)^{1+n}\}/\mathrm{d}(1 - \omega)$.

$$\frac{\partial A}{\partial \omega} = (p - c)\frac{z}{I\omega} \tag{13.23b}$$

If a fixed number J of firms is assumed, a symmetric Nash equilibrium for the industry occurs when $p = \bar{p}$ and $\omega = \bar{\omega}$ and the preceding two equations are solved. This produces equilibrium advertising and price levels given by

$$\frac{\partial A}{\partial \omega} = \frac{\tau}{\omega^3 J^2} \tag{13.24a}$$

and

$$p = \frac{\tau}{J\omega} + c \tag{13.24b}$$

This last expression informs us that the difference between price and marginal cost is inversely related to both the number of firms *and* the advertising intensity. For a fixed number of firms, greater advertising intensity therefore implies lower price–cost margins (monopoly power). This "pro-competitive" result is in contrast with the Kaldor–Bain result noted earlier which is based on a view of advertising as persuasion.

If there is free entry to the industry, and with that zero profits at equilibrium, the added condition

$$(p - c)\frac{I}{J} = F + IA(\omega) \tag{13.24c}$$

also obtains and can be used to determine the equilibrium number of firms. In turn, using (13.24a) and (13.24c) to eliminate p and J from (13.24b) gives

$$\frac{\omega}{A}\frac{\partial A}{\partial \omega} = \frac{F}{AI} + 1 \tag{13.25}$$

At equilibrium, the elasticity of the expenditure function A must equal one plus the fixed-cost ratio of production to advertising. We will return to this condition below.

Optimal Advertising. As usual the aggregate surplus – the sum of consumer and producer surplus – is the welfare criterion. When the expressions developed above are used, this takes on the specific form

$$W = CS + \pi = (v - c)I\{1 - (1 - \omega)^J\} - \frac{\tau I}{4J}\left[\frac{2 - \omega}{\omega}\right]$$
$$+ (1 - \omega)^J\{\omega - 2(1 + \omega J)\} - J\{F + A(\omega)I\} \tag{13.26}$$

The first term on the right-hand side is the aggregate surplus net of variable cost of production, the second term is the disutility incurred as a result of consumers failing to obtain their ideal brands (see equation (13.21′)), and the last term accounts for the fixed costs in both production and advertising. When $(1 - \omega)^J$ is negligible (with large J and $0 < \omega < 1$), this reduces to

$$W = I\left\{(v - c) - \frac{\tau}{4J}\left(\frac{2 - \omega}{\omega}\right)\right\} + J\{F + A(\omega)I\} \tag{13.27}$$

which depends on J and ω. We will use this simpler form in what follows and thereby restrict ourselves to the "large-numbers" case.

The stationarity conditions of W with respect to the advertising level and the number of firms are

$$\frac{\partial A(\omega)}{\partial \omega} = \frac{\tau}{2\omega^2 J^2} \tag{13.28a}$$

and

$$\omega\{F + A(\omega)I\} = \frac{\tau I}{2J^2}\left(I - \frac{\omega}{2}\right) \tag{13.28b}$$

respectively. Eliminating J from these expressions gives

$$\omega\left(1 - \frac{\omega}{2}\right)\frac{\partial A}{\partial \omega} = \frac{F}{I} + A \tag{13.29}$$

It is of interest that the socially optimal level of advertising exposure depends only on the population size I and fixed costs F. While the algebra is rather messy, it can be shown from this relationship that $\partial\omega/\partial F > 0$. Greater levels of fixed production cost imply higher optimal levels of advertising. This result is intuitive, and is consistent with the inverse relationship $\partial J/\partial F < 0$ between fixed costs and product diversity, a comparative statics result obtained in chapter 5, section 5.2.2.

Partial Equilibrium. Suppose that the number of firms (and brands) is exogenously fixed with firms earning positive profits. Then a comparison of the Nash equilibrium and the socially optimal level of advertising requires only that we look at (13.24a) and (13.28a). Dividing these equations gives

$$\left(\frac{\partial A}{\partial \omega}\right)^{e^*} = \left(\frac{\partial A}{\partial \omega}\right)^{0^*}\frac{2}{\omega^{e^*}} \geq 2\left(\frac{\partial A}{\partial \omega}\right)^{0^*} \tag{13.30}$$

where the superscript e refers to market equilibrium values, the superscript 0 refers to socially optimal values, and the asterisk reminds us that these conditions obtain for fixed J only. The rightmost inequality follows from $0 \leq \omega^{e^*} \leq 1$. Because $A(\omega)$ increases in ω at an increasing rate, (13.30) immediately implies that the industry equilibrium level of advertising is *oversupplied* relative to what is socially optimal. This oversupply occurs despite the fact that advertising only serves to supply information.

Full Equilibrium. Suppose now that the number of firms is endogenous. The presence of J^2 in the denominator of (13.24a) and (13.28a) suggests that the above partial equilibrium result will not obtain more generally. This is, in fact, correct as dividing the market equilibrium and optimal solutions (13.25) and (13.29) gives

$$\left(\frac{\partial A}{\partial \omega}\right)^e = \left(1 - \frac{\omega^e}{2}\right)\left(\frac{\partial A}{\partial \omega}\right)^0 \leq \left(\frac{\partial A}{\partial \omega}\right)^0 \tag{13.31}$$

The inequality arises in this expression because $0 \leq \omega \leq 1$. Even with purely informative and pro-competitive advertising the free-entry equilibrium *undersupplies* advertising relative to the social optimum.

Finally, from (13.25a) and (13.28a) we derive the ratio of firms

$$\frac{J^e}{J^0} = 2\left(\frac{1}{\omega^e}\right)^{1/2} \frac{\omega^0}{\omega^e} \frac{(\partial A/\partial \omega)^0}{(\partial A/\partial \omega)^e} \tag{13.22}$$

Since $0 \leqslant \omega^0 \leqslant 1$ this can be written as

$$J^e \geqslant 2J^0 \tag{13.33}$$

so that there is greater brand diversity at the free-entry Nash equilibrium than would be socially optimal. This, the reader may recall, is the same monopolistic competition "brand proliferation" result that was reached in chapter 5, section 5.2.3, under conditions of costless information. Following the analyses in chapter 6, sections 6.2 and 6.3, the reader is cautioned that these results are not robust to a change in the firms' strategy variables, or to a change from the spatial model to one where products are more symmetrically substitutable, or perhaps even to an alternative specification of the advertising technology.

Strategic Advertising. It should be emphasized that the model developed above is static and therefore does not consider possible strategic uses of advertising investments. From the analyses in chapters 10 and 11 the reader can nonetheless anticipate the conditions for strategic over- and under-supply of advertising capital in the dynamic game. In a standard asymmetric model, with an incumbent and potential entrant, the focus moves to the entrant's expectations about the incumbent's (stage 2) post-entry advertising level. The more intense is the rivalry, and with that the greater is the incumbent's post-entry advertising, the less profitable is the entry. The question usually posed at this point concerns the extent to which *pre*-entry advertising by the incumbent indicates *post*-entry levels.[14] Baldani and Masson (1981) and Kotowitz and Mathewson (1982) have analyzed two-stage models in which this link between pre-entry and post-entry levels exists and pre-entry levels thus credibly deter entry. A similar two-stage analysis is developed in SE13.4.

E13.5

The Dorfman–Steiner Relationship

Perhaps the most frequently used analysis of the joint price–advertising decision is that of Dorfman and Steiner (1954). They posit a Nash-in-price demand function

$$z = z(p, a)$$

for the firm, where $\partial z/\partial p < 0$ as usual, $\partial z/\partial a > 0$, and a is expenditure on advertising.[15] (More generally, we can think of a as any demand-increasing cost

---

[14] Cubbin (1981) *assumes* that entrants' expectations of post-entry advertising are based on pre-entry levels and from this concludes that advertising is a "barrier to entry."

[15] Notice that it is the advertising *expenditure a* which shifts the demand schedule here. It is frequently argued that the advertising *message*, not expenditure, is the essential shift parameter. However, we adhere to the original Dorfman–Steiner development at this point. The implicit assumption, then, is that the price per unit advertising message is a constant equal to unity.

(see Demsetz, 1964).) Firm profits are

$$\pi(p, a) = pz(\beta, a) - c(z(p, a)) - a \tag{13.34}$$

If zero conjectures in p and a are assumed, the stationarity conditions are

$$p \frac{\partial z}{\partial a} = \eta_p \tag{13.35a}$$

$$\frac{a}{pz} = \frac{\eta_a}{\eta_p} \tag{13.35b}$$

where η_a and η_p are respectively advertising expenditure and price elasticities of demand. Since at the profit maximum $\eta_p = (p - c')/p$, where c' is the marginal cost, we also have

$$\frac{\partial pz}{\partial a} = \frac{p - c'}{p} \tag{13.35c}$$

Conditions (13.35a) indicate that advertising is employed just to the point where its marginal revenue product equals the price elasticity. From (13.35b) it is seen further that the firm's ratio of advertising to sales (revenue) is equal to the ratio of advertising to price elasticities. Note, in passing, that if $z(\cdot)$ has the Cobb–Douglas form in p and a, so that η_a and η_p are constants, then the firm's ratio of advertising expenditure to sales is a constant. Schmalensee (1972a), in a review of empirical studies of advertising, finds evidence of constant firm and industry advertising-to-sales ratios (over time).

The Dorfman–Steiner stationarity conditions, and (13.35c) in particular, have often been used to argue for a causal link between the advertising-to-sales ratio and price elasticity and, in turn, the price–cost margin. The conclusion drawn from this link is that increased advertising-to-sales ratios increase monopoly power (see, for example, Scherer, 1980, pp. 386–9). This is, of course, a misleading conclusion: advertising and price (the endogenous variables) are, instead, determined simultaneously in the general solution of these equations as a function of (the exogenous parameters of) demand and supply.[16]

13.3   Taste-altering Advertising

To complete any study of advertising as information it is interesting, as a contrast, to set out a model in which advertising acts simply as persuasion to alter consumer tastes without imparting any information about the product. The key points of comparison are conveniently revealed in a monopoly case developed by Dixit and Norman (1978) and our attention is restricted to that (see also Dixit and Norman, 1979; Fisher and McGowan, 1979; Shapiro, 1980).

Demand and Preferences. Let $z(p, \theta)$ be the market demand function, where p is price and θ is advertising *messages*, with $\partial z/\partial p < 0$ and $\partial z/\partial \theta > 0$. This demand is assumed to arise from an aggregate quasi-linear utility function $u(z)$.

[16] For an extension of the Dorfman–Steiner analysis to stationarity dynamics see SE13.1.

Without advertising, $u' \equiv \partial u(z)/\partial z$ provides the observed inverse demand function facing the monopolist. Finally, define $\bar{u} \equiv \partial u(z; \bar{m})/\partial z$, which is the inverse demand when advertising is fixed at specific level $\theta = \bar{m}$. Following traditional terminology, $\bar{m}$ is called the *standard* for advertising and $\bar{u}$ is said to indicate *true* consumer preferences.[17]

Welfare Optimum. How is aggregate surplus related to the monopolist's advertising decision? An answer begins with the aggregate surplus identity

$$W(p, m; \bar{m}) \equiv \bar{u}(z(p, \theta); \bar{m}) - pz(p, \theta) + \pi(p, \theta) \qquad (13.36)$$

$$= \bar{u}(z(p, \theta); \bar{m}) - cz(p, \theta) - z\theta$$

where c is the constant unit production cost and a is the cost per message. Let $p^c(\theta)$ indicate the monopolist's profit-maximizing (equilibrium) price as a function of θ and write W in terms of θ as

$$W = \bar{u}(z(p^c(\theta)), \bar{m}) - cz(p^c(\theta), \theta) - a\theta \qquad (13.37)$$

Note that the surplus depends on the choice of θ, assuming that, whatever message level is chosen, the monopoly chooses the price $p^c(\theta)$ to maximize its profits. In general $p^c(\theta)$ does not maximize W. The relationship between these choices is revealed by differentiating (13.37) to give

$$\frac{dW}{d\theta} = (\bar{u}' - p^c)\frac{dz}{d\theta} - z\left(\frac{dp^c}{d\theta}\right) + \frac{d\pi}{d\theta} \qquad (13.38)$$

At the welfare optimum θ is chosen such that $dW/d\theta = 0$; at the profit maximum θ is such that $d\pi/d\theta = 0$. Let $\theta^c > 0$ indicate this latter (equilibrium) value. Equation (13.38) informs us that advertising is excessively supplied by profit-maximizing firms: $dW(\theta^c; \bar{m})/d\theta < 0$ when the sum of the first two terms on the right-hand side is negative at θ^c.[18] In this regard, first observe that the sign of $dp^c/d\theta$ will be positive when advertising causes demand to be less elastic and it will be negative when advertising increases the demand elasticity. Both possibilities are reasonable; not much can be said beyond that. To make the strongest case here, let us assume for the moment that $dp^c/d\theta$ is positive, making the second term $-z(dp^c/d\theta)$ negative.

What about the first term on the right-hand side of (13.38)? It seems natural that advertising is demand increasing, and so the *total* derivative $dz/d\theta$ will be positive. This leaves the sign of $\bar{u}' - p^c$ to be established.[19] If it is assumed that the "true interests" of consumers are those occurring with demands where $\theta = 0$, then $u' < p^c$ and the first term is negative. All things considered then, the monopolist over-supplies advertising.

The chain of reasoning leading to this over-supply result is somewhat circular:

---

[17] If, alternatively, we were to think of advertising as informative in the sense developed above, then we would take $\bar{u}'$ to be increasing in θ, but that imposition is not made here.

[18] If the firm were a (competitive) price-taker then p^c would be constant function and the second of these terms would be zero. This possibility is not permitted as we deal with a monopolist. Alternatively, when the demand function is separable, $z(p, \theta) = f(p)\xi(\theta)$ and the profit-maximizing price will be independent of θ and the second term will again be zero.

[19] Again, $\bar{u}'$ is the marginal utility of z at the advertising level $\bar{m}$. $\bar{u}'$ will equal p^c only when $\bar{m}$ is also the level of advertising chosen by the monopolist.

if, instead, we had assumed that the consumer's "true interests" are best served when advertising levels are high, then $\text{sgn}(\bar{u}' - p^c)$ would have been positive and, depending on the relative magnitudes of the terms, advertising levels might turn out to be below the socially optimal level. That is, to a large extent the prior choice of the $\bar{m}$ standard dictates the result. In this sense the analysis is dependent on our (personal) standard and *ad hoc*.

13.4   Scale Economies in Advertising

It is frequently argued that the presence of increasing returns to advertising acts to create inefficiencies much in the same way that increasing returns does in production: it reduces product variety below the level which is socially optimal.[20] Since the analyses that have been undertaken to this point have assumed either constant or diminishing returns in advertising, the validity of this frequent argument has not been considered. This is not a difficult analysis, however, as the basic tools are available from chapter 5, section 5.3, where the link between scale economies in production and optimal product diversity was analyzed. It is only necessary here to extend that analysis to incorporate advertising.

13.4.1   The Model

Using the notation of chapter 5, section 5.3, assume again that aggregate utility has the quasi-linear form

$$u(z, y) = u(v) + y \tag{13.39}$$

where $v = \Sigma_j v_j(z_j, \theta_j)$, z_j is firm j's output, θ_j is the number of advertising messages it supplies, and y is consumer (aggregate) income. The utility value v_j of j's product is increasing not only in the number of physical units taken by consumers but also in the level of the firm's advertising. These advertising messages are assumed to affect utility by supplying information which reduces the consumers' cost in using the advertisers' brand. In the usual way the inverse demand for z_j is given by $p_j = \partial u / \partial z_j$, or

$$p_j = u'(v)\{v_j'(z_j, \theta_j)\} \tag{13.40}$$

where $u' \equiv \partial u / \partial v$ and $v_j' \equiv \partial v_j / \partial z_j$. Firm j's revenues are, in turn, $R_j = p_j z_j$ or

$$R_j = u'(v)\{v_j'(z_j, \theta_j)z_j\} \tag{13.41}$$

It eases the calculations to let v_j have a constant elasticity form: $v_j = v_{0j}\theta_j^\gamma z_j^\alpha$ where $v_{0j} > 0$, $\gamma > 0$ is the (constant) utility value elasticity of advertising, and $\alpha > 0$ is the utility value elasticity of quantity.[21] (While these

---

[20] In addition, Bain (1956, ch. 4) and many of his followers have argued that the minimum efficient scale of the firm is made larger as a result of economies of scale in advertising. This larger efficient scale then increases market concentration and, in turn, creates monopoly welfare losses. See Comanor and Wilson (1967, pp. 424–5), Needham (1976), and Scherer (1980, p. 260) for similar comments.

[21] Spence (1980) uses a similar specification.

parameters are positively related to the usual advertising and price elasticities of demand respectively, they are not identical.) In turn $v_j' z_j = \alpha v_j$ and, letting $v_j \equiv \alpha v_j$ we can rewrite j's revenues as

$$R_j = g(v)v_j(\theta_j, z_j) = g(v)(\alpha v_{0j}\theta_j{}^{\gamma} z_j{}^{\alpha}) \tag{13.42}$$

with $v = \Sigma_j v_j$ and $g(v) = u'(\Sigma_j v_j/\alpha)$. For later use, observe that $g(v)$ is decreasing in v and $v_j(\cdot)$ is increasing in both θ_j and z_j. Finally, the firm's profit function can be written as the difference between revenues and cost:

$$\pi_j = g(v)v_j(\theta_j, z_j) - c(z_j) - a(\theta_j) \tag{13.43}$$

Here, $c(z_j)$ is firm j's production cost and $a(\theta_j)$ is the advertising expenditure function.

Returns to Scale. As in chapter 5, section 5.3 it is instructive to treat the profit maximization in two stages. In the first, values of z_j and θ_j are found which minimize the firm's cost for any given v_j. This solution defines an *indirect cost function*

$$\phi(v_j) = \min_{z,\theta} \{c(z_j) + a(\theta_j)\} \tag{13.44}$$

In the second stage v_j is chosen to maximize $g(v)v_j - \phi(v_j)$, with proper consideration being given to rivals' reactions. The ratio of the firm's profits to its revenues, which is commonly called a measure of the firm's **advantage**, can be written as

$$\frac{\pi}{R} = 1 - \frac{1}{g(v)}\left\{\frac{\phi(v_j)}{v_j}\right\} \tag{13.45}$$

Note that a larger profit-to-sales ratio indicates a greater advantage. With Cournot–Nash conjectures, $g(v)$ and v_j are increasing functions of z_j at equilibrium. As a result, firms with greater output will have a greater equilibrium advantage when $\phi(v_j)/v_j$ is decreasing in v_j (that is, average costs are decreasing in the v output). This requires that the elasticity of $\phi(v_j)$ with respect to v_j is less than unity. This elasticity is thus a (local) measure of the gains to size and reflects scale economies in *both* advertising and production.[22]

13.4.2 Constant-elasticity Case

In addition to the constant-elasticity form $v_j = v_{0j}\theta_j z_j$, suppose that the cost functions are given by $c(z_j) = c_0 z_j{}^{1/\beta}$ and $a(\theta_j) = a_0\theta_j{}^{1/\delta}$, where β and δ are positive constants. The elasticity of ϕ with respect to v_j is then

$$\eta_\phi = \frac{\{\partial\phi(v_j)/\partial v_j\}v_j}{\phi(v_j)} = \frac{1}{\alpha\beta + \gamma\delta} \tag{13.46}$$

This (constant) measure of scale economies in the v output has both advertising and production cost effects.[23] Substituting this expression in (13.45) it is seen

[22] This relationship was first developed by Spence (1980); see also Yarrow (1985).

[23] With the cost functions assumed, (13.44) becomes the usual Cobb–Douglas cost minimization exercise with $z^{1/\beta}$ and $\theta^{1/\delta}$ as factors. The exponents of these factors in the associated production function (for v) are thus immediately seen to be $\alpha\beta$ and $\gamma\delta$ respectively. Equation (13.46) indicates that the sum of these exponents determines returns to scale in the standard way. Note finally that this means that the ratio of advertising cost to total cost is constant and equal to $\gamma\delta/(\alpha\beta + \gamma\delta)$.

that size advantages $(\mathrm{d}(\pi_j/R_j)/\mathrm{d}z_j > 0)$ occur when $\eta_\phi < 1$, and conversely. Thus, four parameters create a size advantage when it exists: the returns to scale in both production (β) and advertising (δ) and the demand elasticity parameters α and γ. The impact of β on size advantage is as usual (recall chapter 5, section 5.3.1). The impact of the δ advertising scale economies is immediately seem in (13.46): advertising scale economies and the advertising sensitivity parameter δ enter multiplicatively in creating size advantage. The more sensitive demand is to advertising messages the more likely it is that the advertising scale economies will produce a size advantage.[24] Note, finally, that the overall advertising effect $\gamma\delta$ is additive with the overall production effect $\alpha\beta$ in producing size advantages and each can augment or offset the other in this regard.

E13.6

Advertising Scale Economies: Some Evidence

From (13.46) it is seen that whether or not increasing returns to advertising are the source of a size advantage turns on empirical evidence. In reviewing the literature and in original studies, Simon (1970), Schmalensee (1972a), and Ferguson (1974) found no support for such scale economies, either from time series of cross-sectional statistical evidence. Peterman (1965) and Blank (1968) specifically found a lack of evidence of quantity discounts or price discrimination in favor of large-scale television advertisers. (Some discounts were reported, however, but these served only to equalize unit message costs.) Lambin (1975, 1976) concluded that the evidence from his survey of European consumer-good markets supported *decreasing* returns to advertising, since there was generally decreasing advertising effectiveness with increasing message frequency and audience size. Brown (1978) is perhaps the most recent of the several studies that report evidence of advertising scale economies. Finally, we note that some dispute on these issues still remains because of econometric problems; for example, Comanor and Wilson (1979) and Albion and Farris (1981) criticize the empirical work in this area for failing to allow all inputs to vary and for failing to conduct controlled experiments.

Comanor and Wilson (1967, 1979) also suggest, without systematic empirical support, that the increasing returns in advertising arise because of imperfections in the capital market which permit large firms lower costs of capital. Krouse (1982, 1986) investigated this capital market size advantage, finding it to be without foundation in systematic studies and pointing to the theoretical errors in anecdotes generally offered in support of imperfections (recall also the comments in chapter 12, section 12.5.2).

Supplementary examples

SE13.1   Time-optimal Advertising Stock

A (somewhat) dynamic version of the Dorfman–Steiner model of monopoly

---

[24] Since neither $g(v)$ nor $v_j(z_j, \theta)$ are market observables, it is difficult to relate the demand parameters α and γ to observable demand elasticities.

advertising (recall E13.5) has been discussed by Nerlove and Arrow (1962). At the center of their model is an advertising stock variable S_t. With a constant depreciation rate $\delta > 0$ and *advertising expenditures* a_t, the path of the stock over time is governed by the transition equation

$$S_t = \delta S_{t-1} + a_t \tag{13.47}$$

Nerlove and Arrow presume that the stock enters demand as a shift parameter:

$$z_t = z(p_t, S_t) \tag{13.48}$$

with $\partial z / \partial S_t > 0$. The exact mechanism giving rise to this shift is not developed. Note that the demand function $z(\cdot)$ is stationary over time.

The monopolist maximizes the present value of its profit stream, choosing a *time-dated plan* of prices and stocks.[25]

$$\pi_0 = \sum_{t=1}^{\infty} \rho^t [p_t z(p_t, S_t) - c(z(p_t, S_t)) - (S_t - \delta S_{t-1})] \tag{13.49}$$

where $c(\cdot)$ is the production cost function, $a_t = S_t - \delta S_{t-1}$ from (13.47) and $\rho^t = (1 + r)^t$ is the period t discount factor with constant interest rate r. For an interior maximum the stationarity conditions are

$$\frac{\partial \pi_0}{\partial p_t} = \rho^{t-1} \left\{ \frac{\partial z}{\partial z_t} + \left(p_t - \frac{\partial c}{\partial z_t} \right) \frac{\partial z_t}{\partial p_t} \right\} = 0 \tag{13.50a}$$

$$\frac{\partial \pi_0}{\partial S_t} = \rho^{t-1} \left\{ \left(p_t - \frac{\partial c}{\partial z_t} \right) \frac{\partial z_t}{\partial S_t} - 1 + \rho \delta \right\} = 0 \tag{13.50b}$$

for all $t = 1, 2, \ldots$ Some rearrangement of these two conditions yields

$$\frac{\eta_s}{\eta_p} = \frac{(1 - \rho \delta) S_t}{p_t z_t} \tag{13.51}$$

where η_s is the elasticity of demand with respect to S_t and η_p is the usual elasticity with respect to price. While (13.51) is similar to the Dorfman–Steiner result (13.27b), it implies somewhat different behavior for advertising expenditures a_t. If the elasticity ratio is constant, the monopolist chooses a_t to keep the right-hand side of (13.51) constant. Under this rule, the advertising-to-sales ratio would generally vary, declining in the downswing of a cycle and rising in the upswing.

SE13.2 Advertising Technology and Equilibrium

Butters (1977) constructs a model similar to that developed in section 13.2, but with different results. In his simplest case all buyers have the same reservation price v for the product regardless of their location ($\tau = 0$). Sellers randomly send advertisements indicating their price p and location θ to these buyers. If a

---

[25] The second decision variable may be either advertising stock or advertising expenditure as these are linked uniquely by (13.47).

buyer receives no advertisement, or if he receives only those with $p > v$, he buys nothing; alternatively, he purchases the brand which has lowest price from among those with $p < v$. In this way, advertising produces value by allowing mutually beneficial trades to occur when otherwise they would not.

Suppose that α is the constant cost of sending one advertising message to one customer at random. Let $c + \alpha < v$. If the firm sends κ messages to the population of I consumers, and both of these numbers are large, then the fraction of consumers *not* receiving an advertisement will be (approximately) $\exp(-k)$, where $k = \kappa/I$. If all buyers receiving messages – there are $\{1 - \exp(-k)\}/I$ of them – buy some brand, then the aggregate surplus is equal to

$$W = [(v - c)\{1 - \exp(-k)\} - \alpha k]I \tag{13.52}$$

This surplus is maximized by the choice of messages κ, or $k = \kappa/I$ given that I is fixed, given by

$$k^0 = \ln\left(\frac{v - c}{\alpha}\right) \tag{13.53}$$

What is the level of advertising in a free-entry equilibrium? To answer this, Butters first shows that all prices between $c + \alpha$ and v will be advertised. (Why? There is no fixed cost and so a continuum of firms is possible.) Then, letting $h(p)$ be the probability that a message advertising price p will result in a purchase, the zero-expected-profit (free-entry) requirement becomes $(p - c)h(p) - \alpha = 0$ which solves for

$$h(p) = \frac{\alpha}{p - c} \tag{13.54}$$

Suppose now that the firm sets $p = v$. In this case a purchase is made only if an advertisement from the firm reaches a buyer receiving no other advertisement. In turn, the firm will sell $z(v) = \exp(-k)$ units, and in the symmetric zero-profit market equilibrium

$$\exp(-k) = h(p) = \frac{\alpha}{v - c}$$

or

$$k^e = \ln\left(\frac{v - c}{\alpha}\right) \tag{13.55}$$

which is exactly the k maximizing W. In this special case, the equilibrium level of advertising is socially optimal.

SE13.3   Advertising with Imperfect Recall

The advertising model of section 13.2 is based on the assumption that advertising messages provide full information about the products to which they pertain and these messages, and the consumers' product experiences, are remembered forever. More generally, neither advertising messages nor limited product experience will fully inform a consumer about a given product's quality. To further complicate matters, consumers will generally forget these messages and their experiences over time. Schmalensee (1978a) and Kotowitz and Mathewson (1979a, b) develop equilibrium models of advertising in which incomplete information and forgetfulness occur. In Schmalensee's model it turns out that low-quality brands have greater optimal levels of advertising than high-quality brands and market shares are also inversely related to product quality. Schmalensee interprets these results as indicating that advertising is a compensation for (is a substitute for) quality.

We can derive Schmalensee's key results using a simplified version of his model. To begin, let there be two firms producing goods with quality levels ξ_1 and ξ_2 respectively. Like Schmalensee, we hold aside price competition, fixing the common price at p, and assume constant unit costs for the firms of c_1 and c_2. There are I consumers, each purchasing one unit of the product from either firm 1 or firm 2 in each period. Each consumer has two alternatives at each period: purchase the brand taken in the prior period or, if that brand was unsatisfactory, randomly choose from the two brands according to probabilities based on advertising intensities. If a_{1t} and a_{2t} are the respective dollar advertising expenditures of the firms at period t, then the probabilities governing the random purchase at period $t + 1$ are specifically assumed to be $a_{1t}/(a_{1t} + a_{2t})$ for firm 1 and $a_{2t}/(a_{1t} + a_{2t})$ for firm 2. Suppose further that any consumer using brand 1 finds his purchase to be unsatisfactory with probability $1/h_1$ and similarly let $1/h_2$ pertain for brand 2.

The above assumptions are sufficient to define the process by which market shares develop over time. For firm 1 the market share transition equation is given by

$$m_{1(t+1)} = \left(1 - \frac{1}{h_1}\right)m_{1t} + \left\{\frac{1}{h_1}m_{1t} + \frac{1}{h_2}(1 - m_{1t})\right\}\frac{a_{1t}}{a_{1t} + a_{2t}} \quad (13.56)$$

where m_{1t} is firm 1's market share at date t. A similar transition equation obtains for firm 2. Given that the firms do not engage in price competition and the product qualities are fixed, note that the market shares depend only on the relative advertising expenditures: specifically, the firm with the greater advertising will have increasing share. To see this more exactly, assume that a_1^0 and a_2^0 are constant at equilibrium (steady state) values and solve (13.56) for the equilibrium shares

$$m_j^0 = \frac{h_j a_j^0}{h_j a_j^0 + h_k a_k^0} \quad (13.57)$$

where k indicates the rival firm.

The equilibrium advertising levels derive from the repeated play of the Nash-in-advertising game as follows. Profits per period are $\pi_j = m_j^0 I(p - c_j) - a_j$ for firm j. Firm j's stationarity, given the Nash conjecture, is

$$I\phi_j \frac{dm_j}{da_j} = 1 \quad j = 1, 2 \quad (13.58)$$

where $\phi_j \equiv p - c_j$ is firm j's variable margin. Solving these equations simultaneously gives the equilibrium advertising levels

$$a_j{}^0 = \phi_j I h_j h_k \frac{\phi_j \phi_k}{(h_j \phi_j + h_k \phi_k)^2} \qquad (13.59)$$

Note that, when the firms have identical costs $c_j = c_k$, then $\phi_j = \phi_k$ and the firms will have identical *equilibrium* advertising. Using (13.57) yields market shares for the general case

$$m_j{}^0 = \frac{h_j \phi_j}{h_j \phi_j + h_k \phi_k} \qquad (13.60)$$

Suppose that firm 1 is a low-cost low-quality producer relative to firm 2, that is $c_1 < c_2$ and $h_1 < h_2$. Condition (13.59) then informs us that brand 1 is the most intensively advertised: $a_1{}^0 > a_2{}^0$. Consumers choosing their brands randomly will therefore favor the low-quality highly advertised brand 1. Moreover, (13.60) informs us that this favoring can offset the greater repeat purchase of the higher-quality brand: brand 1 has a greater market share if $h_1/h_2 > \phi_2/\phi_1$. Finally, the reader can quickly show that the low-cost low-quality brand is more profitable when $\phi_1(m_1{}^0)^2 > \phi_2(m_2{}^0)^2$. That is, given $\phi_1 > \phi_2$, a higher market share for firm 1 is a sufficient (not necessary) condition for firm 1 to be more profitable.

SE13.4   Strategic Investments in Advertising Capital

Recall from chapters 10 and 11 that in a dynamic game capital investments can be less than in the static counterpart to the game. Fudenberg and Tirole (1986a) have given an example where such under-investment in advertising is used by an incumbent firm concerned with deterring market entry. In their two-stage model, consumers can purchase only from those firms from which they have received advertising messages (otherwise the firm is not known to exist). In the first stage there is an incumbent who advertises. In the second stage a group of previously inactive firms contemplate entry. As a critical ingredient of the analysis, Fudenberg and Tirole build in brand loyalty by assuming that consumers receiving an advertising message in the first period (from the incumbent) do not open themselves to new advertisements and this reduces the demand available to those firms considering entry. Fudenberg and Tirole refer to the captured consumers as being dependent on the incumbent's *stock of goodwill*.[26] As will be made clear below, the incumbent under-invests in advertising (has lower goodwill) if it chooses to create a credible threat to price iow if firms should enter, and it advertises heavily otherwise.

Consider two firms, the incumbent ($j = 1$) and a potential entrant ($j = 2$), and a population I of identical consumers. We think of the demand and cost faced by the firms as giving rise to per capita net revenue functions $R_j(p_j, p_k)$ for each firm, where the p are prices – again, $j, k = 1, 2$ with $j \neq k$. When some individual is informed by the advertising of firm j, but not k, we write $R_j(p_j, 0)$. $R_j(\cdot)$ is assumed to be differentiable in both prices and to be quasi-concave,

---

[26] The captivity might result from consumers with imperfect information about product quality and high search costs, or it might result from a model in which there are brand-specific costs of learning how to use products efficiently. See Schmalensee (1982b) and Spence (1981b) respectively.

increasing in p_j. Assume that $\partial^2 R_j / \partial p_j \partial p_k > 0$.

Each firm's advertising technology is governed by an advertising cost function $A(\omega_j) > 0$, giving the (total) cost of reaching a fraction ω_j of the consuming population. We require that $\partial A / \partial \omega_j > 0$, $\partial^2 A / \partial \omega_j^2 > 0$ and $A(1) = \infty$. The advertising strategy variable is ω_j for each firm.

During the first stage of the game the incumbent monopolist chooses the fraction ω_1 of consumers to receive its advertisement, and a monopoly price $p_1{}^m$; associated earnings are $R_1(p_1{}^m, \infty)\omega_1 I - A(\omega_1)$. To bypass some unnecessary details assume that the incumbent chooses advertising at stage 2 to yield costs A_2 and, if the entrant enters, it also chooses A_2. If entry is assumed, the profit values at the onset of the game are

$$\pi_1 = R_1(p_1{}^m, \infty)\omega_1 I - A(\omega_1)$$

$$+ \rho\{R_1(p_1, \infty)\omega_1 I + R_1(p_1, p_2)(1 - \omega_1)I - A_2\} \tag{13.61}$$

$$\pi_2 = \rho\{R_2(p_1, p_2)(1 - \omega_1)I - A_2\} \tag{13.62}$$

where ρ is the discount factor.

Second-stage Equilibrium. Since the choice of advertising has been held aside at this stage, we look only at the Nash-in-price equilibrium. This equilibrium is contingent on the incumbent's previously chosen advertising level ω_1, as indicated in the following stationarity conditions:

$$\frac{\partial R_1(p_1, \infty)}{\partial p_1} + (1 - \omega_1)\frac{\partial R_1(p_1, p_2)}{\partial p_1} = 0 \tag{13.63a}$$

$$\frac{\partial R_2(p_1, p_2)}{\partial p_2} = 0 \tag{13.63b}$$

Let $p_1{}^0(\omega_1)$ and $p_2{}^0(\omega_1)$ indicate the solution prices, which again are functions of the first-stage advertising level of the incumbent.[27]

Suppose for the moment, that the game was to be played in a static way, with both advertising and price decisions made simultaneously. The solution conditions for this case include (13.63) and $\partial\pi_1(p_1, \omega_1)/\partial\omega_1 = 0$, or

$$R_1(p_1{}^m, \infty)I + \rho\{R_1(p_1, \infty) - R_1(p_1, p_2)\}I = \frac{\partial A(\omega_1)}{\partial\omega_1} \tag{13.64}$$

Note, in contrast with the two-stage game in which the advertising and price decisions are made sequentially, that the static analysis prices are not functions of the advertising choice (although in the usual way they are mutually determined in the solution).

Strategic Choice of Advertising. We now return to the two-stage analysis. In a perfect equilibrium the incumbent understands that its early-on choice of advertising will alter the market-stage choice of prices in exactly the way indicated by equations (13.63). The optimal choice of ω_1 thus solves $d\pi_1\{p_1{}^0(\omega_1), p_2{}^0(\omega_1)\}/d\omega_1 = 0$, or

---

[27] As $0 \leqslant \omega_1 \leqslant 1$ and $\partial^2 R_j / \partial p_j \partial p_k > 0$, then $\partial R_1(p_1{}^0, \infty) > 0 > \partial R_1(p_1{}^0, p_2{}^0)$: the incumbent would ideally choose to price discriminate against its brand-loyal customers, but we have assumed that to be prohibitive.

$$R_1(p_1{}^m, \infty)I$$

$$+ \rho \left\{ R_1(p_1{}^0, \infty) - R_1(p_1^0, p_2^0) + (1 - \omega_1) \frac{\partial R_1(p_1{}^0, p_2{}^0)}{\partial p_2} \frac{\partial p_2{}^0}{\partial \omega_1} \right\} I = \frac{\partial A}{\partial \omega_1}$$

$$(13.65)$$

Since $\partial p_2{}^0/\partial \omega_1 > 0,[28]$ and we have assumed $\partial R_1/\partial p_2 > 0$, the left-hand side of (13.65) is strictly greater than the left-hand side of (13.64). Thus the solution $\omega_1{}^0$ to the dynamic game conditions (13.65) exceeds the solution ω_1^* to the simultaneous-decision static game.

Fudenberg and Tirole refer to the advertising over-investment of the perfect equilibrium relative to the static game as the **fat-cat effect**. If the incumbent chooses (on some unexplained rationale) to allow entry, it will advertise heavily in the first period to increase its captive market and thus "soften" the entrant's entry. They also note a possible **lean and hungry look**: should the incumbent choose (again, on some unexplained rationale) to deter entry then it would under-invest in advertising. To show this derive

$$\frac{d\pi_2}{d\omega_1} = \rho \left\{ (1 - \omega_1) \frac{\partial R_2}{\partial p_1} \frac{\partial p_1{}^0}{\partial \omega_1} - R_2 \right\} I$$

$$(13.66)$$

The right-hand side of this expression is made-up of two effects. The first term, involving $\partial p_1{}^0/\partial \omega_1$, is the strategic effect (recall chapter 10, section 10.3.1) of advertising on market price. Depending on the magnitude of this effect and R_2, the sign of $d\pi_2/d\omega_1$ can be either positive or negative. When the strategic effect is relative large, $d\pi_1/d\omega_1 > 0$ and decreases in the incumbent's advertising lead to decreases in the entrant's profit. In this case entry deterrence would require under-investment.

SE13.5   Some Empirical Evidence on Advertising

Strickland and Weiss (1976), Comanor and Wilson (1979), Martin (1979), Pagoulatos and Sorenson (1980), and Ornstein (1987) have extensively reviewed the hypotheses linking advertising, concentration, and profitability that have been forged from the early work or Kaldor and Bain. In brief, that tradition proceeds as follows. Extensive brand advertising develops strong brand loyalty. A low price elasticity for the brand results, in turn causing higher profits (price–cost margins) and even greater advertising. Despite the high profitability, new entry is forestalled by a web of entry barriers that accompany the high level of advertising, including those related to advertising scale economies and the capital requirements necessary to meet the advertising levels of existing firms. The barriers to entry promulgate further market concentration and lead, in turn, to increased collusion and still greater profitability and efficiency losses.

On brand loyalty, Massey and Frank (1965) have reported insignificant differences between price (and advertising) elasticities from groups of brand-loyal (repeat) and nonloyal (nonrepeating) buyers. Lambin (1976) concluded

---

[28] This assumes that the incumbent's reaction function is steeper than the entrant's reaction function on the price plane – recall chapter 3, section 3.1.5, and chapter 10, section 10.2.1.

from an extensive survey of European consumer product industries that brand loyalty (repeat buying) is very sensitive to product prices and perceived qualities, and generally unrelated to industry-wide advertising levels. In addition, two indirect forms of testing the advertising to brand loyalty have been suggested: examination of (a) the relationship between advertising level and market share stability, with greater stability suggesting greater brand loyalties, and (b) the relationship between advertising levels and the rate of new product introductions, with fewer introductions implying greater loyalty. In this regard, Telser (1964), Reekie (1974), and Lambin (1976) report negatively, showing that advertising levels are unrelated to market share *in*stability. Buzzell and Nourse (1967), and Porter (1978) also found negatively, showing that high advertising levels were linked with a *greater* number of new production introductions.

On the relationship between advertising and the price elasticity of demand, Albion and Farris (1981) report a positive relationship between these two in a cross-section of brands. Comanor and Wilson (1974) estimated long-run elasticities for 33 industries, 28 of which had the correct sign. These 28 yielded a rank correlation of +0.44 between the calculated elasticity and the advertising-to-sales ratio. In a similar analysis using a sample of European industries, Lambin (1976) reported an insignificant negative correlation (using advertising expenditures, and not the advertising-to-sales ratio).

On the relationship between advertising and concentration, in an early series of studies Telser (1964) (using Internal Revenue Service data and a linear functional form) found no relationship, Kamerschen (1972) (repeating Telser's study with a nonlinear form) found a significant relationship, and Mann et al. (1967) (using SIC four-digit industry data) found a significant relationship. Miller (1972) and Brush (1978) obtained results similar to those of Mann et al. In contrast, Ornstein (1976, 1977) and Demsetz (1974, 1979) have argued that on average, firms attain greater price–cost margins because of superior efficiency (lower cost production and distribution). There are two implications of this efficiency: (a) through the Dorfman–Steiner relationship (13.35c) it implies a greater advertising intensity, and (b) as the superiority should lead to larger firms, industry concentration will increase. In short, Ornstein and Demsetz argue that any correlation between advertising and concentration is jointly determined and should be interpreted as evidence of competition among firms, some of which are superior (have lower unit cost for products of given quality). The correlation, they stress, is not evidence of an anticompetitive causal link from advertising to concentration. Ornstein further argues that the efficiency view is supported by the fact that the concentration–advertising correlation is comparable across consumer and producer goods industries.

On advertising and profitability, Weiss (1969) and Comanor and Wilson (1967, 1974) are the first major studies reporting a statistically important relationship. Using profits after taxes as a percentage of stockholder's equity, Comanor and Wilson found a consistently significant relationship with advertising expenditures to sales in 41 industries. Weiss, and later Bloch (1974) point out that the correct measure of advertising is the accumulated stock arising from prior advertising as well as current expenditure, with due consideration given to depreciation. (In addition, this requires an adjustment to profits by adding back expenditures.) Bloch (1974), Ayanian (1975), and Demsetz (1979) find no relationship between profit rates and advertising intensity after such a correction. Siegfried and Weiss (1974), using a much higher depreciation rate for advertising than these three studies, still find a significant profitability–advertising intensity correlation.

Finally, it should be noted that nearly all the above studies and results have been disputed in one way or another with respect to the model specification, representativeness of data, econometric technique, interpretation of results, etc. Ornstein (1987) and Clarke (1985) provide comprehensive reviews.

14 Signals, Brand Name, and Quality

When pre-purchase quality determination costs are high, incentives generally exist for sellers to use advertising to transmit false or misleading information and, in turn, palm off low-quality products at high-quality prices. More generally, sellers can be expected to advertise in such a way that at the margin the returns from misinformation are just equal to the returns from information. Advertising that has half-truths and fails to note unfavorable aspects of a product and terms of sale is thus not unexpected.[1] While this possibility for deceptive advertising was dismissed in chapter 13, it is now the center of attention.

Several market practices are commonly thought to minimize the likelihood of such moral hazard. The first is based on formal product guarantees which are enforceable at law. As such guarantees are not generally used, we ask about the conditions under which they can and cannot reliably act to assure quality. A second market practice involves a variety of informal (or implicit) guarantees related to the firm's price and its stock of firm-specific assets. The excess of price over cost and the firm's nonmarketable assets can act as quality assurance bonds to be forfeited by the firm with misrepresentations of quality. In this regard, it is of note that the capital value of advertising expenditures, generally called *brand name*, is firm specific and nonsalvageable with palming off. With this second solution we ask about the levels of price and brand name which can assure product quality. A final market practice is based on the notion that consumers learn about a seller's inclinations to provide low quality by observing past market behavior. Firms, knowing that consumers learn in this way, then signal their type by their time sequence of quality supply decisions. Whether they signal their type correctly or falsely depends in part on the way in which consumers form expectations and in part on the conditions of demand and cost.

---

[1] It is frequently noted that the advertisements for over-the-counter pain relievers are ambiguous and misleading. See, for example, testimony in hearings before the Subcommittee on Monopoly, Select Committee on Small Business, US Senate: *Advertising of Proprietary Medicines* (1971). Similarly, and in the same source, it is noted that there is no evidence that other over-the-counter medicines have any effectiveness as sleep aids and sedatives even though they are advertised for that purpose.

An understanding of the market solutions to costly information and the associated moral hazard depends on clearly distinguishing pre-purchase quality determination costs (**pre-costs**) and post-purchase quality determination costs (**post-costs**). For example, with high pre-costs and low post-costs the period of time during which advertising misinformation may provide profitable opportunities is very short. Higher post-costs will, other things being equal, lengthen that period and heighten the deception problem. Using the terminology of Nelson (1970), it is now common to refer to **search** goods, where qualities are typically determined by inspection (low pre-costs), and **experience** goods, whose qualities are typically determined only after purchase and use (high pre-costs, low post-costs).

A substantial amount of attention has been given to market situations with experience goods. von Weizsacker (1980a, b), Klein and Leffler (1981), Shapiro (1982), Dybvig and Spatt (1983), and Milgrom and Roberts (1986) have examined models where pre-costs are high but consumers can determine product quality accurately after purchase *and* each consumer is informed of every other's evaluation (with a very short lag). The result of these conditions is that firms generally find it unprofitable to misrepresent the quality of their products in the long run. Models of this kind are analyzed in sections 14.2–14.4.

For many varieties of goods consumers are frequently not able to accurately evaluate quality after purchase. Such high post-cost situations frequently occur with products used in conjunction with others and it is difficult to separate their contribution in the measured output. In addition, post-cost will be high when the quality of the product, or expert professional service (legal, medical, etc.), is not uniform but varies under ill-defined conditions. Not only will consumers be unable to evaluate quality exactly and at low cost after purchase in these cases, they will generally not be able to share that information with other consumers without incurring high cost. Darby and Karni (1973) define goods such as these, where both pre- and post-costs are high, as having **credence** qualities (see also Smallwood and Conlisk, 1979, Rogerson, 1983). This case is considered in section 14.5.

While our primary interest lies in the more usual informal contracts that arise to assure product quality, we first ask about the conditions under which formal quality guarantees which are enforceable by law will result in market equilibria without quality misrepresentations.

14.1   Guarantees as Signals of Quality

From a buyer's pre-purchase viewpoint, it is usual to think of product quality as a random variable. Two sources of this randomness are of particular interest. First, in any production run successive units of the product may vary in quality because of random elements in the manufacturing process. By allocating more resources to "quality control" the firm may alter the distribution of quality produced, with smaller dispersion and greater average quality requiring higher costs of control. Despite the firm's best efforts, diminishing returns will surely set in and make some residual randomness of this kind optimal. Added to this randomness is an observational uncertainty: because of rising information costs, the consumer's perception of quality will generally be based on imperfect information. Even if some product were to have precisely the same quality level in every unit produced and sold, this second source of randomness will obtain to a degree depending on such things as advertising levels, brand sampling costs, and consumer-to-consumer communication costs.

Whatever the source of randomness, can a seller's guarantee of compensation should its product quality actually fall below specified level reduce the buyer's perception of an adverse trial?

14.1.1 Competitive Equilibrium with Guarantees

Consider $j = 1, 2, \ldots, J$ identical competitive firms producing a homogeneous product. To avoid side issues, suppose that the product can have only one of two quality states, say 1 or 0. Suppose further that, using adjustments in the manufacturing process, each firm can (continuously) control the probability h with which it produces quality 1. These adjustments are not without cost and we let $c(h)$ represent the (constant) unit cost of the firm's output when a technology which yields probability h is adopted. Let 1 indicate the higher level of quality, which makes it natural to require that $dc(h)/dh > 0$.

On the demand side, consumers are assumed to differ in a way that can be reflected by a single parameter θ. When some consumer purchases a product with quality 1 his elementary utility is written $u_1(y - p; \theta)$, where y is *ex ante* income and p is the purchase price of the product. Similarly, $u_0(y - p; \theta)$ is the utility derived from a product of quality 0. For each θ and any *ex post* income $\hat{y}$, $u_1(\hat{y}; \theta) > u_0(\hat{y}; \theta)$ as an implication of high quality.

There is, under the usual conditions, a level of income compensation that sellers could use to offset the quality difference. We suppose that this takes the form of a refund guarantee r payable to the consumer if a product of quality 0 is received. After purchase the quality is assumed to be observable at zero cost to a disinterested third party, and one way or another the guarantee is assumed to be enforced by this third party at zero cost. For this case, a consumer of type θ has (pre-purchase) expected utility

$$EU(\theta) = h^e u_1(y - p; \theta) + (1 - h^e)u_0(y - p + r; \theta) \qquad (14.1)$$

where h^e is the probability assessed by the consumer that quality 1 will occur. While h^e will generally be a function of the *actual* probability h, it is instructive for the moment to hold that dependence aside. In addition, note that it is assumed that probability beliefs are homogeneous in the cross-section of consumer types, that is h^e applies to all individuals.

E14.1 ━━

Third-party Product Guarantees

Suppose that sellers do not offer refund guarantees, but instead consumers purchase an insurance policy from an independent third party which pays v dollars in the event that a low-quality product is found after purchase. The premium to be paid for such a policy will be denoted by αv, where $\alpha > 0$ is called the coverage rate. How much coverage will the consumer purchase?[2]

Consider some specific individual such that $u_0(x) = u_1(x - l)$, that is, the low-quality product imposes a loss of l dollars in income to the individual. In this case expected utility has the simplified form

$$\bar{u} = h^e u(y - \alpha v) + (1 - h^e)u(y - l - \alpha v + v)$$

where the subscript to the utility function is dropped for convenience. The stationarity condition for maximum $\bar{u}$ is

$$\frac{u'(y - l + (1 - \alpha)v)}{u'(y - \alpha v)} = \frac{h^e}{1 - \alpha h^e} \frac{\alpha}{1 - \alpha}$$

If the consumer receives a low-quality product the insurance company nets $\alpha v - v$ dollars; otherwise it captures the entire premium αv. For this example, we will assume that $h^e = h$; the actual and expected probabilities of obtaining a high-quality product are equal. Suppose further that insurance is supplied competitively, with free entry and zero profits to insurers. Zero expected profits require

$$-(1 - \alpha)v(1 - h^e) + h^e \alpha v = 0$$

or

$$(1 - \alpha)(1 - h^e) = \alpha h^e$$

Insurance is supplied with **actuarially fair** premiums when the costs of the policies offered just equal their expected value.

For the case where premiums are actuarially fair, the stationarity conditions for $\bar{u}$ are

$$u'(y - l + (1 - \alpha)v^0) = u'(y - \alpha v^0)$$

where v^0 is the optimal premium. When the consumer is strictly risk averse then $u''(\cdot) < 0$ and therefore

$$y - l + (1 - \alpha)v^0 = y - \alpha v^0$$

which solves for

$$v^0 = l$$

That is, under the conditions imposed, consumers will *completely* insure themselves against the loss arising from low product quality. Compare this with the general insurance result developed earlier in SE7.2.

Market Equilibrium and Socially Optimal Guarantees. As questions of product variety are not of immediate concern, it is convenient to assume that consumers are identical. Then, θ has the same value in the cross-section, and an *aggregate* expected utility function (14.1) can be written simply as

---

[2] This section generally follows Spence (1973) and Stiglitz (1983).

$$\bar{U} = h^e u_1(y - p) + (1 - h^e)u_0(y - p + r) \tag{14.2}$$

At a long-run free-entry competitive equilibrium (identical) sellers choose a (quality) probability level h and a level of guarantee which together maximizes $\bar{U}$ subject to the zero-expected-profit constraint. This constraint requires that the equilibrium price is equal to the unit production cost plus the expected refund per unit, or

$$p = c(h) + (1 - h)r \tag{14.3}$$

Substituting this in (14.2) gives

$$\bar{U}^0 = h^e u_1(y - c(h) - (1 - h)r) + (1 - h)u_0(y - c(h) - (1 - h)r + r) \tag{14.4}$$

which is a function of h^e, h, and r. Firms choose h and r; h^e is assumed to be exogenously given and fixed. In turn, the stationarity of $\bar{U}^0$ with respect to h and r, conditional on given expectations h^e, yields the market equilibrium values h^0 and r^0.

Now let h^e be endogenous. There are many possibilities for the manner in which consumers arrive at these probabilities. In the *ideal* case, which we consider for the moment, consumers costlessly observe the quality control probability, making $h^e = h$ and giving the expected utility

$$\bar{U}^* = h u_1(y - c(h) - (1 - h)r) + (1 - h)u_0(y - c(h) - (1 - h)r + \text{r}) \tag{14.5}$$

(Not only is $\bar{U}^*$ the expected utility with zero cost and complete information, it can also be thought of as the *ex post* utility received on average.)

Following Spence (1973), take $\bar{U}^*$ as the welfare standard,[3] and compare the market equilibrium solution for h and r from the stationarity of $\bar{U}^0$ with the ideal solution based on the stationarity of $\bar{U}^*$. Consumer expectations h^e generally differ from the equilibrium probability as a reflection of costly and incomplete market information. The difference suggests that the equilibrium probability will not be welfare optimal. Whether or not the refund compensation can be adjusted in a way to offset the utility lost with the lack of information remains as the question.

Optimal Insurance. An interior *welfare* optimum satisfies both optimal insurance and optimal quality conditions based on $\bar{U}^*$:

$$u_1'(y^*) = u_0'(y^* + r^*) \tag{14.6a}$$

$$c'(h^*) = r^* + \frac{u_1(y^*) - u_0(y^* + r^*)}{h^* u_1'(y^*) - (1 - h^*)u_0'(y^* + r^*)} \tag{14.6b}$$

where $y^* = y - c(h^*) - (1 - h^*)r^*$, the primes indicate partial derivatives, and

---

[3] The welfare optimum is thus an "ideal" in the sense that it ignores the real costs of information. When we compare the market equilibrium solution with the welfare optimum we are therefore not comparing things which are both possible, but only one concrete possibility with an (unrealizable) ideal. See Demsetz (1972) for critical comments on this method.

the two equations are the stationarity conditions with respect to r and h respectively. Again, $\bar{U}^*$ is the zero-information-cost utility with $h^e = h$. The first condition (14.6a) is the usual requirement that the optimal refund (compensation) is such that it equalizes the marginal utility of income over all contingencies. The second-order condition (14.6b) requires that, at the margin, the costs of producing h just equal its expected utility to consumers.

Equilibrium Solution. In contrast, the competitive equilibrium occurs where $\bar{U}^0$ is maximized. If we let the consumers' expected probabilities depend on the actual probabilities chosen by the firms, we write $h^e(h^0)$; the stationarity conditions of $\bar{U}^0$ with respect to r and h, respectively, are

$$u_1'(y^0) = u_0'(y^0 + r^0) \frac{(1 - h^0)h^e(h^0)}{h^0\{1 - h^e(h^0)\}} \tag{14.7a}$$

$$c'(h^0) = r^0 + \frac{u_1(y^0) - u_0(y^0 + r^0)}{h^e(h^0)u_1'(y^0) + \{1 - h^e(h^0)\}u_0'(y^0 + r^0)} \frac{\partial h^e(h^0)}{\partial h} \tag{14.7b}$$

where superscript zero indicates solution values for h and r and $y^0 = y - c(h^0) - (1 - h^0)r^0$. Comparing (14.6b) and (14.7b) we quickly see that, given r^0, the equilibrium probability h^0 is suboptimal unless $h^e(h^0) = h^0$.

E14.2 ───

Product Guarantees with Risk Neutrality

Suppose that the elementary utilities are (linear) risk-neutral:

$$u_1(x) = x \tag{14.8a}$$

$$u_0(x) = x + \mu \tag{14.8b}$$

where μ is the income which just compensates the individual who receives a product of quality 0 rather than 1. In this case, the consumer's expected utility (at the price giving zero expected profit) simplifies to

$$\bar{U}^0 = y - c(h) - (1 - h)r + (1 - h^e)(r - \mu)$$

$$= y - c(h) - r(h^e - h) - (1 - h^e)\mu \tag{14.9}$$

and, with zero-cost information so that $h^e = h$,

$$\bar{U}^* = y - c(h) - (1 - h)\mu \tag{14.10}$$

Two things are of note in these utilities. First, r enters linearly in $\bar{U}^0$ so that the stationarity condition (14.6a) is inapplicable. Second, r does not enter into $\bar{U}^*$ at all and therefore is irrelevant to the welfare maximum.

At the competitive equilibrium (14.6b) still obtains and takes the special form

$$\frac{\partial c(h^0)}{\partial h} = \mu \frac{\partial h^e(h^0)}{\partial h} + r^0 \left\{ 1 - \frac{\partial h^e(h^0)}{\partial h} \right\} \tag{14.11}$$

When consumers over-estimate good quality ($h^e > h$) then, by inspection of

(14.9), $r^0 = 0$ will result.[4] In this case we have

$$\frac{\partial c(h^0)}{\partial h} = \mu \frac{\partial h^c(h^0)}{\partial h} \tag{14.12}$$

In contrast, $\bar{U}^*$ has a maximum with respect to h when

$$\frac{\partial c(h^0)}{\partial h} = \mu \tag{14.13}$$

When $h^c > h$ and r^0 is zero, this condition for optimality differs from the equilibrium condition (14.11) by the presence of $\partial h^c(h^0)/\partial h$. If $\partial h^c(h^0)/\partial h < 1$ then $h^0 < h^*$ (assuming that $\partial^2 c(h)/\partial h^2 > 0$), and conversely.

Perhaps the most disturbing aspect of the simple model that has been constructed to this point is the exogeneity of consumer expectations. Notwithstanding the fact that the difference between perceptions of quality and that actually supplied by the firm is critical to the results, we have not addressed the manner in which consumers form their expectation. That, however, is an issue on which several useful notes can be made.

14.1.2 Signaling Equilibrium with Guarantees

At the time of purchase, suppose that consumers know both the product's price and the guaranteed refund if they should receive low quality. They do not, however, observe product quality, but instead base their demand on probability estimates of that quality. In this regard, the question that immediately comes to mind is whether consumers can accurately infer quality from the market observable price and guarantee.[5] If p and r are systematically related to h in an equilibrium of the kind developed above, then a sequence of (temporary information conditional) equilibria, over which consumers discover that relationship, might lead to a (final) equilibrium with consumers being well informed. Specifically, our intent here is to show that the refund guarantee level r can act as a **signal** from which consumers can correctly infer quality (pre-purchase). It will be apparent from the development that r serves in this signaling role because guarantees are costly and, more exactly, these costs are inversely related to the level of the quality parameter h chosen by any firm.[6] For reasons which will be clear as the end of this analysis is reached, price will not be useful as a signal of quality.

---

[4] When $h^c < 0$ the solution for r is unbounded from above and the problem is ill formed. Part of the difficulty arises from the fact that h^c is not a function of the guarantee. Since large refunds for low quality would not be used by firms unless they consistently supplied high quality, we would expect consumers to use the level of r as an indicator of high h and accordingly adjust h^c. This is discussed further in section 14.2.

[5] We assume here that quality can be costlessly demonstrated to a disinterested third party judge and guarantees can be enforced costlessly.

[6] The original analyses of such signaling equilibria are by Arrow (1973), Spence (1973), and Riley (1979); see also section 14.4.

The Model. To make the analysis somewhat more realistic, suppose that firms generally differ in the level of quality (measured by h) that they choose for their products. In addition, assume now that consumers base their estimates of quality on the firm's refund guarantee, believing that a product with guarantee r has a probability $h^s(r)$ of high quality. (The superscript s indicates the signaling case.) A consumer of type θ then has expected utility

$$\bar{U}(\theta) = h^s(r)u_1(y - p; \theta) + \{1 - h^s(r)\}u_0(y - p + r; \theta) \qquad (14.14)$$

when choosing a product offering the pair (p, r).

In the absence of fixed costs firms will spring up to satisfy every demand for variety, so that consumers of every θ type will have a product tailored to their specific taste. At a free-entry competitive equilibrium in which firms supply every θ type, the expected utility (14.14) will be maximized subject to zero expected profits. Substituting the zero-profit condition (14.13), this results in

$$\bar{U}(\theta) = h^s(r)u_1(y - c(h) - (1 - h)r; \theta)$$
$$+ (1 - h^s(r))u_0(y - c(h) - (1 - h)r + r; \theta) \qquad (14.15)$$

as the unconstrained criterion. The probability h^0 and guarantee r^0 are chosen to maximize this expression, with the price p then following to give zero expected profits. At this equilibrium, suppose that $h^s(r) \neq h^0$; that is, the consumers' quality expectations based on the guarantee differ from the equilibrium quality. This information conditional equilibrium would be temporary since we expect that, not having their expectations confirmed, consumers would revise their estimates.

Signals. What basis for revision might be used? The stationarity conditions of (14.15) with respect to h and r are helpful in this regard. These are

$$\{h^s u_1'(\cdot; \theta) + (1 - h^s)u_0'(\cdot; \theta)\}\{c'(h^0) - r^0\} = 0 \qquad (14.16a)$$

and

$$\frac{\partial h^s}{\partial r}\{u_1(\cdot; \theta) - u_0(\cdot; \theta)\} + (1 - h^s)h^0 u_0'(\cdot; \theta) - (1 - h^0)h^s u_1'(\cdot; \theta) = 0 \qquad (14.16b)$$

respectively. Equation (14.16a) is critical. Since the first of the two multiplicative terms in this equation is generally nonzero, $c'(h^0) = r^0$ is required for stationarity; let $h^0 = g(r^0)$ be the associated inverse. If we assume that $c'(h) > 0$ and $c''(h) > 0$, then g is a function establishing a one-to-one relationship between r^0 and h^0, and r^0 will be a **signal** of the unobserved h^0 in the sense that greater guarantee levels of r will signal greater quality h.[7] If we further assume that consumers detect and learn this relationship over time, then the expectation function $h^s(r)$ will converge to $g(r)$. On this presumption we can make the $h^0 = g(r^0)$ substitution in (14.16) to give the stationarity conditions of a **signaling equilibrium**:

$$u_1'(y^s; \theta) = u_0'(y^s + r^s; \theta) + \frac{(\partial h^s/\partial h)\{u_1(y^s; \theta) - u_0(y^s + r^s; \theta)\}}{h^s(1 - h^s)} \qquad (14.17a)$$

$$c'(h^s) = r^s \qquad (14.17b)$$

---

[7] For emphasis, it is the properties of h's *cost* $c(h)$ which allows r to signal h.

Compare these equations with the corresponding conditions for socially optimal guarantees and quality in (14.6). Despite the fact that consumers are fully informed at the signaling equilibrium, the optimality conditions are, nonetheless, generally not met. The source of the suboptimality is the requirement that $c'(h^s) = r^s$ at the signaling equilibrium, which contrasts with the somewhat more complex relationship (14.6b) between marginal cost and the guarantee level at the optimum.

An inspection of the equilibrium and optimality conditions, however, does reveal one interesting set of circumstances where the two conditions simplify and become identical. Suppose that the difference between the consumer valuation of high and low quality can be measured in income terms. Specifically, let μ measure this income indifference so that

$$u_1(x) = u_0(x + \mu)$$

In this case, the optimality condition $u_1'(y^*) = u_0'(y^* + r^*)$ implies $r^* = \mu$; that is, optimality is obtained when the refund guarantee exactly restores each consumer's loss from a low-quality purchase. In turn, it is straightforward to verify that the optimally conditions (14.6) are identical with the signaling equilibrium conditions (14.17).

Signaling Equilibrium. Several aspects of the signaling equilibrium are of special note. First, that the equilibrium is reached at all is predicated on the fact that consumers learn the relationship $r = c'(h)$. The wide variety of consumers and the fact that this cost *function* is identical in the cross-section of firms means that at any temporary (incomplete information) equilibrium there are many (r^0, h^0) pairs, one for each distinct θ type, available as a basis for estimating c'. Thus the ease with which these data points can be collected across markets, and the details of the individual's learning process, will be important in determining the speed with which, and the likelihood that, the temporary equilibria approach the final signaling equilibria.

Price as a Signal? Finally, it is of particular interest to indicate why it is that the guarantee r can be a signal of quality, yet price, which in the cross-section of products is also positively related to quality in each equilibrium, cannot be a signal. Suppose that the consumers' expectation of h increases with price p. This would provide *every* seller with an incentive to raise p to signal greater h, for there is no cost in doing so. As price is increased regardless of quality, p and h will in fact not be correlated in equilibrium and the consumers' expectations will not be confirmed. For this reason price fails to be a signal of h.

E14.3 ──

Properties of Product Warranties

Product warranties promise some form of payment from the issuer contingent on the quality-related performance of the covered product. Priest (1981) observes that warranties are pervasive, perhaps the most common form of written contract in developed economies. He also notes several empirical facts about the use of warranties.

1 They are generally issued by the product manufacturer and distributor and not by a third-party insurer.
2 They generally provide incomplete insurance.
3 The level of warranty insurance is generally unrelated to the actual quality (performance level) of the product.

An explanation of facts 1 and 2 is offered in chapter 7, SE7.2, and in E14.1 using insurance preferences based on risk aversion and attempts by sellers to extract surplus by self-selection methods. These analyses do not explain 3. Moreover, arguing that warranties are product quality signals implies a positive relationship between the level of warranty and product quality which, while true in some situations, is also inconsistent with the general observation 3.

As an explanation of 3, Oi (1967), Kambhu (1982), and Cooper and Ross (1985) developed a theory of warranties based on two types of incentive problem. First, in most cases buyer behavior can influence the performance of a product and, when it is not economic for sellers to demonstrate to a disinterested third party that due care is taken by the buyer, a significant likelihood of moral hazard is created by warranties. Second, when buyers have high pre-costs, the incentives for sellers to maintain high quality are affected by the warranty. Cooper and Ross specifically show that this "double" moral hazard and the possibility that due care by the buyer and product quality can be either substitutes or complements in the determination of the probability that the product will perform as warranted provide an explanation for 3.

14.2   Inferring Quality from Market Price

Economists generally think of competition as a "mechanism" for allocating resources. In this, it is usual to let prices play the lead part and transmit the information about the underlying value of the commodities and services involved. The ability of prices to play this role is based on the attempt by buyers and sellers to act on the basis of the information content of the prices. Competition among those who would buy some commodity, because their research indicates that the commodity has higher quality than is generally perceived, drives up its price. In turn, this information on quality is transmitted by the price system to those who would trade in the commodity but do not have direct access to the research information.

To see more particularly how this process works, we follow Grossman and Stiglitz (1976) and suppose that the equilibrium value of a competitive industry's output depends in part on two information sources: a (possibly) random quality variable ξ and an unobservable random variable ε. Suppose further that each consumer's valuation of the commodity in question depends on the linear combination $\xi + \varepsilon$. In turn, the equilibrium price is random: $\hat{p} = p(z; \xi + \varepsilon)$, where z is some aggregate quantity supplied. Alternatively, the associated demand is random at any given price $z = z(p; \xi + \varepsilon)$. The *ex ante* quantity demanded from competitive sellers will depend on the price and, in turn, on the observed value of ξ.

For the moment let $\varepsilon \equiv 0$, so that there is only one information source. Think now of two consumer types: *informed* consumers, who make up a fraction α of the market, observe quality, while the remaining $1 - \alpha$ *uninformed* fraction do not observe quality. The parameter α is common knowledge. Presumably there is a cost in making the observation, and uninformed consumers choose to avoid it. Let $z(p, \xi)$ indicate the demand of the informed consumers, with $z(p, 0)$ similarly associated with the uninformed. In market equilibrium $\alpha z(p, \xi) + (1 - \alpha)z(p, 0) = z^*$, where z^* is the total supply of the commodity. From this expression it is apparent that different levels of ξ will generally produce different equilibrium prices. If the equilibrium p to ξ relationship is one to one, the uninformed consumers can be expected, after some period of time, to discover this link and the market price will convey all available information.

In the above analysis it is assumed that an equilibrium exists under the circumstances described. That need not be the case. If, at the onset, there are no informed consumers ($\alpha = 0$) and information observation costs are not prohibitive, some fraction of the consuming population will choose to make the observation. In this case, $\alpha = 0$ cannot be an equilibrium value. However, as long as there are some informed consumers, market prices will convey the information ξ. That fact is problematic, however, for no consumer will have an incentive to incur the cost of acquiring ξ if he can (with zero cost of waiting for a temporary equilibrium) then costlessly infer it from market price. An equilibrium value for α does not exist for this simple situation.

Several ways have been suggested to make the above situation more realistic and, at the same time, avoid the problem of nonexistence. We might, for example, suppose it to be costly to infer quality from price (an "inversion" cost). As an indirect way of incorporating this cost, let us reformulate the model in such a way that market price conveys the quality information only imperfectly, with noise ($\varepsilon \neq 0$). In turn, let the aggregate supply at any p and ξ be a random variable, which we indicate by $\hat{z}$. The randomness arises from ε. Then, the equilibrium price depends both on the specific realization of $\hat{z}$ that obtains and on ξ. In this case, the uninformed consumer cannot infer complete information on quality from price, for price is jointly determined: large values of p might arise because of large values of ξ, or because the value taken on by $\hat{z}$ is small, for example. If it is assumed that the price function can be inverted costlessly, the best that uninformed consumers can do in this case is to know ξ only conditional on values of $\hat{z}$.

To follow this case somewhat further, assume that uninformed consumers do in fact form probability estimates of $\hat{z}$ and that in turn they determine a probability distribution on the quality value $\xi(p, \hat{z}) + \varepsilon$ of the good. From this, each uninformed consumer can determine his *expected* utility of various purchase amounts and finally calculate his demand $z(p, 0; \hat{z})$. Informed consumers observe p and ξ, and continue to have demand $z(p, \xi; \hat{z})$. Thus for each realization of $\hat{z}$ there will be a market price p^0 derived from the clearing condition

$$hz(p^0, 0; \hat{z}) + (1 - h)z(p^0, \xi; \hat{z}) = z \qquad (14.18)$$

where z on the right-hand side is the realization of $\hat{z}$. Assuming that uninformed consumers form rational expectations also requires

$$p^0 = p(\xi, \bar{z}) \tag{14.19}$$

where $\bar{z}$ is the expectation of $\hat{z}$.

Given the cost to each consumer of observing quality, at market equilibrium each will be just indifferent to being informed or not. If there were no informed consumers, p^0 will convey no information and it will generally be worthwhile for some individuals to incur the expense associated with observing ξ. At the other extreme, if all consumers were informed, p^0 will convey much about ξ and it will generally pay some individuals no longer to purchase quality information, but instead to infer it from the market price. As some consumer switches from purchasing to not purchasing information, the market price becomes a little more noisy (less informative) and this reduces the incentive for others to switch. A **noisy equilibrium** is such that it will not be profitable for any consumer to drop from the informed to the uninformed group, and conversely.

E14.4

Noisy Equilibria with Security Analysis

When information is costly, equilibrium prices will be noisy in the sense that they do not fully reflect available information. If they did, those who acquired the information would not receive adequate compensation. The costly information noisy price equilibrium thus leaves a market role for those who are skilled in information technologies. That is the beginning point for Cornell and Roll (1981), who develop a mixed strategy equilibrium in which information on securities is sold and used by some traders while others choose their securities randomly.

The Cornell–Roll analysis is based on the following static payoff matrix of table 14.1. There are two traders, 1 and 2, who can either use a security analyst's portfolio recommendation or choose a portfolio randomly. (In the payoff matrix one trader plays rows and its rival plays columns. The listed payoffs are for the row player.) The normal rate of return (gross) from a security portfolio is $r > 0$ and the basic transaction cost (in rate of return) is $c_0 > 0$. These rates obtain when both (all) traders select their portfolio randomly and incur no particular information-acquisition costs. When a trader uses the analyst's portfolio selection he incurs the information cost $c > 0$. When just one trader uses the analyst's information, he has a competitive advantage and receives above-normal returns $ar > r$ while his uninformed counterpart receives below-normal returns $r/a < r$ – that is, $a > 1$. Is the cost of information c sufficiently low to allow security analysis to be a viable service?

If risk-neutral traders are assumed, a mixed strategy equilibrium requires

$$h(r - c - c_0) + (1 - h)(ar - c - c_0) = h\left(\frac{r}{a} - c_0\right) + (1 - h)(r - c_0) \tag{14.20}$$

Table 14.1 Investment Strategy Payoffs

	Analyst	*Random*
Analyst	$r - (c + c_0)$	$ar - (c + c_0)$
Random	$r/a - c_0$	$r - c_0$

where h is the probability that analysis will be used. Solving for that mixing probability gives

$$h = \frac{r(1 - a) + c}{r(2 - a - 1/a)} \tag{14.21}$$

If h is zero, then there will be no analysis and the market price will contain no relevant information. Alternatively, if analysis is used by every trader, each would be incurring that cost without gaining any advantage. For *both* informed and uninformed traders to exist in equilibrium the mixing probability must satisfy $0 < h < 1$, which means that the relationship between gross returns, advantage, and information cost must be such that[8]

$$r(a - 1) > c > r\left(1 - \frac{1}{a}\right) \tag{14.22}$$

The equilibrium also requires that both sides of equality (14.20) are zero, or that

$$a = \frac{c}{c_0} - 1 \tag{14.23}$$

$$h = \frac{(r - c_0)(c + c_0)}{rc} \tag{14.24}$$

The level of information technology determines the costs of security analysis, and the competition among analysts and among traders will drive down the price of analysis to the zero profit and trading gain equilibrium. In the mixed strategy equilibrium the informed individuals using security analysts will outperform those who choose securities randomly in *gross* returns. However, on average the *net* returns to all individuals will be equal. This result is consistent with the empirical evidence of Fama (1970, 1976).

14.3 Experience Goods: A Reputation For Quality

If the quality of any product could be costlessly determined prior to purchase, the firm's choice of product quality at any date would have no implication for its choice at any later date. At each moment, the firm would simply choose the level of quality which maximizes its value, myopically, and it would do this without any attempt to build reputation or misrepresent its product's quality.

A problem of moral hazard arises when the costs of pre-purchase quality

---

[8] The denominator in (14.21) is negative. Thus the numerator must also be negative *and* greater than the denominator for $0 < h < 1$. These last two conditions yield the inequalities in (14.22).

determination are not trivial. In this case an opportunistic firm may attempt to palm off low quality (produced at low cost) as high quality (sold at a high price). Relative to a full information equilibrium for the industry, the value of such a firm is maximized by reducing quality, as this lowers production costs without foregoing the high-quality price. When there is not a period-to-period link in quality decisions (no firm reputation for producing high or low quality), it will be optimal for the firm to palm off at every market date. If consumers cannot determine the quality of products, every firm will have the same incentive to deceive consumers in this fashion. The usual lemons equilibrium (recall chapter 13, section 13.1) will occur when further unilateral degradation of quality is unprofitable for any firm, perhaps because it becomes less costly to determine very low quality prior to purchase or because quality degradation itself becomes more costly.

14.3.1   Reputation and Brand Name: Complementary Roles in Quality Assurance

Klein and Leffler (1981) develop a theory of reputation and brand name capital in competitive markets which circumvents the moral hazard associated with unobserved quality (see also Shapiro, 1982, 1983; Cooper and Ross, 1983, 1984). In their analysis firms that palm off low-quality goods at high prices immediately, and universally, become known as opportunistic and are thereafter unable to sell any of their wares. Assuming that consumers know the cost functions of firms, they could, given the prices charged, place themselves in the firm's position and calculate the relative value of (a) the long-lived income stream associated with producing high quality and maintaining a good reputation, and (b) the windfall to palming off. If such calculations are made, it is easy to derive sufficient conditions for a premium price, higher than the competitive price of high quality, which would motivate production of the high-quality good *and* not completely dissipate the consumers' surplus from the purchase of high quality.

The existence of this premium price means that firms selling high quality will earn positive profits. This, however, is inconsistent with free entry at equilibrium. Klein and Leffler's solution to this inconsistency is particularly interesting:

> . . . Competition to dissipate the economic profits being earned by existing firms must therefore occur in nonprice dimensions. However, the zero profit equilibrium is consistent with only a very particular form of profit absorbing nonprice competition. The competition involves firm-specific capital expenditures. This firm-specific capital competition motivates each firm to purchase assets with (nonsalvageable) costs equal to the capital value of the premium rental stream earned when high quality is supplied at the quality assuring price. That is, . . . the investment leading to zero profits must be highly firm specific and depreciate to zero if the firm cheats and supplies [low quality]. Such firm specific capital costs could, for example, take the form of sunk investments in the design of a firm logo or an expensive sign promoting the firm's name. . . . The competition process also forces the firm-specific capital investments (brand name) to take the form of assets which provide the greatest direct service value to consumers. (Klein and Leffler, 1981, p. 622)

Brand name investments would not be made if pre-costs were zero and product quality was perfectly observable. Thus, although the brand name investments have value to consumers, the important aspect of their existence is that, ignoring any information role, that value is less than the investment cost of the assets involved (otherwise they would have been undertaken by the competitive firms and included in any equilibrium under full quality information).

The value of the quasi-rent received by a firm, when it palms off, is reduced by the forfeiture of the brand-specific investment. This means that firms holding assets which are specific to their enterprise (that is, have low value to other users) have high costs of palming off. Competition in price among such firms then lowers the price premium required to guarantee quality.

Brand name capital is such that the firm anticipates a normal investment return with repeat sales to its customers, but less than normal if it palms off and loses its trade. Investments that are known by customers to be nonsalvageable in this way thus assume the role of a forfeitable bond and, along with any forfeitable price premia stream, act as an implicit guarantee of quality. In the presence of such brand name capital and price premia, consumers will not need to incur their own search and quality determination costs. Rather, they simply observe whether the necessary brand name and price premia have been established.[9]

E14.5

Advertising Capital as Brand Name

A brand name can be created by investments of many kinds. Advertising that does not provide specific product or price information (and therefore does not improve demand or costs), nonmarketable information from research and development, tangible firm-specific assets, and organizational capital come immediately to mind.

One key implication of the above analysis is that competitive investments need not be limited to assets which give consumers utility service with a present value greater than the salvage value of the assets. There are a variety of examples: luxurious store fronts and furnishings and ornate signs may be used by firms even when yielding only small "direct" consumer service flows. These assets instead inform customers of the size of sunk capital costs and, in turn, the opportunity costs if the firm palms off on quality. Both informational services and the "direct" utility-producing services are in this way relevant considerations to the firm in deciding upon the best form of its brand name capital investments.

---

[9] With experience goods, those with high pre-costs and low post-cost, buyers know the quality of each good previously bought from extant firms, but they will not know the quality of goods offered by entrants. Schmalensee (1982b) has noted that the buyers' aversion to risk (about quality) can make entry difficult and enable incumbents to sustain high profits without inducing entry. He analyzes this possibility, but his model has the characteristic that buyers systematically misjudge quality. Farrell (1986b) focuses on the incentives that new entrants have to cheat by providing goods of low quality while representing them otherwise. Since entrants do not have brand name capital, there is what he calls a moral hazard barrier to new entry. For further details see SE14.2.

Advertising is a particularly conspicuous firm-specific sunk cost. Not only does it reduce the gains from palming off and permit consumers to use a lower price premium as quality assurance, consumers know that such investments can be profitable only if the firm's quasi-rent stream includes a price premium sufficient to prevent cheating. So-called *noninformative advertising* (the "Marlboro man" for example) can be understood in this way. In addition to providing basic information that the product exists, such advertising informs the consumer that the firm has a large sunk cost. That highly paid celebrities endorse a product is also evidence that the firm has made large investments. Since the crucial variable is the consumer's estimate of the firm's advertising capital *stock*, the analysis explains why firms advertise that they advertise ("as seen on the Johnny Carson Show").

14.3.2   A Reputation for Quality

In the above equilibrium the firm produces high quality because it can sell it at a high price for many periods. The equilibrium price is just high enough that the firm will not sacrifice the profits from high-quality production for a one-period windfall from palming off low quality at a high price.

Additional details can be derived from a somewhat more systematic analysis of the game situation, and it is to that which we turn in this section. The underlying analytical structure we will use is that of the *reputation model* first set out in chapter 9, section 9.6 (in an entry deterrence context). Our understanding is helped somewhat by separating the complementary quality assurance roles of price and brand name investments. Thus for the moment we hold the brand name in the background and focus on the determination of quality-assuring price premia.

Reputation Model. To begin, consider a continuum of identical price-taking firms. Suppose that the active producers have incurred a fixed cost $F > 0$. These firms can, again, produce goods of two quality levels, high (1) and low (0). It is natural to assume that $c_1(z) > c_0(z)$, that is, each firm's cost of producing every output level is strictly greater for high quality than for low. To assure certain solutions, further assume $c_1'(z) > c_0'(z) > 0$ and $c_1''(z) > c_0''(z) > 0$: the cost functions are increasing and convex, with the marginal cost of high quality being greater than that for low quality at every level of output.

Some technical complications are avoided if consumers are considered to be identical and exist as a continuum. Each such consumer has a reservation demand price v_1 for the first unit of the high-quality good. If $v_1 - p > 0$, the high-quality good will be purchased. At most one unit is purchased, as it is also assumed that the utility of the second unit is less than the individual's reservation price for every positive price. Similarly, the individual receives utility v_0 from the low-quality good and, without loss of generality, it is assumed that $v_0 = 0$ and therefore $v_0 - p < 0$ for *all* positive prices, so that consumers would not knowingly purchase low quality.

Finally, markets are assumed to be organized and operated in such a fashion that consumers observe prices and output quantities, but high pre-costs mean that they cannot directly observe product quality. Post-costs are zero, however, so that after purchase each discovers exactly the quality of the good taken. It greatly simplifies the bookkeeping to assume that each buyer's evaluation of a purchased good is immediately communicated to all other buyers. Thus, once some firm produces low quality and palms it off as high quality (at a high-quality price) it becomes, in Klein–Leffler terminology, a *notorious cheater*. Moreover, this reputation is permanent, with every buyer refusing to purchase from such an opportunistic seller ever again.

Boundary Price Schedule. Let the revenues and costs accrue one period after production decisions are made, so that a firm which palms off will have a present value based on surviving just one period and equal to

$$\pi_0 = \rho\{pz - c_0(z) - S\} > 0 \qquad (14.25)$$

Here, $\rho = 1/(1 + r)$ is the discount factor, p is the market price taken by the competitive firm, and S indicates sunk costs due to brand name investments (which we assume to be zero for the moment, but include here for later use). The costs S will be forfeited on palming off. That there is a single price p, which does not distinguish between high and low quality, is a result of the fact that (pre-purchase) consumers cannot observe quality. If, alternatively, the firm chooses to produce high quality it receives an (infinitely long) net revenue stream with present value [10]

$$\pi_1 = \frac{pz - c_1(z)}{r} \qquad (14.26)$$

What strategy should the firm pursue? That choice depends on the relative values of π_0 and π_1. If it is assumed that consumers know the high- and low-quality cost functions of the firms, and observe both p and z, they can also determine whether $\pi_0 > \pi_1$, or conversely. In this case, the firms will find high-quality production more profitable *and* consumers will know that this is the case when the market price p and the firm's output z together satisfy the inequality

$$\frac{pz - c_1(z)}{r} \geq \rho\{pz - c_0(z) - S\} \qquad (14.27)$$

or

$$p^*(z, S) \geq \frac{c_1(z) + r\{c_1(z) - c_0(z) - S\}}{z} \qquad (14.28)$$

When price and output are such that the strict inequality holds in this expression, consumers can (accurately) expect high quality from the firm. When the equality holds price and output are uninformative of quality. If the inequality does not hold then low quality can be expected. As a result $p^*(z, S)$ separates price and output pairs into low- and high-quality regions and is called the **boundary price schedule**. [11]

---

[10] We assume here that demand and cost functions are identical (stationary) for all periods, and we address only stationary strategies and equilibria.

[11] Allen (1984) terms this the "moral hazard curve."

14.3.3   Reputation Equilibria

For the moment we continue to focus on the case where brand name investments measured by sunk costs S are zero. The purchase strategy of consumers set out above is summarized as follows:

1 Consumers refuse to purchase from a cheat.
2 Consumers refuse to purchase from any firm whose price and output pair lies "below" $p^*(z, S = 0)$.
3 Consumers purchase randomly from the remaining firms with the lowest price p such that $v_1 \geq p \geq p^*(z, S = 0)$.

The price, output and quality strategy of producers must be fashioned in response to this purchasing behavior of consumers. For example, if some firm has been discovered to behave opportunistically in the past, then its optimal strategy in the present is to produce nothing. Similarly, if a firm were to choose a price p and output z such that $p < p^*(z, S = 0)$ and/or $p > v_1$ that would be unprofitable, for again it would be unable to sell anything.

Consumers believe that sellers who have not behaved opportunistically in the past will sell high quality in the present. Because consumers believe this, it is optimal for the firm not to palm off at any date and build a reputation for nonopportunistic behavior. Coming full circle, because firms act in this way the consumers' beliefs are rational. This is, once more, the *self-fulfilling expectations* aspect of a reputations equilibrium as first noted in chapter 9, section 9.6.

The Folk theorem (recall chapter 9, section 9.8) informs us that there will be many perfect equilibria for this game. These will include mixed strategies formed over the prices between c_0 and c_1 and all forms of "switching" strategies featuring abrupt shifts between quality levels. Here, the strategy space is a priori limited to pure strategies of constant (over time) quality and symmetric equilibria: low quality or high quality will be uniformly played by all firms. Of course, low quality (lemons) will be the equilibrium if the discount rate is high enough (recall chapter 9, section 9.6) or the game is of finite length. Our interest here is otherwise, with the conditions under which high quality results.

High-quality Equilibrium. To derive the equilibrium under these conditions it is sufficient to consider a single typical firm producing high quality and to take as given the price $\bar{p}$ charged by all rivals. That is, each firm can be thought to

$$\max\{pz - c_1(z)\} \tag{14.29}$$

subject to the restrictions

$$p^*(z, S = 0) < p < v_1 \qquad \text{implies } z = 0 \tag{14.30a}$$

$$p > \bar{p} \qquad \text{implies } z = 0 \tag{14.30b}$$

$$p = \bar{p} \leq v_1 \qquad \text{implies } z = \bar{z} \tag{14.30c}$$

$$p < \bar{p} \leq v_1 \qquad \text{implies } z \leq \infty \tag{14.30d}$$

where $\bar{z}$ is the total number of consumers divided by the endogenously determined number of firms (the equal market share output of the firm). At a free-entry equilibrium the price and output levels must also satisfy a zero-profit condition

$$p^e = \frac{c_1(z^e)}{z^e} \tag{14.31}$$

Thus, at equilibrium we must have

$$p^0 = \bar{p} = p^e \tag{14.32a}$$

$$z^0 = \bar{z} = z^e \tag{14.32b}$$

$$\bar{p} = p(J, \bar{z}) \tag{14.32c}$$

All firms have profit-maximizing prices and these prices must be equal; moreover, the price and optimal production of each identical firm must yield zero profits and with a fixed number of firms J the quantity $\bar{J}_z$ and price $\bar{p}$ satisfy the industry demand function.

The difference between the above equilibrium and the usual competitive equilibrium is the additional quality assurance constraint (14.30a) that $p > p^*(z, S = 0)$. Given the stationary demand and cost function and our concern with only stationary symmetric strategies, the role of that constraint and quality reputation can be illustrated graphically at each instant.

Equilibrium Without Brand Name Capital. The standard long-run average cost $AC(z)$ and marginal cost $MC(z)$ are shown in figure 14.1. We assume for the moment that the average cost schedule has a unique minimum as shown.

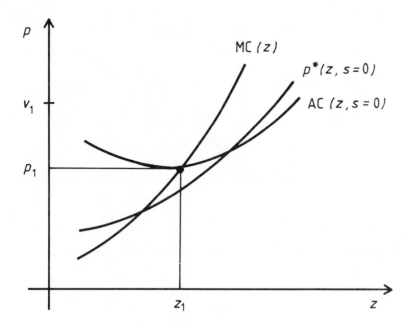

Figure 14.1
Quality assurance without brand name

Following Allen (1984) the boundary price schedule $p^*(z, S = 0)$ is also indicated, with all price and output pairs lying above that schedule assuring consumers that high quality is being supplied. For the case shown in the figure, each firm would produce high quality at output level z_1, with price p_1 obtaining in the long-run equilibrium. This is the usual first-best competitive equilibrium, since the $p^*(z, S = 0)$ constraint (14.30a) is nonbinding. Notice that the equilibrium price and industry output is fixed because AC has a minimum. The minimum, along with the fact that industry demand is not perfectly inelastic, determines the equilibrium number of (identical) firms.

Equilibrium with Brand Name. When the minimum of the firms' average cost lies above the boundary price schedule the standard (unconstrained) competitive equilibrium results. Figure 14.2 illustrates an alternative case where the quality assurance constraint is binding. Note first that the usual equilibrium price and quantity at the minimum of $AC(z, S = 0)$ would inform consumers that low quality is being produced, which is infeasible as an equilibrium in the present circumstances. Rather, the firms' profit-maximizing strategy is to increase price and output from (p_1, z_1), keeping the marginal cost of high quality equal to price. Thus the minimum price at which high quality can be produced occurs where marginal cost intersects the boundary price schedule. This intersection is labeled (p_2, z_2) in the figure. This point is not yet a free-entry equilibrium, for which $p^*(z, S = 0)$ equal to $AC(z, S = 0)$ each firm earns positive economic profits.

Klein and Leffler's solution here is to note that the firms compete in nonprice aspects of their trade, acquiring brand name with firm-specific investments.[12]

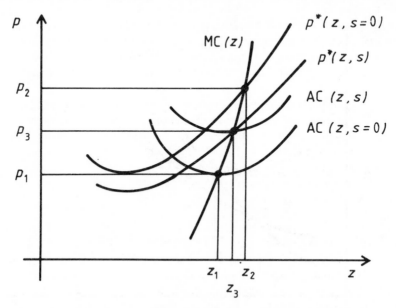

Figure 14.2
Quality assurance with brand name

---

[12] Allen (1984) considers details of the existence and uniqueness of the quality assurance equilibria with and without brand name investments.

The effect of these additional sunk costs is twofold: first, the average cost schedule shifts upward; second, following (14.28) $p^*(z, S)$ shifts downward. The competition in brand name investments ends when zero profits for each firm, as illustrated by the new intersection between the average cost schedule $AC(z, S)$ and $p^*(z, S)$ at (p_3, z_3). (The vertical distance between $AC(z, S = 0)$ and $AC(z, S)$ is the average cost of the brand name investments.) The level $S > 0$ of brand name investments is just sufficient to cause $p_3 = \min AC(z, S) = MC(z) = p^*(z, S)$. We remark again that a key aspect of these firm-specific assets is that the value they impart to consumers is less than their cost, since otherwise they would be undertaken as part of the original average cost schedule.

Reputation Equilibria, Once Again. In the above equilibrium consumers' expectations about a firm's product quality derive from the firm's reputation – the quality chosen by the firm in the previous period. When the firm chooses high quality, and receives the high-quality price at its start, it sustains the reputation for high quality as long as there is no incentive to opportunistically palm off low quality for a one-period gain. Consumers believe that the firm will continue to produce high quality and because the consumers believe this it is in the best interest of the firm to do so. That, in turn, makes the consumers' beliefs rational because the firm's strategy requires that it continue with its previous quality. This is, again, the circular story of a self-fulfilling expectations, or reputations, equilibrium.

Suppose, to the contrary, that reputation did not count in the above way and that regardless of the firm's prior quality consumers expected cheating in the current period. In this case the firm would have no incentive to supply high quality (it could not obtain the high-quality price) and once more expectations are fulfilled. It is interesting to note that this lemons equilibrium would be the one to obtain in the finite version of the above model, as the unraveling argument of Selten's chain store paradox then applies (recall chapter 9, section 9.6).

The above discussion draws attention to the fact that the Klein–Leffler analysis is fundamentally a *reputation* model built on a self-fulfilling equilibrium. The reader is now well aware that there is an alternative way of making history matter in dynamic models, with a signaling model built on asymmetrical incomplete information and the perfect Bayesian equilibrium concept. Milgrom and Roberts (1986) develop this approach to product quality supply and that is the subject to which we next turn.

14.4 Experience Goods: Quality-signaling Equilibria

Think now of experience goods sold under conditions of asymmetric incomplete information. Again, at any market date sellers can provide high quality or low quality. The usual advantage of selling low quality arises because of the experience nature of the good: consumers cannot determine quality pre-purchase and therefore will generally pay a price in excess of the value they place on low quality, depending on the relative probability they place on obtaining high or low quality. The seller can therefore produce low quality, at a low cost, and sell it *for one period* at the same price as it could sell a high-quality product. Once more, it is assumed that a single episode of palming off in this way reveals the seller forever as a low-quality supplier. Is this one-period gain to palming off greater than the disadvantage of being revealed in this way?

Suppose that consumers judge the seller to be of two possible types: either nonopportunistic, in which case it always supplies the high-quality good, or opportunistic, in which case it sells a product of high or low quality depending on the relative present value at any date of palming off or not palming off. The reader will recall from the discussion in chapter 9, section 9.7, that there are three equilibrium possibilities in an asymmetric information, incomplete information game. In section 9.7 the mixed strategy semi-separating equilibrium was developed as a model of entry deterrence for a two-stage game; the *pooling* and *separating* equilibrium were developed for a similar situation in chapter 10, section 10.5.

With these simplified analyses as background it is instructive to develop a more general T-period game here in the described context of quality supply. The resulting perfect Bayesian equilibrium must consider three phases. In the early-on markets the opportunistic seller pools with the non-opportunistic seller: high quality is supplied with probability 1 as the opportunistic seller uses the nonopportunistic ploy; it does not palm off in an attempt to (falsely) signal its type. As the number of remaining markets decreases and the value of the ploy to the opportunistic seller becomes less, it begins to play a mixed strategy with strictly positive probability for both palming off and not palming off, and some separation occurs, that is, when palming off the opportunistic seller reveals itself as such. As the number of remaining periods becomes even smaller the value of the ploy to the opportunistic seller becomes even less; it palms off with increasing frequency and separation occurs with greater likelihood. Finally, as the game nears (or reaches) the end, the ploy has no value and the opportunistic seller always palms off.

Model Notation. The perfect Bayesian equilibrium described above is derived by backward recursion, beginning in the final period-T market. Some notation is helpful in developing the details of the recursion sequence. With the exception of a finite horizon and the incompleteness of information this is similar to that used in the reputation model in section 14.3 and can be set out briefly: there are $t = 1, 2, \ldots, T$ periods, v is the reservation demand price of the aggregate consumer, $0 \leqslant \rho \leqslant 1$ is the (constant) one-period discount factor, $c_1 < v$ is the (constant) cost of producing a high-quality product and $c_0 < c_1$ similarly pertains to the low-quality good, and h_t is the probability (belief) assigned by the consumer at date t that the seller is *not* opportunistic.

Last Period T. This is simple. With experience goods consumers develop their beliefs based on their prior market experience. With no future market period, there is no advantage for the opportunistic seller in sustaining a high-quality ploy at date T: it palms off by choosing low quality. The nonopportunistic seller, myopic by definition, always ignores the gains to deception and it produces high quality even in this circumstance. Consumers also know that the opportunistic seller palms off at this terminal date, but they do not know for sure whether or not the seller is opportunistic (given that it has not already revealed itself by palming off) and therefore will pay a price equal to $p_T = h_T v$.

Next-to-Last Period $T - 1$. The opportunistic seller calculates its two-period optimal strategy knowing that consumers use the market results of prior periods as a basis for forming their beliefs about the quality obtaining in any market. This means that at $T - 1$ the quality choice of the opportunistic seller will not affect consumer beliefs on the $T - 1$ market and hence the price that can be then received. This provides the opportunity to palm off, in which case it gains $c_1 - c_0$ now but it is revealed as opportunistic and therefore receives nothing at the next period T. Alternatively, the opportunistic seller may produce high quality at $T - 1$ and then palm off at T. The maximum gain from this delay strategy will occur if consumers are certain that the seller is nonopportunistic and thus would pay $p = v$ for the product. In this case, the delay strategy has present value $\rho(v - c_0)$. The opportunistic seller will therefore palm off at $T - 1$ if the one-shot cost saving is such that[13]

$$c_1 - c_0 \geq \rho(v - c_0) \tag{14.33}$$

Using a similar reasoning it will produce high quality (with probability 1) if the cost saving is such that

$$c_1 - c_0 \leq \rho(h_T v - c_0) \tag{14.34}$$

where $p = h_T v$ is the maximum price that consumers will pay, given their period-T probability belief h_T. That leaves the opportunistic seller to randomize its quality decision in the intermediate interval[14]

$$\rho(h_T v - c_0) \leq c_1 - c_0 \leq \rho(v - c_0) \tag{14.35}$$

Suppose that the opportunistic seller decides *not* to palm off in this last interval. Consumers, using Bayes updating of their belief concerning the seller's type, then revise their probability as

$$h_{T,m} = \frac{h_{T-1}}{h_{T-1} + (1 - h_{T-1})\gamma_{T-1}} \tag{14.36}$$

where γ_{T-1} is the $T - 1$ probability with which the opportunistic seller chooses to use the nonopportunistic ploy. (We use the subscript m to indicate that the posterior probability is conditional on being in the mixed strategy interval at the prior date.) If consumers knew that the seller was nonopportunistic, and always produced high quality, they would pay v; if they knew that the seller was opportunistic and randomized with probability γ_{T-1}, they would pay $\gamma_{T-1} v$. The price that is paid, given their uncertain belief h_{T-1} and the common knowledge that the seller will use a mixed strategy, is therefore $p_{T-1,m} = h_{T-1} v + (1 - h_{T-1})\gamma_{T-1} v$.

When randomizing, the seller chooses γ_{T-1} in such a way that it is indifferent

[13] The boundary (equality) condition here requires some careful thought (see Milgrom and Roberts, 1982b). We will bypass these technical considerations and leap to the result that indifference in this case leads the opportunistic seller to palm off with probability 1.

[14] In the randomization, the opportunistic seller will supply high quality with probability 1 at the lower boundary and it will palm-off with probability 1 at the upper boundary.

to the opposing quality decisions, that is, γ_{T-1} is chosen to have the cost-savings condition given by (14.34) holds as an equality. Using (14.34) in this expression gives

$$c_1 - c_0 = \rho\left\{\frac{h_{T-1}v}{h_{T-1} + (1 - h_{T-1})\gamma_{T-1}} - c_0\right\} \qquad (14.37)$$

which solves for the mixing probability

$$\gamma_{T-1} = \frac{h_{T-1}}{1 - h_{T-1}}\left\{\frac{\rho v}{c_1 - c_0(1 - \rho)} - 1\right\} = \frac{h_{T-1}}{1 - h_{T-1}}(\delta - 1) \quad (14.38)$$

where the rightmost equality defines $\delta \geqslant 1$. Notice that δ is identical for all dates and is determined by the fundamental cost, discount factor, and consumer value parameters. Substituting (14.38) in (14.36) and simplifying gives

$$h_{T,m} = 1/\delta \qquad (14.39)$$

At the boundary between the intervals where the seller pools and mixes strategies it produces high quality with probability 1. This is nonrevealing and therefore the consumer beliefs which define the boundary are $h^*_{T-1} = h_{T,m} = 1/\delta$. If $h^*_{T-1} \geqslant 1/\delta$, then the opportunistic seller pools. Finally, the present value $V_{T-1,m}$ of the mixed strategy at $T - 1$ is derived as follows:

$$V_{T-1,m} = \gamma_{T-1}(p_{T-1,m} - c_1) + (1 - \gamma_{T-1})(p_{T-1,m} - c_0)$$
$$+ \gamma_{T-1}\rho(h_{T,m}v - c_0) + (1 - \gamma_{T-1})0$$

Using the expression for $p_{T-1,m}$, (14.38), and (14.39), this simplifies to

$$V_{T-1,m} = \delta h_{T-1}v - c_0 \qquad (14.40)$$

The period-$(T - 1)$ actions of the opportunistic seller are summarized in figure 14.3 – again, the nonopportunistic seller never palms off. There are three possibilities depending on the size of the cost advantage, the discount rate, the reservation demand price, and the consumers' prevailing beliefs.

1 When (14.33) holds, the opportunistic seller "pools with" the nonopportunistic seller with probability 1: they act alike and there is no palming off. As all things are common knowledge, except the seller's type, consumers can also observe whether condition (14.33) prevails. When it does, they know that high quality will be forthcoming and will pay $p = v$. Because of the pooling, the noncooperative seller does not reveal its type.

2 When (14.34) holds, the opportunistic seller "separates from" the nonopportunistic seller, by palming off, with probability 1. As consumers can again calculate in the same way that the seller can, but they still do not know the seller's type, the market price $p = h_{T-1}v$ will obtain. After the low quality is observed, the opportunistic seller is revealed and it gives up its trade forever.

3 When (14.35) holds, the opportunistic seller uses a mixed strategy: it chooses not to palm off (pool) with probability γ_{T-1} or to palm off (separate) with the complementary probability. The mixed strategy is, in this sense, semi-separating and semi-revealing.

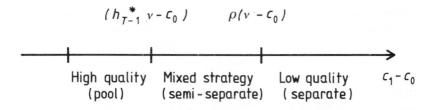

Figure 14.3
Strategies at $(T - 1)$

Period T − 2 and, by Induction, all Periods. There are again three cases to consider depending on whether or not the opportunistic seller palms off with certainty or uses a mixed strategy. The task before us is to delineate the conditions (in terms of model parameters) leading to these three cases and, in comparison with the $T - 1$ results, advance a conjecture about the general conditions which delineate these cases at any date. The conjecture is then to be proven by induction.

Separation: $c_1 - c_0 \geq p(v - c_0)$. Using the same logic as at $T - 1$, the opportunistic seller palms off and reveals itself. In fact, this same logic applies to every market date and is therefore a general condition for the separating equilibrium to obtain uniformly over time. Note that, for ρ sufficiently close to unity, this condition cannot be met. Conversely, if ρ is much less than unity (the future is greatly discounted) then the condition holds and there is separation.

Semi-separation: $\rho V_{T-1,m} \leq c_1 - c_0 \leq p(v - c_0)$. The opportunistic seller uses a mixed strategy in this interval. The boundary between the mixing and pooling strategies occurs at that probability $h^*_{T-2} = h_{T-1}$ where

$$\rho V_{T-1,m} = \rho(\delta h^*_{T-2} v - c_0) = c_1 - c_0$$

or

$$h^*_{T-1} = 1/\delta^2 \qquad (14.41)$$

Pool: $c_1 - c_0 \leq \rho V_{T-1,m}$. The logic of this case is the same as at $T - 1$: the opportunistic seller is better off selling high quality (pooling) at $T - 2$ and then (at worst) mixing strategies at $T - 1$. Using the same steps that produced (14.38) gives the mixing probability γ_{T-2} as

$$\gamma_{T-2} = \frac{h_{T-2}}{1 - h_{T-2}} (\delta - 1) \qquad (14.42)$$

Note that if the opportunistic seller chooses high quality when mixing at $T - 2$, it will also find itself in the mixed strategy interval at $T - 1$. Thus the present value of the mixed strategy at $T - 2$ is

$$V_{T-2,m} = \gamma_{T-2}(p_{T-2,m} - c_1) + (1 - \gamma_{T-2})(p_{T-2,m} - c_0)$$
$$+ \gamma_{T-2}\rho V_{T-1,m} + (1 - \gamma_{T-2})0$$

Following the same steps used in deriving $V_{T-1,m}$ we obtain the $T - 2$

present value of the opportunistic seller, given that it plays a mixed strategy at $T - 2$:

$$V_{T-2,m} = \delta^2 h_{T-2} v - c_0 \tag{14.43}$$

Inspection of (14.41) and (14.43) leads us to conjecture that the present value of mixing at any date $t > 0$ is $V_{T-t,m} = \delta^t h_{T-t} v - c_0$ and the boundary probability between mixing and pooling is $h^*_{T-t} = 1/\delta^t$. The reader can show by induction that these conjectures are true. The general t-period results are illustrated in figure 14.4.

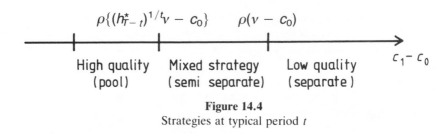

Figure 14.4
Strategies at typical period t

For $\delta > 1$, the opportunistic seller pools with probability 1 at any period when consumer beliefs are such that $h^*_{T-t} \geq 1/\delta^t$. In figure 14.4, for example, note that the larger is h_{T-t} the greater is the pooling interval. Also, when ρ is sufficiently close to unity (so that the future has greater value), δ is approximately equal to v/c_1 and $h^*_{T-t} = (c_1/v)^t$. For large t the boundary probability is close to zero and the interval in which the opportunistic seller signals with the mixed strategy is larger relative to the pure pooling strategy.

14.5 Product Quality and Credence Goods

Reputation also plays a part in assuring product quality with credence goods, although the role is somewhat different than that with experience goods. Because of the high post-costs with credence goods, the likelihood is greater that low-quality sellers can palm off their goods at the high-quality price for a sustained period without detection. Significant communication costs among consumers, as we assume here, also lengthens this period of deception since the identification of a low-quality producer by any one consumer means that that seller does not become a "notorious cheater." Instead, with credence goods there will be a continuous arrival and departure of consumers for both high- and low-quality goods depending on the incidence of errors that occur as consumers use probabilistic information from their experience and communications to infer quality. The impact of such errors on firm size and choice of quality are of concern here. The process by which consumers stop or continue their trade with any seller lies at the center of this analysis, and it is to that which we turn first.[15]

---

[15] This analysis generally follows Smallwood and Conlisk (1979) and Rogerson (1983).

14.5.1   Consumer Dynamics

For convenience assume that any seller's product quality can take on only one of two levels, high (1) or low (0). Let there be I identical consumers of these goods, with each consumer taking one unit or none at any market date. Because of high pre-costs, consumers do not know the quality of any good prior to purchase, although they can identify different sellers using trademarks. Because of high post-cost, consumers derive limited information on any brand from experience and therefore their quality evaluation is only probabilistic. At the onset it is assumed that the pre-purchase probability distribution on quality held by each consumer is uniform across brands. For a high-quality good let α be the probability that consumers falsely infer low quality and, similarly, for the low-quality good let β be the probability that high quality is falsely inferred. Finally, it seems natural to assume that consumers are more likely to infer high quality from a truly high-quality product than to infer high quality when the good is in fact of low quality, that is, $1 - \alpha > \beta$ or $\alpha + \beta > 1$.

Brand Loyalty Rule. Each consumer evaluates his purchase based on its performance in use with probability of error given by either α or β. Following Rogerson (1983), suppose that each consumer remains loyal to his current brand from market date to market date provided that the fraction of high-quality evaluations from his prior purchases remains above a pre-determined threshold level.[16] In turn, denote the probability that any consumer remains loyal to a high-quality product over t market dates by $\omega_1{}^t$, and similarly let $\omega_0{}^t$ pertain to low-quality products. Clearly, $\omega_1{}^t$ is nondecreasing in α and $\omega_0{}^t$ is nondecreasing in $1 - \beta$. Since the probability of any consumer observing high quality is greater for a good actually of high quality, then $\omega_1{}^t > \omega_0{}^t$ for each date t.

Suppose that a constant number $\bar{I}_1$ of *new* consumers arrive at each high-quality firm at each market date. This means that, on average, $\omega_1{}^t \bar{I}_1$ consumers have remained loyal to each high-quality firm for τ periods and $\sum_{t=1}^{T} \omega_1{}^t \bar{I}_1$ consumers will have remained loyal on average since the beginning of the market T periods earlier. Thus

$$z_1 = \bar{I}_1 \left(1 + \sum_{t=1}^{T} \omega_1{}^t \right) \tag{14.44a}$$

is the expected total number of consumers, those remaining and those newly arrived, carrying on trade with each high-quality firm. Over the long haul, as T becomes large, $\sum_{t=1}^{T} \omega_1{}^t$ will be approximately constant, as will z_1. Since $\bar{I}_1$ new consumers arrive at each date and z_1 is constant, then $\bar{I}_1$ consumers must also leave the high-quality firm at each date in the long haul. This means that the *quit rate*, the fraction of consumers to quit the firm on average at each market date, is

$$q_1 = \frac{1}{1 + \sum_{t=1}^{T} \omega_1{}^t} \tag{14.44b}$$

Similarly, the firm size

$$z_0 = \bar{I}_0 \left(1 + \sum_{t=1}^{T} \omega_0{}^t \right) \tag{14.45a}$$

---

[16] This threshold may vary with the number of trials.

and quit rate

$$q_0 = \frac{1}{1 + \Sigma_{t=1}^{T} \omega_0{'}}$$ (14.45b)

pertain to the low-quality suppliers.

Indicate the new consumers arriving at different firms by $\bar{I}_1 = \delta \bar{I}_0$ where $\delta \geqslant 1$; that is, δ times as many new consumers arrive per period at a high-quality firm as at a low-quality firm. The size of δ depends on the *reputation* of high-quality firms created from generally available (but imperfect) market information. For $\delta > 1$, the reputation effect favors high-quality firms relative to their low-quality counterparts. Finally, since $\omega_1{'} \geqslant \omega_0{'}$ for all t, it follows that $q_1 \leqslant q_0$: in the long haul, the quit rate for high-quality suppliers is less than that for low-quality suppliers. The reputation effect and the higher quit rate for low-quality firms lie at the core of the results to be derived.

14.5.2   Firm Size and Type

Using (14.44a) and (14.45a), we obtain the relative number of customers trading with high- and low-quality firms as

$$m^* \equiv \frac{z_1}{z_0} = \frac{\bar{I}_1/q_1}{\bar{I}_0/q_0} = \frac{q_0}{q_1} \delta \geqslant 1$$ (14.46)

where the inequality follows from the reputation effect ($\delta \geqslant 1$) and the relative quit rates ($q_1 \leqslant q_0$). Note that m^* reflects the impact of reputation and quit rate as they operate to reward high-quality producers with more customers.

What about the number of firms producing high and low quality? An approximate answer to this question can be developed using two simplifying assumptions. First, because of the prohibitive switching cost, suppose that on entry the firms commit to one quality level or the other for all time.[17] Second, suppose that the time discount rate is small enough so that firms have an interest only in their steady state profit levels.

With these assumptions, whether or not any entering firm chooses to produce high quality then depends on the relative profits given by

$$\pi_1 = (p - c_1)z_1 - S$$ (14.47a)

$$\pi_0 = (p - c_0)z_0 - S$$ (14.47b)

where $c_1 \geqslant c_0$ indicates that the (constant) marginal cost of producing high quality is greater than that for low quality and S is the common sunk cost. A comparison of these expressions shows that $\pi_1 \geqslant \pi_0$ iff the market price $p \geqslant p^*$ where

$$p^* = \frac{m^* c_1 - c_0}{m^* - 1}$$ (14.48)

---

[17] That is, we look for pure strategy equilibria with stationary strategies. This is not as restrictive as it may seem, for an equilibrium in the game where firms are limited to stationary strategies is also an equilibrium for a game in which nonstationary strategies are also allowed. Moreover, Denardo (1967) has shown that when one firm finds that all others are choosing stationary strategies, it can do no better by adopting a nonstationary strategy than by adopting a stationary strategy.

In the terminology of section 14.4.1, p^* is the *boundary price*. The advantage of producing high quality occurs through the reputation effect of m^*: high-quality firms sell more units. The disadvantage is that these units cost more to produce. Differentiating (14.48) gives $dp^*/dm^* = (c_0 - c_1)/(m^* - 1)^2 \leqslant 0$. As the reputation effect becomes larger, m^* is larger and the boundary price becomes less, and conversely. Note finally from (14.48) that as the market price rises above c_1 the gains from producing high quality (having the increased sales from high quality) become greater. For some price these gains offset the disadvantage of the higher cost (c_1 relative to c_0) so that it becomes profitable to a high-quality producer.[18]

Supplementary examples

SE14.1   Signaling Pigs in a Poke

The original signaling model of Arrow (1973) and Spence (1973) was concerned with labor markets. In their analyses individuals differ in their productivity and it is prohibitively expensive to sort them directly. Each will therefore receive wages on the basis of average productivity. It is then supposed that educational level reveals the productivity of the individual without affecting it: better-educated (and more productive) individuals signal employers of this and command a greater wage rate.[19] Resources spent on education therefore provide a signal which affects the distribution of worker output, but importantly it does not change the level of that output. In this situation resources are inefficiently allocated.

Barzel (1977) has argued that institutional arrangements will arise to economize on the sorting resource loss. He gives an example using medical insurance as follows. Consider a collection of individuals whose expected medical expenses are identical. In this case medical insurance is sold at a uniform premium (recall E14.1). Suppose now that (data collection and analysis) technology is developed which permits it to be learned that these expenses vary in the cross-section of individuals. In an Arrow–Spence signaling arrangement we would expect that individuals who know that they have better health would spend resources to signal insurance companies, for example, by submitting to a graduated medical examination whose cost per grade varied inversely with the health of the individual. Because of their signal, they would command lower premiums. As in the education example we also suppose that, except for the premium change, other things are unaffected by the adoption of the (examination) signal. The decrease in the premiums to those who are healthy simultaneously brings about a premium increase for others. There is, with this sorting, only a redistribution of income from the less healthy to the more healthy, and no overall change in healthiness.

---

[18] Rogerson (1983) derives conditions for a symmetric market equilibrium in pure strategies where high-quality firms operate at a fixed capacity constraint, the last entering firm has high quality and causes $p = p^*$, and the reputation effect determines firm sizes.

[19] As in all signaling models, the cost of providing the signal must be inversely related to the quality being signaled. Here, the costs of any given level of education are less for the more productive so that, other things equal, they acquire a greater education.

Barzel notes that medical insurance is commonly offered to whole groups, for example, all employees of a given firm, members of a union, or students at a college. An important aspect of the group policy is that no medical examination, and no sorting of individuals by healthiness, is required. Individuals qualify simply by their membership. The purpose of the group policy, Barzel argues, is to avoid the sorting/signaling costs of the examinations. He also suggests other "pig-in-a-poke" cases:

> . . . most dramatic of these is DeBeer's sale to dealers of bags of assorted diamonds, each bag fetching a price ranging from fifty thousand to a quarter million dollars. A single prospective buyer is offered, and usually chooses to buy, a bag (sometimes several bags) at the price set by DeBeers. Had the contents of a particular bag been available for appraisal by all buyers, each probably would have spent resources to determine the properties of the diamonds. The ultimate resource allocation presumably would hardly be affected. The actual form of sale avoids this extra resource cost. Indeed, the moment the seal on a bag is broken, the bag as a whole loses part of its market value. . . . It should be recognized, however, that some additional costs have been incurred. For instance, DeBeers has had to establish such a reputation that prospective buyers can be confident that the ultimate value of the bag exceeds it price. Thus, an individual buyer does not need to spend resources to investigate a questionable offer. The incentive for DeBeers to engage in this peculiar form of trade seems to be that buyers are now in a position to spend on the actual purchase of the diamonds the amount they otherwise might have spent on collecting information (Barzel, 1977, p. 304)

Similarly, what about the oranges, apples, and potatoes sold in opaque plastic bags at the grocery market?

SE14.2   Quality, Barriers to Entry, and Introductory Promotions

With experience goods, consumers know the quality of previously used brands but not that of untried brands, and in particular they do not know the quality of brands to be offered by new entrants to the market. Schmalensee (1982b) and Farrell (1986b) have considered the possibility that this asymmetry in knowledge between tried and untried products will create a barrier to new entry. Recognizing that there are incentives for an opportunistic entrant to palm off low quality, just as in the analyses of product quality supply by extant firms in sections 14.3 and 14.4, Farrell notes that consumers with rational expectations will be inclined not to purchase entrant brands and this creates a "moral hazard barrier to entry." Such a barrier, he notes, is positively related to the surplus being received by buyers from extant brands (they forego this when taking a brand from the entrants). Thus incumbents can control the height of the entry barrier by offering greater surplus that otherwise. The entrant is not without recourse in all of this, as it may convince buyers of its intention to supply high quality and remain in the industry (to not "hit and run") by a commitment built on foregoing profits in early stages, that is, by using introductory promotions. Our interest here is in setting out the nature of the moral hazard barrier more completely and in clarifying the conditions under which introductory promotions will be effective as a counter-strategy. We generally follow Farrell (1986b).

Model Details. As this analysis is only an entry variant of the models of earlier sections, most of the details are familiar. The timing of entry's being new, however, does require some additional comment. We consider two market periods ($t = 1, 2$), two firms (an incumbent and entrant) selling an experience good, and to possible product quality levels from which the firms can choose, as before high (1) and low (0). Let $v > 0$ again be the consumers reservation demand price for high quality and let low quality have zero value. (Thus a brand known to be of low quality will not be taken at any positive price.)

At the onset the incumbent's quality is assumed to be given by prior decision and to be unalterable throughout the play; the entrant's one-time decision on quality is open to our consideration. Regardless of that decision, the experience nature of the good means that consumers will not know that quality for sure until after the good is tried. The incumbent's quality is known during the first period to those who previously purchased from it, and heard of its brand from other users, and that history of usage provides it with an advantage. During the second period both firms will have prior users – the entrant's clientele may be relatively small or zero if it is unsuccessful in avoiding a low-quality image.

Incentive for Opportunism. Let $\pi(z)$ be the period 2 equilibrium level of profits of the entrant given it has *first-period* sales of z. However specified, this profit level depends on industry demand and cost conditions and all rules of the period 2 market game. The effect of z in separating informed from uninformed consumers at period 2 defines its state variable role in π (recall chapter 10, E10.1, for further details).

At period 1 it is helpful to distinguish revenue and cost components of profits. Let $c_1(z)$ be the entrant's cost of producing high quality at output level z and let $c_0(z)$ similarly pertain to the costs of low-quality production: then $c_1(z) > c_0(z) > 0$ for $z > 0$. Whatever the specific rules of play in the period 1 market competition, let $p(z)$ be the price received when the entrant's output is z. Note that this inverse demand schedule does not depend on whether high or low quality is selected by the entrant, as the experience good's quality cannot be observed prior to purchase.

High or Low Quality? Using the above notation the entrant's present value on producing high quality is

$$V_1 = p(z)z - c_1(z) + \rho\pi(z) \tag{14.49}$$

where ρ is the one-period discount factor. If low quality is provided then that present value is

$$V_0 = p(z)z - c_0(z) \tag{14.50}$$

High-quality production has two requirements: that it be the preferred choice ($V_1 \geq V_0$) *and* that it be profitable ($V_1 \geq 0$). These requirements take the specific forms

$$\rho\pi \geq c_1 - c_0 \tag{14.51a}$$

and

$$pz - c_1 + \rho\pi > 0 \tag{14.51b}$$

respectively. The output z is understood to be an argument in these profit and cost functions, but is suppressed for notational convenience. When considering entry with full information, (14.51b) is the only relevant requirement for high-quality production (low quality, with zero value to consumers, would not be possible with full information). With the lack of full information, however, the preference condition (14.51a) acts as an additional restriction on entry.

High quality can be produced only if there is some *scale of entry* z which simultaneously satisfies both (14.51a) and (14.51b). Otherwise, consumers with rational expectations, and calculating with the same skill as the entrant, will understand that low quality is being supplied: this is the moral hazard barrier to entry.

As an example of this barrier, consider the possibility of *hit-and-run* entry. This occurs when, for all feasible z, (a) $V_0 > V_1$, so that low quality is preferred, (b) $\pi = 0$, and (c) $V_1 > 0$ for some z. If these conditions are simultaneously met, then low-quality production for one-period hit-and-run entry will be the only possibility for the entrant. Given that the rules of the game are common knowledge, however, consumers will be able to make the same calculations as the entrant. Thus they will rationally expect low quality and that will foil hit-and-run entry.

The Scale of Entry. In contrast with the above situation, suppose that $\pi(0) > 0$ and $\pi(z)$ increases at a slower rate in z than does the cost difference $c_1(z) - c_0(z)$. This will be the case, for example, when the cost difference between high and low quality is sensitive to the rate of output and information is passed among consumers rapidly so that π is relatively unaffected by the scale z. Whatever the specific conditions, in this case the quality preference condition (14.51a) will be satisfied below the minimum scale $\bar{z}$ which solves $\rho\pi(\bar{z}) = c_1(\bar{z}) - c_0(\bar{z})$. In turn, entry will occur with high quality at that scale $0 < z^* \leq \bar{z}$ which maximizes V_1 (assuming that the maximum present value is positive). There is also the converse case, where $\pi(z)$ increases at a faster rate in z than does the cost difference and large-scale entry at high quality is more likely. This will generally occur when information about quality is slow to diffuse among consumers, leaving π more sensitive to the z scale, and the difference in cost of quality arises principally from fixed cost.

Once more, consumers knowing the same facts as firms and acting with rational expectations can use the scale of the entrant's first-period output as an indication of the quality it produces. In this sense the scale of entry, large or small depending on the proportionality of π and the cost difference to z, is a quality commitment overcoming the moral barrier to entry. Scales of entry z which are inconsistent with high quality, that is, do not satisfy (14.51a) and (14.51b) jointly, will leave the moral hazard barrier to entry intact.

Introductory Promotions. It seems intuitive that entrants use introductory promotions – schemes which effectively lower first-trial prices – to overcome the hesitancy of buyers to try an unknown product. The way in which such promotions work is not immediately obvious: note that the price at period 1 does *not* appear in either of the two conditions (14.51a) and (14.51b) determining the decision to enter either with high or low quality.[20] However, there is an indirect effect as period 1 price determines the scale of entry. When p is lowered by introductory promotions this increases the scale of entry. If large scale acts as a commitment in the manner outlined above, then a large promotion will be successful. Alternatively, if the scale which acts as a commitment is relatively small, then the introductory promotion will be commensurately small.

SE14.3 Optimal Fraud

Darby and Karni (1973) define credence goods as those with qualities which make both pre- and post-costs high. Such qualities arise when a good is utilized in combination with other goods and it is difficult to determine their separate contribution in the measured output.

Automotive repair services are popular example of goods with credence qualities. When there are additional significant costs of buying diagnosis and actual repair services from different vendors, the consumer does not separate these purchases and there is a possibility that fraudulent information and repairs will be offered. The incentives for fraud, and the level of its provision, can be seen in a simple competitive firm model. We use the following notation: p is the price of repair services, z is the level of repair services prescribed by the firm, v is the expected present value of future repair services for a given customer, and $c(z)$ is the firm's cost of providing service level z. The firm's expected profit for a particular customer is given by the profit if the diagnosis is accepted times the probability of its acceptance plus the present value of future net sales times the probability the consumer will in fact return:

$$\pi = \{pz - c(z)\}\{1 - f(z)\} + v\{1 - h(z)\} \qquad (14.52)$$

where $f(z)$ is the cumulative probability that the customer will refuse repair services z and $h(z)$ is the probability that he will transfer his future trade elsewhere. It is assumed that f and h are differentiable functions with $f'(z) > 0$ and $h'(z) > 0$. At the expected profit stationarity with respect to z,

$$\{p - c'(z)\}\{1 - f(z)\} = \{pz - c(z)\}f'(z) + vh'(z) \qquad (14.53)$$

Let z^* solve this condition for an expert buyer who can accurately assess the relationship between repair services and their future value. For fraud to occur, the gain at the margin to selling additional repair services must exceed the marginal cost of the services, or

---

[20] This is in contrast with the reputation and signaling models of quality supply discussed in sections 14.3 and 14.4, where price directly guaranteed quality.

$$\{p - c'(z^*)\}\{1 - f(z^*)\} = \{pz^* - c(z^*)\}f'(z^*) + vh'(z^*) \qquad (14.54)$$

This inequality, and the incentive to fraud, obviously occurs where the costs of diagnosis are significant.[21]

The central problem in fraud is the existence of credence qualities: consumer ignorance and the additional cost of separate diagnosis and repair provide the motivation for a service firm to defraud its customers. To determine an equilibrium, and the optimal amount of fraud, Darby and Karni focus on market arrangements which minimize the total costs of obtaining any given level of service.

---

[21] Darby   anad   Karni   (1973,   pp.   74–6)   show   the   comparative   statics   result $dz/dv = h'(z)/(d^2\pi/dz^2) < 0$ (since the denominator is negative by the second-order maximum conditions). The greater is the expected value of future business from a customer the less likely is fraud. Tourists and casual customers will be defrauded to a greater extent.

Bibliography

Abreu, D. (1983) Repeated Games with Discounting: a General Theory and an Application to Oligopoly. Ph.D. dissertation. Princeton, NJ: Princeton University.

Acs, Z. and Audretsch, D. (1988) Innovation in large and small firms: an empirical analysis. *American Economic Review*: 678–90.

Adams, W. and Yellen, J. (1976) Commodity bundling and the burden of monopoly. *Quarterly Journal of Economics*: 475–98.

Akerlof, G. (1970) The market for lemons: qualitative uncertainty and the market mechanism. *Quarterly Journal of Economics*: 488–500.

Albion, M. and Farris, P. (1981) *The Advertising Controversy*. Boston, MA: Auburn House.

Alchian, A. (1982) Property rights, specialization and the firm. In J. F. Weston and M. Granfield (eds), *Corporate Enterprise in a New Environment*. New York: KCG Productions.

Alchian, A. and Demsetz, H. (1972) Production information costs, and economic organization. *American Economic Review*: 777–95.

Alessi, L. (1983) Property rights, transaction costs and X-efficiency. *American Economic Review*: 64–81.

Allen, B. (1969) Concentration and economic progress. *American Economic Review*: 600–4.

Allen, B. (1971) Vertical integration and market foreclosure: the case of cement and concrete. *Jornal of Law and Economics*: 251–74.

Allen, B. (1982) Some stochastic processes of interdependent demand and technological diffusion of an innovation exhibiting externalities among adopters. *International Economic Review*: 595–608.

Allen, B. and Hellwig, M. (1986) Bertrand–Edgeworth oligopoly in large markets. *Review of Economic Studies*: 595–608.

Allen, F. (1984) Reputation and product quality. *RAND Journal of Economics*: 331–27.

Anderson, J. (1984) Identification of interactive behaviour in air service markets: 1973–76. *Journal of Industrial Economics*: 489–508.

Anderson, S. (1987) Spatial competition and price leadership. *International Journal of Industrial Organization*: 369–98.

Appelbaum, E. (1979) Testing price taking behaviour. *Journal of Econometrics*: 283–94.

Appelbaum, E. (1982) The estimation of the degree of oligopoly power. *Journal of Econometrics*: 287–99.

Archibald, G. (1961) Chamberlin versus Chicago. *Review of Economic Studies*: 2–28.

Archibald, G. and Rosenbluth, G. (1975) The "new" theory of consumer demand and monopolistic competition. *Quarterly Journal of Economics*: 568–90.

Archibald, G., Eaton, B. and Lipsey, R. (1986) Address models of value theory. In J. Stiglitz and G. Mathewson (eds), *New Developments in the Analysis of Market Structure*. Cambridge, MA: MIT Press.

Areeda, P. and Turner, D. (1975) Predatory pricing and related practices under section 2 of the Sherman Act. *Harvard Law Review*: 697–733.

Areeda, P. and Turner, D. (1976) Scherer on predatory pricing: a reply. *Harvard Law Review*: 891–900.

Armentano, D. (1972) *The Myths of Antitrust*. New York: Arlington House.

Arrow, K. (1962) Economic welfare and the allocation of resources for inventions. In R. Nelson (ed.), *The Rate and Direction of Innovative Activity*. Princeton, NJ: Princeton University Press.

Arrow, K. (1963) Uncertainty and the welfare economics of medical care. *American Economic Review*: 465–91.

Arrow, K. (1965) *Aspects of the Theory of Risk Bearing*. Helsinki: Yrjo Jahnssonin Saatio.

Arrow, K. (1973) Higher education as a filter. *Journal of Public Economics*: 193–9.

Arrow, K. (1975) Vertical integration and communication. *Bell Journal of Economics*: 173–83.

Arrow, K. and Hahn, F. (1971) *General Competitive Analysis*. San Francisco, CA: Holden Day.

d'Aspremont, C., Jacquemin, A., Jaskold-Gabszewicz, H. and Weymack, J. (1983) On the stability of dominant cartels. *Canadian Journal of Economics*: 17–25.

d'Aspremont, C., Jaskold-Gabszewicz, H. and Thisse, J. (1979) On Hotellings's stability in competition. *Econometrica*: 1145–50.

Atkinson, A. and Stiglitz, J. (1976) The design of tax structures: direct vs. indirect taxation. *Journal of Public Economics*: 55–75.

Aumann, R. (1960) Acceptable points in games of perfect information. *Pacific Journal of Mathematics*: 381–417.

Aumann, R. (1981) Survey of repeated games. In M. Shubik (ed.), *Essays in Game Theory and Mathematical Economics in Honour of Oscar Morgenstern*. Mannheim: Bibliographisches Institut.

Aumann, R. and Shapley, L. (1976) Long-term competition: a game theoretic analysis. Unpublished manuscript. Heilbron: Hebrew University.

Ausubel, L. and Deneckere, R (1987) One is almost enough for monopoly. *RAND Journal of Economics*: 255–74.

Averch, H. and Johnson, L. (1962) Behavior of the firm under regulatory constraint. *American Economic Review*: 1053–69.

Axelrod, R. (1987) *The Evolution of Cooperation*. New York: Basic Books.

Ayanian, R. (1975) Advertising and rates of return. *Journal of Law and Economics*: 479–506.

Azariadis, C. (1983) Employment with asymmetric information. *Quarterly Journal of Economics*: 157–72.

Bailey, E. and Malone, J. (1970) Resource allocation and the regulated firm. *Bell Journal of Economics and Management Science*: 129–42.

Bailey, E. and Panzar, J. (1981) The contestability of airline markets during the transition to deregulation. *Law and Contemporary Problems*: 125–45.

Bailey, M. (1954) Price and output determination by a firm selling related products. *American Economic Review*: 82–93.

Bailey, M. (1972) Research and development costs and returns: the U.S. pharmaceutical industry. *Journal of Political Economy*: 70–85.

Bain, J. (1949) A vote on pricing in monopoly and oligopoly. *American Economic Review*. 448–64.

Bain, J. (1951) Relation of profit rate to industry concentration in American manufacturing, 1946–1950. *Quarterly Journal of Economics*: 293–324.

Bain, J. (1954) Economies of scale, concentration, and the conditions of entry in twenty manufacturing industries. *American Economic Review*: 68–79.

Bain, J. (1956) *Barriers to New Competition*. Cambridge, MA: Harvard University Press.

Bain, J. (1959) *Industrial Organization*. New York: Wiley.

Bain, J. (1960) Price leaders, barometers, and kinks. *Journal of Business*: 193–203.

Baker, J. and Bresnahan, T. (1984) Estimating the demand curve facing a single firm: estimates for three brewing firms: Working Paper. Stanford, CA: Department of Economics, Stanford University.

Balcer, Y. (1981) Equilibrium distributions of sales and advertising prices over space. *Journal of Economic Theory*: 196–218.

Baldani, J. and Masson, R. (1981) Economies of scale, strategic advertising and fully credible entry deterrence. Working Paper: Ithaca, NY: Department of Economics, Cornell University.

Baldwin, W. and Childs, G. (1969) The fast second and rivalry in research and development. *Southern Economic Journal*: 18–24.

Banks, J. and Sobel, J. (1987) Equilibrium selection in signalling games. *Econometrica*: 647–62.

Baron, D. (1970) Price uncertainty, utility, and industry equilibrium in pure competition. *International Economic Review*: 463–80.

Baron, D. (1972) Limit pricing and models of potential entry. *Western Economic Journal*: 298–307.

Baron, D. (1973) Limit pricing, potential entry and barriers to entry. *American Economic Review*: 666–74.

Baron, D. and Myerson, R. (1982) Regulating a monopolist with unknown costs. *Econometrica*: 911–30.

Barro, R. (1973) Monopoly and contrived depreciation. *Journal of Political Economy*: 598–602.

Barton, J. (1972) The economic basis of damages for breach of contract. *Journal of Legal Studies*: 277–304.

Barzel, Y. (1968) Optimal timing of inventions. *Review of Economics and Statistics*: 348–55.

Barzel, Y. (1977) Some fallacies in the interpretation of information costs. *Journal of Law and Economics*: 291–306.

Basar, T. and Ho. Y. (1974) Information properties of the Nash solutions of two nonzero-sum games. *Journal of Economic Theory*: 370–87.

Baumol, W. (1979) Quasi-permanence of price reductions: a policy for prevention of predatory pricing. *Yale Law Journal*: 1–26.

Baumol, W. and Bradford, D. (1970) Optimal departures from marginal cost pricing. *American Economic Review*: 265–83.

Baumol, W. and Klevorick, A. (1970) Input choices and rate-of-return regulation: an overview of the discussion. *Bell Journal of Economic and Management Science*: 162–90.

Baumol, W. and Willig, R. (1981) Fixed costs, sunk costs, entry barriers, public goods and the sustainability of monopoly. *Quarterly Journal of Economics*: 405–31.

Baumol, W., Panzar, J. and Willig, R. (1982) *Contestable Markets and the Theory of Industry Structure*. San Diego, CA: Harcourt, Brace, Jovanovitch.

Baxter, N. (1967) Leverage risk of ruin and the cost of capital. *Journal of Finance*: 395–404.

Beckman, M. (1970) Equilibrium vs. optimal market areas. Discussion paper No. 16. Providence, RI: Brown University.

Bellman, R. (1957) *Dynamic Programming*. Princeton, NJ: Princeton University Press.

Belton, T. (1987) A model of duopoly and meeting or beating competition. *International Journal of Industrial Organization*: 399–417.

Benavie, A. (1972) *Mathematical Techniques for Economic Analysis*. Englewood Cliffs, NJ: Prentice-Hall.

Benham, L. (1972) The effect of advertising on the price of eyeglasses. *Journal of Law and Economics*: 337–52.

Benoit, J. (1984) Financially constrained entry into a game with incomplete information. *RAND Journal of Economics*: 480–98.

Benoit, J. and Krishna, V. (1985) Finitely repeated games. *Econometrica*: 905–22.

Benston, G. (1985) The validity of profits-struture studies with particular reference to the FTC's line of business data. *American Economic Review*: 37–67.

Bergson, A (1973) On monopoly welfare losses. *American Economic Review*: 863–70.

Bergstrom, T. (1979) Cournot, Novshek, and the many firms. CREST Discussion Paper No. 21. Ann Arbor, MI: University of Michigan.

Bernhardt, I. (1977) Vertical integration and demand variability. *Journal of International Economics*: 213–29.

Bernheim, B. (1984) Rationalisable strategic behaviour. *Econometrica*: 1007–28.

Bernheim, B. (1985) Strategic deterrence of sequential entry into an industry. *RAND Journal of Economics*: 1–11.

Bertrand, J. (1883) Revue de la théorie mathématique de la richesse sociale et des recherches sur les principles mathématiques de la théorie des richesses. *Journal des Savants*: 499–508.

Bierman, J. and Tollison, R. (1970) Monopoly rent capitalization and antitrust policy. *Western Economic Journal*: 385–9.

Biggadike, E. (1976) *Corporate Diversification, Entry, Strategy and Performance*. Cambridge, MA: Harvard University Press.

Bishop, R (1952) Elasticities, cross-elasticities, and market relationships. *American Economic Review*: 779–803.

Blackorby, C., Nissen, D., Primont, D. and Russell R. (1973) Consistent intertemporal decision making. *Review of Economic Studies*: 239–48.

Blackstone, E. (1975) Restrictive practices in the marketing of electrofax copying machines and supplies: the SCM corporation case. *Journal of International Economics*: 189–202.

Blair, R. (1974) Random input prices and the theory of the firm. *Economic Inquiry*: 214–26.

Blair, R. and Kaserman, D. (1978a) Vertical integration, tying, and antitrust policy. *American Economic Review*: 397–402.

Blair, R. and Kaserman, D (1978b) Uncertainty and the incentive for vertical integration. *Southern Economic Journal*: 266–72.

Blair, R. and Kaserman, D. (1980) Vertical control with variable proportions: ownership integration and contractual equivalents. *Southern Economic Journal*: 1118–28.

Blank, D. (1968). Television advertising: the great discount illusion, or tonypandy revisited. *Journal of Business*: 10–38.

Bloch, H. (1974) Advertising and profitability: a reappraisal. *Journal of Political Economy*: 267–86.

Boiteux, M. (1960) Peak load pricing. *Journal of Business*: 157–79.

Bolton, P. and Bonano, G. (1987) Resale price maintenance and competition in post-sales services. Mimeo. University of California, Davis.

Bond, E. and Samuelson, L. (1984) Durable good monopolies with rational expectations and replacement sales. *RAND Journal of Economics*: 336–45.

Bondt, R. (1976) Limit pricing, uncertain entry and the entry lag. *Econometrica*: 939–46.

Borch, K. (1962) Application of game theory to some problems in automobile insurance. *Astin Bulletin*: 208–21.

Borenstein, S. (1985) Price discrimination in free-entry markets. *RAND Journal of Economics*: 380–97.

Bork, R. (1978) *The Antitrust Paradox*. New York: Basic Books.

Bound, J., Cummins, C., Griliches, Z., Hall, B. and Jaffe, A. (1984) Who does R&D and who patents? In Z. Griliches (ed.), *R&D, Patents, and Productivity*. Chicago; IL: University of Chicago Press.

Bowley, A. (1924) *The Mathematical Groundwork of Economics*. Oxford: Oxford University Press.

Bowley, A. (1928) Bilateral monopoly. *Economic Journal*: 651–9.

Bowman, A. (1957) Tying agreements and the leverage problem. *Yale Law Journal*: 19–36

Boyer, K. (1974) Informative and goodwill advertising. *Review of Economics and Statistics*: 541–8.

Boyer, K. (1979) Degrees of differentiation and industry boundaries. In T. Calvani and J. Siegfried (eds), *Economic Analysis of Antitrust Law*. Boston, MA: Little, Brown.

Boyer, M. and Moreaux, M. (1983) Conjectures, rationality, and duopoly theory. *International Journal of Industrial Organization*: 23–41.

Bradburd, R. (1980) Conglomerate power without market power: the effect of conglomeration on a risk averse quantity adjusting firm. *American Economic Review*: 483–8.

Bradburd, R. and Over, A. (1982) Organizational costs, sticky equilibria, and critical levels of concentration. *Review of Economics and Statistics*: 50–8.

Braithwaite, D. (1928) The economic effects of advertising. *Economic Journal*: 16–37.

Bramness, G. (1979) The general conjectural model of oligopoly – some classical points revisited. Unpublished paper. Coventry: University of Warwick.

Brander, J. and Eaton, J. (1984) Product line rivalry. *American Economic Review*: vol. 74.

Brander, J. and Lewis, T. (1986) Oligopoly and financial structure: the limited liability effect. *American Economic Review*: 956–70.

Brander, J. and Spencer, B. (1983) Strategic commitment with R & D: the symmetric case. *Bell Journal of Economics*: 225–35.

Braun, E. and MacDonald, S. (1982) *Revolution in Miniature: The History and Impact of Semiconductor Electronics* (2nd edn). Cambridge: Cambridge University Press.

Brennan, T. (1986) Understanding "raising rivals' cost". Antitrust Division Working Paper 86–16. Economic Analysis Group, US Department of Justice.

Bresnahan, T. (1981a) Competition and collusion in the American automobile industry: the 1955 price war. Working Paper. Stanford, CA: Department of Economics, Stanford University.

Bresnahan, T. (1981b) Departures from marginal-cost pricing in the American automobile industry: estimates for 1977–1978. *Journal of Econometrics*: 201–27.

Bresnahan, T. (1981c) Duopoly models with consistent conjectures. *American Economic Review*: 934–45

Bresnahan, T. (1982) The oligopoly solution concept is identified. *Economics Letters*: 87–92.

Brock, W. (1983) Contestable markets and the theory of industrial structure. *Journal of Political Economy*: 1055–66.

Brock, W. and Scheinkman, J. (1985) Price-setting supergames with capacity constraints. *Review of Economic Studies*: 371–80.

Brodley, J. and Hay, G. (1981) Predatory pricing: competing economic theories and the evolution of legal standards. *Cornell Law Review*: 738–803.

Brown, D. and Heal, G. (1979) Equity, efficiency and increasing returns. *Review of Economic Studies*: 571–86.

Brown, D. and Heal, G. (1980) Two-part tariffs, marginal cost pricing, and increasing returns in a general equilibrium framework. *Journal of Public Economics*: 25–49.

Brown, G. and Johnson, M. (1969) Public utility pricing and output under risk.

American Economic Review: 119–28.

Brown, R. (1978) Estimating advantages to large scale advertising. *Review of Economics and Statistics*: 428–37.

Brozen, Y. (1971) Bain's concentration and rates of return revisited. *Journal of Law and Economics*: 351–69.

Brozen, Y. (1974) Entry barriers, advertising and product differentiation. In H. Goldschmidt et al. (eds), *Industrial Concentration: The New Learning*. Boston, MA: Little, Brown.

Brush, B. (1978) Errors in the measurement of concentration and the advertising – concentration controversy. *Southern Economic Journal*: 978–86.

Buchanan, J. (1952) The theory of monopolistic quantity discounts. *Review of Economic Studies*: 199–208.

Bulow, J. (1982) Durable-goods monopolists. *Journal of Political Economy*: 314–32.

Bulow, J. and Pfeiderer, P. (1983) A note on the effect of cost changes on prices. *Journal of Political Economy*: 182–5.

Bulow, J., Geanakoplos, J. and Klemperer, P. (1985) Multimarket oligopoly: strategic substitutes and complements. *Journal of Political Economy*: 488–511.

Burns, M. (1986) Predatory pricing and the acquisition costs of competitors. *Journal of Political Economy*: 266–96.

Burstein, M. (1960a) The economics of tie-in sales. *Review of Economics and Statistics*: 68–73.

Burstein, M. (1960b) A theory of full-line forcing. *Northwestern University Law Review*: 62–95.

Butters, G. (1977) Equilibrium distribution of prices and advertising. *Review of Economic Studies*: 465–92.

Buzzell, R. and Nourse, R. (1967) Product innovation in food processing, 1954–1964. Unpublished Manuscript. Cambridge, MA: Division of Research, Graduate School of Business, Harvard University.

Bylka, S. and Komar, J. (1975) *Cournot–Bertrand Mixed Oligopolies*. New York: Springer-Verlag.

Capozza, D. and VanOrder, R. (1977) Pricing under spatial competition and spatial monopoly. *Econometrica*: 1329–38.

Carlton, D. (1979) Vertical integration in competitive markets under uncertainty. *Journal of Industrial Economics*: 189–209.

Carruthers, N. (1981) Location choice when price is also a decision variable. *Annals of Regional Science*: 29–42.

Carson, R. (1975) On monopoly welfare losses: comment. *American Economic Review*: 1008–14.

Cave, J. (1985) A further comment on preemptive patenting and the persistence of monopoly. *American Economic Review*: 256–8.

Caves, R. (1982) *American Industry: Struture, Conduct and Performance* (5th edn). Englewood Cliffs, NJ: Prentice-Hall.

Caves, R. and Murphy, W. (1976) Franchising: firms, markets and intangible assets. *Southern Economic Journal*: 572–86.

Caves, R. and Porter, M. (1976) *Essays on Industrial Organization in Honour of Joe Bain*. Cambridge, MA: Ballinger.

Caves. R. and Porter, M. (1977) From entry barriers to mobility barriers: conjectural decisions and contrived deterrence to new competition. *Quarterly Journal of Economics*: 241–61.

Caves, R. and Pugel, T. (1980) *Intraindustry Differences in Conduct and Performance*. Monograph 1980–2, Series in Finance and Economics. New York: NYU Graduate School of Business.

Caves, R., Crookell, H. and Killing, J. (1983) The imperfect market for technology licenses. *Oxford Bulletin for Economics and Statistics*: 249–67.

Caves, R., Porter, M., Spence, A. and Scott, J. (1980) *Competition in an Open Economy: A Model Applied to Canada*. Cambridge, MA: Harvard University Press.

Chamberlin, E. (1929) Duopoly: value when sellers are few. *Quarterly Journal of Economics*: 63–100.

Chamberlin, E. (1933) *The Theory of Monopolistic Competition*. Cambridge, MA: Harvard University Press.

Chamberlin, E. (1951) Monopolistic competition revisited. *Econometrica*: 343–62.

Chandler, A. (1969) The structure of American industry in the twentieth century. *Business History Review*: 257–69.

Chari, V. (1983) Involuntary unemployment and implicit contracts. *Quarterly Journal of Economics*: 107–22.

Cheng, L. (1984) Bertrand equilibrium is more competitive than Cournot equilibrium: the case of differentiated products. Working Paper. Gainesville, FL: Department of Economics, University of Florida.

Cheng, L. (1985) Comparing Bertrand and Cournot equilibria: a geometric approach. *RAND Journal of Economics*: 146–51.

Chiang, R. (1982) Imperfect price discrimination and welfare. *Review of Economic Studies*: 155–81.

Chiang, R. and Spatt, C. (1982) Imperfect price discrimination and welfare. *Review of Economic Studies*: 155–81.

Cho, I. and Kreps, D. (1987) Signalling games and stable equilibria, *Quarterly Journal of Economics*: 179–221.

Clarke, D. (1976) Econometric measurement of the duration of advertising effect on sales. *Journal of Marketing Research*: 345–57.

Clarke, R. (1983a) Duopolists don't wish to share information. *Economics Letters*: 33–6.

Clarke, R. (1983b) Collusion and the incentives for information sharing. *Bell Journal of Economics*: 383–94.

Clarke, R. (1985) *Industrial Economics*. Oxford: Blackwell.

Clarke, R. and Davies, S. (1983) Market structure and price-cost margins. *Economica*: 277–87.

Clarke, R., Davies, S. and Waterson, M. (1984) The profitability – concentration relation: market power or efficiency? *Journal of Industrial Economics*: 435–50.

Clarkson, K. (1977) *Intangible Capital and Rates of Return*. Washington, DC: American Enterprise Institute.

Coarse, R. (1937) The nature of the firm. *Economica*: 331–51.

Coarse, R. (1960) The problem of social cost. *Journal of Law and Economics*: 1–44.

Coarse, R. (1972) Durability and monopoly. *Journal of Law and Economics*: 143–9.

Coen, R. (1982) Industry revenues outpace GNP in '81. *Advertising Age*: March 22, 10, 66.

Collins, N. and Preston, L. (1969) Price–cost margins and industry structure. *Review of Economics and Statistics*: 271–86.

Comanor, W. (1968) Vertical territorial and customer restrictions. White Motor and its aftermath. *Harvard Law Review*: 1419–38.

Comanor, W. (1985) Vertical price fixing and market restrictions and the new antitrust policy. *Harvard Law Review*: 98–106.

Comanor, W. and Kirkwood, J. (1985) Resale price maintenance and antitrust policy. *Contemporary Policy Issues*: 9–16.

Comanor, W. and Leibenstein, H. (1969) Allocative efficiency, X-inefficiency, and the measurement of welfare losses. *Economica*: 304–9.

Comanor, W. and Smiley, R. (1975) Monopoly and the distribution of wealth. *American Economic Review*: 177–94.

Comanor, W. and Wilson, T. (1967) Advertising, market structure and performance. *Review of Economics and Statistics*: 423–40.

Comanor, W. and Wilson, T. (1974) *Advertising and Monopoly Power*. Cambridge, MA: Harvard University Press.

Comanor, W. and Wilson, T. (1979) Advertising and competition: a survey. *Journal of Economic Literature*: 453–76.

Connolly, R., Hirsch, B. and Hirshey, M. (1986) Union rent-seeking, intangible capital, and the market value of the firm. *Review of Economics and Statistics*: 567–77.

Cooper, R. (1984) On allocative distortion in problems of self-selection. *RAND Journal of Economics*: 568–77.

Cooper, R. and Hayes, B. (1984) Multiperiod insurance contracts. Cowles Foundation Papers No. 673. New Haven, CT: Yale University.

Cooper, R. and Ross, T. (1983) Monopoly provision of product quality with uninformed buyers. Unpublished Paper. New Haven, CT: Yale University.

Cooper, R. and Ross, T. (1984) Prices, product qualities, and asymmetric information: the competitive case. *Review of Economic Studies*: 197–208.

Cooper, R. and Ross, T. (1985) Product warranties and double moral hazard. *RAND Journal of Economics*: 103–13.

Cooper, T. (1986) Most-favored-customer pricing and tacit collusion. *RAND Journal of Economics*: 377–88.

Cornell, B. and Roll, R. (1981) Strategies for pairwise competitions in markets and organizations. *Bell Journal of Economics*: 201–13.

Cournot, A. (1983) *Recherches sur les Principes Mathématiques de la Théorie des Richesses*. Paris: Hachette (reprinted 1960).

Cowling, K. (1976) On the theoretical specification of industrial structure–performance relationships. *European Economic Review*: 1–14.

Cowling, K. and Cubbin, J. (1972) Hedonic price indexes for cars in the U.K. *Economic Journal*: 963–78.

Cowling, K. and Mueller, D. (1978) The social costs of monopoly power. *Economic Journal*: 727–48.

Cowling, K. and Waterson, M. (1976) Price–cost margins and market structure. *Economica*: 267–74.

Crandall, R. (1968) Vertical integration and the market for repair parts in the United States automobile industry. *Journal of International Economics*: 212–34.

Crawford, V. (1982) A theory of disagreement in bargaining. *Econometrica*: 607–37.

Crawford, V. and Sobel, J. (1982) Strategic information transmission. *Econometrica*: 1431–51.

Crew, M. and Kleindorfer, P. (1976) Peak load pricing with a diverse technology. *Bell Journal of Economics*: 207–31.

Crew, M. and Kleindorfer, P. (1978) Reliability and public utility pricing. *American Economic Review*: 31–40.

Cubbin, J. (1974) A measure of apparent collusion in oligopoly. Warwick Economics Research Paper No. 49.

Cubbin, J. (1975) Quality change and pricing behaviour in the U.K. car industry. *Economica*: 43–58.

Cubbin, J. (1981) Advertising and the theory of entry barriers. *Economica*: 289–98.

Cubbin, J. (1983) Apparent collusion and conjectual variations in differentiated oligopoly. *International Journal of Industrial organization*: 155–63.

Cummings, F. and Ruther, W. (1979) The Northern Pacific case. *Journal of Law and Economics*: 329–50.

Cyert, D. and DeGroot, M. (1973) An analysis of cooperation and learning in a duopoly context. *American Economic Review*: 24–37.

Dansby, R. and Willig, R. (1980) Industry performance gradient indices. *American Economic Review*: 249–60.

Darby, M. and Karni, E. (1973) Free competition and the optimal amount of fraud. *Journal of Law and Economics*: 67–88.

Dasgupta, P. (1983) The theory of technological competition. In J Stiglitz and F. Mathewson (eds), *New Developments in the Analysis of Market Structure*. Cambridge, MA: MIT Press.

Dasgupta, P. and Stiglitz, J. (1980a) Uncertainty, industrial structure and the speed of R&D. *Journal of Economics*: 1–28.

Dasgupta, P. and Stiglitz, J. (1980b) Industrial structure and the nature of innovative activity. *Economic Journal*: 266–93.

Davidson, C and Deneckere, R. (1984) Horizontal mergers and collusive behavior. *International Journal of Industrial Organization*: 117–32.

Davidson, C. and Deneckere, R. (1986) Long-run competition in capacity, short-run competition in prices and the Cournot model. *RAND Journal of Economics*: 404–15.

Davies, S. (1979a) *The Diffusion of Process Innovations*. Cambridge, MA: Cambridge University Press.

Davies, S. (1979b) Choosing between concentration indices. *Economica*: 67–75.

Demsetz, H. (1959) The nature of equilibrium in monopolistic competition. *Journal of Political Economy*: 21–30.

Demsetz, H. (1964) The welfare and empirical implications of monopolistic competition. *Economic Journal*: 623–41.

Demsetz, H. (1968a) The cost of transacting. *Quarterly Journal of Economics*:

33–53.

Demsetz, H (1968b) Why regulate utilities? *Journal of Law and Economics*: 158–76.

Demsetz, H. (1969) Information and efficiency: another viewpoint. *Journal of Law and Economics*: 1–22.

Demsetz, H. (1970) The private production of public goods. *Journal of Law and Economics*: 293–306

Demsetz, H. (1973a) Joint supply and price discrimination. *Journal of Law and Economics*: 389–415.

Demsetz, H. (1973b) Industry structure, market rivalry and public policy. *Journal of Law and Economics*: 1–9.

Demsetz, H. (1974) Two systems of belief about monopoly In H. Goldschmidt et al. (eds), *Industrial Concentration: the New Learning*. Boston, MA: Little, Brown.

Demsetz, H. (1979) Accounting for advertising as a barrier to entry. *Journal of Business*: 345–60.

Demsetz, H. (1982a) Barriers to entry. *American Economic Review*: 47–57.

Demsetz, H. (1982b) *Economic, Legal and Political Dimensions of Competition*. Amsterdam: North-Holland.

Denardo, E (1967) Contraction mappings in the theory underlying dynamic programming. *SIAM Review*: 165–77.

Deneckere, R. (1983) Duopoly supergames with product differentiation. *Economic Letters*: 37–42.

Deneckere, R. and Davidson, C. (1985) Incentives to form coalitions with Bertrand competition. *RAND Journal of Economics*: 473–86.

De Neef, P. (1979) *Two-part tariffs and nonlinear prices*. Louvain la-Neuve: Université Catholique de Louvain.

De Vane, A. and Saving, T. (1983) The economics of quality. *Journal of Political Economy*: 979–1000.

Diamond, D. (1984) Financial intermediation and delegated monitoring. *Review of Economic Studies*: 393–414.

Diamond, D. (1985) Reputation acquisition in capital markets. Unpublished manuscript. Chicago, IL: Department of Economics, University of Chicago.

Dickson, V. (1983) Collusion and price–cost margins. *Eonomica*: 39–42.

Diewert, W. (1978) Duality approaches to microeconomic theory. IMSSS Technical Publication No. 281. Stanford, CA: Stanford University Press.

Dixit, A. (1979) A model of duopoly suggesting a theory of entry barriers. *Bell Journal of Economics*: 20–32.

Dixit, A. (1980) The role of investment in entry deterrence. *Economic Journal*: 95–106.

Dixit, A. (1982) Recent developments in oligopoly theory. *American Economic Review*: 12–17.

Dixit, A. (1986) Comparative statics for oligopoly. *International Economic Review*: 107–22.

Dixit, A. (1987) Strategic behavior in contests. *American Economic Review*: 891–8.

Dixit, A. and Norman, V. (1978) Advertising and welfare. *Bell Journal of*

Economics: 1–17.

Dixit, A. and Norman, V. (1979) Advertising and welfare: reply. *RAND Journal of Economics*: 728–30.

Dixit, A. and Stiglitz, J. (1977) Monopolistic competition and optimum product diversity *American Economic Review*: 297–308.

Dixon, H. (1984) Approximate Bertrand equilibria and strategic precommitment. D. Phil, thesis. Oxford: Oxford University.

Dixon, H. (1985) Strategic investment in an industry with a competitive product market. *Journal of Industrial Economics*: 56–68.

Dolbear, F., Lave, L. and Bowman, G. (1968) Collusion in oligopoly: an experiment on the effect of numbers and information. *Quarterly Journal of Economics*: 240–59.

Domsimoni, M.-P., Geroski, P. and Jacquemin, A. (1984) Concentration indices and market power: two views, *Journal of Industrial Economics*: 419–34.

Dorfman, R. and Steiner, P. (1954) Optimal advertising and optimal quality. *American Economic Review*: 826–36.

Douglas, A. and Goldman, S. (1969) Monopolistic behaviour in a market for durable goods. *Journal of Political Economy*: 49–59.

Dreze, J. and Hagen, K. (1978) Choice of product quality: equilibrium and efficiency. *Econometrica*: 493–513.

Dybvig, R. and Spatt, C. (1983) Does it pay to maintain a reputation? Consumer information and product quality. Mimeo. New Haven, CT: Yale University.

Easterbrook, F. (1981a) Maximum pricing fixing. *University of Chicago Law Review*: 886–910.

Easterbrook, F. (1981b) Predatory strategies and counter-strategies. *University of Chicago Law Review*: 263–337.

Easterbrook, F. (1984) The limits of antitrust. *Texas Law Review*: 1–40.

Eaton, B. and Lipsey, R. (1975) The principle of minimum differentiation reconsidered: some new deveopments in the theory of spatial competition. *Review of Economic Studies*: 27–49.

Eaton, B. and Lipsey, R. (1976) The non-uniqueness of equilibrium in the Loschian location model. *American Economic Review*: 77–93.

Eaton, B. and Lipsey, R. (1978) Freedom of entry and the existence of price profit. *Economic Journal*: 455–69.

Eaton, B. and Lipsey, R. (1979) The theory of market pre-emption: the persistence of excess capacity and monopoly in growing spatial markets. *Econometrica*: 149–58.

Eaton, B. and Lipsey, R. (1980) Exit barriers and entry barriers: the durability of capital as a barrier to entry. *Bell Journal of Economics*: 721–9.

Eaton, B. and Lipsey, R. (1981) Capital, commitment and entry equilibrium. *Bell Journal of Economics*: 593–604.

Eaton, B. and Wooders, M. (1985) Sophisticated entry in a model of spatial competition. *RAND Journal of Economics*: 282–97.

Eaton, J. and Kierzkowski, H. (1985) Oligopolistic competition, product variety, entry deterrence, and technology transfer. *RAND Journal of Economics*: 99–107.

Economides, N. (1981) Symmetric oligopoly in differentiated products. Discussion Paper No. 208. New York: Columbia University.

Edgeworth, F. (1881) *Mathematical Physics*. London: Kegan Paul (reprinted 1974).

Edgeworth, F. (1897) La teoria pura del monopolio. *Giornale degli Economisti*: 13–31.

Ekelund, R. (1970) Price discrimination and product differentiation in economic theory: an early analysis. *Quarterly Journal of Economics*: 268–78.

Elzinga, K. (1970) Predatory pricing: the case of the Gunpowder Trust. *Journal of Law and Economics*: 223–40.

Elzinga, K. and Hogarty, T. (1973) The problem of geographic market delineation in anti merger suits. *Antitrust Bulletin*: 45–81.

Encaoua, D. and Jacquemin, A. (1980) Degree of monopoly, indices of concentration and threat of entry. *International Economic Review*: 87–105.

Encaoua, D., Geroski, P. and Jacquemin, A. (1984) *Strategic Competition and the Persistence of Dominant Firms: a Survey*. Boston, MA: MIT Press.

Engle, J., Blackwell, R. and Kollat, D. (1978) *Consumer Behavior*. Hindsdale, IL: Dryden.

Erkkila, J. (1986) Copyright law, photocopying and price discrimination: comment. In J. Palmer (ed.), *Research in Law and Economics*, vol. 8. Greenwich, CT: JAI Press.

Fama, E. (1970) Efficient capital markets: a review of theory and empirical work. *Journal of Finance*: 383–417.

Fama, E. (1976) *Foundations of Finance*. New York: Basic Books.

Fama, E. (1980) Agency problems and the theory of the firm. *Journal of Political Economy*: 288–307.

Farrar, D. and Phillips, C. (1959) New developments on the oligopoly front: a comment, *Journal of Political Economy*: 414–17.

Farrell, J. (1986a) A note on inertia in market share. *Economic Letters*: 73–5.

Farrell, J. (1986b) Moral hazard as a barrier to entry. *RAND Journal of Economics*: 440–9.

Farrell, J. (1987) Cheap talk, coordination, and entry. *RAND Journal of Economics*: 34–9.

Farrell, J. and Saloner, G. (1985) Standardization, compatibility and innovation. *RAND Journal of Economics*: 70–83.

Farrell, J. and Shapiro, C. (1988) Dynamic competition with switching costs. *RAND Journal of Economics*: 123–37.

Faulhaber, G. (1975) Cross-subsidization: pricing in public enterprises. *American Economic Review*: 966–77.

Fellner, W. (1960) *Competition Among the Few*. New York: Kelley.

Ferguson, C. (1969) *The Neoclassical Theory of Production and Distribution*. Cambridge: Cambridge University Press.

Ferguson, J. (1965) Tying arrangements and reciprocity: an economic analysis. *Law and Contemporary Problems*: 522–80.

Ferguson, J. (1974) *Advertising and Competition: Theory, Measurement, Fact*. Cambridge, MA: Ballinger.

Fershtman, C. and Judd, K. (1984) Equilibrium incentives in duopoly. CMSEMS Working Paper No. 640. Evanston, IL: Northwestern University.

Fisher, F. (1961) The stability of the Cournot oligopoly system: the effects of speeds of adjustment and increasing marginal costs. *Review of Economic Studies*: 125–35.

Fisher, F. (1985) The social costs of monopoly and regulation: Posner reconsidered, *Journal of Political Economy*: 410–16.

Fisher, F. (1987) On the misuse of the profit–sales ratio to infer monopoly power, *RAND Journal of Economics*: 384–96.

Fisher, F. and McGowan, J. (1979) Advertising and welfare: comment. *Journal of Economics*: 726–7.

Fisher, F. and McGowan, J. (1983) On the misuse of accounting rates of return to infer monopoly profits. *American Economic Review*: 82–92.

Fisher, F. and Temin, P. (1973) Returns to scale in research and development. *Journal of Political Economy*: 56–70.

Fisher, F., Griliches, Z. and Kaysen, C. (1962) The costs of automobile model changes since 1949. *Journal of Political Economy*: 433–51.

Fisher, F., McGowan, J. and Greenwood, J. (1983) *Folded, Spindled and Mutilated: Economic Analysis and U.S. vs. IBM*. Cambridge, MA: MIT Press.

Fisher, I. (1898) Cournot and mathematical economics. *Quarterly Journal of Economics*: 210–26.

Florence, P. (1972) *The Logic of British and American Industry* (3rd edn.) London: Routledge and Kegan Paul.

Forchheimer, K. (1908) Theoretisches sum unvollstaendigen Monopole. *Schmollers Jahrbuch*: 1–12.

Fouraker, L. and Siegel, S. (1963) *Bargaining Behavior*. New York: McGraw-Hill.

Fox, E. (1981) The modernization of antitrust: a new equilbrium. *Cornell Law Review*: 1140–92.

Freeman, C. (1974) *The Economics of Industrial Innovation*. Harmondsworth: Penguin.

Friedman, D. (1979) In defense of long-haul/short-haul discrimination. *Bell Journal of Economics*: 706–8.

Friedman, J. (1963) Individual behavior in oligopolistic markets: an experimental study. *Yale Economic Essays*: 359–417.

Friedman, J. (1969) On experimental research in oligopoly. *Review of Economic Studies*: 399–415.

Friedman, J. (1971) A non-cooperative equilibrium for supergames. *Review of Economic Studies*: 1–12.

Friedman, J. (1977) *Oligopoly and the Theory of Games*. Amsterdam: North-Holland.

Friedman, J. (1983) *Oligopoly Theory*. Cambridge: Cambridge University Press.

Friedman, J. (1986) *Game Theory with Applications to Economics*. New York: Oxford University Press.

Friedman, J. and Hoggart, A. (1980) *An Experiment in Non-cooperative Oligopoly*. Greenwich, CT: JAI Press.

Friedman, M. and Savage, L. (1972) The utility analysis of choices involving risk. *Journal of Political Economy*: 279–304.

Fudenberg, D. and Maskin, E. (1986) The Folk Theorem in repeated games with discounting or incomplete information. *Econometrica*: 533–55.

Fudenberg, D. and Tirole, J. (1982) Capital as a commitment: strategic investment to deter mobility. *Journal of Economic Theory*: 227–56.

Fudenberg, D. and Tirole, J. (1984) The fat-cat effect, the puppy-dog ploy, and the lean and hungry look. *American Economic Review*: 361–6.

Fudenberg, D. and Tirole, J. (1986a) *Dynamic Models of Oligopoly*. New York: Harwood Academic.

Fudenberg, D. and Tirole, J. (1986b) A signal-jamming theory of predation. *RAND Journal of Economics*: 366–76.

Fudenberg, D., Gilbert, R., Stiglitz, J. and Tirole, J. (1983) Preemption, leapfrogging and competition in patent races. *European Economic Review*: 3–31.

Galbraith, J. (1936) Monopoly power and price rigidities. *Quarterly Journal of Economics*: 466–8.

Galbraith, J. (1967) *The New Industrial State*. Boston, MA: Houghton Mifflin.

Gale, D. and Hellwig, M. (1986) Incentive compatible debt contracts. *Review of Economic Studies*: 647–64.

Gallini, N. (1984) Deterrence by market sharing: a strategic incentive for licensing. *American Economic Review*: 931–41.

Gallini, N. and Winter, R. (1985) Licensing in the theory of innovation. *RAND Journal of Economics*: 237–51.

Gal-Or, E. (1985) Information sharing in oligopoly. *Econometrica*: 329–43.

Gal-Or, E. (1986) Information transmission: Cournot and Bertrand equilibrium. *Review of Economic Studies*: 279–92.

Gal-Or, E. (1987) First-mover disadvantges and private information. *Review of Economic Studies*: 279–92.

Garvin, D. (1983) Quality on the line. *Harvard Business Review*: 33–41.

Gaskins, D. (1971) Dynamic limit pricing: optimal pricing under threat of entry. *Journal of Economic Theory*: 306–22.

Gaskins, D. (1974) Alcoa revisited: the welfare implications of a secondhand market. *Journal of Economic Theory*: 254–71.

Gelman, J. and Salop, S. (1983) Judo-economics: capacity limitation and coupon competition. *Bell Journal of Economics*: 315–25.

Geroski, P. (1982a) Interpreting a correlation between profits and concentration. *Journal of Industrial Economics*: 305–18.

Geroski, P. (1982b) Simultaneous equations models of the structure–performance paradigm. *European Economic Review*: 145–58.

Geroski, P. (1983) Some reflections on the theory and application of concentration indices. *International Journal of Industrial Organization*: 79–94.

Geroski, P. (1986) Do dominant firms decline? In D. Hay and J. Vickers (eds), *The Economics of Market Dominance*. Oxford: Blackwell.

Geroski, P. and Jacquemin, A. (1984) Dominant firms and their alleged decline. *International Journal of Industrial Organization*: 1–27.

Ghemawat, P. and Nalebuff, B. (1985) Exit. *RAND Journal of Economics*: 184–94.

Gilbert, R. (1981) Patents, sleeping patents and entry deterrence. In S. Salop (ed.), *Strategy, Predation and Antitrust Analysis*. Federal Trade Commission.

Gilbert, R. and Harris, R. (1981) Investment decisions with economies of scale and learning. *American Economic Review*: 172–7.

Gilbert, R. and Newbery, D. (1982) Pre-emptive patenting and the persistence of monopoly. *American Economic Review*: 514–26.

Gilbert, R. and Newbery, D. (1984a) Uncertain innovation and the persistence of monopoly: comment, *American Economic Review*: 238–42.

Gilbert, R. and Newbury, D. (1984b) Pre-emptive patenting and the persistence of monopoly: reply. *American Economic Review*: 251–53.

Goldberg, V. (1979) The law and economies of vertical restrictions: a relational perspective. *Texas Law Review*: 91–129.

Goldberg, V. and Morirao, S. (1973) Limit pricing and potential competition. *Journal of Political Economy*: 1460–6.

Goldberger, A. (1964) *Econometric Theory*. New York: Wiley.

Goldman, S. and Uzawa, Y. (1964) A note on separability in demand analysis. *Econometrica*: 387–98.

Gollop, F. and Roberts, M. (1979) Firm interdependence in oligopolistic markets. *Journal of Econometrics*: 313–31.

Gorman, W. (1976) Tricks with utility functions. In M. Artis and N. Nobey (eds), *Essays in Economic Analysis*. Cambridge: Cambridge University Press.

Gorman, W. (1980) A possible procedure for analyzing quality differences in the egg market. *Review of Economic Studies*: 1–30.

Gort, M. and Klepper, S. (1982) Time paths in the diffusion of product innovations. *Economic Journal*: 650–3.

Gort, M. and Konakayama, A. (1982) A model of diffusion in the production of an innovation. *American Economic Review*: 1111–20.

Gould, J. (1977) Price discrimination and vertical control: a note. *Journal of Political Economy*: 1063–71.

Gould, J. and Preston, L. (1965) Resale price maintenance and retail outlets. *Econometrica*: 302–12.

Grabowski, H. (1968) The determinants of industrial research and development. *Journal of Political Economy*: 292–306.

Graitson, D. (1980) On Hotelling's stability in competition, again. *Economic Letters*: 1–6.

Green, J. and Porter, R. (1984) Noncooperative collusion under imperfect price information. *Econometrica*: 87–100.

Green, J. and Stokey, N. (1983) A comparison of tournaments and contest. *Journal of Political Economy*: 349–64.

Greenhut, J. and Greenhut, M. (1977) Nonlinearity of delivered price schedules and predatory pricing. *Econometrica*: 1871–5.

Greenhut, M. and Ohta, H. (1972) Monopoly output under alternative spatial pricing techniques. *American Economic Review*: 705–13.

Greenhut, M. and Ohta, H. (1976) Related market conditions and interindustrial mergers. *American Economic Review*: 267–77.

Greenhut, M. and Ohta, H. (1979) Vertical integration of successive oligopolists. *American Economic Review*: 137–41.

Greenwald, B. and Stiglitz, J. (1985) Externalities in economies with imperfect information and incomplete markets. *Quarterly Journal of Economics*: 63–81.

Griesmer, J., Levithan, R. and Shubik, M. (1967) Toward a study of bidding processes, part IV: games with unknown costs. *Naval Research Logistics Quarterly*: 415–33.

Griliches, Z. (1961) Hedonic price indexes for automobiles: an econometric analysis of quality change. In *Price Statistics of the Federal Government*. New York: National Bureau of Economic Research.

Griliches, Z. (1971) Hedonic price indexes revisited. In Z. Griliches (ed.), *Price Indexes and Quality Change*. Cambridge, MA: Harvard University Press.

Grossman, G. and Shapiro, C. (1984) Information advertising with differentiated products. *Review of Economic Studies*: 63–81.

Grossman, G. and Shapiro, C. (1987) Dynamic R&D competition. *Economic Journal*: 372–87.

Grossman, S. (1980) The role of warranties and private disclosure about product quality *Journal of Law and Economics*: 461–83.

Grossman, S. (1981) Nash equilibrium and the industrial organisation of market with large fixed costs. *Econometrica*: 1149–72.

Grossman, S. and Hart, O. (1980) Takeover bids, the free-rider problems, and the theory of the corporation. *Bell Journal of Economics*: 42–64.

Grossman, S. and Hart, O. (1983) An analysis of principal–agent problem. *Econometrica*: 123–56.

Grossman, S. and Perry, M. (1986) Perfect sequential equilibria. *Journal of Economic Theory*: 97–119.

Grossman, S. and Stiglitz, J. (1976) Information and competitive price systems. *American Economic Review*: 246–53.

Grote, J. (1974) A global theory of games. *Journal of Mathematical Economics*: 223–36.

Guasch, J. and Sobel, J. (1980) Monopoly and product selection. *Economic Letters*: 81–3.

Guesnerie, R. and Seade, J. (1982) Nonlinear pricing in a finite economy. *Journal of Public Economics*: 157–79.

Hadar, J. (1966) Stability of oligopoly with product differentiation. *Review of Economic Studies*: 57–60.

Hahn, F. (1962) The stability of the Cournot oligopoly situation. *Review of Economic Studies*: 329–31.

Hahn, F. (1977) Exercises in conjectural equilibria. *Scandinavian Journal of Economics*: 210–26.

Hahn, F. (1978) On non-Walrasian equilibria. *Review of Economic Studies*: 1–17.

Haldi, J. and Whitcomb, D. (1967) Economies of scale in industrial plants. *Journal of Political Economy*: 137–49.

Hall, R. (1971) The measurement of quality change from vintage price data. In Z. Griliches (ed.), *Price Indexes and Quality Change*. Cambridge, MA: Harvard University Press.

Hamberg, D. (1966) *R&D: Essays on the Economics of Research and Development*. New York: Random House.

Hannah, L. and Kay, J. (1975) *Concentration in Modern Industry: Theory, Measurement, and the U.K. Experience*. London: Macmillan.

Hanoch, G. (1975) The elasticity of scale and the shape of average costs. *American Economic Review*: 492–7.

Hansen, R. and Roberts, R. (1980) Metered tying arrangements, allocative efficiency, and price discrimination. *Southern Economic Journal*: 73–83.

Harberger, A. (1954) Monopoly and resource allocation. *American Economic Review*: 77–87.

Harris, C. J. and Vickers, J. S (1985a) Perfect equilibrium in a model of a race. *Review of Economic Studies*: 193–209.

Harris, C. J. and Vickers, J. S. (1985b) Patent races and the persistence of monopoly. *Journal of Industrial Economics*: 98–111.

Harris, M. and Raviv, A. (1979) Optimal incentive costs contracts with imperfect information. *Journal of Economic Theory*: 231–59.

Harsanyi, J. C. (1967) Games with incomplete information played by Bayesian players, I. *Management Science*: 159–82.

Harsanyi, J. C. (1968a) Games with incomplete information played by Bayesian players, II. *Management Science*: 320–34.

Harsanyi, J. C. (1968b) Games with incomplete information played by Bayesian players, III. *Management Science*: 486–502.

Hart, O. (1983) Optimal labor contracts under asymmetric information: an introduction. *Review of Economic Studies*: 3–36.

Hart, O. (1985a) Monopolistic competition in the spirit of Chamberlin: a general model. *Review of Economic Studies*: 529–46.

Hart, O. (1985b) Monopolistic competition in the spirit of Chamberlin: special results. *Review of Economic Studies*: 889–908.

Hart, P. (1983) Experience curves and industrial policy. *International Journal of Industrial Organization*: 95–106.

Hathaway, N. and Rickard, J. (1979) Equilibria of price-setting and quantity-setting duopolies. *Economic Letters*: 133–7.

Haugen, R. and Senbet, L. (1978) The insignificance of bankruptcy costs to the theory of optimal capital structure. *Journal of Finance*: 383–93.

Hause, J. (1977) The measurement of concentrated industrial structure and the size distribution of firms. *Annals of Economic and Social Measurement*: 73–107.

Hausman, J. (1981) Exact consumer's surplus and deadweight loss. *American Economic Review*: 662–75.

Hay, D. (1976) Sequential entry and entry deterring strategies in spatial competition. *Oxford Economic Papers*: 240–57.

Hay, G. (1982) Oligopoly, shared monopoly and antitrust law. *Cornell Law Review*: 439–81.

Hayes, B. (1984) Unions and strikes with asymmetric information. *Journal of Labor Economics*: 57–83.

Heal, G. (1977) Guarantees and risk-sharing. *Review of Economic Studies*: 549–60.

Henning, J. and Mann, M. (1978) Advertising and oligopoly: correlations in search of understanding. In D. Tuerck (ed.), *Issues in Advertising*. Washington, DC: American Enterprise Institute.

van Herck, G. (1982) Corporate monopoly power and risk. *European Economic Review*: 115–24.

Herstein, I. and Milnor, J. (1953) An axiomatic approach to measurable utility. *Econometrica*: 291–7.

Hillman, A. and Katz, E. (1984) Risk-averse rent-seekers and the social costs of monopoly power. *Economic Journal*: 104–10.

Hines, H. (1957) Effectiveness of entry by already established firms. *Quarterly Journal of Economics*: 132–50.

Hirsh, B. and Link, A. (1987) Labor union effects on innovative activity. Unpublished manuscript. University of North Carolina.

Hirshleifer, J. (1958) Peak loads and efficient pricing: comment. *Quarterly Journal of Economics*: 451–62.

Hirshleifer, J. (1972) Price Theory and Applications (1st edn). Englewood Cliffs, NJ: Prentice-Hall.

Hoggatt, A. (1967) Measuring the cooperativeness of behaviour in quantity variation duopoly games. *Behavioural Science*: 109–21.

Holahan, W. (1975) The welfare effects of spatial price discrimination. *American Economic Review*: 498–503.

Holahan, W. (1978) Cartel problems: comment. *American Economic Review*: 942–6.

Holmstrom, B. (1979) Moral hazard and observability. *Bell Journal of Economics*: 74–91.

Holt, C. and Scheffman D. (1985) The effects of advance notice and best-price policies: theory, with applications to *Ethyl*. Thomas Jefferson Center Working Paper, University of Virginia.

Holt, C. and Scheffman, D. (1987) Strategic business behavior and antitrust. Unpublished manuscript. Washington, DC: Federal Trade Commission.

Holthausen, D. (1979) Kinky demand, risk aversion and price leadership. *Internationl Economics Review*: 341–8.

Horowitz, I. (1962) Firm size and research activity. *Southern Economic Journal*: 298–301.

Horowitz, I. (1984) The misuse of accounting rates of return: comment. *American Economic Review*: 492–3.

Hotelling, H. (1929) Stability in competition. *Economic Journal*: 41–57.

Houthakker, H. (1960) Additive preferences. *Econometrica*: 244–57.

Inaba, F. (1980) Franchising: monopoly by contract. *Southern Economic Journal*: 65–72.

Ireland, N. (1972) Concentration and the growth of market demand. *Journal of Economic Theory*: 303–5.

Ireland, N. (1980) The anology between parameter uncertainty and parameter changes. *Economics Letters*: 301–8.

Ireland, N. (1983) Monopolistic competition and a firm's product range. *International Journal of Industrial Organization*: 239–52.

Irwin, M. and McKee, R. (1968) Vertical integration and the communication equipment industry: alternatives for public policy. *Cornell Law Review*: 446–72.

Ishii, Y. (1977) On the theory of the competitive firm under price uncertainty: a note. *American Economic Review*: 768–9.

Iwata, G. (1974) Measurement of conjectural variations of oligopoly. *Econometrica*: 947–66.

Jacquemin, A. (1972) Market structure and the firm's market power. *Journal of Industrial Economics*: 122–34.

Jacquemin, A. and Thisse, J. (1972) *Strategy of the Firm and Market Structure: an Application of Optimal Control Theory in Market Structure and Corporate*

Behaviour: London: Gray-Mills.

Jaskold-Gabszewicz, H. and Thisse, J. (1979) Price competition, quality, and income disparities. *Journal of Economic Theory*: 340–59.

Jaskold-Gabszewicz, J. and Thisse, J. (1980) Entry (and exit) in a differentiated industry. *Journal of Economic Theory*: 327–38.

Jensen, H., Kehrberg, E. and Thomas, D. (1962) Integration as an adjustment to risk and uncertainty. *Southern Economic Journal*: 378–84.

Jensen, R. (1982) Adoption and diffusion of an innovation of uncertain profitability. *Journal of Economic Theory*: 182–93.

Johnson, A. and Helmberger, P. (1967) Price elasticity of demand as an element of market structure. *American Economic Review*: 1218–21.

Johnston, J. (1974) *Statistical Cost Analysis*. New York: McGraw-Hill.

Jones, W. (1978) The two faces of Fortner: comment on a recent antitrust opinion. *Columbia Law Review*: 39–47.

Joskow, P. (1983) A welfare analysis of industry product variety. Unpublished paper. New Haven, CT: Yale University.

Joskow, P. and Klevorick, A. (1979) A framework for analyzing predatory pricing policy. *Yale Law Journal*: 213–70.

Jovanovic, B. (1981) Entry with private information. *Bell Journal of Economics*: 649–60.

Just, R. and Chern, W. (1980) Tomatoes, technology and oligopoly. *Bell Journal of Economics*: 584–602.

Kahn, A. (1971) *The Economics of Regulation*: New York: Wiley.

Kahn, C. (1986) The durable goods monopolist and consistency with increasing cost. *Econometrica*: 275–94.

Kaldor, N. (1935) Market imperfection and excess capacity. *Economica*: 33–50.

Kaldor, N. (1950) The economic aspects of advertising. *Review of Economic studies*: 1–27.

Kalecki, M. (1939) *Essays in the Theory of Economic Fluctuations*. London: George Allen and Unwin.

Kalish, L., Hartzog, J. and Cassidy, H. (1978) The threat of entry with mutually aware potential entrants. *Journal of Political Economy*: 147–53.

Kambhu, J. (1982) Optimal product quality under asymmetric information and moral hazard. *Bell Journal of Economics*: 483–92.

Kamerschen, D. (1966) An estimation of the welfare loss from monopoly in the American economy. *Western Economic Journal*: 117–29.

Kamerschen, D. (1972) The statistics of advertising. *Rivista Internazionale di Scienze Economiche e Commerciali*: 1–25.

Kamerschen, D. and Lam, N. (1975) A survey of measures of monopoly power. *Revista Internazionale di Scienze Economiche e Commerciale*: 1131–56.

Kamien, M. and Schwartz, N. (1972) Uncertain entry and excess capacity. *American Economic Review*: 918–27.

Kamien, M. and Schwartz, N. (1974) Product durability and monopoly and competition. *Econometrica*: 289–301.

Kamien, M. and Schwartz, N. (1975) Cournot oligopoly with uncertain entry. *Review of Economic Studies*: 125–31.

Kamien, M. and Schwartz, N. (1982) *Market Sturcture and Innovation*. New York: Cambridge University Press.

Kamien, M. and Schwartz, N. (1983) Conjectural variations. *Canadian Journal of Economics*: 191–211.

Kamien, M. and Tauman, Y. (1986) Fees versus royalities and the private value of a patent. *Quarterly Journal of Economics*: 472–91.

Kaserman, D. (1978) Theories of vertical integration: implications for antitrust policy. *Antitrust Bulletin*: 484–510.

Katz, M. (1983) Nonuniform pricing, output and welfare under monopoly. *Review of Economic Studies*: 37–56.

Katz, M. (1986) An analysis of cooperative research and development. *RAND Journal of Economics*: 527–43.

Katz, M. and Shapiro, C. (1985) On the licensing of innovations. *RAND Journal of Economics*: 504–20.

Katzner, D. (1970) *Static Demand Theory*. New York: Macmillan.

Kaysen, K. and Turner, D. (1965) *Antitrust Policy, an Economic and Legal Analysis*. Cambridge, MA: Harvard University Press.

Kelly, T. (1970) The Influences of Firm Size and Market Structure on the Research Efforts of Large Multiple-Product Firms. Ph.D. dissertation. Oklahoma State University.

Kessel, R. (1958) Price discrimination in medicine. *Journal of Law and Economics*: 20–53.

Kessler, F. and Stern, R. (1959) Competition, contract, and vertical integration. *Yale Law Journal*: 1–129.

Kihlstrom, R. and Levhari, D. (1977) Quality, regulation and efficiency, *Kyklos*: 214–34.

Kirman, W. and Masson, R. (1980) Excess capacity credibility and entry deterrence. Unpublished paper. Ithaca, NY: Cornell University.

Kitch, E. (1972) The yellow cab antitrust case. *Journal of Law and Economics*: 327–36.

Kleiman, E. and Ophir, T. (1966) The durability of durable goods. *Review of Economic Studies*: 165–78.

Klein, B. (1980) Transaction cost determinants of 'unfair' contractual arrangements. *American Economic Review*: 356–62.

Klein, B. and Leffler, K. (1981) Non governmental enforcement of contracts: the role of market forces in assuring quality. *Journal of Political Economy*: 615–41.

Klein, B., Crawford, R. and Alchian, A. (1978) Vertical integration, appropriable rents, and the competitive contracting process. *Journal of Law and Economics*: 297–326.

Klemperer, P. (1987a) The competitiveness of markets with consumer switching costs. *RAND Journal of Economics*: 138–50.

Klemperer, P. (1987b) Markets with consumer switching costs. *Quarterly Journal of Economics*: 375–94.

Koenker, R. and Perry, M. (1981) Product differentiation, monopolistic competition, and public policy. *Bell Journal of Economics*: 217–31.

Kohler, R. (1971) The myth of predatory pricing: an empirical study. *Antitrust Law and Economics Review*: 105–23.

Kohn, M. and Scott, J. (1982) Scale economies in research and development. *Journal of Industrial Economics*: 239–49.

Kotowitz, Y. and Mathewson, F. (1979a) Advertising, consumer information, and product quality. *Bell Journal of Economics*: 566–88.

Kotowitz, Y. and Mathewson, F. (1979b) Information, advertising and welfare. *American Economic Review*: 284–94.

Kotowitz, Y. and Mathewson, F. (1982) Advertising as a barrier to entry. Working paper. University of Toronto.

Koutsoyiannis, A. (1979) *Modern Microeconomics*. London: Macmillan.

Krattenmaker, T. and Salop, S. (1986) Anticompetitive exclusion: raising rivals' costs to achieve power over price. *Yale Law Journal*: 210–95.

Kreps, D. and Scheinkman, J. (1983) Quantity precommitment and Bertrand competition yield Cournot outcomes. *Bell Journal of Economics*: 326–37.

Kreps, D. and Spence, M. (1984) Modelling the role of history in industrial organization and competition. In G. Fewel (ed.), *Contemporary Issues in Modern Microeconomics*. London: Macmillan.

Kreps, D. and Wilson, R. (1982a) Sequential equilibria. *Econometrica*: 863–95.

Kreps, D. and Wilson, R. (1982b) Reputation and imperfect information. *Journal Economic Theory*: 253–79.

Krouse, C. (1972) Complex objectives, decentralization, and the decision process of the firm. *Administrative Science Quarterly*: 544–54.

Krouse, C. (1973) On the theory of optimal investment, dividends and growth in the firm. *American Economic Review*: 269–79.

Krouse, C. (1976) Measuring allocative efficiency. *Journal of Finance*: 685–700.

Krouse, C. (1979) The optimality of risk allocation in competitive production and exchange. *Southern Economic Journal*: 762–77.

Krouse, C. (1982) The capital barriers to entry. In J. F. Weston (ed.), *Corporate Enterprise in a New Environment*. New York: Little, Brown.

Krouse, C. (1984) Brand name as a barrier to entry: the Realemon case. *Southern Journal of Economics*: 495–502.

Krouse, C. (1985) Competition and unanimity revisited, again. *American Economic Review*: 1109–14.

Krouse, C. (1986) *Capital Markets and Prices: Valuing Uncertain Income Streams*. Amsterdam: North-Holland.

Krugman, P. (1980) Scale economies, product differentiation and the pattern of trade. *American Economic Review*: 950–9.

Kuhn, H. W. (1953) *Extensive Games and the Problem of Information*. Princeton, NJ: Princeton University Press.

Kwoka, J. (1984) Does the choice of concentration really matter? *Journal of Industrial Economics*: 445–53.

Kydland, F. and Prescott, E. (1977) Rules rather than discretion: the inconsistency of optimal plans. *Journal of Political Economy*: 473–91.

Laffer, A. (1969) Vertical integration by corporations, 1929–1965. *Review of Economics and Statistics*: 91–3.

Laffont, J. and Maskin, E. (1980) A differential approach to dominant strategy mechanisms. *Econometrica*: 1507–21.

Laitner, J. (1980) Rational duopoly equilibria. *Quarterly Journal of Economics*: 641–62.

Lambin, J. (1975) What is the real impact of advertising? *Harvard Business Review*: 139–47.

Lambin, J. (1976) *Advertising, Competition, and Market Conduct in Oligopoly over Time*. Amsterdam: North-Holland.

Lambin, J., Naert, P. and Bultey, A. (1975) Optimal marketing behaviour in oligopoly. *European Economic Review*: 105–28.

Lamson, R. (1970) Measured productivity and price change. *Journal of Political Economy*: 105–28.

Lancaster, K. (1966) A new approach to consumer theory. *Journal of Political Economy*: 132–57.

Lancaster, K. (1971) *Consumer Demand: a New Approach*. New York: Macmillan.

Lancaster, K. (1975) Socially optimal product differentiation. *American Economic Review*: 567–85.

Lancaster, K. (1979) *Variety, Equity and Efficiency*. New York: Columbia University Press.

Landes, W. and Posner, R. (1981) Market power in antitrust cases. *Harvard Law Review*: 937–96.

Lane, W. (1980) Product differentiation in a model with endogenous sequential entry. *Bell Journal of Economics*: 237–60.

Lanning, S. (1985) Cartel costs, quotas, and regulation. Mimeo. University of Notre Dame.

Lanzillotti, R (1958) Pricing objectives in large companies. *American Economic Review*: 921–40.

Lave, L. (1962) An empirical approach to the prisonner's dilemma game. *Quarterly Journal of Economics*: 424–36.

Lazear, E. (1986) Retail pricing and clearance sales. *American Economic Review*: 14–32.

Lee, E. and Marcus, L. (1968) *Foundations of Optimal Control Theory*. New York: Wiley.

Lee, L. and Porter, R. (1984) Switching regression models with imperfect sample separation information – with an application on cartel stability. *Econometrica*: 391–418.

Lee, T. (1986) Strategic commitment with R&D. *Economic Letters*: 375–8.

Lee, T. and Wilde, L. (1980) Market structure and innovation: a reformulation. *Quarterly Journal of Economics*: 429–36.

Lee, W. (1975) Oligopoly and entry. *Journal of Economic Theory*: 35–54.

Leffler, K. (1981) Persuasion or information? The economics of prescription drug advertising. *Journal of Law and Economics*: 45–74.

Leland, H. (1972) Theory of the firm facing uncertain demand. *American Economic Review*: 278–91.

Leland, H. (1979) Quacks, lemons, and licensing: a theory of minimum quality standard. *Journal of Polical Economy*: 1328–46.

Leland, H. and Meyer, R. (1976) Monopoly pricing structures with imperfect information. *Bell Journal of Economics*: 449–62.

Leland, H. and Meyer, R. (1977) Quality choice and competition. *Bell Journal of Economics*: 127–35.

Lerner, A. (1934) The concept of monopoly and the measurement of monopoly power. *Review of Economic Studies*: 157–75.

Lerner, A. and Singer, H. (1937) Some notes on duopoly and spatial competition.

Journal of Political Economy. 145–86.

Letwin, W. (1956) Congress and the Sherman antitrust law: 1877–1890. *University of Chicago Law Review*: 221–58.

Leung, A. (1983) Essays on the Economics of Technological Progess. Ph.D. dissertation. London: London School of Economics.

Levhari, D. and Pindyck, R. (1981) The pricing of durable exhaustible resources. *Quarterly Journal of Economics*: 365–78.

Levhari, D. and Srinivasan, T. (1969) Durability of consumption goods: competition versus monopoly. *American Economic Review*: 102–7.

Levin, R. and Reiss, P. (1984) Tests of a Schumpeterian model of R&D and market structure. In Z. Griliches (ed.), *R&D, Patents, and Productivity*: Chicago, IL: University of Chicago Press.

Lewbel, A. (1985) Bundling of substitutes or complements. *International Journal of Industrial Organization*: 101–8.

Liebeler, J. (1976) Integration and competition. In E Mitchell (ed.), *Vertical Integration in the Oil Industry*. Washington, DC: American Petroleum Institute.

Liebeler, J. (1978) Market power and competitive superiority in concentrated industries. *UCLA Law Review*: 1231–1300.

Liebenstein, H. (1966) Allocative effiency v. X-efficiency. *American Economic Review*: 392–415.

Liebenstein, H. (1973) Competition and X-inefficiency: reply. *Journal of Political Economy*: 765–77.

Liebowitz, S. (1982) Durability, market structure and new-used goods models. *American Economic Review*: 816–24.

Liebowitz, S. (1986) Copyright law, photocopying and price discrimination. In J. Palmer (ed.), *Research in Law and Economics*. Greenwich, CT: JAI Press, 181–200.

Lindenberg, E. and Ross, S. (1981) Tobin's *Q* ratio and industrial organization. *Journal of Business*: 1–32.

Link, A. (1980) Firm size and efficient entrepreneurial activity: a reformulation of the Schumpeterian hypothesis. *Journal of Political Economy*: 771–82.

Littlechild, S. (1975) Common costs, fixed charges, clubs, and games. *Review of Economic Studies*: 11–32.

Loeb, P. and Lin, V. (1977) Research and development in the pharmaceutical industry. *Journal of Industrial Economics*: 45–51.

Loesch, A. (1954) *The Economics of Location*. New Haven, CT: Yale University Press.

Loescher, S. (1959) *Imperfect Collusion in the Cement Industry*: Cambridge, MA: Harvard University Press.

Long, W. (1982) Market share, concentration and profits: intra-industry and inter-industry evidence. Working Paper No. 43. Federal Trade Commission.

Long, W. and Ravenscraft, D. (1984) The usefulness of accounting profit data. Working Paper No. 94. Federal Trade Commission.

Loury, G. (1979) Market structure and innovation. *Quarterly Journal of Economics*: 395–410.

Luce, R. and Raiffa, H. (1966) *Games and Decisions*. New York: Wiley.

Lunn, J. (1986) An empirical analysis of process and product patenting: a simultaneous equation framework. *Journal of Industrial Economics*: 319–30.

Lynk, W. (1981) Information, advertising, and the structure of the market. *Journal of Business*: 271–303.

Machlup, F. (1949) *The Basing-point System*: *an Economic Analysis of a Controversial Pricing Practice*. Philadelphia, PA: Blakiston.

Machlup, F. and Taber, M. (1960) Bilateral monopoly, successive monopoly, and vertical integration. *Econometrica*: 101–19.

Makowski, L. (1980a) A characterization of perfectly competitive economies with production. *Journal of Economic Theory*: 208–21.

Makowski, L. (1980b) Perfect competition, the profit criterion, and the organization of economic activity. *Journal of Economic Theory*: 222–42.

Maksimovic, V. (1984) Balance sheet composition and value creation in a stochastic oligopoly. Unpublished manuscript. Department of Economics, Harvard University.

Malinvaud, E. (1972) *Lectures on Microeconomic Theory*. Amsterdam: North-Holland.

Mankiv, G. and Whinston, M. (1986) Free entry and social efficiency. *RAND Journal of Economics*: 48–58.

Mann, M. (1966) Seller concentration, barriers to entry, and rates of return in thirty industries. *Review of Economics and Statistics*: 296–307.

Mann, M. (1971) The interaction of barriers and concentration: a reply. *Journal of Industrial Economics*: 291–3.

Mann, M., Henning, J. and Meehan, J. (1976) Advertising and concentration: an empirical investigation. *Journal of Industrial Economics*: 34–45.

Manne, H. (1965) Mergers and the market for corporate control. *Journal of Political Economy*: 110–20.

Mansfield E. (1963) Firm size, market structure, and innovation. *Journal of Political Economy*: 556–76.

Mansfield, E. (1968) *Industrial Research and Technological Innovation*: *an Econometric Analysis*. New York: Norton.

Mansfield, E. (1977) *The Production and Application of New Technology*. New York: Norton.

Mansfield, E. (1985) How rapidly does new industrial technology leak out? *Journal of Industrial Economics*: 217–23.

Mansfield, E., Schwartz, M. and Wagner, S. (1981) Imitation costs and patents: an empirical study. *Economic Journal*: 907–18.

Marfels, C. (1975) A bird's eye view to measures of concentration. *Antitrust Bulletin*: 485–503.

Markham, J. (1951) The nature of significance of price leadership. *American Economic Review*: 891–905.

Markovits, R. (1967) Tie-ins, reciprocity and leverage theory. *Yale Law Review*: 1397–472.

Markovits, R. (1974) Oligopolistic pricing suits, the Sherman Act, and economic welfare, part I. *Stanford Law Review*: 494–539.

Markovits, R. (1975) Oligopolistic pricing suits, the Sherman Act, and economic welfare, part III. *Stanford Law Review*: 304–79.

Markovits, R. (1980) Tie-ins and reciprocity: a functional, legal and policy analysis. *Texas Law Review*: 1363–445.

Marris, R. and Mueller, D. (1980) The corporation and competition. *Journal of Economic Literature*: 32–63.

Marshack, J. and Selten, R. (1974) *General Equilibrium with Price-taking Firms*. New York. Springer.

Marshall, A. (1920) *Principles of Economics*. London: Macmilian.

Martin, D. (1962) Monopoly power and the durability of durable goods. *Southern Economic Review*: 271–7.

Martin, S. (1979) Advertising, concentration, and profitability: the simultaneity problem. *Bell Journal of Economics*: 639–47.

Martin, S. (1983) *Market, Firm and Economic Performance*: an *Empirial Analysis*. Monograph 1983–1 Series in Finance and Economics. NYU Graduate School of Business.

Martin, S. (1988) *Industrial Economics*. New York: Macmillan.

Marvel, H. (1976) The economics of information and gasoline price behavior: an empirical analysis. *Journal of Political Economy*: 1033–60.

Marvel, H. (1982) Exclusive dealings. *Journal of Law and Economics*: 1–26.

Marvel, H. and McCafferty, S. (1984) Resale price maintenance and quality certification. *RAND Journal of Economics*: 346–59.

Maskin, E. and Riley, J. (1984) Monopoly with incomplete information. *RAND Journal of Economics*: 171–96.

Maskin, E. and Tirole, J. (1985) A theory of dynamic oligopoly II: price competition Working Paper No. 373. Cambridge, MA: Massachusetts Institute of Technology.

Mason, E. (1939) Price and production of large-scale enterprise. *American Economic Review*: 61–74.

Massey, W. and Frank, R. (1965) Short-term price and demand effects in selected market segments. *Journal of Marketing Research*: 171–85.

Masson, R. and Wu, S. (1974) Price discrimination for physicians' services. *Journal of Human Resources*: 63–79.

Mathewson, G. and Winter, R. (1984) An economic theory of vertical restraints. *RAND Journal of Economics*: 27–38.

Matthews, S. (1983) Selling to risk averse buyers with unobservable tastes. *Journal of Economic Theory*: 370–400.

Matthews, S. and Mirman, L. (1982) Equilibrium limit pricing: the effects of private information and s demand. *Econometrica*: 381–96.

Matthews, S. and Moore, J. (1984) Monopoly provision of product quality and warranties. Mimeo. Evanstown, IL: Northwestern University.

Maurizi, A. (1972) The effect of laws against price advertising: the case of retail gasoline. *Western Economic Journal*: 321–9.

McConnell, J. (1968) An experimental examination of the price–quality relationship. *Journal of Business*: 439–49.

McGee, J. (1958) Predatory price cutting: the Standard Oil (N.J.) case. *Journal of Law and Economics*: 137–69.

McGee, J. (1966) Patent exploitation: some economic and legal problems. *Journal of Law and Economics*: 135–62.

McGee, J. (1971) *In Defense of Industrial Concentration*. New York: Praeger.

McGee, J. (1973) Economies of size in auto body manufacture. *Journal of Law and Economics*: 239–73.

McGee, J. (1980) Predatory pricing revisited. *Journal of Law and Economics*: 289–330.

McGee, J. (1988) *Industrial Organization*. Englewood Cliffs, NJ: Prentice-Hall.

McGee, J. and Bassett, L. (1976) Vertical integration revisited. *Journal of Law and Economics*: 17–38.

McKenzie, L. (1951) Ideal output and the interdependence of firms. *Economic Journal*: 785–803.

McKinnon, R. (1966) Stigler's theory of oligopoly: a comment. *Journal of Political Economy*: 281–5.

McLean, D. and Round, D. (1978) Research and product innovation in Australian manufacturing industries. *Journal of Industrial Economics*: 1–12.

McLeod, W. (1985) A theory of conscious parallelism. *European Economic Review*: 25–44.

McRae, J. (1978) On the stability of non-replenishable resource prices. *Canadian Journal of Economics*: 287–9.

Meade, J. (1974) The optimal balance between economies of scale and variety of products: an illustrative model. *Economica*: 359–67.

Meechan, J. and Larner, R. (1981) A proposed rule of reason for vertical restraints on competition. *Antitrust Bulletin*: 195–225.

Menge, J. (1962) Style change costs as a market weapon. *Quarterly Journal of Economics*: 632–47.

de Meza, D (1986) Do consumers benefit from quality discounts? *Economic Letters*: 307–10.

Milgrom, P. (1981) Good news and bad news: representation theorems. *Bell Journal of Economics*: 350–91.

Milgrom, P. and Roberts, J. (1982a) Predation, reputation, and entry deterrence. *Journal of Economic Theory*: 280–312.

Milgrom, P. and Roberts, J. (1982b) Limit pricing and entry under incomplete information: an equilibrium analysis. *Econometrica*: 443–59.

Milgrom, P. and Roberts, J. (1986) Price and advertising signals of quality. *Journal of Political Economy*: 796–821.

Milgrom, P. and Weber, R. (1982) A theory of auctions. *Econometrica*: 1090–122.

Mill, J. (1965, reprinted) *Principles of Political Economy*. Toronto: University of Toronto Press.

Miller, R. (1972) Advertising and competition: some neglected aspects. *Antitrust Bulletin*: 467–78.

Mirman, L. and Sibley, A. (1980) Optimal nonlinear prices for multiproduct monopolies. *Bell Journal of Economics*: 659–70.

Mirrlees, J. (1971) An exploration in the theory of optimum income taxation. *Review of Economic Studies*: 175–208.

Mirrlees, J. (1976) Optimal tax theory: a synthesis. *Journal of Public Economics*: 327–58.

Mitchell, E. (1976) *Capital Cost Savings of Vertical Integration*. Washington, DC: American Enterprise Institute.

Mitten, L. (1964) Composition principles for synthesis of optimal multistage processes. *Operations Research*: 610–19.

Modigliani, R. (1958) New developments on the oligopoly front. *Journal of*

Political Economy: 215–32.

Monteverde, K. and Teece, D. (1982a) Supplier switching costs and vertical integration in the automobile industry. *Bell Journal of Economics*: 206–13.

Monteverde, K. and Teece, D. (1982b) Appropriable rents and quasi-vertical integration. *Journal of Law and Economics*: 321–8.

Moulin, H. (1982) *Game Theory for the Social Sciences*. Stanford, CA Stanford University Press.

Mowery, D. and Rosenberg, N. (1979) The influence of market demand upon innovation: a critical review of some recent empirical findings. *Research Policy*: 102–53.

Mueller, D. (1977) The persistence of profits above the norm. *Econometrica*: 369–80.

Mueller, D. and Tilton, G. (1969) Research and development costs as a barrier to entry. *Canadian Journal of Economics*: 570–9.

Mueller, W. (1969) *Public Policy Toward Vertical Mergers*. Pacific Palisades, CA: Goodyear.

Mueller, W. and Hamm, L. (1974) Trends in industrial concentration. *Review of Economics and Statistics*: 511–13.

Muris, T. and McChesney, F. (1979) Advertising and the price and quality of legal sources: the case for legal clinics. *American Bar Foundation Research Journal*: 179–207.

Mussa, R. and Rosen, S. (1978) Monopoly and product quality. *Journal of Economic Theory*: 301–17.

Myerson, R. (1984) Two-person bargaining problems with incomplete information. *Econometrica*: 461–87.

Nabseth, L. and Ray, G. (1974) *The Diffusion of New Industrial Processes*. Cambridge: Cambridge University Press.

Nalebuff, B. and Stiglitz, J. (1983a) Prizes and incentives. *Bell Journal of Economics*: 21–43.

Nalebuff, B. and Stiglitz, J. (1983b) Information, competition, and markets. *American Economic Review*: 278–83.

Narasimham, C. (1984) A price discrimination theory of coupons. *Marketing Science*: 128–47.

Nash, J. (1950) Equilibrium points in *n*-person games. *Proceedings of the National Academy of Sciences*: 48–9.

Neale, A. and Goyder, D. (1980) *The Antitrust Laws of the U.S.A.* New York: Cambridge University Press.

Needham, D. (1969) *Economic Analysis and Industrial Structure*. New York: Holt, Rinehart and Winston.

Needham, D. (1976) Entry barriers and non-price aspects of firms' behaviour. *Journal of Industrial Economics*: 29–43.

Negishi, T. (1960) Welfare economics and existence of an equilibrium or a competitive economy. *Metro-economica*: 92–7.

Nelson, P. (1970) Information and consumer behaviour. *Journal of Political Economy*: 311–29.

Nelson, P. (1974) Advertising as information. *Journal of Political Economy*: 729–54.

Nelon, R. (1963) *Concentration in the Manufacturing Industries of the U.S.* New

Haven, CT: Yale University Press.

Nelson, R. (1981) Research on productivity growth and productivity differences. *Journal of Economic Literature*: 1029–64.

Nelson, R. and Winter, S. (1982) The Schumpeterian tradeoff revisited. *American Economic Review*: 117–32.

Nerlove, M. and Arrow, K. (1962) Optimal advertising policy under dynamic conditions. *Economica*: 129–42.

Neumann, M. (1982) Predatory pricing by a quantity setting multiproduct firm. *American Economic Review*: 825–8.

Neven, D. (1985) Two-stage (perfect) equilbrium in Hotelling's model. *Journal of Industrial Economics*: 317–26.

Ng, Y. (1971) Competition, monopoly, and the incentive to invent. *Australian Economic Papers*: 45–9.

Ng, Y. and Weisser, W. (1974) Optimal pricing with a budget constraint – the case of the two-part tariff. *Review of Economic Studies*: 337–45.

Nichol, A. (1930) *Partial Monopoly and Price Leadership*. Philadelphia, PA: Smith-Edwards.

Nichols, L. (1985) Advertising and economic welfare. *American Economic Review*: 213–18.

Nickell, S. (1978) *The Investment Decisions of Firms*, Cambridge: Cambridge University Press.

Norman, G. (1981a) Spatial competition and spatial price discrimination. *Review of Economic Studies*: 97–111.

Norman, G. and Nicholls, N. (1982) Dynamic market strategy under threat of competitive entry; an analysis of the pricing and production policies open to the multinational company. *Journal of Industrial Economics*: 153–74.

Novshek, W. (1980) Equilbrium in simple spatial (or differentiated product) models. *Journal of Economic Theory*: 313–26.

Novshek, W. and Sonnenschein, H. (1980) Small efficient scale as a foundation for Walrasian equilibrium. *Journal of Economic Theory*: 243–55.

Novshek, W. and Sonnenschein, H. (1982) Fulfilled expectations Cournot duopoly with information acquisition and release. *Bell Journal of Economics*: 214–18.

Oi, W. (1967) The economics of product safety. *Bell Journal of Economics*: 3–28.

Oi, W. (1971) A disneyland dilemma: two-part tariffs for a mickey mouse monopoly. *Quarterly Journal of Economics*: 77–90.

Okuguchi, K. (1969) On the stability of price adjusting oligopoly equilibrium under product differentiation. *Southern Economic Journal*: 244–6.

Omori, T. and Yarrow, G. (1981–3) Product diversification, entry prevention, and limit pricing. *Bell Journal of Economics*: 242–8.

Ono, Y. (1981) Price leadership: a theoretical analysis. *Econometrica*: 11–20.

Ordover, J. and Saloner, G. (1987) Predation, monopolization, and antitrust. New York University, Deparment of Economics Ms. 87–07.

Ordover, J. and Willig, R. (1981) An economic definition of predation: pricing and product innovation. *Yale Law Review*: 8–53.

Ordover, J., Sykes, A. and Willig, R. (1982) Herfindahl concentration, rivalry and mergers. *Harvard Law Review*: 1857–74.

Oren, S., Smith, S. and Wilson, R (1983) Competitive nonlinear tariffs. *Journal of Economic Theory*: 49–71.

Ornstein, S. (1976) The advertising–concentration controversy. *Southern Economic Journal*: 892–902.

Ornstein, S. (1977) *Industrial Concentration and Advertising Intensity*. Washington DC: American Enterprise Institute.

Ornstein, S. (1987) An analysis of advertising, concentration, and profit studies. In T. Copeland (ed.), *Modern Finance and Industrial Economics*. London: Blackwell.

Orr, R. and MacAvoy, P. (1965) Price strategies to promote cartel stability. *Economica*: 186–97.

Osborne, D. (1973) On the rationality of limit pricing. *Journal of Industrial Economics*: 71–80.

Osborne, D. (1976) Cartel problems. *American Economic Review*: 835–44.

Ostroy, J. (1980) The no-surplus condition as a characterization of perfectly competitive equilibrium. *Journal of Economic Theory*: 183–207.

Pagoulatas, E. and Sorenson, R. (1980) A simultaneous equation analysis of advertising concentration, and profitability. *Southern Economic Review*: 728–41.

Pakes, A. (1984) Patents and R&D at the firm level: a first look. In Z. Grilichles (ed.), *R&D, Patents, and Productivity*. Chicago, IL: University of Chicago Press.

Pakes, A. (1985) On patents, R&D, and the stock market rate of return. *Journal of Political Economy*: 390–409.

Pakes, A. (1987) Professor Mueller and the profitability debate: a review of *Profits in the Long Run*. *RAND Journal of Economics*: 355–66.

Palfrey, T. (1982) Risk advantages and information acquisition. *Bell Journal of Economics*: 219–24.

de Palma, A., Ginsburgh, V. and Thisse, J. (1985) The principle of minimum differentiation holds under sufficient heterogeneity. *Econometrica*: 767–81.

Panzar, J. (1973) A model of regulated oligopoly with product variation. Center for Research in Economic Growth, Stanford University.

Panzar, J. (1976) A neoclassical approach to peak load pricing. *Bell Journal of Economics*: 521–30.

Pashigian, B. (1961) *The Distribution of Automobiles: An Economic Analysis of the Franchise System*. Englewood Cliffs, NJ: Prentice-Hall.

Pashigian, B. (1968) Market concentration in the US and Great Britain. *Journal of Law and Economics*: 299–319.

Patinkin, D. (1947) Multi-plant firms, cartels, and imperfect competition. *Quarterly Journal of Economics*: 173–205.

Pauly, M. (1974) Overinsurance and the public provision of insurance: the roles of moral hazard and adverse selection. *Quarterly Journal of Economics*: 44–62.

Pearce, D. (1984) Rationalisable strategic behaviour and the problem of perfection. *Econometrica*: 1029–50.

Peltzman, S. (1969) Issues in vertical integration policy. In J. F. Weston and S. Peltzman (eds), *Public Policy Toward Mergers*. Pacific Palisades, CA: Goodyear.

Penrose, E. (1959) *The Theory of the Growth of the Firm*. Oxford: Blackwell.

Perloff, J. and Salop, S. (1985) Equilibrium with product differentiation. *Review of Economic Studies*: 107–20.

Perry, M. (1978a) Price discrimination and forward integration. *Bell Journal of Economics*: 209–17.

Perry, M. (1978b) Related market conditions and interindustrial mergers: comment. *American Economic Review*: 221–4.

Perry, M. (1978c) Vertical integration: the monopsony case. *American Economic Review*: 561–70.

Perry, M. (1982a) Vertical integration by competitive firms: uncertainty and diversification. *Southern Economic Journal*: 201–8.

Perry, M. (1982b) Oligopoly and consistent conjectural variations. *Bell Journal of Economics*: 197–205.

Perry, M. and Porter, R. (1985) Oligopoly and the incentive for horizontal merger. *American Economic Review*: 219–27.

Peterman, J. (1965) The structure of national time rates in the television broadcasting industry. *Journal of Law and Economics*: 77–132.

Phillips, A. (1963) Industrial capacity – an appraisal of measures of capacity. *American Economic Review*: 275–83.

Phillips, A. (1971) *Technology and Market Structure: A Study of the Aircraft Industry*. Lexington: Heath, Lexington.

Phlips, L. (1974) *Applied Consumption Analysis*. Amsterdam: North-Holland.

Phlips, L. (1983) *The Economics of Price Discrimination*. Cambridge: Cambridge University Press.

Pigou, A. (1912) *Wealth and Welfare* (4th edn). London: Macmillan.

Pigou, A. (1932) *The Economics of Welfare*. New York: Macmillan.

Pitofsky, R. (1978) The Sylvania case: antitrust analysis of non-price vertical restrictions. *Columbia Law Review*: 1–38.

Plott, C. (1982) Industrial organization theory and experimental economics. *Journal of Economic Literature*: 1485–527.

Png, I. and Hirshleifer, D (1987) Price discrimination through offers to match price. *Journal of Business*: 365–83.

Pollak. R. (1971) Additive utility functions and linear Engel curves. *Review of Economic Studies*: 401–14.

Porter, M. (1978) Optimal advertising: an intra-industry approach. In D. Tuerck (ed.), *Issues in Advertising*. Washington, DC: American Enterprise Institute.

Porter, M. (1980) *Competitive Strategy*. London: Free Press.

Porter, M. (1981) Strategic interaction: some lessons from industry histories for theory and antitrust policy. In S. Salop (ed.), *Strategy, Predation and Antitrust Analysis*. Washington, DC: Federal Trade Commission.

Porter, R. (1983a) Optimal cartel trigger price strategies. *Journal of Economic Theory*: 313–38.

Porter, R. (1983b) A study of cartel stability: the joint executive committee, 1880–1886. *Bell Journal of Economics*: 301–14.

Posner, R. (1969) Oligopoly and the antitrust laws: a suggested approach. *Stanford Law Review*: 1562–91.

Posner, R. (1974) Exclusionary practices and the antitrust laws. *University of Chicago Law Review*: 506–35.

Posner, R. (1975) The social costs of monopoly and regulation *Journal of Political Economy*: 807–28.

Posner, R. (1976) *Antitrust Law: an Economic Perspective*. Chicago, IL: University of Chicago Press.

Posner, R. (1977) The rule of reason and the economic approach: reflections on the Sylvania decision. *University of Chicago Law Review*: 1–20.

Posner, R. (1981) The next step in the antitrust treatment of restricted distribution: *per se* legality. *University of Chicago Law Review*: 6–26.

Pratt, J., Wise, D. and Zeckhauser, R. (1979) Price differences in almost competitive markets. *Quarterly Journal of Economics*: 189–211.

Pratten, C. K. (1971) *Economies of Scale in Manufacturing Industry*. Cambridge: Cambridge University Press.

Prescott, E. and Townsend, R. (1984) Pareto optima and competitive equilibria with adverse selection and moral hazard. *Econometrica*: 21–46.

Prescott, E. and Visscher, M. (1977) Sequential location among firms with foresight. *Bell Journal of Economics*: 378–93.

Priest, G. (1971) Cartels and patent license arrangements. *Journal of Law and Economics*: 358–76.

Priest, G. (1981) A theory of product warranty. *Yale Law Journal*: 1297–352.

Primeaux, W. (1977) An assessment of X-efficiency gained through competition. *Review of Economics and Statistics*: 105–8.

Pryor, F. (1972) An international comparison of concentration ratios. *Review of Economics and Statistics*: 136–45.

Pyatt, G. (1971) Profit maximization and new entry. *Economic Journal*: 246–55.

Qualls, D. (1978) Market structure theory and the policy implications of product complementarity. *Industrial Organization Review*: 38–48.

Rader, T. (1972) *Theory of Microeconomics*. New York: Academic Press.

Radner, R. (1985) Repeated principal–agent games with discounting. *Econometrica*: 1173–98.

Ramsey, F. (1927) A contribution to the theory of taxation. *Economic Journal*: 47–61.

Rao, R. and Rutenberg, D. (1979) Pre-empting an alert rival: strategic timing of the first plant by analysis of sophisticated rivalry. *Bell Journal of Economics*: 412–28.

Rasmusen, E. (1988) Entry for buyout. *Journal of Industrial Economics*: 281–99.

Ravencroft, D. (1983) Structure–profits relationships at the line of business and industry levels. *Review of Economics and Statistics*: 38–48.

Reekie, W (1974) Advertising and market share mobility *Scottish Journal of Political Economy*: 143–58.

Reinganum, J. (1981a) Dynamic games of innovation. *Journal of Economic Theory*: 21–41.

Reinganum, J. (1981b) On the diffusion of new technology. *Review of Economic Studies*: 395–405.

Reinganum, J. (1981c) Market structure and the diffusion of new technology. *Bell Journal of Economics*: 618–24.

Reinganum, J. (1982) A dynamic game of R & D. *Econometrica*: 671–88.

Reinganum, J. (1983) Uncertain innovation and the persistence of monopoly.

American Economic Review: 741–8.

Reinganum, J. (1984) Uncertain innovation and the persistence of monopoly: reply. *American Economic Review* 243–6.

Reinganum, J. (1985) Innovation and industry evolution. *Quarterly Journal of Economics*: 81–99.

Rey, P. and Tirole, J. (1986) The logic of vertical restraints. *American Economic Review*: 921–39.

Rice, E. and Ulen, T. (1981) Rent-seeking and welfare loss. *Research in Law and Economics*: 93–106.

Riley, J. (1979) Informational equilibrium. *Econometrica*: 331–60.

Riley, J. (1980) Strong evolutionary equilibria and the war of attrition. *Journal of Theoretical Biology*: 383–402.

Riordan, M. (1985) Imperfect information and dynamic conjectural variations. *RAND Journal of Economics*: 41–50.

Roberts, J. (1986) A signalling model of predatory pricing. *Oxford Economic Papers*: 75–93.

Roberts, J. and Sonnenschein, H. (1977) On the foundations of the theory of monopolistic competition. *Econometrica*: 101–13.

Roberts, K. (1979) Welfare considerations of nonlinear pricing. *Economic Journal*: 66–83.

Roberts, K. (1980) The limit points of monopolistic competition. *Journal of Economic Theory*: 256–79.

Roberts, M. (1984) Testing oligopolistic behaviour: an application of the variable profit function. *International Journal of Industrial Organization*: 367–84.

Roberts, M. and Samuelson, L. (1988) An empirical analysis of dynamic, nonprice competition in an oligopolistic industry. *RAND Journal of Economics*: 200–20.

Robinson, J. (1933) *The Economics of Imperfect Competition*. London: Macmillan.

Robson, A. (1981) Implicit oligopolistic collusion is destroyed by uncertainty. *Economic Letters*: 75–80.

Rogerson, W. (1982) The social costs of monopoly and regulation. *Bell Journal of Economics*: 391–401.

Rogerson, W. (1983) Reputation and product quality. *Bell Journal of Economics*: 508–16.

Rosen, S. (1974) Hedonic prices and implicit markets: product differentiation in pure competition. *Journal of Political Economy*: 34–55.

Rosenberg, J. (1976) Research and market share: a reappraisal of the Schumpeter hypothesis. *Journal of Industrial Economics*: 110–12.

Rosenthal, R. (1980) A model in which an increase in the number of sellers leads to a higher price. *Econometrica*: 1575–9.

Rosenthal, R. (1981) Games of perfect information, predatory pricing and the chain-store paradox. *Journal of Economic Theory*: 92–100.

Rosenthal, R. (1982a) A dynamic model with customer loyalties. *Journal of Economic Theory*. 69–76.

Rosenthal, R. (1982b) A dynamic oligopoly game with lags in demand: more on the monotonicity of price in the number of sellers. *International Economic*

Review: 353–60.

Ross, S. (1973) The economic theory of agency: the principal's problem. *Economic Review*: 134–9.

Rosse, J. (1970) Estimating cost function parameters without using cost data. *Econometrica*: 256–75.

Rotemberg, J. and Saloner, G. (1986) A supergame theoretic model of business cycles and price wars during booms. *American Economic Review*: 390–407.

Roth, A. and Schoumaker, F. (1981) Expectations and reputations in bargaining: an experimental study. *American Economic Review*: 362–72.

Rothschild, M. (1973) Models of market orgnization with imperfect information: a survey. *Journal of Political Economy*: 1283–308.

Rothschild, M. and Stiglitz, J. (1976) Equilibrium in competitive insurance markets: an essay on the economics of imperfect discrimination. *Quarterly Journal of Economics*: 629–50.

Rothschild, R. (1981) Cartel problems: note. *American Economic Review*: 179–81.

Rowley, C. (1972) *Readings in Industrial Economics*. London: Blackwell.

Rubinstein, A. (1979) Equilibrium in supergames with the overtaking criterion. *Journal of Economic Theory*: 1–9.

Ruffin, R. T. (1971) Cournot oligopoly and competitive behaviour. *Review of Economic Studies*: 439–502.

Sah, R. and Stiglitz, J. (1987) The invariance of market innovation to the number of firms. *RAND Journal of Economics*: 98–108.

Salant, D. (1980) Quality, Location Choice and Imperfect Competition. Ph.D. dissertation. New York: University of Rochester, unpublished.

Salant, S. (1984) Preemptive patenting and the persistence of monopoly: comment. *American Economic Review*: 247–50.

Salant, S., Switzer, S. and Reynolds, R. (1983) Losses from horizontal merger: the effects of an exogenous change in industry structure in Cournot–Nash equilibrium. *Quarterly Journal of Economics*: 185–99.

Salinger, M. (1984) Tobin's-q, unionization and the concentration–profits relationship. *RAND Journal of Economics*: 159–70.

Saloner, G. (1982) Dynamic Pricing in an Uncertain Environment. Ph.D. dissertation. Stanford, CA: Stanford University.

Saloner, G. (1987) Predation, mergers and incomplete information. *RAND Journal of Economics*: 165–86.

Salop, S. (1977) The noisy monopolist: imperfect information, price dispersion, and price discrimination. *Review of Economic Studies*: 393–406.

Salop, S. (1978) Parables of information transmission in markets. In A. Mitchell (ed.), *The Effects of Information on Consumer and Market Behavior*. Chicago, IL: American Marketing Association.

Salop, S. (1979a) Strategic entry deterrence. *American Economic Review*: 335–8.

Salop, S. (1979b) Monopolistic competition with outside goods. *Bell Journal of Economics*: 141–56.

Salop, S. (1981) *Strategy, Predation and Antitrust Analysis*. Washington, DC: Federal Trade Commission.

Salop, S. (1986) Practices that (credibly) facilitate oligopoly coordination. In J.

Stiglitz and G. Mathewson (eds), *New Developments in the Analysis of Market Structure*. Cambridge, MA: MIT Press.

Salop, S. and Scheffman, D. (1983) Raising rivals' costs. *American Economic Review*: 267–71.

Salop, S. and Stiglitz, J. (1977) Bargains and ripoffs: a model of monopolistically competitive price dispersion. *Review of Economic Studies*: 493–510.

Salop, S. and Stiglitz, J. (1982) A theory of sales: a model of equlibrium price discrimination with identical agents. *American Economic Review*: 1121–30.

Samuelson, P. (1967) *Foundations of Economic Analysis*: New York: Antheneum Press (originally published 1947).

Sandmo, A. (1971) On the theory of the competitive firm under price uncertainty. *American Economic Review*: 65–80.

Sappington, D. (1982) Optimal regulation of research and development under imperfect information. *Bell Journal of Economics*: 354–68.

Sappington, D. (1983) Limited liability contracts between principal and agent. *Journal of Economic Theory*: 1–21.

Sattinger, M. (1984) Value of an additional firm in monopolistic competition. *Review of Economic Studies*: 321–32.

Saving, T. (1970) Concentration ratios and the degree of monopoly. *International Economic Review*: 139–45.

Saving, T. (1982) Market organization and product quality. *Southern Economic Journal*: 855–67.

Sawyer, M. (1981) *The Economics of Industries and Firms*. New York: St Martin's Press.

Schelling, T. (1960) *The Strategy of Conflict*. Cambridge, MA: Harvard University Press.

Scherer, F. (1965) Firm size, market structure, opportunity, and the output of patented inventions. *American Economic Review*: 1097–123.

Scherer, F. (1967) Market structure and the employment of scientists and engineers. *American Economic Review*: 524–31.

Scherer, F. (1976) Predatory pricing and the Sherman Act: a comment. *Harvard Law Review*: 869.

Scherer, F. (1980) *Industrial Market Structure and Economic Performance*. Chicago, IL: Rand McNally.

Scherer, F. (1982) Demand-pull and technological innovation: Schmookler revisited. *Journal of Industrial Economics*: 225–37.

Scherer, F., Beckenstein, A., Kaufer, E. and Murphy, R. (1975) *The Economics of Multiplant Operation*. Cambridge, MA: Harvard University Press.

Schildkraut, M. (1975) Areas of primary responsibility and other territorial restrictions in channels of distribution under antitrust laws: a legal and economic analysis. *Columbia Journal of Law and Social Problems*: 509–70.

Schmalensee, R. (1970) Regulation and the durability of goods. *Bell Journal of Economics and Management Science*: 57–64.

Schmalensee, R. (1972a) *The Economics of Advertising*: Amsterdam: North-Holland.

Schmalensee, R. (1972b) A note on monopolistic competition and excess capacity. *Journal of Political Economy*: 586–91.

Schmalensee, R. (1973) A note on the theory of vertical integration. *Journal of*

Political Economy: 442–9.

Schmalensee, R. (1974) Brand loyalty and barriers to entry. *Southern Economic Journal*: 579–88.

Schmalensee, R. (1976) A model of promotional competition in oligopoly. *Review of Economic Studies*: 493–507.

Schmalensee, R. (1977a) Comparative static properties of regulated airline oligopolies. *Bell Journal of Economics*: 565–78.

Schmalensee, R. (1977b) Using the H-index of concentration with published data. *Review of Economics and Statistics*: 186–93.

Schmalensee, R. (1978a) A model of advertising and product quality. *Journal of Political Economy*: 485–503.

Schmalensee, R. (1978b) Entry deterrence in the ready to eat breakfast cereal industry. *Bell Journal of Economics*: 305–27.

Schmalensee, R. (1979a) Market structure, durability, and quality: a selective survey. *Economic Inquiry*: 177–96.

Schmalensee, R. (1979b) On the use of economic models in antitrust: the Realemon case. *University of Pennsylvania Law Review*: 994–1050.

Schmalensee, R. (1981) Output and welfare implications of monopolistic third-degree price discrimination. *American Economic Review*: 242–7.

Schmalensee, R. (1982a) Antitrust and the new industrial economics. *American Economic Review*: 24–8.

Schmalensee, R. (1982b) Product differentiation advantages of pioneering brands. *American Economic Review*: 349–65.

Schmalensee, R. (1983) Advertising and entry deterrance: an exploratory model. *Journal of Political Economy*: 636–53.

Schmalensee, R. (1987) Competitive advantage and collusive optima. *International Journal of Industrial Organization*: 351–68.

Schmookler, J. (1966) *Invention and Economic Growth* Cambridge, MA: Harvard University Press.

Schrieves, R. (1976) Firm size and innovation: further evidence. *Industrial Organization Review*: 26–33.

Schumpeter, J. (1939) *Business Cycles*. New York: McGraw-Hill.

Schumpeter, J. (1976) *Capitalism, Socialism and Democracy* (5th edn). London: Allen and Unwin.

Schwartzmann, D. (1960) The burden of monopoly. *Journal of Political Economy*: 627–30.

Seade, J. (1977) On the shape of optimal tax schedules. *Journal of Public Economics*: 203–35.

Seade, J. (1980a) The stability of Cournot revisited. *Journal of Economic Theory*: 15–27.

Seade, J. (1980b) On the effects of entry. *Econometrica*: 479–90.

Selten, R. (1965) Spieltheoretische behandlung eines oligopolmedells mit nachfragetragheit. *Zeitschrift fur die Gesamte Staatswissenschaft*: 301–24.

Selten, R. (1975) Reexamination of the perfectness concept for equilibrium points in extensive games. *International Journal of Game Theory*: 25–55.

Selten, R. (1978) The chain store paradox. *Theory and Decision*: 127–59.

Shaffer, S. (1984) Consistent conjectures in utility maximizing firms with constant marginal costs. *Economic Letters*: 133–7.

Shaked, A. and Sutton, J. (1982) Relaxing price competition through product differentiation. *Review of Economic Studies*: 3–14.

Shaked, A. and Sutton, J. (1983) Natural oligopolies. *Econometrica*: 1469–84.

Shaked, A. and Sutton, J. (1984) Natural oligopolies and international trade. In H. Kierzkowski (ed.), *Monopolistic Competition and International Trade*. Oxford: Oxford University Press.

Shapiro, C. (1980) Advertising and welfare: comment *Bell Journal of Economics*: 749–52.

Shapiro, C. (1982) Consumer information, product quality, and seller reputation. *Bell Journal of Economics*: 20–35.

Shapiro, C. (1983) Premiums for high quality as returns to reputations. *Quarterly Journal of Economics*: 659–79.

Shapiro, C. (1985) Patent licensing and R&D rivalry. *American Economic Review*: 25–30.

Sharkety, W. (1982) *The Theory of Natural Monopoly*. Cambridge: Cambridge University Press.

Sheahan, J. (1956) Integration and exclusion in the telephone equipment industry. *Quarterly Journal of Economics*: 249–69.

Shelton, J. (1967) Allocative efficiency vs. X efficiency: comment. *American Economic Review*: 1252–8.

Shepard, A. (1987) Licensing to enhance demand for new technologies. *RAND Journal of Economics*: 360–88.

Shepard, R. (1953) *Cost and Production Functions*. Princeton: Princeton University Press.

Shepard, W. (1972) The elements of market structure. *Review of Economics and Statistics*: 25–37.

Shepard, W. (1982) Causes of increased competition in the U.S. economy, 1939–1980. *Review of Economics and Statistics*: 619–31.

Shepard, W. (1985) *The Economics of Industrial Organization*. Englewood Cliffs, NJ: Prentice-Hall.

Sherman, R. and Willett, T. (1967) Potential entrants discourage entry. *Journal of Political Economy*: 400–3.

Shillinglaw, G. (1954) The effects of requirements contracts on competition. *Journal of Industrial Economics*: 147–63.

Shilony, Y. (1977) Mixed pricing in oligopoly. *Journal of Economic Theory*: 373–88.

Shleifer, A. and Vishny, R. (1986) Greenmail, white knights, and shareholder's interest. *RAND Journal of Economics*: 293–305.

Sidak, J. (1983) Debunking predatory innovation. *Columbia Law Review*: 1121–49.

Siegfried, J. and Weiss, L. (1974) Advertising, profits and corporate taxes revisited. *Review of Economics and Statistics*: 195–200.

Sieper, E. and Swan, P. (1973) Monopoly and competition in the market for durable goods. *Review of Economic Studies*: 333–51.

Simon, H. (1978a) Rationality as process and as product of thought. *American Economic Review*: 1–16.

Simon, H. (1978b) On how to decide what to do. *Bell Journal of Economics*: 494–507.

Simon, J. (1970) *Issues in the Economics of Advertising*. Urbana, IL: University of Illinois Press.

Singer, E. (1981) *Antitrust Economics and Legal Analysis*. Columbus, OH: Grid Publishing.

Singh, N. and Vives, X. (1984) Price and quantity competition in a differentiated duopoly. *RAND Journal of Economics*: 546–54.

Slade, M. (1987) Conjectures, firm characteristics and market structure. *International Journal of Industrial Organization*: 347–70.

Slawson, W. (1980) A stronger, simpler tie-in doctrine. *Antitrust Bulletin*: 671–99.

Smallwood, D. and Conlisk, J. (1979) Product quality in markets where consumers are imperfectly informed. *Quarterly Journal of Economics*: 1–23.

Smirlock, M., Gilligan, T. and Marshall, W. (1984) Tobin's Q and the structure–performance relationship. *American Economic Review*: 1051–70.

Smith, A. (1937) *An Inquiry in the Nature and Causes of the Wealth of Nations. (Glasgow Edition)*. Oxford: Oxford University Press (originally published 1776).

Smith, R. (1982) Efficiency gains from strategic investment. *Journal of Industrial Economics*: 1–23.

Smith, V. (1971) The borrower–lender contract under uncertainty. *Western Economic Journal*: 52–6.

Smithies, A. (1941) Optimal location in spatial competition. *Journal of Political Economy*: 423–39.

Solomon, E. (1970) Alternative rate of return concepts and their implications. *Bell Journal of Economics*: 37–52.

Sonnenschein, H. (1968) The dual of duopoly is complementary monopoly: or two of Cournot's theorires are one. *Journal of Political Economy*: 316–18.

Spence, M. (1973) Job market signalling. *Quarterly Journal of Economics*: 355–67.

Spence, M. (1975) Monopoly, quality and regulation. *Bell Journal of Economics*: 417–29.

Spence, M. (1976a) Product selection, fixed costs and monopolistic competition. *Review of Economic Studies*: 217–36.

Spence, M. (1976b) Product differentiation and welfare. *American Economic Review*: 407–14.

Spence, M. (1977a) Entry, capacity, investment and oligopolistic pricing. *Bell Journal of Economics*: 534–44.

Spence, M. (1977b) Nonlinear prices and welfare. *Journal of Public Economics*: 1–18.

Spence, M. (1978) Tacit co-ordination and imperfect information. *Canadian Journal of Economics*: 490–505.

Spence, M. (1979) Investment strategy and growth in a new market. *Bell Journal of Economics*: 1–19.

Spence, M. (1980a) Notes on advertising, economies of scale, and entry barriers. *Quarterly Journal of Economics*: 493–507.

Spence, M. (1980b) Multi-product quantity-dependent prices and profitability constraints. *Review of Economic Studies*: 821–41.

Spence, M. (1981a) Competition, entry and antitrust policy. In S. Salop (ed.),

Strategy, Predation and Antitrust Analysis. Washington, DC: Federal Trade Commission.

Spence, M. (1981b) The learning curve and competition. *Bell Journal of Economics*: 49–70.

Spence, M. (1984) Cost reduction, competition, and industry performance. *Econometrica*: 101–22.

Spengler, J. (1950) Vertical integration and antitrust policy. *Journal of Political Economy*: 347–52.

Spiller, P. and Favaro, E. (1984) The effects of entry regulation on oligopolistic interaction: the Uruguayan banking sector. *RAND Journal of Economics*: 244–54.

Spulber, D. (1981a) Capacity, output and sequential entry. *American Economic Review*: 503–14.

Spulber, D. (1981b) Spatial nonliner pricing. *American Economic Review*: 923–33.

von Stackelberg, H. (1934) *The Theory of Market Economy*. New York: Oxford University Press (reprinted 1952).

Stahl, K. (1982) Differentiated products, consumer search, and locational oligopoly. *Journal of Industrial Economics*: 97–113.

Stauffer, T. (1971) The measurement of corporate rates of return: a generalized formulation. *Bell Journal of Economics*: 434–69.

Steiner, P. (1957) Peak loads and efficient pricing. *Quarterly Journal of Economics*: 585–610.

Steiner, P. (1966) The economics of broadcasting and advertising: discussion. *American Economic Review*: 472–5.

Steiner, R. (1973) Does advertising lower customer prices? *Journal of Marketing*: 19–26.

Stern, N. (1972) The optimal size of market areas. *Journal of Economic Theory*: 154–73.

Stewart, M. (1979b) Monopoly and the choice of product characteristics. *Economics Letters*: 79–84.

Stigler, G. (1940) Notes on the theory of duopoly. *Journal of Political Economy*: 521–42.

Stigler, G. (1947) The kinky oligopoly demand curve and rigid prices. *Journal of Political Economy*: 444–6.

Stigler, G. (1949a) *Five Lectures on Economic Problems*. New York: Macmillan.

Stigler, G. (1949b) A theory of delivered price systems. *American Economic Review*: 1143–59.

Stigler, G. (1951) The division of labor is limited by the extent of the market. *Journal of Political Economy*: 185–93.

Stigler, G. (1956) The statistics of monopoly and merger. *Journal of Political Economy*: 33–40.

Stigler, G. (1958) The economies of scale. *Journal of Law and Economics*: 7–16.

Stigler, G. (1961) The economics of information. *Journal of Political Economy*: 213–85.

Stigler, G. (1962) Administered prices and oligopolistic inflation. *Journal of*

Business: 88–98.

Stigler, G. (1963) A note on block booking. *The Supreme Court Review*: 146–50.

Stigler, G. (1964) A theory of oligopoly. *Journal of Politial Economy*: 44–61.

Stigler, G. (1966) *The Theory of Price* (3rd edn). New York: Macmillan.

Stigler, G. (1968) Price and non-price competition. *Journal of Political Economy*: 149–54.

Stigler, G. (1976) The existence of X-efficiency. *American Economic Review*: 213–16.

Stigler, G. (1978) The literature of economics: the case of the kinked oligopoly demand curve. *Economic Inquiry*: 185–204.

Stigler, G. and Becker, G. (1977) Gustibus non est disputandum. *American Economic Review*: 76–90.

Stiglitz, J. (1977) Monopoly, non-linear pricing, and imperfect information: the insurance market. *Review of Economic Studies*: 407–30.

Stiglitz, J. (1982) Self-selection and Pareto efficient taxation. *Journal of Public Economics*: 213–40.

Stiglitz, J. (1983) *Information and Economic Analysis*. Oxford: Oxford University Press.

Stiglitz, J. (1984) Price rigidities and market structure. *American Economic Review*: 352–60.

Stiglitz, J. and Weiss, A. (1981) Credit rationing in markets with imperfect information. *American Economic Review*: 393–410.

Stokey, N. (1979) Intertemporal price discrimination. *Quarterly Journal of Economics*: 355–71.

Stokey, N. (1981) Rational expectations and durable goods pricing. *Bell Journal of Economics*: 112–28.

Strasser, K. (1977) Vertical territorial restraints after Sylvania: a policy analysis and proposed new rule. *Duke Law Journal*: 775–840.

Strickland, A. and Weiss, L. (1976) Advertising, concentration, and price–cost margins. *Journal of Political Economy*: 1109–21.

Sullivan, D. (1985) Testing hypotheses about firm behavior in the cigarette industry. *Journal of Political Economy*: 586–98.

Sullivan, L. (1977) *A Handbook of the Law of Antitrust*. St Paul, MN: West Publishing.

Sultan, R. (1974) *Pricing in the Electrical Conspiracy*. Cambridge, MA: Harvard University Press.

Sumner, D. (1981) Measurement of monopoly behavior: an application to the cigarette industry. *Journal of Political Economy*: 1010–19.

Swan, P. (1970) Durability of consumption goods. *American Economic Review*: 884–94.

Swan, P. (1971) The durability of goods and regulation of monopoly. *Bell Journal of Economics*: 347–57.

Swan, P. (1972) Optimum durability, second-hand markets, and planned obsolescence. *Journal of Political Economy*: 575–85.

Swan, P. (1980) ALCOA: the influence of recycling on monopoly power. *Journal of Political Economy*: 76–99.

Sweezy, P. (1939) Demand under conditions of oligopoly. *Journal of Political*

Economy: 568–73.

Sylos-Labini, P. (1962) *Oligopoly and Technical Progress*. Cambridge, MA: Harvard University Press.

Takayama, A. (1969) Behavior of the firm under regulatory constraint. *American Economic Review*: 255–60.

Tandon, P. (1983) Rivalry and the excessive allocation of resources to research. *Bell Journal of Economics*: 152–65.

Taylor, C. and Silberston, Z. (1973) *The Economic Impact of the Patent System*. Cambridge: Cambridge University Press.

Telser, L. (1960) Why should manufacturers want fair trade? *Journal of Law and Economics*: 86–105.

Telser, L. (1964) Advertising and competition. *Journal of Political Economy*: 551–67.

Telser, L. (1965) Abusive trade practices: an economic analysis. *Law and Contemporary Problems*: 488–505.

Telser, L. (1966a) Supply and demand for advertising messages. *American Economic Review*: 457–66.

Telser, L. (1966b) Cutthroat competition and the long purse. *Journal of Law and Economics*: 259–77.

Telser, L. (1968) Some aspects of the economics of advertising. *Journal of Business*: 166–73.

Telser, L. (1972) *Competition, Collusion and Game Theory* Chicago, IL: Aldine-Atherton.

Telser, L. (1973) Searching for the lowest price. *American Economic Review*: 41–9.

Telser, L. (1979) A theory of monopoly of complementary goods. *Journal of Business*: 211–30.

Theocharis, R (1960) On the stability of the Cournot solution on the oligopoly problem. *Review of Economic Studies*: 133–4.

Thorelli, H. (1954) *The Federal Antitrust Policy*. London: Allen and Unwin.

Timothy, L. and Bona, B. (1968) *State Space Analysis*. New York: McGraw-Hill.

Tobin, J. (1957) Liquidity preference as behavior towards risk. *Review of Economic Studies*: 65–86.

Triffin, R. (1940) *Monopolistic Competition and General Equilibrium Theory*. Cambridge, MA: Harvard University Press.

Tucker, I. and Wilder, R. (1977) Trends in vertical integration in the U.S. manufacturing sector. *Journal of Industrial Economics*: 81–94.

Tullock, G. (1967) The welfare costs of tariffs, monopolies, and theft. *Western Economic Review*: 274–332.

Turner, D. (1962) The definition of agreement under the Sherman Act: conscious parallelism and refusals to deal. *Harvard Law Review*: 655–730.

Turner, D. (1965) Conglomerate mergers and Section 7 of the Clayton Act. *Harvard Law Review*: 1313–95.

Ulen, T. S. (1983) Railroad cartels before 1887: the effectiveness of private enforcement of collusion. *Research in Economic History*: 125–44.

Van Damme, E. (1983) *Refinements of the Nash Equilibrium Concept*. Berlin: Springer.

Varian, H. (1978) *Microeconomic Analysis*. New York: Norton.

Varian, H. (1980) A model of sales. *American Economic Review*: 651–9.

Varian, H. (1985) Price discrimination and social welfare. *American Economic Review*: 870–5.

Vernon, J. and Graham, D. (1971) Profitability of monopolization by vertical integration. *Journal of Political Economy*: 924–5.

Vickrey, W. (1961) Counter-speculation, auctions, and competitive sealed tenders. *Journal of Finance*: 8–37.

Villcassim, N. and Wittink, D. (1985) Manufacturers' use of coupons. Working Paper. Cornell University Graduate School of Management.

Viscusi, W. (1978) A note on 'lemons' markets with quality certification. *Bell Journal of Economics*: 277–9.

Visscher, M. (1973) Welfare-maximizing price and output with stochastic demand. *American Economic Review*: 224–9.

Vives, X. (1984) Duopoly information equilbrium: Cournot and Bertrand. *Journal of Economic Theory*: 71–94.

Vives, X. (1985) On the efficiency of Cournot and Bertrand equilibria with product differentiation. *Journal of Economic Theory*: 179–93.

Wallace, D. (1937) *Market Control in the Aluminium Industry*. Cambridge, MA: Harvard University Press.

Walters, A. (1963) Production and cost functions: an econometric survey. *Econometrica*: 39–52.

Ware, R. (1984) Sunk costs and strategic commitment: a proposed three-stage equilibrium. *Economic Journal*: 370–8.

Warner, J. (1977) Bankruptcy costs: some evidence. *Journal of Finance*: 337–48.

Warren-Boulton, F. (1974) Vertical control with variable proportions. *Journal of Political Economy*: 783–802.

Warren-Bouton, F. (1977) Vertical control by labor unions. *American Economic Review*: 309–22.

Warren-Boulton, F. (1978) *Vertical Control of Markets: Business and Labor Practices*. Cambridge, MA: Ballinger.

Waterson, M. (1980) Price–cost margins and successive market power, *Quarterly Journal of Economics*: 135–50.

Waterson, M. (1982) Vertical integration. Variable proportions and oligopoly. *Economic Journal*: 129–44.

Waterson, M. (1983) Economies of scope within market frameworks. *International Journal of Industrial Economics*: 223–37.

Weiss, L. (1963) Factors in changing concentration. *Review of Economics and Statistics*: 70–7.

Weiss, L. (1969) Advertising, profits and corporate taxes. *Review of Economics and Statistics*: 426–30.

Weiss, L. (1972) The geographic size of markets in manufacturing. *Review of Economics and Statistics*: 245–66.

Weiss, L. (1974) The profits–concentration relationship in antitrust. In H. Goldschmidt et al (eds), *Industrial Concentration: The New Learning*. Boston: Little, Brown.

von Weizsacker, C. (1980a) A welfare analysis of barriers to entry. *Bell Journal of Economics*: 399–420.

von Weizsacker, C. (1980b) *Barriers to Entry: a Theoretical Treatment*. Berlin: Springer.

von Weizsacker, C. (1984) The costs of substitution. *Econometrica*: 1085–116.

Wenders, J. (1971) Excess capacity as a barrier to entry. *Journal of Industrial Economics*: 14–19.

Wenders, J. (1976) Peak load pricing in the electric utility industry. *Bell Journal of Economics*: 232–41.

West, D. (1981) Testing for market pre-emption using sequential location data. *Bell Journal of Economics*: 129–43.

Westfield, F. (1981) Vertical integration: does product price rise or fall? *American Economic Review*: 334–46.

Westoff, F. (1977) Existence of equilibria with a local public good. *Journal of Economic Theory*: 134–9.

Whinston, M. (1986) Exit with multiplant firms. Working Paper No. 1299. Harvard University (HIER).

White, L. (1976) Searching for the critical concentration ratio. In S. Goldfeld and R. Quandt (eds), *Studies in Nonlinear Regression*. Cambridge, MA: Ballinger.

White, L. (1977) Market structure and product varieties. *American Economic Review*: 179–82.

White, L. (1981) Vertical restraints in antitrust law: a coherent model. *Antitrust Bulletin*: 327–45.

Wicksell, K. (1934) *Lectures on Political Economy*, Appendix 2. London: Routledge and Kegan Paul.

Williamson, O. (1965) Innovation and market structure. *Journal of Political Economy*. 67–73.

Williamson, O. (1968a) Wages rates as a barrier to entry. *Quarterly Journal of Economics*: 85–116.

Williamson, O. (1968b) Economics as an antitrust defense: the welfare tradeoffs. *American Economic Review*: 18–34.

Williamson, O. (1971) The vertical integration of production: market failure considerations. *American Economic Review*: 112–23.

Williamson, O. (1973) Markets and hierarchies: some elementary considerations. *American Economic Review*: 316–25.

Williamson, O. (1974) The economics of antitrust: transactions cost considerations. *University of Pennsylvania Law Review*: 1429–96.

Williamson, O. (1975) *Markets and Hierarchies: Analysis and Antitrust Implications*. New York: Free Press.

Williamson, O. (1977) Predatory pricing: a strategic and welfare analysis. *Yale Law Journal*: 284–340.

Williamson, O. (1979a) Williamson on predatory pricing II. *Yale Law Journal*: 1183–200.

Williamson, O. (1979b) Assessing vertical market restrictions: antitrust ramifications of the transaction cost approach. *University of Pennsylvania Law Review*: 953–93.

Willig, R. (1976) Consumers' surplus without apology. *American Economic Review*: 589–97.

Willig, R. (1978) Pareto-superior nonlinear outlay schedules. *Bell Journal of*

Economics: 56–69.

Wilson, C. (1977) A model of insurance markets with incomplete information. *Journal of Economic Theory*: 167–207.

Wolinsky, A. (1983) Prices as signals of product quality. *Review of Economic Studies*: 647–58.

Wolinsky, A. (1984) Product differentiation with imperfect information. *Review of Economic Studies*: 53–61.

Wolinsky, A. (1986) True monopolistic competition as a result of imperfect information. *Quarterly Journal of Economics*: 493–511.

Worcester, D. (1957) Why dominant firms decline. *Journal of Political Economy*: 338–47.

Worcester, D. (1973) New estimates of the welfare loss to monopoly, United States 1956–69. *Southern Economic Journal*: 234–45.

Worcester, D. (1975) On monopoly welfare losses: comment. *American Economic Review*: 1015–23.

Working, H. (1948) The theory of inverse carrying charge in futures markets. *Journal of Farm Economics*: 1–28.

Wu, S. (1964) The effects of vertical integration on price and output. *Western Economic Journal*: 117–33.

Yamey, B. (1970) Monopoly, competition, and the incentive to innovate: a comment. *Journal of Law and Economics*: 169–77.

Yamey, B. (1972) Predatory price cutting: notes and comments. *Journal of Law and Economics*: 129–42.

Yamey, B. (1974) Monopolistic price discrimination and economic welfare. *Journal of Law and Economics*: 377–80.

Yarrow, G. (1985) Welfare losses in oligopoly and monopolistic competition. *Journal of Industrial Economics*: 515–29.

Yu, B. (1981) Potential competition and contracting in innovation. *Journal of Law and Economics*: 215–38.

Zajac, E. (1970) A geometric treatment of Averch–Johnson's behavior of the firm model. *American Economic Review*: 117–25.

Zelek, E., Stern, L. and Dunfee, T. (1980) A rule of reason decision model after Sylvania. *California Law Review*: 13–47.

Zermelo, E. (1912) Uber eine anwendung der mengnlehre und der theorie des schacspeil. *Proceedings of the Fifth International Congress of Mathematicians*. Cambridge, MA: MIT Press.

Zeuthen, F. (1930) *Problems of Monopoly and Economic Welfare*. London: Routledge and Kegan Paul.

Author Index

Subject Index